D1000670

THE WORLD OF
FANTASTIC FILMS

To Clare, who bravely kept me company not just through Superman *and* E.T., *which is easy, but through* Zombie Flesh-Eaters *and* The Evil Dead, *which is not so easy. A living refutation of the theory that people continually exposed to monsters become inured to them, she screamed most satisfyingly to the last.*

WITHDRAWN

PN
1995.9
.F36
N53

THE WORLD OF
FANTASTIC FILMS
AN ILLUSTRATED SURVEY

PETER NICHOLLS

DODD, MEAD & COMPANY
NEW YORK

Copyright© Peter Nicholls
and Multimedia Publications (UK) Ltd 1984.

All rights reserved.
No part of this book may be reproduced in any form without
permission in writing from the copyright owner.

Published in 1984 by Dodd, Mead & Company, Inc.
79 Madison Ave, New York, NY 10016

Distributed in Canada by
McClelland and Stewart Limited, Toronto

First edition

Library of Congress Cataloging in Publication Data

Nicholls, Peter, 1939-
    The world of fantastic films.

    1. Fantastic films – History and criticism. I. Title.
PN1995.9.F36N53   1984   791.43'09'0915   84-10185
ISBN 0-396-08381-1
ISBN 0-396-08382-X (pbk.)

Originated by D S Colour International Ltd, London
Typeset by Text Filmsetters Ltd, Orpington
Printed in Spain by Graficromo SA, Cordoba

Contents

Introduction

This is a book about seven hundred of the most interesting fantasy films ever made.

Fantastic cinema has become the most popular area of movie-making in the world. By the end of 1982, eight of the top twelve money-making films ever released were fantastic: *ET: The Extraterrestrial* (1st), *Star Wars* (2nd), *The Empire Strikes Back* (3rd), *Jaws* (4th), *Raiders of the Lost Ark* (5th), *The Exorcist* (7th), *Superman* (9th) and *Close Encounters of the Third Kind* (12th).

Yet not all that long ago, in 1971, fantastic cinema accounted for only 5 per cent of American box-office takings, if we can accept *Variety's* findings. By 1982 this figure had risen close to an amazing 50 per cent. There is, therefore, a vast amount of money at stake in making fantastic movies, especially since their very nature often means that they are extremely expensive to produce.

There can be a lot of argument about what qualifies a film as "fantastic", and to a degree such judgements will always be subjective. One person's fantasy is another person's reality. In a philosophical sense *all* films, on the other hand, could be defined as fantasy. But for the purposes of this book I take a fairly straightforward definition: a fantastic film is set in a world which differs in one or more important respects from the actual world we live in.

A fantastic film may be set in another world altogether, like *Return of the Jedi*, or in an imaginary future world, like *Blade Runner*, or in an imaginary past world, like *Conan the Barbarian*. (But I have excluded films set in a supposedly historical past, like *Ben-Hur*, or in a plausible and extremely close near-future, like *The China Syndrome*.)

The fantasy element in a film may be just one extraordinary thing in an otherwise "realistic" world. *Jaws* is set in a mundane, present-day America, but in real life Great White Sharks do not swim around Long Island Sound, and they are not so big. This book accepts all "monster movies" as fantasy, no matter whether the monsters are comparatively realistic, as in *The Birds* or *Cujo* or even *Alligator*, or entirely fantastic, as in *Q – The Winged Serpent*.

Different Kinds of Fantasy

Films about the supernatural constitute a special case. Most of us believe that the world we live in is more or less rational, subject to the known laws of nature. The world today is, by and large, secular: that is, non-religious. Thus I have included as fantasy all films about supernatural forces erupting into everyday life (such as *The Exorcist* and *The Omen*). Although I know that plenty of people still believe in the Devil, for the average viewer these films are fantastic.

Most of the films discussed in this book fall into clearly defined categories: science fiction (Chapter Five), monster movies and supernatural horror films (Chapter Six), movies set in an imaginary past and sword-and-sorcery films (Chapter Seven). But obviously there are borderline cases. For example, the James Bond movies are set in a moderately real world, but Bond uses so much science-fiction paraphernalia, and is so often pitted against mad scientists out to conquer Earth, that I have stretched a point and included them.

I have not included those many horror films whose supernatural or SF content is negligible; nor have I included (with only partial exceptions) films whose fantastic happenings turn out to have a rational explanation, such as *Phantom of the Opera* and *The Cat and the Canary*. The main kind of non-fantastic horror film, of course, is the regrettably popular mad-slasher-on-the-loose genre where the behaviour of the villain has a psychological rather than a fantastic explanation. Again, there are borderline cases and room for argument, because my judgement may be seen as subjective. For example, this book does not include *Psycho*, *Psycho II*, *Texas Chainsaw Massacre*, *Dressed to Kill* or *Friday the Thirteenth*; yet it does include *Halloween* and *Funhouse*. (*Halloween* is included because the killer himself seems practically unkillable; he is almost a supernatural force. *Halloween II*, by contrast, is a straight slash-movie. The mad mutant in *Funhouse* is a freak of nature so extreme as to be fantastic, especially as the screenplay implies, indirectly, that he is the progeny of a human and a cow. On the other hand, deformity itself is not fantastic as a general rule, so with regrets I have excluded all versions of *The Hunchback of Notre Dame*. The films, both the 1923 and the 1939 versions, are richly atmospheric, and the events strain our credibility. But, after all, they *could* have taken place in the real world. Again, such judgements are subjective, and one classic film of deformity, *Freaks*, is included in this book for its surreal qualities.)

Having dealt with the categories listed above, we are left with a grab-bag of general fantasy and surrealism, ranging in setting from the comic-strip world of *Popeye*; through the allegorical worlds of *Savages* or *The Seventh Seal* or *The Tin Drum*; through worlds where the fantasies of schizophrenic minds are given an objective reality, such as *Hour of the Wolf* or *The Tenant*; through worlds of inexplicable events, such as *Céline and Julie Go Boating* or *Picnic at Hanging Rock*; all the way through to worlds of surrealist exaggeration, such as *Britannia Hospital* or *The Discreet Charm of the Bourgeoisie*.

Surrealism is perhaps the most difficult case to define as fantasy, because the individual scenes in a surreal film may be quite credible. It is in their bizarre juxtapositions that their fantastic nature often lies. There will be more about this interesting subject later on. It is enough to say here that I have been rather selective with surrealist films, which are often so-called "art-house" films rather than films for a popular audience. Thus I have included representative films made by such directors as Woody Allen, Robert Altman, Ingmar Bergman, Luis Buñuel, Jean Cocteau, Federico Fellini and Jacques Rivette, but I have not included (as I could quite plausibly have done) their entire output. I felt it important in this book not too take too much weight away from the "popular" movies side of the scale. Not that this is an anti-intellectual book – but it is, after all, the popular films that have hitherto been most neglected by the critics, and it is precisely in this area that some of the most exciting work is being done. And, of course, it is the popular films, by definition, that people (probably including the readers of this book) most often go to see.

Confusions

It may seem strange to some readers that monsters, cavemen, starships and demons should all be lumped together in the one book. Nevertheless, though very different, such subjects are all certainly fantastic, and market research has also shown that viewers who are attracted to one such theme are very often fond of the others. (The specialised magazines that deal with fantastic cinema, such as *Cinefantastique*, *L'Ecran Fantastique* and *Starburst*, also jumble these fantastic categories together.)

In practice, of course, fantastic categories overlap considerably. Is *Alien* science fiction, horror or a monster movie? In fact, it is all three. *Demon Seed* is an interesting case. It features a super-computer and in that sense is science fiction, but the feeling is that of a horror film, and the computer is a rapist, which seems quite clearly irrational. Should it be discussed with horror or with science fiction? (For convenience, because it fits into an argument about Luddite movies, I chose the latter, but this was really rather arbitrary.)

This book is about the cinema, and not about television. There is, however, some overlap. Films made for television sometimes achieve theatrical release as well (especially overseas) and some of the very best are just as interesting as conventional feature films. I have included, therefore, a small number of made-for-TV feature films, but I have not included television series as such. You will not find the *Star Trek*, *Dr Who* or *Twilight Zone* television series here, only their movie spinoffs.

The Main Text of the Book

Most of the chapters are structured on a self-evident basis: one on science fiction (a term which is abbreviated to SF for most of the book), one on supernatural horror, and one on general fantasy. But the first four chapters need some explanation.

The most important milestone in the history of fantastic cinema was the year 1968: the year of *2001: A Space Odyssey*, *Planet of the Apes*, *Rosemary's Baby*, *Night of the Living Dead* and several other seminal works of the genre. The emphasis of this book is largely on the cinema of 1968 and afterwards, partly because the earlier history of fantastic cinema has already been told many times, but its recent history – despite the enormous success of the genre – has been comparatively unchronicled. The first seventy years of fantastic cinema, from the pioneering work of the Frenchman Méliès in the late nineteenth century right down to 1967, is summarised by way of discussion of key films (eighty-six of them) in Chapters One and Two. The factors that made the year 1968 a turning point are explained in Chapter Three. In Chapter Four we look at thirteen of the most important directors and producers who have transformed the genre since 1968.

The decision to devote a separate chapter to thirteen of these figures (for the sake of neatness we will regard Monty Python as a kind of *gestalt* individual) is, I am sure, the right one, but it has meant that not all the SF movies are dealt with in the SF chapter, nor all the horror movies in the chapter on horror. Some of the greatest films from all areas of the fantastic genre will be found in Chapter Four.

Up until the last moment I had intended to include a separate chapter on animated feature films, but I was defeated not only by the pressure for space but also by the sense that, for many viewers, cartoon features, no matter how fantastic their content (animated films are fantastic almost by definition), belong in a wholly separate category which is not very usefully discussed in the context of *Star Wars* or *The Exorcist*. I regret the loss of such Disney classics as *Fantasia*, *Sleeping Beauty* and *The Jungle Book*, and of more recent animated features from other studios, such as *Fritz the Cat*, *Fantastic Planet*, *Heavy Metal*, *The Plague Dogs* and *The Secret of NIMH*. I have, however, included films such as *The Muppet Movie* and *Dark Crystal* which use animated models and puppets.

To sum up: Chapters Three to Seven deal almost exclusively with post-1968 films. You will find older films in Chapters One and Two and the Filmography.

The Filmography

More than one third of this book – around 50,000 words – is devoted to the Filmography, which indexes exactly 700 films. For the

Demon Seed *(MGM, 1977), science fiction or horror? Julie Christie is pinned down by an amorous robot.*

The advance of the cannibal zombies from Night of the Living Dead *(Image Ten), one of the key movies that made 1968 a breakthrough year.*

Poster advertising the notorious Zombie Flesh-Eaters *(Variety, 1979), one of the few films covered in this book to be awarded the maximum three-skull squeamish rating.*

period up to 1967 I have necessarily been selective (not severely so); 229 films from the period 1897-1967 are discussed, 90 in the main text and a further 139 in the Filmography. For the period 1968-83 it is fairly comprehensive, with 210 films receiving detailed treatment in the main text and a further 261 in the Filmography. Let me put it this way. If a fantastic film – particularly a post-1967 film – is not in this book, then the chances of its being worth seeking out are not particularly good, so far as I have been able to establish, though surprises are always possible. (I viewed the low-budget and unpromising-sounding *Dead Kids*, also known as *Strange Behavior*, at the last minute, and it proved well worth including.) I cannot claim to have seen every movie from the fantastic genre made either before or since 1968, and if I have missed a "sleeper" that is a potential classic, I do apologise, and hope that you will let me know.

I have, specifically and knowingly, omitted quite a few of the worst exploitation movies, while remaining quite aware that even *Horror of Party Beach* (1964) and *Evilspeak* (1981) have their fans who will be annoyed. But one has to stop somewhere. To have been fully comprehensive would have made this book too expensive for all but a handful of movie buffs to buy.

I have attempted to cover all important fantastic films released up to the end of 1983. Unfortunately, there are some films released in late 1983 in the USA for which no prints are yet available in the UK. The main omissions of which I am aware are *The Man With Two Brains*, *Hercules* (with Lou Ferrigno), *Deathstalker*, *The Keep* and *Amityville 3-D*; however, from reports received, several of these may not have been worth including. *Echtzeit* from Germany and *La Belle Captive* from France also sounded promising, but could not be located, although both were premiered at film festivals during 1983.

All 700 films in the Filmography have been rated for quality (stars) and also for the extent to which they might disturb the squeamish (skulls). See the Filmography for details of what information is given, but three points are worth discussing here: the star ratings, the squeamish ratings and videotape availability.

The Star Ratings

No film rating system can be wholly authoritative, but I have guarded against subjectivity by averaging out the ratings of four experienced critics: my own, and those of Philip Strick (author of *Science Fiction Movies*), Tom Milne (author of several film books, and like Strick one of the best critics who regularly review fantastic films in *Monthly Film Bulletin*), and Ramsey Campbell, English horror novelist and, appropriately, video critic for the magazine *Halls of Horror*.

The system works as follows:

★ Don't waste your time unless you derive amusement from true awfulness

★★ Watch these only if it is raining and there is nothing better to do

★★★ Solid, average film-making – nothing very special, but usually with points of interest

★★★★ A good film, well above average

★★★★★ Must see

To give greater flexibility to the system, we have awarded half stars (★½, ★★★½ and so on) which stand for critical judgements midway between any two of those above.

There is only one drawback to polling opinion from a panel of judges rather than relying on one judge only. This is a slight flattening effect: fewer five-star or one-star judgements. This is because, though each single judge may have quite a generous list of, say, five-star films, one strongly dissenting voice is enough to eliminate quite a few of these. For this reason, readers are advised to note that films with four and a half stars may well be very good indeed. It very occasionally happens that the overall star rating of a film is more or less favourable than my own capsule comment would seem to imply, but this hardly matters. The opinion that will finally matter is your own.

The Squeamish Factor

The squeamish rating is quite different. Most of the films in this book do not have one. I have had to include these "skull" ratings because it is quite common for people to wander into a cinema or hire a videotape in all innocence, only to find themselves confronted with violent and/or disgusting imagery that they may find genuinely disturbing.

To get a "skull" rating the imagery in a given film has to be explicit. What counts is gore, viscera, painful metamorphosis, lingering vomit shots and copious use of such precious bodily fluids as blood and slime.

It would be wrong to suppose that only bad films resort to overtly gory, sensational effects. I have, for example, given John Carpenter's excellent film *The Thing* a maximum rating of three skulls for its squeamish quotient; here the graphic horrors are intrinsic to a sophisticated screenplay. On the other hand, Lucio Fulci's *Zombie Flesh-Eaters*, which also earns the maximum three skulls, has no apparent *raison d'être* beyond the horrors themselves. It is, in large part, a film designed to display, literally, the maximum of blood and guts, and has no aesthetic purpose beyond this.

In other words, the squeamish rating is no guide to quality. It warns people that they may be disgusted or sickened by a film's content. The rating does not apply to films whose horrors are merely implied, no matter how frightening they are, even though some films that rely on atmosphere and tension can be just as disturbing as others whose horrors are displayed up front for everyone to see. But it would be almost impossible to quantify such effects. So a three-skull film, you may be assured, will be disgusting. It may or may not be good, and it may or may not be frightening: disgust is not the same thing as terror.

A tiny minority of the films discussed in this book – no more than ten – are definitely if mildly pornographic. Since I do not regard sex as disgusting, I have not given these films a squeamish rating unless the sex involved is cruel or sadistic.

The system works as follows:

- ☠ The film has moments that are gross but does not linger unduly over them; these are not films for nervous people or young children, but they are really comparatively mild

- ☠☠ These are fairly ripe; the intent to shock is overt and at least partly successful

- ☠☠☠ In the words of *Mad* magazine, "Yecchh!"; these go over the top, and you may need a strong stomach to endure them unflinchingly

Movies on Videotape

There are probably around forty million videotape recorders in the world, of which nine to ten million are in the USA, and another six million in the UK. There are a great many people, for this reason, who very often see a feature film for the first time on videotape rather than in a theatre. Thus the availability of a film on videotape can be quite important, which is why we give this information in the Filmography. Many American films are available in the UK *only* on videotape, never having had cinema release, and to a more limited degree the story is the same the other way around. A large number of the films discussed in this book are available for videotape sale or rental (rental being a more important factor in the UK), and many of them for 16mm film rental as well (but we do not list details). Information about videotape availability given here is accurate up to the beginning of 1984, though some of the tapes listed may recently have been withdrawn by the distributors from their catalogues, or belong to the catalogues of bankrupt companies (but will probably still exist in tape libraries). New films are released on tape every month, so the availability listings in this book will go rapidly out of date, though they will remain useful for showing what *is* available, even if wrong about what is *not* available.

I would be pleased to hear from any readers who notice omissions from this list. I am well aware of the possibility, since some films have their titles changed for videotape release and it is quite easy for them to slip through the net. The goodish SF movie *Who?*, for example, has been issued in the UK under the title *The Man in the Steel Mask*. George Romero's least-known film *Jack's Wife* appears on videotape as *Season of the Witch*, a slightly misleading title presumably designed to entice fans of Romero's zombie films into hiring it as a supernatural thriller, which it is only marginally (it is primarily a kitchen-sink drama about the crumbling world of a suburban housewife).

The videotape version of a film is not always the same as the version used for theatrical release. Not only are cuts sometimes made (see above), but also the reverse sometimes occurs, and a more carefully edited or fuller version of a film is available on videotape. For example, *Star Trek The Motion Picture* has an extra twelve minutes of reinstated footage in its videotape version in the USA. It sometimes happens that violent films which have been cut for theatrical release to receive a more lenient rating from the relevant authorities are released in a fuller version on videotape. This is the case, appropriately enough, with Cronenberg's *Videodrome* in the USA. Sometimes two versions of a film are both available on tape – censored and uncensored. This is true, for example, of *Basket Case* in the USA and *Zombie Flesh-Eaters* in the UK.

Videotape availability is given only for the UK and the USA (which, incidentally, use incompatible systems of recording).

Fantastic cinema has always been central to the history of film, and is one of the most enjoyable of all film genres. In recent years it has become the chosen field of work for an amazing number of very talented filmmakers. I hope that this book serves the dual purpose of reminding you about good films you have already seen, and telling you about other good films that you should see. There are some not-so-good films listed here also, and the book may help to save you from wasting your time on the occasional disaster.

London, February 1984

A frame from the animated fantasy Wizards *(20th Century-Fox, 1977), made by Ralph Bakshi, one of the many animated cartoon features of recent years related to the themes explored in this book.*

The First Fifty Years

Previous two pages: a rare picture of Kong versus the airplanes at the climax of King Kong *(RKO Radio, 1933). Note Fay Wray slumped prettily at his feet.*

Fantastic cinema is almost as old as cinema itself, for the very good reason that fantasy is implicit in the very nature of film. Action can be slowed down or speeded up; people can be made to appear or disappear; scale can be altered, so that people become giants or mannikins; double exposure allows one actor to play two roles simultaneously. The possibilities are endless, and they were realized very early – not long after the first commercial showing of moving pictures in 1894. It was no coincidence that professional stage magicians were among the earliest film-makers.

Film snobs often talk as if special effects were somehow vulgar – at best, the icing on an otherwise realistic cake. It probably makes more sense to regard special effects as competely fundamental to film, the cake itself. After all, the language and grammar of film is nearly all "special effects", but most of the tricks are now so familiar that we pay them no more attention than people just talking pay to nouns, verbs and adjectives. Montage (juxtaposing different images in quick succession), cross-cutting, close-ups, panning and tracking shots, zooms and all the rest of the film-maker's vocabulary, were all in their day special effects. Now we take them for granted, but in the earliest days of film-making they did not exist; the camera was plumped down in the visual equivalent of the front row of the stalls, and there it stayed. This did not last long.

Magic

The Frenchman Georges Méliès, a profess-ional illusionist, realized very early (his first films were made in 1896) that the camera could succinctly create illusions that could be made cheaply available to large numbers of ordinary people. He soon found that he could go much further than was possible on the stage and he was one of the earliest pioneers of double exposure, slow and fast motion – even stop-motion, where the film is exposed one frame at a time, which allows amazing transformations to take place. Most of his films are now lost, but it is still possible to see the first SF film ever made, *A Trip to the Moon* (1902). To a modern viewer, this short film (it was unusually long for the time at around 15 minutes) will of course appear contrived, theatrical and far too whimsical. Méliès was not interested in convincing us that what we saw was really happening – he was recreating the splendid nonsense of the pantomime. But it is not too difficult a feat to project our minds back eighty or so years, and to recapture the extraordinary thrill the film-going public of the time must have felt at the rocket trip through space (a subjective shot, with the face of the Moon racing towards the viewer); the lobster-clawed Selenites (there were chorus girls on the Moon as well); and even the art-nouveau splendours of the Moon Palace. All combine in a surreal pot-pourri which showed clearly that magic had indeed entered the cinema. As it turned out, magic was never to leave it.

An Impossible Voyage (1904) was the second of Méliès' SF films; it was about a train trip to the Sun. Even more absurdly theatrical than *A Trip to the Moon*, it remains an awe-inspiring compendium of special-effect devices which in some cases have remained almost unchanged to the present day: the combination of live action and painted backdrops; multiple exposures; split-screen effects; animation; spectacular disasters using models to stand for reality (the train falls into the sea); and stop-motion transformations.

Méliès failed to keep abreast of popular taste for very long; sadly, by 1908 he was being criticized as childish. In 1913 his company went bankrupt, and by then, anyway, Europe was on the brink of war.

The First World War did not, however, prevent the making of films, and it was in one of the major combatant countries, Germany, that the next advances in fantastic cinema were made.

Gothic cinema arrives

The Gothic tradition had always been stronger in Germany than anywhere else, ever since the Romantic Movement at the beginning of the 19th century. At the heart of the Gothic was a revolt against the rationality and smugness of an increasingly scientific-minded world – a world in which it seemed that everything had an explanation, and order and harmony were to be prized above all.

The Gothic tale typically featured an explosion of madness or horror into the lives of ordinary people, and this was a metaphor for the forces of unreason that simple observation confirmed to exist.

The theme of the Gothic often resolved itself into ancient-versus-modern (as it still does today), and Gothic stories tended to be set in the past, or in some corner of the present where ancient survivals lingered on. As the shadows grew deeper around Europe, the century-old conventions of Gothic fiction came alive again in the cinema, in the Gothic's ancestral home. (The word referred originally to an ancient German tribe, the Goths.)

The first hero of Gothic cinema was Paul Wegener, initially as actor (often in bizarre and fantastic roles), and then as director. *The Golem* (1914), which Wegener directed with his screenwriter Henrik Galeen, tells the old Jewish myth of the monster without a soul, fashioned out of clay by a daring Rabbi in the Middle Ages to defend the ghetto of Prague against a pogrom. In the 1914 film, the Golem is dug up in modern times by workmen excavating for a new synagogue. They mistake him for a statue, but he is brought to life by an antiquarian, with whose daughter the monster falls in love. She is appalled, and the spurned creature, with its brooding immobile, muddy face and soft, living eyes, runs amuck and finally falls from a tower. All that now exists of the film are the stills showing the Golem, played by Wegener.

The film helped to create an appetite for filmed fantasy in Germany. Also, during the war it was safer to film indoors – and studio conditions always emphasise the fantastic over the realistic element of cinema. Wegener went on to make a series of *Märchenfilme* (fairy tales) but he returned to a longer and grander version of the Golem story in 1920. This second *Golem*, which still exists in an 85-minute version, returned to the original story of Rabbi Loew, who creates the Golem to save the ghetto from disaster. The Rabbi is unable, finally, to control his creature, who resembles an incarnation of some juggernaut-like natural force. The Golem breaks through the ghetto gate into the world outside, where a pretty little Aryan girl, significantly, offers him an apple and then plucks the Star of David from his chest, and he once again becomes no more than a dead, clay thing. Young German maidens dance and play on the body, which is then ceremonially carried back into the ghetto by the Jewish leaders. The essence of the story was coincidentally to be repeated in *Frankenstein*.

Expressionism
In the first film, according to Henri Langlois, the power of the film sprang from the contrast between the inhuman Golem and the naturalistic surroundings; in the second, however, the tortuous and bizarre Expressionist sets served to mirror the unnaturalness of the creature.

These twisted settings, which recur occasionally in fantastic films to this day, became very popular for a while, and some film historians see nearly all German silent fantasy as Expressionist, though in fact it was more often a playing of Expressionist against naturalistic effects that gave them their uncanny atmosphere. One truly Expressionist fantasy, however, was *The Cabinet of Dr Caligari* (1919), directed by Robert Wiene.

Caligari is still an extraordinary film. The effect of the heavily stylised, distorted sets with their jagged diagonals and painted shadows, along with the deliberately exaggerated acting, is to create a film that feels like a sinister animated cartoon using live actors. Caligari is the fairground hypnotist whose servant, Cesare the somnambulist (sleepwalker), carries out a series of murders under his instructions. As in *The Golem*, we are able to feel sympathy and revulsion simultaneously at the "monster" Cesare, with his white face, emaciated appearance, and jerky, inhuman movements. Many fantastic

films have "monsters" – they may have the outward look of humans – whose abnormality poses a threat to our normality, yet within whom we are sometimes able to glimpse an innocence that we ourselves, perhaps, have lost. King Kong and the Frankenstein monster are later examples. Cesare's downfall comes when, astonished at the beauty of the woman whom he has been sent to murder, he abducts her instead. He dies of exhaustion after a pursuit by the outraged "normal" people of the town. Caligari, the human manipulator, is the real monster and Cesare is merely his unfortunate creature. This moral reversal is typical of fantasy films, and perhaps lies at their very root. That is, fantasy not only helps us to exorcise our nightmares – it actually causes us to question more deeply what is monstrous and what is not. In the case of *Caligari* the issue was confused by the epilogue, in which Cesare is shown to be the still-living inmate of an insane asylum, and Caligari the benevolent-seeming head of the institution. Apparently, all we have seen has been Cesare's nightmare, and yet the last shot, a close-up of Caligari's face, is enigmatic. The sting in the tale, which suggests that the world may not have been made safe for "normals" after all, is typical of the disquieting end frequently found in the horror film right through to today.

Creatures of the dark
The climax of German Gothic cinema may well have been F. W. Murnau's *Nosferatu* (1922), the first, and in my view the most memorable, of the many adaptations of Bram Stoker's vampire novel *Dracula*. Over the years the film has received a good deal of adverse criticism; even Carlos Clarens, one of the shrewdest of horror historians, compares Max Schreck's performance as the vampire unfavourably to Bela Lugosi's handling of the same role a decade later. But for all the oddities of detail – the roly-poly bourgeois playing of the Jonathan Harker role, for example – it remains one of the soaring classics of fantastic cinema. Clarens may prefer the comparative urbanity of Lugosi's playing, but it is the sheer unhumanness of Schreck's Graf Orlok (Murnau changed Dracula's name) that makes his role so hairraising. Orlok cannot possible be urbane: he seems to exist in some frozen circle of hell, quite cut off from a world in which it might remain important for a Count – vampire or not – to behave like a gentleman. His gaunt, ungainly, scuttling, hook-nosed, rodent-toothed appearance has all the potency of a great archetype. Today, Lugosi's *Dracula* has become tame in retrospect: Lugosi now seems high camp – almost cuddly, with his exaggerated, Middle-European manners and his stilted English; he is a figure of fun. It is not possible to adjust to Graf Orlok; he is so

utterly outside human experience. Visually, he is associated with the dark and damp; his white skin looks like something growing on the wall of a cave; the innocent flower-gathering of the very ordinary young lovers is crudely done, but their chubby inadequacy has its own symbolic strength in the film. The warmth and sunshine that they represent are pitted against the dark and the inhuman (though not necessarily the unnatural, for Orlok is visually linked with many sinister natural forces – notably a scurrying horde of plague-carrying rats) – against the diseased, in short. The important point is this: the film leaves us feeling that the darkness is stronger than the light. Orlok himself is destroyed by the young wife, who lures him to suck her blood until the first light of dawn strikes him through the window. But she dies, and Bremen is nearly destroyed by the plague. *Nosferatu* stands at the head of the whole line of apocalyptic horror: that is, it tells us that ultimately the "normal" is not the norm at all – that it may lose out against the forces of repression, disease, despair and violence. The placidity of our lives is terribly vulnerable. The film is set in 1838, but the message was appropriate enough for the Weimar republic, and even today it may be a valuable counterpoise to the smugness of our idea of progress.

Early science-fiction films

The idea of progress itself produced another major line of development in the fantastic film. If the Gothic strand represents the monsters of darkness – creatures from our archaic past – erupting into the sunlight, the science-fiction strand represents the future. But film-makers were not generally prepared to accept the Utopian elements in science fiction – the idea that as the world steadily progressed, it would become a better place – and the First World War, where death on an unparallelled scale had been unleashed, partly through the new technology, knocked much of the optimism out of science-fiction projections of the future.

The image of the machine that would save us was metamorphosing into the image of the machine that would enslave us. Quite early on, the German cinema had shown signs of being disturbed at the advance of science. One of the biggest hits of the First World War period was Otto Rippert's serial *Homunculus* (1916), an ambitious project in six one-hour episodes. The Homunculus was an artificial man, created in a laboratory, and in appearance not a monster at all – rather handsome, in fact. Designed as a supremely ethical superman, he is so appalled at discovering his true origin that he becomes evil, wreaking his various unpleasant designs throughout the series until his death (by stroke of lightning) at the end. Lightning is an important symbol in the iconography of hor-

ror, both science-fictional and Gothic – it can be life-giving, as in *Frankenstein*, or death-dealing (or death-announcing), as in the storms that so regularly portend the crisis of a horror film.

The first great SF film – it remains one of the very greatest even today – is Fritz Lang's *Metropolis* (1926). Some few earlier films, notably the Russian *Aelita* (see filmography), had sequences set in the future, but there had been nothing so full-blooded as *Metropolis*, the archetypal film of the future.

Lang was already one of the most important figures in fantastic cinema. A friend of Robert Wiene, he had worked on the script of *Caligari*; in 1922 he made the extraordinary *Dr Mabuse* (see filmography); and in 1923-4 he directed the long two-part *Die Nibelungen* (in filmography), the most spectacular fantasy film yet made.

It is Lang's sheer commitment to the science-fiction aspects of the film that makes *Metropolis* so startling even today. The future is evoked not only in gigantic cityscapes but in tiny details, whereas even today many

Max Schreck plays the pallid, rodent-featured vampire in Nosferatu *(Prana Film, 1922), the first screen adaptation of the novel* Dracula, *and still perhaps the best.*

films set in the future (*Death Watch*, for example) are content with one or two futuristic elements in an otherwise contemporary-seeming story. The love story at the heart of *Metropolis* has perhaps lost its power to enthrall, but the visual imagery remains archetypal: the shuffling workers in the underground city; the soaring towers of the upper city; the robot duplicate of Maria, created by the mad scientist Rotwang to deceive her upper-class lover; the thirty thousand extras used in the crowd scenes, including the great disaster spectacle of the lower-city flood.

Metropolis created visual equivalents for many of the great ideas of science fiction: men dwarfed by inexorably working machinery and subjugated to it, and the contrasts between the world of feeling and the world of technological progress – cold, powerful and rational. Few SF films made since have not owed a debt to *Metropolis*, right down to *Blade Runner*.

Fun in Hollywood

By the time that *Metropolis* was released in America, Hollywood had discovered fantastic cinema for itself, with early films of importance including the regrettably now lost 1910 version of *Frankenstein* and the surviving 1920 John Barrymore version of *Dr Jekyll and Mr Hyde* (both in filmography). Later on, the uncanny German style of symbolism was to be imported into Hollywood and there domesticated, but the main products of the 1920s were rip-roaring fantastic adventures of a distinctly American kind. One of the first

Brigitte Helm played the screen's first and sexiest robot in Metropolis *(Ufa, 1926), shown here with her gesticulating creator Rotwang, played by Rudolf Klein-Rogge. Note his gloved right hand, whose deformity recurred many years later with another mad scientist, Dr Strangelove.*

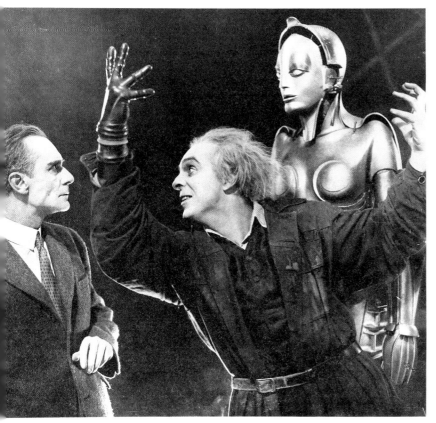

was *The Thief of Bagdad* (1924), starring the incomparable Douglas Fairbanks.

In this first version of the often filmed story, the hero is the thief himself (later he became a prince who befriends the thief). In a nice fetishist opening he meets the Caliph's daughter (Julanne Johnson) and expresses his love for her by taking her shoe. To prove his worthiness, he must perform many tasks. In fact, the film is very much a celebration of the Protestant work ethic. Title cards include HAPPINESS MUST BE EARNED, and BY TOIL THE SWEETS OF LIFE ARE FOUND. Fairbanks is a swashbuckler with a heart of marshmallow: I CAN BEAR A THOUSAND TORTURES, ENDURE A THOUSAND DEATHS – BUT NOT THY TEARS. He is up against a wicked magician and his lovely associate (Anna May Wong).

Rather slow-paced by later Hollywood standards, the film sags a bit in the middle, but the effects still look pretty good: the magic rope, the rose that forms out of sand, several rather lethargic monsters (conquered a little too easily), and most famous, of course, the magic carpet and the white, flying horse (a remarkably convincing creature played by a real horse with wings strapped on).

Hollywood, knowing it was on to a good thing with monsters, made a silent version of Conan Doyle's *The Lost World* in 1925, which is still very watchable. It also ushered in a whole new genre of fantasy cinema, the dinosaur movie. The many plausible monsters were the work of the famous early master of stop-motion animation, Willis O'Brien, who was the first person to perfect the technique of photographing miniature models of monsters a frame at a time, and combining the results with live action. Thus, at the end of the film, when Professor Challenger's story of his adventures in the hidden plateau in South America is doubted by the snooty Royal Society in London, Challenger – played with hairy panache by Wallace Beery – produces the perfect squelch, a live brontosaurus. This creature then escapes, and rampages around London (a scene repeated *ad infinitum* in movies since, usually in Tokyo), causing much chaos around Tower Bridge. Harry Hoyt's direction is slow and wordy (it is amazing how many words could appear in the titles of silent movies), but the monsters save the day.

Hollywood supernatural gothic

It was around 1927 when Hollywood finally decided to compete with the Germans at making shadowy, menacing, Gothic horror films, but American hard-headedness still shied clear of the utterly supernatural. A popular literary genre of the time specialized in bizarre mysteries which turned out to have a rational explanation, and that is exactly what happened with *London After Midnight* (1927). This brought together again two of

Hollywood's major talents, the director Tod Browning and Lon Chaney, the famous character actor. Chaney plays the vampire who with his ghostly, white-faced daughter creates terror around London. The supernatural sequences, and the grotesque Expressionist sets, are said to have been very effective, but the film is now lost. We can see from still photographs, though, Chaney's ghastly appearance: thin wires around his eyes caused them to bulge horribly, and his mouth is stretched open in a rictus of mirthless glee. The whole affair turns out to have been a hoax by a police inspector anxious to trap a murderer. The film was remade by Browning in the sound era as *Mark of the Vampire* (1935), with Bela Lugosi in the title role, and here, too, the unearthly sequences (for all their revealed fraudulence) are astonishingly good – and never wholly explained. How does the pale-faced Luna fly? This version still exists.

Three years following *London After Midnight*, Tod Browning returned to the vampire theme with the most famous of all such films, *Dracula* (1930). As supposed classics go, it is a bit feeble – or at any rate, it has not weathered well. Lugosi's performance is dreadfully hammy, and the plummy, torpid, middle-European accent he gives Dracula must surely have seemed like self-parody even then. Dwight Frye, on the other hand, is splendidly shrill and obsessive as Dracula's lunatic disciple, Renfield. The opening sequences in Dracula's castle, where the unfortunate Renfield becomes the fly in the vampire's web, has a good, Gothic chill about it, with disturbingly sinister camerawork by the German Karl Freund, and, of course, nearly all the best lines. As the eerie howl of a wolf echoes outside, Lugosi intones, "Listen to them…children of the night…what music they make!" But the long London sequence that follows is merely stagey, and dreadfully coy about the horrors, most of which – including the staking of Dracula through the heart – occur discreetly off-screen.

Hollywood, however, had become really enthusiastic about horror films by now, and the boom had begun. The years 1930 to 1936 were a good time for Hollywood Gothic. In addition to those discussed below, there is comment in the filmography on *The Mummy, Island of Lost Souls* and *Doctor X* (all 1932); *The Invisible Man* (1933); *Mad Love* and *The Werewolf of London* (both 1935); and *The Devil-Doll* (1936). There were others as well.

One of the most popular films of the period was Rouben Mamoulian's remake of *Dr Jekyll and Mr Hyde* (1931), usually considered the best version of this rather Calvinist story of guilt, sin, punishment and the emergence of the beast within. (Mr Hyde, the brutal, lustful *alter ego* of prim, repressed Dr Jekyll, can be regarded as part of the werewolf tradition of fantasy cinema. Although he does not liter-

ally become a wolf, he does develop rather a lot of hair and teeth. The image of Hyde as a slavering brute has the same metaphoric force as similar images in werewolf movies though, curiously, the audience's sympathy goes more readily to the wolf than to the man. The latter is seen as being partly to blame for his predicament; the former is an "innocent" victim of the workings of some kind of original sin.) Mamoulian's film is notable for the transformation scenes, achieved by using make-up that became slowly visible to the camera as infra-red light was directed on to the actor's face – a technique that may have been devised by cameraman Karl Struss. The studio would not reveal how the trick was performed for many years.

As usual, Jekyll is a pompous bore, and all the filmic interest is with Hyde. Fredric March gives a full-bloodedly obscene performance, and, unlike Spencer Tracy in the 1941 remake, seems to thoroughly enjoy being reduced to his primitive animal instincts. The scenes with bad girl Miriam Hopkins have a genuine erotic charge. The film is stylish, and makes good use of sound (an early use of heartbeats on the soundtrack), but, as usual in the many versions of this story, the overall effect is a bit stilted and hollow (studios seem to have regarded it as rather "literary" which it is not).

Hollywood scientific Gothic

Dr Jekyll and Mr Hyde offered a quasi-scientific explanation for what was fundamentally a supernatural horror story, and this became almost the Hollywood norm. Even today, much filmed science fiction is generically horror rather than SF. The scientific elements are a perfunctory device (as in, say, *Tarantula* or *Squirm*) for creating a Gothic threat. Curiously enough, this was not wholly true of the great original in this field. *Frankenstein* (1931) was not the first film about monstrous simulacra of humans created by science (*Homunculus* in 1916 probably deserves that honour), but it became the template for those that followed. Everybody remembers the dark elements of the story, but equally important was the Promethean reaching out for higher things by Colin Clive as Baron Frankenstein – a sense of the huge importance of science and its intellectual ecstasies ("It's alive!") reinforced by the great laboratory in the mill, with its crackling electricity. Baron Frankenstein is *not* seen as a madman – he is merely a little neurasthenic.

Mary Shelley's original story has never received an adequate screen treatment (though the television film *Frankenstein: The True Story* – see filmography – did include the chilling final sequence in the arctic snows). In the 1931 *Frankenstein*, the least excusable change was to have the brain of a lunatic put in the skull of the artificial man, thus giving an all-too-obvious reason for his later homicidal behaviour, which would be more interesting if seen as resulting from the painful injuries to his innocence.

The director, James Whale, was then mainly known for his work on the stage. A highly intelligent man, he made the most of this, his third film and first horror piece, and became (to his dismay) type-cast as Hollywood's top horror director. The film also made a star out of the bit-player Boris Karloff, who was tested for the part (in Jack Pierce's now famous make-up, the best known monster make-up in cinema) after Bela Lugosi turned it down. The film was made to cash in on the success of Lugosi's *Dracula*, by the same studio, and Lugosi's declining of the part (because nobody would see his face) was the first of many disastrous decisions he was to make in his tragically second-rate career. Karloff, on the other hand, soared to prominence on the basis of this one film, and stayed there ever afterwards.

Filmed with admirable restraint, *Frankenstein* has moments of uncanny effectiveness even today, notably the creature's first, gradual appearance, and the later scene where he drowns the little girl. Unfortunately, clumsy censorship (in most versions) conceals the fact that the drowning was accidental; thus the one scene that stressed the creature's pristine innocence was destroyed.

This innocence was better portrayed in the sequel, *Bride of Frankenstein* (1935), which remains on the whole the best of the Frankenstein films. It, too, was directed by Whale and starred Karloff. A specially touching scene is that where the monster stumbles lurchingly into the hovel of a blind hermit, and warms to the domestic simplicities of the hermit's life – including the smoking of a cigarette. Karloff's performance, considering how much of his face was rendered rigid with make-up, is extraordinarily expressive.

Bride of Frankenstein is more a black comedy than a horror film. In an ironic prologue, sometimes omitted, Elsa Lanchester plays Mary Shelley ("frightened of thunder, fearful of the dark") explaining to her husband ("My Mary is an angel", says the poet) and to Lord Byron (who makes up the "elegant three") how the monster escaped the conflagration at the end of the previous film. "That wasn't the end at all..." cuts almost directly to a gloating Una O'Connor saying "Insides is always the last to be consumed", and then to the creature's unexpected re-appearance.

Whale's stroke of genius was to cast Elsa Lanchester in a second role, the artificial woman who is to be a mate for the creature "created from cadavers out of rifled graves". The moment when she is brought to life is one of the great climaxes of fantastic cinema, set in a towering laboratory with elaborate electrical apparatus (designed by Kenneth Strickfaden) hissing and spluttering. There is

the horrified scream with which she first greets the monster; her wild-eyed, weirdly coiffeured appearance; the mechanical, inhuman jerking of her neck as she turns her head; the guttural hiss like a maddened cat as the creature prepares to pull the lever that will destroy them. This is an extraordinary piece of scene-stealing, particularly because, though bizarre, the Bride is not unlovely.

The film is made even more baroque by the uneasy camerawork (which gives the impression of fluidity, though there are few tracking shots), and most of all by the inclusion of a new character, a genuine mad scientist this time. Dr Pretorius, played by Ernest Thesiger, is a grimacing, sardonic figure ("Do you like gin? It is my only weakness... The creation of life is enthralling; enthralling, is it not?"). In fact, his inclusion may be the film's only weakness. Played too

The great Lon Chaney as the wide-eyed, grinning vampire in the lost film London After Midnight *(MGM, 1927). Edna Tichenor is his lovely, mysterious daughter.*

In one of the immortal performances of fantastic cinema, Elsa Lanchester plays the artificial woman created by Baron Frankenstein. Here she is about to reject the pathetic, amorous advances of Boris Karloff as the creature in The Bride of Frankenstein *(Universal, 1935).*

obviously for laughs, he weakens the audience's commitment to the story as believable, especially in the scene where he reveals his homunculi: the little king, queen, bishop and others that he has grown from seed and keeps in bottles.

As an essay in the purely fantastic, *Bride of Frankenstein* is one of the few genuine classics of the genre. It has many bold moments: the subdued references to Christ's crucifixion throughout, notably in the scene where the captured creature is tied to a wooden beam and stoned; the wedding bells on the soundtrack as the Bride comes to life; and, above all, the use of lightning to symbolize both the potency and the unpredictability of science.

Universal studio made five sequels to these first two films; they are almost uniformly disappointing. Karloff starred only in the first of these: *Son of Frankenstein* (1939). The last one, *Abbott and Costello Meet Frankenstein* (1948), a lunatic parody, is surprisingly by far the best.

Soon after Karloff's success in *Frankenstein*, he was borrowed by MGM to star in a totally different role: the sinister oriental Fu Manchu, in *The Mask of Fu Manchu* (1932). This was exactly the sort of pulp adventure classic imitated so well by *Raiders of the Lost Ark* fifty years later and, like the latter film, featured a heavy mix of pseudo-science and

occultism that is symbolized by the skull and the laboratory apparatus on Fu's workbench. His plan, of course, is to conquer the world, for which he requires Genghis Khan's death mask and sword as symbols to arouse the modern equivalent of the Mongol hordes. Pitted against Fu is his old nemesis Nayland Smith (Lewis Stone) who at the end uses Fu's own massive electrical apparatus (more effects by Strickfaden) to destroy his generals. The film is fondly remembered by fetishists everywhere for the exotic torture apparatus, the huge Nubian slaves, and Myrna Loy (Fu's wicked daughter) whipping and then caressing one of Lewis Stone's helpers. Also memorable are Karloff's lisp, the tarantulas, the zombie serum, and the statue of Genghis Khan that comes to life. All this was pacily directed by Charles Brabin and Charles Vidor, with excellently bizarre sets designed by Cedric Gibbons.

The first monster classic

There had been monsters before: dinosaurs in *The Lost World*, the creature in *Frankenstein* (but the latter was a deformed man rather than a beast). It was *King Kong* (1933) that set up a matrix for the monster genre in which many monster films are moulded even today.

Film director Carl Denham (Robert Armstrong) has heard of a great location – a mysterious Skull Island where a huge wall conceals something worshipped by the natives. When they get there, Ann (Fay Wray) is kidnapped as a sacrifice to the "god" of the natives, who turns out to be a mountainous gorilla called Kong. The clean-cut hero (Bruce Cabot) pursues Kong, who has retreated behind the wall with Ann (whom he seems to like). They battle prehistoric monsters (many of the crew are killed) but Ann is saved and, when Kong pursues her, he is knocked out by gas grenades and trussed up by a delighted Denham, who plans to exhibit him in New York. But during the grand opening, Kong breaks his chains and escapes, rampaging around Manhattan seeking Ann, on whom he is fixated. He finds her and carries her to the top of the Empire State Building, where he is finally shot down by a squadron of biplane fighter aircraft, and crashes to the street many storeys below.

In outline it all sounds silly, but the sure touch of the screenplay, and of the directors Merian C. Cooper and Ernest B. Schoedsack, give the story an amazing dignity. When the film plays on television today, many who tune in to jeer stay on to weep.

The film has created a myth, a new way of seeing the old dichotomy between Nature and Civilization. Kong is not sentimentalized; he is savage and frightening, but also regal. His squalid death invariably arouses pity and shame in an audience. The squalor is made worse by the film being set in the Depression years, in which we see a miserable populace of New York eager for any marvel that will temporarily make them forget their own problems. The scene where they expect to see a convincing fake, and are actually confronted with a magnificent reality, is wonderfully done. The intensity of the visual imagery is such – especially the terrible contrast between Kong's baffled defiance and the brutal, buzzing little engines of war that shoot him down at the end – that it allows the film to get away with lines which in another context would seem inflated: notably the line from the cynical exploiter Denham, the film's capitalist symbol, who remarks at the close: "No, it wasn't the airplanes; it was Beauty killed the Beast."

And indeed, beauty and bestiality form one of the film's many polarities, but even more important is innocence versus sophistication, and nature versus technology. Other possible readings of the subtext are to see Kong as representing the exploitation of the black races, and even (during the exhibition where he is chained in a cruciform position) as representing a kind of misunderstood Christ. These themes are, indeed, evoked in passing, but tactfully, and they are not central.

Much of this would not have worked without Willis O'Brien's stop-motion animation of Kong and the other monsters. We have already met O'Brien as the effects genius who helped make *The Lost World*, but he was never to excel his work in *King Kong*, and nor were any of his successors. Despite the undoubted talents of animators like Ray Harryhausen, Jim Danforth and David Allen, none of them has come close to O'Brien's achievement, which was, quite simply, to make Kong seem real.

The surrealists

While the commercial form of fantastic cinema was being shaped, first in Germany and then in Hollywood, it was receiving a rather different kind of input from several noncommercial, intellectual film-makers in Europe. Yet it was not so very long before the influence of the artistic movement of surrealism was making its way into the commercial cinema as well.

Surrealism as a separately definable movement grew up around 1924, evolving in part from the earlier Dada movement, which stressed the absurd in art. With hindsight, we can see that several aspects of surrealism had existed even earlier, though not under that name, notably in the French symbolists of the nineteenth century.

This is not the place to embark on a lengthy definition of what precisely can be defined as surrealism and what not. But we can point to four familiar qualities of surrealism that create at least some of its characteristic atmosphere, and we can locate all of these in one film, the first truly surrealist feature, *L'Age d'Or* (1930), directed by Luis Buñuel. The surrealist painter Salvador Dali is given a co-writing credit with Buñuel, but in fact he had little to do with the film, though he was a genuine co-writer on Buñuel's first, surrealist short film, *Un Chien Andalou* (1929).

These are the four qualities:
(i) Surrealism is bizarre. There is no acknowledgement of the primacy of "reality", and by implication, there is no such thing as "reality" anyway. Both within scenes, and in the juxtaposition of different scenes, there is a strong element of the grotesque, the absurd, the apparently arbitrary. Thus in *L'Age d'Or* ("The Golden Age") Gaston Modot, the passionate hero, hurls first a giraffe and then a bishop in full regalia from a window (grotesqueness within a scene): the film then dissolves to a medieval castle from which are emerging four aristocratic orgiasts, clearly modelled on the Marquis de Sade and his friends (arbitrariness of juxtaposition); the de Sade figure looks exactly like Christ (grotesqueness within a scene).
(ii) Surrealism pays homage to dreams, and to the workings of the subconscious mind; it is clearly post-Freudian. Much of *L'Age d'Or* has the mysteriousness of dreams, and Modot's imaginings are given a kind of

dream-reality. For example, he imagines the women he loves (Lya Lys) sitting on a spotlessly clean lavatory and we cut to a shot of lava bubbling from a volcano (make of this what you will; his imagination is clearly heated).

(iii) Surrealism is subversive, against repression, slaps the faces of the bourgeois, and is politically, religiously and sexually radical. *L'Age d'Or* is full of examples of all these, some quoted above. Near the beginning, a boatload of dignitaries arrives at a beach where some kind of important celebration is about to take place, But this is interrupted by the orgasmic cries of two guests (Modot and Lys) rolling in mud in a passionately sexual embrace. In a later scene, Modot is called from a tryst to answer the telephone, and Lys, frustrated, sucks lasciviously on the toe of a classical statue. Buñuel was successful in his attempt to shock. The film was banned for a great many years.

(iv) Surrealism looks at its subjects, with a wide-eyed, concentrated stare, as single-mindedly as a child might. No matter how innocent or inappropriate the object of the gaze might appear, the hypnotic intensity of the scrutiny gives it a kind of abstract significance. We do not know what it means, but we know it means something, and later we may find out. Thus *L'Age d'Or* begins with a documentary-style shot, in close-up, of three scorpions struggling together. This seems to have nothing to do with what follows (a bandit, played by Max Ernst, witnessing the arrival of four archbishops on a rocky shore, followed by a shot of their skeletons in the rocks) but the effect of the image nevertheless pervades the film. It is as if all of life has the matter-of-fact, insect-like cruelty of the scorpions. Surrealism, in fact, is very often cynical, and evokes images of a kind of cosmic, absurd cruelty that wounds us not deliberately but indifferently.

L'Age d'Or has flaws, and it is easy to find parts of it pretentious, but it must surely be one of the most important fantastic films ever made.

All of these qualities of surrealism re-emerge again and again in fantastic cinema, first of all in consciously artistic films made for the intelligentsia, and later in commercial films – especially horror movies. Some examples of the former are *Zéro de Conduite* (1933, see filmography), Cocteau's *Orphée* (1950) and Rivette's *Céline and Julie Go Boating* (1974). Horror films that use surrealistic devices very consciously include Lynch's *Eraserhead* (1976), Borowczyk's *The Beast* (1975) and Jodorowsky's *El Topo* (1971). But many other horror films are surrealist also, especially, for some reason, Italian *giallos* like Argento's *Inferno* (1980) and Fulci's *The Beyond* (1981). Others would include Cohen's *It's Alive* (1973), Coscarelli's *Phantasm* (1978) and Raimi's *The Evil Dead* (1982). Polish

directors seem especially to thrive on surrealist imagery, examples being practically everything Polanski has made, Zulawski's *Possession* (1981) and Skolimowski's *The Shout* (1978). It is also very strong in the German cinema.

In short, what Buñuel innocently began has become probably the most important influence in fantastic cinema after the German Gothic. Sometimes the influence is direct, sometimes it is because the language of surrealism has become part of the way we think, familiar to millions who may never have heard of André Breton or Buñuel through, for example, television commercials.

Curiously enough, two of the most obviously surrealist films of the 1930s had no direct link with the surrealist movement, though their directors were probably aware of its existence. These were Carl Dreyer's *Vampyr* (1931/2) and Tod Browning's *Freaks* (1932).

Abnormal vision

Vampyr is described by the critic William K. Everson as "the one undisputed masterpiece of the genre" and, somewhat hesitantly, I do not dispute this. The hesitation is because most of the available prints are of poor quality, and it is hard to tell to what extent their washed-out appearance is the fading due to generations of reduplication, and to what extent it is the deliberate bleached look Carl Dreyer gave to the film.

Vampyr is based rather remotely on Sheridan Le Fanu's classic story "Carmilla" (filmed several time since—see *Blood and Roses* in filmography) about a female vampire. It has little direct terror, but a suffocating, claustrophobic sense of the unnatural pervades it. The film has a slow, inexorable, dreamlike quality that immediately suggests its strong relationship to surrealism, as does its emphasis on inexplicable events: a policeman's shadow walks off and leaves him; a peasant waiting to catch a ferry becomes for the moment a figure of Death holding his scythe; a crooked old man enters the hero's bedroom at night and whispers "She must not die"; the hero dreams of being trapped in a coffin and slowly carried to the burial ground (the camera is within the coffin staring helplessly out along with the hero); the vampire (unlike the beautiful original of the story) is a withered old woman; her human accomplice, the doctor, is finally trapped mysteriously in a cage in a flour mill, and suffocated with the fine white powder that bleaches the screen completely, recapitulating the strange pallor of all the previous events.

The words of the prologue prepare us for this dreamlike quality: "There exist certain beings whose very lives seem bound by invisible chains to the supernatural. They crave solitude. To be alone and dream – their imagination is so developed that their vision reaches beyond that of most men." Thus the

Madness may be in the eye of the beholder, some surrealistic films suggest. In Carl Dreyer's Vampyr *(Tobis-Klangfilm, 1931/32), a peasant waiting to catch a ferry appears to a hyper-sensitive observer – and to the audience – as an image of Death himself.*

almost somnambulistic, curiously passive hero is not the innocent observer who walks into most vampire films; it is as if his very personality creates the fantastic horrors that entrap him. Of these, the most terrifying touch is the most subtle. In a shot often to be imitated, but whose essence has never been recaptured, Sybille Schmitz, who has been bitten by the vampire, lies in bed looking tortured and weak. She slowly turns her head, and as she does so, her expression changes from innocence to sensual malignance as she passes her tongue across her teeth. No fangs, no special effects, but a disturbing moment.

Here then is another of the great focal points of fantastic cinema: the film which established so brilliantly the link between the fantasies of the mind and the way in which external reality is seen. The whole film was shot in the half-light of dawn and dusk, in a never-never world of quietness and mist. Rudolph Maté's camerawork is compelling, unlike his later direction. (Among his Hollywood films was *When Worlds Collide.*)

Vampyr is about abnormal vision. So, in a very different way, is *Freaks.* Like *L'Age d'Or*, but unusually for a Hollywood film, it was banned for many years. This was largely because it uses circus freaks (real ones, including genuine Siamese twins and several hydrocephalics, some of them deformed so grossly that it is difficult to imagine how they came to be alive at all, such as the man whose body stops at the base of his rib cage) to pose the simple question, what is normal? Olga Baclanova plays the attractive, normally sized circus trapeze star who is worshipped by Hans (Harry Earles), a dwarf engaged to marry another midget (played by his real-life sister, Daisy Earles). When the trapeze artist discovers that Hans is wealthy, she agrees to marry him, and later attempts to poison him. The circus freaks find out, and they take a terrible revenge.

The story is melodramatic, but it is trium-

phantly justified by the poignancy with which the film's point is so succinctly made: that normality is in the eye of the beholder. It is the lovely trapeze artist and her strongman boyfriend who are psychologically abnormal, because they are affectless: that is, they do not have ordinary human feelings. In contrast, the freaks very quickly come to seem like ordinary people, except that they are a little more vulnerable. This justifies Browning's decision, for which he was much criticized, to use real freaks. It is, in fact, a very *humane* movie, and oddly enough, it manages to make the freaks appear normal without either patronizing or sentimentalizing them.

They are, of course, very conscious of belonging to a specialized group, but no more than other oppressed groups in the real world: blacks, women, homosexuals and so on. Their cheery chant "One of us, one of us, gooble garble, one of us" as the loving cup is passed around at the wedding ceremony is not welcomed by Olga Baclanova, appalled at the very thought of being one of them. "Freaks!" she screams. Of course, the film is too tidy, in a way, in that a freak is exactly what *she* becomes: the other freaks in the Grand-Guignol ending pursue her through mud and rain (the limbless ones rolling and wriggling towards her in a moment of awe-inspiring, dark surrealism) and transform her into a chicken-woman, covered with feathers, with one bright, staring eye. This had been judged to be in bad taste – too grotesque in a film that is otherwise touchingly persuasive about normality in the most unexpected surroundings, but such a criticism is perhaps a little pompous. The film is designed as a black comedy rather than a tragedy, and the shock ending with its amusingly appalling image – one of which Salvador Dali might have been proud – is surely more wickedly funny than anything else.

This is probably Browning's best film – much better than *Dracula*, certainly. Its compassion and relaxed friendliness towards the freaks no doubt comes from his own early days in the circus. Interestingly, the film (apart from its surgically implausible end) is only fantastic because we *think* of freaks as being fantastic; the whole thrust of the film is to force us to redefine fantasy. MGM did not see it that way. Horrified at the film, they cut it heavily, perhaps by as much as 25 minutes, and inserted a mealy-mouthed and inaccurate prologue about famous "freaks" of history, which stunningly lists several fictional characters among them! We may never know what was lost. The original may have been more disturbingly dark; it certainly included a scene of the strongman being castrated, a point which it is now rather difficult to deduce from the film.

As to the morality of using real freaks in movies, students of such ethical questions

Director Tod Browning had a genuine affection for the deformed circus people he starred in the film Freaks (MGM, 1932). It is obvious from this photograph, taken on the set, that the affection was mutual. Freaks is a sensitive film, but the British censors banned it for a quarter of a century.

would do well to study Browning's film in relation to two that are much more recent: Brian De Palma's *Sisters* (1972) and Michael Winner's *The Sentinel* (1976). The latter case, where the freaks are used to symbolize a world of monstrous evil, is pure sadistic exploitation of the worst kind; the former case, however, is arguably acceptable. Again the freaks stand for the "abnormal", but this time in a context where the film's "normal" heroine is being brought face to face with her own abnormality.

The years of Good Taste

There were few radical or genuinely original fantasy films made in the decade 1939-1948. The horror boom had burst (as the real horrors of war approached) and that genre was largely represented by perfunctory sequels to much better films. What was new was an increasing sophistication in special effects, a greater overall polish, a move in many cases from black-and-white to colour film stock, and a general emphasis (whose complex sociology cannot be elucidated here) on good taste. The *frisson* was replacing the fright; ghosts tended to appear only discreetly, and primarily to upper-class persons; the devil was more whimsical than evil; science fiction disappeared almost altogether; werewolves were likeable, tormented souls and the new horror king was pudgy, sad-eyed Lon Chaney Jr: a proper attitude to the supernatural was wisecracking sophistication (see *I Married a Witch* in filmography). What was usually missing was the idea of the fan-

tastic as being any sort of projection of internal fears or torments. Perhaps the world of that day held enough external fears. Also, the darker side of life (Hollywood version) was tending to appear in the so-called *film noir* rather than in outright fantasies; that is, in B-movies about police, gangsters, doomed love and revenge.

Oz and Arabia

On the other hand, fantasy still had an important role to play in the brightly exotic side of life, and never more so than in the fantastic worlds of *The Wizard of Oz* (1939) and *The Thief of Bagdad* (1940).

Wizard of Oz is not a great film, but it is joyous and has deservedly become a classic, though it was a semi-flop at the time, taking twenty years to recover its very high production cost of $2,777,000. The screenplay was fundamentally a committee job (eight or more people working on it), but the result was quite true to the sometimes dark and often grotesque vision of L. Frank Baum, who wrote the original novel in 1900.

The real stars of the film are the three vaudevillians who played the Tin Man, the Scarecrow and the Cowardly Lion: Jack Haley, Ray Bolger and Bert Lahr, particularly the latter, whose delivery, honed by years on the stage, derives full comic weight from each drawled syllable. The other star – not Judy Garland as Dorothy, who even then played sadness more convincingly than happiness, and was too old for the part – was A. Arnold Gillespie, for many years head of

MGM's special effects team. The effects, from the Kansas tornado through to the flying monkey-men, are still wonderful. The Munchkins (more than two hundred midgets here, according to one source) are an appropriately fantastic introduction to Oz; there is a very professional performance from the terrier who played Toto (earning a mere $125 for her owner); and several of the songs are terrific. This is a rare instance of a film whose classic status has largely come about through replays on television.

The 1940 remake of *Thief of Bagdad* was the other special effects extravaganza of the period. Here some of the music (dreadful songs) was more of a hindrance than a help, but all is saved by the childlike sense of wonder the film miraculously maintains. (Its production, featuring family squabbles among the Kordas, repeated changes of director, and the moving of the entire production from England to Hollywood after the outbreak of war, was enormously complex.) In this new· version of the film, the romantic lead, the prince, is no longer the thief. That part was taken by the young Indian actor Sabu whose smile is so very infectious, and it is he who has most of the fantastic adventures. The special effects deservedly won an Oscar, and it is they (plus the lush, fairy-tale sets) that give the film its sparkling, brightly-coloured atmosphere of fantasy (foremost among them: the mechanical flying horse, the giant djinn, the monstrous spider that Sabu battles, and the flying carpet). It is all exactly the kind of high-spirited, escapist flim-flam that people wanted to see during the war years. Conrad Veidt makes a good, smouldering evil magician.

Dr Cyclops (1940), also in Technicolor, which was still a comparatively new process, was one of the very few science-fiction films of the 1940s, and the pseudo-science is really only an excuse to tell a fundamentally Gothic tale. A pebble-lensed mad scientist (Albert Dekker, looking suspiciously Japanese, at a time when Americans were beginning to worry about the Yellow Peril) works in the jungle, is very short-tempered, and can shrink living creatures. He uses his shrinking rays (powered by radium!) on some nosy colleagues, and much of the film is devoted to these unfortunate Lilliputians evading chickens and a cat, and attempting to dispose of the now (to them) gigantic mad doctor. It is all done with commendably straight-faced direction from Ernest Schoedsack (who made *King Kong*), much helped by Hans Dreier and Earl Hedrick, designers of the gigantic sets whose effect was to make the protagonists appear tiny. The film is half-forgotten now, but it is almost as good as *The Devil-Doll* (1936, see filmography) in the shrinking-people line. Nothing, however, can touch *The Incredible Shrinking Man* (1957) for the evocation of tiny-person paranoia.

More of this later.

Smooth surfaces

All That Money Can Buy (1941) is a good example of the wise-cracking whimsicality with which Hollywood was now approaching supernatural themes. The film was based on Stephen Vincent Benet's much-anthologized short story "The Devil and Daniel Webster", about a young New England farmer who sells his soul to Mr Scratch (the Devil) in return for seven years' prosperity. When the debt is called in, the farmer refuses to pay up, and a court case follows with the celebrated lawyer Daniel Webster (Edward Arnold) defending his client before a ghostly jury of dead American traitors. Walter Huston's performance as the Devil is cheerfully cocky, and the film is polished and entertaining, but barely a ripple from the uneasy depths ruffles its smooth surface. This was to be the pattern for many sophisticated fantasies of the war years and after, as for example *The Uninvited* (1944), which is highly spoken of in some critical histories as Hollywood's first serious attempt at a real ghost story.

A current cliche tells us that modern horror films suffer from being too literally horrible (guts and gore everywhere), and that things were done better in the old days, when horror was conveyed by subtlety and implication, and the cold chill that resulted was because the viewer's own imagination was allowed to conjure up sinister shapes that were only hinted at.

The weakness of this viewpoint is clearly seen in *The Uninvited*, which is all atmosphere and no substance. Set in a pulp-romance hinterland of *Rebecca* country, it features Ray Milland and Ruth Hussey as the brother and sister who move into a haunted house on the Cornish coast. The house features a menacing room where everybody feels miserable; a haunting, evanescent per-

Judy Garland as Dorothy, Jack Haley as the Tin Man and Ray Bolger as the Scarecrow in The Wizard of Oz *(MGM, 1939) – a film that retains its magic two generations later.*

In the most spectacular special effects sequence of The Thief of Baghdad *(United Artists, 1940) poor Sabu, who plays the Thief, is menaced by the foot of a giant djinn, who is played by the black actor Rex Ingram. Other versions of the film were made before and since, but this is the definitive account of the swashbuckling, magical romance.*

fume of mimosa; weird sobbing at night; and, it turns out, not one but two ghosts (one good, one bad). The climax features an actual ghostly appearance of ectoplasm looking vaguely like wisps of cotton wool, and the explanation of all this (unhappy wives, family secrets etc.) is appropriately woman's-magazine stuff. The lushly romantic score by Victor Young serves only to reinforce the sense one has that this rather talky movie, for all the smoothness and apparent sophistication of its content, has as much to do with real life as the novels of Barbara Cartland. Hollywood fantasy of this period was becoming bland and cosy. Instead of the wonder, the exaltation and sometimes the real menace that characterizes the best of fantasy, Hollywood was offering *ersatz* substitutes that neither disturb nor exhilarate.

Domesticating the monstrous

This was also true of the 1940s addition to the iconography of the horror film proper. The Americans had already been given Dracula, Frankenstein's creature and The Mummy as folk heroes performing in the ever more mechanical charades being put out by Universal. To this list was now added the Wolf Man. Lon Chaney Jr's spaniel-eyed portrayal of this unfortunate creature in *The Wolfman* (1941) nearly reduced the status of Gothic Monster to Household Pet, and was a key point in Hollywood's domestication of threatening forces from beyond the grave or outside the sphere of normality to familiar, predictable friends. In spite of – or perhaps, because of – these factors, the film was a

great success, and did much to create the details of the werewolf myth, which owe little to folk-legend and much to the German writer Curt Siodmak, who co-wrote the screenplay. The most famous, of course, is the gypsy doggerel intoned by Maria Ouspenskaya: "Even a man who is pure in heart/ And says his prayers by night/ May become a wolf when the wolfbane blooms/ And the autumn moon is bright".

The hollowness of the werewolf story, perhaps, is its fatalistic view that a good chap, through no fault of his own, can become a beast. There is not much dramatic pith in this arbitrary cosmic injustice. The beast-in-man idea is done far more interestingly in *Cat People* (see below) where the beast stands for something already implicit in the person. One critic (R. H. W. Dillard in *Horror Films*, 1976) thinks differently, and says "the film is a retelling of the story of the Fall", but his main piece of evidence (hero Larry Talbot stole apples as a child) is flimsy. Anyway, intellectual subtexts do not work if the surface text has no richness. The film is stilted, and is almost crippled by Jack Pierce's weak werewolf make-up, which makes Chaney look like a Russian peasant with a woolly cap and bad teeth.

More ghosts

The bigger-budget Hollywood fantasy productions of the 1940s eschewed monsters, but retained an interest in ghosts. *Portrait of Jennie* (1948) is a better film than *The Uninvited*, and its romanticism strikes deeper. It tells the literally haunting story of an artist

(Joseph Cotten) who is deeply attracted to a young girl (Jennifer Jones) whom he keeps meeting, often in the park, when nobody else is around. It is only after several meetings that he realizes she is growing up at an unnatural speed, at first a schoolgirl and only months later a beautiful young woman. They fall in love. She is, of course, a ghost, and various remarks she makes reveal that she imagines herself to be living in what, to Cotten, is the distant past. Learning that the "real" Jennie was drowned in an accident at Cape Cod, he insanely attempts to prevent her long-passed death there in a frightful hurricane (which in the original black-and-white release print was tinted green, and ended in full Technicolor). His attempt to cheat destiny fails.

The film was directed by William Dieterle, who also made *All That Money Can Buy*. Its strength is in the intensity of emotion it draws out of the leading players (Jennifer Jones's nervous, vulnerable, unworldy charm being a key element), and in the thematic power of a story which is in essence about the impossibility of recapturing childhood innocence. Cotten's despairing efforts to be with Jennie are attempts to pass the angels with the flaming swords and re-enter the Garden of Eden. The full-bloodedly plangent emotions of the film touch the heart for a variety of cleverly-worked reasons. The fact that Jennie does not know she is a ghost is the foremost of these, but also central is Cotten's inadequacy as an artist: romantic and derivative with only his portrait of Jennie having any real power. The film won an Oscar for its special effects, but was not a huge commercial success, perhaps because it is fundamentally a rather European film about unhappiness and failure. It is sensitively made and compelling, however, and over the years has quietly assumed the status of a minor fantasy classic.

So, too, has an unusual English essay in the well-bred ghost-story film, *Dead of Night* (1945), featuring six brief, supernatural tales, linked by a strange story of an architect's recurrent nightmare which at the very end (sometimes missed, because the final credits have already rolled) turns out to be possibly true. Two of the best stories are directed by Cavalcanti: "Christmas Party" where a girl comforts a sobbing child in another room near where the party is being held, only to learn that he had been murdered years ago by his sister; and "The Ventriloquist's Dummy", the most famous of the episodes, where Michael Redgrave plays the nervous ventriloquist who descends into madness as his dummy comes to life; eventually the ventriloquist speaks and acts with all the mannerisms of the dummy who has possessed him. But the strongest of all is probably "The Haunted Mirror", directed by Robert Hamer, in which a rather suburban couple in the twentieth century are influenced by an old

mirror within which a powerful and sinister nineteenth-century atmosphere is reflected, eventually both firing and destroying the soul of the boring young modern husband.

The film is extremely restrained, though atmospheric in its depiction of largely upper-middle-class horrors. Horror films were heavily censored in the UK from 1937 to 1950 (given an "H" certificate to restrict them to people of sixteen or over), or as in the case of *Freaks* and *Island of Lost Souls*, banned outright. The release of "H" certificate films was totally banned between 1942 and 1945, so the making of *Dead of Night* (while the war was still on) was an act of courage, and it is not surprising if parts of it seem so tasteful today as to be almost prissy. The endeavour was a success, and the censor rewarded an obviously good film by merely giving it an "A" certificate – it could be seen by younger people in the company of adults.

Val Lewton

This book has been looking at sometimes good but usually fairly conventional fantasies produced by the commercial cinema in the 1940s. But in the middle of all this was one small oasis of the unusual: the low-budget, low-key horror movies produced by Val Lewton for RKO Radio between 1942 and 1945, and made by a small, fairly autonomous unit, saving money where possible by using little-known contract actors and already existing studio sets. Lewton worked with three directors on these films: Jacques Tourneur (*Cat People*, 1942; *I Walked with a Zombie*, 1943; *The Leopard Man*, 1943); Mark Robson (*The Seventh Victim*, 1943; *The Ghost Ship*, 1943; *Isle of the Dead*, 1945; *Bedlam*, 1946); and Robert Wise (*The Curse of the Cat People*, 1944; *The Body Snatcher*, 1945). Though all of them have uncanny moments, four of the films are not fantasy at all: *Leopard Man*, *Ghost Ship*, *Body Snatcher*, *Bedlam*. The remainder operate a little precariously on the ambiguous borderline between true fantasy (magic is at work in the world) and psychological melodrama (the mind can conjure up strange shapes). Three of these films, all excellent, are discussed in the filmography. Here I discuss the work of Jacques Tourneur, who arguably was the most successful of the three directors in imprinting his own personality on films which were essentially designed by an intelligent committee.

The first point to note about all nine Lewton productions, including those directed by Tourneur, is that they reinforce the pattern we have already outlined in 1940s Hollywood fantasy: good taste, restraint, a certain staginess. (The exception, the creature movies from Universal, were a little more direct – *Wolfman* reveals its rather slender horrors almost face on.) But for all the praise that has been lavished on Lewton's films for their tactfulness, it is not for this reason they are remembered. Rather, it is a kind of breathless, claustrophobic, shadowy quality – a sense of impotence in the face of ill-defined menaces that may be purely subjective, but which nevertheless create a neurotic, high-strung tension, and finally even terror.

Cat People, photographed like many of the best Lewton films in a highly-wrought style of chiaroscuro – lots of shadows and highlights – by Nicholas Musuraca, tells of a woman fashion designer (Simone Simon), with a Serbian background, who fears that she may be a were-cat; she falls in love and marries, but will not give herself sexually to her husband because the orgasmic release may bring about her transformation into a beast, a panther creature. The sexual element is hinted at, rather than explained in so many words. She goes to see a psychiatrist, who seems to understand her nature. Meanwhile, the husband is attracted to another woman. The other woman is menaced (though not actually hurt) by a half-glimpsed panther; the psychiatrist, attempting to seduce the wife, is attacked by a cat-creature and wounds it with his sword stick before he dies of his injuries. The film ends with Irena, the wife, releasing a panther from the zoo – it is immediately hit by a car – and then dying.

Fundamentally, all this is the lurid romanticism of a story from a pulp-magazine like *Weird Tales*, but much has been done (the use of a picture by Goya and a poem by John Donne, for example) to make it "artistic". The strength of the film is in its symbolic representation of sexual repression, though the Freudian elements are perhaps a little obtrusive, with phallic symbols like sword-canes and keys protruding randomly whenever Irena is around. Also, Tourneur is a masterful evoker of atmosphere, most notably in the scene where Alice (the other woman) is swimming in a deserted indoor pool and suddenly feels menaced (her robe is torn to shreds, apparently by claws), and the scene where again she senses herself followed walking through the park; a careful build up of tension ends in what appears to be the hiss of an attacking cat – but it is only the air-brakes of an approaching bus, on which she escapes.

Like *Cat People*, *I Walked with a Zombie* implies a supernatural explanation for events, but allows the psychological explanation as a let-out for rationalist audiences. The film has one of the several deceptively garish titles imposed on Lewton by RKO (he delighted in finding literate solutions to the quandaries such coarse titles placed him in). In fact *I Walked with a Zombie* is delicate, almost insubstantial in its evocation of eeriness. The story, which is consciously modelled on Charlotte Brontë's *Jane Eyre*, tells of a nurse hired to care for the trance-like wife of a plantation owner in Haiti. The black islanders believe she is a zombie, a member of the living dead, and the film's most extraordinarily atmospheric sequence shows the nurse and the somnambulistic wife walking at night through rustling cane-fields, past hanging voodoo symbols, to seek help from the local witch-doctor who, in an about-turn of amazing implausibility, turns out to be the wife's mother-in-law. She has been feeding the superstitious fears of the natives as a way of persuading them to take orthodox medical treatment!

The film uses its many black actors with a dignity unusual for the time. Darby Jones is compelling as the tall, sombre zombie – not at all a creature to be pitied – who looms up before the white-gowned women as they drift through the sugar-cane. He watches, again, as the wife is carried into the sea at the end, having been killed by the drunken brother-in-law who loves her. He seems an immobile symbol of a way of being that is ultimately untouched by the melodramatic goings-on of a white world that has only briefly and accidentally brushed against his. It is never established whether or not the wife is genuinely a victim of voodoo, or merely insane. More important, perhaps, is the subtext established by the strongly conflicting images of the film – an ethereal, death-like whiteness on the one hand, and the pulsing voodoo drums on the other, which seem to stand for a life of sexual repression versus a life of sexual warmth.

The Lewton films have been technically influential in showing how a fantastic atmosphere can be created with minimal resources. Possibly, however, they have been still more influential in their linking of fantastic mythologies to the (perhaps) equally superstitious iconography of post-Freudianism. These dark mysteries, flickering at the nervous edges of our everyday vision, come to reflect a turmoil within the human mind.

Meanwhile, back in Europe

It may seem surprising that in Germany the war years bred an appetite for the light fantastic, just as they did in Hollywood. The twenty-fifth anniversary of the famous Ufa studio was due in 1943, and *The Adventures of Baron Münchausen* (1943) was a big-budget spectacular designed to celebrate the event.

Rudolph Erich Raspe's tall stories about the eccentric baron were extraordinarily popular in German-speaking areas and even beyond, and film versions have been made many times, beginning in 1909 in France. The two best Münchausen films are probably this German one of 1943 and the Czech version, featuring a blend of animation and live action *Baron Münchausen* (1961). The director of the German film, the Hungarian Josef von Baky, makes splendid use of the melancholy, pastel tones of Agfacolor in this wry, erotic, adult fantasy. The film begins at a twentieth-century costume ball whose host, Münchausen, turns out to be extremely old (though he looks young and handsome). He has been given the secret of eternal life by the magician Cagliostro for whom he once performed a favour. The film flashes back to the events of Münchausen's youth, which is packed with witty incident, by no means all fantastic. When magical effects do occur, they are treated with a nice matter-of-factness: riding a cannonball into a Turkish fort; a runner who can speed from Turkey to Vienna and back in an hour; a trip to the Moon where people's heads live separate lives from their bodies; a hunting horn whose solemn note gets frozen inside it, to emerge later as it warms by the fire; a ring of invisibility; a picture that comes to life. A swordfight in Venice features flashing light-sabres that outdo those of *Star Wars*. Münchausen is more successful erotically than the plump and ageing Casanova who appears in the film, and does very nicely with Catherine the Great, Elizabeth D'Este of Venice and other great ladies. Elegant, stylish, free-spirited, a touch cold-blooded, the film seems cautiously to belong to the anti-Nazi cause, though its political references (such as reminiscences of revolution in Mexico) are heavily coded.

Around the same year, there were problems in making films in France under the German Occupation, and critics, when some of these works were exported after the war, saw French cinema of the period as "dipping into the world of fantasy, films without hope of the future", as Richard Griffith wrote in *The Film Till Now* (1960 edition). Of *L'Eternel Retour* (1943), directed by Jean Delannoy from a script by playwright and artist Jean Cocteau, a retelling in modern dress of the Tristan and Isolde legend, the critic Richard Winnington wrote: "The pervading mood of defeatism sublimating itself in death...must have made it a pleasure for the Nazis to give permission for this production...the whole dolorous bag of tricks...often superbly beautiful in its execution, but rotted." But he was writing during the sombre years of social realism, when fantasy was often seen as indecent escapism.

This tale of doomed love is enlivened by delicately fantastic images throughout: the black scarf fluttering from the boat, the streaming blonde hair of the lovers (seen by several critics as another sign of Nazism – in fact, Isolde was played by Madeleine Sologne, whose husband was Jewish and in hiding).

L'Eternel Retour now seems a little like a five-finger exercise, made to prepare Cocteau for his own two great fantasy films of the post-war years: *Beauty and the Beast* (1946) and *Orphée* (1950). Both films were quite successful, but they make no concessions to commercialism. Both are very consciously works of art. *Beauty and the Beast*, in fact, begins exactly like a Flemish painting though soon it moves into a more sinister world of fairy-tale as first the father and then the heroine enter the mysterious castle of the Beast, where she expects to sacrifice herself to the creature to save her weak father from the same fate. The castle is a strange, haunted place, with candelabra held by living arms projecting into the dark corridors; there is living statuary, too. The Beast is not quite the vision of ugliness that the old story insists on; his leonine head is almost majestic, and he has a gentleness about him that makes his final transformation to fairy-tale prince perhaps less surprising than it might have been. At the end, in a superbly over-the-top sequence of high romance, he flies through the sky with Beauty to some paradise for sanctified lovers. As an exercise in romantic symbolism, the film is not especially erotic – Cocteau's vision of women tends to be idealized, decorative and other-worldly; he himself found fulfilment in other men, and the Beast/Prince is played by his long-time lover, Jean Marais. But it makes up for this in the consistency of its allegorical texture, stylized, sometimes calm, sometimes macabre, always alive and inventive.

Beauty and the Beast is a film in which all else is subdued to the creation of a world of fantasy. *Orphée* is at once more consciously "literary" and more relevant to everyday life. It seems less cohesive, to be remembered largely for its moments of high fantasy: the black-clothed motorcycle outriders of Death; the mirror whose surface dissolves, giving entrance into the limbo of the dead; the winds of Hell which move people as in a slow-motion dream; the car-radio which plays fragments of poetry (by Apollinaire) as messages from the other world to Orphée. The story retells the myth of Orpheus in modern terms, and sometimes it has a sense of straining for effect and significance. The poet, loved both by his wife Eurydice and by Death herself is, as played by Jean Marais, a little too wooden to explain the intensity of the love he arouses. But as a film about the interpenetration of the visible and the invisible worlds (which is how Cocteau saw it), it remains remarkable, and the "zone" behind the mirror is an extraordinary achievement, quite unlike any stereotypes the viewer might have about Hell, yet somehow convincingly hellish. It is for his eloquence as a designer that Cocteau is likely to be remembered, rather than for his perhaps too-elevated and too-literary views of love and death, which remain those of an armchair romantic for whom a symbol (the rose, the mirror) seems as real as the thing itself.

The year of *Orphée* (1950) revealed the modest beginnings of a different sort of fantastic cinema. The post-war world of progress, technology and the Bomb was creating another kind of mythology altogether.

1950-1967: The SF Boom and After

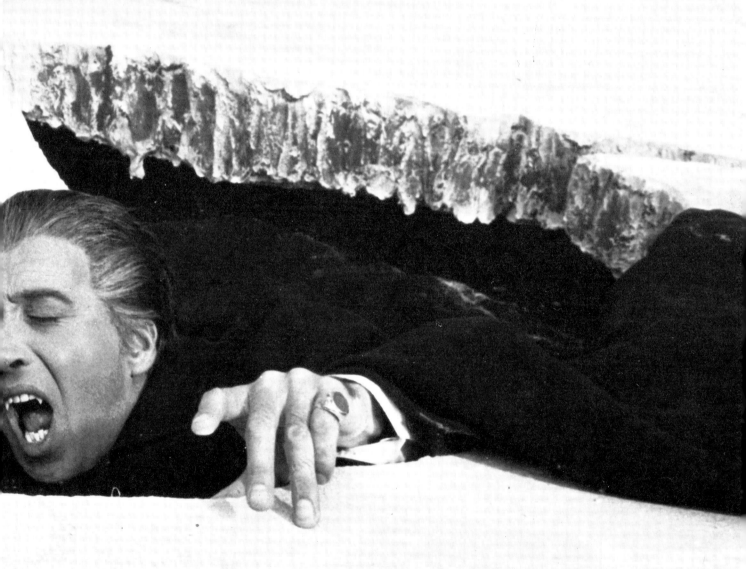

Previous two pages: one of the highlights of fantastic cinema 1950-1967, for many viewers, was the series of Dracula movies from Hammer films, starring Christopher Lee. Here we see Dracula about to crash through the ice at the climax of Dracula – Prince of Darkness *(1965).*

Raymond Massey as the visionary Oswald Cabal, in his observatory in Everytown, declaims about the glories of Man's destiny in outer space. The film is Things to Come *(United Artists, 1936), the major SF film of the 1930s.*

Sherlock Holmes attached great significance to the failure of a dog to bark. The equivalent phenomenon in fantastic cinema was the almost total disappearance of science fiction during precisely the period when SF (in magazine form) was coming of age and finding a devoted audience (to this day, SF fans refer to the 1940s as the Golden Age). Yet the most passionately held of all SF beliefs – that Man would one day conquer space and reach other worlds – received almost no cinematic credence during the 1940s, despite the enormous technological strides being made in the real world during that period – advances that included the use of rocket propulsion on a large scale, and the atom bomb. Indeed, outside the radium gun of *Dr Cyclops*, science of any kind was barely visible in movies of the period. The 1950s were to change all that.

Before looking forward into the technological turmoil of the 1950s, it would be helpful to remember the high points of past SF movies. Even in 1950, *Metropolis* (1926) remained the most toweringly successful futuristic film. *Bride of Frankenstein* (1935) and *The Invisible Man* (1933, see filmography) were the outstanding films giving portraits of the Scientist as Over-Reacher, bringing destruction down upon himself. *King Kong* (1933)

was far and away the best of all monster movies of the non-supernatural variety. By the end of the 1930s, SF was moving down-market into the lurid, melodramatic space fantasies of the serials: *Flash Gordon* (1936) and *Buck Rogers* (1939) are discussed in the filmography.

At a very much more dignified, not to say pompous, level than that of *Flash Gordon*, the 1930s did produce one memorial to the outward urge that was to stand as a solitary beacon for many years: *Things to Come* (1936). This was scripted by H. G. Wells from his own 1933 utopian novel, *The Shape of Things to Come*. The yearning for other worlds would not receive cinematic expression again until *Destination Moon* (1950, see filmography), and even then it had a certain morose flatness about it.

There is nothing morose about *Things to Come*, the most lavish SF production of the 1930s. Rather, it has a soaring if somewhat theatrical exhilaration, in its story of a war-torn future coming slowly (and fortunately, thought Wells) to be ruled by a technocracy of scientists, who then – under the forceful guidance of the visionary Oswald Cabal (Raymond Massey) – seek to send humanity into space, using a gigantic, electric Space Gun. (For years SF fans laughed at this

device as being scientifically bogus, but it appears not dissimilar in principle to the electromagnetic catapult being considered seriously in the 1980s by space engineers at the Massachusetts Institute of Technology and elsewhere.) Nostalgic revisionists who yearn for the good old days try to interfere with Cabal's scheme, arguing (more or less) that if God had meant us to leave Earth he would have fitted us with rockets. A mob whipped up by the revisionist demagogue (significantly a sculptor – the arts versus the sciences again, with Wells having very little time for the former) attempts to prevent the firing of the spacecraft, but it is sent off just in time, followed by a wonderfully overblown but somehow moving speech by Massey, which ends: "Man has no rest and no ending. He must go on, conquest beyond conquest ...at last out across immensity to the stars. And when he has conquered all the deeps of space and all the mysteries of time, still he will be beginning."

The film suffers badly from its preachy script, and from the director's apparent inability to handle actors. William Cameron Menzies had previously been an admirable production designer, and it is in his design that this film has its strength, although poor miniature work mars some otherwise impressive special effects. Wells took a close, paternal interest in the film. Part of the problem seems to have been his determination to avoid stereotype: "You may take it that whatever Lange (sic) did in *Metropolis* is the exact contrary of what we want done here", he records himself as having said. Bad advice.

Apart from the heart-lifting finale, the best parts of the film come early: they are the clouds of foreign bombers sweeping in over the coast just as they were to do in real life five years later, and the dreadful subsequent bombardments. (These scenes were felt to be quite fantastic at the time – real science fiction.) The war continues sporadically into the 1960s until the good life is restored by the Airmen, stern scientific types who quell the local British warloads with Peace Gas!

After a gap of more than a decade since *Buck Rogers*, Man went into space again in *Destination Moon* (1950), which is usually regarded as the forerunner of the interest in SF movies that was to continue until the real-life Moon landing in 1969. Though dull, *Destination Moon* was at least technologically convincing, and it made a profit. A more significant landmark was another film from the same producer, George Pal: *When Worlds Collide* (1951). A modest disaster movie, it shows a handpicked group of survivors leaving in a spaceship just before Earth is destroyed by collision with another planet. The destruction sequences largely use stock footage, though there is rather a jolly shot of a submerged Manhattan hit by a tidal wave. The spaceship takes off, enjoyably, along a railway track laid on a ramp. The film ends with humanity's representatives – the new Adams and Eves – stepping off the ship to face a new world that looks like a very big, colourful painting – which is what it was. It is a likeable, rather silly film, directed only competently by Rudolph Maté, once Dreyer's cameraman on *Vampyr*.

Here come the aliens

The idea of people going out into space had an opposite, of course – the idea of people, or things, coming from space to visit us. This

This spaceship is a new Noah's Ark, which will save a tiny proportion of humanity from the catastrophe described in the film's title: When Worlds Collide *(Paramount, 1951). Note the old-fashioned idea that rockets would be launched on railway tracks.*

has become a major SF theme in its own right, down to *Close Encounters of the Third Kind* and beyond. Some of the more monstrous visitations from space will be discussed later on in the section on creature features. The first "realistic" visit was in Robert Wise's *The Day the Earth Stood Still* (1951). Michael Rennie plays the soft-spoken alien visitor who moves into a small Washington rooming-house in the guise of an ordinary human being – which is what he looks like. His servant, on the other hand, is not ordinary at all: a giant, gleaming, metallic robot called Gort. Most of the humans that Klaatu, the alien, encounters are militaristic swine, but he also meets a nice Mum and her small boy. Finally he is shot but, like Christ, he is returned to life (by his robot colleague) and blackmails us earthlings by telling us that we will all be blown to smithereens unless we give up being aggressive to one another. I have always found this simple-minded and authoritarian approach strange coming from Wise, who is normally impeccably liberal. But given the story's premises, he makes a good, gripping film of it all, and the modest SF effects (including the flying saucer, modelled on alleged descriptions which were very much in the news at the time, for this was the beginning of the flying-saucer boom) are well achieved. The film is considered a classic, but it is surely less than that. It was made, of course, at the height of the Cold War between Russia and America, and perhaps Wise's natural fear of imminent holocaust may excuse his toying with this somewhat intemperate scheme for eliminating the nuclear risk.

Two years later aliens returned once more, this time in force, in *The War of the Worlds* (1953). George Pal was producer again – one of the very few producers who specialized in SF and fantasy – and the director was Byron Haskin, who was also to do a lot of work in this field. He had previously worked in special effects, so he knew about the technical problems.

The original novel of the same title by H. G. Wells was set in England, but the movie was re-located in California. Indeed, little of the Wellsian atmosphere remains. Wells had been concerned to show the fragility of the human psyche and our social and religious institutions in the face of a monstrous invasion, and there is a great deal of idiocy and hysteria among the population in the book. People behave much more nobly in the film, though some of the idiocy remains, as in the rather good scene (not in the book) where a minister walks towards the Martian spacecraft with his Bible aloft, intoning the twenty-third psalm, only to be rapidly fried in a death ray. The film uses a great deal of religious imagery, and implies at the end that it was only God's intervention that saved mankind, a point that would have in-

furiated Wells.

The people in *War of the Worlds* are not very interesting, and the love interest is banal, but the Martians are terrific. We only once see a Martian in the flesh (he's a leathery creature with one huge eye), but the Martian fighting machines – sinuously gliding saucers with serpentine, metallic necks from which green rays emerge – are memorable. The occasional visibility of the wires supporting the models does not seem to matter much. The destruction of Los Angeles is one of the high moments. Though the film is not a patch, in its comparative simple-mindedness, on the sophistication of the original it does at least reinforce Wells's main theme: the vulnerability of the civilization we so smugly assume to be rock solid.

Space opera
With some daring, Hollywood now took the next thematic leap in filmed science fiction. Men had been seen leaving Earth, and aliens arriving on Earth. Why not imitate the most popular area of pulp SF, and set the story on another world altogether? There were certain problems, of course, one being financial. Much more money has to be spent on special sets for off-world movies than for those set on Earth. Such movies, therefore, were only made when the powers-that-be had decided that SF movies were already established as a

Producer George Pal decided, perhaps wisely, not to show the physical appearance of the Martian invaders in The War of the Worlds *(Paramount, 1953), except in one very brief sequence. Ann Robinson as the heroine is about to get a very nasty shock when she turns around.*

commercial proposition.

SF stories featuring adventures in space or in other worlds were already known to the fans as space operas, a term created as analogous to soap operas and horse operas (westerns). The first post-war space-opera film was *This Island Earth* (1955). It is a fast-moving, flamboyant movie that came closer than anything previously in the cinema to capturing the lurid excitements of pulp-magazine SF stories. A very strange, dome-foreheaded person called Exeter (Jeff Morrow) entices nuclear scientist Cal (Rex Reason), by ingeniously sending him weird electronic parts through the post and arousing his interest, to join a secret project. After a while Cal grows suspicious of what is going on at this strange, deserted mansion in the desert, but is kidnapped, along with a female colleague (Faith Domergue), by a flying saucer as he flees. Exeter, it seems, is actually an alien, using the expertise of Earth scientists to help construct an atomic screen to save his home planet, Metaluna, from a space bombardment carried out by their enemies, the Zahgons. The two humans are taken to Metaluna where they are to be brainwashed, but in a fit of conscience Exeter decides to send them home again. This requires outwitting some formidable mutants with lobster-like claws and heads shaped like uncovered brains. Exeter gets them home again, sacrificing his life in the process.

If there is a subtext it is, as the critic Philip Strick has pointed out, that there is so much nastiness out there in space we might be better off pursuing a policy of planetary isolationism. So the logic of the film insists, but its exciting imagery tells a different story of wonder and garish colour. The Metalunan sequences contain some of the best SF imagery in cinema, as meteors rain down upon the planet's pitted, ruined surface and the sky is ablaze with the light of warfare. As vivid adventure – admittedly at a juvenile level – *This Island Earth* remains even today one of the better SF movies.

However, inarguably the greatest SF film of the period is *Forbidden Planet* (1956), whose narrative is every bit as exciting as that of *This Island Earth*, and with considerably more depth – not surprisingly, as the plot was stolen from Shakespeare's *The Tempest*. In the Shakespeare play a ship is wrecked on the shores of Prospero's magic island; in *Forbidden Planet* a spacecraft

Leslie Nielsen as the spaceship captain, with two of his crew, is alarmed at the strange reception they are given by Dr Morbius (Walter Pidgeon) on the remote planet of Altair-IV. The film is Forbidden Planet *(MGM, 1956), and the creature with the gun is Robbie, the cinema's most popular robot prior to* Star Wars.

needing repair lands on the planet Altair-IV, on which lives an Earth scientist, Morbius (Walter Pidgeon), and his daughter (Anne Francis). These are the Prospero and Miranda of the story. The servant sprite, Ariel, has been amusingly transmuted in this version to a robot, Robbie. But it is Caliban who gives the story its resonance – here he is the invisible monster that threatens the lives of the spaceship crew.

The monster turns out (after a genuinely enthralling period of uncertainty during which various baroque pieces of evidence click into place) to be the Monster from the Id, a projection of all the suppressed jealousies and rages of the outwardly rational Morbius, a man who cannot face his own internal conflicts. When his daughter shows sexual interest in the spaceship captain (Leslie Nielsen), the sleeping monster is aroused and once more menace stalks the planetary surface. In an image straight from William Blake, the daughter's tame tiger, having hitherto lain down, in effect, with the lamb, suddenly leaps upon her. The symbolism is powerful, as is the design of the hidden city of the Krell (the race which used to inhabit the planet) whose mysterious power-machines stretch for many kilometres within the planet; this apparently bottomless cavern of whirring machinery itself comes to seem a correlative to the inside of Morbius's brain. As the Krellian machines begin to overload and the Id Monster begins to claw its way through many feet of supposedly impervious alloy while the daughter commits herself to her new lover and the father's brain is almost bursting, the overall effect is stunning. Seldom has a fantastic movie worked so successfully on so many levels: as adventure, as allegory of technological power and its proper use, and as allegory of internal torment and incestuous jealousy. Unfortunately, the casting is not as strong as the conceptual design of the film, but none of the actors disgrace themselves. The effects are splendid, the alien city of the Krell, especially, being one of the most successful evocations of scientific might in SF-movie history.

Time travel
To end this section on travels beyond the here-and-now, we turn to time-travel. George Pal, obviously feeling himself to be on to a good thing with the novels of H. G. Wells after *The War of the Worlds*, adapted another. The result was *The Time Machine* (1960). Again the effect was weakened by using a rather conventionally handsome, inflexible actor as hero: *War of the Worlds* had Gene Barry; *The Time Machine* has Rod Taylor. And once again, the intellectual complexity of the original was pared down to straightforward adventure. The best sequences of the film show the time traveller going into the future, pausing occasionally to watch London changing. Gene Warren and Tim Barr won an Oscar for the well-crafted special effects here. In fact the design is quite successful throughout, but Wells' grim allegory of evolution, in which the working class has become troglodytes who feed cannibalistically upon the capitalist classes they serve, in an act of grotesque symbiosis, is lost. Here the Morlocks are no more than stereotyped, hairy ape-people. The film is not without its moments: the diseased, white sphinx statue of the original is still there, for example. But overall it is an appalling vulgarization of a great novel, and is one of the instances that caused SF fans to wonder if SF cinema would ever rise above its preoccupation with adventure and spectacle to produce something to excite the mind.

Science fiction as anti-science
Fantastic cinema has always been better able to cope with horror, to which imagery and atmosphere are central, than with science fiction, which in its literary form relies on quite complex intellectual structures. These structures are not only built up within single stories or books, but they are carried on from book to book as a series of elaborate intellectual conventions that have a kind of floating existence, independent of particular works. Film-makers, however, are unwilling to trust the kind of sophistication that this assumes in an audience, and thus they often waste valuable time in explaining what hardly needs to be explained or, more commonly, they avoid all elaborate situations where any subtlety of explanation is necessary.

But there is one extremely common thought-structure in science-fiction cinema that is paradoxically unusual in SF literature. This is, that science itself is not to be trusted. Again and again the scientist is seen as somebody who unleashes horrors on the world, or conversely is quite unable to deal with horrors that already exist because he over-intellectualizes; meanwhile the military, for example, steps in and takes direct action. Thus we have the situation where SF movies are fundamentally conservative (there are exceptions, of course), to the point where SF becomes just another form of Gothic. Instead of Gothic being equated with irrational forces, and science fiction with rational forces, the cinema conventionally sees *both* genres as dealing with creatures of darkness, and science as just another form of magic. (Thus in *Forbidden Planet* it is the scientist, Morbius, who is modelled on Shakespeare's magician, Prospero; and it is from the scientist's mind, amplified by the powers of a now-dead scientific race, that the horrors erupt.)

All of this may be a salutary reminder to us that we should not necessarily put our faith in men in white coats, and it was a very natural reminder in an age where the primary miracle of science seemed to be the atomic bomb, but it also contributed to the paranoia of modern life, and this paranoia reached a peak in the 1950s.

The Thing (1951, also known as *The Thing from Another World*) is a good example. It is a basically simple film, complexly directed. A mixed scientific and military group find what appears to be an alien spacecraft deeply embedded in the arctic ice. In attempting to reach it with explosives they ignite it, and it burns away, but the body of an alien is found close by. When thawed out, this comes back to life and, seeking the blood it needs to raise its young from spores (it is a vegetable life form) it murders several of the group. Eventually it is killed by electrocution.

The film is very crisply directed. Although the directorial credit went to former editor Christian Nyby, it is generally understood that this was done as a favour to Nyby to help him become accredited as a director and that most of the real direction was carried out by the film's very famous producer, Howard Hawks. It certainly has many typically Hawks features: fast, wisecracking conversation; overlapping dialogue; a ballsy woman who can give men as good as she gets; and the very confident evocation of menace. The creature (played by James Arness) has unconvincing make-up – it does not even look like the "intellectual carrot" it is described as being – but is wisely kept as a shadowy shape for most of the film. Although the film is cleverly directed for maximum suspense (there is a scene where the Thing is waiting on the other side of a door that is still pretty scary), its main power is as a film about the claustrophobic tension of people under siege, even if there is plenty of comic relief, including an extraordinary fetishistic scene where Nikki (Margaret Sheridan) ties up Hendry (Kenneth Tobey) so that she can talk to him without his running his hands all over her body.

It is the film's military men who save the day; they are down-to-earth, practical types, Carrington (Robert Cornthwaite), the scientist, is a cold-blooded fool who recommends talking to the Thing rather than killing it. He is shown to be quite wrong. When practising what he preaches, he is very nearly killed. In the cold-war context of the period, this looks very much like propaganda of the shoot-first-and-ask-questions-afterwards variety, and it may not be too far-fetched to see the Thing as symbolizing the perceived intelligent inhumanity of the Russian threat. This would give an extra dimension to the film's famous last lines, from the radio journalist broadcasting the story to the world: "Tell the world … to watch the skies. *Keep watching the skies!*" This is an appropriate enough message to an American people worried about the arrival of Russian bombers.

The Thing was based on a famous SF story by John W. Campbell Jr entitled "Who Goes There?", but it dropped the most important part of the original story: that the monster had the ability to change its shape, and thus it was able to kill people and take their place without anyone being the wiser. (This became the central image of the 1982 John Carpenter remake of the film.)

It is curious that this scary metamorphic ability should have been eliminated from the film, for it is the perfect symbol of the worst fear of the Cold War: that America was being undermined by Communist agents *who looked just like us*. The McCarthyist paranoia of the period was, in fact, reflected in a number of films that featured aliens manipulating humans or disguising themselves as human.

When loved ones become monsters...

The first of these was a small-scale film, partly made for children, entitled *Invaders from Mars*, directed by William Cameron Menzies (who had once made the big-budget SF film *Things to Come*), and released in May 1953. A small boy wakes up at night to see a flying saucer arrive and burrow into the ground in his back yard. The next day his father goes to investigate, and comes back oddly changed: emotionally remote and rather violent. He has a mark on the back of his neck. (All of this is filmed from a child's-eye view, with adults tending to loom rather menacingly.) The boy goes to the police, only to find that the police chief has the same mark on the back of his neck. The nightmare continues when his mother arrives, similarly cold and alien. In fact the psychological reverberations of this image go deep; it is surely a fundamental fear that a person's nearest and dearest are basically alien, that they have no love for you, that they belong to another world that you can never join. Fortunately the boy manages to convince an astronomer that his story is true, and after much melodrama and a confrontation (slightly disappointing) with the presiding Intelligence of the Martians, the ship is blown up. In the American version of the film, the closing sequence reveals that it was all a dream – apparently a recurrent dream, for the saucer lands again at the very end. In the European version this material was cut, and the story is told as "real". The film has wonderful moments, and indeed a kind of dream-like quality throughout (the back yard is like a picture from a story-book). A very good moment is the opening up of the sand to reveal the Martian lair beneath, into which the boy and a friend both fall. The original screenwriter, John Tucker Battle, was so furious when the dream-ending was added that he had his name removed from the credits, but in some ways it fits the unearthly quality of the story.

A better known film is *It Came from Outer Space* (1953), released one month later. It was the first of many SF films director Jack Arnold was to make with producer William

WALTER WANGER
CREATES
THE ULTIMATE
IN
SCIENCE-FICTION!

INVASION OF THE **BODY SNATCHERS**

FILMED IN
SUPERSCOPE

ALLIED ARTISTS presents

KEVIN McCARTHY · DANA WYNTER

One of the now rare lobby cards that used to decorate the foyers of cinemas. This one shows Kevin McCarthy finding a "pod" – a vegetable alien in the process of taking on a human appearance – in the classic Invasion of the Body Snatchers *(Allied Artists, 1956). Even though the film was in black-and-white, the lobby cards were in colour.*

Alland, mostly for Universal. For many years it was believed that the Ray Bradbury treatment on which the film was based had been substantially changed by screenwriter Harry Essex, but research by Bill Warren, published in his book *Keep Watching the Skies!*, has shown that the final film adheres quite closely to the famous fantasy writer's own detailed script.

This was one of the first big 3-D movies. It is a strongly atmospheric film, making good use of the desert setting to which Jack Arnold was to return again and again in later SF works. There is something other-worldly and mysterious about the American desert that renders believable almost any strange event that might occur there. The desert itself looks almost like a landscape from some other planet (and was often so used, as in *Robinson Crusoe on Mars*, 1964 – see filmography). It was also a cheap location, not too far from Hollywood.

The story is simple. An astronomer sees what he takes to be a meteor land in the desert, but he finds that it is a spacecraft. Nobody will believe him, but one by one local townspeople are mysteriously changed; the aliens have removed people and are masquerading in their place; eventually his own girlfriend is taken over. It is a haunting little film, sometimes weakly acted, sometimes implausibly melodramatic, but it has many memorable sequences. Interestingly, the

aliens are not hostile invaders. They are frightened beings who want nothing more than to repair their craft and leave as soon as possible.

And then I kissed her...

The best film about aliens taking over people's bodies is Don Siegel's *Invasion of the Body Snatchers* (1956). People in a small Californian town are being taken over, and their relatives and friends realize that something is wrong but do not know what. A doctor, returning to his old home town, is caught up in the nightmare, especially when he finds (with friends) a not quite human, unfinished-looking body lying on a pool table. It turns out that the duplicates are grown from alien pods, like some kind of weird vegetable. But before he can take firm action it is already too late; too many of the townspeople are now not really people at all.

The film is mainly notable for its remorseless quality. What begins as a curious mystery comes closer and closer to terminal nightmare for Doctor Bennell (Kevin McCarthy), as first acquaintances and then friends are taken over and, finally, his lover, as he discovers when he kisses her – or kisses "it". All the horror of alienation from other people, of paranoia (your mother might be a "thing"), of the loss of personality, are present in the film. These would be symptoms, in ordinary life, of schizophrenia. What we effectively have is a situation that forces madness as the only sane response.

Many commentators have insisted on reading the film politically ("the Commies are coming"), and this is certainly valid, but like all good symbols the pod-people stand for more than just one thing; they stand, for example, for the loss of emotion and by implication for the loss of the possibility of love or any human warmth. This is a truly apocalyptic film, because it faces up to the implications of its own central idea in a way that the otherwise similar *Invaders from Mars* and *It Came from Outer Space* did not. Siegel's direction is quietly daring; the film moves very fast, but it gradually changes in style from a low-key, sometimes jokey realism to a more intense, nightmare style later on, ending in the highly stylized shot that everyone remembers of Kevin McCarthy running along a freeway trying to stop the puzzled drivers of passing cars to warn them of the threat to mankind – a dreadful, almost iconographic image of impotence. To soften the film, it was originally released with framing sequences at beginning and end showing McCarthy in hospital (these were additions, shot long after primary shooting was over), and ultimately managing to convince at least one person, a fellow doctor. These sequences are very often dropped from the prints exhibited today, on the grounds that Siegel was never committed to them in the first place.

The image of a human possessed by something inhuman is tremendously strong, almost archetypal in fact. It has never lost its appeal in SF movies and stories, though there was only one more interesting use of the theme in 1950s movies, and that was minor, though bizarre. *I Married a Monster from Outer Space* (1958) took up, in its enjoyably tasteless way, the one question previous films on the theme had politely evaded. What would it be like to have sex with, ugh, a "thing", without knowing it when you began? The bridegroom is duplicated by an alien just before his wedding (short of women, the aliens are in search of breeding stock). Audiences are invariably breathless when handsome Tom Tryon (later to write horror novels himself, in real life) goes out to smoke a cigarette before consummating the marriage; a flash of lightning renders his face momentarily transparent, and the alien features can be seen beneath. Fortunately (phew!) his ruse is discovered and so, rather later, is his spacecraft in which the bodies of many local men are stashed. As the bodies are released, the duplicates dissolve into writhing knots of eel-like, wriggling strands – probably the most inventive low-budget aliens ever put into a film. Actually, by this time we are beginning to feel a bit sorry for the lonely, sex-starved aliens, who have become a bit like the wall-flower who can't persuade a girl to dance with him at the local hop. The film is well

directed, and with a straight face, and it features some moody camerawork. It may well be the best film ever made with a really bottom-of-the-barrel exploitation title.

Creature features

I Married a Monster, of course, puts as much emphasis on the alien appearance as on the human disguise, and in this respect it is a good example of the most popular of all 1950s fantastic genres, the monster movie, or as it used to be called at the drive-in cinema, when I was a teenager in Australia, the creature feature. These had been going strong throughout much of the 1950s, and monster-oriented SF was probably more popular than space-oriented SF. (Some films, of course, like *Forbidden Planet* and *This Island Earth*, had both.)

There is a point to my reference to drive-in cinemas. To a degree, monster movies were deliberately created as erotic aids. In the UK, where drive-ins were unknown, it has never really been possible for people to see monster movies as they were, perhaps, meant to be seen: through the slightly misted windscreen of a car loaded with two or three teenage couples, a flagon of cheap red, and a lot of aphrodisiac gasps as the monsters made their presence felt. Nobody could get the full horrific force of *I Married a Monster from Outer Space* while sitting respectably in a cinema; you needed to be in a car with a girl who wasn't too sure about you anyway giving you a speculative glance whenever the lightning flashed.

The Thing, which made a lot of money, initiated this round of monster movies (there had been previous ones of course, but not many; the most famous was *King Kong*). Then there was a strange gap for a couple of years (filled in only by a few low-budget horrors: *Superman and the Mole Men*, 1951, for example) until *The Beast from 20,000 Fathoms* (1953, see filmography), which was not particularly good. But the dam burst in 1954.

An interesting thing about the monster boom of the 1950s is that the monsters were not supernatural. These films insisted that monsters could *really* exist in the real world, perhaps as almost prehistoric survivals in forgotten corners, more commonly as mutants created by radioactivity from nuclear-weapon testing, or even the actual Hiroshima bomb.

But the first of the 1954 monster movies was an example of the former group. *The Creature from the Black Lagoon* (1954) was an archaic survival located in the remote headwaters of the Amazon. A humanoid creature with gills and, apparently, some intelligence, he is graceful and swift in water, menacing and ungainly on land. Although the effect could not have been created more simply – a man in a suit – this memorable creature became one of the favourite mons-

Stunt man Ricou Browning (he could hold his breath for five minutes) plays the amphibious Gill-Man in Revenge of the Creature *(Universal, 1955), the second of the three films starring this unfortunate prehistoric survival. Here, escaped from a marine park in Florida, he terrorizes the locals.*

ters of the 1950s. The story is that a small team of explorers (one a woman, played by Julie Adams) finds this living fossil and captures it. It escapes, but later kidnaps the woman, in which it is erotically interested. By far the best scenes are underwater, particularly that in which the creature swims below and parallel to the woman (she does not know it is there), mimicking the lazy movements of her body in what is almost a mime of sexual intercourse. In most ways the film is quite conventional, but these and other underwater sequences, excellently directed by Jack Arnold, lift it out of the ordinary. (Steven Spielberg acknowledged his debt to the film when he made *Jaws.*) At the end, of course, the woman is saved. The film was

made in 3-D, and was so successful that a sequel was shot and released a year later: *Revenge of the Creature.* In this the Creature is recaptured and exhibited in an ocean park in Florida, where scientists try to teach him to speak. Eventually he breaks out, kills a man, does a lot of lurking, abducts another lady and is shot. The film does not exploit the pathos in the situation of a natural creature locked up in glass-and-concrete surroundings (the situation treated archetypally in *King Kong*) and is really rather second-rate. This was again directed by Jack Arnold, and in 3-D. The second sequel, *The Creature Walks Among Us* (1956), was not shot in 3-D (the boom was almost over), and is distinctly minor. It was made by John Sherwood whose

best monster movie was *The Monolith Monsters* (1957, see filmography).

Gigantism

The best monster movie of 1954, and one of the best of the decade, was *Them!*, directed by Gordon Douglas. The film was remarkable for jettisoning the more melodramatic aspects of the creature feature, and adopting a low-key, semi-documentary approach (rather like that of the police thrillers of the time) which adds greatly to the realism of the unlikely story. Nuclear tests in the desert create giant, mutated ants, most of which are destroyed in their nest by poison gas, but the queen ant and one male escape, and a new nest is created in the storm drains of Los Angeles. The New Mexico police sergeant, Ben (well played by James Whitmore), who originally discovers the ants, follows them to Los Angeles, and is killed by them while rescuing two small boys trapped in the drain.

The best parts of the film are at the beginning (the mystery of unexplained deaths in the desert is well done, and a subplot involving a little girl terrified by the smell of formic acid is very vivid) and the end (the famous sewer scenes, later reprised in an act of homage by Larry Cohen in *It's Alive*). But there are good moments throughout, especially the evidence given by a supposedly insane aircraft pilot and a babbling wino, both of whom have seen the ants in action. The ants themselves were created with full-scale mechanical models (they are about eight feet long), and while not brilliantly achieved, are quite acceptably convincing.

Nuclear testing also created the monster in one of the most classically bad creature features ever made, *Godzilla, King of the Monsters* (1954), the film that launched Japan's Toho studios on its long and sometimes laughable career of SF movies, mostly about giant creatures.

Godzilla was quite an influential film in America, too, but it was not released there until 1956, at which time it featured cleverly edited-in sequences shot by an American director and featuring Raymond Burr as a reporter, in order to make the film slightly more acceptable to Western audiences. In fact, it was a hit. Like all subsequent Toho creature features, the monsters were played by men in rubber suits. Stop-motion animation, the alternative technique, was simply too expensive. Godzilla was created by the Japanese effects expert Eiji Tsuburaya, who was to make many more monsters before his death in 1970, including *Rodan* in 1956 (see filmography), the film that was to confirm that Toho had struck a rich vein.

Godzilla (the Japanese call him Gojira) is a 400-foot long amphibious dinosaur with fiery breath (not too far removed from the traditional dragon) who makes a mess of Tokyo, munches on trains, and creates the chaotic wasteland that is in fact the opening scene. (Most of the film is flashback.) A reclusive scientist finally eliminates him with an oxygen-destroyer which, for some reason, by depleting sea water of oxygen, disintegrates the creature entirely into its constituent atoms, and the scientist too. However, a first cousin, also called Godzilla, was revived to star in at least twelve sequels, some better, many (including the deplorably lunatic *Godzilla vs the Smog Monster*, 1971) even worse. In most of the sequels Tokyo is squashed again but as the years passed Godzilla's temperament softened. He became a Japanese folk-hero, who grumpily defended them against the ravages of even more villainous monsters.

The understandable Japanese sensitivity to nuclear weapons was quite an important factor in the making of the earlier films, but later the atomic-testing = creation-of-monsters equation was not so prominent. The appalling innocence of these comic-book type Japanese monster movies has won them many devoted fans in the West.

Meanwhile, back in the USA, the actions of irresponsible scientists were also continuing to create monsters, usually based on various members of the family of *Arthropoda*. Of these, the class *Arachnida*, genus *Mygale*, was to star in another desert-based film directed by Jack Arnold: *Tarantula* (1955). Leo G. Carroll, in rather a good performance, plays the scientist trying to develop a new nutrient, which causes gigantism in animals (more meat to feed people with). It also causes acromegaly, a deformity of bone structure, in people, and poor Carroll winds up with a face so twisted as to be barely human. An escaped laboratory spider gets bigger and bigger, conveniently leaving pools of venom at the scenes of its depradations, so that its presence can be deduced before it is even seen. Moody photography early on creates plenty of atmosphere in the desolate locations, but at the end (air force planes destroy the spider with napalm) it's merely silly.

More monsters of the id

A more imaginative and even lower-budget form of monster emerged in *Fiend Without a Face* (1957), in the shape of small creatures that look like human brains, hop wildly about, and attach themselves to people's spinal columns by drilling holes in their necks, through which they suck nervous tissue. At first they are creatures of pure energy, resulting from ill-judged experiments in the amplification of thought-waves. But it is when they materialize that the film really comes to life, giving the lie to the theory that it is always better to suggest than merely to show. There can be no purer surrealism in cinema than the sight of these twitching brain-things, besieging a house full of people, leaping and plopping like possessed frogs. The whole thing has the bizarreness of some mad, medieval allegory, like a triptych by Hieronymus Bosch. The ultimate in anti-intellectual films – there can be few movies where the villains are carnivorous brains – it has understandably developed a cult following.

Sometimes the film industry is like a symbol of the Freudian model of the human mind. The industry's super-ego sees to it that its big-budget productions are respectable, but hidden behind the walls and down in the basement lurks the industry's id, the concealed subconscious, which every now and then explodes into action and throws up images so bizarre as to call into question the rationality of human existence. The continued vitality of fantastic cinema has been largely due to these strange, disreputable leaks from areas of the industry that people would sooner not know about, and *Fiend Without a Face* is a particularly crazed example. Though set in North America, the film is actually a British production.

By 1958 the monster-movie boom was beginning to run out of steam, and smaller companies were beginning to take over from the major studios in this area, as with Roger Corman's unbelievable *Attack of the Crab Monsters* (1957). This is discussed in the filmography along with other monster productions of the period. These include: *The Mysterians* (1957), *Twenty Million Miles to Earth* (1957), *Most Dangerous Man Alive* (1958), *Caltiki – The Immortal Monster* (1959), *Gorgo* (1959), *The Tingler* (1959) and *The Wasp Woman* (1959).

But though temporarily submerged, the monster movie was by no means dead, and it returned triumphantly in 1963, with a lavish production from a major studio: Alfred Hitchcock's *The Birds*.

Monsters that don't look like monsters

The Birds is set in a quiet township on the Californian coast. Out of a clear sky, literally, comes a murderous assault from seagulls, crows, finches – the entire bird kingdom. The birds are not monstrous in appearance; they are just birds. But in other respects they are every bit as much monsters as the giant ants in *Them!*, and the film follows the conventions of the monster movie closely. These conventions move in pre-ordained stages as rigid as the conventions of Greek tragedy, if not as dignified: the establishing of a peaceful normality; the first hints of menace that disturb the calm; the slow build up of tension; the first witnessed attack; and eventually, the apocalyptic finale in which, in the old days, the monster would meet its end (or their end, if there were more than one), but in which, since *The Birds*, the menace more commonly spreads out, possibly to engulf the world. That is to say, *The Birds* marked a turning point in the cinema's attitude towards the vul-

nerability of our lives, and the possibly vengeful power of nature. Humanity's position at the top of the evolutionary tree has looked very shaky in many movies since. The message of post-*Birds* monster movies is usually that mankind has had its chance and muffed it. Something else will take over.

There is very much more to Hitchcock's movie than fierce birds, of course. There is a subplot involving the way in which people put other people in mental cages, on which the bird plot ironically comments. There is the interesting manner in which the too-perfectly groomed heroine, something of a bird herself as played by Tippi Hedren, seems to precipitate events by her arrival in the town, which coincides with the growth of passion within her for a man. There is a Freudian subtext here. But it is the birds – whose attacks are masterfully choreographed, with a combination of real birds and models designed by Walt Disney's old colleague Ub Iwerks – that everyone quite properly remembers. It is a masterly film.

Since *The Birds*, a new genre of monster movie has opened up, in which the monsters are existing animal species that suddenly, apparently irrationally, turn upon man – rather than giants or prehistoric survivals or aliens. Among such species, and the films in which they have starred (the list is restricted to films discussed elsewhere in this book) are: sharks (*Jaws*), whales (*Orca*), piranha (*Piranha*), ordinary ants as opposed to giant ones *(Phase IV)*, roaches (*Bug, Creepshow*), locusts (*Exorcist II*), earthworms (*Squirm*), spiders (*Kingdom of the Spiders*), bees (*The Swarm*), frogs (*Frogs*), cats (*Inferno, The Uncanny*), dogs (*Mephisto Waltz, Devil Dog, Cujo*), wolves (*Wolfen*), rats (*Pied Piper, Ben, Willard*), bats (*Chosen Survivors, Nightwing*), buffalos (*White Buffalo*), rabbits (*Night of the Lepus*), trees (*Evil Dead*) and even tomatoes (*Attack of the Killer Tomatoes*). In fact, some of these creatures *are* mutants, and others are supernaturally inspired, but in every case they look – more or less – like ordinary, familiar species.

A supernatural monster

Supernatural monsters, as opposed to existing or scientifically created monsters, were rather rare in films of the 1950s. In the filmography you will find the Scots laird who is trapped in the shape of a giant frog in *The Maze* (1953), and the witchcraft-created flying stone eagles in *Night of the Eagle* (1962), but the most interesting appeared in a splendidly sinister, quiet little film called *Night of the Demon*, also known as *Curse of the Demon* (1957). It was directed by Jacques Tourneur, who proved here that he did not require the assistance of producer Val Lewton in order to create first-class work in the fantasy genre.

The film is based on a nasty, scholarly hor-

The poster advertising Night of the Demon (Columbia, 1957) suggests an ambiguity in the film ("victim of his imagination...?") hardly supported by the picture of the demon in the middle. Note that this mild and sensitive film received an "X" certificate.

ror story by the English writer M. R. James, "Casting the Runes", and despite its American hero (Dana Andrews) the film is very English too. Niall MacGinnis gives a brilliantly relaxed, jovial, almost likeable performance as the warlock with the power to unleash demons upon those who cross him. First he slips them a parchment covered with runes; if it blows away (and the parchment flutters and dances in its efforts to escape), the victim is doomed. Only if he hangs on to the parchment and then passes it on to another, will he be saved. The warlock, Karswell, is investigated by an American psychic researcher, a sceptical fellow, who finds it difficult to believe the mounting evidence of Karswell's powers.

The film opens with the demon (a well animated monster built by Wally Veevers) pursuing and then dismembering an unfortunate professor. Tourneur has stated in interviews that he would have preferred to show his horrors by suggestion only, as he did in the old days with Val Lewton, and that his philistine producer forced the demon upon him. Well, maybe so, but structurally it works very well for us actually to see the creature, which closely resembles the medieval woodcut that we are later shown. It puts the audience in the position of non-sceptics, and there is an added *frisson* for us in watching the American take what *we* know are unwarranted risks. (There is something of a critical con-

spiracy to argue otherwise: Carlos Clarens, the most respected critic of horror films but a frightful snob, writes: "...they inserted some atrocious shots of a demon at the very outset...it is a tribute to the director's skill that his movie survives such a monumental blunder." Subsequent critics have mostly followed Clarens like sheep.) In fact, the demon is so well integrated into the film that it seems very likely that Tourneur was mistaken in his memory, or perhaps he wanted to impress the intellectuals. Our knowledge of its existence serves to make Dana Andrews' headlong rush through woodlands halfway through the film, pursued by a glowing ball of light (the beginnings of the demon's manifestation, as we already know) an intensely frightening *tour de force*. This scene follows another, beautifully rendered, where Andrews has broken into Karswell's country seat, and in a dark room meets a domestic cat that suddenly metamorphoses into a panther.

At the end, Karswell has the parchment passed back to him in a train just entering Clapham Junction station. He *knows* this has been done, but the paper blows away, and he pursues it down the railway tracks in a stunning sequence of nightmare, never quite catching it. The demon materializes and so (for the sake of rationalists among the audience) does a train; whatever the cause, he is thoroughly demolished.

Grant Williams, the now tiny hero of The Incredible Shrinking Man *(Universal, 1957), stares longingly at the garden into which he will soon be small enough to slip. A little later he will disappear altogether.*

The film is consistently witty, uncanny, blending the domestic and the mysterious with great élan. Karswell has such charm (which Dana Andrews, as the investigator Holden, lacks) that there is a sense in which we feel that he is being unjustly persecuted, and though he is really a wicked old fellow we are somewhat appalled at his violent demise. One of the film's best scenes shows him entertaining local children with clown's magic tricks, and a moment later conjuring up real magic (a violent storm) for Andrews.

Night of the Demon, a true classic of the genre, is delicately poised between two fantastic traditions: the English ghost story tradition with its subtle intimations of disturbing forces at the fringe of one's vision (this is a tradition of horrors of the mind), and the later tradition of the violently unnatural that can uncaringly or cruelly maim us (this is a tradition of horror of the body).

Horror of the body

During and after the Vietnam war, the image of our bodies as intensely vulnerable to decay and mutilation reached its climax (some would say its nadir) in the work of George Romero, David Cronenberg and others. Such images, however, did not spring up by parthenogenesis; they were the wild children of an already exisiting family of images, a family with a history.

Mention has already been made of the scientist in *Tarantula* whose work dreadfully deforms him, when he is forcibly injected with his own serum. He is an early example of a long cinematic line of victims of technology, people who are rendered into monsters, whose bodies are changed or damaged, sometimes subtly, sometimes horribly. The saddest of all monsters is the one that was once exactly like you or me.

We can take five out of a number of possible examples in the late 1950s and the early 1960s. The first, from a small, newly revived British studio, Hammer, is *The Quatermass Xperiment* (1955), known in America as *The Creeping Unknown*.

The film was based on the television serial *The Quatermass Experiment*, the first of three serials by Nigel Kneale broadcast on BBC Television between 1953 and 1959, featuring Professor Quatermass who comes up against scientific mysteries of an extremely Gothic variety. All three were later filmed by Hammer.

The strange spelling, *The Quatermass Xperiment*, was a gimmick. The big "X" in "Xperiment" referred to the "X" censor's certificate they correctly expected to be given for the film's horror content. Richard Wordsworth played the astronaut who returns from space with a strange fungal infection which eventually takes over his entire body, turning him into a kind of blob that is electrocuted by Quatermass as it clings to the wall of Westminster Abbey. By far the best parts of the film involve the earlier stages of Wordsworth's appalling metamorphosis: he gives a splendidly tortured performance as the man barely able to communicate his humanity (he only speaks two words) even to his wife. His arm is the first part to change; there is a good moment when it absorbs a cactus growing in a pot, and he has to conceal the half-arm half-cactus beneath his trench coat.

The special effects are really rather poor, though Les Bowie (Hammer's top effects man for many years) performed miracles on the tiny budget. But Wordsworth's shambling, pathetic performance is memorable, and the film set the studio on its feet and encouraged it to follow on with many more man-into-monster films. (The direct sequels – see filmography – were *Quatermass II*, 1957, and *Quatermass and the Pit*, 1967.)

The subtext – science can reduce men to beasts – was crude enough, though rendered more compelling by the fact that the supposed hero, Quatermass (not very well played by Brian Donlevy), is unsympathetically hard-headed, and quite prepared to continue with the space programme no matter what the cost in human suffering.

A film that evoked the paranoia of man-injured-by-technology with greater precision and flair, was the excellent *The Incredible Shrinking Man* (1957), the best of Jack Arnold's SF films for Universal. It is based on a screenplay by Richard Matheson (his first) from his own novel, *The Shrinking Man*.

Grant Williams plays the man who, after passing through a radioactive cloud (a classic

of pseudo-science, this) begins to shrink. The paranoia, however, swells, by stages. First, it is sexual, as his size relative to that of his wife continues to diminish; she comes to seem a looming and gross creature, and her behaviour to him is patronizing. (Later he is to have a rather sentimentally conceived affair with a circus midget.) As he becomes smaller still, he moves into a doll's house, and when attacked by the family cat, beats a hasty retreat to the cellar. This prosaic basement, seen from his shrinking perspective, becomes a surrealist jungle of terrors, with monstrous waterfalls (a leaking boiler) and a giant spider. He is like a down-market Lear in a suburban blasted heath, struggling with madness, but continuing his odyssey with amazing strength of will. His insistence on his humanity even when microscopic is touching: clinging to humanness is one of the hallmarks of the man-into-monster film. At the end, he slips through a grating on the cellar window into the garden where he finally shrinks away altogether as the wind plays through the autumn leaves – a more satisfying close than the melodramatic end of the novel where he shrinks into another universe to continue his adventures. The effects of miniaturization (achieved as usual in this sort of film by building giant sets) are very good.

Less disturbing, but crudely enjoyable, was the grotesque film *The Fly* (1958), directed by Kurt Neumann and starring Al (David) Hedison as an unfortunate scientist. As SF it is just as absurd as *Shrinking Man* (there was very little real science in SF movies of the period), but as a surrealist nightmare, the story of a man who (through an error in an experiment in matter transmission) exchanges his head and arm for the head and leg of a fly, it is quite successful. Surprisingly lavish production values and a robustly forthright approach to the idiocies of the story make the whole thing good fun, and there is a sympathetic shudder from the audience when the fly-headed scientist puts his new head in a steam press and commits suicide. That is not the end, however; afterwards we see a fly (with the scientist's now tiny head) trapped in a spider's web shouting "Help me" in a little high-pitched scream. As the critic John Brosnan has pointed out, this raises the question: if both fly and scientist have the scientist's brain, where is the fly's brain? A box-office success, the film spawned two sequels, *Return of the Fly* (1959) and *Curse of the Fly* (1965), neither especially distinctive.

The Fly went as far as any film of the period in evoking the horror of the body in terms of disgusting metamorphosis. But changes to the body could be much more subtle, and this was the case with *The Damned* (1961, *These are the Damned* in USA), made in England for Hammer by the celebrated director Joseph Losey, who was

The doctor's daughter in Les yeux sans visage *(Lux, 1959) always wears a mask to hide her scarred face. Yet somehow the actress, Edith Scob, contrives to play the role very expressively, even "without a face".*

undergoing hard times after his exile from Hollywood as an undesirable Communist-sympathizer during the McCarthy period.

In a secret government experiment, children have been exposed since birth to radioactivity. Their home is a hidden re-search installation in caverns off a cliff-face on England's south coast. Now highly radioactive themselves, their education is carried out by closed-circuit television. They have an amazingly low body temperature. They have been created as the possible progenitors of a new race of mankind after the present race is destroyed in the ex-pected nuclear holocaust. The image of these icy youngsters is both literally and metaphor-ically chilling; they do not completely under-stand their own predicament, which is that the only world in which they can safely live out their lives is a world destroyed by atomic war.

The film opens in a seedy resort town terrorized by roaming gangs of youths – thus evoking an image of social breakdown at the outset – and it is a couple fleeing such a gang (sadistically led by Oliver Reed in one of his earliest roles) who stumble across the impris-oned children, and without understanding their own danger (they are fatally contamin-ated) try to help them escape. A scientist just as cold-blooded as the children lets this hap-pen, and has the couple shot from a helicop-ter that hovers above them like a hawk, in a visually haunting scene, as they try to escape by boat. The distributors, alarmed at the poli-tical implications and at the fact the film was not categorizable as straight horror, delayed the film's release for several years, cut the British release print from 96 to 87 minutes and cut the American print to 77 minutes – Americans being presumably more suscep-tible to all this Commie propaganda.

Even in its ruined state, the film remains a stark, ironic, stylish study in human manipula-tion, with a number of strong visual symbols – notably the stern, abstractly humanoid sculp-

tures made by the woman played by Viveca Lindfors who, when she begins to guess what is happening within the bird-haunted cliffs, is ruthlessly executed by the scientist, while her statues look on in silent reproach.

Breaking the rules

In all of these films dealing with the horrible things that can happen to the human body (almost invariably because of scientists doing nasty or silly things), there was an unwritten law. You could show physical deformity; you could show mental anguish; but you could not show physical torment. Then along came an eccentric Frenchman, who had once directed a bloodcurdling documentary about abattoirs (*Le Sang des Bêtes*, 1949), who broke all the rules by using slaughterhouse imagery in a film about people. *Les Yeux sans visage* (1959), directed by Georges Franju, is really too consciously artistic a film to fit comfortably into the horror category, but the American distributors decided to emphasize the Sadean aspects of the story by retitling the film *The Horror Chamber of Dr Faustus*. (The French title literally means *Eyes Without a Face*, which is how it was known in the UK.)

Yeux sans visage does, in a sense, fall into a familiar category: the mad surgeon film (*Mad Love* and *Frankenstein* are others). All such films play in a remote sort of way on our fear of the surgeon's knife, but Franju, in a convincing clinical sequence, went one step further and showed the surgeon operating. The story deals with the terrible guilt he feels at his daughter's facial disfigurement in a car accident for which he was responsible. He uses his nurse, who is also his lover, to decoy or kidnap beautiful women and bring them to his clinic, where he literally removes the skin from their faces and attempts to graft a new face on his daughter. The grafts do not take. Eventually the daughter collapses under the strain of all this, stabs the nurse, and releases half-crazed experimental dogs on her father, the master they hate. In synop-sis, the film does indeed sound like a sadistic exploitation movie whose only interest today might be its adumbration of the more visceral horror which was only to enter the cinema in a widespread way a decade later. In fact, *Yeux sans visage* is both more and less than this. Less, because the surgical sequences are not, in fact, unbearable at all; they are executed with moderate tact, and to a grave-ly classical musical score by Maurice Jarre; far more shocking scenes (admittedly in a very different context) are regularly shown in television documentaries. More, because the emotional centre of the film is not the surgery – it is the wistful, haunting performance of Edith Scob as the masked daughter whose face we do not see, and the delicate imagery with which she is associated. (Scob's feat of acting "without a face" is extraordinary.) The

Sinister Robert
Helpmann as Dr
Coppelius,
manufacturer of
magical dolls and
spectacles to watch
them through, in Tales
of Hoffman (London
Films, 1951).

film revolves around the twin poles of tenderness and cruelty (father and daughter love
each other deeply), and as all good films about the horror of the body must be, it is in
part about the horror of the mind. (The
daughter retreats, finally, into madness). It is
also a film about victims – the father as much
as the daughter. It is sad that, when the film
has been imitated, its Grand Guignol horrors
rather than its poetry and its psychological
tenderness have been used as a model.

Extravaganzas

Fantasy is a term that is often associated with
childhood, and it may strike some readers as
paradoxical that so many of the fantasies discussed above were made for adults only. Of
course, even children's fantasies traditionally
have a dark side, and many are the local
libraries that have attempted to ban the fairy
stories of the Brothers Grimm and others as
"unsuitable for children" although they were
designed for them. However, even during
the SF and monster boom of the 1950s, the
major studios in the UK and the USA did not
abandon fantasies made for all the family,
and it is worth looking at some of the key
moments in this line of development.

No matter how bright and colourful these
fantastic extravaganzas were, the dark side
of life still showed itself. Perhaps fantasy can
only be nurtured upon the polarities of dark-

ness and light – light may mean nothing without the piquant contrast of its opposite. This
was especially true of the fantasies of the
British producer/writer/directors Michael
Powell and Emeric Pressburger, who
worked on nineteen films together. (Powell
appeared earlier in this book as one of
several directors of the 1940 remake of *Thief
of Bagdad.*) They were a flamboyant pair,
and many of their films were unusually bizarre and stylized for the period. Their out-
and-out fantasies were *The Red Shoes* (1948)
and *The Tales of Hoffman* (1951), the former
revolving around a ballet, and the latter
being a filmed version of an opera by Offenbach.

In *The Red Shoes*, Moira Shearer plays the
young ballerina whose life is totally domin-
ated by the sinister impresario Lermontov;
she is torn between him and a struggling
young composer. The high romance of the
telling is intensified by the luridly glowing
Technicolor of the film, which must have
been seen as something of a contrast to the
grey austerity of post-war Britain. Although
clearly meant as a film for all the family, it is,
in fact, a rather heightened, symbolic study
of the destruction of lives in the cause of art.
This morbidity is emphasized by the film's
centrepiece, the Ballet of the Red Shoes
(which run away with and totally exhaust
their wearer) in which Shearer dances, and
which comments so clearly on the action of
the story. Stylishly fantastic, in its preoccupation with death as (apparently) the true end
of art, the film is reminiscent of the symbolically doom-laden films of Jean Cocteau.

Much the same sort of comment can be
made about the hugely enjoyable, lush, decadent *Tales of Hoffman*. This is an opera that
was obviously congenial, in its *fin-de-siècle*
world-weariness, to the psychological make-
up of its directors. What is so much fun about
the amazingly sinister worlds they create is
that they are, at bottom, so very British –
even jovial. There are three acts in the
opera, each of which has Robert Rounseville
as the young man who falls in love with a
beautiful woman, only to find the gaunt figure
of Robert Helpmann as his Evil Genius – like
a medieval, allegorical figure of Death himself – coming between him and the consummation of his desires. In each episode,
the morbid excesses are so melancholy and
Gothic – such swishings of cloaks and heav-
ings of sighs and clapping of hands to fore-
heads – that one can almost hear Powell and
Pressburger giggling behind the scenes as
they manipulate their puppets. The most
striking of the three sequences, in fact, centres on precisely this image: Helpmann here
plays Dr Coppelius, the grotesque old
spectacle-maker, who gives Rounseville
some glasses that cause him to believe that a
life-size puppet is a living, breathing woman.
We, the audience, are allowed to alternate

our vision between what Coppelius sees (a limp scarecrow in the arms of a lovesick lunatic) and what Rounseville sees (a goddess). It is an aristocratically cynical view of human folly, as indeed are the voluptuously swooning events of the entire opera. (Though the film possesses, in the person of Pamela Brown, a bracingly British commonsense as well.) *Tales of Hoffman*, the most disheartening of fantasies in its subject matter, usually sends its audiences home cheerful. (Michael Powell was to make good use of all this cinematic experience with love, death, sex and spectacle, when he made the remarkable *Peeping Tom*, 1960, a non-fantasy horror film about a shy, impotent, homicidal voyeur who specializes in filming the frenzies of fear in his female victims before he kills them – perhaps a cynical comment on the whole horror-film genre.)

Fantasy for children

Not many people know that Dr Seuss, author of *The Cat in the Hat* and other moving poems for children, once wrote an excellent motion picture. *The 5,000 Fingers of Dr T* (1953) is regarded by some people as the invisible fantasy classic of the 1950s. Almost everybody who sees it likes it, but almost nobody sees it. Prints exist, but they are very seldom shown. The film presents itself as a small boy's nightmare, and Dr Seuss was astute enough to know that children are more interested in nightmares than dreams. Hans Conreid plays the sadistic piano teacher who kidnaps children (especially those who are lazy about practising their scales) and uses them as slaves in the fantastic kingdom he rules. It really is a very odd film indeed. The musical numbers sometimes slow it down, but the warped inventiveness of the sets alone should ensure it some sort of immortality among *aficionados* of the fantastic; they were the work of the art director, Rudolph Sternad. Particularly notable is the world's largest piano, on which the 5,000 fingers of the 500 kidnapped children have to toil.

From 5,000 to 20,000. I had always assumed that the rush of filmed adaptations of Jules Verne novels in the 1950s must have been because his books came out of copyright fifty years after his death in 1905. That does not, however, explain the release of *20,000 Leagues Under the Sea*, a Walt Disney production, in December 1954. It seems at least a month too early.

Whatever their motivation, the Disney studios must have been delighted with the enthusiastic response to the film, which proved once and for all (though it was not their first live-action feature, which was *Treasure Island*, 1950) that the way ahead for Disney was in live-action movies, as animated features became ever more expensive to produce. Often considered Disney's most successful non-cartoon fantasy, *20,000 Leagues*

may have been a little over-rated, though Richard Fleischer's direction is more than adequate, and the set-pieces – especially the celebrated battle with the giant squid – are well staged. Also in the film's favour is a good performance from James Mason as the obsessed Captain Nemo, an anarchist hero alone against the world, who uses his submarine (the *Nautilus* is a magnificent piece of Victoriana in its internal decor) to sink warships. On the debit side is the character of Ned Land, the harpoonist – badly scripted, and badly played by Kirk Douglas, as a noisy vulgarian. Partly because of Douglas, much of the sombre, Byronic quality of the original novel is lost, though James Mason's darkly intelligent performance helps here.

The film ends with Nemo's suicide, as his atomic submarine explodes in a symbolic mushroom cloud. Verne's submarine, of course, was not nuclear-powered, but the Disney version of the story is the one most people remember (the original novel is extremely long and in many ways dated), and the amusing result was that when the first real-life nuclear submarine was named *Nautilus*, the US Navy's homage to Verne was inaccurate. The giant squid was built by Bob Mattey, a genius at mechanically operated special effects, and many years later Steven Spielberg, remembering the squid, hired Mattey to build "Bruce", the mechanical shark used in the filming of *Jaws*. Twenty-eight men were needed to operate the squid, which worked by a mixture of hydraulics, compressed air and electronics.

Animated creatures

The most famous animated creature in film history was not the giant squid; it was King Kong. Willis O'Brien was the man who built that. In 1946 O'Brien was working on another giant-ape movie (*Mighty Joe Young*) and hired a young assistant, Ray Harryhausen. During the 1950s it became clear that Harryhausen had inherited O'Brien's mantle as premier stop-motion animator in the film business – a position which, in the eyes of many, he continues to hold today.

Stop-motion animation is done by photographing models, a frame at a time, to give the illusion when the film is projected that they are in motion (the models are normally constructed around flexible armatures), and then optically combining the results (often using a technique called travelling matte) with live action. When live action is combined with the animated miniature, tricks can be played with scale, so that a model less than a foot high can appear to loom up like a colossus.

O'Brien, who died in 1962, lived long enough to see some of his former pupil's success, though most of the early films on which Harryhausen worked were comparatively minor. Two are discussed in the filmography:

The Beast from 20,000 Fathoms (1953) and *Twenty Million Miles to Earth* (1957). But in 1958 Harryhausen, along with the producer with whom he nearly always worked, Charles Schneer, had a breakthrough film, *The Seventh Voyage of Sinbad.* Very much an exotic fairy-tale, largely aimed at children but with a love interest as well, it turned out (the old cliche is appropriate) to appeal to children of all ages from nine to ninety. The time was obviously ripe for this sort of romantic fable based loosely on traditional mythologies. The Italians had just had a big success with a truly dreadful film, featuring muscleman Steve Reeves, called *Hercules* (1957, see filmography), and many Hercules films were to follow, each with at least one monster for the giant-thewed hero to subdue. *Hercules* was very successful in the USA, too.

Seventh Voyage is amusing, but from the beginning the trouble with Harryhausen's fantasy films, no matter who directed them (this time it was Nathan Juran), has been the weak, highly episodic scripts. These seem to be dashed off rather mechanically to link together already-planned sequences featuring people versus monsters. In this case the animated creatures include a Cyclops (a one-eyed giant with hairy, satyr-like legs), a dragon, a roc (a monstrous bird with two heads), a four-armed snake-woman and a sword-fighting skeleton. The Harryhausen-animated bits are great fun, and often very well done, but somehow his films seldom achieve the really magical. The screenplays are blunderingly literal-minded, and the actors (especially Kerwin Mathews as Sinbad) come from a long way down the hierarchy and were presumably hired cheap. Films of this kind are adroit, but rather crude, too. It may be paradoxical to suggest it, but although they have devoted much of their lives to the craft, Harryhausen and Schneer seem to have no more than a novice's appreciation of what elements constitute true fantasy. For one thing, *Seventh Voyage* never suggests anything by implication, by creating subtleties of atmosphere. The whole point of animated fantasies of this sort is typically to *show* the fantastic straight on and in a good light – and in this case, in colour. (This was the first colour film made as a showcase for stop-motion animation sequences.)

There are great difficulties in combining animation with live action. One feels for poor Mathews, who had to learn a sword-fight stroke-perfect, and use it against empty air (the skeleton he fights was added afterwards), while looking (a difficult job even for more accomplished performers) as if some-

One of Ray Harryhausen's most spectacular creations: the brass giant Talos in Jason and the Argonauts *(Columbia, 1963) pursues the crew of the* Argos.

thing was there. By this time, Harryhausen had christened his animation process Dynamation; its unusual feature (though it was by no means a Harryhausen exclusive) was that in the optical combination of live action and animation he would sometimes have live action in the background, then the animated model in the mid-ground, and more live action in the foreground. Even comparatively sophisticated audiences, used to animated figures against a real background, were impressed by this sandwiching effect, which certainly heightened the illusion of reality. On the other hand, the models in *Seventh Voyage* have a slightly mechanical feel to them, as they almost always do in this kind of film. This is partly because every individual frame of animation is entirely still, whereas in ordinary films individual frames are very often blurred. When a succession of individually motionless frames is run through a projector, a stroboscopic effect can be produced. This is to do with the way in which our brain perceives images and runs them together to produce the illusion of motion. No matter how smoothly the animation is achieved, the end result can still be jerky because of strobing.

Schneer and Harryhausen had taken a risk with *Seventh Voyage of Sinbad*. The conventional wisdom of the time held that Arabian Nights fantasies, like *The Thief of Bagdad*, were now old hat. The last success in the field had been *Sinbad the Sailor* with Douglas Fairbanks Jr in 1947 (see filmography). More recent examples had flopped. So it was a great relief when the film did extremely well. A factor that certainly helped was the energetic musical score by Bernard Herrmann, one of his best.

Harryhausen worked steadily at a variety of fantasy projects with Schneer over the next few years. They included *The Three Worlds of Gulliver* (1959) and *Mysterious Island* (1961), both in the filmography. His next major mythological project, however, was *Jason and the Argonauts* (1963). It is probably his best film. Unfortunately, it did not do as well at the box-office as its predecessor, so the sequel that seems to be promised by the ending was never made. Don Chaffey's direction is professional, and the animation is Harryhausen at his most meticulous. Indeed, even the screenplay has its moments, especially the amusingly acid dialogue of Zeus, as he watches the earthlings blundering around, from his perch in Olympus.

The story (which had already been used as the basis of the Italian *Hercules* a few years earlier) involves Jason's collecting a crew of heroes together, and setting off to steal the Golden Fleece from Colchis, to use it as a rallying point for the people in his efforts to get rid of a tyrannical king. Nigel Green makes a very jolly Hercules, but Nancy Kovack is a listless Medea, and Jason

(Todd Armstrong) is deplorably lacking in charisma. Nevertheless, this is the film in which Harryhausen comes closest to capturing the elusive magic that he has so often missed, both before and since. There are moments, as when the vast, creaking, brass statue of Talos comes to life, or when the screeching harpies persecute the old blind seer, where the film does evoke a primal innocent world in which the natural and the supernatural co-exist; where behind the next hill horrors, miracles or even gods might lurk.

Other effects sequences are a bit more knowing and modern, though well carried off: the fight with the seven-headed hydra (which seems like something out of an SF monster movie), the rising of Poseidon from the waves to hold apart the clashing cliffs through which the ship must pass, and the ultimate fight with the skeleton grown from the hydra's teeth. (There are not quite enough of them.) Children love the film, and for all one's intellectual talk about the vulgarizing of mythology and the crudity of the screenplay, there is no denying that Harryhausen contrived to bring a lot of sparkle, excitement and fun back into the world of fantastic cinema, which was beginning to lose sight of these qualities.

All the fun of the fair

Most of the key points in the development of fantastic cinema up to the turning-point year of 1968 have already been touched on, even though we have barely reached the 1960s. The early 1960s were mostly years when proven formulae were being repeated, though the horror film was to hold a few surprises, and in Europe and Japan a new generation of intellectuals was discovering the symbolic possibilities of fantasy film.

But first, a quick survey of the period's best loved fantastic romps: all the fun of the fair for the whole family. The next fantasy of any quality from Disney studios was *Darby O'Gill and the Little People* (1959). It launched Sean Connery's career, but it flopped. It is not a very distinguished film, but it deserved to do a little better. In Ireland, an old man, recently sacked from his job and depressed, meets up with leprechauns; these sections are a bit cute, but full of verve, with extremely clever effects. Where the film scores, unusually for a Disney production, is in its moments of terror: an innocent pony transformed into a demon horse; a green, wailing banshee foretelling death; and the arrival of the Costa Bower, the Death Coach, streaming through the sky, coming to carry off the old man's daughter. Some well scripted sleight of hand involving three wishes saves the situation at the last moment, and the kids in the audience (some of whom may have really been scared) could breathe again.

7 Faces of Dr Lao (1963) was produced by

*Tony Randall plays six
of the major roles in
George Pal's fantasy
7 Faces of Dr Lao
(MGM, 1963). Here he
models a rather
old-fashioned hair
style, as Medusa.*

George Pal, who was taking a short break from science fiction. The film's theme – the allegorical circus that comes to town and changes the lives of the inhabitants – has been quite popular over the years. This film was based on a novel by Charles Finney which has a lot in common with the later novel by Ray Bradbury filmed as *Something Wicked This Way Comes*.

Dr Lao (a little old Chinese) is played by Tony Randall, who also plays five of the circus's menagerie of mythological persons: Merlin, Apollonius, Pan, Medusa and the Abominable Snowman. A librarian is seduced by Pan; a bullying wife is turned to stone; and local bad guys release from a goldfish bowl a tiny snake which turns into the Loch Ness Monster (animated by Jim Danforth, a young disciple of Harryhausen). The sophisticated allegory of the original novel is cleaned up, de-sexed, and reduced to uncontroversial, down-home, Middle-American moral preaching.

The film was nominated for an Oscar for best special effects, but it lost out to Disney's *Mary Poppins* (1964), in which the eccentric, plump harridan-witch of a nanny in Travers' original books is put through the Disney nice-making machine and comes out as crisp, lovely Julie Andrews. The film's story concerns the magical nanny taking two slightly neglected middle-class children on a series of fantastic adventures to cheer them up. The live-action fantasy (flying over London by umbrella power is one, with wonderful mattes painted by Peter Ellenshaw) is much more successful than the cartoon fantasy sequences, which are crude. There are certainly good moments, some involving Dick Van Dyke who tries desperately hard but not too successfully to sound like a cockney chimney sweep. But the sentimental moralising, and the sheer randomness of the fantasy sequences, prevent the film reaching classic status so far as film buffs are concerned. The film-going public, apparently, thinks differently. It was, and is, one of Disney's most successful films.

However, *Mary Poppins* may be a better film than the gargantuan children's fantasy that followed three years later – the most expensive children's film ever made: *Doctor Dolittle (1967)*. This is more than two and a half hours long and, partly because of Leslie Bricusse's soggy script and lyrics, drags along like a cripple. The zany good humour and charm of the original children's story is sanitized out of existence, and most of the cast looks embarrassed, except for Richard Attenborough as the circus proprietor. "Talk to the Animals" is the only good song, and the legendary beasts (the two-headed pushmi-pullyu and the giant snail) are only so-so. It was a disaster for 20th Century-Fox, and an

Rex Harrison, altogether more dapper than the original chubby Doctor Dolittle of the children's books, can talk to any animal – even a giant snail – in Doctor Dolittle *(20th Century-Fox, 1967). The film dragged a little, but it still won L. B. Abbott an Oscar in 1968 for best special effects.*

unusually bad film for the director, the generally competent Richard Fleischer, who had made *20,000 Leagues Under the Sea.*

Fleischer had also made, the previous year, a much more interesting fantasy, which survived its ridiculously melodramatic script and hammy acting through its miraculous special effects (infinitely better than those of *Dolittle*). The film was *Fantastic Voyage* (1966), which, creating a new world record for absurd pseudo-science and arbitrary plotting, told of the miniaturized medical crew of a tiny submarine which is inserted into the blood stream of a gravely ill scientist-defector from Czechoslovakia who has secrets to impart. The shrunken crew is to operate by laser on the poor chap's brain-clot from inside his head. Pursued by malevolent white corpuscles and sabotaged by fiendish double-agent Donald Pleasence while being distracted by the breasts of Raquel Welch (the least plausible crew member), they eventually achieve their aim and exit the body through a tear duct to loud cheers from the audience, mere seconds before resuming their full stature. (Sadists in the audience wonder what would have happened if they had still been inside.) The film is, however, memorable for Dale Hennesy's gaudy, surrealist sets which masquerade as lung tissue, nervous tissue, ear drums et al. They really are very good indeed. One of the mysteries of science fiction is how the normally responsible Isaac Asimov was persuaded to write the book of the film.

Corman's assembly-line horror

When the cinema of horror was temporarily abandoned a few pages back, it was mostly low-budget, black-and-white, and about monsters. At the beginning of the 1960s the budgets were lower than ever, but everything else was changing. As monsters flew out the window, doomed, epicene neurotics (most of them Vincent Price) were plodding hauntedly through the door. The day of the Gothic costume-drama had arrived, and its prophet was a brisk young fellow called Roger Corman. As we have seen, the Gothic was a familiar element in fantastic cinema from the beginning, but oddly enough, no matter how medieval the plot-lines, most such Gothics had been set in more-or-less contemporary times. Then Corman, with his screenwriters Richard Matheson and Charles Beaumont (both popular fantasy writers with a number of books published), discovered Edgar Allan Poe.

The first, though not the best, of Corman's Poe adaptations was *House of Usher* (1960). Like the subsequent adaptations, it was designed by Daniel Haller (who later became a middling director himself) and photographed by Floyd Crosby in Pathecolor, a process which emphasized the blue-green end of the spectrum while underplaying the red-yellow end, thus giving the film a ghastly patina, echoing the morbid lifestyle of the rambling old mansion's decadent occupants. Most of Corman's Poe films have a subtext in which a place – usually an ancient house, cobwebbed and decaying – comes to stand for all the traps of old memories, sins, regrets. The camera that wanders down the gloomy corridors is effectively tracking through Vincent Price's unaired mind. In his Poe films,

Corman abandoned his usual speedy cutting and vigour for a hypnotic, rather ponderous style which seems to float lethargically through nightmares that are not so much terrifying as excruciatingly claustrophobic. Yet audiences loved them, and a number were produced. Those discussed in the filmography are *The Pit and the Pendulum* (1961), *The Premature Burial* (1962), *Tales of Terror* (1962), *The Raven* (1963), *The Terror* (1963) and *The Tomb of Ligeia* (1964). Of these, the last was the most accomplished, along with *The Haunted Palace* (1963) and *The Masque of the Red Death* (1964).

The only element of Poe in *The Haunted Palace* is the title. The story is taken from the lurid pulp classic "The Case of Charles Dexter Ward" by H. P. Lovecraft. By this time Corman had perfected his technique of the gliding, inexorable camera prying more and more deeply into the mysteries of dark places. A curse lies over the village of Arkham, now populated by deformed, mutant beings as a result of witchcraft many years before. In the cellar of the Curwen mansion, down deep in a stone pit, lives a demonic creature, one of Lovecraft's elder gods – or perhaps an alien being from another world – whose malign influence infects those who live there. Vincent Price, who inherits the house, is gradually possessed by the spirit of his ancestor, the burned witch. Once again the subtext tells of the past reclaiming the present; it also reveals a new psychological element: a Freudian, repressed "thing" that we have eventually to confront. All this is pretty rich stuff, and despite the garish conventions of pulp horror that Corman never seems to have struggled against too hard (including some ludicrously hammy overacting), his powerful pictorial sense makes this (and his other Poe movies as well) an authentically *cinematic* experience.

The Masque of the Red Death is considered by many to be Corman's most effective work in this area, and it is certainly his most stately and grandiloquent. It is, however, all so remote and stagey that it is difficult to take too seriously the plight of a palace-full of decadents dancing the night away, while malignant, tortured dwarfs hop about and Death stalks the red-lit room in the guise of Plague (also in the guise of Vincent Price). Curiously, a masque, in the old Elizabethan sense, is exactly what it is: more of a venomous ballet than a story. The evocative use of colour is stylized to an extraordinary degree. A footnote: in this as in most Corman movies, women are glamorous, often-corrupt *icons*. His image of femaleness is disquietingly asexual, cool and unvoluptuous. There are no erotic delights in the world of Corman's nightmares, and precious little warmth of any kind.

Corman had not entirely abandoned science fiction while all this was going on.

One of his best and most modest films was *X – The Man with X-Ray Eyes* (1963), starring Ray Milland as Doctor Xavier, who invents a serum that will allow him to see within his patients. It works all too well, and his insight into the horrors that go on inside perfectly ordinary-seeming people drives him close to madness. Nor does it end there. Soon his vision is penetrating to the heart of the cosmos – the deepest mysteries of things. All this is (cheaply) symbolized visually by using black contact lenses, which have the paradoxical effect of making him appear sightless. Getting a job as mind-reader in a tatty carnival does not help, and eventually, echoing Oedipus Rex many centuries earlier, he takes decisive action after hearing an evangelist preaching "If thine eye offend thee, pluck it out!" It is all done in the best possible taste.

Corman's own genius is not unlike that of Dr Xavier's in the film. He can see right through the tat of conventional horror cliches to the lethal metaphor that lies hidden beneath. He makes good horror films because they all have something to say, beyond the immediate nightmares they so melodramatically describe.

The birth of the "giallo"

In Italy, the word "giallo" has come to refer to a horror film with moments sufficiently gross – usually images of mutilation – to bring an average audience to the brink of nausea. Many people – not necessarily sadists – enjoy this, in much the same way as people enjoy riding on roller coasters: in both cases it is a test of *machismo* to survive.

This innocently ghoulish sub-genre largely grew out of the work of Riccardo Freda (see *Caltiki, the Immortal Monster* in filmography), and the ex-cameraman Mario Bava. Bava has made some very bad films, but one of his first (*Black Sunday*, 1960) is a minor horror classic. It is not an enormously violent film, but society's tolerance level for physical horror has risen alarmingly since 1960, and it seemed pretty bloodthirsty at the time.

The film's prologue introduces a then-unknown actress, Barbara Steele, about to have a metal mask nailed to her face by torturers of the Inquisition. She is a witch, and centuries later she returns (along with a male colleague), with holes still in her face, revived by the blood of a passer by. The romantically complex story is vividly photographed in a very stylish black-and-white, and the film is memorable not for the story (which involves the vampiric witch trying to take the place of her still living, look-alike descendant), but for haunting individual images: a ghostly coach seeming to float through a misty wood; a corpse struggling from its muddy grave; and above all the huge-eyed, high cheek-boned, luminously exotic face of Barbara Steele herself, impassively contemplating the horrors of the Pit.

Her remoteness and her curiously bizarre beauty – the eyes are *too* large – were to make her an icon of horror pictures, the very symbol of Woman as vengeful, alien and "other".

So began a revival of the Gothic costume-drama in Italy, at the same time as in the United States, and England too (see below). But the Italian line of development has now become a distinct style of its own: highly episodic, visually startling, grotesque, surreal and sadistic. *Black Sunday* stands at the head of this tradition.

Hammer horror

The horror film was evolving even faster in England than elsewhere. Several years earlier than the films described above, Hammer was conducting a small but influential revolution. It all began with *The Curse of Frankenstein* (1957), a cheap little film, with lots of bright, primary colours. It used a flaky-looking, pasty, surprisingly minimal make-up for the creature (Christopher Lee), because the make-up in James Whale's earlier version of the story was copyright. But the thing it did that caused a public outcry was to show, full-frontally as it were, the horrors that most previous films had only suggested. Graphic horror had arrived – though in retrospect this particular example looks quite sweet and innocent – and it is still here today.

The film was not very good, though it was quite interesting for Peter Cushing's interpretation of the Baron (it was to become one of his most popular roles, many times reprised) as the urbane dandy, self-containedly moving from aristocratic drawing rooms to the shambles of his laboratory with no apparent sense of incongruity.

A much better film from the same studio was *Dracula* (1958, known as *Horror of Dracula* in the USA), made by the same director. (Terence Fisher is regarded by some critics as an *auteur*, by others as a rather unimaginative and literal-minded journeyman. I incline towards the latter view.)

Just as Roger Corman introduced blues and greens as the new colour of American horror, Hammer introduced red for British horror – the colour of blood. Lots of blood. Christopher Lee made a striking and spirited debut as a vampire, his formal bearing contrasting nicely with the bestial hiss in which he specialized; this is a more full-blooded film (sorry) than Tod Browning's rather pallid version of 1930. One new feature was the emphasis on the sexuality of the vampire (to which his female victims eagerly responded), and as the 1960s approached – a period in which the UK was thought by some of its more outraged residents to be mimicking the decline and fall of the Roman Empire – Hammer kept pressing ever-harder towards the edges of what was permissible in this direction. In sequels to *Dracula*, the

effect of his toothy caress is often, fairly obviously, to bring about an orgasm in the bosom-heaving recipient. Thus the horror film was developing yet another subtext: vampirism = pleasure = sexual possession = infection = death. When you come to think of it, it is a message that might please the most devoutly puritan. It is easy to joke about Hammer films, but the fact is that *Dracula* came as a genuine shock to viewers – much more than *Curse of Frankenstein* – and its rococo sensuality, while unsubtle, opened the doors to quite new ramifications of the horror genre.

Peter Cushing played Van Helsing, so this was the second film in a row in which Lee and Cushing starred together. Both are highly professional, though perhaps Lee has greater depth and versatility (not that he has often been given a chance to display it), and they made a strong team. The era of Karloff was ended; even Vincent Price was coming to seem old-fashioned. Horror cinema was developing a new pantheon.

The irony, of course, is that within a decade Hammer's costume dramas would themselves come to seem old-fashioned and repetitive. Certainly they milked the Dracula-Frankenstein formulae for all they were worth (see filmography for over a dozen sequels). Ultimately, most of Hammer's films were not highly original, and many of them leave something of a bad taste in the mouth. Some better ones are looked at in the chapter on post-1968 horror, but two of their mid-1960s films are worth mentioning here. The first is *The Plague of the Zombies* (1966), a forerunner of yet another change in horror iconography, where zombieism (the horror of decay) was to replace vampirism (the horror of sexuality) in the fickle public taste, which would be an accurate measure, if only we could quantify it, of what social and political fears are uppermost in any one period. *Plague of the Zombies* is the best film, if not the first, to show the cliche of clutching dead hands reaching up out of the soil from the grave below. In fact it is a clever, well designed movie, whose central image is of a plague in a small Cornish village; this is connected with the local squire's use of zombie slave labour in his tin mines – quite an interestingly radical comment on the relation of capitalists to the working class.

One Million Years BC (1966), also made by Hammer, should be mentioned for quite another kind of resurrection: that of the prehistoric-monster-anachronistically-existing-alongside-cavemen movie. These were to remain popular (though nearly always appallingly bad) for the next decade, and they still turn up occasionally. Harryhausen designed a job-lot of monsters for this film – the pterodactyl is the best – but its real joy, for lovers of camp fantasy, is the love affair between John Richardson of the warlike Rock Tribe and scantily-clad Raquel Welch of the peace-loving Shell People. They are Romeo and Juliet in animal skins, the handsomest cave people ever seen. The obligatory volcano provides a rousing finale. The film closely followed its original, a curiosity called *One Million BC* (1940), on which D. W. Griffith is alleged to have worked.

And on the artistic side...

Most of this book is devoted to fantasy as a definably separate genre: that is, to films that draw upon, and occasionally expand, an existing tradition. Most of the writers and directors who work in this field are very conscious of belonging to a generic tradition. But fantasies can be created by anybody, and it sometimes happens that directors from quite different traditions find it appropriate to draw upon the world's fund of fantastic imagery – not just from films, but from books and poems and paintings – for non-generic purposes of their own.

Such a director is Ingmar Bergman, who uses a great deal of visionary and fabulous imagery in his films, much of which is taken directly from literature, art and myth. Most of Bergman's films could be defined as marginal fantasy, but I have restricted the choice to six: *The Face* (1958, aka *The Magician*) and *The Devil's Eye* (1960) are in the filmography; *Hour of the Wolf* (1968) and *Fanny and Alexander* (1982) appear in Chapter Seven on post-1968 fantasy. Here we can make brief mention of two seminal films: *The Seventh Seal* (1957) and *The Virgin Spring* (1960).

The Seventh Seal is an allegory, beautifully photographed in black-and-white by Gunnar Fischer. Max von Sydow is the Knight, riding with his sardonic squire across the ravaged landscape of a Dark-Ages Europe that is suffering from plague and anarchy at the time of the Crusades. Early in the morning he meets the figure of Death on the beach; later he confesses in Church but it is Death who hears him (and points out to the Knight that God may not be there to hear his prayers – a viewpoint that seems all too possible when we see the squalor and misery through which the Knight travels); he meets Death

The director of Dance of the Vampires *(MGM, 1967), Roman Polanski, also stars as the meek assistant of the vampire hunter; here he nervously carries out his duties. This film was a burlesque of vampire movies, but Polanski also gave fantastic cinema two serious films, at around the same time:* Repulsion *(1965) and* Rosemary's Baby *(1968).*

again at the end, but tries to refuse (with a dignity that seems almost crazy in the circumstances) to submit to the inevitable. The film ends with the Knight and his Lady, along with others, capering behind the cowled skeleton in the grotesque (yet not wholly joyless) Dance of Death.

Priest become rapists, witches are burned, torment is everywhere; only an innocent troupe of actors remains relatively unscathed. Bergman has weighted the scales in this thesis film, whose subject is belief in God, and the difficulties of reconciling such a belief with human suffering. Its beautifully composed – if rather studied – *tableaux* are visually very striking; they often echo old paintings and engravings. *Seventh Seal's* imagery added much to the visual iconography of fantastic cinema.

So too did the imagery of *The Virgin Spring*. (Ironically it was even unofficially remade as one of the most brutally sadistic exploitation movies ever filmed, Wes Craven's *Last House on the Left*, 1972.) *Virgin Spring*, which is based on a medieval ballad, tells of a young, fresh girl raped and murdered, and the violent vengeance taken by her father. After the revenge a spring gushes forth from the spot where she died. There are minor fantastic elements throughout, for the film is set in a period poised between belief in pagan gods such as Odin and a belief in Christianity. The film's visual symbolism gives a kind of credence to both faith-systems in images of a telling simplicity. The film vividly evokes an age when the natural and the supernatural worlds – the visible and the invisible – seemed more adjacent than they do now.

Ghosts and Freud

Keen intelligence and an educated eye for fantastic symbolism were not, of course, confined to Sweden. They are very evident in two very interesting English-language films about hauntings – by no means traditional horror films: *The Innocents* (1961) and *The Haunting* (1963). Both, significantly, are adapted from sophisticated and ambiguous originals: *Innocents* from Henry James's *The Turn of the Screw*, and *Haunting* from Shirley Jackson's *The Haunting of Hill House*; both were made by maverick intellectuals, Jack Clayton in the former case and Robert Wise in the latter. Both films are so tactful in revealing their ghosts that it is almost possible to believe that there are none – that we are witnessing the projections of troubled minds; and both rely heavily upon the careful building-up of an uneasily electric atmosphere, clouded with enigma. Yet the films are rather different.

The Innocents had much going for it: the crystalline photography of Freddie Francis (who went on to direct many horror films himself for Hammer), and a screenplay

worked on by two strong writers, John Mortimer and Truman Capote. The story tells of a governess in a beautiful country house caring for two young children, who may or may not be possessed by the evil spirits of Miss Jessel, the previous governess, and her brutal valet-lover Quint. We, the audience, see their ghosts (dimly and at a distance), but it may be that we are looking through the eyes of the governess (a wonderfully genteel, nervous, repressed performance from Deborah Kerr), and it may also be that she is a frustrated spinster who conjures up imaginary images of sexual evil for entirely Freudian reasons.

The contrast between sunlit gardens and moody shadows wonderfully reflects the psychological drama, but strongest of all are the individual, baroque images: a fat, black beetle crawling between the lips of a fallen statue of Cupid in the garden; the goodnight kiss from the young boy, Miles, which somehow becomes indecently sexual; the unsettling ballad he recites at night just before the windows inexplicably fly open. The music is haunting, too, with a song of dead love, "O Willow, Waly" presenting a leitmotif at the beginning, picked up later by Miss Jessel's tinkling music-box. *Innocents* is one of the classics of fantastic cinema. A disquieting film, it shrewdly alternates between traditional Gothic imagery (dark shadows creeping into a ring of candlelight) and bright matter-of-factness in its presentation of the otherworldly. The performances Clayton coaxed from the children have an impeccable, middle-class creepiness.

Wise's *The Haunting* is a less subtle film whose Freudian elements are more up-front, but it has many strong moments. Psychic researchers investigating a haunted house experience an increasingly menacing atmosphere; the uncanny manifests itself in sounds and intimations rather than outright ghosts. The house may really be haunted, or the manifestations may be poltergeist phenomena springing from the disturbed mind of one of the investigators (an obsessed anthropologist, a neurotic virgin, a lesbian psychic and the obligatory crude sceptic). The labyrinthine interior of this twisted old house becomes (as so often in this kind of film) an image of the contortions and mazes of the mind. For a ghost story without ghosts, the film is amazingly scary, its most horrific moment being the enormously·violent pounding on a door which begins to buckle inwards towards the terrified investigators huddling within.

Japanese ghosts

There is a strong tradition of the supernatural in Japan, which often appears in films. The greatest of these was made years earlier than the period we are now considering: *Ugetsu Monogatari* (1953, see filmography), but two more excellent Japanese fantasies were released in 1964: *Kwaidan* and *Onibaba*. The former, directed by Masaki Kobayashi, is based, curiously enough, on four tales written by an American author, Lafcadio Hearn. One sequence of this anthology film ("Yuki-Onna", the story of a female ice-demon who marries a human) was released as a separate short film in the West. The three remaining stories are all extremely eerie and atmospherically photographed. The story of the blind musician who unknowingly plays music for the dead, and then (having discovered what he did) refuses to give a repeat performance, is the most memorably black episode. As a punishment, the ghosts tear off his ears.

Onibaba, directed by Kaneto Shindo, is set in a sixteenth-century Japan reeling from monstrous civil wars. A mother and a daughter scratch a living, in the heart of a wide sea of placidly waving, man-high reeds, by robbing the bodies of dead soldiers, which are then dumped into a mysterious hole. The mother steals a demon-mask from a disguised Samurai (whom she lures into falling to his death in the hole), and wears it to frighten her daughter away from the sexual liaison she had begun with a lazy, layabout neighbour. But the mask possesses the mother, and she cannot take it off. When it is finally ripped from her, the face beneath is horribly disfigured – apparently from smallpox, but perhaps by the demon. This is a strong, uncanny film, which displays a quiet pity towards its protagonists, who are victims as much as monsters; yet the constantly moving, rustling reeds seem to reflect the insubstantiality of their way of life, and its inevitable collapse. The demon mask is a grotesquely effective symbol of the vengeful spirit of the harridan mother, and also of the cruel wars that were depopulating Japan.

The quiet 1960s

The 1960s were not especially sparkling years for fantastic cinema. Before 1968 only an individual film here and there (several are discussed above) stands out as a lonely island in a sea of the ordinary. (Some more of these are discussed in the filmography, including the preposterously maze-like Polish fantasy *The Saragossa Manuscript*, 1965, and the frightening, but sometimes funny, early work of Roman Polanski: *Repulsion*, 1965, and *Dance of the Vampires*, 1967.)

The 1960s were a period of intense activity in other areas of cinema, however, with a new generation of European directors (especially in France) creating radical shifts of taste in what the public was prepared to accept. These were the so-called New Wave directors, and every now and then they entered the realms of surrealism and fantasy. One of these was François Truffaut and we end this teasing out the first seventy years' threads of fantastic cinema's tapestry by considering his very odd essay in marginal science fiction: *Fahrenheit 451* (1966).

The original novel by Ray Bradbury – a tale about a repressive future where all books are burned (at 451° F) – was a kind of science fiction. The Truffaut film topples over into fantasy – which did not win it many friends among SF readers. Yet on its own offbeat terms, the film is interesting. Oddly, it is much kinder to the paternalistic, book-destroying society (books only make you miserable anyway, it is believed) than was Bradbury's novel. Montag (Oskar Werner) is the book-burning "fireman" who becomes a secret convert to literature (abandoning his television-drugged wife for the naughty book-reading girl next door – both parts played in a piece of enigmatic symbolism by Julie Christie); he is rather attractive as he hurtles around town in his bright red fire-engine, burning books (including *Mein Kampf*) left, right and centre. When he leaves the city to join the revolutionaries (each of them has memorised a book and wanders around reciting it), the film seems to tell us that he has only exchanged one form of chilling pointlessness (the friendly but cool city that has no spirit or character) for another (zombie-like book-people tramping greyly through the snow, chanting their books in the monotone of uncomprehending zealots). Perhaps this strange picture is the revenge of a film-maker upon literature. It is a sad little film, and rather uneven, as if at times Truffaut had just lost interest, but poignantly beautiful in its best moments. It is well photographed by Nicolas Roeg, a young cameraman who went on to become one of the most distinguished of fantasy-film makers himself. But that was after 1968, the year that brought the entire genre back to life.

No longer would fantastic cinema be the exclusive property of the people who haunt low-budget horror-film cinemas, or of the other people who attended art-houses where they could see films by Bergman and Buñuel. After 1968, fantastic cinema would be for the first time a truly popular genre with an ever-increasing mass audience.

1968: The Breakthrough Year

Previous two pages: an archetypal science-fiction image from the archetypal SF movie, Stanley Kubrick's 2001: A Space Odyssey *(MGM, 1968). The success of this key film began a new boom in SF cinema.*

The traffic problems outside Paris are worse than usual in Jean-Luc Godard's Weekend *(Ascot Cineraid, 1967). Jean Yanne and Mireille Darc are here rather irritated at the delay to their weekend plans.*

For most of the 1960s, fantastic cinema had been going through a very quiet period – and, incidentally, not making much money for the film studios. Of the few real hits in the genre between 1960 and 1967, most were fringe fantasy rather than centrally fantasy. The major commercial successes were *Dr No* (1962), *The Birds* (1963), *Dr Strangelove* (1963), *Mary Poppins* (1964) and *You Only Live Twice* (1967). Apart from Mary Poppins' ability to levitate, there was not much in the way of hard-core supernatural or science-fiction effects in any of these. But everything was to change in 1968, the year of the big breakthrough.

Curiously enough, the first signs of a renewed interest in fantastic cinema came from the French rather than from Hollywood. Fantasy has always been popular with French intellectuals, and it was two of the most intellectual of New-Wave film directors, with two films copyrighted 1967 but released later, who surprised the world by showing that science-fiction scenarios could be taken seriously by "artistic" directors.

Apocalypse on the roads

Jean-Luc Godard's *Weekend* remains a disturbingly effective and blackly amusing fantasy when viewed today. It begins realistically enough with a highly sexed couple setting off for a dirty weekend in a car. Unfortunately, most of Paris also seems to be driving into the country at the same time, and an extraordinary sequence follows, of minor traffic jams and dented fenders escalating into a conflagration of violence and death on the roads. One of the most surreal tracking shots in cinema history moves slowly along a line of jammed cars, revealing more and more blood, death and destruction as it goes. At the beginning of this long shot we are still in the real world; by its end we have reached a kind of motorized apocalypse. It also seems that left-wing guerrilla forces have revolted (while philosophical characters dressed in eighteenth-century costume roam the countryside reading aloud), and by the end of the film the survivors are plunged into a scenario of civil war and cannibalism. (After all, by 1968, social unrest was endemic in the Western world, and this was the year in which student riots practically tore Paris apart, making Godard's film even more relevant at the moment of release.) *Weekend* is an absurdist tale, but it is also highly political, exhibiting a kind of crankily comic Marxism. Possessions (symbolized by the car), technology and consumerism have corrupted this lunatic world. A girl whose lover has been killed when their car collides with a tractor screams at its working-class driver that, as opposed to him, "We can screw on the Riviera or in ski resorts!" in manic if irrelevant exultation, since her partner lies dead beside her. After a particularly bloody crash, a barely surviv-

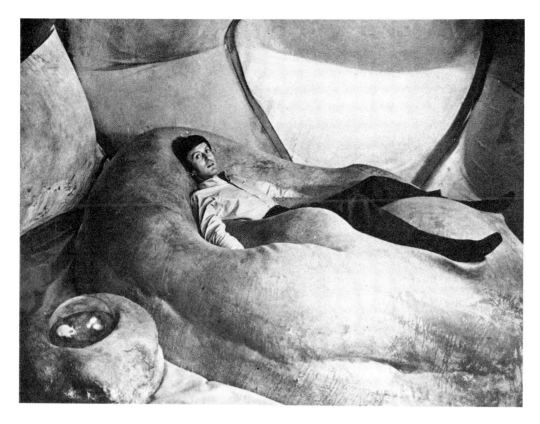

Claude Rich, along with an enigmatic mouse, is about to take a ride in the cinema's strangest time machine, in Alain Resnais' eccentric SF movie Je t'aime, Je t'aime *(Fox Europa, 1967), perhaps the most complex time-travel film ever made. The soft, organic contours of the machine in which Rich lies foreshadow the sensuality, but not the frustration, of the experiences he will have in the past.*

ing woman screams through the blood, "My Hermes handbag! My Hermes handbag!" The film is sometimes visually memorable: hysterical people run through a flock of unbelievably white sheep, scattering them like the parting of some frothy Red Sea. A perverse sexual anecdote at the beginning, featuring the unusual conjunction of an egg and a vagina, is mirrored at the end, where the running white and yolk dripping over the heroine's private parts seem a deranged metaphor for a fantasy society (our own) gone quite wrong. This is not a film for children. Unfortunately, Godard's New-Wave devotees were bewildered by the science-fiction elements, and the science-fiction fans were not tuned in to French intellectual imagery, so the film, falling between two stools, has never had the recognition it deserves despite all its pretentious excesses.

Time paradoxes

Alain Resnais's film *Je t'aime, Je t'aime* ("I love you, I love you") also puzzled the intellectuals, for here Resnais had moved from the subjective use of time travel (in the memory) of *Last Year at Marienbad* (1961, see filmography) to the actual use of a bona fide science-fiction time machine. It looks like a cross between a womb and a pumpkin; it is a very organic time machine indeed. A failed suicide is asked to take part in a scientific experiment, and go back for one minute into his own past. But does the soft, womblike time machine bring about a rebirth or a miscarriage? The first part of the trip is to the warm amniotic fluid of the sea and to a love affair; thereafter it is very difficult to dis-

tinguish between "actual" events and desired or hallucinatory events, much as in the extraordinary novels of Philip K. Dick. This is a moving, rather unhappy film, though it has good jokes too (as when the time-travelling hero enters a telephone booth to dial TIME), which suggests that the paradoxes of time are difficult to cope with, and that the past may not be easily changed. Yet some changes may be possible. Viewers should watch the white laboratory mouse very carefully indeed in the last minutes of the film, one of the saddest and most resonant closing scenes in cinema.

I include *Je t'aime, Je t'aime* (the repetition of the phrase has a subtle meaning in the film) as a breakthrough movie because of its intrinsic quality, not because it was a smash hit. Indeed, it was not released in the UK until 1971, when it was dismissed by influential critic Penelope Gilliatt largely on account of the alleged unattractiveness of hero Claude Rich's legs.

Sex on other worlds

The other breakthrough French movie of 1968 was, on the contrary, a major popular success, and it did much to resuscitate science fiction in the minds of commercial movie-makers. This was Roger Vadim's *Barbarella*, starring the director's then-wife Jane Fonda.

A lot of people thought *Barbarella* was nothing much more than an over-prolonged sex joke. Certainly the dopy and sexually ignorant role played with naive panache by Fonda was the not very subtle core of the movie. Barbarella is a kind of innocent, much

One of the most memorable symbols of fantastic cinema's exotic side was Jane Fonda as the innocent sex goddess in Barbarella *(De Laurentiis/Paramount, 1968); soon she will be propositioned by half the population of a corrupt alien planet. Note the internal decor of her spacecraft. This was the third important SF movie made in France within twelve months.*

coupled-with Candide figure, moving through the corrupt world of a wicked planet and its city Sogo, from which she had been instructed by the World President to rescue a missing scientist. Puritanical critics resented the blatant sexism (not, it could be argued, anti-feminism) of the film, and its aimless, episodic plot (derived from the French comic strip by Jean-Claude Forest) was seen as betraying the intellectual incisiveness of which science fiction is capable in favour of a lazy opulence.

But the fact is that *Barbarella* succeeds in precisely the area where science fiction is supposed to excel: it creates a sense of wonder. The planet on which the story is set remains one of the most truly alien creations in cinema, with bizarre surprises around every corner: small sinister children with steel-toothed carnivorous dolls; a blind angel; an ice yacht; rock people; exotic spacecraft; and the writhing monster Matmos over whom

the city is built. All of this was genuinely exotic, and a tribute to the production design of Mario Garbuglia and the wildly fantastic sets of art director Enrico Fea. Claude Renoir's light-filled photography was also excellent.

Some of the sex jokes are pretty dumb and schoolboyish (the intellectuals' favourite soft-core pornography writer, Terry Southern, was one of eight credited writers), but the scene featuring sexual intercourse via the fingertips remains truly amusing. Guest star David Hemmings played the young revolutionary in this encounter. *Barbarella* was an early production by Italian super-producer Dino De Laurentiis (see next chapter), and the success of its bizarre settings and big-name actor cameos probably served to warp his subsequent career by turning him away from the primacy of plot – witness the failure of *Flash Gordon* a decade later, which did not manage to reproduce the innocent lunacy of its comic-strip origins.

A science-fiction weepie

1968 was the year of science fiction in the English-speaking world as well. The quietest science-fiction film of the year was *Charly*, directed efficiently, though without charisma, by journeyman Ralph (*Requiem for a Heavyweight*) Nelson. *Charly* had one very important advantage. Unlike most science-fiction movies (which tend to be made from original screenplays), *Charly* was based on a genuine science-fiction classic, Daniel Keyes' beautiful story "Flowers for Algernon".

The story (which the film follows quite closely) tells of a mentally-retarded handyman who is the subject of a scientific experiment designed to increase intelligence (the experiment has already been carried out, apparently successfully, on the mouse Algernon). Cliff Robertson gives, as usual, an intelligent and sensitive performance, this time of a man with the mind of a child slowly coming to full adult life and knowledge (and falling in love with his doctor, played by Claire Bloom). The main interest of the story is that the operation turns out to be only a temporary success. The now brilliant Charly has to come face to face with the knowledge that all he has gained will be lost again. His moment of realization is certainly touching, and there is a horrible fascination in watching his IQ being slowly stripped away, but it may be that the original story was never quite as good as the claims made for it. Certainly, blown up on the big screen, its elements of sentimentality seem over-inflated, and they're milked for all they're worth. But for all the easy manipulation of an audience's ready

sympathies, this quite likeable though sometimes wooden movie does have something serious if not profound to say about human intelligence and emotion, and the way they are linked. After decades in which screen science fiction mostly meant monsters, *Charly* was a very definite step in the direction of (relative) maturity.

A satirical blockbuster

Superficially more childish, but in fact more grown-up, was *Planet of the Apes*, one of the two commercial American SF blockbusters of the year. Curiously enough, the French had a hand in this one too, for it was based on *Monkey Planet*, a not especially remarkable satirical novel by the popular French novelist, Pierre (*Bridge on the River Kwai*) Boulle. The director, Franklin J. Schaffner, probably had no real affinity with science fiction, though he later made another SF movie, *The Boys from Brazil*. What Schaffner could do, with forcefulness and insight, was to show the clash of strong, self-willed men with the worlds in which they find themselves, other examples of his work being *The War Lord* and *Patton*. Charlton Heston is the tough guy here, leader of a small band of astronauts which crashlands on an apparently alien planet, where the dominant races are all apes (gorillas, chimpanzees and orangoutangs, each with a different cultural function). Humans are a subnormal slave class.

The resulting story has become deservedly famous, especially for the wonderfully adroit use in its closing stages of the old science-fiction cliché, the half-buried Statue

Cliff Robertson is the retarded handyman in Charly *(Cinerama, 1968), here receiving a lesson from nice doctor Claire Bloom. At the moment he is not very bright, but later – for a brief time – he will be a genius.*

Three judicial orang-outangs are about to consider a difficult case in Planet of the Apes *(20th Century-Fox, 1968). The chief orang-outang, Dr Zaius, was played by Maurice Evans. Note the amazingly mobile facial make-up, designed by John Chambers.*

of Liberty. It projects from the sand like an eroded memory, and shows that this alien planet is really Earth in the far future. The harsh settings (actually Arizona and Utah desert landscapes) are notably effective, as are the now celebrated ape make-ups by John Chambers, who entered the special-effects pantheon through his creation of these brilliantly mobile and convincing masks.

Where the film comes unstuck is, perhaps, through being over-ambitious. The script tries to have it both ways. At times ape society is seen as a satirical reflection of all the worst excesses of human society: its racism, its snobbery, its casual, unthinking cruelty. At other times, conversely, the apes' sensitivity is supposed to throw a cold light on human insensitivity: we are meant to wonder if perhaps the apes have made a better fist of things than we ever did. (This aspect of the film was stressed in the four sequels – see filmography – whose view of ape life is consistently more sentimental than that of the original.) But this is to quibble. The firmly directed, fast-moving story sweeps away most of these objections, and while the black jokes may not make coherent sense overall, most of them work individually. In fact, *Planet of the Apes* is quite disturbing; there is nothing comfortable about it; indeed, its cold view of human/ape evolution was a real step forward in relation to the intricacy of the sub-

jects that science-fiction cinema was prepared to contemplate. The old idea that *laissez-faire* capitalism and the American way of life was bound to be the cultural norm for millennia to come was given a severe bruising by this film, and its popular success showed that maybe the old taboos ("never suggest that mankind is not the peak of creation") could be profitably broken. The decade of Vietnam (during which this film was made) was stimulating a useful self-doubt among people everywhere.

If audiences were prepared to swallow this pill – without too much sugar-coating on it – then perhaps the tough-mindedness of so much science fiction in written form could be imported into the cinema as well. This mood of greater maturity was to continue – waveringly – for another decade before being swept away by the entertaining simplicities of *Star Wars* in 1977.

The greatest SF film ever made?
The greatest science-fiction film of 1968, and according to the diehard fans who have not been seduced by the glowing fantasies of Spielberg and George Lucas in subsequent years, the greatest science-fiction film ever made, was Stanley Kubrick's *2001: A Space Odyssey*. This was another film featuring intelligent apes, and presenting a wry and chilling view of human evolution.

In a way, the film's success was surprising. It received quite a hostile critical reception when it first appeared, and was only saved by the crowds of young people who – largely because of word-of-mouth publicity rather than any orchestrated campaign – flocked to see it after an initial period when it looked like being a flop. It remains one of the most intellectually audacious science-fiction films ever made, and a rare example of a film of considerable complexity and obscurity becoming a hit. Most science-fiction blockbusters have story lines no more complicated than a fairy tale, but Kubrick had a metaphysical statement to make, and he wished to make it through imagery (the film is very non-verbal) rather than conventional narrative. Arguments still proliferate about the film's meaning, partly because of the novelization (written after the film was made) by Arthur C. Clarke, the celebrated SF writer who collaborated with Kubrick on the screenplay. The film, in fact, was rather remotely based on one of Clarke's short stories, "The Sentinel", and its central idea – that humanity is a childlike and rather primitive race whose evolution may need to be directed by some kind of outside force (symbolized in the film by the presence of gigantic black monoliths) is one that has always been close to Clarke's heart. But for all Clarke's metaphysical yearnings, his narrative style has always been straightforward, and his novelized version of the film spelt out in prosaic detail many of the points which Kubrick had (one presumes deliberately) left opaque and mysterious. In other words, the book of the film reduces its meaning from a multiplicity of possibilities to just one.

Despite the general belief that it was the presence of Clarke – a senior and respected SF writer – that ensured the film's genre purity, I suspect that the driving force throughout was Kubrick's. He had always had a strong visual orientation as a film-maker – he used to be a photographer – and *2001* remains his most remarkable visual achievement. From the film's beginning in prehistoric times on Earth when the black monolith first appears, to the near-future technological sequences, the spaceship sequences, the hallucinatory passage through the stargate and the final surreal sequence in an elegant, archaic bedroom, its visual strength and complexity is flawlessly achieved. All this took money, and the then cost of six-and-a-half million dollars probably remains (allowing for inflation) the highest sum ever spent on sets and special effects for a film. (The space sequences in the *Star Wars* films would have cost much more if the painstaking matte process used by Kubrick had been employed to make them – but the result is that the process work remains visible in *Star Wars* – a slight outline around the spacecraft – and invisible in *2001*.)

Kubrick's use of the wide screen is superb, and for sheer spectacle *2001* has never been surpassed. It cries out to be seen in a properly equipped cinema with a 70mm print, loses some of its potency in a 35mm print, and most of it when seen on videotape.

The story is now so well-known that it hardly needs recounting. What is interesting is its cold pessimism. There are very few cases on record of really pessimistic films becoming smash hits, yet *2001* managed it. Pessimism, of course, is in the eye of the beholder, and in the violent and secular world of the late 1960s, there may have been a certain appeal in the thought that the mess we have made of things could yet be redeemed by some kind of alien intervention. *2001*, in fact, can be seen as proposing a new religious belief for a technological age, with God – by a kind of weird semantic juggling – being redefined as an enigmatic alien who will intervene. But even here the film is not especially optimistic. The first intervention of 'God' – teaching ape-men about the use of tools, in this case a large animal bone – is instantly followed by an act of murder. Yet there is still something very moving about the shot, perhaps the greatest visual metaphor in cinema, when the bone thrown high into the air in slow motion becomes a modern spacecraft – a million years of technological evolution encapsulated in one soaring image.

The greatest coldness of the film is in its near-contemporary sequences, with most of the human figures seen as banal, uncommunicative, sometimes almost autistic. The casting of Keir Dullea (who first came to prominence in *David and Lisa*, 1963, an experimental film where he played a disturbed teenager almost unable to communicate) was an act of perverse genius. In some ways Dullea simply reprises his earlier role, and his extreme coolness here is reinforced by the clinical, sterile settings in which he is placed. All the near-future settings have the crisp anonymity of – as the film actually implies – a new Hilton Hotel. At the end, when Dullea dismantles HAL, the disturbed computer, he seems no more than an array of transistorised relay switches himself, while HAL (sadly crooning "Daisy, Daisy, Give Me Your Answer Do") is the one who seems human.

Then follows the light show – loathed by the critics in 1968, but loved by young audiences during this period of flower power, hippiedom and psychedelic art. The legend of the time was that *2001* should only be viewed while stoned or, better yet, freaked out on LSD. But this psychedelic rite of passage, which ultimately brings Dullea face to face with his sterile, luxurious dying self (an image of the sterile, luxurious world he inhabits?) is not the end. The final image shows Dullea transmuted to a foetus hovering above Earth. Mankind, for all its potential (as all

The image of a vast space ship floating awesomely and in complete silence through deep space against a background of stars has become central to the iconography of SF cinema. Such special effects were first perfected in 2001: A Space Odyssey *(MGM, 1968).*

babies have potential) has yet to achieve its growth. We have got everywhere but nowhere. Yet, perhaps because of our warm feelings towards babies, the final image is less chilling than almost everything that precedes it. In the mood of self-doubt that had hit the West, especially Americans, so very hard during the Vietnam dispute, the self-flagellation of *2001* may have seemed not only acceptable but somehow almost joyous. I think it fair to assume that as a lament for the sterility of human achievement, *2001* is the work of a single hand, and that hand was Kubrick's, not Clarke's.

A film about pain

While 1968 was chiefly notable for its great advances in cinematic science fiction, the genre of supernatural horror was also undergoing radical changes. One of the most important milestones in this area was a film that was released comparatively quietly: *Witchfinder General*, known in America as *The Conqueror Worm*. The paradox is that this low-budget production of the British Tigon company (keenly exploiting the commercially successful area of costume horror pioneered in the UK by Hammer Films) was not strictly speaking a fantastic film at all, since there is no evidence that the witches whose dreadful persecution is the film's subject matter had any real supernatural powers.

Nonetheless, the film has a brooding, implacable, sinister atmosphere – very much

the atmosphere of fantastic cinema generally in its darker moments. Vincent Price plays the historical figure Matthew Hopkins, who travelled the coutnry executing supposed witches under powers given him by the Roundhead parliament during the Civil War. The brilliant 24-year-old director Michael Reeves, whose third and last film this was, died of a barbiturate overdose the next year. (See the filmography for his two previous films, *Revenge of the Blood Beast* and *The Sorcerers*.) Reeves had trouble persuading Vincent Price to moderate his usual slightly jokey, over-the-top approach to portraying villains, but he finally succeeded, and the result is Price's greatest role, severe, obsessive, cruel and low-key.

The reason for selecting *Witchfinder General* as a "breakthrough" film is for its unsettling violence. In his appalled horror at the historical sadism of Matthew Hopkins, Reeves went further than any commercial director before him in the kinds of brutality he decided could be shown on the screen. But there is no *wallowing* in horror, no actual enjoyment of what the film purports to condemn, as is so common in the visceral horror films of today. Rather, there is a sombre assessment of the reality of pain, and its ability to corrupt both givers and receivers. Nonetheless, it is a deeply disturbing film, even in the cut version which is the only one to have been shown in the UK. (The torture of the heroine with needles through the kidney is now barely visible, and the dismemberment of Hopkins with an axe is mercifully curtailed.)

In *Witchfinder General*, the cruelty is artistically justified, even necessary, but its significance in the history of cinema is, in part, that it was one of the key films that opened the way to ever more explicit gore at the horror end of the fantastic movie spectrum.

Bringing it all back home

Witchfinder General was a costume drama, but one of the changes which made 1968 a key year was the bringing of supernatural horror films very much closer to home. Horror used to be distanced in both time and place, as a general rule – often to a never-never land such as Transylvania. But two films in 1968 located supernatural horror right at the heart of modern America.

The best-known at the time was Roman Polanski's adaptation of Ira Levin's novel, *Rosemary's Baby*. Though not a deeply original film, it was made with assurance and flourish, and successfully portrayed the ter-

rible situation, worse than paranoia, where the persecuted person really *is* being persecuted but nobody believes her. Rosemary and her actor husband move into a pleasant old apartment in a New York brownstone. The affable, eccentric neighbours, unknown to Rosemary, belong to a cult of Satan worshippers. They quickly pervert Rosemary's husband (John Cassavetes), who betrays his wife, allowing her to have sexual intercourse with the devil himself while in a drugged sleep. This is all the most appalling tosh, but the central situation (woman betrayed by ambitious husband) is real enough, and the sense of loving vulnerability defiled is powerfully portrayed by Mia Farrow, whose bony, pretty, bruised appearance is just right for the part. Abused and suffering, she undergoes a variety of torments, none of them especially frightful, but each one helping to build up to a veritable crescendo of uneasiness. The ultimate exploitation is of mother love (that great American verity) itself. Rosemary finally gives birth to the De-

Mia Farrow, the persecuted wife in Rosemary's Baby *(Paramount, 1968), is here considering infanticide – not surprisingly, since the baby's father is the Devil. Inevitably, however, mother love wins out in this entertainingly paranoid melodrama directed by Roman Polanski.*

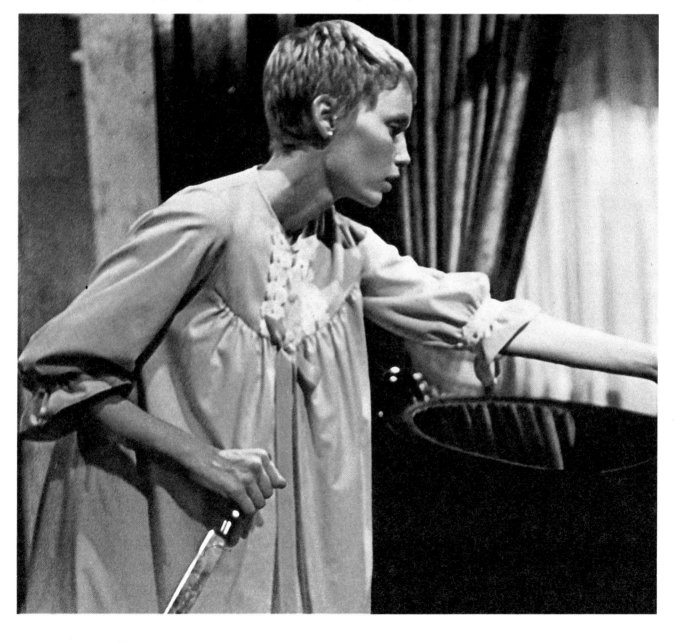

THEY WON'T STAY DEAD!

George Romero's Night of the Living Dead *(Image Ten, 1968) is a very intelligent film, but this poster emphasises its exploitation elements: "bloodthirsty lust for HUMAN FLESH!".*

vil's child, and accepts it, putting it to her breast. This is a nasty, clever, entertaining movie about the abuse of women – a kind of feminist document in its perverse way.

America devours itself

In retrospect, the most subversive horror movie of 1968 – a film whose implications are far more unsettling than any of the implausible nonsense of *Rosemary's Baby* – was a low-budget black-and-white affair made on a shoestring by an advertising-film director based in Pittsburgh, a locale hardly famous for its flourishing film industry. The entire film was cheaper to make than some one-minute advertisements; it cost $114,000. Yet, over the next few years, George Romero's *Night of the Living Dead* became one of the most famous cult movies ever made, playing primarily at the sort of midnight movie houses frequented by students and other social outcasts. It was greeted at first with stunned disgust by the critics, who saw in it the obvious seeds of the decline of the West. Columbia would not dis-

tribute it (hardly surprising) and even AIP (whose main product was low-budget horror fare for drive-in cinemas) would not accept it unless Romero was prepared to reshoot it with a happy ending. He refused to do this.

The story could not be simpler. Dead people are rising from their graves and feasting on the living; as Hoberman and Rosenbaum put it in their useful book *Midnight Movies*, it offers "the most literal possible depiction of America devouring itself". A sister and brother laying flowers on father's grave are the first victims. The brother's teasing of the nervous sister ("'They're coming to get you, Barbara, they're coming to get you") is followed abruptly by his own demise. The sister escapes to a lonely farmhouse already occupied by a young black man who has also been attacked, and some others. Throughout a long night (and several deaths later, including the appallingly bloody attack on a mother by a zombified daughter) the farmhouse is besieged. The sole survivor, Ben, the black man, staggers out of the door the next morning into what he presumes to be safety. But numbed and shocked by his experiences, he looks rather like a zombie himself, and he is instantly shot by a posse of local rednecks.

What makes the film so unusual is not only its graphic display of literally visceral horror, but its refusal to throw the audience any sop of good cheer. This is a truly apocalyptic story of a quiet, workaday America abruptly on the verge of total dissolution. Not surprisingly, the more intellectual critics instantly saw a political message in the whole thing. After all, 1968 was the fourth year in a row of terrible urban riots around America; Robert Kennedy had just been assassinated; society was in a ferment. This cheap, grainy film, with much of the look of a newsreel shot at the battlefront, was somehow all the more convincing for not being glossy. The day of the urbane, exotic, polite vampire had gone, and horror cinema had opened its doors to the living dead: shambling, pitiful, decaying mirror-images of ourselves, with only one thought in mind: to feast upon us, their (so to speak) parents. Whoever comes to write the much-needed social history of the Western world as decoded from its movies will have rich material to study in the changing images of horror depicted in genre movies (see Chapter Six).

The fact that Ben in *Night of the Living Dead* is black is never overtly made an issue. He is just another working stiff trying not to be eaten. But the society which produces the zombies (who are never given an adequate "rational" explanation) also produces the tough guys (themselves ordinary working men) who shoot him down quite casually at the end. Who, then, are the "living dead"? The zombies? Their pathetic and sometimes apathetic victims? Or the vigilantes out to get them?

Only one thing about this film is sure. The traditional, "cosy" horror film where the status quo is restored at the end, and evil neatly demolished with a wooden stake, would never again look really convincing. Hitchcock's *The Birds* was one of the first films which envisage the horror continuing, spreading, overwhelming society as we know it. Romero (whose film contains visual references to *The Birds*) rammed the point home with a violence which an appalled Hitchcock would have been too much of a gentleman ever to contemplate.

Musical fantasy

1968 was primarily the year of science fiction and horror. In the gentler pasturelands of fantasy cinema, the only portent of any importance was an amusing, lively musical comedy, *Finian's Rainbow*, about a leprechaun (played by Tommy Steele) who upsets life in a small southern town in part by turning white people black as an act of mischief. Apart from some mild social satire, there was nothing groundbreaking about this affable film version of an old Broadway hit whose songs really weren't very good. It was just another vehicle for an ageing but still spry Fred Astaire, as the miser searching for the pot of gold. The significance of *Finian's Rainbow* could not, perhaps, be seen at the

time. It was the work of a very young director who had been to film school, a clever chap with an education who had not risen through the old Hollywood grind. His name was Francis Ford Coppola. As it happens, Coppola has not since been much involved, directly, with fantastic cinema. He is best known for *The Godfather* and *Apocalypse Now*. But he was one of a group of bright young kids – since christened "the movie brats" – who have turned fantastic cinema completely upside down. For example, he gave his burly patronage to a skinny and shy colleague called George Lucas, whose first film, *THX 1138* (1970), he was later to produce. *Finian's Rainbow*, a charming but not wholly successful movie of the old school, was the first faint signal of a revolution that was 'to rock Hollywood to its very foundations.

Another door had been opened – one of the many doors of 1968 through which a new vigour and ebullience was to enter fantastic cinema – and to keep it flourishing for at least the next fifteen years.

The cynical lesson to be learned was this: in 1968 fantastic cinema had proved its worth in box-office dollars. Film is an art form that thrives on hard cash. Without the help of the money men, artistic growth in the cinema is next to impossible. 1968 made it possible.

We do not usually associate chief Movie Brat Francis Ford Coppola with fantastic cinema, but one of his earliest films, Finian's Rainbow *(Warner Bros, 1968), was fantasy through and through. Fred Astaire plays the old miser seeking the pot of gold at rainbow's end, who has a lot of trouble with a leprechaun.*

Key Directors and Producers Since 1968

More directors and producers of fantasy film have attracted a cult following since 1968 than ever before. I have selected twelve as perhaps the most important, ranging from the internationally celebrated, such as Steven Spielberg and Stanley Kubrick, to those whose coterie following is not yet so well publicised and substantial, such as Larry Cohen and David Cronenberg. To make the number up to lucky thirteen, I have added another name – not a real person, it is rumoured – that of Monty Python, who has perhaps the most devoted cult following of all. My apologies to those fantasy film-makers, not included in this chapter, whose major work was for the most part before this period: Mario Bava, Ingmar Bergman, Luis Buñuel, Roger Corman, Charles Schneer, Terence Fisher, Roman Polanski and Robert Wise, for example. If the Pantheon of thirteen could have been doubled in size, I would have included (from the more recent period) the following: Woody Allen, Lindsay Anderson, Dario Argento, John Boorman, Joe Dante, Tobe Hooper, John Landis, David Lynch, George Miller, Nicolas Roeg, Andrei Tarkovsky, Lewis Teague and Peter Weir. These are the men (no women, alas) who, together with those who are the subject of this chapter, have done the most work in forging the genre of fantastic cinema into the extravagant variety of forms it assumes today, and their achievements are chronicled elsewhere in this book.

Robert Altman

Previous two pages: spectacular special effects by John Dykstra made the space sequences of Star Wars *(Lucasfilm, 1977) very convincing, and helped create the most successful SF cult the cinema has ever seen.*

Altman (born 1922), the director of *M.A.S.H.* and *Nashville*, is not an easy artist to summarize. He has always been a fiercely unpredictable lone wolf – like many of his heroes – in the film business. But surprisingly, the one category in relation to which his work is seldom discussed is the fantastic. Yet at least five of Altman's films are indubitably fantasy, and he himself said in an interview: "...all these films of mine are science fiction".

The first of Altman's fantastic films – excluding *Countdown* (1968), a story about astronauts – was *Brewster McCloud* (1970). This features Bud Cort as the owlish Texan kid who has trouble coping with work, sex and life generally, and becomes preoccupied with building wings instead. The poor, earthbound boy yearns to fly. His path keeps crossing that of enigmatic Sally Kellerman, who appears to be a dewinged angel of rather lustful tendencies. She has some connection with a series of homicides that take place wherever he goes, always connected with birds (or bird droppings). It is a very birdish, feathery film all round. Ultimately Cort does fly, triumphantly circling inside the Houston Astrodome, before crashing like some exhausted Icarus to the ground. The film is funny, bizarre, inconsequential in its development, and usually inventive. The theme of obsessives following their dreams was to be one of the few constant notes in Altman's subsequent career.

A connected Altman theme, the relation of truth and illusion, was probed altogether too artily in the next of his fantasies, *Images* (1972). Susannah York plays the writer of children's books suffering from ever-advancing schizophrenia. Her hallucinations are given the same visual weight as the "reality" of the film, and since she has a lot of them, and since they involve basic plot points such as homicide, the audience is understandably confused.

A less intense but more disturbing film is *3 Women* (1977). Fantasy fans may best remember Sissy Spacek as *Carrie*, and Shelley Duvall as the terrified wife in *The Shining*. Here Spacek plays a shy, clumsy girl who latches onto the apparently more sophisticated woman played by Duvall, and moves into her apartment. Both work in the wholly unreal surroundings of a geriatric clinic. Duvall gives a memorably, luridly hateful/sad performance as the woman wholly definable (so it seems) by her possessions – her clothes, her neat, fussy flat. She yearns for a boyfriend who might equally appear to have stepped straight from a T.V commercial, but when it comes down to it is prepared to have sweaty, down-market sex with the local adulterer. Spacek attempts suicide, suffers severe concussion, and is hospitalized. So far, no fantasy, except for the haunting third of the three women, played by Janice Rule, who drifts around aimlessly preoccupied with

Amidst his birds, Rene Auberjonois also adopts an avian pose, in Brewster McCloud *(Lion's Gate, 1970), a very feathery film.*

painting mythopeic, erotic murals whose scaly, serpentine femaleness pervades the whole film.

But when Spacek recovers, the fantasy starts. She begins to take on Duvall's personality, developing confidence, poise and a hard brittleness. Duvall, appalled but unable to resist, becomes at the same time drained of personality, first waiflike and later (metaphorically) almost invisible. This apparent psychic vampirism is a disturbing *tour de force*. As a fantasy of the mutability of personality, *3 Women* (whatever its exact meaning, which is certainly not paraphrasable) is as startling in its way as, say, the overt science fiction of *Invasion of the Body Snatchers*.

Altman's next fantasy was, in fact, SF: *Quintet* (1979). It is a cold, remote, almost unapproachable film in many ways. Yet it is purer science fiction than many a genre piece such as *Star Wars*. In the future (time unspecified), seal-hunter Essex (Paul Newman) tramps through a desolate landscape of snow with his pregnant wife (Brigitte Fossey) towards a derelict but still inhabited city. Maybe some catastrophe has taken place (a new Ice Age seems to have begun), or maybe humanity is dying out through sheer apathy. (Fossey's unborn baby will be the first child in many years.) The people of the city, dressed in furs (technology is frozen, too) and appearing medieval rather than

futuristic, are all obsessed with a board-game called Quintet. A "real" version of this game also exists, a tournament where players lose because they are killed in actuality. During one such move, Essex's wife is inadvertently killed.

Events become complicated after that, but in the end Essex (after killing several players himself, including a woman who seems to love him) walks northward into the snow; he has the romantic and unlikely notion (symbolised by the goose in flight that is a recurrent image in the film) that there may be a better place, elsewhere. He will almost certainly die. The film seems to say that Essex, an uncorrupt man still in touch with nature, has to leave the city because society there is decadent and death-obsessed. Underneath, one wonders whether Essex's romanticism is not just as sterile in its way as the city, where at least the Game provides a simulacrum of warm, passionate life even if death is its object. Indeed, the Game *is* life. There are few films that give a three-dimensional plausibility to a future society, but this one does. (*Blade Runner* is another.)

This fleshing out of an alternate culture (a kind of creativity that is at the heart of SF) surfaced again the next year in a very unexpected context. *Popeye* (1980) came as a complete surprise. A Disney-financed film, based on a comic-strip, and made by Altman? It seemed impossible. Yet in many

Sissy Spacek (below) and Shelley Duvall are two of the 3 Women *(Lion's Gate, 1977), here seen in an empty swimming pool, decorated by the mythopoeic murals of the third woman, played by Janice Rule. The weird relationship of the women is mythic as well.*

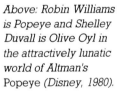

Above: Robin Williams is Popeye and Shelley Duvall is Olive Oyl in the attractively lunatic world of Altman's Popeye *(Disney, 1980).*

Left: Paul Newman is Essex, the seal hunter who has entered a cold, decaying city of the future in Quintet *(Lion's Gate, 1979). Here he is learning to play Quintet, the occasionally lethal game of the title.*

ways it was a triumph.

In the opening, Popeye (battling through heavy seas in a row-boat) arrives at a small fishing village of spindly, precarious houses. All is not well in Sweethaven, which is being tyrannized by the brutal Bluto (Paul Smith), but the place is full of life: a clumsy, accident-prone life, it's true. Popeye seems at the outset more "human" and less of a comic-strip stereotype than the Sweethaven inhabitants, but as the story progresses he is somehow drawn into this bizarre world and comes to stand as its emblem: jutting jaw, swivelling pipe, grotesquely muscled lower arms and sweet temperament. It is a performance of genius from Robin Williams, who manages to subdue his own powerful personality and allow the semi-coherent Popeye to take on an air of reality. The paradox of the film is the way in which human actors playing cartoon figures come to seem as deeply real as "real" people.

Altman's films have always been known for their sense of bustling life, abundant, muddled, almost spilling over the edge of the screen. (Many people dislike his work because the soundtrack can be so confusing, with background noises and snatches of seemingly irrelevant conversation competing for our attention against the main action.) The result this time is a boundless vitality exactly right for this fantastic fairy tale about a sailor searching for his long lost Pappy, finding him (he turns out to be a villain), and also finding a baby, Swee'pea.

The old Altman themes, which have sometimes seemed over-intellectualized previously (as in *Quintet*), emerge quite naturally in this far-from-intellectual film: dreams and obsessions, truth and illusion, sweetness and savagery, and the adjustment of one's self to things as they are. Shelley Duvall (Olive Oyl) is an absurdly close replica of the original comic-strip character. She has the film's most touching moments: her wispy little song about Bluto (to whom she is engaged), purporting to praise him but feebly coming down to his only possible recommendations ("He's large", and "He's mine"); and the moment when, while scolding Popeye, her lips manage with a coquettish precision "accidentally" to brush his. Altman's baby grandson, Wesley Ivan Hurt, plays wide-eyed Swee'pea with all the confidence of an experienced trouper. Harry Nilsson's cleverly naive-seeming songs would not work very well on their own, but are just right for the story, as is Jules Feiffer's vinegary screenplay.

For all that life has its sour moments in Sweethaven, it *is* a haven, not just for Popeye, but in a curiously touching way for many of the fantasies of the great American dream. As one critic (Tom Milne) has said, perhaps Sweethaven is the place Essex is forlornly seeking at the end of *Quintet*.

Cubby Broccoli

Albert R. "Cubby" Broccoli (born 1909) may not be a great film producer – the case is arguable – but he is certainly a smart operator. In partnership with Harry Saltzman for fifteen years, and working alone since November 1975, Broccoli revolutionized fantastic cinema by showing the money men that it could be profitable. He thus opened the door to the multi-million-dollar financing of fantasy movies, without which the genre could not have reached the dizzying heights (and some of the abysmal depths as well) of today.

Broccoli did this by producing a series of super-spy adventure movies starring James Bond, a swashbuckling killer and lover, originally the creation of the best-selling novelist Ian Fleming. From the beginning, the Bond movies have never been hardcore fantasy; they are the kind of fringe fantasy that was first popularised in the Fu Manchu movies of the 1930s – movies that tend to feature mad scientists out to control the world and an assortment of implausible scientific gadgetry. While purporting to take place in the real world, most of the Bond films are – to varying degrees – science fiction. They are also fantastic in the psychological sense; that is, they create fantasies of potency, of urbanity, of guilt-free mayhem, impossible in the real lives of ordinary people.

Not all the Bond movies could be rigorously described as "fantastic" in the sense that term is used throughout this book, and I restrict myself here to only six. The plots of Bond movies are repetitive. Almost invariably, they feature an evil genius holding the world to ransom. In *Dr No* and *You Only Live Twice*, it is spacecraft belonging to the great powers that are interfered with and kidnapped: the same applies to *The Spy Who Loved Me*, only this time it is submarines. *On Her Majesty's Secret Service* threatens the world with a virus that kills plants and animals, and *Moonraker* with a nerve gas that kills people. All these plot devices are patently SF. *Live and Let Die*, on the other hand, is the only one of the series to feature supernatural fantasy.

Dr No (1962) was the first Bond film, and it set the pattern: a guest star playing at being sinister up to the hilt; Bond himself (Sean Connery in those days), handsome, sardonic, wisecracking, amoral, brilliantly efficient; several beautiful girls for Bond to have sex with. (One of these is almost always killed in the later films, though in the earlier ones the obligatory sacrifice is sometimes that of a male friend, this time the Jamaican Quarrel.) Joseph Wiseman, who played Dr No, remains one of the best villains in a Bond movie, ruthless, polite, and both metaphorically and literally metallic (he has hands of steel).

None of the movies is artistically great, though all, to a degree, are entertaining. They are not really films with a narrative structure: they are fantastic episodes of violence strung loosely and sometimes indigestibly together. Thus there is seldom a sense of a Bond film growing and intensifying towards a genuine climax; they are, in fact, nothing *but* climaxes, each set-piece exciting, none wholly satisfying, because none of them has a sense of completeness or inevitability. All of this was much more obvious in the later films. *Moonraker* and *The Spy Who Loved Me* are good examples of narrative structure so arbitrary as to appear entirely random. *Dr No* lacked some of the surface gloss of the subsequent films, but on the other hand it had a stronger narrative thrust and also gained through having its tongue-in-cheek quality moderately restrained; Bond at the outset was more of a real character, less a bundle of affectations. He was, incidentally, crueller as well.

In the minds of many, James Bond is still Connery, an intelligent, *macho* actor who made the part very much his own. He played the role in the first five Broccoli-Saltzman Bond movies, dropped out for *On Her Majesty's Secret Service* (where the part was played with bare competence by Australian actor George Lazenby) to return for the seventh (non-fantasy) – *Diamonds are Forever*. The fifth of these, *You Only Live Twice* (1967), was notable for its elaborate sets, designed in a spacious, clinical, rather expressionist style by Ken Adam, one of them at the then extraordinary cost of one million dollars (this was the rocket launching pad inside the volcano). Adam worked on seven of the Bond films from *Dr No* up to *Moonraker*, after which set decorator Peter Lamont took over as production designer.

Connery's withdrawal from the series (apart from his 1983 comeback in the non-fantasy, non-Broccoli remake of *Thunderball* entitled *Never Say Never Again*) sealed its aesthetic fate. Lazenby had been a disappointment (in an otherwise above-average film), and the subsequent choice of Roger Moore (three years older than Connery) as Connery's heir proved fatal to the balance between action and irony. Now the films were strictly played for laughs, to suit Moore's personality – that of a dapper, slightly soft lounge-lizard, far too cheerful to be a killer.

The remaining fun, such as it was, lay in seeing what ever-more-spectacular effect (often involving some absurdly cumbrous piece of high-tech killing equipment) would cap the previous one. Opening sequences were sometimes so strong that the remainder of the film would prove an anti-climax. The

Baron Samedi (Geoffrey Holder), the voodoo Lord of the Dead, rises menacingly from the grave in the imaginative James Bond movie Live and Let Die *(Eon/United Artists, 1973), the first of the series to star Roger Moore.*

best example, at the beginning of *The Spy Who Loved Me* (which was the first Bond film for which Broccoli was the sole producer), had Bond on skis pursued by Russians to the brink of a quite enormous precipice in the Alps. Without pausing, Bond skis over the edge and drops like a stone for hundreds of metres, but then, just as his death seems certain, a parachute emblazoned with a Union Jack opens and he floats patriotically to the invisible ground below. (The audience generally assumed that this stunt was a clever fake by the special-effects boys. In fact, it was a genuine leap by a brave lunatic called Rick Sylvester, who skied in midwinter off the top of El Capitan rock in California's Yosemite Valley, a sheer drop of two-thirds of a mile.)

The first film in which Moore played Bond was in many respects only so-so: *Live and Let Die*. The villain here was a black man (played uneasily by Yaphet Kotto, who was worried about black dignity being impugned), and the setting was in and around the Caribbean. What is done tremendously well is the voodoo element – especially the tall, skeletal, half-comic, half-deathly figure of Baron Samedi (Geoffrey Holder) who seems unkillable, and reappears at the end, just when everything seems settled, sitting on the cow-catcher of Bond's fast-moving express train and laughing creepily. This was a moment (they are rare) when a Bond film captured a strongly disquieting image of the uncanny. The trick of the unkillable killer

was tried again with the steel-toothed figure of "Jaws" (Richard Kiel) in *The Spy Who Loved Me* and *Moonraker* (where true love reforms him), but Jaws' invulnerability is no more than a running gag. By now the films were effectively formula slapstick. None the less, Broccoli (who had a real creative input into the films, for better or for worse) has been one of the most influential producers in fantastic cinema. He found a formula and he made it work. It does not matter to Broccoli if intellectuals sneer at these movies, providing that the masses still go to them. Much of the audience consists of children, and part of Broccoli's achievement (later developed further by George Lucas) was in taking fantastic cinema back to the area of family movies and away from adult-only horrors.

As a footnote to Broccoli's career: he once made a film specifically for children. Based on a novel written (surprisingly) by the author of the Bond books, it was *Chitty Chitty Bang Bang* (1968), made with the Bond-movies team. Dick Van Dyke starred as the eccentric inventor who creates a flying car, Gert Fröbe is the evil Baron Bombast who steals it (he was better as Goldfinger in 1964), and Sally Anne Howes is Van Dyke's girlfriend called (oh dear) Truly Scrumptious. The flying-car effects are jolly but phoney-looking; the songs are terrible, and the entire two-and-a-half hours finally collapse under their own weight. It flopped, and it was back (successfully) to the Bond drawing-board for Broccoli.

John Carpenter

John Carpenter (born c.1948) is one of the new generation of young directors to come out of film school – the same school as George Lucas. Though his first feature, *Dark Star* (1974), which was actually an expanded form of his film-school thesis, was well received at festivals, it was years before it gained any sort of wide distribution, and he did not become generally known to the public until *Halloween* (1978).

Dark Star has a cult following, especially among undergraduates. It is an amazingly good film for $60,000, better than films that have cost literally one hundred times as much. Unlike so much SF on the screen, it is obviously made by people who love and understand the genre. The co-writer, editor, effects-man and star was Dan O'Bannon, who was later co-writer of *Alien* and, less spectacularly, *Dead and Buried* (see filmography). On a spaceship whose mission is to destroy unstable stars the captain is frozen and the crew nearly psychotic. A captured alien (looking like a mean beach ball with claws) has escaped, the computer is on the blink, and there is a rather prissy, intelligent, talking bomb that wants to go off and can only be dissuaded, temporarily, by a philosophical argument about phenomenology. The plot (part parody, part genuine SF) defies synopsis, but its realization (despite some messiness in the middle) is achieved with wit, precision and painstaking special effects that often look pretty good despite the shoestring budget. The apocalyptic ending ("Let there be light!" the bomb decides) has the hippy surf-loving crew member blissfully board-riding through space and burning up in a planetary atmosphere, while another – an autistic, star-gazing mystic – meets his ecstatic end in a passing asteroid shower.

Carpenter had to wait a while before getting a fully professional directorial assignment, and passed the time writing screenplays. The one that was finally made (*Eyes of Laura Mars*, 1978, see filmography) was much changed from his original conception, and he does not like it. Then he was allowed to direct a modest thriller from his own screenplay: *Assault on Precinct 13* (1976). It is a tense and witty reworking of the theme of Howard Hawks's western *Rio Bravo* set in a contemporary urban wasteland, and featuring a killer gang of youths. It is not fantasy, but it did give him a second start in fantasy, for when the film was enthusiastically received at the London Film Festival, producer Irwin Yablans was present, and this led to the making of *Halloween*.

The rest is history. Quite big history, as a matter of fact, for the film continues to hold the record for biggest profit on smallest outlay (it cost around $320,000 and has made

well over ·one hundred times that). In essence it is a very simple piece of work. In a small midwestern town, an escaped lunatic in a Halloween mask kills a babysitter and two of her friends (the fake scariness of Halloween is in the background of the whole piece); he almost kills a second babysitter, Laurie, a part played realistically and matter-of-factly

Left: one of the best known images in horror cinema, Nick Castle as the masked, homicidal Shape in the hugely successful Halloween *(Falcon International, 1978).*

A sinister ghost ship from the dead past glides out of the mist in Carpenter's The Fog *(Avco Embassy, 1979).*

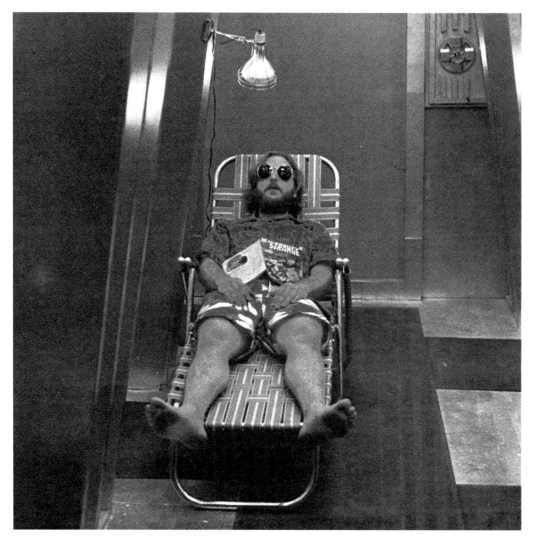

Left: the new captain, Doolittle (Brian Narelle), finds out that there is little to do on a long spaceship voyage except read comics, in the cult comedy-SF success Dark Star (Harris Enterprises, 1974). Until, that is, the alien escapes and the talking bomb goes mad.

Right: in a previous film Kurt Russell had played Elvis Presley, but in Escape from New York (Avco Embassy, 1981) he is Snake Plissken, the tough-guy hero who turns a future Manhattan – now a sanctuary for criminals – upside down.

by Jamie Lee Curtis (the daughter of Janet Leigh, herself murdered by a homicidal maniac in *Psycho*), but she escapes. Afterwards she is attacked again, but she manages to wound him with a knitting needle; he attacks again and this time she apparently kills him with his own knife; but yet again – a real shock, this – he comes back at her, and is repeatedly shot. Later, the spot where the body fell is empty.

This is a virtuoso piece of story-telling that claims no metaphysical significance for itself at all. (Carpenter, in interviews, is characteristically insulting about any work by his colleagues that he regards as inflated or pretentious; he says he would have been happy in the old studio system.) This film appears to be shockingly violent, but in fact it is not. The irony is that its success *did* lead to a torrent of genuinely violent stalk-and-slash movies featuring women as the victims of crazed killers, and the blame for this unnervingly sadistic phenomenon has been laid at Carpenter's door. This would seem much more unfair had not the sequel to *Halloween* (*Halloween 2*, 1981, not directed by Carpenter, but co-produced and co-written by him) been exactly the kind of nasty exploitation movie that *Halloween*'s imitators are.

Halloween 2 is not fantasy, but in a sense *Halloween* is, for the looming, unkillable Shape comes to seem no mere lunatic, but an incarnation of all the supernatural evil forgotten by the people who make a joke out of Halloween today.

With this success, Carpenter had reached the big time. Yet with his next two films he did not quite know what to do with the bigger budgets he was given. *The Fog* (1979) is an interesting little supernatural thriller about the living-dead crew of a ghost-ship that returns to wreak vengeance on the tiny Californian port whose people were responsible for their deaths a century ago. Very consciously a "story", it reminds us of the tradition of story-telling at the very beginning, with John Houseman as the old sea-dog telling a ghostly yarn to frightened children. Then, in the best sequence of the film, uncanny events take place in the town: glass breaks, car horns erupt, a petrol pump starts gushing – a series of beautifully choreographed incidents at exactly midnight in the sleeping street. But as the film moves on from eeriness and fog to the all-too-solid phantoms looking for victims, it collapses into purely conventional B-movie scares, and incidentally leaves a lot of loose plot ends hanging. There are some nice

Right: Kurt Russell again, in The Thing (Universal, 1982), as MacReady, a member of an Antarctic research unit, who is wondering what has been cut out of this block of ice. Soon he will wish that he never found out.

sequences, though.

Escape from New York (1981) is science fiction, supposedly Carpenter's favourite genre, and the one he was brought up on. In the near future, Manhattan has become a walled colony of criminals and outcasts, free to do what they like inside, but locked away from the outside world by massive barriers. Unfortunately, the President of the USA crashes inside the walls in a plane, and ex-criminal Snake Plissken (Kurt Russell) is sent in to bring him out. The film is atmospheric, as Snake weaves his way through the exotically tough, low-life society inside this sanctuary of free enterprise, but it is episodic, with little narrative thrust, and slightly lacklustre climaxes. Tremendously good fun, it is nevertheless a disappointment, for by now people were expecting remarkable things with each new Carpenter film.

Life began to look even grimmer for Carpenter after his next film, a remake of Howard Hawks' production of *The Thing from Another World*. It did not completely flop, but it was not the success that Universal needed to recoup the production costs, which were said to have been $15 million. However, *The Thing* (1982) may prove to be one of the great milestones in fantastic cinema, and its comparative failure at the box-office could be a testament to its ambitious breaking of new ground. Audiences may well have been puzzled by the story (which is far more sophisticated than that of most filmed SF), and they were certainly revolted at the awesomely disgusting special effects.

But these effects (the monstrous guises adopted by the Thing) were not merely a grotesque icing on the cake; they were integral to the story.

The original film of *The Thing* (see Chapter One) is an acknowledged classic, but has possibly been over-praised. Certainly it jettisoned the most interesting element of the story on which it was based: that the Thing (which has been frozen in the Antarctic ice for sixteen million years) has the capacity to mimic exactly any life form it is able to absorb. It was one of the first in a series of science-fiction "shape-shifters" that have seldom found their way into movies (though they appeared in the SF film that Carpenter loved best as a child: *It Came from Outer Space*). Anyway, the Hawks movie reduced the Thing to a bloodsucking carrot, but Carpenter and his screenwriter Bill Lancaster (Burt's son) stayed close to the original story.

The film is an object lesson in building tension and atmosphere economically. It opens with a beautifully photographed scene of a husky fleeing across the snow, being pursued by a Norwegian helicopter trying to shoot it. It makes its way to an American research base. Why are the Norwegians trying to kill the nice doggie? We are instantly hooked. Building slowly, but giving extraordinary value when it reaches its climaxes, the film goes on from this mysterious opening to detail the slow growth of the horror of loss of personality, and of alienation from those close to you. (It is a recognized nightmare of small children that a friend or a parent turns around, and is alien, distant, a Thing with No Face.) The Thing begins taking everybody over, and there seems no way of knowing who is real and who is a monstrous replica built out of the Thing's protoplasmic ability to look like anything at all, and its undoubted intelligence. Its various overt manifestations (in the first instance as a dog turned literally. inside out, hissing, spitting, oozing, sprouting wildly whipping tentacles) are quite extraordinary, but they are never allowed to dominate the basic situation of a group of ordinary men trapped in a nightmare. That is, the film (as in Hawks's original) gives due credit to humanness as well as monstrosity. But so bizarre is the Thing that many viewers could see no further, which may be why the film was not instantly recognized as the undoubted classic it is. Rob Bottin, a young make-up artist who had also worked on *The Fog*, performed miracles, with his large team of technicians, in creating the various effects. Most spectacular, perhaps, is the moment when electrodes are applied to a recent corpse in the attempt to stimulate a heartbeat; suddenly the body's torso grows teeth and bites the doctor's arms off; its neck stretches obscenely and lowers the corpse's head to the floor; its head extrudes an enormously long tongue which whips around a table leg and pulls itself along; then it grows legs like a spider and scuttles away. One of the characters speaks surely for the audience as well when he looks aghast at one of the Thing's incarnations and says (quite in character), "Ya gotta to be fuckin' kidding!"

Carpenter's speciality has always been to capture the feelings of groups (sometimes individuals) who are trapped and isolated. This could, if repeated often enough, be both gloomy and paranoid, except that he is also excellent at showing courage and level-headedness *in extremis*, so his films are not particularly downbeat. *The Thing*, which ends with two survivors too exhausted to care any more if one or other of them is actually a monster (a terrible thought is that *both* could be), is not exactly cheerful; yet they *have* survived, and there is something touching about this momentary camaraderie in front of a hellish scene of flames licking in the snow.

Carpenter is a genuine *auteur*, though his films do not have the unmistakable style of, say, a Cronenberg, or even the unmistakable themes of, say, a Spielberg. He always emphasizes narration, using an unobtrusively fluid camera style and tight editing. He has also written the music for all the films discussed here (except *The Thing*), and very good music it is, too. He has worked with much the same team on his films, notably the very efficient producer Debra Hill (still an unusual job for a woman), the cameraman Dean Cundey, and the production designer, his old high-school friend Tommy Lee Wallace.

Wallace was given a chance to direct the second sequel to *Halloween*. (He had turned down the first.) *Halloween III: Season of the Witch* (1983) was produced by Carpenter and Hill. Wallace was given the writer's credit as well as the director's, but in fact the original screenplay was the work of British writer Nigel Kneale, author of the *Quatermass* stories.

Unlike its two predecessors (which it has nothing to do with, apart from taking place on Halloween), this is *not* a stalk-and-slash movie. Mad Irishman Dan O'Herlihy, infuriated at the degeneration of Halloween into a commercial festival, decides to revenge himself by using technological witchcraft to renew the bloody, sacrificial quality of the original Celtic festival. Using microchips made from a stolen Stonehenge monolith to lend occult power to his devices, he creates Halloween masks (advertised with conscious irony on TV with an infuriating commercial jingle) which, when triggered, erupt inwards into spiders and snakes and cause general murderous mayhem. With them, he will be able to destroy a fair proportion of America's youth on the night of Halloween.

Kneale resigned because Dino De Laurentiis, whose production company was financing the film, wanted more bloody horror sequences, so as "not to disappoint the kids", according to one report. In fact, though the film does have some spectacular, Grand Guignol, visceral horror, it has by no means lost the wittily eerie atmosphere that Kneale had wanted. An unnerving feature is the use of politely sadistic android killers by O'Herlihy to deal with interference. Even the heroine (in the almost obligatory twist ending) turns out to have been replaced by an android. It's all innocently nasty fun for people with a strong constitution, and the goriest scene (displaying the masks' powers on a horrid little boy) is not just decorative: it carries a powerful charge central to the film's theme. This fully functional use of a fantastic element is a typical Carpenter touch, and while Wallace certainly shows promise, there is plenty in the film to suggest that Carpenter's firm hand had something to do with it. Disquieting moments where things seem not quite right, in the town in which O'Herlihy's toy factory is situated, are subtly achieved and directly comparable to Carpenter's earlier work.

Carpenter works hard and fast. His latest film, *Christine* (1983), was actually scripted, filmed and released within a year of publication of the Stephen King novel (same title) on which it is based. It is an excellent film, but by no means a great one. There are special problems in transferring a best-seller to the screen, because it exists already as a series of images in the minds of the public. Carpenter treats with respect, but a curious remoteness, the story of a possessed, evil car (a 1958 Plymouth Fury lovingly rebuilt twenty years later by a teenage wimp). There is little attempt to involve us directly in the action with, say, subjective camerawork or cutting; we do not feel personally threatened. Most of Christine's victims are thoroughly nasty types. Keith Gordon gives a most accomplished performance as the pimply, gangly youth transformed by Christine's influence into a darkly good-looking young man. He is both her lover and her saddest victim, falling literally prey to the great American myth of the machine as god. The special effects are amazingly good: the car's ability to reconstruct itself from rusty junk to gleaming sleekness being masterfully achieved by Roy Arbogast, who also did the mechanical effects on *The Thing*, as well as on *Return of the Jedi*. All this cost money, but some of the best effects are cheap, especially the car radio that turns itself on to play rock-'n'-roll oldies from the fifties when bent on vengeance. This is the film of an old-fashioned, skilful story-teller. A very intelligent but modest film-maker, Carpenter may never make movies that directly reflect his rather enigmatic personality; he is not an *auteur* in that sense. But he is likely to go on

giving us well-made genre movies that, occasionally, transcend their formulae to vibrate uneasily within us.

One aspect of Carpenter may be a strength or weakness, it is hard to tell: he seems to be a Manichean. That is, he seems to believe in Evil as existing outside humanity, as an absolute force which has the same integrity as Good. In *Christine* he took away the possible psychological reasons for the car's behaviour (infected by the nastiness of a previous owner perhaps), and in a bravura opening sequence shows it as wholly malicious while still on the assembly line. In Carpenter's movies there is usually a Shape or a Thing – a Malevolence out there, waiting to get us. One of the paradoxes of fantastic cinema is that many of us want the catharsis of imagining ourselves being got. And there is one element of comfort in his films: while Evil may be formidable, it is not irresistible. Carpenter also believes in the strength of humans to cope with it.

Above: this is a tiny Manhattan, being prepared for a special effects sequence in Carpenter's Escape from New York *(Avco Embassy, 1981).*

Below: John Stockwell, left, is the best friend and Keith Gordon, right, is Arnie, the wimp whose life is about to be transformed by the evil power of the old car he finds rotting in a front yard. The film is Carpenter's Christine *(Delphi/Columbia, 1983), and Christine is a 1958 Plymouth Fury.*

Larry Cohen

There is plenty of room for argument about Larry Cohen. His films, when they are mentioned at all, tend to be dismissed as the lowest kind of hackwork. *It's Alive* (1973), one of the most successful films of its year at the box-office, appears in a book called *The Best, Worst, and Most Unusual Horror Films* in the "Worst" chapter, and is awarded one star out of ten. I would be tempted to give it nine stars out of ten.

Cohen (born 1938) ought not to be confused with three screenwriters with similar names (one of them the Lawrence D. Cohen who wrote *Carrie*). He is, however, the whiz-kid who created eight television series including the SF series *The Invaders*, wrote at least twenty-nine television episodes and plays, and then left the television business (still a young man) just as he was becoming rich. He is also the Larry Cohen whose exposé movie *The Private Files of J. Edgar Hoover* (1976) was not played on American network television because it was thought to be too slanderous. (It incidentally reveals the probable identity of "Deep Throat", the anonymous tipster who broke open the Watergate scandal.)

Larry Cohen, who has his own small production company, Larco, writes, produces and directs all his own films. There is a case for seeing him as the most original, subversive and eccentric of all the Hollywood independents. Since his subversion is normally carried out by way of low-budget horror films, he is not seen as a real threat to the establishment, but his four (to date) fantasy/horror films repay viewing, and viewing again, for the extraordinary mileage he gets out of what in other hands would be bottom-of-the barrel exploitation plot ideas.

His fantasy movies are *It's Alive* (1973),

Demon (1976, originally titled *God Told Me To*), *It Lives Again* (1978) and *Q – The Winged Serpent* (1982). There is no space here to describe them in detail – and you wouldn't believe me, anyway – but a few high spots should be mentioned.

It's Alive is a film about a toothed, carnivorous, mutant baby who starts life by bloodily demolishing the entire staff of the hospital delivery theatre. Most critics have been so appalled at this schlock premise (fortunately we only see the aftermath) that they have not examined what Cohen does with the idea. This is completely different from any other of the many monstrous-child movies. The title itself refers back to Frankenstein's cry of triumph when the monster first comes to life; and, as in *Frankenstein*, the whole film examines the pathos of the abnormal. The baby's father moves inexorably from horrified rejection to passionate protection of his offspring, which makes its own way home. The film ends with a sequence in the storm drains of Los Angeles (in homage to *Them!*) which is sufficiently brilliantly directed for one part of it to have been repeated almost shot-for-shot (probably coincidentally) in *E.T.*, where again the abnormal creature is hunted by the full force of a repressive society and blinded by searchlights – easy enough to do when the audience knows the creature is good (*E.T.*), but a tour de force of sympathy-arousal in Cohen's case. *It's Alive* is also consistently witty, as in the scene where heavily armed policemen surround a perfectly ordinary baby, guns at the ready, on a surburban front lawn. The baby looks astonished.

It Lives Again extends the imagery in a successful sequel, probing even further the rifts in family life and society at large that a mutant offspring may not only reveal but come to symbolize.

Demon is a thriller about a mad sniper who turns out to have been under the mental control of a messianic, androgynous creature, child of an alien father and a human mother, who turns out in a genuinely astonishing finale to have an unexpected relationship to the police detective who has been hunting him. It is almost impossible to describe this film. Only Cohen could (a) invent a male Christ-figure with a vagina, and (b) produce a screenplay in which this bizarre image is completely central. Also, any other director would have put the emphasis on the monster, but Cohen puts it on the policeman, in an extraordinary study of Catholicism, guilt, and the perversion of the instinct to have children.

Demon is not the sort of film to appeal to conventional horror-film audiences. For one thing, Cohen demands a good deal of intelligence from his viewers: the religious allegory is worked out not only in imagery (pentecostal flames flickering around the new

The low-budget, seldom glimpsed, carnivorous baby from Larry Cohen's It's Alive *(Larco/Warner Bros, 1973) was the creation of Rick Baker. At one point it was animated by pulling it along on a string!*

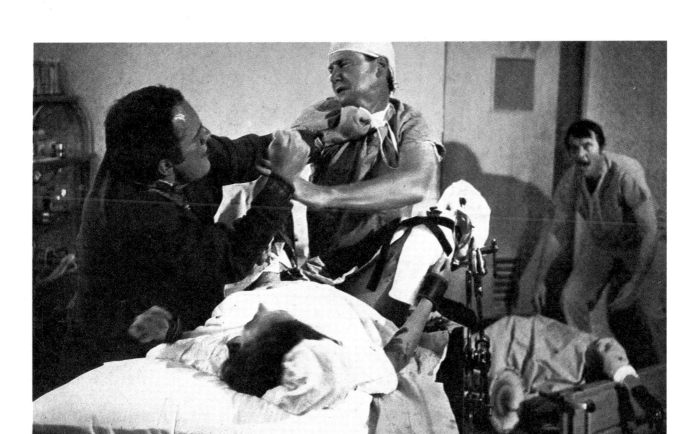

Messiah's head), but in long passages of dialogue, and in knowing reference (the Messiah has twelve disciples – business men – one of whom betrays him to the police). Neither Christian nor Jew is likely to be pleased at the direction of all this symbolism – an unfeeling, harsh God.

In every Cohen film, the viewer is first asked to swallow a grotesquely fantastic central image, and then finds to his astonishment that the central drama of the film lies with the human characters. Cohen continually turns our expectations upside-down.

The very title *Q – The Winged Serpent* (at one stage it was to be called simply *Q*) points to the ambiguity of the film. Q is an incarnation of Quetzalcoatl, the Aztec god, who appears as a huge, flying reptile terrorizing New York and appropriately making its nest on the Aztec pyramid atop Manhattan's Chrysler building. Ritual murders featuring the complete removal of skin from bodies ("Last night I saw a woman flayed, and you would hardly believe how much it altered her person for the worse", as Jonathan Swift once wrote) are connected with the monster's appearance. But Q can also be identified as a small-time jewel thief, Jimmy Quinn (played with extraordinary conviction by Michael Moriarty as a timorous, narcissistic opportunist) who in his own way makes sacrifices to the winged god whose lair he has stumbled on. The almost likeable human monster Quinn coalesces (metaphorically) with the literal monster in one of the wittiest films for years, which once again quietly subverts

conservative views about how society works, and filmgoers' views about how B-movies work, in very much the same breath.

Cohen always gets tremendously good performances from his actors. But more important, he is a genuine *auteur* who, even though he chooses to work in the most derelict slums of genre cinema, has shown the big boys just how ambitious fantastic movies can be. May Cohen's brand of schlock continue for years!

Above: mayhem in the delivery room in It's Alive.
Below: Quetzalcoatl returns to its roost on top of Manhattan's Aztec-style Chrysler building, in Cohen's Q – The Winged Serpent *(Larco, 1982).*

David Cronenberg

David Cronenberg (born 1943) is a comparatively young Canadian film director around whom controversy swirls. On the one hand, he is seen as the cynical maker of disgusting, exploitative "splatter" movies – the kind that (on tape) have been christened "video nasties" in the UK and are sometimes seen as ushering in an age of moral collapse as bad as anything since Rome under Caligula. On the other hand, he is the daring, intellectual iconoclast who has chosen deliberately disturbing, subversive metaphors to show society that it is in an age of moral collapse as bad as anything since Rome under Caligula.

To give an idea of what sort of person he might actually be, it is worth quoting at length from a recent, unpublished BBC radio interview:

"When people ask me, 'Why do you make horror films?' I immediately have to go back to Aristotle and his theory of catharsis as being a justification for high tragedy, or even comedy. For me, horror films are films of confrontation, not films of escape at all, but in a horror film one confronts things that you might not really want to cope with in your real life, in a kind of a safe, dreamlike way. But you will meet these things eventually: I'm talking about ageing, death, separation.

"That's the metaphorical level that horror films work on. All of my films, I'm aware of it now, are very body-conscious, because for me the body is really the source of horror in human beings; it is the body which ages and the body which dies. It really is very Cartesian of me, I suppose, because to me the mind/body split is the source of the mystery, and also the horror, which I think ultimately we have to confront. You see people whose minds are perfectly together while their bodies begin to distort, begin to change, begin to age, begin to rot, whatever: that to me is horror...I don't want to give my audience a chance to get too distanced. That's why my films are very urban and very contemporary in their setting."

Pretty impressive for an *ad lib* answer in an interview. Yet Cronenberg may be conscious of an inadequacy in this sort of argument. Max Renn, the hero of *Videodrome* (1982), uses the catharsis argument (he runs a cable-television channel that specializes in violence and pornography) during a scene set in a talk-show interview, and there Cronenberg shows it as an obviously glib response from a man unwilling to confront his deeper motivations.

From the beginning of his career, Cronenberg's films have been intentionally shocking. His first two features were made non-professionally, but they received a minimal showing at film festivals. *Stereo* (1969) is a story about surgically induced telepathy, and the unhappiness it leads to in experimental subjects. It was made cheaply with a voice-over narration. *Crimes of the Future* (1970) was a little more expensive, and it had synchronous sound. The premise of the film is mildly tasteless, and its execution extremely so. A cosmetics additive has triggered a disease that kills all women of child-bearing age and most of the younger ones. Five-year-old Tania Zolty plays a surviving child who is kidnapped by a group of paedophiles desirous of impregnating her. The sequences that disgusted even the comparatively sophisticated audiences at film festivals were those dealing with unpleasantly gooey fluids leaking from the noses and eyes of affected women, which contain a powerful chemical that impels people to sniff and lick at them. The "crimes" of the title are mostly various forms of sexual fetishism.

Cronenberg, who was later to be dubbed "the King of Venereal Horror", seemed to have been aiming at the title from the beginning. It was, however, his first professional feature, *Shivers* (1975), also known as *They Came from Within* and *The Parasite Murders*, that earned him the sobriquet.

Shivers is a deeply black comedy, set in an upper middle-class apartment building. It begins with a maddened-seeming doctor in his consulting room apparently trying to rape a young female patient. In fact he forces her on a table, disembowels her, and pours acid into the resulting cavity. Not quite as disgusting as it sounds, it was nevertheless electrifying, more especially as there turns out to have been method in his madness. It seems the doctor has developed a parasite (they are around six inches long and look like slugs – he is trying to destroy one here) which it is intended should live symbiotically with man and take over some of his bodily functions. In fact, the main effect of the parasite is aphrodisiac. Infected persons are sexually maddened, or eaten away from within, or both. What the film gives us, on a small scale, is sexual apocalypse, directed with lunatic conviction and a series of extremely revolting variations on the theme of parasitic infection. Soon the apartment building resembles one of the less enlightened areas of Dante's *Inferno*, and the film ends as, with manic gaiety, the building's occupants climb into their cars and drive out to infect first Canada and then the world.

Basically *Shivers* is a film about a form of VD with very big germs. The grossness of the film is almost beyond belief, but the initial reaction of revulsion is quite inadequate, though it is as far as many critics got. It could be argued that this bizarre cinema of disgust opened up areas of reality that had been barely touched upon before in film, and provided metaphors with which to explore them.

However, his second feature, *Rabid* (1976), is structurally too close to *Shivers* to represent any particularly interesting new departure. Marilyn Chambers (previously best known for her roles in hardcore pornographic films) plays the innocent victim of a new technique in plastic surgery, which as a side effect creates a retractable, penis-shaped syringe in her armpit. (Synopsizing these films in cold blood makes them sound quite absurd; in fact, Cronenberg is skilled at making his audiences take various bizarre premises for granted.) Chambers feels compelled to attack people occasionally with her syringe, for now she needs blood to stay alive. Her victims develop a rabies-like disease which creates homicidal mania, and once again the apocalypse hits society, only this time we see it in action in the larger world. The development of the film is rather predictable, but it has incidental moments of some subtlety. The central image of the innocent, phallus-wielding killer-woman is powerful, but so densely loaded a metaphor it is hard to tell exactly what its function is.

The Brood is a far more startling exercise (not that *Rabid* was conventional by any standards other than Cronenberg's). Oliver Reed plays a pop psychologist who has written a trendy textbook called *The Shape of Rage*. The hero's wife is a patient of the therapist; she is mentally disturbed. Her husband begins to investigate the therapist's practices and is appalled to find physical stigmata among his ex-patients, including a monstrous lymphosarcoma on the neck of one ex-patient. A mysterious series of murders, which, it transpires, are being carried out by inhuman dwarf-children, seem to be linked to the psychologist's work. It becomes clear that the bodies of people in therapy are being literally metamorphosed by their mental conditions (hence the concealed meaning of the book title), and this theory is proved appallingly accurate when the husband visits his ex-wife, who raises her nightdress to reveal that she is breeding dwarf creatures in yolk-sacs extruded from the vicinity of her vagina. In a moment that contrives to be both horrible and touching, she bites open the new sac, and licks the latest of her brood clean, like a mother cat with a kitten. The brood members are literally the children of her rage, and the murders have been willed by her. This metaphor for mental disturbance, where the internal monsters of the mind are given literal reality, is stunning.

The Brood is not a brutal film, though it is disturbing. It seems to be partly fuelled by a furious animus against the neglect of children. Cronenberg has confessed that it is the most autobiographical of his films (this was before *Videodrome*). He has sardonically referred to it as "my *Kramer vs Kramer*" (he was involved in a custody battle for the child of his first marriage at the time). His sarcastic comment is in fact quite true; all the domestic, human emotions of *Kramer vs Kramer* are here, but stretched out and distorted on some ghastly mental rack.

In *Scanners* (1980), horrific opening and closing sequences frame a grotesque story that is more science fiction than horror, and

Samantha Eggar, in a fit of snarling, maternal protectiveness, clutches the most recently "born" of her brood to her breast, in David Cronenberg's The Brood *(Mutual/Elgin, 1979). The "baby" is the living, external manifestation of her internal rage.*

Dick Smith created the special effects for the alarming, climactic scene of Cronenberg's Scanners *(Filmplan International, 1980), in which Michael Ironside, left, duels telepathically with his brother, played by Stephen Lack, right.*

suggest that Cronenberg's satirical interests go well beyond the venereal. Once again, the villains behind the scenes are the scientific manipulators, this time a group trying to create an army of "scanners" by giving pregnant women a drug that will ensure telepathic babies. But the two oldest telepaths (brothers, it turns out) are both in their way corrupted by their talent, though one fights on behalf of human society, and the other on behalf of what is effectively a new race of super-beings. The narrative line is a little incoherent, and the film is mainly notable for its accomplished set pieces: the notorious exploding head of the beginning, the disturbed telepathic sculptor who ekes out an autistic existence within his own sculptures, the scene where an ordinary telephone booth becomes a battleground between the hero and a giant laboratory computer, and the final telepathic duel (make-up effects by Dick Smith being all swollen, pulsing veins and hideous distortions) which ends with the wrong brother apparently the survivor, but speaking with the right brother's voice. It is, in fact, the visual equivalent of some pulp E.S.P. novel of the 1940s – something like A. E. van Vogt's *Slan* or James Blish's *Jack of Eagles*.

Cronenberg finally found the perfect

metaphor for all his complex obsessions in *Videodrome* (1982). His most ambitious, expensive film up to that time, it was said to be aimed at a wider audience than the smallish band of cult followers he had so far collected. It flopped badly, as it was almost bound to, for the intellectual intricacy of the film was hardly going to endear him to a juvenile audience largely reared on the pabulum of traditional horror cliches, more especially as *Videodrome* is a full-blooded attack on precisely those sadistic elements in horror films that the audience may have been attracted to in the first place. It is a stroke of paradoxical daring to make a pulp exploitation movie which takes the dubious morality of pulp exploitation movies as its actual theme. It may look rather too much like having your cake and eating it too, but it just about comes off.

Max Renn (played with cold, nervous conviction by James Woods) runs a tatty cable-television station specializing in sex-and-violence programming. His sidekick Harlan, who pirates programmes from satellite broadcasts, discovers a strange channel, Videodrome, that seems to show genuine scenes of sadism – a kind of snuff-movie channel – and Renn becomes obsessed with it. But when he comes across sado-masochistic behaviour in real life, in the person of his new girlfriend Nicki Brand (played with serene perversity by pop star Deborah Harry), a television talk-show hostess, he is unhappy. She on the other hand is excited (sexually and intellectually) by the output of Videodrome, which appears to emanate from Pittsburgh, and she goes off in search of it. When next seen she is a face and a body on the TV screen. Events are too complex for proper synopsis, but the gist of the story is that Videodrome imagery literally changes the brains of its viewers, inducing a kind of cancer that results in powerful hallucinations. The second half of the film, in which Renn is surrounded by appallingly plastic phenomena where objects become flesh, and flesh hardens into objects (in a typical black pun, his hand become a hand gun), is possibly explicable as one continuous hallucination. Certainly reality and Videodrome-induced fantasy are seamlessly joined. This is part of the point, of course – a trick played on the audience in order to make them think about the very real question of where media-reality stops and real-reality takes over. Videodrome has been invented by a Marshall McLuhan type guru who is apparently dead, but living on in a vast cassette library cared for by his daughter (named Bianca O'Blivion!); "I am my father's screen", she pronounces with religious resonance.

The most startling images concern Renn's television, which softens and deforms and becomes flesh, and his stomach, which develops a vaginal-looking slit which, it turns out, can accept video cassettes. This sounds

– and is – over the top, but one must admire a film-maker who does not flinch from any metaphor, no matter how grotesque and how difficult to incorporate into an ordinary narrative. It is no wonder that the film left its audience bemused.

In my view (a minority judgement), this is a deeply angry, deeply moral film. It tackles questions of some sophistication in a genre context which is not, finally, flexible enough to deal with them all; but what a brave attempt! Among the questions: Do horror films corrupt? Can sadism be programmed? Is McLuhan's distinction between "soft" and "hard" media valid or useful? Could it be that television will prove to be the ultimate aversion therapy? Does the religious phrase "the Word made Flesh" have a new connotation in the world of the media? (There is a lot of complex transsubstantiation imagery here.)

All this is done with considerable wit and – amazingly – realism. The tacky ambience of down-market television broadcasting is brilliantly evoked, and the television motif is wittily achieved in many areas of the film's design. It is all much too intellectual for schlock-movie fans, and too schlocky for intellectuals, and if Cronenberg keeps making films like this, then his audience will always be very limited.

Almost immediately afterwards, however, he proved that, if he forced himself, he *could* work within the conventional movie system. One imagines that if he had not proved this, the financing of each new film would have become more and more difficult. His adaptation of Stephen King's novel, *The Dead Zone* (1983), is not a typical Cronenberg movie, but it is an extremely clever adaptation. Christopher Walken plays the teacher involved in an accident who, after his recovery from a very prolonged coma, proves to have powers of telepathy and precognition. These powers are very disquieting, both for him and for people with whom he comes into contact. The story of a sensitive man feeling himself progressively dehumanized and placed apart by a talent he loathes and wants nothing to do with is evoked with a warmth that may surprise those familiar with the rather chilling quality of Cronenberg's previous work. He made the film with many of his usual team, including cinematographer Mark Irwin and production designer Carol Spier.

One hopes that this proves to be the breakthrough film that Cronenberg needs. It is well-made, subtle, true in essence to its literary source and deserves success. It is also, in the opinion of some, ever so slightly characterless. It would be a pity if the price Cronenberg had to pay for media success was the loss of personality.

For those with the stomach to tolerate the distortions and metamorphoses of the flesh and the spirit that have characterized Cronenberg's previous work, he is one of the great *auteurs* of fantastic cinema. He has remained true to his slightly Manichean vision, and has continued to subvert the smugness of society by producing appalling images of what distortions of life may lurk beneath its repressive surface. He belongs to that small group who have fashioned the B-movie into a secret weapon for exposing the soft underbelly of Life in the West.

The metamorphosis of human flesh is the dominant image of Videodrome *(Filmplan International/Universal, 1982). In this blown up frame from the film, we see James Woods' hand and arm coalescing with his gun, to create (in a typical Cronenberg visual pun) a hand-gun.*

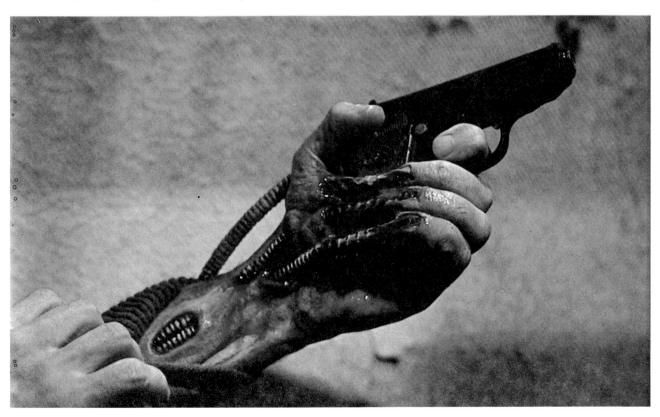

Dino De Laurentiis

Dino De Laurentiis has appeared three times already. He produced *Barbarella* (1968), and his production company financed *Halloween III: The Season of the Witch*, produced by John Carpenter, and *The Dead Zone*, directed by David Cronenberg. He is something of an enigmatic figure in film-making. Generally dismissed as a philistine, insolently nicknamed Dino De Dum Dum by a British cinema magazine, he has nevertheless been described by Cronenberg, who is nobody's yes-man, as "...a very interesting man, one of the last of the Old Style moguls...It's pretty exhilarating working with him, because he obviously loves to solve problems; there's a great deal of energy and dynamism going on around him." On the other hand, John Milius, who directed *Conan the Barbarian* for De Laurentiis, said "His methods are...unsound. Dino's just like bad weather, he'll pass, but meanwhile you contend with it."

Contrary to popular myth, the films he produces are by no means always aesthetic disasters. Indeed, at the beginning of his career De Laurentiis was a name to conjure with among intellectuals, for he produced two of

In some scenes of the De Laurentiis-produced Flash Gordon *(Starling-Famous, 1980), the action seems to have been designed by a collective of Italy's bondage freaks. Typical family fare of the last decade?*

Federico Fellini's early masterpieces: *La Strada* (1954) and *Nights of Cabiria* (1956). He still sometimes finances ambitiously artistic films, such as Ingmar Bergman's *The Serpent's Egg* (1977).

The execration of De Laurentiis by fans of fantastic cinema began with *King Kong* (1976), but he had been making fantasy films for a long time before that. An early example is *Danger: Diabolik* (1968), directed by the unevenly brilliant Italian, Mario Bava. This, like *Barbarella* (made around the same time), was based on a European comic-strip; it stars John Phillip Law as a super-criminal who can scale walls with the agility of a monkey. The film is colourful and spoof-like. Diabolik makes love, for example, in a soft nest of bank notes. His apparent demise, after molten, radioactive gold is poured over him, is followed by a close-up of the resulting statue's eyes...one of which winks.

It may have been the commercial success of *Barbarella* and *Diabolik* that set De Laurentiis on the wrong path, towards brightly coloured comic-strip action, seasoned with parody, and the use of special effects that

make remarkably little effort to look like anything realistic. His cardinal crime with *King Kong*, and *Flash Gordon* (1980), was not to take the subject matter seriously. In both cases his directors were given a screenplay by Lorenzo Semple Jr, writer of the very camp *Batman* series for television. But the illusion of reality is central for lovers of fantastic cinema; they do not want to be constantly reminded that they are watching a fiction. Semple's insistence on parody has the effect of making the stories seem unreal.

Both films made money, however, and it may be that the tastes of fantasy fans are not representative of what the public wants. The remake of *King Kong* is among the twenty most popular fantasy films ever made. De Laurentiis approaches film-making very much as manufacturers approach soap powder: as a product to be packaged. In some cases his advertising budget has been almost as big as his production budget, and this advertising has not always been wholly honest.

For example, a mechanical model of Kong built by the Italian effects engineer Carlo Rambaldi (who later worked on *E.T.*) was given tremendous publicity. Electronically controlled, forty feet tall, it was the star of the film, we were told. In fact, the model simply did not work, and appears in only one scene. (The separately-built, giant mechanical hands used for some close-ups were much more usable.) For nearly all the film, Kong is played by effects whiz-kid Rick Baker in an ape suit, which he described as "…a piece of shit; there are big seams and gaps – you can see it in the film." People angered by this kind of shoddiness, the big money going on promotion while short-cuts were taken in the over-hasty production, may have judged the film too harshly. Jessica Lange in the Fay Wray role takes quite an amusing liberated-woman approach to Kong: she treats him as a very large male chauvinist pig who is not without charm, and the film has several good moments. But compared with the melancholy, resonant power of the original *King Kong*, this remake looks tacky.

De Laurentiis was obviously much struck with the huge success of Spielberg's *Jaws*. His next two American productions were *The White Buffalo* (1977) and *Orca… Killer Whale* (1977). Both featured outsize monsters, one of which actually lived in the ocean. *The White Buffalo* was an incoherent mess, directed by J. Lee Thompson (who had once made the competent *Guns of Navarone*, but in recent years had sunk to the depths of *Planet of the Apes* sequels). The sad thing is that the story, about old enemies Crazy Horse and Wild Bill Hickok both haunted by a monstrous, spectral white buffalo, was sufficiently bizarre and interesting to have had a chance of coming off. It was the buffalo built by Rambaldi (one sometimes wonders how he gained his repu-

tation as an effects genius) that sank the film. It advanced jovially in great lolloping jumps, a bit like a very large March Hare, and in one preposterous sequence its wheels are repeatedly visible on screen.

Orca, too, had sadly flat direction, and rather a lame story, about the revenge of a whale whose mate and child have been slaughtered by Richard Harris (the one notable scene shows the birth of a baby whale at the moment its mother is being hauled out of the water). It bites Bo Derek's leg off, burns down a seaport and causes a mystical Eskimo to revise his values rapidly in the direction of suburban conservatism.

Flash Gordon goes wrong in the same way as *King Kong*, only more so. The rushed effects work (Van Der Veer studios had less than nine months to put together over six hundred blue-screen composites of live-action and matte paintings) shows all too clearly. The flying hawkmen look like, and are, people with cardboard wings flapping on wires. Sam Jones (an unknown and therefore presumably inexpensive actor) plays Flash with all the emotional expressiveness of a cigar-store wooden Indian. Only the set decorators and costumers show any flair: the film is a paradise for leather-and-spike-gear fetishists, and looks as if it resulted from a convention of all the kinkiest designers in

Richard Harris versus a vengeful killer whale in Orca…Killer Whale *(Famous, 1977), the De Laurentiis-produced attempt to cash in on the success of* Jaws. *Harris is not going to win this one.*

An uncomfortable moment for Arnold Schwarzenegger in Conan the Barbarian *(Dino De Laurentiis, 1981).*

a popular series of violent, vigorous and colourful pulp-magazine stories. De Laurentiis seems never to have lost his childlike trust in pulp literature as the best source for popular movies. The original stories were very much sword-and-sorcery, and part of the trouble with the film is that its respected director, John Milius, loves swords but has no interest in sorcery. (In interviews he significantly expresses complete disinterest in the craft of special effects. This may be why the effects team was allowed to get away with a large but totally unconvincing mechanical snake.) There is, however, a very effective wolf witch who lives in a desolate mountain valley; a genuinely eerie sequence, this. And there are some good mound-spirits. But the familiar Milius obsessions (rites of passage, rituals of physicality, the martial arts, and above all, the nature of true manliness) are dominant. The film is curiously remote and stylized in its treatment of violence – almost Japanese, one might say, but Milius does not have the visual strength of a Kurosawa. It has a kind of brooding, detached quality, though, and Milius must be admired for his refusal to *wallow* in violence, even though there is room for dismay about his insistence on its mystic elements. The dancer Sandahl Bergman makes a splendidly spirited woman swordfighter, and Arnold Schwarzenegger (a bodybuilding champion) is carefully directed so that, although wooden, he does have a dour dignity as the massive-thewed avenger, Conan. It is a pity that individually praiseworthy elements do not cohere into a whole. It is rumoured that De Laurentiis took twenty minutes out of the film, and this may well have damaged it. (He is said to have diminished the gory elements, no doubt with one eye on the family audience.)

It does seem, though, as if De Laurentiis has learned to take fantasy more seriously, or at least to trust his directors more. *The Dead Zone* (1983) is a distinguished film, and even *Amityville II: The Possession* (1982) has its moments. Designed as a chronological prelude to the earlier picture, *The Amityville Horror* (not a De Laurentiis effort), it is an attempt to cash in on that film's undeserved success (see Chapter Five). In fact, it is more vigorous and has the courage of its B-grade convictions, with a remarkably nasty performance from Jack Magner as the possessed teenage boy who seduces his sister and murders his parents while his face goes green and lumpy. Unabashedly stealing several key scenes from *The Exorcist* (pleas for help as stigmata on possessed body, transfer of demon to exorcising priest), the film is luridly energetic Grand Guignol.

By pumping many millions of dollars into the genre, De Laurentiis has been a potent influence on the evolution of fantastic cinema. Good or bad, he is a film phenomenon to be reckoned with.

Italy. As for the story – old style space opera of the zaniest kind, taken quite closely from the original *Flash Gordon* serials (see filmography) – it is all done so tongue-in-cheek and charmlessly that it holds no interest at all. One must bitterly regret that the film was not directed, as originally planned, by Nicolas Roeg.

De Laurentiis's next major fantasy effort was an altogether more distinguished film, *Conan the Barbarian* (1981), loosely based on

Brian De Palma

Brian De Palma (born 1944) is still a young director. He has had the labels "promising" and "talented" attached to him for many years now, but he has yet to produce a sufficiently consistent body of work for it to be clear how important he is to the thriller or fantasy genres within which he mostly works.

A cinephile, De Palma regularly pays homage in his films to the work of great directors of a previous generation – especially Howard Hawks and Alfred Hitchcock – and for this reason his talent has been dismissed by some as purely derivative. Yet his most Hitchcockian film, *Sisters* (1972), remains his most original. It was also his first major work.

Sisters is a brilliantly structured thriller with strong fantasy elements. It is a story of voyeurism that opens with a TV game show of the Candid Camera type, in which a young man is embarrassed to see a young woman (apparently blind) undressing in front of him. The young man later takes home the actress (Margot Kidder) who plays this role, and makes love to her. The following morning he is shockingly murdered by her jealous "sister", but the murder is witnessed by a woman journalist who lives across the courtyard (recalling Hitchcock's *Rear Window*). Nobody believes her story. The ensuing events are too complex for synopsis here, and they are

told in a bravura manner, with a particularly clever use being made of split-screen. It turns out that Danielle once had a Siamese-twin sister (we have seen the scar of the surgical removal) who committed suicide. She is a schizophrenic; the dead sister, Dominique, lives on within her. If this were all, we would have a clever sting-in-the-tail thriller of a moderately conventional kind. The brilliance is in the way the reporter, Grace (Jennifer Salt), is drawn closer and closer to this psychodrama, eventually (by way of a hallucinatory flashback sequence) *becoming* the twin sister herself. It is a tremendously well-wrought metaphor, whose implications go even further than anything Hitchcock managed in *Vertigo* and *Psycho*, the other two films to which *Sisters* constantly alludes, right down to the use of a swirling musical score by Hitchcock's old composer, Bernard Herrmann. It is not a better film than either of these, but it is extremely daring. All the women in the film are oppressed by the social and psychological pressures put upon them, and it is this that creates the Siamese sisterhood between a homicidal schizophrenic and the unhappy "liberated" reporter. This is a case where horror/fantasy cliches (nightmares of staring freaks, intimations of monstrousness) are used to make a point that

Piper Laurie gives a riveting performance as the religious-maniac mother in Brian De Palma's Carrie *(United Artists, 1976), here about to give her daughter (Sissy Spacek) a nasty shock while she comforts her about the unfortunate events at the high school prom.*

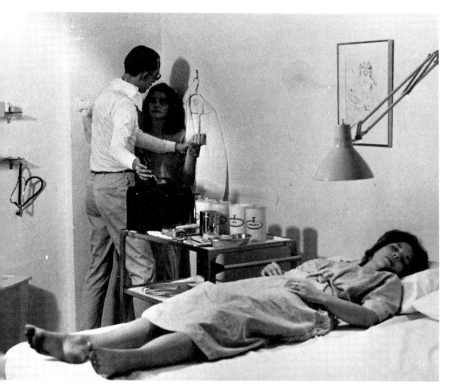

The journalist played by Jennifer Salt (right) develops a psychic sisterhood with the madwoman played by Margot Kidder (left), better known to us as Lois Lane, in De Palma's disturbing thriller about fantasies of personality, Sisters *(Pressman-Williams, 1972).*

her mental powers directing a load of kitchen cutlery; her mother is repeatedly transfixed with knives and becomes a human replica of the icon of St Sebastian which occupies a prominent place in the household. Carrie herself dies in the inferno that follows, but one last shudder remains in the film's final sequence, when she reaches out from the grave to clutch at a friend placing flowers there. But this is simply, it turns out, a nightmare.

De Palma's style is quite the opposite of, say, John Carpenter's. Where Carpenter's direction is self-effacing, De Palma's draws attention to itself with visual pyrotechnics. These are often admirably achieved, but the trouble is that by drawing attention to themselves as dramatic effects they also draw attention to the fictional nature of the story. Nonetheless, it is a very well-constructed film, which on subsequent viewings proves to have surprisingly brief moments of fantasy/horror, but many long, careful minutes of preparation. Spacek's performance is memorable, but the Carrie figure is perhaps sentimentalized from the book: cleaned up too much, too easy to like. The book had a genuine minatory charge. This, by becoming a film feeding the power-fantasies of basically nice kids who don't want sand kicked in their faces, eliminates the disgust of the story. Disgusting things are done to Carrie, but the things *she* does are meant, by and large, for us to applaud rather than be disgusted by. Still, the film remains an important cinematic document about sexual repression, here linked overtly to destruction by and within the mind.

It is very much a minority judgement to say so, but in some ways the next fantasy, *The Fury* (1978), did the things *Carrie* should perhaps have done rather better. The story is again of adolescents (two of them this time) oppressed and exploited by the adult world, using gigantic mental powers to fight back. But this time the theme of power corrupting is stronger; the innocent and the only-partly guilty suffer as badly as the villains from the teenagers' ability to cause blood to flow from every imaginable orifice of their victims. It was precisely this that offended some of the gentler critics, who saw the film as a nasty exploitation movie playing on fantasies of sadism. But if fantastic powers do exist, they could well be used arbitrarily and cruelly, and corrupt the once innocent users. The film is again a display of pyrotechnics, but this time they are more functional, as in the case of the nice lad who becomes a levitating monster, hovering hatefully above his own desperate father, thick veins pumping in his tortured forehead, or the sweet girl who is driven to cause the villain's head to literally explode in the amusingly ghastly finale. The story is melodramatic and often deeply silly, but it has a kind of schlock plausibility.

resonates well beyond the horror genre, and says something important about real life. Indeed, by concentrating on the abnormal, the film throws the whole question of normalcy open.

Next to this, *Phantom of the Paradise* (1974) is very lightweight, but still enjoyable. It is a rock-opera parody of *Phantom of the Opera*, featuring an impresario (Paul Williams) who has made a Faustian deal for eternal life, and the vengeful composer (William Finley) whose music he has stolen and whose face has been hideously deformed in a record-press. Deliberately lurid and over-the-top, the film mainly works on the level of spoof, featuring a series of garish deaths as just the kind of decorative motif that might help sell pop records. The main interest is in the switch of emphasis; here the wicked, eternally young impresario is able to out-manoeuvre the slightly timid phantom just about every time.

De Palma's real breakthrough film was *Carrie* (1976), an adaptation of a novel by Stephen King that, like the book, was an enormous popular success. Carrie (Sissie Spacek) is a shy, plain, gawky adolescent who has suffered a terribly repressive upbringing from her religious-maniac mother (Piper Laurie), a woman who loathes sexuality yet is obsessed by it. Carrie has telekinetic powers, and when a cruel practical joke is played on her at the very moment of her first social success at the high-school prom (a bucket of pig's blood is poured over her head) she unleashes a murderous mental fury, and half the school is killed. Returning home to seek comfort, she is attacked by her mother with a knife, and again lets fly, with

More and more, De Palma seems to be moving from fantastic horror to thrillers where the horror is socio-psychological, as in *Dressed to Kill* (1980) and *Scarface* (1983). There is very little sign of any less dependence on imitating his predecessors in these two films, and there is room to wonder whether the promise of originality in *Sisters* may have been illusory.

Blow Out (1981) is a well photographed thriller, but it exploits its distinguished original (Antonioni's *Blow-Up*, 1966) rather than using it as a stepping stone to an original vision. (The story deals with a sound recordist, John Travolta, who accidentally records the sound of an assassination.) The implausible cynicism of the end, in which Travolta uses the screams of a woman to whom he was attracted (recorded as she dies) as soundtrack on a schlock horror movie, sums up the speciousness of the whole endeavour (by being a trick point almost unbelievable in human terms). The prime point of interest for fantasy fans remains the knowingly bad film-within-a-film, which sums up in all its exploitative second-rateness exactly what can go wrong with the horror genre, and perhaps displays a certain amount of self-disgust on De Palma's own part.

Given the ambiguous nature of De Palma's relationship to fantasy/horror, it is difficult to predict where he will go next. But it would be surprising if he went on to become a truly creative *auteur* within the genre. His approach is too manipulative.

Above: William Finley is the inefficient revenger, a masked and mutilated composer, in Phantom of the Paradise *(Pressman-Williams/20th Century-Fox, 1974).*

Right: Andrew Stevens as the teenage boy, corrupted while his telepathic powers are exploited by government agents, in The Fury *(Yablans/20th Century-Fox, 1978). When the veins on his forehead swell, nasty things happen.*

Stanley Kubrick

Malcolm McDowell is the hoodlum rapist in Kubrick's A Clockwork Orange (Polaris/Warner Bros, 1971), about to be brainwashed by the equally brutal operatives of the totalitarian state. His eyes are clamped open while he undergoes aversion therapy: forced to watch filmed scenes of horror.

The most spectacular fantastic film of Stanley Kubrick (born 1928) was *2001: A Space Odyssey*, which has already been discussed in another context. But it was not his first fantasy film. That went by the extraordinary title of *Dr Strangelove: Or, How I Learned to Stop Worrying and Love the Bomb*. Made in 1963, it still remains the last word on cold-war tensions, and makes contemporary films on the same theme (*Wargames*, for example) look feeble by comparison. Kubrick's achievement was to diagnose, through the grotesque caricatures of black comedy, the most alarming and least discussed possibility of nuclear politics: that the leading protagonists may be appallingly attracted by precisely that vision of Armageddon which it is their job to prevent. We see it in the mad scientist Dr Strangelove (one of Peter Sellers' three roles), for whom the idea of a cleansing holo-caust is sexually exciting (the hoarse voice and twitching limbs are superbly done); we see it in the lunatic general played with slit-eyed conviction by Sterling Hayden; and we see it *par excellence* in the final sequence, where Slim Pickens as the Texan nuclear-bomber pilot rides the Bomb itself, like some bucking bronco, with cries of triumph down to its target, while Vera Lynn's plangent voice swells sonorously, thrillingly, in the background. One leaves the cinema ashamed because Kubrick has succeeded in making the spectator, too, want to see this glorious destruction: it is here, precisely, that the film achieves its major, unnerving success.

After *2001*, Kubrick returned to near-future fantasy as a way of making another dark commentary about the directions of social evolution. In *A Clockwork Orange* (1971), he

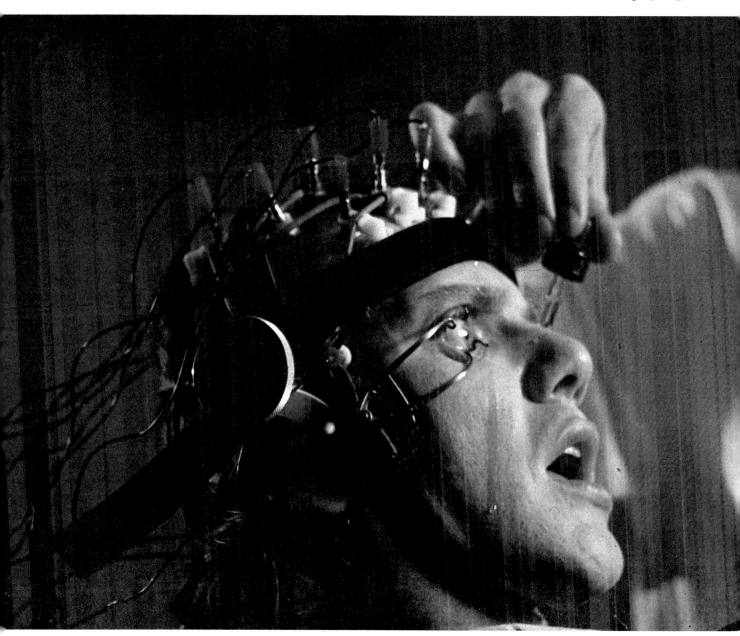

even works the same trick of playing uplifting music against a scene of horror – this time a brutal rape and murder carried out by one of the roving youth gangs which populate tomorrow's urban society while "Singin' in the Rain" is sung. Anthony Burgess's satirical novel, on which the film was based, obviously resulted from a creative chemistry compatible with Kubrick's own, for the whole film has an amazing sureness of touch – the feeling of a personal statement – that is rare in film adaptations of novels. The futuristic settings are tawdrily, luridly fantastic and contorted – pointing in their grotesqueness towards the dehumanization that has already been symbolised in the boisterous, brutal, "fun-loving" rape. But Kubrick typically lures his audiences into metaphysical traps, seducing them into states of mind that are then shown to be vacuous or inadequate. We are just about ready to campaign for a renewal of capital punishment to cope with hooligans like Alex (the gang-leader eerily portrayed with lascivious, wide-mouthed glee by Malcolm McDowell), when our sympathies are caused to veer towards him. Aversion therapy of the most vicious kind is practised on him by the authorities of this totalitarian society; his eyes are clamped open as scenes of torment are shown to him over and over again, while Beethoven's Ninth Symphony is drummed into his ears. Sexuality is made to seem vile to him, and when he leaves (cured?) he is also effectively impotent. But there is yet another twist to Kubrick's manipulation of our emotions, for ultimately it proves more convenient to the powers-that-be for people like Alex to behave like beasts, and he is restored to his original state.

The film is highly stylized, in a way that evokes the warping of an entire society, and not just the protagonists. The bizarre sets were the work of designer John Barry, later shrewdly chosen by George Lucas to design *Star Wars*, which features cultures almost as alien as that which Kubrick presents as being just around the corner.

All of Kubrick's films so far seem pessimistically designed to show where humans can go wrong. A theologically inclined critic might even argue that Kubrick's basic subject is Original Sin. But Kubrick is not without empathy for the sinner, and he often shows us the attraction of the sin; it is one of his favourite ploys. Therefore he may not have been the most appropriate director to film Stephen King's novel *The Shining*, where Evil is inherent in a place (in this case, a remote resort hotel in the Rocky Mountains), and people are its innocent victims. (Perhaps somebody like John Carpenter, who later filmed King's *Christine* and who regularly deals with the idea of Evil as an *external* force, would have been more suitable.)

All this probably accounts for the consensus view that *The Shining* (1980) is largely a failure. Certainly it is an uneasy film, a little more strained than most of Kubrick's work, but there is a case for arguing that, though the film is bad King (jettisoning many of the story's fantasy horror elements), it is very good Kubrick indeed. One cause of disappointment is that Kubrick shifted the emphasis from the telepathic son, Danny, to the alcoholic writer-father, Jack (the out-of-season caretaker played, with wild-eyed despair and bravado, by Jack Nicholson, in a performance so mannered as to have alienated many critics). But this fits Kubrick's vision of the world; now the hotel becomes a metaphor for the inside of Jack's skull, rather than a self-sufficient chamber-of-horrors. Nevertheless, the hotel remains the centre of the vision, and Kubrick's visual sense is as vividly in evidence as ever, as he uses a Steadicam camera (which can create the appearance of an unearthly, smooth gliding) to move along endless vistas of corridor and opulent rooms, filled occasionally by waves of blood or sinister children (that only Danny can see) or bartenders and corpses (that only Jack can see), but as often as not empty and echoing, like Jack's tortured mind. (The film, aside from its other sterling qualities, is the most anguished account of the psychology of writer's block in cinematic history.) Jack's wife Wendy (Shelley Duvall) is a matter-of-fact woman, protected from the hotel's visual phenomena until the end, though very vulnerable to the mental collapse of her husband, of which they are a symbol.

Like all Kubrick's work, *The Shining* is a subtle and complex film, and it would take many thousands of words to tease out its various strands of meaning: the image of increasing coldness, for example, reflected in the ever-bluer colours, which are emphasized by the film stock used; the image of Jack as a Minotaur in a modern equivalent of a Cretan labyrinth, half man, half maddened bull; the image of communication breaking down, within the family, within the maddened repetitions of a typed manuscript, within the blizzard that isolates the hotel from outside help.

The film is definitely not a conventional horror picture, and its public acceptance suffered for this reason. (Twenty-five minutes were cut in desperate last-minute editing before it opened in the UK, in an effort to make the film look more conventional.) However, almost contemptuously, as if to show he could do it if he wanted to, Kubrick puts in one superb, generic-horror sequence, where Jack embraces a mysterious woman who emerges from a hotel bathroom, and she changes to a rotting corpse in his arms.

None of Kubrick's films have proved instantly accessible. *2001* did not pick up its vast audiences until months had passed. It may be years in the case of *The Shining*,

Shelley Duvall is the terrified wife in The Shining *(Hawk/Warner Bros, 1980), waiting for her insane husband (Jack Nicholson) to break down the door with an axe. So much for a quiet winter in a rural hotel.*

George Lucas

In 1964 a short, skinny kid from the rural Californian town of Modesto entered film school at the University of Southern California. Fifteen years later he was a multi-millionaire. He was still skinny and shy.

His name is George Lucas (born 1944), and for a time it looked as if his first feature film, *THX 1138* (1970), was going to be his last. It was produced by Lucas's friend Francis Ford Coppola as part of the output of his new company Zoetrope, of which young Lucas was vice-president. (At around that time, Lucas was developing a screenplay about Vietnam; later on Coppola asked him to direct it, but Lucas was busy making *Star Wars*, so he reluctantly handed the project over to Coppola, who made the film himself. It was called *Apocalypse Now*.)

THX 1138 has plenty of action, but fundamentally it is an art-house movie. THX 1138 is the name of a man, living in a repressive, totalitarian future society where people have numbers, not names, and are kept sedated by drugs so that they behave themselves. THX's friend LUH, a woman, suggests to him that they stop taking the pills, and to THX's surprise he starts to feel sexual desire, probably for the first time. LUH becomes pregnant, and THX is sent for punishment and brainwashing to the White Limbo. The centre of the movie, visually very intense, is this stark, clinical whiteness which seems to absorb the human warmth of all those exposed to it. Others kept in Limbo tell THX that there is no escape, but he walks out anyway. After outwitting authorities in a bike chase (a sequence to be reprised years later in *Return of the Jedi*), he reaches a less populous sector of this underground society, where he is attacked by hirsute dwarfs (to be reprised later as the Jawas in *Star Wars*).

Some of the best sequences in George Lucas's film, THX 1138 *(American Zoetrope/Warner Bros, 1970), take place in the futuristic White Limbo where dissidents against state conformity are brainwashed.*

Then he finds a ladder, and climbs to the surface. There he stands, in real wind, confused and exhilarated, as he faces a blinding sunrise.

There was nothing very original about Lucas's screenplay (written with Walter Murch). Most of the ingredients were standard stuff for SF dystopias, and many of them first appear in stories written more than sixty years ago by Wells, Zamiatin, Huxley and E. M. Forster. But the visual treatment was very strong indeed: the bleak sets, the crowds of shaven-headed, drugged conformists bustling through the corridors, the sex-and-violence shows on TV to keep the masses quiet.

Lucas, a fast learner, took the moral of the film's failure. Do not make films that are bound to appeal only to minority tastes. (He still likes the film, and indeed it remains one of his best, but it hardly made any money, even when it was re-released in the days of Lucas's fame.)

With this major black mark against him, Lucas had trouble selling his next idea: a rock'n'roll movie set in the 1950s, about bored car-driving teenagers in a small town just like the one he grew up in. Eventually Universal agreed to back it, and *American Graffiti* was released in 1973. An excellent film, it was a deserved smash hit. Things were looking up.

Even then, it was not easy for Lucas to get *Star Wars* off the ground, especially on the basis of a thirteen-page treatment, as it was obviously going to be very expensive to shoot, and it did not resemble any previous Hollywood hit. Universal passed on it (there must have been some post mortems there), but Alan Ladd Jr at 20th Century-Fox took a chance on it. The huge success of the finished film is now history, and the movie itself hardly needs describing.

The blend of mythology and science fiction in *Star Wars* (a fairy story in extraterrestrial settings) was not accidental. Lucas researched traditional stories very carefully before setting to work (he wrote the film himself), and he was also interested in the work of Jung, the celebrated psychologist who analysed the archetypal elements of myths in relation to our psychic needs.

It never does to underestimate George Lucas. He is not an especially articulate person, and he is guilty of commercial shrewdness. This has led intellectuals to suppose that he is just a cunning money man, with good intuition about popular taste. In fact, Lucas is a very *conscious* craftsman, and his successes have not been accidental or intuitive. Nor, on the other hand, are they the result of cold calculation alone. There is a passionate openness about his best work – it is obvious in his first two features – and for all his slightly blank, introverted manner in public, it is fair to suppose on the basis of the evidence before us that he is very much a man of feeling.

Star Wars was a nightmare to make. The effects work was stunningly difficult, and would have been impossible without the extremely able team that Lucas (who also has great talent on the production side) gathered together. The team included John Dykstra for the optical effects (he developed a special camera for the film, which was linked to a computer and allowed the exact and controlled repetition of camera angles, enabling a great deal of time to be saved in the miniature photography); and John Stears, one of the most professional men in the business (he worked on most of the James Bond movies), who did the mechanical effects. P. S. Ellenshaw, a comparatively untried young man, painted the mattes (imaginary backgrounds later to be combined with live action). (He is a third-generation matte-painter: his father won an Oscar for the effects of *Mary Poppins*, and his step-grandfather did the mattes for *Things to Come*.) The make-up department was run by Stuart Freeborn, and a later addition when Freeborn fell ill was a then almost unknown young man, Rick Baker, who has since become the first person to win a special Oscar for make-up, for *An American Werewolf in London*.

Lucas cast three unknowns in the major roles and they were very effective, though only one of them (Harrison Ford) is really an actor of the first rank, and he alone has established a firm career independently of the *Star Wars* films. To balance out the unknowns, Alec Guinness and Peter Cushing were brought in for vital cameo roles. Guinness's role of Obi-Wan Kenobi, the mystical Jedi Knight, proved enormously popular. This was partly because Guinness is capable of stealing a scene by moving a face muscle only three millimetres, and partly because the yearning for spirituality in a secular world paid off handsomely for Lucas, who had written into the film a rather nebulous, pantheistic, cosmic Force, and this was associated with Guinness's role.

The story of *Star Wars* is partly fairy tale (princess is abducted by evil wizard) and partly rite of passage (young man grows to maturity). Lucas was at pains not to promote the film as pure science fiction. Its opening words – "A long time ago in a galaxy far, far away..." set it up as fantastic rather than futuristic, a tale told to children perhaps. (Lucas's readiness to appeal directly to the child in everyone was perhaps his greatest act of daring; it could so easily have backfired.) To eliminate the kind of sexuality he felt would distract attention from the heroic elements of the film, he even had Carrie Fisher (Princess Leia) tape her breasts flat.

Lucas was dreadfully worried during the making of the film, especially when the budget escalated from $3.5 million to $10 million. But, as everybody knows, it soon became the most successful film ever made, and even today it is second only to *E.T.* An essential factor in the film's popularity was the stirring, martial musical score by John Williams, who has since become the most successful composer of film music in history (his first popular achievement had been the music of *Jaws*).

The really extraordinary outcome was George Lucas's decision to retire at the moment of his triumph. He had only directed three films. But he has by no means disappeared from the world of fantastic cinema; he has merely changed roles. For one thing, the special-effects unit he set up for *Star Wars*, which he christened Industrial Light and Magic, continues to play a central role in creating fantastic miracles on screen, in other people's films as well. And, secondly, he continues to act as executive producer and writer on his own projects. So far there have been three of these, two of them being the second and third parts of the *Star Wars* trilogy: *The Empire Strikes Back* (1980) and *Return of the Jedi* (1983). Lucas wrote the original story of both these, but he now realized that he needed help on his screenplays. (For one thing, he was no master of dialogue.) For *The Empire Strikes Back*, Lucas commissioned a first draft from Leigh Brackett (author of a number of excellent space operas) but she died of cancer immediately after delivery. The screenplay was revised by an unknown, Lawrence Kasdan, who has since become an important director in his own right (*Body Heat*, *The Big Chill*).

The Empire Strikes Back is more polished than *Star Wars*; it has better dialogue and even more spectacular effects. Yet it does not quite have the raw vigour of its predecessor. There is something ever so slightly calculating about it, though it remains excellent entertainment, with its striding Tauntauns, its implausibly gnome-like guru, Yoda, and its Freudian revelation (later confirmed) that villainous, heavy-breathing Darth Vader might be Luke Skywalker's father. One element missing is narrative thrust; the film is too episodic. Part of the trouble, too, is that, although *Star Wars* came as a complete surprise, this time around audiences knew what to expect and, of course, they got it. It is hard to tell whether it would have been a better film if Lucas rather than Irvin Kershner had directed; his signature is still visible everywhere in the film, which he is reputed to have controlled very closely indeed.

Fans may argue which is better: *Star Wars* or *Empire Strikes Back*. Few are likely to propose *Return of the Jedi* as the best of the trilogy. Here, for the first time, a certain tiredness seems to have crept in, all too ob-

Left: a mounted Imperial stormtrooper from George Lucas's Star Wars (Lucasfilm, 1977). Location shots in Tunisia were used to represent the desert planet, Tatooine.

Below: one of the nasty creatures employed by Jabba the Hutt to make life difficult for nice people, in Return of the Jedi (Lucasfilm, 1983), a film remarkable for its vast numbers of sometimes rubbery alien life-forms.

*The impish Jedi
Master, Yoda (with the
voice of Frank Oz),
gives Luke Skywalker
(Mark Hamill) a lesson
in the use of the Force,
in* The Empire Strikes
Back *(Lucasfilm, 1980),
the first sequel to* Star
Wars.

vious in what is a virtual reprise of the destruction of the Death Star in *Star Wars*. And the revelation that Princess Leia is actually Luke Skywalker's sister may have been one domestic revelation too many, though it conveniently freed her for the waiting arms of Han Solo. All the principals had lost some of their youthful charm with the passing of the years, Carrie Fisher now looking positively matronly in some sequences. And yet the film is still excellent value for money, filled with an entertaining variety of grotesque aliens (some of them looking rather rubbery, it is true), and with a chase on flying, rocket-propelled motorcycles that is certainly the best effects sequence of its kind ever made. The invention of a new alien race, the Ewoks, rather gives the game away, however. The success of the previous two films (including much of the enormous spin-off in marketing clothes, dolls, toys, soap etc.) had obviously depended heavily on the presence of quite young children who would nag their parents to take them not once or twice, but repeatedly. The Ewoks, designed to look like a cross between puppies and teddy bears, are surely a cynical wooing of this kiddie audience. Richard Marquand's direction, incidentally, is self-effacing and efficient. Lucas gave him some freedom, but "I had to understand the rules of *Star Wars*, the givens, which are very rigid".

Even though *Return of the Jedi* has disappointed some, there had been ample evidence two years earlier that Lucas's creative talents (at least at that stage) were by no means played out. *Raiders of the Lost Ark* (1981) was co-produced and co-written by George Lucas (the other writer was Kasdan again), and directed by Steven Spielberg. It may be the best swashbuckling adventure movie ever made. The interesting thing about *Raiders*, apart from its intrinsic merits, is that Spielberg and Lucas seem to have taken it on almost for fun, as a kind of therapy after more elaborate productions. Lucas did not oversee the shooting of the film on the spot, however, He trusted Spielberg and was right to do so. But Lucas's creative input cannot be written off, either. The film was a dazzling and genuine partnership. Planned as a kind of high-grade B-movie in memory of the great serials of the past, it wound up being comparatively expensive at $22 million.

Harrison Ford is supremely well cast as the unshaven tough-guy hero, quick-thinking and unscrupulous, but his part would not have worked so well if he had not played opposite Karen Allen, whose spunky heroine precisely balances it. The film is an object lesson in pacing and editing, piling incident upon incident with superb precision so that the audience positively gasps at the snowball effect, which continues just long enough to go beyond excitement into wit. The film works so well because it goes very close to being over-the-top but carries off its balancing act and never sinks into spoof. It is literally breathtaking.

The main fantasy element, of course, is the lost Ark itself. Taking a leaf out of Erich von Däniken's book, Lucas envisages it as the repository of occult and possibly alien electrical powers, though the scene where these powers messily dissolve a whole slew of Nazis is not the best part of the film. But overall, from Aztec treasures to Egyptian snakepits, the film remains a wonderfully good-humoured recreation of the pulp adventures of the past, renewing all their fabulous absurdity for another generation. Perhaps, as somebody once said, Lucas's greatest strength (maybe Spielberg's, too) is that he never lost touch with his own adolescence. *Raiders of the Lost Ark* is on the one hand a careful string of effects designed by a couple of knowing millionaires, but on the other hand (and it would not work otherwise), it is

a film of glowing, pristine innocence. This is not really a paradox. With Lucas the knowingness goes into the craftsmanship, but the innocence resides in the love of the myth itself.

The influence he has had, not just on fantastic cinema but on modern cinema generally, is incalculable. For one thing, by keeping his last three films as independent productions, he has completely out-manoeuvred the intricate structure of Hollywood financing, and may well point the way to the final collapse of the old system. For another thing, whether or not you regard the *Star Wars* trilogy as the greatest fantasy ever made (and I do not), you must give it credit for encouraging the financing of other, major fantasy projects that otherwise may not have got off the ground: films as different as, say, *Excalibur* and *Blade Runner*. If fantasy cinema has a saviour, George Lucas is it. By shifting its emphasis away from adult complication to childlike simplicity, he may also prove to be its destroyer, but I doubt it. We must wait and see.

Not since the heyday of Humphrey Bogart has an unshaven, sardonic hero been as popular as Harrison Ford became as the whip-wielding, archaeologist star of Raiders of the Lost Ark *(Lucasfilm, 1981), co-produced and co-written by George Lucas.*

"Monty Python"

British television comedy received a good shot in the arm with *Monty Python's Flying Circus*, a weekly half-hour programme that ran for several seasons during the early 1970s. Its style was partly in the tradition of surrealism-with-funny-voices made famous a generation earlier with *The Goon Show*, partly in the tradition of university undergraduate revue, the background of most of the performers. It was satirical and disrespectful, but not so much about immediate political targets as about the general absurdity of modern life. The programme elevated the *non sequitur* to a new status in comedy, and also specialized in blending the intellectual and the dead-common, as in the famous sequence where a number of charladies go to visit Jean-Paul Sartre in Paris. ("Is Mr Sartre free?" "He's been asking himself that for years now.")

The team consisted of writer-performers Graham Chapman, John Cleese, Eric Idle, Terry Jones and Michael Palin, and also Terry Gilliam who produced the blackly comic animated cartoons, which often consisted of such cosmic injustices as giant feet (God's?) appearing from the sky and squashing people, or huge white kittens des-

troying London. When the series ended, the group reassembled from time to time to make movies. *And Now For Something Completely Different* (1971) was merely a re-hash of their television sketches for the American market. The first original film was *Monty Python and the Holy Grail* (1974), followed by *Monty Python's Life of Brian* (1979) and *Monty Python's The Meaning of Life* (1983). *Jabberwocky* (1977) and *Time Bandits* (1981) were primarily the creation of Terry Gilliam with the help of Michael Palin and other members of the Python team; but they are so much imbued with the Python spirit that they deserve to be considered part of the Python oeuvre.

Monty Python and the Holy Grail closely followed the television series, chronologically and stylistically. It was directed by Gilliam and Jones (one or other of whom directed each of the later films as well). Basically, it was no more than a series of revue sketches strung together by an inconsequential story about the Holy Grail. It featured a lot of amusingly idiotic knights, of whom everybody's favourite was the one who wanted to keep on fighting after his arms and legs were cut off.

Poor Graham Chapman plays Brian, the man mistaken for the Messiah (front right cross), in Monty Python's Life of Brian *(HandMade, 1979). Fortunately, Eric Idle (front left cross) is about to cheer up all the crucified victims with a rousing song.*

(Squalid black comedy featuring mutilations and various forms of violent death had been part of the Python routine ever since a famous sketch they performed satirizing Sam Peckinpah. The only difference is that the move to the big screen allowed a more frankly nasty approach, which reached its apex, or perhaps nadir, with a sequence in *Monty Python's The Meaning of Life*, in which a grotesquely fat man enters a restaurant, eats a vast meal, pausing every now and then to vomit violently, and eventually explodes, showering neighbouring tables with entrails and half digested food. Python's love of deliberately bad taste has a lot to do with the middle-class insistence on good manners, which clearly the whole team feel to be one of the most oppressive aspects of English society.)

Holy Grail also features a quite remarkable animus against the Middle Ages: dirty, unjust, cruel and disgusting is how the period is always represented. It is, in fact, Python's favourite setting, and the next film, *Jabberwocky*, was also medieval. Michael Palin was the only member of the Python team to play a substantial role: he is a Candide-like innocent who gets peed on and abused, and generally has a terrible time in the big city. The film strains vigorously for effect, but the script is too disjointed. Masochistic flagellants, squires squashed to death under beds of passion, beggars who cut their feet off: they all blur together. Palin has a hand in slaying the Jabberwocky (a good, horrific monster this, based on the Tenniel drawing in *Alice Through the Looking Glass*) and becomes a hero despite himself. All the ironies are rather cheap and easy, but it's fun.

Monty Python's Life of Brian, on the other hand, has a well-structured screenplay, and is all the funnier for it. Brian, born in Bethlehem, joins the Judean People's Front (an ill-organized anti-Roman terrorist group), then in trying to evade capture poses as a boring prophet and is taken by the crowd as the Messiah. After many alarming events he is crucified, but a cheerful thief being crucified next to him leads all the victims in a rousing chorus urging them always to look on the "Bright Side of Life". The story is constantly hilarious and inventive, and in the course of its tastelessness makes many accurate though not specially biting jibes at the nature of religious hysteria and political persecution. It isn't really very blasphemous. It displays a comic ensemble at the height of their creative powers. All the Python group play half-a-dozen different roles. There is a very silly scene with an alien spaceship.

The most coherent and charming Python movie is *Time Bandits*, a violent little fable for children, at the end of which a small boy watches unmoved as his appallingly materialistic parents are reduced to ashes. The film opens with a moment of fantasy spirited

enough to delight anyone who has anything of the child still within them. A lonely boy is in bed and hears noises in the wardrobe. It is an ordinary, boring, suburban house. But out of the wardrobe leaps a huge knight in full armour on a rearing, frothing horse. It is a great image, and could stand next to anything by, say, Jean Cocteau. The whole film gains immeasurably from taking its fantasy elements moderately seriously. The story tells of Kevin, who joins a band of six disreputable dwarfs who can travel through time, for they have stolen a map belonging to the Supreme Being which shows where the time-warps are. (One of the dwarfs, Fidgit, was played by Kenny Baker who had deservedly found fame as R2D2 in the *Star Wars* trilogy.) Amazing adventures follow. It is not a great film, but surprisingly, perhaps, for such sophisticated creators, it does have a sense of wonder about it.

The Python group have now gained a cult following in the USA as well as the UK, and will no doubt remain popular until they cannot tolerate each other long enough to make fresh movies every now and then. Sadly, the best comedian (John Cleese) has played the smallest role in the films. *Meaning of Life* goes back to the series-of-sketches format: some are feeble, some merely disgusting, but several are very good indeed, notably the scene showing Cleese giving a sex-education lesson to a class of public-school boys, using his wife (a respectable looking woman) as a demonstration model. Overall the film is sufficiently gory and violent to earn a two-skull rating in the filmography!

Peter Vaughan plays a not-very-intelligent ogre in Time Bandits *(HandMade, 1981), a film for naughty, adventurous children directed by Monty Python alumnus Terry Gilliam.*

George Romero

Night of the Living Dead (1968), discussed in Chapter Three, was the cult movie that launched the directing career of George Romero (born 1940). But unlike, for example, John Carpenter and George Lucas, who started small but moved into big-budget productions, Romero has continued to work, with his Pittsburgh-based production company, on the low-budget fringes of "respectable" film-making. This may have been a good thing, creatively. It has meant that he could continue to set his stories in those silent-majority areas of life, neglected by most film-makers, in which he seems most at home.

After *Living Dead*, Romero's next fantasy was surprisingly low-key. *Jack's Wife* (1972, also distributed as *Season of the Witch* and *Hungry Wives*) is a kitchen-sink drama about a dissatisfied, middle-aged woman (excellently played by Jan White) whose life is oppressively suburban; her husband is something of a lout. Seeking some sort of outlet for her femaleness, she decides half-jokingly to take up witchcraft. The world of tatty occultism which she then enters is not really endorsed by Romero as containing genuinely magic elements, but the possibility remains. This is a passionately feminist film (which may surprise people who know Romero only through his zombie stories), quite affecting in its evocation of the ways in which a rather inarticulate woman can be imprisoned by her social context. But its best moments are not those dealing with the dreary details of suburban *angst*, but those dealing with the hallucinations of violence that reappear throughout the film, ending in a scene of genuine violence. Even when Romero moves away from the *film noir*, it is the dark motifs he evokes best. The satire is a bit heavy-handed, and the one possibly fantastic manifestation (a cat) will be a severe disappointment to anybody expecting to find Romero in bloodily supernatural form. Those

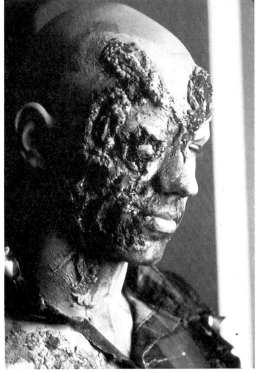

Above: one of the features of Romero's Dawn of the Dead *(Laurel, 1977), sequel to* Night of the Living Dead, *is the ghoulish, decaying, zombie make-up by Tom Savini.*

Right: a skull-like Spectre peers through a small boy's window in Romero's homage to the old E. C. horror comics, Creepshow *(Laurel, 1982). It was built by Tom Savini from foam latex overlaid on a human skeleton.*

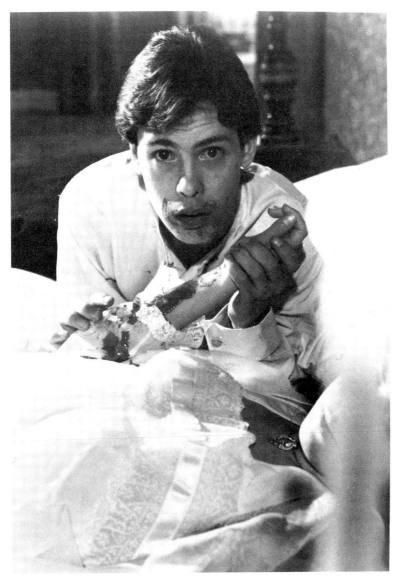

John Amplas plays Martin, the disturbed, vampiric teenager in Romero's Martin *(Braddock/Laurel, 1976). Here, in the film's most unsettling sequence, he drinks blood from the arm of his first victim, a woman in a train, after drugging her.*

with less specific expectations may find a modestly original little movie, well worth watching.

The Crazies (1973) is back in zombie-land, only this time the murderous creatures are still alive, though transformed into homicidal maniacs by the effects of a secret biological weapon that has been accidentally released. First we see the local townspeople murdering one another, and then (our sympathies being given a sudden twist) we see the army stepping in, rather brutally, to contain the plague. The film focuses on the efforts of a small group of survivors (some of whom may be infected) to evade the military patrols. There are good moments that result from the unpredictable effects of the bacteria; the madness is sometimes rather sweetly harmless. However, the sweetest of all, a little old lady sitting knitting in an armchair with a contemplative smile, skewers a visiting soldier through the belly with one needle without dropping a stitch. The theme of innocent people suffering a ghastly apocalypse is well carried out, but formulaic. It is not as good as *Living Dead* on the same subject.

Martin (1976) was a stronger and more adventurous film, the first since *Living Dead* to suggest that Romero might really deserve a place as an American *auteur* of the first rank. It begins with a conventional but extremely vivid horror sequence of a teenage boy in a train attacking a woman in a sleeping compartment, drugging her, then cutting her arm to drink her blood. It looks, in short, like the nastiest kind of sadistic exploitation movie, but it does not continue that way. Martin (John Amplas), who is obviously mentally ill, is believed by his elderly cousin (Rumanian by birth) to have inherited the family curse: vampirism. Martin half believes this himself, and occasionally has hallucinations (black-and-white sequences in an otherwise colour film) in which he envisages his vampiric behaviour romantically, in very much the style of the old B-movies. These are in stark contrast to the rather seedy surroundings of the grimy industrial quarter of Pittsburgh where Martin lives and works. There seems a chance that his severe disturbance may cure itself; it is clearly connected with feelings of sexual inadequacy, and his sexual initiation by a local bored housewife seems to be freeing him of his obsession, but when the housewife commits suicide (for reasons unconnected with Martin) his cousin assumes that she is another of Martin's victims, and stakes the boy through the heart.

The film attempts almost too much: an examination of the vampire stereotype, of popular superstition, of the problems of growing up, of the romanticising of evil, of the repressiveness of families, all in a rather melodramatic context. But it lives up to its ambitions in long sequences, if not throughout, and there are many pleasures in both the visual treatment and the often witty script.

The film Romero's fans eagerly awaited was the second in his announced zombie trilogy. *Living Dead* was the first. *Dawn of the Dead* (1977), also known as *Zombies*, may not have been quite what they were expecting. The whole of Romero's career since his first film had concentrated on the problems of isolated people trying to cope with a monstrousness within them (as in *The Crazies* and *Martin*) that they were trying to eradicate. Clearly, unlike the stereotyped image many people still had of him, Romero had become an old softie whose heart was with the monsters. It should therefore have surprised nobody that *Dawn of the Dead* reversed the emphasis of its gory predecessor, and presented the zombies as victims rather than the malevolent creatures they had been before.

There is still plenty of gore in *Dawn of the Dead*, but much of it is the zombies', as they are attacked first by SWAT teams, then by the four main protagonists who have holed up in a suburban shopping mall, and finally by a gang of sadistic bikers. It's true the zombies continue to bite when they can reach their intended victims, but they are so slow and shambling (looking like slightly spaced-out consumers as they dawdle around the shopping mall, still dressed in their "civilian" uniforms as nuns, or nurses, or businessmen) that they make a comparatively easy target. And this time around the visceral horrors, although excessive, have a kind of comic-book luridness that is strangely inoffensive, partly because Tom Savini's gory effects are so grossly over the top.

Dawn of the Dead, in fact, is a satirical allegory of the consumer society. Bikers and the other survivors who fight them are united in a meaningless desire for consumer goods even as the world crumbles around them. Presumably the film is intended to pose the question, which of us are really the zombies? But the question is put without subtlety, though one has to admire the way in which Romero produces an impeccably liberal message while exploiting precisely the mow-'em-down comic-strip action which the film's liberal elements purport to condemn. But when all that is said, it is a film by a true film-maker who knows how to get the most out of his material, and there are few sequences without incidental delights for viewers who are not too squeamish.

Creepshow (1982) unfortunately develops this comic-strip aspect of Romero's filmic character at the expense of his undoubted intelligence, and more surprisingly, at the expense of his expertise at scaring the hell out of us. *Creepshow*, an anthology film with five stories scripted by the young horror guru Stephen King, is no more than a jolly romp, never jollier than when King himself (he acts in the film) is infected by wildly proliferating plant life after unwisely handling a meteor, and becomes an extremely depressed shrub. It is hardly fair to criticise *Creepshow*, a conscious homage to the nastily amusing E.C. horror comics of the 1950s (see also *Tales from the Crypt* and *The Vault of Horror* in filmography) for being rather like a crude comic itself. One can conclude, however, that either Romero and King nostalgically inflated the artistic virtues of their horror-comic originals, or else the imitation – with its broad, cartoonist's strokes and its careful telegraphing of the scary bits – did not quite come off.

The two final stories, whose grossness is controlled to rather better point, save the film. "The Crate" (which stars John Carpenter's wife Adrienne Barbeau in a wonderfully observed cameo as an alcoholic faculty wife, making Elizabeth Taylor in *Who's Afraid of Virginia Woolf* look like an amateur) has a splendidly voracious, ill-tempered monster that lives in a box under the stairs. "They're Creeping Up on You" stars E.G. Marshall as the unpleasant businessman in a sterile, squeaky-clean apartment, who is attacked (in the only truly nasty sequence of the film) by a large number of cockroaches who stand for precisely the kind of squalid, miserable, exploited life that he has made his money from.

The verdict on Romero must, in the Scots style, be "not proven". At his best an enormously vigorous original, he lapses rather too easily into self-indulgent fun, whose conscious bad taste makes him a kind of down-market, blue-collar, Pittsburgh Monty Python.

Roger, played by Scott H. Reininger, wakes up not feeling very well – but definitely feeling hungry – after a zombie bite in Dawn of the Dead *(Laurel, 1977).*

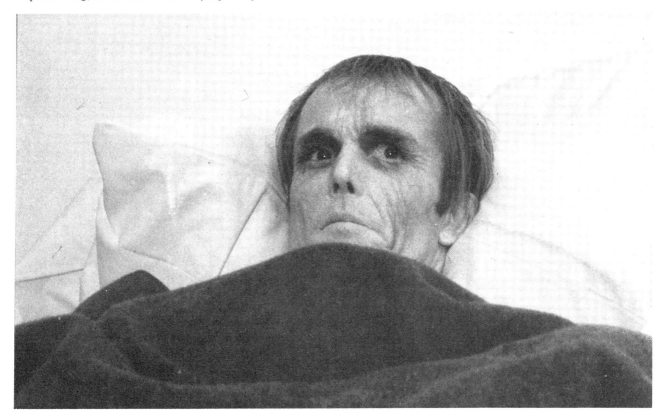

Ridley Scott

Ridley Scott (born 1938) is the sole director in this chapter to have made only two fantasy films. He has been more influential than other directors of equally limited fantasy output, like David Lynch and Nicolas Roeg, not only because he is more mainstream but because he did something new in SF movies: he created a genuine feeling of foreignness. He is a master of elaborately *different* settings, in which places removed from us in space or time are not simply sketched in, with a couple of alien-seeming artefacts. They are vividly, solidly realized in the round. After Scott, the design of SF movies can never be the same again.

When Scott graduated from London's prestigious Royal College of Art, he was taken on by BBC Television as a set designer and sent on a production course. His first full-scale television work was to direct two episodes of *Z-Cars*, a low-key, realist police series. After three years, Scott set out on his own, filming commercials. He became something of a legend in the advertising business.

It was almost an accident that he was given a feature to direct, after well over a decade as an ad-man, but the result attracted a lot of attention. *The Duellists* (1977) is an offbeat and colourful historical romance, set in France during the Napoleonic era, about two soldiers (one working-class, the other aristocratic) whose enmity is such that they fight a series of duels over a period that stretches through most of their adult lives. It is based on a deeply ironic novella by Joseph Conrad. All Scott's training in making things look good in commercials paid off, for the film is a ravishing series of *tableaux*, beautiful to look at, and to some extent functional in that the gorgeous settings themselves comment ironically on the "points of honour" that come so close to wrecking these two men's lives. I stress this film, even though it is not a fantasy, because making things *look* interesting was to be Scott's primary contribution to SF cinema.

Alien (1979) is a monster movie, based on a script by Dan O'Bannon (already introduced as the writer and effects creator of John Carpenter's first film *Dark Star*). The script was picked up by Walter Hill and David Giler, both celebrated screenwriters themselves (Hill is also a first-rate director now) for their independent company, Brandywine Productions. There has since been a lot of ill feeling about the screenplay, which the Writer's Guild adjudged should be credited to O'Bannon alone, though a comparison of various stages of the screenplay shows a tremendous input from Hill and Giler.

It is worth lingering a moment on the matter of screenplay, because *Alien* brought up very starkly a question that is relevant to a number of recent blockbuster SF films. To what extent can one regard now-classical SF situations as being in the public domain? Hill, Giger and Ridley Scott probably did not know A. E. van Vogt's novella "The Black Destroyer" (1939), which was later incorporated into a novel, *The Voyage of the Space Beagle*, one of the lunatic pulp classics of SF. In fact, the resemblances between *Alien* and that story are suspiciously close; so too are the resemblances between *Alien* and an old B-grade monster movie called *It! The Terror from Beyond Space* (1958, see filmography).

Alien is, effectively, an up-market B-movie. It is well scripted, well acted, has a

Swiss surrealist artist H.R. Giger designed this weird looking, long abandoned spacecraft in Ridley Scott's Alien *(Brandywine-Shusett/20th Century-Fox, 1979).*

tremendously frightening monster and looks extraordinarily convincing. But there is little to the story beyond monster-kills-crew, last-survivor-evades-monster. A potentially interesting subplot, added by Hill and Giler, about a robot science officer who wants to keep the alien alive, because he wishes to see the result (intellectually intriguing) between a head-on confrontation of two advanced races, is undeveloped; it ends in a vividly nasty scene where the robot is unmasked and then unheaded. Down to horror again, in other words.

Nevertheless, the film is excellent SF in its atmosphere. The *Nostromo* (the name is another reference to Joseph Conrad) looks like a real, *working* spacecraft and not like a shiny set. There is a genuinely mysterious feeling of "otherness" about the planet on which the derelict spaceship is found, and the alien itself. Much of the credit for the design goes to H. R. Giger, a Swiss surrealist illustrator, who was brought into the project

on the basis of some drawings of monsters in one of his books; one of these formed the basis for the alien being itself. Giger's designs, a strange blend of skeletal hardness and curved, organic, slightly phallic forms, were something quite new in SF cinema. Michael Seymour's production design, Carlo Rambaldi's creation of the mechanical effects for the alien, and Roger Dicken's brilliant concepts for the earlier stages of the alien's growth were all important to the film.

The various stages of the alien's development were well worked out from the SF point of view. It was envisaged as a sort of biological weapon (maybe artificially created) programmed to destroy other organic forms, such as humans, and to use them as a fresh meat supply for its young. Unfortunately, this last point was rather lost when one horrific scene was cut from the release version. This showed Dallas and Brett (the captain and a crew member we had already thought dead) hanging helplessly paralysed in a kind of co-

Some of the key sequences of Scott's futuristic Blade Runner *(Warner Bros, 1982) are set inside Los Angeles' historic old Bradbury building. Here, centre and right, Daryl Hannah and Rutger Hauer play the two lethal replicants confronting J. F. Sebastian (William Sanderson), left, whose eccentrically cluttered apartment this is.*

coon for use as food by the hatching alien eggs.

Scott's direction is impeccable, not just in the building up of tension, but in the realism he evoked for a basically silly story – especially the underplayed, convincing delivery of dialogue by the crew. He obtains an especially good performance from Sigourney Weaver as the hardbitten, slightly unsympathetic woman survivor, although conventionally-minded fans would have preferred a more charmingly feminine person in the role (which would have destroyed the film's edgy quality).

Many people assumed that *Alien* was a one-off from a slightly arty director who would now return with relief to the mainstream of cinema. They were completely wrong. Scott's next venture was science fiction again, but far more sophisticated than 95 per cent of all previous filmed SF.

Blade Runner (1982) was based on Philip K. Dick's classic *Do Androids Dream of Electric Sheep?* an almost surrealist novel about the relationship between man and machine, appearance and reality, tenderness and cruelty in an entropic future Earth that is slowly going to seed (and is almost devoid of animal life), with most of its population emigrated to other planets.

The screenplay jettisoned many elements of Dick's novel, at a fairly late date in filming in some cases, leaving some puzzling sequences. The film, for example, does not make clear that the rarity of real animal life has led to a thriving trade in robot simulacra of animals, which in turn renders baffling a sequence in which the empathy-quotient of a suspected android is tested by asking questions about dead animals.

These androids (called replicants in the film) are artificial human slaves who have escaped (passing as real humans) to revenge themselves on the human race, and especially upon the scientist-entrepreneur who created them. Harrison Ford, grim, unshaven and Bogartian, plays the bounty-hunter whose task it is to locate and destroy these dangerous creatures, who have superhuman strength and high intelligence.

The film has been cut in such a way that its subtext is almost invisible. I do not suppose that more than one in a hundred viewers took the point (also ambiguous in the original novel) that Rick Deckard, the slayer of androids, may without knowing it be a specialized android himself. He has, in common with the androids that he hunts, a curiously intermittent deficiency in human feeling. There is a subtle point being expressed here about what actually makes us human, and about destruction making us less human. For an SF movie, *Blade Runner* is very adult.

Despite various incoherences in the narrative development, and an appallingly sentimental scene tacked on by the studio at the end so as not to make the whole effect seem too pessimistic (Deckard goes off into the sunset with his android lover), *Blade Runner* is quite extraordinary science fiction. Its strength is the wonderful fullness of the way a near-future Los Angeles is visualized: crowded, tacky, sometimes only half-visible through rain and steam, blending high technology with near-universal decay and heavily orientalized (have the Japanese won a war?).

Visually the film is enormously exciting, but not in an obvious way. Scott makes heavy use of chiaroscuro – the bizarre sets are shadowy, dimly lit, with shafts of light producing unexpected illuminations. The replicants are wonderfully done, too, with two almost unknown actors, Rutger Hauer and Daryl Hannah, as replicants on the run – all animal grace, physical perfection, bubbling with a kind of frenetic gaiety, yet also curiously mechanical and capable of bursting into an oddly inhuman, scarifying violence, with no more visible emotion than somebody else might feel in squashing a fly. The inhuman image is most perfectly captured when Daryl Hannah conceals herself amid a crowd of life-size clockwork dolls, and suddenly erupts into a violent attack on Deckard which is simultaneously a narcissistic display of gymnastics. It is an uncanny scene, partly cut for American release but restored in the more vicious British version. The film is indeed disturbing for the squeamish, but the violence is unavoidably intrinsic to its central point.

Scott's masterly direction evokes an alien world which has evolved visibly from our own. (Los Angeles is weirdly futuristic, yet some of the main sequences are set in a rococo apartment house which even now is one of the oldest buildings in LA.) Once again he worked closely with an artist to help visualize the details; this time it was Syd Mead, a well-known industrial designer, whose gouache renderings were vividly brought to life by the production designer Larry Paull, whose own input was also very important.

Unlike *Alien*, *Blade Runner* is more than a magnificent *mise-en-scène;* this time settings and narrative cohere into a striking whole, a film of thoughtful, intricate substance, partly sustained by a convincing performance from Harrison Ford (though there are flaws: the unfortunate voice-over narration by Ford in the style of Chandler's gritty private eye, Marlow, strikes a false note.)

Scott's sense of both the exotic and the mundane qualities to be found in alien worlds (they are even present in *The Duellists*, which after all is set in an alien world of the past) makes him one of the most creative of all fantastic-cinema directors. He plans to work further in the field. The results should be interesting.

Steven Spielberg

Steven Spielberg (born 1947) is the most successful film-maker in history, currently running just a little way ahead of George Lucas. According to the figures published by *Variety*, Spielberg has directed four of the top twelve money-makers of all time. *E.T.* (first), *Jaws* (fourth), *Raiders of the Lost Ark* (fifth) and *Close Encounters of the Third Kind* (twelfth). These four films have made over one billion dollars worldwide.

Spielberg's name came to public notice, in a modest way, with his first feature, *Duel*, which was made for American television and broadcast on 13 November 1971. However, it was not his first professional work. Spielberg had tried to enter the film school at the University of Southern California on the basis of amateur movies he had made. He failed; they had taken George Lucas, John Milius, and were about to take John Carpenter, but they would not take young Spielberg. But eventually, at the age of 21, after haunting the lot at Universal Studios and making a 35mm documentary about hitchhiking called *Amblin'*, he was given a job as one of three directors making a television pilot for a new fantasy series called *Night Gallery*. In 1971 he had seven episodes for various television series aired, but *Duel* (which was an actual movie, and not just an episode) was what caught people's eyes. There was no immediate excitement; although *Duel* was well received, it was not until 1973 that it gained release as a cinema film in Europe (with added

footage, increasing the length from 74 to 90 minutes). That was when it started winning festival prizes and rave reviews, and suddenly Spielberg's career had taken off.

Duel is a text-book Monster Movie – one of the best ever made – with a very unusual monster, a large, rather decrepit-looking lorry. The script was by Richard Matheson, based on a story he had written himself. Dennis Weaver plays the man whose car is repeatedly attacked for no particular reason by a lorry he has overtaken. It is definitely the lorry that is the "monster" and not its driver, who is never fully seen. It is the truck itself that seems malevolent, its headlights (as it lurks in ambush) like the glowing eyes of some great dinosaur, its engine like the growling of a vast beast. The film has almost no dialogue. It is pure cinema, brilliantly edited, about an ordinary man in the street (like nearly all of Spielberg's subsequent heroes), being driven to the brink of madness by a violent attack out of nowhere. The idea of horror erupting out of a clear sky is basic to the monster movie, and it has never been better done. Even the ending has a wonderful logic, when the lorry finally leaps voraciously, not on Weaver but on his car, and goes over a cliff in the attempt; in the one moment of overt fantasy, the lorry utters a bellôwing death cry as it plunges to its death.

Spielberg made two more feature movies for television in 1972 and 1973, *Something*

Dennis Weaver plays the persecuted car driver in Steven Spielberg's Duel *(Universal, 1971-72). Here he looks nervously in his driving mirror to see if the monster truck is still following.*

Evil and *Savage*. Both were competent, neither was extraordinary, and neither received cinema release. *Something Evil* was a supernatural story about the possession of a young girl; *Savage* was a run-of-the-mill private-eye story. But after the European success of *Duel*, Spielberg was given a cinema feature to direct: *Sugarland Express* (1974), starring Goldie Hawn and William Atherton as the jailbird couple on the run in an effort to save their baby boy from being adopted. Well-made, sentimental, but with only lukewarm promotion it quietly sank out of sight.

Spielberg's professional career had now been going for five years and it would have taken a remarkable prophet to predict that one day he would turn the film business upside down. He was only one of a number of bright kids, but he had a reputation for shooting on time and within budget. That was about all. Then he received his big chance, which was *Jaws* (1975). It is a wonderfully adroit exercise in manipulating an audience's fear, but one doubts if his heart was really in it; terror is not Spielberg's special interest. Furthermore, it presented massive technical problems, many of them to do with recalcitrant model sharks (three of them, each 24 feet long) that kept threatening to sink in heavy seas. The 52-day shooting schedule stretched agonizingly to 155 days. Everybody making the film in the rather remote resort of Martha's Vineyard came to feel trapped, and the budget kept on being massively revised upwards. One way and another, it is suggested, there was a lot of ill feeling and ten-

sion between the young director and various colleagues. But when the film became a smash hit, things must have felt very different – especially now that Spielberg was in the situation, at last, to make the sort of films he wanted to make.

Jaws is technically a superb piece of filmmaking. Everything about it is classy: especially John Williams' sinister music (Spielberg had first worked with him on *Sugarland Express*) and Verna Fields' tight editing. Williams and Fields won Oscars; rather unfairly, Spielberg did not.

With hindsight one can see that the characteristically Spielbergian parts of the movie were not the scary bits, well done as they were, but the casting of scrawny Richard Dreyfuss as the sardonic, slightly wimpish shark expert; the humorously affectionate portrayal of middle-class types; and the overriding obsession of the fisherman, played by Robert Shaw in a style that owed a lot to Captain Ahab in Melville's *Moby Dick*. In his next film, Spielberg was to combine the obsessive and the scrawny suburbanite in one figure, that of Roy Neary (Richard Dreyfuss again), the electrical linesman who is compulsively attracted to the flying saucers in *Close Encounters of the Third Kind* (1977).

Close Encounters is certainly one of the three or four best SF films ever made. And yet the science in it is not particularly good or particularly interesting. It is the mythic qualities of the film that make it so haunting: the child's toys coming to life when the

Jobeth Williams is the mother trying to save her children (Oliver Robbins and Heather O'Rourke) from being swallowed up by a closet that has become a gaping oesophagus in the final supernatural assault of Poltergeist *(MGM, 1982), a Spielberg production.*

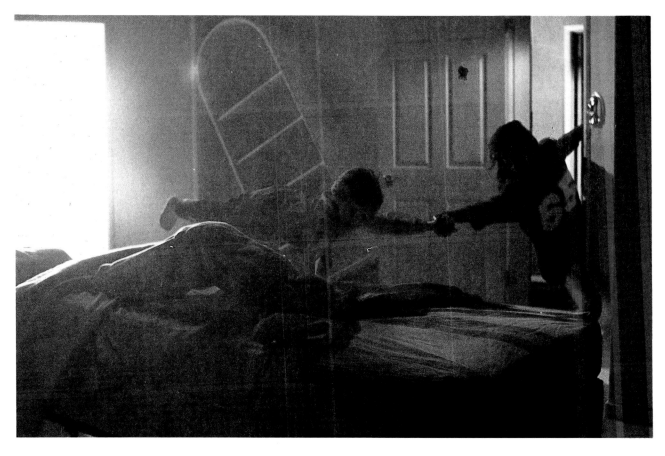

saucer passes overhead; the little group wait-ing on a lonely road to see some definitive sign (it is a *religious* experience we are seeing here), the visual image of a mountain that casts a glamour over the minds of the two protagonists. The world "glamour", with its connotations of magic, is exactly right, for above all *Close Encounters* is a fairy-tale, not just in a loose, metaphoric sense, but quite specifically. Fairies (the legends tell us) are slim, ethereal beings with musical voices who enchant chosen humans and entice them into their saucer-shaped mounds where time almost comes to a halt, so that when they re-join the human race, maybe seven or four-teen years later, it is as if only a night has passed in fairyland. Spielberg's aliens are slim, ethereal beings who speak in musical tones and cast a spell over their victims, some of whom are enticed into the aliens' circular homes, where they no longer age.

The other subtext, closely related, con-cerns religious experience. Roy Neary is similar, surely, to those saints who, vouch-safed a transcendental glimpse of God (like St Paul on the road to Damascus), gave up their ordinary lives and devoted themselves passionately to their vision in the hope of re-ceiving another divine visitation. At the end (as can be seen in medieval paintings), they are taken to Heaven in a glowing apotheosis, surrounded by light, thus being repaid for their sacrifice of all earthly things and their eschewing of the lusts of the flesh. All of this is in the film.

Spielberg's genius was to recognize that these archetypal myths are fundamentally as compelling as ever in the late twentieth cen-tury, but that the forms they take are no longer satisfying. It is not feasible any more to make a successful big-budget spectacular about fairies or about God. So he found a new incarnation for the old archetypes, and appears to have done so with a kind of wholesome innocence. There is nothing knowing or calculated in the atmosphere of *Close Encounters*. Its passion and yearning for some transcendental otherness (quite the

The most popular sequence of the anthology film Twilight Zone The Movie *(Warner Bros, 1983), produced by Spielberg and John Landis, was the final one, directed by George Miller. This tells of a scary gremlin (designed by Ed Verreaux) on an aircraft wing, which is seen by only one passenger.*

reverse of the commitment to scientific rationality that is generally if wrongly supposed to be characteristic of SF) can sweep the most sceptical viewer off his mental feet.

Not only is the basic narrative extraordinarily strong, it has texture, too. The film is humorous (Neary's transcendental vision clicks into focus as he watches the telly; he builds icons out of mashed potato), affectionate (wide-eyed child actor Cary Guffey is superbly used as an open-hearted surrogate for the child in each of us), and spectacular (the majestic appearance of the Mother Ship over Devil's Tower in Wyoming is as close to an epiphany – a manifestation of God – as any of us are ever likely to experience in the cinema).

After its huge success, Spielberg issued a "revised edition" of *Close Encounters* (1980), and by watching it one can see vividly how big the risk had been. Because, strangely, second time around he got it wrong; he went too far. Neary's obsession now appears in darker colours, and his treatment of his family is less humorous and more disturbing; at the end, he enters the Mother Ship to the strains of the old Jiminy Cricket song from *Pinocchio*, "When You Wish Upon a Star", in an unsuccessfully daring bit of kitschy taste which vulgarizes the experience. And the inside of the ship, to be blunt, is less than terrific. The revised edition does, however, produce one new, memorable image: an ocean liner stranded, by puckish aliens, in the middle of the Gobi Desert.

Spielberg's next film, *1941* (1979), was not a fantasy except for its surrealistically high budget. It flopped, being one of several astronomically expensive spectaculars made by movie brats at the time (Cimino's *Heaven's Gate* was another) that caused some radical re-evaluations in Hollywood. Films with this sort of budget are now rare. A comedy about panic in Los Angeles not long after the Japanese attacked Pearl Harbor, *1941* is full of loonily destructive special effects and rather heavy-handed slapstick humour. Its failure may have taught Spielberg a valuable directorial lesson.

At any event, *Raiders of the Lost Ark* (1981) was shot by Spielberg with amazing speed and efficiency, and for a reasonable sum of money. The film has already been discussed in the earlier section dealing with George Lucas. It proved again that both Spielberg and Lucas excel not so much at truly futuristic fantasy as at the re-creation of proven fantasy formulae from the past. *Raiders* is a homage to the swashbuckling serials of the 1930s and 1940s, but created with a dash and a polished finish that was signally lacking from most of its tatty originals. *Raiders* is one of the best movies ever made about going to the movies.

In the late 1970s Spielberg began working as a film producer as well as a director. Perhaps his most interesting production was *Poltergeist* (1982), directed by Tobe Hooper (*Texas Chainsaw Massacre*) from a screenplay co-authored by Spielberg himself. There was much gossip about this film, for Spielberg was on the set a great deal and the suggestion was made that he effectively directed it himself. This is not strictly true, but film buffs did get a lot of fun from figuring out which sequences had the authentic Spielberg touch, and which looked obviously like the work of Hooper.

The obviously Spielbergian aspect of *Poltergeist* is the dark side of *Close Encounters*. A child of a suburban family is again ensnared by mysterious powers; toys come to life (but this time malevolently); much is made again of the television set as the focus of family life but this time the young daughter is literally swallowed up by it. The whole section is humorous, well observed, uncanny rather than terrifying.

The bits that look most like Tobe Hooper's work are generically much closer to the traditional horror film. The suburban house is built over an old Indian cemetery, and its

This rare shot appears in Close Encounters of the Third Kind (Special Edition) *(Columbia/EMI, 1980), but not in the original film. Aliens have dumped an ocean-going steamer in the middle of the Gobi Desert.*

occupants' lives are violently distorted by some kind of dark, malign revenge from beyond the grave (in one case the distortion is literal, when a young parapsychologist in the house watches appalled in a mirror as his face appears to rot away in the film's most disturbing moment). The climax of the film features the earth itself literally vomiting up corpses, in a Grand Guignol episode that seems to have nothing to do with the rather remote but touching sequences involving the little girl trapped in another dimension. This is not a film to be watched for its overall coherence, but it does have good moments.

Spielberg's vision of a world of childhood that is innocent and open, that makes no distinction between the fantastic and the real, that has triumphs and traumas that can barely be comprehended by adults, has been foreshadowed by much of his previous work. But it had its fullest, most plangent treatment in a comparatively modest little film called *E.T. The Extraterrestrial* (1982) which became the most popular film ever made only weeks after its release.

Spielberg, not a conscious intellectual, would probably be sarcastic about comparison with the poet Wordworth, but for both the world of childhood is central to their vision of adult life. Wordsworth quite simply saw children as being closer to God than is possible for grown-ups, and the actual process of growing up he saw as a slow corruption and darkening of their vision. To be an adult is to have lost not just one's innocence but also one's joy. He says of what he calls the "vision splendid", "At Length the Man perceives it die away, /And fade into the light of common day". To grow up is to become confined: "Shades of the prison-house begin to close/ Upon the growing Boy". Spielberg's genius is to teach this lesson over again, but to render it acceptable by giving it a commonplace, twentieth century context where children are not just vessels of the pristine light but also cheeky kids.

Just as *Close Encounters* restructures an ancient fairy-tale, so *E.T.* restructures *Peter Pan*, Wordsworth and – in the most daring (and rather vulgar) stroke of all – the death and resurrection of Christ.

E.T. is himself a child, a lost alien whose family have accidentally deserted him. He makes friends with Elliott (E.....t) who is himself lonely and fatherless. E.T. is the secret, magic friend of childhood. But the adult world intrudes (almost always seen with a child's-eye view, the emphasis on legs and bodies with the faces too high up to be visible), and E.T. (a soft-eyed, charming, ungainly, pleasantly reptilian creature) finally dies. It is not a direct crucifixion – nobody has killed him – but the nature of our fallen world has caused him to sicken. Fortunately, he rises from the dead, and in a sequence of transcendent joy he teaches the children

how to fly (so many Peter Pans on bicycles) and soar to freedom high above the repressions of the adult world. It is all enormously well done, and people who resist the undoubted charm of the film have the embarrassment of enduring accusations of hardheartedness from the tearful majority.

It is difficult to analyse Spielberg's appeal. It is as if he has somehow made all the films Walt Disney should have made and did not; but they are more thoughtful, sharper, less marshmallowy, and most of all, both wry and tender. (Spielberg has many times testified to his early and continuing devotion to Disney movies.)

The sentimental side of Spielberg's filmmaking, only just controlled in *E.T.*, finally overbalanced in his contribution to the anthology homage to the popular television series: *Twilight Zone The Movie* (1983), which he also co-produced. Spielberg's episode (the second, "Kick the Can") starred Scatman Crothers as the new inmate of a senior citizen's home who teaches the other old people how to become children again. Wordsworth would have known better than this but Spielberg apparently didn't, and the story is not only saccharine but untrue to the uniqueness of childhood that Spielberg had established in earlier films. It is not saved by the decision of the newly-created children to return to old age, knowing that childhood still exists within them.

Overall, *Twilight Zone* is disappointing but it does have a marvellously effective prologue directed by John Landis ("Ya wanna see something really scary?" asks a hitchhiker to the affable fellow who has given him a lift, and proceeds to show him). The third episode, directed by Joe Dante and based on an SF classic by Jerome Bixby called "It's a GOOD Life", is technically innovative and constantly alarming in its tale of a not very nice child with appalling mental powers. (He can make cartoon monsters come to life, and could end the universe if he wanted to.) The final episode, well directed by the comparative newcomer from Australia, George (*Mad Max*) Miller, is the best, featuring a nervous passenger on an aircraft who can see something nasty on the wing, invisible to everybody else on the plane. Because the audience can see it too, we are skilfully sucked into the centre of his ludicrously spiralling paranoia.

Spielberg's technical expertise, allied to his seldom erring instinct for mythologies that keep their power in a secular world, has already worked miracles both commercial and aesthetic. It would be no surprise at all if his future accomplishments were even greater than those in the past, for he is thoughtful, extremely talented, and true to his own vision, and also, most importantly, he is still rather young. His next twenty-five years will be interesting to watch.

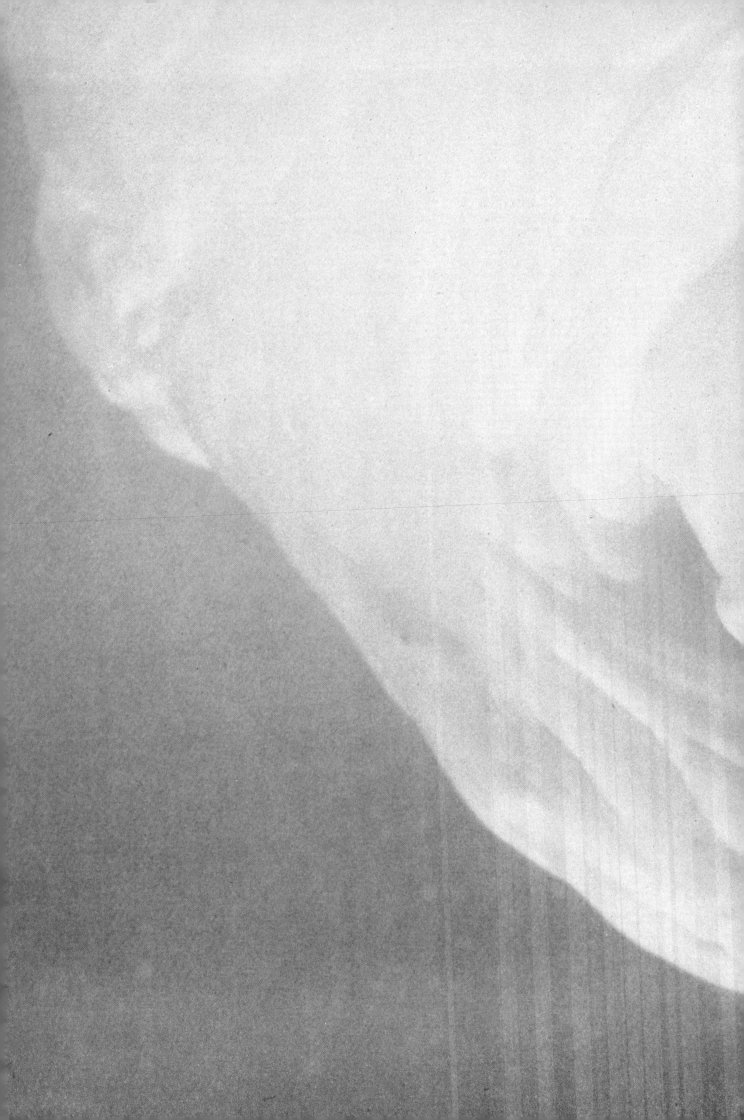

Science-Fiction Films
Since 1968

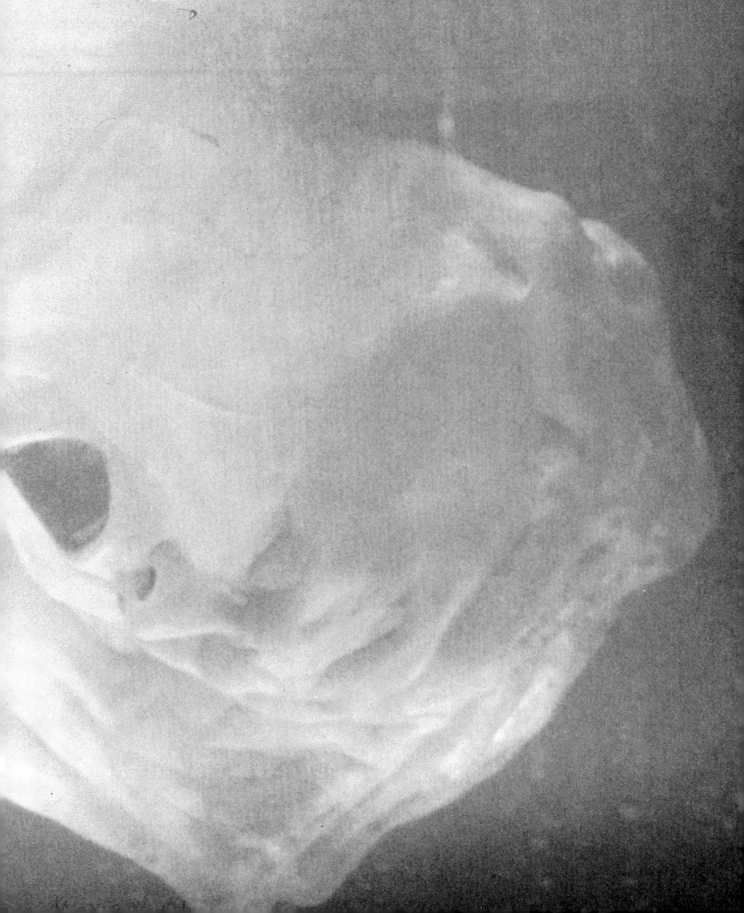

Some of the best-known SF films of the recent period – *Close Encounters of the Third Kind*, *Star Wars*, *Flash Gordon* – have already been discussed, and they were a fairly cheerful lot on the whole. But SF films, from 1968 to the present, have been full of forebodings as well. One of the main themes has been the fear that technology might run wild, whether biologically (*Boys from Brazil*, *Android*) or electronically (*Demon Seed*, *Forbin Project*). Another question is, what will life be like after the holocaust (*Zardoz*, *Mad Max*)? Or will the future see us trying to kill ourselves with lunatic sports (*Rollerball*, *Westworld*, *Death Race 2000*)? At least we can amuse ourselves with weird, lethal aircraft (*Firefox*, *Blue Thunder*). Or we could experiment with the strange powers of the mind (*Altered States*, *Brainstorm*) that we might need to cope with enigmatic alien creatures (*Solaris*, *Strange Invaders*). Some alien visitors, of course, will be quite innocuous, perched in front of their televisions (*Man Who Fell to Earth*). And if all else fails, we can go out and have adventures at the other end of the galaxy (*Star Trek The Motion Picture*, *The Black Hole*, *Spacehunter*). Life may be dangerous, in the future, but apparently it won't be dull.

In the good old days, we all knew that it was robots we should fear. Unfortunately, however, SF writers had missed the boat; in the real world, it was computers, not robots, that were taking over. Quickly pulling itself together, only ten years or so too late, the SF-movie people hastily started creating computer villains, of whom the archetype was HAL in *2001: A Space Odyssey*. Two years later, in *The Forbin Project* (1970), it was Colossus, the super-computer built by Dr Forbin (rather a cold fish himself) to control the US military networks. Designed to eliminate waste, Colossus rapidly figures out that nuclear warfare would be massively wasteful, and joins forces electronically with his opposite number in Russia. Together they rule the world, with all the father-knows-best charmlessness of any Orwellian dictator, and at the end (after various plots against them have failed) they look like running things indefinitely.

The subtext, of course, is that it is better to retain all the idiocies that make us human, even at the risk of nuclear war, than to surrender our autonomy to machines with no feelings. Colossus is given a sexual education of a sort when Forbin tells it that he needs regular sexual fulfilment to function properly. Colossus watches, through moving cameras, Forbin's relationship (actually non-sexual to begin with – it was all a ploy) with a lady scientist, and seems dubious of its utility. It is quite a neat little film, and the scenes showing the giant computer in vast caverns beneath the Rockies do evoke the feeling of awesome power.

Sex-crazed computers

The household robot in *Demon Seed* (1977) is more directly lascivious, more of a rapist than a voyeur. It is merely one terminal of yet another loony super-computer that threatens to run amuck. But when its inventor hastily shuts most of the computer down, this single terminal retains autonomy, and subjects the inventor's wife (Julie Christie) to a calculatedly fetishistic ordeal, imprisoning her in her house and finally, in a scene of the most

Farrah Fawcett has a hang-up about robots, and this one seems completely to have lost its head about her, in Saturn 3 *(Transcontinental/ITC, 1980) – one of several lascivious-machine films in the past decade.*

astonishing tastelessness, impregnating her. (So much for the common belief that machines are impotent.) Julie Christie is quite upset, as well she might be, for the artificially-inseminated ovum is put in a special incubator and eventually hatches into the cutest little metallic-scaled baby ever seen. In a fit of mother love, Ms Christie stops her husband taking to it with a hatchet, and then its scales fall away and a perfectly normal baby emerges. Everyone is frightfully relieved for several seconds until the baby intones, rather mechanistically, "I live". (Subtext: the Luddites were right. First machines put you out of work, and then they ruin your sex life.) The film is not as bad as it sounds.

One film about a philoprogenitive computer would seem to be enough, but nobody told Stanley Donen that, nor his scriptwriter, Martin Amis. The result was *Saturn 3* (1980), which *is* as bad as it sounds. Actually it was John Barry, production designer on *Superman* and other SF spectaculars, who initiated the project, but he fell ill (dying soon after) and Donen took over. Harvey Keitel plays the mad scientist who hijacks a space shuttle, and invades a research station on one of Saturn's moons where Farrah Fawcett and Kirk Douglas idyllically alternate between romping in bed and designing hydroponic systems to feed Earth's starving millions.

Keitel builds a robot with a computer brain that unfortunately inherits his neurotic instability, and sexual chaos ensues as everyone, robot included, tries to do interesting things to Fawcett's body. The scientific logic of the story is sieve-like, the sadism is repugnant (the robot likes to tear living things apart), and only Keitel makes any pretence at acting. On top of all that, the film is deeply derivative, echoing, for example, the protracted search for the dangerous monster in *Alien*, in not dissimilar surroundings.

People dwarfed by machinery

Ever since *Metropolis* (1926), the image of little people dwarfed by great big machines has been at the heart of SF cinema. Along with that goes a less obvious image, of the people who tend machines taking on machine-like characteristics themselves. It is as if the logic and rationality required to construct a technological world has dried up the warmer human emotions. Whether or not this is true in real life – it is an arguable thesis – it remains central to SF cinema, even television's *Star Trek*, whose plots so often centre on Spock, half soppy human, half cold, unemotional Vulcan.

An interesting and quite subtle illustration of all this is Robert Wise's underestimated *The Andromeda Strain* (1970), which was

Bruce Dern plays the last surviving hippie eco-freak; he attempts to save Earth's only oasis of plant life, which grows aboard the spaceship Valley Forge, *in Douglas Trumbull's* Silent Running *(Universal, 1972).*

Previous two pages: William Hurt goes through the ultimate metamorphosis after a series of experiments into new states of consciousness in Ken Russell's Altered States *(Warner Bros, 1980). The special effects were created by make-up supremo Dick Smith.*

based on a novel by Michael Crichton, who has since become an SF movie director himself. The film tells of an American satellite that crashes in New Mexico, followed shortly afterwards by the death of nearly everyone in the vicinity (except the old town drunk and a baby). Apparently, it carries an unknown micro-organism picked up in space – but then again, it may be something to do with germ-warfare experiments. In any event, an enormously elaborate isolation centre hollowed out beneath the desert turns out to have been prepared by the US government in readiness for just such a happening, and most of the film consists of the efforts of a hastily assembled research team wandering through its dazzlingly antiseptic rooms, trying to pin down the cause of the plague, and to find a solution.

The shiny, austere machinery in this centre completely dwarfs the scientists, who themselves seem like micro-organisms in some gigantic, technological body – and are so treated at the end when this body attempts to eliminate them as possible intruders. It is a strong image, as is the visual insistence on the scientists' own humanity being diminished by their clinical surroundings. They come to seem machine-like too. Even the baby is encapsulated in a polythene incubator. It is a cold film, but more intelligent than it was given credit for being at the time. It is one of the best SF movies about human irrelevance.

The unfeeling future

Woody Allen's SF comedy *Sleeper* (1973) is a totally different sort of film, but it too takes as its theme a future where human feelings have become, by our standards, minimised. (Orgasm is achieved by entering a special Orgasmatron – it only takes a few seconds – and old-fashioned sex is unknown.) Woody Allen plays the ordinary little guy (a would-be hip musician) from the twentieth century who wakes up from a two-hundred-year frozen sleep and finds himself in this clinical future. There is a lot of slapstick, quality variable, and the film alternates between genuine SF jokes (about sex, robots, artificial food) and contemporary satire (political radicals, Greenwich Village *angst*). Some of the nicest jokes are about the continuities rather than the differences: the McDonald's fast-food franchise is still in operation, and a VW beetle, unused for centuries, still starts. But why is it assumed in 90% of all SF films made that future governments will be totalitarian? Perhaps belief in the capitalist system runs shallower than everyone thinks.

Silent Running (1972) views the future with a pessimism so profound as to be ludicrous. We are asked to believe that all plant-life on Earth has been destroyed, largely by pollution, and that only the vast spaceship Valley Forge, with its external hydroponic domes (a kind of Hanging Gardens of Space), still contains trees and flowers. Then the totalitarian government of Earth orders the destruction of these. Bruce Dern (in the conventionally neurotic performance he always gives) is very upset, murders his botanist colleagues (who don't really love plants anyway, so forfeiting much audience sympathy) and saves

The second film directed by special-effects wizard Douglas Trumbull came more than a decade after the first. Brainstorm (MGM-UA, 1983) stars Christopher Walken as the scientist who develops a machine that allows its wearer to read the thoughts and emotions of other people, and record them on tape. It is a spectacularly cumbrous device.

vegetable life for posterity by sending the gardens drifting off into space where nobody can see them anyway.

The film was directed by the special-effects genius Douglas Trumbull (*2001: A Space Odyssey*, *Close Encounters* and many others), and it looks good, as one would expect. But the story is puerile, and riddled with bad science: sound travelling in vacuum, the spacecraft orbiting near Saturn where there would not be enough sunlight for the plants. The sociology is fatuous, too: why keep plants in space when you could keep them under glass on Earth for a tiny fraction of the cost, and having done so, why bother destroying them? Nice imagery (the swimming hole set in the space gardens, the three cute robots playing cards, the symbolic penitent's robe worn by Dern) does not save this mish-mash. Trumbull's next film as director, *Brainstorm* (1983), showed the same weakness in intellectual structure.

Medical ethics

At least the capitalist system is still alive and well in Peter Hyams' *Outland* (1981), though it is helped by a corrupt government. The suicide rate is suspiciously high in a claustrophobic mining base on one of Jupiter's moons, and it is a tired government security man (Sean Connery) who investigates. It turns out that workers are being slipped illicit drugs which give pleasure *and* increase productivity, but the side-effects are to cause mental breakdown. Good-guy Connery, who wants to put a stop to this unethical behaviour, comes up against the full weight of the capitalist system, including hired killers. The sets are good, the acting is fair, and as an adventure story it is all quite enjoyable, being basically a remake of *High Noon* in that nobody will support the Federal Marshal against the bad guys. Although the film's ambitions are clearly modest – no deep intellectual points are made – it succeeds where more elaborate movies have failed, in giving a believably detailed texture to a little slice of the future. Yes, one feels, that is how a mining station out near Jupiter might really be. This a better film than Hyams' previous SF attempt, the wholly implausible *Capricorn One* (1977 – see filmography).

Medical ethics also come to the fore in an earlier film: *The Terminal Man* (1974), directed by Mike Hodges and based on a novel by Michael Crichton, who had also written *The Andromeda Strain* (Crichton is a doctor of medicine himself).

George Segal plays the unfortunate victim of an experiment in surgical therapy for erratic behaviour. Since a car accident, he has been subject to intermittent fits of violence. Doctors implant many tiny terminals in his brain (the film's title is a pun) which will measure brain rhythms, and initiate a calming effect when they become erratic. The experiment predictably fails (the brain has even more fits in order to have its pleasure centres stimulated by the resulting jolts). Segal escapes, commits mayhem, and is finally shot down like a dog. Despite its obvious aspirations to some kind of artistry (music by Bach, a long quotation from T. S. Eliot's "The Waste Land"), the film is rather crude. The unfeeling doctors are painted almost uniformly black (except for moderately nice Joan Hackett), and visual symbolism is used like a bludgeon. All the sets (both inside and outside the hospital) appear distinctly hostile to organic life: they are gleaming and antiseptic. Doctors and orderlies loom menacingly, presented as narcissistic vulgarians one and all. The symbolism backfires, however, because it is difficult to feel sympathy for an experimental guinea pig who is pictured so coldly that we can have no interest in him as a person. Segal is given few lines to speak that might humanise him; he is a mildly tormented "thing" and his fate is of little interest. Director Hodges makes his point so heavy-handedly that the ship sinks under the weight.

Similar comments can be made about a later film, *Coma* (1977), though this time the roles were reversed. Michael Crichton was now the director, and the film was based on a best-seller by somebody else (Robin Cook). *Coma* is made with a good deal of style and assurance, with a fine performance from Genevieve Bujold as the young woman doctor who slowly comes to suspect that something is rotten in the big hospital where she has begun to work. Patients are becoming comatose after operations, always in the same operating theatre. Finally she learns that the hospital administrators have a nefarious scheme to use patients – especially the lonely ones with few friends to investigate what has happened – as living repositories of fresh organs that can be sold to other hospitals for use in spare-part surgery. An audience that can swallow this can swallow anything; as melodrama it is just about watchable, as near-future SF it is terrible. The film received some publicity through being approved by some sections of the Women's Movement, who were pleased that for a change an adventure film featured a resourceful, independent woman (except that she still requires her boyfriend's assistance at the end, when she is about to be comatosed herself). It is all terrible tosh, but it has one or two nice images of bodies, frozen and slung up like sides of beef, or gently suspended, living but comatose, in decorative rows swinging gently in mid-air. The metaphor (medicine = the meat trade) is, however, crude, and cannot please those of Dr Crichton's old colleagues still in practice.

And more dystopias still

A Utopia is a Good Place. A Dystopia is a Bad

Place. Science-fiction futures in the optimistic nineteenth century tended to be Utopias; but the twentieth century, living with such scourges as the Bomb, pollution, unemployment, and two World Wars, besides such minor irritants as television, Freudian psychology and Heisenberg's Uncertainty Principle, has concentrated on the Dystopia.

A common feature of modern Dystopias is to imagine a world so devoid of natural fulfilment for ordinary people that, as if they were vultures of the mind, they can only get sustenance from avidly devouring the disasters of others. Such a future is presented in *Death Watch* (1979), a French film made by Bertrand Tavernier who chose – eccentrically, some might think – to shoot the film in Glasgow as the nearest he could get to the City of the Future.

The film is based on a good SF novel by the British writer D.G. Compton (*The Continuous Katherine Mortenhoe*), and is fairly true to it. The time is not far from now. The medical profession (clearly more successful than as presented in the last two films discussed) has almost eradicated death. There is, therefore, considerable public interest in Katherine Mortenhoe (Romy Schneider), who programmes computers to write romantic fiction as a profession, because she is dying of a rare disease. Roddy (Harvey Keitel) is an investigative journalist for television who is detailed to follow her (without revealing his identity) and beam back pictures of her dying for the popular television programme *Death Watch*. To do this without being caught, it is necessary that his eyes should be surgically modified to operate a TV camera implanted in his skull.

The film is almost tremulously oversensitive. So keen is Tavernier to capture the human pathos of this vile situation (a vileness which Roddy feels himself) that all the emphasis is on the slightly soap-opera nuances of the relationship between Roddy and Katherine, and almost no energy is expended on making the future believable. A rather perfunctory evocation of urban blight is not enough. Much energy, on the other hand, is spent in exploring the morbidity of a situation which is, after all, self-evidently morbid; it hardly needs the point to be rammed home. (It turns out that Katherine is not really ill at all; her symptoms are being caused by the phoney "medicine" she has been given. By the time that we learn this, Roddy has blinded himself in a fit of guilt, and she, naturally enough, commits suicide.) It is terribly downbeat stuff, in a French sort of way, and about as fair to the media as *Coma* was to doctors. What happened to the good old days when satire depended on the *subtlety* of its malice?

Soylent Green (1973) is crudely pessimistic as well, though it does offer the sad joy of Edward G. Robinson's excellent last perform-ance, as a dying old man in a future where such people are coaxed into euthanasia centres, so that they can expire peacefully while listening to Muzak and watching films of the flowery fields that no longer exist in the world outside. (Robinson was dying in real life as well.) This particular future is suffering terribly from overpopulation, but the film's producers panicked at including the main point of the original book, *Make Room! Make Room!*, that the Catholic Church's prohibition of contraception was one important cause of too many people being born (the author of the book, Harry Harrison, was furious). Anyway, the film's Dreadful Revelation is that a popular foodstuff of the future, Soylent Green, is partly made of reprocessed human meat – complete idiocy, since the name, as invented by Harrison (who did *not* invent the cannibalism theme), is obviously derived from soy beans and lentils, a far more plausibly economic food source in a period which, through necessity, would be largely vegetarian.

The film is set in Manhattan, in the year 2022, and its strength is the vividness with which the teeming, festering city is pictured – not just the crowds, but the lifestyles that result from the crowding and the minimal expectations of life that people might have in that sort of situation. But the tawdry thriller plot is very run of the mill. The director, Richard Fleischer (*Doctor Dolittle*, *Fantastic Voyage*), is a man who seems to have terribly bad luck, or bad judgement, about his screenwriters.

Fortunately, these grey futures were not the only fantasies produced by SF cinema. The objection to them is not that life should be cheerful – after all, the future may indeed be rather unpleasant – but that there is something about dystopian themes that seems to bring out thunderously crude symbolism in screenwriters and directors. But of course there have been some other, rather good, dystopian films made since 1968. Three of the best were discussed in the previous chapter – they are all variations on the theme of futures in which we will be brainwashed – George Lucas's *THX 1138*, Stanley Kubrick's *A Clockwork Orange* and David Cronenberg's *Videodrome*.

After the holocaust

A theme which would seem more depressing still is life after the collapse of civilisation as we know it – after the Bomb, or plague, or something simpler like the oil running out. Oddly enough, such films can have their cheerful moments too.

One of the first in the period after 1968 was, however, surprisingly grim: *Beneath the Planet of the Apes* (1969), the first sequel to *Planet of the Apes*. Another time-warped astronaut arrives at the ape planet (our own in the distant future), encounters friendly chimps, and then wanders into underground ruins which turn out to be parts of a New York that was apparently smashed by nuclear war. These ruins are inhabited by creepy looking telepathic mutants who actually have a powerful nuclear weapon of their own, which they worship. Once the film stops copying its predecessor and heads off in its own direction down in the derelict subways, it develops a certain harsh conviction, especially when Charlton Heston, hero of the previous picture, turns up again. He is, by now, half-crazy and venomous. In fact, during a final shoot-out between apes and mutants, he detonates the Doomsday weapon. For those who are a bit tired of Heston as the brawny, clean-living good guy (as he mostly was in the previous film) this is a moment to applaud.

A Boy and His Dog (1975), however, is an altogether tougher proposition. It was put together by a strange team: director L. Q. Jones (well-known bad-guy character actor) and SF writer Harlan Ellison. With another actor, Alvy Moore, Jones had started a small production company specializing in low-budget horror films, of which the best had been *Brotherhood of Satan* (1970, see filmography). As so often in Hollywood, it is the small independents who will take risks with material that the major studios would be frightened of touching. Ellison's award-winning story (same title) quietly assumes that, after a nuclear war, conventional human priorities will certainly differ, in ways that

might seem very offensive to us.

Don Johnson is the boy, Vic. His dog, a shaggy mongrel called Blood, is in telepathic communication with Vic, and we hear his mental voice, too – crisp, world-weary and middle-aged – as spoken by Tim McIntire. This works very well. Their partnership is symbiotic: Vic finds meat for Blood, and Blood finds girls for Vic to rape. All this happens in a wasteland of dried mud and dust into which the tops of buried buildings occasionally project, relics of the pre-war days.

The title, with its evocation of innocent boyhood days before the adult responsibilities of love and maturity, is not entirely ironic. The terrible world Vic and Blood inhabit, brief, violent skirmishes for food being everyday stuff, is all they know and it's not too bad. They can even go to the movies – scratched, yellowing old prints projected in a tumbledown shanty. In one good scene Vic and Blood are lying on their backs, silhouetted against a splendid sky, wholly content. As if this world were a paradise with infinite possibilities, Blood asks, "What do *you* wanna do tonight?"

Into this bedraggled Eden comes a female serpent, Quilla June. Vic is about to rape her, but she seduces him and then persuades him to come underground where another quite different life goes on. There he finds a stern, repressive, agrarian society, policed by a robot killer dressed as a country yokel. People are painted with grotesquely cheerful clown make-up. Vic has been lured there

The Humungus leads the barbarian hordes attacking a desert fortress in a near-future Australia, in Mad Max 2 *(Kennedy Miller Entertainment, 1981). The part was played by a Swedish body-building champion, Kjell Nilsson, in a costume of a kind only to be found in very specialist shops.*

because they need his sperm (to be milked from him mechanically, he learns to his consternation) to impregnate the local girls. Eventually he escapes with Quilla June, who now loves him, and rejoins Blood above. Blood is hungry. Vic looks at Blood and looks at Quilla June. We cut to Blood, now replete, saying "She had marvellously good taste." The cannibalistic ending was Ellison's but the gag was not; he hated it for its unfeeling crudity, which he regarded as sexist.

It is not a great film, but it is one of the most imaginative SF movies we have yet seen, and one of the most plausibly brutal, too.

A new wizard of Oz
Another inventive film – too crammed with ideas for its own good – is *Zardoz* (1973). A huge stone head with a cruel smile sinks slowly from the sky and hovers over a landscape across which horsemen with gunbelts and loincloths are riding. Rifles fall in a torrent from its mouth. In a booming voice this god, Zardoz, orders the horsemen (the Exter-

minators) to kill all lesser beings. This seems to be the stereotyped, brutalised future that has followed some huge disaster. Civilization is dead. But is it? Where does the head come from?

It turns out that it comes from the Vortex, writer-director John Boorman's version of the Emerald City, and the stone head is just as phoney as the great mask used by the Wizard of Oz. The unlikely Dorothy, in this scenario, is Sean Connery's Zed, toughest of the Exterminators; his whole body is a weapon. He travels (in the head) to the Vortex, where he finds more than can be summarized here: Immortals, a crystalline Tabernacle (repository of all human knowledge), Renegades doomed to eternal old age, Apathetics who wish they were dead, women (like those in *A Boy and His Dog*) who need him for breeding purposes because the Immortals are impotent. Zed is an innocent monster in this sophisticated, decadent world of high technology, and at the end, he exultantly destroys it in a prolonged fusillade of rifle fire that is greeted with joy

The film is Rollerball *(United Artists, 1975), and the action is fast, furious and often lethal in the gladiatorial sports craze of the title. Steel-studded gauntlets are predicted as a popular futuristic fashion here, too – see also the still from* Mad Max 2 *on page 119.*

by the death-hungry Apathetics.

Other themes include the natural superiority of women to men, the doom that awaits any slave-holding society and the clash of cultures. All this complex material is incorporated in a story with a good deal of fustian, some brilliant images and some very forced ones as well, and a curiously gentle, luminous visual style, all misty pastels, photographed by Geoffrey Unsworth (who also photographed *2001: A Space Odyssey*). It is a gravely flawed but fascinating film.

Look before you cross the road

Mad Max has become a cult hero. Originally, he was a hero with an American accent, because the strenuously Australian *Mad Max* (1979) was redubbed by nervous American distributors. The second time around, he was too popular for this softening process to be necessary, and in *Mad Max 2* (also known as *The Road Warrior*) he speaks in his natural, pleasant Australian drawl. The creators of the futuristic mayhem that caused all the fuss were unknown director George Miller, unknown producer Byron Kennedy, and unknown actor Mel Gibson. On the basis of the Mad Max films, Gibson is now well on the way to becoming a superstar, and Miller was invited to film the fourth episode of Spielberg's production *Twilight Zone*. It turned out to be the best. (Byron Kennedy was killed in a helicopter crash in 1983.)

Mad Max and its sequel are set in a post-holocaust Australia some time after the oil wars have left the world in a mess. Gasoline has become a valuable medium of exchange, and status is conferred by burning it up on the roads. Australia seems largely populated by roving biker gangs and the equally brutal police force that opposes them. It is only at the end of *Max Max* that policeman Max Rockatansky goes mad – or at least extremely violent – when his wife and baby have been nastily slaughtered by a biker gang that he had antagonised. The film is a laconically single-minded hymn to, and dirge for, death on the roads. Men identify with their machines ("I'm a fuel-injected suicide machine" cries one in an ecstasy of excitement seconds before his demise). Bikers and cops are indistinguishable except for their uniforms (based respectively on punks and rockers). The film arguably has the most tautly directed action sequences of any low-budget film ever made.

Mad Max II is more ambitious. Here post-apocalypse tough guys besiege a desert fortress held by fur-clad and fractionally more civilized families. (The besiegers – the Indians, so to speak – were christened by the film crew, according to their physical appearance, the Smegma Crazies, the Mohawk Bikers and the Gay-Boy Berserkers. The people in the fort were the Gucci Arabs.) The fort people have gasoline, with

which they hope to move to a place called Paradise (a splendid Australian in-joke: in real life, this is a sleazy resort town, Surfer's Paradise). Max Max, now a loner, assists the fort people, and finally defeats the leader of the invaders, a steel-studded, jockstrap-wearing brute called the Humungus. Max is helped in this by an appealing little killer called the Feral Kid, who has a metal boomerang he uses for slicing people up.

All this fits into a thrillingly directed action film that seldom allows the viewer to draw breath, except to laugh at the poker-faced Australian-style jokes. It is an intensely colourful, intelligent exploitation film, and probably no more than that. Nevertheless, Miller has successfully created a true cinematic mythology, even if it is in the style of a lurid comic-strip.

The post-holocaust movie, in fact, has proved to be one of the more vital SF film forms. There is a kind of exhilaration in imagining the greyness of our society, with all its bureaucratic worries, going up in smoke and remaining only as the odd rusted girder or faded magazine – especially if the emphasis is not on the holocaust itself but the new beginnings afterwards. These are nearly always seen as having vitality and energy along with cruelty and barbarism, and interesting oppositions along these lines are often set up. Other relevant films from the period are *Glen and Randa* (1971), *The Ultimate Warrior* (1975), *Damnation Alley* (1977), *Virus* (1980), *The Last Chase* (1981), *Malevil* (1982) and *Battletruck* (1982). All these are discussed in the filmography.

Killer sports

A lunatic sub-genre of the future Dystopia film is the give-them-bread-and-circuses,

Matthew Broderick is the young computer genius in John Badham's WarGames *(MGM-UA, 1983), shown here with his girlfriend, played by Ally Sheedy, as he is about to link up – unintentionally – with the giant nuclear-war-control computer at NORAD.*

killer-sports film. Two of these came out in 1975. The cheap one, *Death Race 2000*, was made to cash in on the publicity for the expensive one, *Rollerball*. Actually, the low-budget shocker from New World pictures, produced by the shrewd old king of exploitation, Roger Corman, was the better film. Directed with verve by Paul Bartel, it tells of a car race across the USA in the year 2000, the winner being the one who kills the most pedestrians on the way. The nation's favourite is "Frankenstein" (David Carradine) whose body, it is rumoured, is so smashed up that most of it is now artificial. Sylvester Stallone (then unknown) had a cameo as the evil Machine Gun Joe. The script is amusing and, because the film does not take its absurd premise too seriously, it's all good, dirty fun.

Rollerball, directed by Norman Jewison, takes itself very seriously. James Caan is the sports hero who stars in the game of the title: a cross between roller derby, Roman gladiatorial sports and skittles with the players as nine pins, and a heavy steel sphere projected at great speed being the ball). So popular has he become that he is now a menace to the totalitarian government (consisting of a loose amalgam of industrial corporation heads), which does not believe in allowing cults of the individual to spring up. They change the rules, and make the game ever more vicious. In the climactic game the ring is littered with mangled corpses, but (three cheers for individualism!) James Caan survives. The film's sociology is extremely naive, its symbolism is leaden, and, of course, it exploits precisely that unhealthy attraction to ritualised violence that it purports to condemn. Fortunately, its basic silliness does not allow the scenes of violence to carry any more disquieting a message than that of a Tom and Jerry cartoon.

A much better film about surrogate violence is *Westworld* (1973), which was the feature-film directorial debut of Michael Crichton; he wrote the screenplay, too.

Westworld is part of a Disneyland of tomorrow, along with Medievalworld and Romanworld. But Disney-style technology has moved on a long way, and these three areas offer surprisingly convincing simulacra of the real thing, though many of the "people" who live in the old-time Wild West township are actually robot duplicates. They're cleverly made, though; visitors who stay in the local inn can make love to robot whores and have shoot-outs with robot gunmen in the secure knowledge that in both cases they will come out on top.

Yul Brynner plays the gunslinger robot who runs amuck and leads a robot revolt. The fantasies of *machismo* being lived out by the tourists (mostly men – the women seem to go to Romanworld) turn into nightmare. The lethal, implacable Brynner robot seems indestructible as he stalks a tourist (Richard Benjamin) through the corpse-littered streets, not even pausing when his face is destroyed by acid (in a memorable image, which abruptly reminds us that he is indeed a robot, though he looks so human), revealing the whirring cogs and flickering circuits beneath.

As a film about the absurdity of male fantasies, it is very good; as a film about the revolt of the technological world against the humans who created it, it is predictable, but good fun. This is more than can be said about the disappointing sequel, *Futureworld* (1976), which is set in another, newly-built sector of the same amusement complex. Peter Fonda and Blythe Danner play the journalists assigned to the grand opening, where they uncover a plot to replace vital politicians with robot doubles. There are some entertaining sequences, mostly derivative from the first film, but overall it is rather a mess.

Computer games

Several recent films have dealt with teenagers who are adroit at computer-game skills, including *Tron* (see Chapter Seven), and one episode of *Nightmares* (see filmography). But by far the most successful at the box-office was *WarGames* (1983), directed by John Badham (*Saturday Night Fever, Dracula*).

WarGames is set in a very near future. A bright kid, who uses his home computer terminal to sneak around the electronic circuits of other people's computers without permission, accidentally taps the big one, designed to mastermind nuclear war. Not realizing what he has done, he starts playing games with it – war-games scenarios of the kind games enthusiasts often play in real life – but unfortunately the computer takes the whole thing seriously, and before we know what has happened, the world is on the brink of war between the Soviets and the USA. All this is set up in a witty first half-hour, which promises great things. But sadly, after that, the film slumps into a rather Disneyesque chase-movie, and loses credibility.

The NORAD computer in its underground headquarters at Cheyenne, Wyoming, is convincing enough – good graphic design here. What is not convincing is the bunch of stereotypes that the film alleges are running it. If American war strategy is really in the hands of overacting hysterics like these, then we're all in trouble. Ultimately, the film's anti-nuclear message ("The only winning move is not to play") is gravely compromised by its central image, in which such warfare, by being reduced to pretty flashing lights on a kind of scoreboard, is trivialized. The ending, in which the militaristic types turn out to be nice, paternal fellows who ruffle the boy's hair, is nauseating. As the sardonic British critic Steve Jenkins punned, this is a film about the nuclear family. It should be said that Matthew Broderick performs very winningly as the clever kid.

Questions of identity

Newcomers to the genre often suppose that an SF story must be about technology. This is wrong. Some of the questions that SF tackles best are psychological and philosophical. Because it allows bizarrely new perspectives, science fiction can give us new insights into traditionally difficult areas of thought.

The masterly Russian film *Solaris* (1972), adapted from a philosophical SF novel by the Polish writer Stanislaw Lem, illustrates the point perfectly. It is, however, a very long film (165 minutes), paced more slowly than we are used to in the West, and it is only fair to say that some of its viewers have left baffled and sometimes bored. When dragged back for a second viewing, they usually like it better.

The film opens on Earth, at a country homestead outside Moscow, where we meet Kelvin, the space scientist about to leave on a mission. We learn that he has difficulty in expressing his love for his father. This prologue (all dampness,, greenness, rippling sedges, water meadows, a galloping horse) is very evocative, and establishes the sense of transience and mutability that is to permeate the film. The director, Andrei Tarkovsky (surely the greatest of living Russian film-makers) has learned the secret of surrealist vision: that if you stare at an object long enough, it attains an intense significance. So it is with the wildly running horse. So it is later with a winter landscape by Breughel, and with all the images of screens, glasses, windows, obstructions to vision.

Solaris is the name of a strange planet, around which a space-station is in orbit. When the new conscript, Kelvin, arrives there, he finds it shabby, badly maintained and apparently untenanted. Later, however, two very uncommunicative fellow scientists are found, lurking and frightened, in their laboratories. They are accompanied by strange, half-glimpsed figures. Beneath the station we see the ever-changing ocean of Solaris. We learn that the planet may be sentient – one giant, living thing. But how would such a godlike creature communicate?

Kelvin soon finds out when he wakes one morning in his cabin to find his wife next to him. It all seems the most natural thing in the world, and for a moment he simply accepts her presence. Then he remembers where he is, and that his wife had committed suicide.

Attempting to exorcise this phantom (for so Hari appears to be – perhaps she is a "message" sent by Solaris), he tricks her into a space shuttle and fires it off. From within we hear inhuman sounds, and witness the screeching metal buckling outwards as with alien strength she tries to escape before she is jettisoned. But soon another Hari materialises.

There is no space here to describe the whole film; it is too rich and densely textured. It is enough to say that the second Hari comes to realize that she is a copy, recreated from Solaris's reading of Kelvin's mind. But at the same time she feels herself to be quite real, proving her humanity paradoxically at one point when she attempts suicide (for a second time?) to save Kelvin further distress. (The gruelling scene where she drinks liquid oxygen must be the envy of many horror-film directors.)

One day Hari is simply not there any more. Perhaps her function as "message" from Solaris was ended. The sensitive, bear-like Kelvin is stunned. In a completely unexpected ending, we see him descend to the planet's surface where a temporary island has been cast up by the protean ocean. On this island is a pleasant old Russian house. It is raining. Dimly visible within, seen through the window streaming with water, is Kelvin's father who does not see and cannot hear his son reaching out. It is a poignant, powerful image that perfectly sums up the themes of this extraordinary film.

One of the questions of identity in *Solaris* is this: if a dead wife, who now exists only in a man's mind, is made flesh again and given autonomy, in what cognitive sense can she be said to be *not* the man's wife? A different but comparable question is posed by the film *Who*? (1974), even in the title. A key American scientist is terribly injured in an accident on the East European border. Later he is returned to the West by the Communists

Donatas Banionis as the Russian astronaut, Kelvin, is more disturbed than happy to be re-united with his dead wife, Hari (Natalia Bondarchuk), in the Russian SF classic Solaris (Mosfilm, 1972), directed by the great Andrei Tarkovsky.

David Bowie (right) is the alien, Newton, the corrupted hero of Nicholas Roeg's The Man Who Fell to Earth (British Lion, 1976). This rare still comes from the film's only traditional SF sequence, the flashback to Newton's native desert planet, where he is saying farewell to his wife before leaving for Earth.

Beneath their human disguises, this is what the aliens look like in the enjoyable SF nostalgia trip, Strange Invaders (Orion/EMI, 1983). Vaguely reminiscent of E.T.?

H. G. Wells (played by Malcolm McDowell, who is about a foot too tall) visits modern San Francisco in his time machine in Time After Time *(Orion/Warner Bros, 1979). He is quite pleased to find a special Wells display at the local museum.*

who have patched him up, but so badly was he hurt that they have provided him with a metal face and a metal hand.

American security investigators are worried. How do they know the Russians have not slipped them a counterfeit? This maimed person – he looks like a robot – may be a double agent. The entire film is about the attempt to establish his identity. It is not quite as gripping as the first-rate SF novel (same title) by Algis Budrys on which it is based, but it did not deserve to be consigned to obscurity upon its delayed and muffled release.

The sad thing about the film is that, as a man machine, the scientist shows more feeling than he ever showed (if indeed it is he) as a man, as revealed in a touching scene with an ex-lover. Subtext: the human political world is machine-like; the prosthetic monster

may be more human than us. Eventually he becomes a farmer, all questions of identity being rendered irrelevant, as in a sense they were all along. This is a taut, efficient little metaphysical thriller. (Clever viewers are given just about enough information to solve the mystery – provided that they are gifted with a sense of irony.)

The return of the pod people

It is odd how often SF movies ask the question, when is a person not a person? Perhaps the question has a keener edge, when asked in the twentieth century – a time when we see Man as an impermanent element in an evolutionary spectrum – than it would have had in previous centuries when Man was seen as existing at the top of the hierarchy of created life. Older horror dealt with the re-emergence of the beast; newer horror deals with the *loss* of the beast: that is, with the loss of the animal warmth that we think of as part of being human. We have a fear that whatever species replaces us, or whatever we evolve into, may be a creature of intellect, lacking both love and anger. We have already seen this symbolised in *Invasion of the Body Snatchers* (1956), and it is even clearer in Philip Kaufman's remake of the same film in 1978.

Leonard Nimoy (*Star Trek*'s Spock) plays a new character in the old story, a psychiatrist, who while discussing Californian therapies for tinkering with personality, says "People are changing; they're becoming less human." Kaufman's pod people are definitely of the 1970s. They are not so much political symbols as sociological symbols, and the film reflects this shift of emphasis with its geographical shift from a cohesive small town to the alienation of the big city – where it is difficult at the best of times to tell who is a pod and who isn't. The psychiatrist, naturally enough, is one of the first to be replaced with a pod; it is a nice irony.

The film is not as strong as its original, but it is an ingenious remake all the same, working quirky variations on the theme. The special effects are good and the inside jokes are amusing (Kevin McCarthy materialises out of the darkness, reprising his role in the original film, still shouting his warning; Don Siegel plays a taxi driver). On the other hand, a certain fussiness in the direction sometimes dissipates the strength of the narrative.

Strange Invaders (1983) was a relatively low-budget film that arrived without any advance fanfare, yet looked on the way to becoming a cult favourite within weeks. It was made by Michael Laughlin, whose only previously directed film was *Strange Behavior* (1981, see filmography), a modestly intelligent exploitation horror pic that received almost no critical attention at all. *Strange Invaders* is a hugely affectionate replay of the themes of 1950s SF/horror movies. It takes as its premise that body-snatching invaders without human feelings might have real trouble in producing efficient replicas of human beings. A township in the mid-west is taken over by these creatures in 1958, and the result is a community (they are studying human customs in a twenty-five-year research project) that seems frozen in the Eisenhower period – not so much "They Came from Outer Space" as "They Came from the *Saturday Evening Post*". Despite their menace, there is something likeable about their inadequacies. Beneath their human masks they look rather like *E.T.*, and it is appropriate that the human who first exposes these bug-eyed monsters is himself an entomologist. This is a fun movie, full of visual and verbal gags, and interestingly updating the 1950s paranoia it purports to satirise. (In the 1950s it was the Commies who scared Americans; now the sinister post-Watergate conspirators come from their own government.)

The most alarming problem of identity posed by the film is that the entomologist has in fact been married to one of these aliens (they are now separated) without realizing she was an alien, apparently regarding her blank manner as normal in a wife. An unusually upbeat ending, for this kind of film, allows all the people the aliens took over twenty-five years ago to return, looking puzzled but pleased. And they, too, of course, will have problems in modern America.

Alien anomie

We have seen the horror of loss of identity when it is stolen from us by aliens. But what of the reverse case? *The Man Who Fell to Earth* (1976) is the story of an alien whose identity is stolen from him by us. This interesting, difficult film was directed by Nicolas Roeg, who had already proved his mastery of fantastic cinema in *Don't Look Now* (1973, see Chapter Six).

David Bowie gives an extraordinary, frail, vulnerable performance as the human-seeming alien who, like Icarus, falls to Earth in the opening sequence and starts a new life here. (The image of Icarus, the mythical drowning boy whose wings melted when he flew too close to the Sun, pervades the film.) His fall is also a recapitulation of the original Fall, when innocent Adam ate the fruit and committed the first sin.

The alien's reason for coming here is quite clear in Walter Tevis's original novel, but is deliberately obscured in the film. We know it is connected with his desire to help his compatriots on their dying, desert planet, but that is all. A vision of his family on this planet is one of the few directly science-fictional images in the film. Anyway, he is lonely, and there is something about him that attracts other lonely people.

The film is long. It has been accused of pretentiousness, and it is certainly wilfully obscure in places, but the sum total of its images is powerful, and like *Solaris* it all makes more sense on a second viewing. The story is told in a non-linear way, disjointed both in space and time (the alien is capable of a kind of psychic time travel). Eventually, he is corrupted by Earth. His story is strongly reminiscent of the legend of Howard Hughes: the transition from keen, young inventor (the alien patents a number of extraordinary new devices) to ruined recluse (at the end, Bowie is a gin-sodden wreck).

It is the visual images and their surprising juxtapositions that make the film: the scene where he reveals his alien nature (by the simple device of removing contact lenses to reveal the alien eyes beneath), causing his girlfriend to wet herself with fright; or the serried ranks of television sets with which the alien barricades himself away from direct human experience.

Less interesting, though surprisingly similar in theme, is Nicholas Meyer's *Time After Time* (1979). This tells of the young H. G. Wells who has invented a time machine, stolen by a friend of his who turns out to be Jack the Ripper. The machine returns to the nineteenth century empty, and Wells (Malcolm McDowell) uses it to pursue the homicidal maniac (David Warner) to San Francisco in the 1970s. The film tells us that the 1970s are just right for the mad, affectless killer, as our violent world is attuned to his sadistic psychology. Wells on the other hand, is as lost as if he were actually an alien, a Martian perhaps, and, like David Bowie in the previous film, he seems to be losing his sense of self.

There is something too conventionally self-lacerating about the naive view that we live in an age of unparalleled cruelty, just right for Jack the Ripper. It is historically crude and false, as is the film. Ingenious moments, and a charming performance from Mary Steenburgen as the not-quite-liberated bank clerk who falls for Wells, do not save this film from its conceptual tawdriness. We are asked to believe, at the end, that she returns to the nineteenth century with Wells, where she became the Mrs Wells of history, which seems ludicrous to anyone who knows about Wells's private life.

Clones and androids

There has been a lot of talk in the popular scientific press about clones, and even androids. A clone is an artificially produced, genetically identical duplicate of a person. (Identical twins are naturally occurring clones.) An android, in science fiction, is an artificial construct of flesh – not always a robot – that is human-like in appearance and perhaps even in psychology. By far the best SF film about androids was *Blade Runner* (see Chapter Four), but it was preceded by several others.

One of these was *The Stepford Wives* (1975), a crude but sometimes funny satire about men who want their women to be perfect little housewives. Katharine Ross plays the professional photographer who moves with her husband and family to a pleasantly suburban small town in Connecticut, away from the hurly burly of Manhattan. Bit by bit she uncovers a conspiracy by the local men to have their wives murdered and replaced by biddable robots who tell them what great studs they are, dress fifteen years out of date, have enormous breasts, and keep the kitchen squeaky clean. Paula Prentiss livens the film up as the newcomer's best friend Bobby, but most of the story consists of rather silly variations on an extremely silly theme, taken from the novel by Ira Levin. This film degrades men. (It does not do much for the

dignity of womanhood either.)

At least the science is better in *The Boys from Brazil* (1978), also based on a novel by Ira Levin, but this time about clones, who are more plausible than androids. There is a perverse enjoyment in watching Gregory Peck in a rare role as a villain – the evil Nazi Doctor Mengele, now based in South America. The basic idea is quite interesting: cell tissue from Adolf Hitler has been kept alive and cloned. The resulting boy babies have been adopted by various families around the world. The idea is to obtain a new Hitler, but to do this, stage two of the plan requires that their fathers should be assassinated. The real Hitler's father died when he was a boy, and they wish to duplicate his environment as closely as possible.

The interesting point is that the film does *not* support the kind of mindless genetic determinism that supposes a clone would grow to have an identical psychology to that of his "parent" (genetically a brother rather than a father). In fact, one of the young Adolfs saves the day for the hero, a Jewish Nazi-hunter (Laurence Oliver), though not without some sinister Hitlerian twitching. The plot, however, is ridiculously melodramatic, and the acting is uniformly hammy – disgracefully so in the case of Olivier.

The low-budget production *Android* (1982) is an altogether more gripping thriller. It was a directorial debut for Aaron Lipstadt, who made the film for Roger Corman's New World company, which over the years has produced several movie diamonds amid all its exploitation junk. Unusually, the film was scripted by its star, another newcomer, Don Opper. He is obviously an SF fan, for his film contains a far more sophisticated use of conventional SF tropes (images, ideas, symbols, metaphors) than most of the more lavish SF films made by the big companies.

Opper plays an android (in this case, part flesh, part metal) who works as a research assistant in a remote space laboratory run by Dr Daniel, a long-haired, sinister scientist played by Klaus Kinski. We do not know that Max is an android at first, but we do know that he is extremely innocent – rather like Voltaire's Candide. His whole life seems to consist of playing computer games and watching sex-instruction tapes and old movies. He does imitations of Jimmy Stewart (in *It's a Wonderful Life*) in private. Then the real world intrudes in the shape of three runaway criminals, two men and a woman.

One of the film's better moments concerns his first sexual experience with this woman: "Max, you're a doll", she tells him. But there is much, much more: the replay (a little differently) of the scene in *Metropolis* where the female robot is awakened; the grim moment when the endearing, shambling Max is temporarily re-programmed to become an unfeeling killer; the clever way in which his

basic idea is that the human brain contains within it the entire history of Man's evolution (no argument here). But the film reverses cause and effect. It's one thing to argue that our genetic being is reflected in the nature of our consciousness, and quite another thing to say that by altering our consciousness we can alter our genetic being, and hence our bodily shape. It is all a bit like arguing that if LSD was given to a chicken, out of sheer hallucinogenic chagrin it would instantly revert to being an egg.

People with no interest in science presumably don't worry about this sort of thing, but it genuinely spoils the enjoyment for those people who *do* know and are consequently unable to suspend their disbelief. The film tells of a scientist who eats magic mushrooms, has mystic experiences, neglects his wife, enters a sensory-deprivation tank, devolves to an ape-man, kills a goat in the zoo, becomes human again, has bad moments when bits of his body ripple and change, finally devolves to primordial ooze, and is eventually saved by the love of a good woman. It is, of course, *Dr Jekyll and Mr Hyde* updated with psycho-babble, Russell pyrotechnics, and some rather creepy make-up by Dick Smith, who since *The Exorcist* (and before) has specialized in making people look monstrous.

The supersonic Russian fighter plane of the title in Firefox *(Malpaso/Warner Bros, 1982) gets into a dogfight. But all is well, Clint Eastwood is at the controls; all he has to do is think in Russian, for the aircraft works by thought control.*

innocence is not over-emphasised, so that he is actually able to learn quite fast; the amusingly black revelation of Dr Daniel's true nature (similar to a scene in *Alien*); and Max's final, joyful departure for Earth with his new android mate (an extremely attractive Bride of Frankenstein), in the guise of a fully fledged human. It is a minor film, but witty and sometimes enchanting.

Powers of the mind

Most SF is about technological power, but some is about strange powers of the mind. Ken Russell's *Altered States* (1980) is an example. Like much of Russell's work, it applies a lunatic vigour to a great many currently trendy ideas, and makes of them a highly-coloured pot-pourri. The perfume of this concoction, however, is of dubious quality. The

Right: beautiful, bald Persis Khambatta is an exotic new crew member of the starship Enterprise *in* Star Trek The Motion Picture *(Paramount, 1979), here incarnating the alien being, V'ger.*

Below: the lifestyles on plague planet Terra Eleven are pretty derelict; this cross between a sailing ship and a train is one of the posher modes of transport in Spacehunter: Adventures in the Forbidden Zone *(Delphi/Columbia, 1983).*

It is more fun, though, than Douglas Trumbull's *Brainstorm* (1983), which incorporates that old SF favourite, the machine that can read thoughts and emotions. The film changes format and becomes bigger during the sequences in which we are seeing what is happening inside people's heads, but these are oddly static and conventional, considering Trumbull's reputation as a wizard in the area of special effects. The film falls to pieces in three ways: the tired old plot of the military wanting to exploit a civilian invention as a weapon (numbingly predictable); the fixing of the broken marriage of scientist and wife by the use of the machine to reach each other's minds (ghastly sentimental flashbacks to weddings, and of course the screen the audience watches can only show pictures, not emotions, so we never quite get the point); and worst of all, the tape-recording of a woman's thoughts as she dies (this tape is supposed to represent a metaphysical breakthrough into the nature of a cosmic reality so compelling that a weak person could be

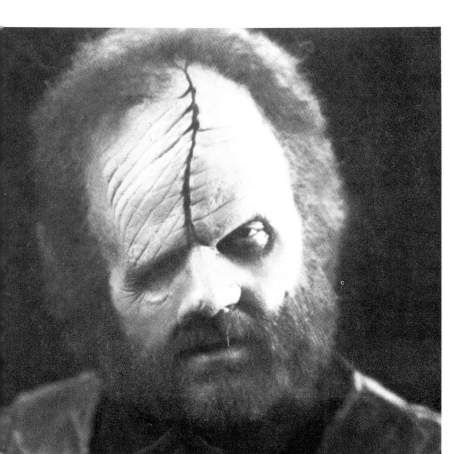

In the lurid melodrama Battle Beyond the Stars (New World, 1980), the mutant henchmen of warlord Sador are a nasty bunch, who all appear to have undergone a rather primitive form of brain surgery.

killed by it, but in fact it consists of little people moving about in soap bubbles). Natalie Wood, who plays the wife, was drowned during the production; the film was greatly delayed as a result, and some awkward rescripting was required so that a large part of the film could be shot around her presence without her actually being there.

Big machines

People like technological menaces, hence two recent films about flying super-weapons in which it is the machine itself that is the star. Clint Eastwood's *Firefox* is about a neurotic ex-Vietnam pilot who steals a super-plane from the Russians (it is very fast and works by thought control) and flies it away. It would have been a better film if John Dykstra's plane effects had not been so obviously phoney. Dykstra won a great reputation on *Star Wars* as a man who could matte miniature spaceships against a background of space and make them look real. It did not work here, largely because the trick is more difficult to pull off against a blue sky rather than the blackness of space.

Blue Thunder (1982), a film by John Badham released almost simultaneously with his *WarGames*, is in many ways a carbon copy of *Firefox*; veteran haunted by Vietnam horrors, lethal aircraft (this time a super-helicopter), lots of aerial battles. The movie is well made, crisply edited, wholly illogical and morally repugnant. It exploits precisely those scenes of cold-blooded violence that it

supposedly deplores. The plot (more post-Watergate paranoia) has the US government fomenting race riots so that it can test out the killer plane, designed for riot control. In the attempts of the good policeman (Roy Scheider) to prevent this, he manages to put the helicopter through exactly the sort of paces for which it was designed.

Space, the final frontier

The biggest and best-loved SF machines of all are the ones that go out into space. Spaceship movies have, of course, been among the most popular of recent fantasies, but we have already considered the best of them in Chapter Four, under the heading of Key Directors. These include *Star Wars*, *Dark Star*, *Close Encounters* and *Alien*. We have also looked at the great paradigm space movie, the one that began the boom, *2001: A Space Odyssey*. Outside these few key movies, there are perhaps five others worth looking at here.

The biggest disappointment was *The Black Hole* (1979). Advance publicity promised a visual feast, but in fact the special-effects work was not of high enough quality to save the puerile script – which was, in effect, a reprise in space of *20,000 Leagues Under the Sea*. The script gives the appearance of having been put together by a cynical committee who knew nothing of science fiction, but knew what Walt Disney's rules were. Thus we have a Captain Nemo figure (Maximilian Schell) who lives in a derelict spacecraft moored close to a black hole (it is red, presumably so that we can see it better). He is served by a small army of goose-stepping robots. There are two nice robots (as in *Star Wars*) who have funny voices (Roddy McDowall, Slim Pickens). Astronauts enter this craft and have a bad time. A meteor strike is the most absurd visual effect, and it is never explained why the ship does not suffer explosive decompression when it is punctured by a meteor the size of a house. At the end, everyone is sucked into the black hole, which turns out to be an entirely metaphysical vortex, producing Dante's Inferno for Schell and some sort of kitschy cathedral for the surviving good guys. It is sad that the film was the swansong of Peter Ellenshaw, the matte artist and special effects supervisor who had contributed so much to Disney studios.

There were always going to be problems in transferring the slightly tatty ethos of television's *Star Trek* to the big screen. The original stories had minimal special effects, concentrated on a jolly but stereotyped view of character, and every week gave a neat lesson about ethical behaviour thinly disguised in allegorical SF terms. It was all precisely engineered to the strengths and weaknesses of the small screen, and no matter how carefully the big-screen script was constructed, either it would be untrue to the flavour of the original (and upset the series' many fans) or else the magnification would reveal the many flaws, Robert Wise directed *Star Trek: The Motion Picture* (1979) in a way that gave maximum value to the technological romance of the film – long, contemplative, gliding shots of various forms of mysterious space hardware – but he had problems with the story. This was based on two of the original television episodes, "The Doomsday Machine" about an implacable alien force heading straight towards Earth, and "The Changeling", about an old Earth space probe that has developed a form of autonomous life. There are many things wrong with the film, but one has to admire Wise's nerve in telling a tale which effectively ends in a coruscating act of sexual intercourse between man and machine. The latter is *Voyager VI*, now known as the alien creature V'ger, temporarily and partially incarnate as bald, lovely Persis Khambatta. I will not attempt to recount the events that lead to this touching apotheosis.

Many fans believed that the sequel, *Star Trek: The Wrath of Khan* (1982), was the better film. It was certainly cheaper. Wise's effort had cost Paramount an amazing forty million dollars – although the cost was finally recouped. The sequel, which was filmed by Paramount's television unit rather than a conventional film crew, came in at a mere ten million. It did enormously well for the studio, but its popularity was undeserved. It was filmed in flat television style with muddy colours, and little weight was given to the symbolic possibilities of the melodramatic plot, which were many: Kirk is reunited with his abandoned son; Spock dies disappointingly though decorously after sacrificing himself for the crew; a space pirate called Khan believes himself to be Captain Ahab; Project Genesis, a device that turns planetary wastelands into paradise, can also be used as a terrible weapon; Chekov is mind-controlled into disloyalty because an alien earwig is implanted in his brain; and Captain Kirk quotes Dickens: "It is a far, far better thing I do..."

Enthusiasts claim that the film is good because the story is paramount, but the trouble is, the story's implications are given short shrift by the hurried episodic style, which has none of Wise's visual flair. The much-touted humanistic values of *Star Trek* amount here to little more than Kirk's soft-faced gloom whenever he is placed in a moral dilemma, and a lot of sentimental stuff about self-sacrifice that could come straight out of a sermon. Surely there is more to humanism than a marshmallow endorsement of such woolly, uncontroversial precepts.

Old-fashioned space opera

There was, however, some old-fashioned entertainment to be derived from two unambi-

tious space operas of the period. *Battle Beyond the Stars* (1980) was the cynical, typical attempt by Roger Corman's New World studios to exploit the success of *Star Wars*, *Star Trek* et al. The film, cheekily, is a replay in space of the popular western *The Magnificent Seven*, right down to Robert Vaughn repeating his role as the world-weary gunslinger. Instead of bandits besieging a village, we have an alien warlord besieging a planet, but the principle is the same. Richard Thomas (John-Boy Walton of the television series) is the young hero who collects an ill-assorted group of interstellar thugs to dispose of the warlord. Of these, the most memorable are the reptilian mercenary, the metal breast-plated huge-bosomed Valkyrie ("You haven't seen anything until you see a Valkyrie go down"), the heat-eating Kelvin, and Robert Vaughn. It is all rather perfunctory, but the space battles are surprisingly good for a small budget, and the script by John Sayles is fun. (Sayles is the brightest of the young genre scenarists, and was also responsible for *Piranha*, *The Howling* and *Alligator*.)

Finally, let me recommend the underestimated *Spacehunter: Adventures in the Forbidden Zone* (1983), a film made in somewhat eye-straining 3-D. Peter Strauss plays a kind of down-market Indiana Jones (laconic, unshaven, cynical), a salvage pilot who sees an opportunity to make big bucks by saving three captured Earthwomen on the post-holocaust planet of Terra Eleven. The planet is populated by hairy scavengers, mutants, bat people, barracuda women, a mad half-cyborg warlord, and a winning tomboy played by Molly Ringwald, who, since she never bathes, doesn't smell very nice. It is all very entertaining, especially the artefacts on the planet, all of which seem to be made from scrounged bits and pieces of scrap metal, remnants of civilization before the plague. Particularly good is the rickety schooner with tattered sails that runs on a railroad, and the sad moment where the hero's sexy partner, who is dying, turns out to be a robot. All the bits and pieces of the movie are thoroughly second-hand, but they are cheerfully put together, and the seedy dialogue crackles along very successfully.

The more exciting SF adventure films there are, the better: they are great fun to watch in their own right, and they create a climate of opinion in which, every now and then, a studio can attempt something more ambitious and thought-provoking. It is sad that ambition of this kind – as shown in *Blade Runner* or *The Man Who Fell to Earth* for example – is still comparatively rare. Tired old formula movies, crammed with bad science (like *The Black Hole*, which seems to have been made by people who did not know what a black hole was), are still the rule rather than the exception.

Horror Films Since 1968

Previous two pages:
Nosferatu The
Vampyre *(Gaumont,
1979). Klaus Kinski
plays the title role, in
this new version by
Werner Herzog,
looking only fractionally
more friendly than Max
Schreck in the original
movie of 1922 – see
picture on page 14.*

Just as they were for science fiction, the 1970s were breakthrough years for horror in the cinema. The success of *Rosemary's Baby* in 1968 had something to do with this, and many horror films were made right through the 1970s, but the biggest commercial breakthrough was that of *The Exorcist* in 1973. Before that, most horror films were the product of comparatively small production companies like New World, American International, Hammer and Amicus. After 1973 the big boys began to get into the act. By 1983, the boom seemed to be subsiding, but for the previous decade audiences were inundated with monstrous children (*The Omen, Eraserhead, To the Devil a Daughter*), possessed houses (*Burnt Offerings, Amityville Horror, Inferno*), doomed psychics (*Don't Look Now*), beast-people (*American Werewolf in London, The Howling, Cat People*), bloodthirsty ghouls (*House by the Cemetery, Evil Dead*) and monsters (*Piranha, Wolfen, Alligator*). The late 1970s were the years of visceral horror, more graphic than anything that had previously appeared on the screen, and the result, especially in the UK, was a good deal of public concern, though not very much well-informed debate. But our story begins with the slow death of the costume Gothic.

The British Gothic cinema was still active in the late 1960s, but there were signs that it was losing heart. Most of these films were costume dramas set in the nineteenth or early twentieth century, but after *Rosemary's Baby* the public was beginning to want its horror films set in the here-and-now, and mostly in urban settings at that.

Blood from the Mummy's Tomb (1971), directed by Seth Holt, was one of Hammer's more stylish period productions. Set in the recent past, it was based on a novel by Bram Stoker (author of *Dracula*) called *Jewel of the Seven Stars*, and does not feature the lurching, bandage-swathed figure of their previous Mummy films. The story centres on the ancient artefacts needed for the resuscitation in London of the Egyptian Queen whose spirit has already been intermittently possessing the body of the heroine.

A metal cobra, a jackal's skull, a statuette of a cat – each is involved in a startling and messily jugular death, and each time the severed stump of the dead Queen's wrist sympathetically oozes blood. A particularly strong scene shows the stigmata of rips and scratches appearing on a screaming woman's face, as if by magic, while the image continually cuts away to the impassive gaze of the stone cat. All this is directed with a fine frenzy, in a number of bizarre, expressionist compositions, which are artistic almost as often as they are arty. The finale, where a house falls in, leaving only the girl alive, is witty. Swathed in bandages (because of the accident) she lies in bed, and we never do find out if she is now the lovely heroine or the evil Queen. (Holt, who was 48, died during filming, and the last few scenes were directed, uncredited, by Michael Carreras.)

Most Hammer films of this period was quite weak, especially the Dracula films set in modern London (see, for example, *Dracula AD 1972* in filmography). The Lesbian-oriented Karnstein trilogy, which began with *The Vampire Lovers* (see filmography), was also appalling. But just when it seemed that they had played out the vampire theme altogether, Hammer came up with what may be the best of the lot, an underrated film, *Vampire Circus* (1971).

Sexual equations

Vampire Circus is not so much a good film, as a good bad film. That is, it is not good in the conventional ways in which films are good. The script is ragged, the acting often wooden. What it has is an iconography as conventionalized and ritualistic as that of a Japanese Noh play, especially in the choreography of the bloody finale. When vampires snarl, they always throw their heads back; their mouths when lifted are always surrounded by a formal ring of red after they have fed. This is almost a vampire ballet. The film opens with the staking of a vampire count who pronounces a curse on the children of the villagers with his dying breath. Fifteen years later plague has struck the village, armed guards outside prevent people leaving, and the Circus of Night (and "one hundred delights") comes to town.

The circus performs genuine magic. A panther becomes a man; when the cat woman performs an erotic dance, the tiger shudders with delight in its cage; two bats wheel and turn in the air, and become two beautiful young people, still flying. (One of them, Lalla Ward, was to become Dr Who's assistant in the popular British television series.) The villagers think all this is a clever fake, but we, the audience, know better; in a curious about-turn, we accept the fantasy that they reject. The editing provides more magic. A vampire kills a victim, who gasps as he dies, and the gasp becomes the gasp of pleasure as the pretend-vampires (who are really real vampires) float above the circus audience. Clever stuff. The hall of mirrors with one mirror that is a magic door to the castle crypt half a mile away is good too.

This enjoyable, gory masque about appearance and reality gives all the vitality and enchantment to the vampires, and all the plodding idiocy to the villagers, who stand for us. The villagers' final victory, we feel, is the triumph of philistines over the artist, of cuckolds over seducers. (In this, as in other Hammer films, the vampire's reign is specifically related to unfaithful wives and fornicating daughters, both of whom regularly expire in bliss.)

Hammer's films were generally becoming worse, but their last cinema production to date had a certain sordid interest. This was *To The Devil a Daughter* (1976). The screenplay is extraordinary for the lengths it goes to in its desire to produce the most perverse sensationalism possible – at the cost of all logic, if necessary. The makers were fortunate in their casting of Nastassia Kinski – she must have been extremely young at the time – as the young woman at the centre of events. Kinski has a polymorphous, powerful sexuality that effortlessly ranges from attractive innocence to voluptuous corruption, and she needs the whole gamut in this movie. We first meet her as a nun; we later find that the order to which she belongs is headed by a satanist (Christopher Lee) and that she is the daughter of Ashtaroth. The children of Ashtaroth are born to willing mothers who have their thighs bound together, to prevent normal egress of the foetus; it bursts bloodily through the abdominal wall. We actually see most of this occurring in a scene of unparalleled nastiness for the period. (It points forward to the chest-bursting scene of *Alien*.)

Kinski is not just the daughter of Ashtaroth, she is also the wife (we see her mounted from above, below and behind by Lee, who is the god's avatar in a golden mask). Finally, in a scene one can hardly credit passing the censor, she becomes Ashtaroth's mother when the creature (small and reptilian) crawls onto her belly and is pushed by her back down into her genital passage. Richard Widmark is the likeable writer of horror stories who saves her at the end, and one wonders what he's let himself in for. As a film, it is not very good. As a sociological symptom, it points forward to many of the horror-film obsessions that were to follow: the monstrous child, the perverting of religion, and the equating of sex with both energy and evil. (That is, it is presented as *attractively* distasteful.) Kinski could be the Barbara Steele of the 1980s – she has something of the same icon-like quality. She was also well used in *Cat People*, later on.

Cute horror

So Hammer expired (as a producer of feature films) in a blaze of nausea, appropriately enough. But other low-budget horror films were being made in the UK in the early 1970s. One of the most successful was *The Abominable Dr Phibes* (1971), directed by Robert Fuest, who specialised in trendy, camp fantasy, such as *The Avengers* on television (see *The Final Programme*, *The Devil's Rain* in filmography). The film is a spoof, starring Vincent Price in the sort of tongue-in-cheek role he obviously most enjoys. He plays the dreadfully mutilated Dr Phibes, avenging himself on the doctors who failed to save his wife's life in a series of bizarre murders which recapitulate the plagues of ancient Egypt. These have a Grand Guignol, comic-book air about them which renders them more amusing than disturbing, and they are the point of the film, apart from Price's own melodramatic performance: mugging, playing the organ, talking hollowly through a vocal synthesizer plugged into a hole in his neck, and living chastely with the beautiful and blank Vulnavia (Virginia North) in an art-deco paradise. (This was a period, in the UK, of spoof movies like *Modesty Blaise*, 1966, and its successors. I find their attempt to have it both ways – to be both shocking and cutely lovable – rather revolting, but many people like them.) The inferior sequel was *Dr Phibes Rises Again* (1972, see filmography).

There was an air of "it's all a game" about the Amicus anthology films, also. These were *Dr Terror's House of Horrors* (1964), *Torture Garden* (1967), *The House that Dripped Blood* (1970), *Tales from the Crypt* (1972), *Asylum* (1972), *The Vault of Horror* (1972) and *From Beyond the Grave* (1973). They are all discussed in the filmography.

Fertility cults

Considering the enormous popularity, in their day, of books abut pagan fertility rituals – such as Sir James Frazer's *The Golden Bough*, Robert Graves's *The White Goddess*, and the best-seller of all, Margaret Murray's *The Witch-Cult in Western Europe* – and considering the vast spin-off of this interest in the form of occult novels, it is surprising how seldom the theme of pagan survivals into modern times has entered the cinema. The most notable example, *The Wicker Man* (1973), was so hacked about and badly distributed that it appeared to have been suppressed by influential witches. With a screenplay by well-known playwright Anthony Shaffer, one might have expected that the film would be aimed at the art-house audience, but instead it was cut from 102 to 87 minutes, pushed down-market, and then instantly sunk from sight for many years. The result was that its very invisibility magnified its virtues, and it developed a cult reputation as perhaps the greatest modern horror film. Now that the film can occasionally be seen again (and it is available on videotape, heavily cut in the UK but full-length in the USA), it can be judged more coolly as interesting but flawed.

Edward Woodward plays the policeman called to a remote island off the Scottish coast to investigate the case of a missing girl. A virginal, puritanical, middle-aged Christian, he is both attracted to and appalled by the easygoing life on the island, presided over by Lord Summerisle (Christopher Lee, in probably his best role), and slowly realizes that the bawdy songs, the naked dances, the odd touches of ritual mean that the islanders are pagans. He suspects that the missing girl may

The Kinski family have left their mark on horror movies of the 1970s (see picture on pages 132/133). This is Nastassia, daughter of Klaus, about to receive (willingly) the embraces of Ashtaroth in To The Devil a Daughter *(Hammer, 1976), the last feature, to date, from the celebrated studio.*

be intended as a human sacrifice (everybody denies knowing her). Eventually he finds her (having joined a May-Day procession dressed as the Fool), but it is he, it turns out, who is to be the sacrifice, and the girl was merely the lure. Suspended in a man-shaped wicker cage, he is burned to bring fertility to the island and ensure a good harvest. It is a genuinely shocking ending to an otherwise fairly quiet film. Visually the film has conviction, in many nice, small touches, and the islanders do not (as in most films of remotely comparable theme) look as if they come from Central Casting. But the ironies are perhaps a little obvious, as both the policeman's faith and the islanders' faith are weighed in the balance and found wanting. Unlike most films about witches, this one does not suggest that somewhere a genuine Satan is manipulating events (the Devil is never mentioned) – or a genuine God, if it comes to that. It is rather a cruel film, only fantastic in its imagery (Jungian rather than Freudian), and in its suggestion that sacrificial rituals are so close to the surface of human consciousness, perhaps in the form of a race memory, that they may erupt again at any time. (Few anthropologists believe any longer that a witch or mother-goddess fertility cult *ever* existed in Europe in historical times, but the idea of witchcraft as a genuine religion has become a potent modern myth, in both books and films. To evince a belief in the powers of witchcraft is now trendy, and almost respectable. George Romero's film *Jack's Wife* looked at the phenomenon.)

More witchcraft
An earlier film, *Blood on Satan's Claw* (1970), is more typical of the conventional treatment

of witchcraft in horror films. Here the witchcraft is directly organized by ·the Devil. The film is set in the seventeenth century. A ploughman, in the promising opening, digs up a strange, demonic head with one rolling blue eye. That night a girl sees something nasty in the bedroom, and emerges stark mad with a claw where her hand should be. A talon is picked up in the fields by a nubile young thing who instantly turns nasty and tries to seduce the vicar. Soon she is running a witch cult that is joined by most of the local young people – there is a lot of naked dancing in the woods. One of them grows on her leg a patch of hair ("Satan's skin") which is surgically removed and kept in a bottle. It is all filmed with some imagination by Piers Haggard, mostly on location – all misty fields and woodlands. The final appearance of the demon is badly muffed. It is not an important film, but possession by an ancient spirit of evil was certainly to be an important theme.

Possession
Stories about possession are, to a degree, stories about moral responsibility. It could be quite convenient to claim that you did some dreadful thing because you had been possessed by an evil spirit or demon; it would lift the guilt from your shoulders. Nevertheless, some of the acts done by possessed people in films of this kind symbolize what they might want to do anyway. Possession films can also be stories about repressed desires. But one of the earlier possession films, oddly enough, was in part political.

This was *The Possession of Joel Delaney* (1971). An upper-class young man (Perry King), with a fashionable, over-protective older sister (Shirley MacLaine), becomes possessed by the spirit of his dead friend, a homicidal Puerto Rican youth, who – it is somewhat blandly suggested – went bad because Puerto Ricans live in such rotten conditions in New York. (The insistent contrast between the slums of Spanish Harlem and the comfortable apartments of the wealthy is at the centre of this socio-political revenge fable.) He beheads his girlfriend, and evinces an incestuous interest in his sister (which serves her right, because rather primly she has been doing the same to him) before being gunned down by the cops. The film is notable for two cliches which have been used repeatedly since: the severed head in the fridge, and the final scene where the evil spirit leaves its old tenement of flesh and enters a new one. The film closes with the sister smirking evilly and fingering a switch-blade. While not particularly good, the film may prove to be historically significant.

Lock up your daughters

The Exorcist (1973) became instant legend. It is the most popular horror film ever made. The film is efficiently if not brilliantly directed by William Friedkin, who takes his time about setting up a family's normative, suburban life-style in a nice part of Washington, before destroying this peaceful, middle-class oasis by introducing the demonic possession of the young daughter, Regan, a girl just on the brink of puberty, played by Linda Blair.

It begins with strange noises upstairs (rats?), and goes on quietly enough, if portending the sexual imagery to come, with Regan urinating on the carpet during a dinner party. Symptoms of the demon's entry start to snowball. In no time at all, Regan's face is hideously contorted; she levitates; she vomits green mess over a priest; her head performs 360° turns on her shoulders; she speaks different languages in a strange, gruff voice (that of veteran character actress Mercedes McCambridge); she masturbates violently and painfully with a crucifix; and she uses foul language with the clergy. She also kills one of her mother's friends. This, of course, in symbolic terms, is what all suburban mothers feared their teenage daughters would do in the mid-1970s, a period when the alienation of children from parents was the number-one sociological talking point in the USA. Thus the film could simultaneously attract teenagers (delighted at seeing someone get away with it) and parents (worst fears confirmed). In retrospect, one can see how the film could hardly fail.

Graphic scenes of sex and deformity had been done before in horror films, but these were mostly not considered to be reputable and they were not made by major studios with large budgets to spend on effects. For the mass audience, *The Exorcist* was some-

thing new.

Intellectual Catholics may have been amused to observe that *The Exorcist* was a perfect modern example of an ancient heresy, the Manichean, in that it implies that the struggle between God and Satan is a battle between equals, and it sees the body as always, potentially, the temple of evil. All of this would be more repugnant if one could take it seriously. It is certainly disturbing that a public, that was in theory largely agnostic, should take so readily to the proposition that absolute Evil exists in the world. This is always a dangerous view; it leads in the end to the idea of pogrom as virtuous, and in its determinism it lessens any need we may feel to change ourselves. ("The Devil made me do it.")

Indeed, in this film Evil actually has primacy over Good. One priest, the Exorcist, is killed; the other is nearly powerless, and only succeeds by taking the demon into himself while committing suicide.

The film is too simplistic to be first-rate, but the entertainingly nasty make-up effects by Dick Smith, the dean of Hollywood make-up artists, were successful. So too was the moody photography of the sinister prologue in Iran, and the romantic chiaroscuro in which the Exorcist is largely seen.

Consensus opinion holds that *Exorcist II: The Heretic* (1977) was a disastrous sequel. For example, Consumer Guide's *The Best, Worst and Most Unusual Horror Films* (1983), my bible in these matters, puts *Exorcist II* into the "Worst" chapter. I therefore expect, along with my film-rating panel, to be execrated for suggesting that Boorman's sequel was more interesting than the original film.

John Boorman had already demonstrated

The May Day celebrations on Summerisle are about to get rough in The Wicker Man *(British Lion, 1973). Behind the jester's mask is the face of Edward Woodward; he is attempting to save Geraldine Cowper from being sacrificed. Nice try, wrong victim. Woodward himself will burn in the pagan ceremony of the "wicker man".*

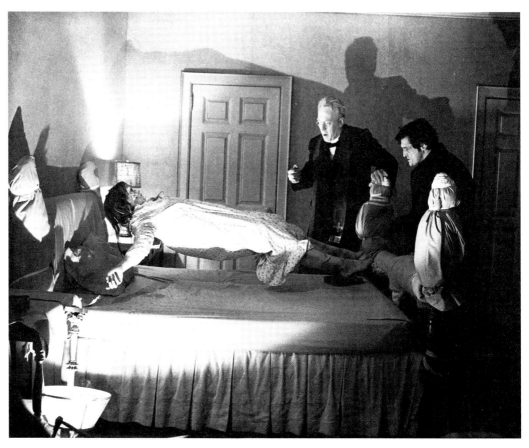

The exorcism is not going too well in The Exorcist *(Warner Bros, 1973). The possessed Regan (Linda Blair) continues to levitate and growl obscenities, watched by the exorcist (Max von Sydow, centre) and his assistant (Jason Miller, right).*

his intellectual ambition and his tendency to over-reach in *Zardoz* (see Chapter Five). He did much the same here. Richard Burton plays Father Lamont who is investigating the death of Father Merrin, the Exorcist of the previous film. It is four years later. Regan, now apparently cured, is nevertheless still disturbed and undergoing psychiatric treatment. At this time Regan learns that she has healing powers. Through an electronic device that allows a partial melding of minds, Father Lamont finds that Regan is still in intermittent contact with her ex-possessor, who turns out to be Puzuzu, the African locust god. In a complex story, Lamont goes to Africa, has visions of Puzuzu, meets a witchdoctor – or is he an ordinary doctor? – who was once possessed by Puzuzu, returns to America, decides that Regan is in danger, returns with her to the now abandoned Washington house where it all happened first time around, and is subjected to hallucinations where Regan splits into good-Regan and bad-Regan. Bad-Regan tries to seduce him, but he has the strength to tear her heart out. Locusts attack, the house collapses, but Regan and Lamont walk out unharmed.

Worried about the people who laughed at this final scene during early screenings, Warner Bros asked Boorman to recut the film. In this second version, the one that was shown abroad, Lamont is killed at the end. Other minor changes of emphasis were also made. The second version did much better.

Where did Boorman go wrong? He says, "The sin I committed was not giving the audi-

ence what it wanted in terms of horror. There's this wild beast out there which is the audience. I created this arena and I just didn't throw enough Christians into it."

The film does have moments of incoherence, and an over-melodramatic performance from Burton, but it also has a thought-provoking intellectual structure. Boorman had denied the Good-Evil dualism of the first film, and sees Good and Evil as co-existing in an uneasy balance, each one needing the other, it seems, to make it meaningful. As part of this, the Evil side of the equation is subtly seductive, not merely ugly as in the first film. Puzuzu is linked with images of great energy and sometimes beauty, as well as with hordes of all-devouring locusts. Puzuzu, in short, is given dignity. The film is full of precarious tensions between different ways of thought: science/magic (priest/psychiatrist), faith/doubt, nature/the unnatural, healing/destroying. Lamont, the good priest, has moments when he is infected by the Evil he is out to destroy, as when he nearly causes a plane to crash.

The visual images of the film are very strong: the primitive African cliff-village, all muddy browns; the locust plagues (shot by Oxford Scientific Films); the demon-flight on the wind; the extraordinary make-up effect when the possessed Regan (all warty and horrible) becomes voluptuous Regan (glowing and lascivious and lovely) in one smooth, continuous take. This is a complex, teasing, hesitant, exploratory sort of film that breaks all the genre rules. It has its absurd moments, but one has to admire its metaphysical ambition, and its refusal to settle for stereotypes.

More rotten kids

The Omen (1976) was the other up-market horror hit of the period. The son of the new American Ambassador to the UK (Gregory Peck) is a changeling, a spawn of the devil, but his mother (Lee Remick) does not know. When he grows up, he will become the Antichrist. In the meantime he is protected by a sinister nanny (Billy Whitelaw) and a big, black dog. Drunken priests and loony photographers who try to warn Peck about his son suffer impalements and beheadings. Bad omens proliferate. The kid looks sanctimoniously angelic, but he won't go to church. He is dragged there, finally, by Dad, who intends sticking him with a bunch of magical daggers, but the cops arrive in time to shoot the father. We see the son at his father's funeral, finally, standing next to the President of the USA.

The Omen is inoffensively nasty, prettily filmed and in good taste, with Gregory Peck looking appropriately sober and concerned – but what on earth is it *about*? One possible subtext is: never adopt children. Another is: when the little dears look angelic they've got mischief on their mind. A third is: evil is something foreign (Italian and English) and does not grow from *within* America.

Bourgeois values are not threatened by the film in any way except perhaps in the secret pleasure the audience derives from the bad kid's victory at the end, and the suggestion that all will not be well with the Presidency. But even that was a commonplace American thought in 1976. This glossy, glazed attempt to rework the traditional horror picture (big stars, nice photography) for a respectable audience was commercially successful, but as a film it does not amount to much.

The sequel, *Damien Omen II* (1978), was cheaper and a bit livelier. It was certainly gorier, as Damien, now a handsome teenage boy adopted by a politically powerful American family, grows into knowledge of his powers, and polishes off any sign of resistance (crows peck out eyes, elevator-cables cut people in half, and in the visually most inventive sequence, a man drowns in a frozen lake, struggling wildly just beneath the ice that he cannot break through). As fantasy the film is so-so, the best sequence being Damien's beating up a bully at military school, using his telekinetic powers. As an anthology of murders, it gives devotees of extravagant demise their money's worth. Indeed, the film points forward to such exploitation pictures as *Friday the 13th* whose only *raison d'être* is the presentation of successive homicides.

The second sequel (*The Final Conflict*, see filmography) is stunningly inadequate. The series ended with a whimper, not a bang.

Bad medicine

A lurid alternative to the spiritual possession of people by Evil is straightforward physical possession. *The Manitou* (1977) is so grotesquely inventive, along these lines, that it should really have been much better than it is. Susan Strasberg plays the unfortunate young woman in San Francisco who develops a tumour on her neck and, distrusting her doctor, asks the advice of an old friend, a phoney fortune teller played with tawdry dash by Tony Curtis. It turns out that the foetus-like growth houses a tiny Indian Medicine Man, Misquamacus, who is four hundred years old and very angry. The growth enlarges, and Misquamacus (deformed by an X-ray treatment given to the tumour) hatches out. Fortunately, in the meantime, Curtis has found a good medicine man (Michael Ansara) to fight the bad one. This battle, on the astral plane, is largely signified by flashing lights. When Curtis harnesses the manitou (spirit) of the hospital computer, Misquamacus (a truly sinister apparition) is defeated. Most of the effects are pretty awful (a supposedly flayed man is actually wearing what looks like a wrinkled, red polythene body suit), but they make up in quantity for what they lack in quality.

An interesting sub-genre features objects rather than people being possessed, very often cars, as in *Crash!* (see filmography). My favourite of these, until *Christine* (see Chapter Four) came along and topped them all, was *The Car* (1977). Most critics hated it, but I enjoyed the surrealist effect of its offering absolutely no explanation for anything that

British child actor Harvey Stephens plays the Antichrist in The Omen *(20th Century-Fox, 1976). Here he watches something unpleasant happen to his mother. This was one of the many monstrous-child movies of the period, along with* The Exorcist.

happens. The Car is a big, black limousine with smoked-glass windows (but it has no driver) that roars around the town of Santa Ynez killing people. It revs its engine menacingly when it is lying in wait, rather like the truck in Spielberg's *Duel*. That is the whole of the story. After all, most explanations in horror films are unbelievably thin, and it is refreshing to have a film that simply presents its horror as emerging out of a clear blue sky. The Car is even allowed to kill the heroine, by driving clear through her house – another nice, surreal touch, for we always think of houses as being, symbolically, fortresses.

Bad places

Houses need not be good. One of the oldest possession themes of all is the house possessed of evil. In *Burnt Offerings* (1976) a mansion near the sea is rented for the summer by a couple (Oliver Reed and Karen Black) with their son (Lee Montgomery) and Auntie (Bette Davis). Locked away upstairs is the landlord's invisible, invalid mother, whose meals are left for her on a tray. Bad things happen, flamboyantly choreographed by director Dan Curtis, except to the wife, Karen Black, who eerily falls in love with the house. It turns out (this is quite a good touch) that the house feeds on suffering, and when

A huge limousine, possessed of evil, lies in wait for another victim. In the pleasant, sunlit countryside where much of the action of The Car *(Universal, 1977) takes place its arbitrary menace appears surrealistic.*

Auntie dies and Dad inexplicably attacks Son, the paintwork starts renewing itself and the mansion begins to look quite spruce. It will not let them escape, and when Oliver Reed goes upstairs to confront the previously invisible old lady he finds... well, as twist endings go, it is not too bad. The film loses points from Oliver Reed's over-acting, and the director's self-indulgently showy visuals, constantly straining for effect (and consequently disrupting our concentration), but Karen Black gives a performance of real depth which deserved a better setting.

The old New York brownstone in *The Sentinel* (1976) has masturbating, lesbian ballet dancers on the ground floor, Burgess Meredith with a canary and a sinister twinkle on the first floor, the heroine's dead father having sex with fat prostitutes on the second floor, and one very baffled lady (Cristina Raines) who has just moved in. She is a glamorous fashion model, but she starts to get migraines. There is an old blind priest in the attic, as well.

She is even more baffled when the rental agent tells her that nobody else lives in the house, because she has just had dinner with a whole bunch of inhabitants (all deceased murderers, we later learn). It comes as no surprise to discover that the house is actually a gateway to Hell (an idea done better in

Lucio Fulci's *The Beyond*, see below), but it seems to be gilding the lily, scriptwise, to have her learn that her boyfriend is a murderer too. All ends well; she banishes the hordes of Hell (in a particularly despicable piece of casting, these are played by horribly deformed people – circus freaks) and becomes a nun, the house's new Sentinel.

The film is an object lesson in how not to make an exploitation movie (it was quite expensive, too). Scene after scene is cynically set up purely to manipulate the sado-voyeurism of the audience but, because the story is windily incoherent, nobody cared and the film flopped. There is more to fantastic horror than a series of arbitrary *frissons*, and the film indeed displays a leaden literal-mindedness, not untypical of director Michael Winner's work before and since.

Much more demure than this – too demure – was *The Changeling* (1979, see filmography), while the strongest exercise by far in the same sub-genre was *The Shining* (1980, see Chapter Four). The most commercially successful, and the most stereotyped, of these late 1970s haunted-house films was *The Amityville Horror* (1979). In *Burnt Offerings* the house seduced the wife; here it is a suburban husband (James Brolin) who is the target.

Built on an ancient Indian burial site, and the scene of an inexplicable domestic massacre a year before, the house is confusingly malign in a variety of ways. We are left uncertain whether it is angry Indians, recent ghosts or just suburban *angst*. that causes James Brolin to stop going to work, and begin staring contemplatively at his axe. Margot Kidder is efficient in the thankless role of the wife. An irrelevant priest, badly overplayed by Rod Steiger, is attacked by hordes of flies in an evil room, and later struck blind in church. No sternly inexorable exorcist, he. Blood drips down the stairs, Kidder ages rapidly (in about five seconds), black tides swill around the cellar (suggesting a fourth explanation for events, a malfunctioning septic tank), and the audience wonders why on earth the family do not just get out. Finally they do.

The film is made in a blandly functional, almost documentary style, which is meant to convince us that this is the record of a true story (the claim made for the original book). *Amityville Horror*, in fact, is one of the small sub-genre of fantasy films that pretend not to be fantasy films.

Fact or fiction?

Robert Wise, for example, goes to some lengths to persuade us that *Audrey Rose* (1979) is an account of a phenomenon that actually exists. The film's subject is reincarnation, which here is a variation on the theme of possession. The little girl of a rich family suffers hysterical fits in which she

appears to relive the death of another little girl in a fiery car accident. The father of the dead girl, who has spent years learning about reincarnation in India, approaches the parents of the living girl with the information that their daughter is in fact the reincarnation of his. Anthony Hopkins plays this part with his characteristic manner of muted hysteria.

Naturally, the parents are horrified at the encroachments of this lunatic, but bit by bit the mother comes to believe there may be something in his story. Eventually, in this wholly incredible soap opera, there is a court hearing that turns on the question of whether or not reincarnation actually exists. The little girl's father allows her to be hypnotised (against the mother's will) to give evidence, and in this state she relives Audrey Rose's death again, and dies herself. The film plays cynically upon our fears about the safety of children, and the ending would be unforgivable, were it not so silly. The sentimental finale about how her little soul lives on is, however, quite vile.

Wise directs with his customary shrewdness – he has probably never made a wholly bad film. He was clearly tempted to leave the whole reincarnation question ambiguous, and it would perhaps have been better if he had. It would then have become a very strange film indeed, about the gullibility of conventional parents unable to cope with wholly unexpected claims made on their child. But the little girl's burned hands cannot readily be explained away, and a *bona fide*, well-made reincarnation movie is what we undoubtedly have.

Audrey Rose was adapted from a novel by

Moving into a Manhattan apartment can be dangerous. This one is in an old house whose other occupants come from Hell, which lies immediately beneath. Here Cristina Raines seems put out to find two fat, demonic prostitutes on the landing, in The Sentinel *(Universal, 1976).*

Frank De Felitta, who has made a speciality of truth-is-stranger-than-fiction books. Another of these was filmed as *The Entity* (1981). It tells the supposedly true story of Carla Moran (very well played by Barbara Hershey), a single mother living with her three children, who is sexually attacked by an invisible assailant. The attacks continue over several evenings. The psychiatrist from whom she seeks help believes she is conjuring up the attacks from her own repressed sexuality, and that her bruises are simply hysterical stigmata. At different times both her son and her lover witness attacks. A group of parapsychologists attempts to trap the entity by spraying it with liquid helium, but it escapes.

The film is interesting in that it bluntly confronts the idea that is suggested by so many horror films but seldom spelt out: that the attack of the Beast is willed by its victims, that the horrible Shape is an external manifestation of internal torments. But having produced the idea, it then proceeds to weigh the scales against the psychiatrist who believes in it, so that the film becomes no more than an intelligently made creature feature about the violation of a lonely but courageous woman. Miss Hershey's performance, however, does contrive to suggest that in some small back room of the mind her defilement may be welcome and, to this degree, the film is disturbing. As to the claims made by this and other films for documentary truth, believe them if you will, but such claims are so much a tradition of yellow journalism that they should be treated with caution and, in any case, the film is in no sense deepened by its supposed truth. On the contrary, a rather sordid element of exploitation is added to a story that is already morally dubious in its treatment of repeated rape as a theme designed to entertain.

Return of the repressed monster

Deadly Blessing (1981) is the first "respectable" film made by *enfant terrible* Wes Craven, director of the brutal *Last House on the Left*, which is not at all funny, and the slightly less brutal *The Hills Have Eyes*, which is. The theme of *Deadly Blessing* is religious and sexual repression breeding monsters. A group of puritanically fundamentalist farmers, the Hittites, do not welcome the marriage of one of their own to a sexy outsider (Maren Jensen). Carefully staged shock murders take place, beginning with the husband, and including one of the wife's scantily clad (and most unHittite) friends. We believe, of course, that the Hittites are responsible, but this is a red herring: it is the local young woman artist, painter of weirdly distorted canvases and (it turns out) a hermaphrodite, who is the killer. The Hittites' feeling that an "incubus" was at work seems to have been merely the result

of the kind of religious fanaticism that will always symbolize evil as an actual monster, something external to humanity. But a very badly executed twist ending has a perfectly real incubus rising up through the floorboards and snatching the wife away, thus rather pointlessly endorsing the Hittite world view after all. It is not clear what all this is supposed to mean, and it became even less clear when many versions of the release print were trimmed by the distributors to excise the incubus scene (thus cutting out the fantasy element altogether).

The irony of the peaceful, lovely, rural scenery concealing all these Gothic goings-on is quite well done, and the set-pieces – especially the tarantula falling into a girl's open mouth during a dream sequence – are efficient. But the film's fundamental timidity (Craven was perhaps trying to prove that he was a good boy now) is nicely symbolized by the scene of the phallic snake crawling unseen between the parted thighs of the wife in the bath. This routinely nasty exploitation stuff is wholly defused by the fact that through the murky bath water we can see (unintentionally) that the demure Miss Jensen is wearing knickers.

Ghost Story (1981) is another film about a cohesive social group (not religious zealots this time, but four upper-class old men in a small New England town) repressing forces, such as sexuality, that might disturb the social order, only to have these forces erupt with obscene violence into their lives. Half a century ago these four accidentally killed a sophisticated young woman who had been behaving in a way that both aroused and humiliated their shyly burgeoning manhood. The body, in the back of a car, was pushed into a lake. It seemed that they saw her look back at them, still alive, as the car sank. Disturbed by guilt, they nevertheless live out mostly peaceful and conventional lives until they are old; the disturbance comes out in the form of the creepy ghost stories they tell one another at their regular meetings.

Now, a lifetime later, a lithe, lovely young woman has almost driven the son of one of these men mad, and caused a second son to fling himself from a window. Soon the same woman, whom we now recognize to be a vengeful spirit, comes to the town and starts to destroy the old men. We, the audience, are allowed to share the vision that drives all these people mad, and it is disappointingly conventional – she merely appears as a rotting corpse. It is an unpleasant, even scary image (as so often in these films, the make-up wizardry of Dick Smith was responsible), but it has no particular dramatic resonance.

In fact, the failure of the film is mystifying, for it is based on a subtle, ironic book written by Peter Straub – one of the most unusual horror novels of the century. This should have provided a good basis for director John

Irvin to work with, especially as he had previously shown, with his excellent television adaptation of John Le Carré's *Tinker, Tailor, Soldier, Spy*, that he knew a thing or two about showing ageing men confronted by resurrected secrets from the past. And he could hardly have had four more professional old actors to work with than Fred Astaire, Melvyn Douglas, Douglas Fairbanks Jr and John Houseman.

It was probably a mistake to eliminate the main point of the original novel, which was that the vindictive woman, a compound of elegant sophistication, raw sexuality and decay, was in fact a nature spirit, a shape-changing fiend – something altogether more primal and terrifying than the standard ghost who appears in the film. In jettisoning the more bizarre fantastic aspects of the story, Irvin somehow eliminated its psychological strength as well. The conservative, proudly traditional way of life of the four old men should have been seen as a house of cards, appallingly vulnerable to the monstrous affront and the *vigour* of the supernatural invasion. The pretty old picture-postcard town should have represented a quite inadequate bulwark against the ancient things that roam America's primeval woodlands.

Ghost Story is one of the saddest episodes of missed opportunities in the history of fantastic film. The powerful themes of the original are shrunk to a conventional soap opera about guilty secrets. Sad, too, is the fact that Alice Krige, who plays the woman, was not really given the opportunity to do much, although even as it stands her performance is by a long way the best thing in the film. Very little is done, even with the material that lies so close to hand: the ghost's ability to switch in a moment from warm young flesh to rotting death should have a special meaning for four men whose own bodies bear upon them the marks of inevitable dissolution.

Predestination

John Irvin made little of much. Nicolas Roeg's peculiar talent is to make a great deal out of very little. Typically, Roeg's films are based on the slightest of source material. *Don't Look Now* (1973) is based on a short story by Daphne Du Maurier. The comparatively simple incidents of the story are transmuted by Roeg into a hauntingly complex work, a web of uncanny displacements in time and space that suggests a geometry of meaningful connections hidden behind the mundane geography of our lives.

Donald Sutherland plays the art historian, a restorer of churches, who at the film's opening is studying colour slides of a church interior in Venice. As a strange red blot oozes across the slide he unexpectedly rises to his feet with a howl of anguish, and rushes outside to where his little daughter, dressed in red, lies drowned in a small lake. He and his wife (Julie Christie) go to Venice in the hope that he may lose himself in work. They meet two very eccentric middle-class English ladies who claim psychic powers and are told that the dead daughter is sending them a message; the wife half believes them. Everywhere the husband travels in Venice he sees flashes of red in the corner of his eye, the identical red to his daughter's raincoat. Within the same church which we saw on the slide, the husband nearly falls to his death. When the little girl was drowning, her brother rode over a pane of glass on his bicycle, and it shattered. In Venice, too, glass shatters more than once. The couple go to bed to make love, but intercut with this they are getting dressed to go out. Time is telescoped. The husband sees his wife standing on the prow of a funeral barge on a Venetian canal when she is supposed to be in England; he does not know that with his intermittent second sight he is witnessing his own subsequent funeral. The two kind old ladies laugh inexplicably when they are alone, after telling the wife they have seen her daughter in a red mackintosh. Are they frauds?

Venice is a gloomy labyrinth, out of season, shrouded. Bodies are pulled out of the canals. Someone is committing Jack the Ripper murders. In a church the wife lights a candle, the husband tries to make the electric light work. In Venice the streets go in wrong directions and you end up where you began. He follows the red raincoat into the church where we began, and the death which has been insistently adumbrated since the opening death of the daughter is, this time, his, for the red raincoat turns around and it is an old, mad, female dwarf with a cleaver. A spreading stain of blood engulfs the screen which is, in a way, a colour transparency itself.

I am suggesting, in this impressionistic account, that Nicolas Roeg has few peers in the art of dazzling editing, so that juxtapositions flare out with meaning. He makes motion pictures as if he were the first director in the world to discover colour film, with a joyful freshness in the exultant way he exploits this private discovery.

Don't Look Now is a very tantalising title. Because "now" may be then? Because "looking" is paradoxically what the film is about? Why should we not look now? The theme of the film is not so much telepathy, or precognition, as it is predestination. I do not believe in predestination, but I confess that never before in the cinema has it been so convincingly evoked, from the very opening scene which has the seeds of every other scene within it. It is not a film about ghosts as such; it is a film that evokes an invisible world where our fate is already known, intimations from which occasionally enter ours. By creating a network of meanings and associations, the film convinces us that in some

Thanks to Dick Smith's make-up, lovely Alice Krige does not appear at her best in this scene from Ghost Story *(Universal, 1981). During most of the film she looks very nice; it must be one of those days.*

alternate, fantastic reality pieces of a predestined jigsaw are being put together. These may be pulp metaphysics, but they are brought to life with the most amazing flair.

Supernatural semiotics

There seems to be a general if undiscussed agreement among film-makers that vampires are more refined and cultured than werewolves, and infinitely more presentable than zombies. This is strange because, like zombies, vampires are undead (which is quite different from being alive), and like werewolves they symbolize the ravenous beast within. Indeed Christopher Lee's Dracula specializes in animal snarls and bestial hisses, and the original Nosferatu, Max Schreck, looked more like a rodent than a human.

Vampires, werewolves and many zombies have one thing in common: they feast upon the bodies of the living. Another thing they have in common is that they are infectious. One bite is often enough to do the job. In other words, we are all extremely vulnerable to the possibility of becoming vampires, werewolves or zombies ourselves. On the one hand these monstrous creatures are ineffably "other", but on the other hand they are us.

But the distinctions are as interesting as the similarities. Perhaps vampires are regarded as more aristocratic (many of them are members of the nobility) because they feast not upon flesh but upon blood. Blood is the most spiritual of bodily essences, and the drinking of it is quite a rarefied thing to do – almost a religious ceremony at times, a perverse communion. Perhaps that is why vampires are seen as more gentlemanly than their rougher, flesh-eating cousins. Blood is an image of sexuality, for it is the colour of lips, and of strawberries, of life itself. Vampires, therefore, are sexy.

Werewolves are much less sexy, and they tend to be middle-class rather than upper-class. Many of them in everyday life are professional people, doctors, university students and so on. Zombies, as I have suggested in previous discussions, are working class. They shamble; they are poorly dressed and inarticulate; they suffer from skin diseases. They are the least sexy of all, because they represent death.

Thus the sociology of horror movies is the sociology of our everyday lives. It is surely significant, then, that the past few decades have witnessed an inexorable move away from vampire films. The public is investing heavily in werewolves and zombies. A temporary boom on Wall Street did coincide with the release of an upper-class vampire movie, *The Hunger* (1983), and I am sure there was a connection, but by and large increasing unemployment and economic depression has resulted in more zombies (the baffled jobless) and werewolves (social democrats to a man).

We do not need to linger upon the vampire movies of the 1970s and 1980s. The main development was that the vampire came to town – or indeed the big city. One of the best urban vampire movies was the cheaply produced *Count Yorga, Vampire* (1970), set in modern Los Angeles. The Count is played with cheerful relish by Robert Quarry, who vampirizes a number of young girls, who then show alarming symptoms: one of them eats a cat. Their boyfriends raid the place, and one disposes of the Count with a broom-handle through the heart and saves his girlfriend in what turns out not to have been the nick of time. Her smile of thanks, in the final freeze-frame, is fanged.

At the intellectual end of the market was a German film directed by Werner Herzog, *Nosferatu the Vampyre* (1979), a beautiful, dreamy remake of *Nosferatu*. For surprisingly long stretches of the film, Herzog submerges his own characteristic concerns in a loving recreation of Murnau's imagery, now in colour and sound, with the soft-spoken, death-yearning Klaus Kinski accurately made up to look like Max Schreck. At times this comes close to pastiche, with Kinski, and also Isabelle Adjani as Lucy Harker, giving stylized performances; Roland Topor as Renfield is allowed to over-act quite dreadfully, and other parts are played naturalistically. Adjani is often like a one-woman tableau from Victorian melodrama, as her mouth forms a perfect "O" of a frozen scream, her hands raised in the air, or when she faints like some fading flower.

Herzog's more familiar concerns come to the fore in the scenes set in Wismar (but photographed in Delft). The stifling bourgeois atmosphere of this town is shattered when Dracula's plague ship arrives, releasing literally thousands of diseased rats. As the coffins of the newly dead accumulate in the town square, a macabre, lively *Totentanz*, a Dance of Death, takes place as the surviving townspeople eat their Last Supper. The cohesion of society is fragmented at a stroke. Adjani floats somnambulistically through all this as she approaches her own melancholy sacrifice. Herzog provides a new ending to the film, also, with the now infected Jonathan Harker riding off maniacally through twirling sand devils and clouds to carry doom to the rest of the world. Thus vampire film becomes political apocalypse.

Less interestingly, the same Schreck make-up (the two front teeth pointed, rodent-style, rather than the incisors) appeared in a quite different vampire story, the made-for-TV *Salem's Lot* (1979), based on a best-selling novel by Stephen King. Horror fans were eager to see this, for it was directed by Tobe Hooper, of *Texas Chainsaw Massacre* fame. Alas, the deadening propriety of television took its toll, and there is not much that is disturbing, though one or two television taboos are mildly contravened: children are placed in jeopardy (there is an excellently creepy vampire, until very recently a small boy, who floats with a nasty smile outside his brother's window), and in an entirely non-fantastic scene a cuckolded man takes a humiliating revenge on his wife's lover. This last is the most typically Hooper sequence. It has all the sordid sweatiness of real human fear, and it makes the vampire sequences look a bit hollow in comparison. David Soul is a very colourless hero, in a predictably wet bit of television casting. The film never quite captures the all-embracing quality of the novel, in which a whole town is convincingly destroyed.

The Hunger (1983) was made by Tony Scott, brother of Ridley. His technique as a director of television commercials is all too evident in this attempt to sell vampirism through chic imagery, as if it were soap, and blood is just another colour to highlight a pastel decor. Catherine Deneuve is the beauti-

ful, ageless woman vampire whose lovers share her immortality for centuries before suddenly growing old. She lives in Manhattan, picks up victims at trendy discos, and shares her life with David Bowie who, in the best sequence (make-up by Carl Fullerton) changes from youthful beauty to extreme old age in a single afternoon. Backlit dust motes floating in dark rooms, gauzy curtains fluttering, blood elegantly spurting in buckets full. It is all rather nasty, and generates no internal logic. The promising attempt to combine supernatural with scientific themes fizzles out (research into ageing seems to dovetail with the vampire's immortality). A Lesbian seduction scene seems stolen from *Daughters of Darkness* (see filmography). Corpses randomly come to life. Confusingly edited sequences seem to suggest a transfer of personality between Deneuve and her woman victim, played by Susan Sarandon. The links between vampire decadence and the decadence of New York's swingers are left notional. It is a slick film, not entirely hollow, but its ambitions though discernible remain

This rare still shows the dwarf killer, played by Adelina Poerio, in the final scene of Don't Look Now *(British Lion, 1973). This is the only time we see her face; previously the red duffel coat has made her seem to be the ghost of Donald Sutherland's daughter.*

David Bowie's ageing process was assisted by Carl Fullerton's make-up in The Hunger *(MGM-UA, 1983)*. His beautiful vampire lover, Catherine Deneuve, we are asked to believe, is thousands of years older still.

unrealized. There is a vulgar crudity behind it all that is very apparent in a shock transition from vampiric blood to a rare steak being severed with a knife.

The beast within

Most recent vampires have been so lethargically world-weary, as if they knew that the late twentieth century was not really their milieu, that it is a relief to turn to beast-people, who seem more at home in the modern world.

Joe Dante, who had already made a very promising debut with *Piranha* (see below), was responsible for an excellent little werewolf film called *The Howling* (1980), whose witty script is packed with reference to earlier werewolf films. Dr Waggner (Patrick Macnee) has a therapy centre in rural California, where traumatized newscaster Karen White (Dee Wallace), who was about to be weirdly murdered but suffered amnesia and cannot remember what was weird about the murderer, has gone for a rest cure. What she gradually learns, in a splendidly swelling avalanche of incident, is that all the other guests at the colony, including Dr Waggner, are werewolves. The make-up effects include an astonishing real-time transformation of man into wolf (using no camera tricks, only hydraulics, bladders, prosthetics) that lasts for minutes. These were devised by a brilliant crew that included Rob Bottin, who later did the incredible transformations for John Carpenter's *The Thing*. The special effects are capped only by the remorseless series of wolf references (cartoons of *Little Red Riding Hood*, references to disc-jockey Wolfman Jack, and even a copy of Allen Ginsberg's

poem *Howl*), and by the fearful one-liners. The most nauseating of these is werewolf Eddie saying "I'm going to give you a piece of my mind" to Karen before reaching a claw into a bullet hole in his distorted head, and handing her a lump of brain tissue. Ugh.

It is a good, breezy film, with a great punch-line at the end (a *very* unusual television interview), and a total consciousness of what its subtext (about violent instincts) is all about. I said before that werewolves were not generally sexy, but an exception must be made for the Barbara Steele look-alike Elisabeth Brooks, who plays the woman (or bitch) werewolf that seduces Karen's husband. Dog-fashion, of course.

Also thoroughly amusing, and in many ways comparable, was John Landis's *An American Werewolf in London* (1981), which confidently walks the tightrope between spoof and genuine horror throughout. In effect, the film is a reprise of the theme of Henry James's novels: American innocence collides with European decadence. Two college kids from the USA meet a werewolf on the Yorkshire moors. One is killed (though he keeps on returning as a mutilated spectre, more decayed every time, who not surprisingly complains volubly about his lot). The other, David (David Naughton), is bitten. The transformation scenes, designed by Rick Baker, take the state of the art one step further even than *The Howling*. They are both incredible and convincing. In modern horror films these metamorphoses – all popping joints, lengthening bones and writhing muscles – become the *subject* of the film. The central figure is no longer the human, nor the animal he becomes, but the agonized half-and-half thing who belongs to neither world, like a victim of God's wrath in the Hell of Hieronymus Bosch.

Jenny Agutter plays completely straight and very touchingly the nurse who loves David. He has terrible trouble convincing anyone that he has become a *bona fide* werewolf, and causes a good deal of carnage before the message gets through. London locations, seen with a satirical American eye, are used casually but well. This is very much a fable for today, right down to the songs: "Blue Moon", "Bad Moon Rising", "Moondance". Beast imagery appears in more than one context. Jack, the calmly talking friend, sophomoric even in death, is the death-in-life beast; then there are the Nazi beasts of a horrifying dream sequence, with the faces of monsters and the uniforms of soldiers, who gun down a nice family watching the Muppets on television in a suburban living room. There are even the real beasts, the puzzled wolves in the zoo, who find our hero stark naked in their cage one morning. Landis had obviously learned a thing or two about making films since *National Lampoon's Animal House*, his earlier filmic essay about the Beast in Man.

Paul Schrader's ambitious remake, *Cat People* (1982), looks rather arty alongside the two confident comedies just discussed. It is a film without any sense of humour at all. Everything is supercharged with a lithe but languid sexuality in this steamy romance, set, second time around, in New Orleans. The original *Cat People* (see Chapter One) had been content to hint at what could be shown full frontally by 1982. Schrader, whose films specialize in Calvinist themes, has here not one but two repressed puritans meeting their destinies: Nastassia Kinski, luminously feline as the virgin who will become a giant cat should she ever sleep with anyone but her equally feral brother (Malcolm McDowell) who incestuously desires her, and zookeeper Oliver (John Heard), a misogynist who prefers animals to people. Everything, then, is set up for the amazingly perverse finale where, with a bit of bestiality thrown in and Nastassia roped to the bed, the two both get what they want. Only a stern protestant like Schrader is capable of perversity quite as feverish as this. It is the godhaunted who are most possessed by devils.

Horror fans mostly hated the film, and certainly it is rather a torrid muddle, with its ochre-tinted prologue evoking strange fertility rites in Africa, its solitary descent into visceral horror (McDowell as panther in cage tears a man's arm off), its rite-of-passage dream scene (back in the red African dust again), and its symbolic last shot (the zookeeper reaches out to his lover, now a panther in a cage, and she growls enigmatically). But it has a febrile intensity that is sometimes interesting. Despite a more con-

ventional love story thrown in (another woman loves Oliver, apparently quite healthily) the subtext seems to be in part: sex is what animals do, and if you do it, then you're an animal. The second subtext is that it might be better to be an animal, for animals do not have guilt and *angst*.

The pathos of the human monster

Death Line (1972), released in America as *Raw Meat*, and directed by the little-known Gary Sherman (see also *Dead and Buried* in filmography), was generally dismissed as just another low-budget exploitation movie. Since then, however, it has developed a small cult reputation. In the late nineteenth century, construction workers building an underground extension to London's Tube system were buried in a cave-in. Late-night travellers are being murdered (in the present) in London's Russell Square Tube station, near the British Museum. Survivors of the buried workers, we discover, are living the life of troglodyte cannibals. All of this would have been quite conventionally silly were it not for the sequences that show the last survivor (the others have died from a leprous disease which has also affected him) mourning over his dead family. It is an abrupt change of perspective, with real pathos, that makes us feel like Cro Magnon man suddenly realizing that the Neanderthals may not have been so bad after all.

A much more considerable movie, *The Elephant Man* (1980), questions the whole concept of monstrousness versus normality much more deeply. It was a theme that the director, David Lynch, had already explored in the underground classic *Eraserhead* (see below), but this was his first opportunity to express himself in the world of commercial cinema.

Elephant Man, like *The Entity*, but far more responsibly, purports to be based on a true story. John Hurt plays the hideously deformed freak in the 1880s, who is exploited in circus sideshows. He is then rescued by a surgeon, who gives him a private room in the London Hospital, but who ironically exploits him very much as before, by displaying him to astounded colleagues, and then to visiting socialites. The film carefully and tactfully delays its revelation of the nature of John Merrick's deformity for some time; when we see it (a convincing and, in a curious way, low-key make-up design by Christopher Tucker) it is all too clear why he is called the Elephant Man.

The true revelation, of course, is that of the man inside the monster. We are staggered, in a tenderly wrought scene, when we learn that he can even speak. Hurt's carefully judged performance hovers on the edge of sentimentality, but stays just on this side, as we become ever more aware of his real sensitivity. There is melodrama and pessimism

Right: Don McLeod plays T. C. Quist, one of a large family of werewolves in Joe Dante's The Howling *(Avco Embassy, 1980).*

Below: the emotional centre of An American Werewolf in London *(Lycanthrope/ Polygram, 1981) is the prolonged, agonizing metamorphosis of David Naughton into a werewolf – an astonishingly realistic sequence, here caught at mid-point, designed by Rick Baker, who won an Oscar for it.*

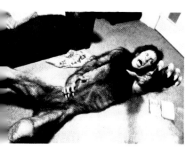

of course; he is kidnapped at one point, and his abnormality causes panic and derision among most of the people who see him. The film is very good in its understanding of unthinking cruelty, and of the almost primal reflex that causes us to shy away from abnormality like this. ("There but for the grace of God go I"); we simply do not know how to cope with it.

The cruelty of society is mirrored in the cruelty that society itself suffers. In wonderfully evocative black-and-white photography, the grimy cityscapes of the late industrial age, all steam and coal smoke and heavy machinery, constitute one of the inhumanities of the story. How can decency thrive in this world? The subtext is generally taken to be the reverse of the usual: that is, inside the monster, humanity is latent and can be coaxed up into the light. But more traditionally and pessimistically, it also says that inside all of us normals there is an Elephant Man struggling to get out.

Tiny budget creativity

I have already suggested, discussing George Romero and Larry Cohen in Chapter Three, that many of the advances in fantastic cinema come from the lowly independents, who are less constrained by stereotyped conventions, and by questions of good taste (because their films can make a profit without reaching the family market). They can be very nearly as subversive and iconoclastic as they want.

The tradition of surrealism has stayed very much alive at the low-budget end of the market also. Indeed, the short cuts necessary in cheap filming encourage the startling juxtapositions of surrealism. Film stock is not cheap, and the smooth continuities of commercial cinema require high shooting ratios

to achieve. Then again, low budget films are often the work of *auteurs*, people who can do much as they like without a committee of financiers looking gloomily over their shoulders. Such film-makers are often young, hungry and ambitious, and their films may reflect the slightly desperate vigour such a state induces.

The most extraordinary of these cheap, surrealist fantasias was David Lynch's *Eraserhead* (1976). It tells the story of Henry, played with a wild-haired, staring-eyed, autistic quality by John Nance. He is inadequate, polite, withdrawn, almost wholly incapable of ordinary social contacts. He lives in a squalid bed-sitting room, and has a marginal relationship with a skinny, hysterical girl whose family, human rejects living in an urban wasteland, alternate between total passivity and a violent mania that borders on epilepsy. He is told he has fathered a child on this waif (Mother: "She's having a baby." Daughter, distraught, "Mother, they're not *sure* it's a baby!"), and she moves in with him. The baby is a mutant, mewling horror – quite unnervingly convincing – that looks like a skinned rabbit. It is tightly wrapped, like a mummy, in swaddling clothes. The girl cannot tolerate the baby and leaves. Industrial noises permeate the room. The central images are of slime and ooze and small, wriggling things. Henry drifts through this nightmare trying to care for the child. From behind a radiator a pallid chubby-cheeked vaudeville girl emerges to dance, squashing foetus-like worms as she does so. Henry sleeps with the nymphomaniac across the hall, and the bed turns into a swamp. The baby comes out in horrible spots. Henry nurses it. Then, ultimately maddened, he begins to cut open its swaddling clothes with

John Heard in bed with Nastassia Kinski in Cat People *(RKO-Universal, 1982). Kinski is the one who looks like a panther.*

scissors. The bandages turn out to be part of its body, which bursts open revealing a mess of entrails that begin to foam and fill the room. A miniature apocalypse ensues, and a quiet man by a window (his face in the dim light looks horribly burned) again pulls the lever that he pulled at the beginning, and everything explodes. This man may be God.

The film is nauseating and compulsive. The industrial and human desolation that it evokes, and the disgust it shows for the body, for sex and procreation, is not for the squeamish. Yet all this is shown with a kind of objective pity, even a warped beauty. We cannot assume that the disgust shown in the film reflects any hatred of the body on Lynch's part. One of the many points of this strange film may be political: that bodily disgust is in part born from human deprivation. The pessimism is not total. Henry is not a person without decency.

Don Coscarelli's *Phantasm* (1978) is interesting, too – a better film than his more commercial *Beastmaster* (see Chapter Seven). *Phantasm* is about the dreadful experiences of a teenage boy at the local mortuary, where the Tall Man lives. In the grounds, the Lady in Lavender murders a man who had thought he was going to make love to her. Mike (Michael Baldwin) visits the mortuary at night and is chased by a caretaker who is then killed by a silver sphere that whizzes through the air, clamps to his forehead, and inserts a spike into his brain. Mike chops off the Tall Man's finger, and takes it home. It comes to life and becomes a fearful, buzzing insect-monster. Back in the mortuary, horrible dwarfs ooze yellow blood. The Tall Man is an alien making homunculi from dead bodies. Mike passes through a space gate to another planet where dwarfs are shuffling

across a desert. A second person is killed by the Lavender Lady who is really the Tall Man. Mike wakes up and finds it was all a dream, brought about by his brother's recent death in a car smash. But in the next room the Tall Man is waiting in the mirror...

Cheerfully episodic, wholly surrealist, largely incoherent, it was ignored or loathed by most critics. But I think the point is that life is *not* logical, that we impose meaning on the world only to keep from mental collapse; underneath, bizarre and arbitrary things are happening. Around the next corner the Tall Man may be waiting for any of us. What is so pleasing is that Mike accepts this lunacy, and actually manages to survive it, for a while. He is no helpless pawn of fate.

Basket Case (1981) is a much more coherent film, and on the surface a more conventional one. It, too, is largely cheerful, despite the total seediness of its fleabag-hotel setting. The affable hero carries with him a wicker basket, inside which his monstrous Siamese-twin brother (surgically removed and thrown into a garbage bag as dead, many years before) is living. Occasionally the hero feeds his brother Belial with hot dogs. Horrible chomping sounds come out of the basket. We flash back to the monster sitting on his aunt's knee while she reads him a passage from Shakespeare about Caliban. Belial, all head, teeth and arms, has a likeable personality. With huge gusto he revenges himself, with lots of comic-book gore, on the doctors who parted him from his brother. But at the end sexual jealousy raises its head, Belial rapes his brother's girlfriend (an experience telepathically shared by his appalled brother), and he and his brother fight and fall to their deaths through the window.

bodies, instant rot, insane laughter (the women develop a much stronger sense of humour once they become ghouls), shock cuts, hands reaching through walls, things in ·the cellar, blood dripping from the plumbing. It is a maniacally confident homage to, and parody of, the entire genre of the splatter movie that has the audience laughing and scared out of its socks simultaneously. Middle America's dark suspicion of what college kids are really like is triumphantly confirmed: the younger generation *are* monsters.

This is all achieved with considerable wit that makes up-market shockers like *The Omen* look positively cosy by comparison. It is notable that low-budget horror films seldom offer consolation. In each of the last four films discussed there is an apocalyptic ending; evil spreads; American society is being ripped asunder by forces it will not recognize but can no longer contain. This, at bottom, is what all these films are about.

Nasties

Videotapes of *The Evil Dead* have been seized and destroyed by the police in the UK, and something resembling public hysteria was whipped up, condemning so-called "video nasties", especially on the grounds that irresponsible parents may make them available to their children. (In fact, *The Evil Dead* can legally be shown in British cinemas – it has passed the censor – and was premiered in this country at the London Film Festival.) Legislation in the UK in 1984 proscribes graphically horrible films from being sold or rented in videotape format even if they have been approved for theatrical release.

Almost nobody has spoken out in public to point out that there are fine distinctions to be made in this moral minefield. Films like *I Spit on Your Grave*, with scenes of graphic mutilation and prolonged sexual sadism *in a supposedly realistic, almost documentary context*, might very properly be condemned, and banned. These are films exploiting the dark cowardice of sado-voyeurs. But when the context is avowedly fantastic – when the graphic mutilations appear, so to speak, within the inverted commas provided by the film's deliberately fabulist nature, then surely the question is very different.

In the case of *The Evil Dead*, for example, the action is so highly conventionalised, so fantastically theatrical, that its undisputed violence is closer to that of a Tom and Jerry cartoon than the brutality of *I Spit on Your Grave*. The latter typifies the really obscene form of "nasty" in its emphasis on gloating observation: long scenes of perverse rape, and later of castration, for example. Fantastic cinema seldom places any emphasis on sexual mutilation – no example springs to mind – while the nasties proper place enormous emphasis on this kind of brutality specifically,

A scarred man sits by a window and pulls on a mysterious crank-handle at the beginning and end of Eraserhead *(David Lynch, 1976). In the credits he is called the* Man in the Planet *(the actor is Jack Fisk). He may be God.*

The theme of the monstrous family (which is only the normal family seen in a distorting mirror) occurs again and again in low-budget horror films, especially in the USA, where the myth of the family as the central repository of human values is so very strong. Horror films sometimes present the reverse case: the family as claustrophobic and repressive, a breeding ground for violence and isolation. The family, in this style of subtext, stands for alienation.

A further example of insane creativity on a miniscule budget caused a furore with its deliberate shock tactics: *The Evil Dead* (1982). Made semi-professionally by a recent college graduate, Sam Raimi, it also reversed conventional values with its story of clean-cut college kids holidaying in a remote rural shanty, and becoming possessed by demons. No taboo is left unturned; there is something to offend everyone. A woman is raped by a tree (sexist exploitation); dismemberment becomes a moral imperative, because the ghouls can only be destroyed if cut up (sadism); strong men become whimpering cowards (realism); the sole survivor is demoniacally attacked from behind in the closing seconds (not playing fair); we see this from a demon's-eye viewpoint (illegitimate audience identification).

The film is a fantasia of metamorphosing

and on women as sexual victims and/or revengers generally. The "rape by a tree" scene in *Evil Dead* is a very brief, notably absurd sequence in admittedly bad taste; the rape scenes in nasties proper tend to be disgracefully prolonged. In practice, the graphic violence of fantastic cinema is not notably sexist, and even when it is sexist, it is very seldom sexual (no theoretical explanation immediately offers itself for this).

In Chapter Four David Cronenberg (author of a number of graphically horrible films himself) was quoted as saying that the horror of the body, the horror of decay, is a legitimate and important theme that fantastic cinema is peculiarly well suited to contemplate. Art must be able to incorporate ugliness or violence in some manner, and the wholly theatrical, rigid conventions of Grand-Guignol visceral horror surely provide an acceptably "distanced" way of registering the body's vulnerability. After all, our viscera are separated from the outside world by the thinnest of partitions, and it may not hurt us to be reminded occasionally of what lies beneath the skin.

Fantastic "nasties" deal with the violation of bodies, of minds, of normality. But in only a few of these films are the audience implicitly invited to join with the oppressor, the violator. The novelist Gene Wolfe said to me, in an interview, "I think that all of us have a desire to experience the worst so that we can tell ourselves that we can survive the worst. That is part of the appeal of horror." The audiences at graphic horror films may be quite innocent of sadism. They are voluntarily undertaking a rite of passage, which is just as likely to be cleansing and cathartic as it is to be corrupting. The entertainment to be derived from these films need not be sick; the source of the entertainment is our knowledge that the events we are witnessing *are* a fiction, just as riding a roller coaster is not the same as actually plunging over a cliff. Our relief at this, along with the knowledge that we can go home afterwards and have a cup of tea, constitutes a major part of our response. But for this reason, the nasties in fantastic cinema – very obviously fictions – should not be categorized in the same pigeon hole as the nasties presented in the realist mode.

Are Italians sadists?

In recent years Grand Guignol has become a speciality of the Italians, especially the directors Dario Argento and Lucio Fulci. Argento is the superior craftsman. His *Suspiria* (1976) is a stylish exercise. Jessica Harper plays the American girl attending a ballet school in a German provincial town. The proprietors of the school are a coven of witches hell-bent, it seems, on murdering and mutilating their students. The film opens with the heroine, Suzy, leaving a German airport through sliding

glass doors. As she goes through, into the wintry night outside, her scarf blows back up around her face as if directed by some invisible strangler, but it is only the wind. Set-piece follows set-piece. Girls are picturesquely murdered in art deco settings; one of them has her head bisected by a pane of coloured glass. Maggots rain from the ceiling. The vast halls of the Academy glow with coloured light. We hear a stone bird flapping around the town square; then the blind man whom it seems to be attacking has his throat torn out by his own guide dog. A student falls into a room surrealistically billowing with great coils of baling wire. The dead body of a girl with pins in her eyes is animated by an invisible witch. Art-nouveau irises on a wall hold the secret to hidden passages. Pounding rock music assaults the ears, but in the few silences whispers can be heard. The Academy is run by Helena Marcos, who is hundreds of years old and looks it. She is the Mother of Whispers. She is stabbed with a glass dagger (a quote from Argento's previous *Bird with Crystal Plumage*) plucked from the tail of an ornamental peacock. The labyrinthine building majestically collapses as Suzy escapes. We have been in the country of slow-motion, Gothic nightmare, lost without a map.

The flamboyance of *Suspiria* was sustained

It is typical of exploitation movies to use posed advertising material that does not appear in the film. This publicity shot for The Evil Dead *(Renaissance, 1982) is more tranquil than most of the events that do take place in the film.*

in the sequel, *Inferno* (1980), which is largely set in a New York apartment house, ancient residence of the second of the three mothers, the Mother of Darkness. Here, however, the bravura is faltering, the killings more random. We cannot, this time around, identify with any one character, because one by one they are demolished not long after they have been introduced. There is a straining for effect in the killings (people attacked by cats, eaten by rats, strangled by the wires of an electronic voice-box) that comes close to being ludicrous. Mario Bava did the special effects, and was responsible for the most haunting scene, where a girl wandering through a dank cellar comes across a well in the floor. Insanely entering it to retrieve a dropped brooch, she finds herself swimming in an underground room, sumptuously furnished. Through the rippling blue water we see paintings, carpets, grand settees. It is a moment of authentic magic in a film that takes magic as its subject. Argento is not interested in linear narrative. For him, magic is arbitrary and inexplicable. The result is a fragmentation so extreme as to defy analysis of what it all might mean.

A director with guts

Lucio Fulci makes the sort of movie that nice people do not go to see. Perhaps mercifully, most people do not even know about them. He is the sick innocent of Italian "giallo"; his childlike wish is to show successive horrors each one of which is worse than you could ever have imagined. He is the master of what Stephen King, wearing his critic's hat in *Danse Macabre* (though he does not mention Fulci), calls "the gross-out". The crude delight Fulci so transparently takes in his special effects probably has a very long history; I should imagine the theatre of the Dark Ages was not above using animal entrails as usefully revolting props.

Fulci's *Zombie Flesh-Eaters* (1979) features members of the living dead with table-manners so revolting as to make Romero's look like gentlemen by contrast. In a neat turn on *Jaws*, one of them even makes a meal of a shark. Viewers of the uncensored version can witness the gouging out of an eye in loving close-up. The soil of the tropical island where all this happens has heads and arms bursting upwards as thick as weeds at passers-by.

City of the Living Dead (1980) carries physical horror into the realms of frank disbelief. A girl is buried alive and her careless rescuer swings a pick through the coffin within millimetres of her face in a series of thunderous blows. A dead priest glares, red-eyed, at a young woman who obligingly vomits up all of her intestines at him. The local idiot boy is fascinated – not to say transfixed – by a power drill. Zombie hands reach out from the sides of the frame to pluck off

the backs of people's heads (it happens more than once) and paddle about in the brains beneath.

The Beyond (1981) is quite ambitious. A New Orleans hotel is built over one of the gates of Hell; by some Lovecraftian geometry it is linked up by a short flight of stairs to the mortuary of the hospital some miles away, where killer zombies abound. A strange blind woman lives in a fine house that in daylight is decayed and empty; later, she is mutilated by her own guide dog. Supernatural spiders live in the library. The survivors at the end walk through the cellar into the desert of Hell itself which reflects the oil painting we saw at the beginning (the sheer nerve of this sequence is admirable).

There are signs, in fact, that in his repulsive way Fulci is becoming a force to be reckoned with. *The House by the Cemetery* (1981), where the sinister Dr Freudstein plays with corpses in the cellar – indeed, he is one himself – is at moments both witty and inventive. The unfortunates who live in this house all contrive to finish up in the cellar (one of them taking an alarming short cut through the floor), and there is also an especially vicious vampire bat to be coped with. The treatment of children in the film is surprisingly tender, especially the scenes of the little boy making friends with a blank little girl (long dead), who lives in the timeless limbo to which he escapes from the cellar at the end. The film's epigraph is taken from Henry James.

I am tempted to defend Fulci's bottom-of-the-barrel sado-exploitation films for their macabre jollity, all *papier mâché* and sheep's guts, and the director's ill-advised but admirable insistence on breaking every rule of coherent narrative in order to create the illogicality of nightmare. But upon mature consideration, I will not.

It is not only the Italians who like this sort of stuff. There is a strong case for arguing that the first of the "nasties" proper were two 3-D films made (in Italy) by American *enfant terrible* Andy Warhol, who, feeling too languid to direct them himself, handed the job over to Paul Morrissey – both writing and direction. These were *Blood for Dracula* (1973, see filmography) and *Flesh for Frankenstein* (1973), now usually known as *Andy Warhol's Frankenstein*. This bloodthirsty parody features ponderously improvised, smart-ass dialogue; pornography, as the stud villager Joe Dallesandro sodomitically carries on the class struggle with Baron Frankenstein's wife (also his sister) in bed; internal organs strung everywhere in the Baron's laboratory; a handsome monster with the head of the local virgin boy who wanted to be a monk; and vast quantities of gore. As the necrophile Baron inserts part of his person into the abdominal slit he has carved into one of his latest victims (she is to be the

Above: Irene Miracle goes swimming in the cellar of a mysterious house in Inferno *(Intersound/20th Century-Fox, 1980). Right: apologies to the squeamish! This is what so-called "video nasties" tend to look like. The cellar this time is in Lucio Fulci's* The House by the Cemetery *(Fulvia Film, 1981). The little boy (unidentified in the credits) escapes, into Limbo.*

monster's wife), he says to his assistant (summing up the intellectual level of the film) "To know death, Otto, you have to fuck life in the gall bladder". This is my candidate for the worst line in any horror film to date.

This decadent joke against the decadents did extremely well at the box-office (people enjoyed the three-dimensional intestines dangling in their faces) and had something to do with rendering splatter movies acceptable to fashionable persons.

The film everyone hates

I do not want to protract the discussion of graphic horror to the point of tedium, but there is one further example that has a certain sordid interest as the film that everyone hated, *Possession* (1981). It was made in Berlin by Andrzej Zulawski, a Polish exile living in Paris. The intellectual critics hated it, the sleaze critics hated it, the UK police force hated it (and placed it on the list of proscribed videos), and the public stayed away

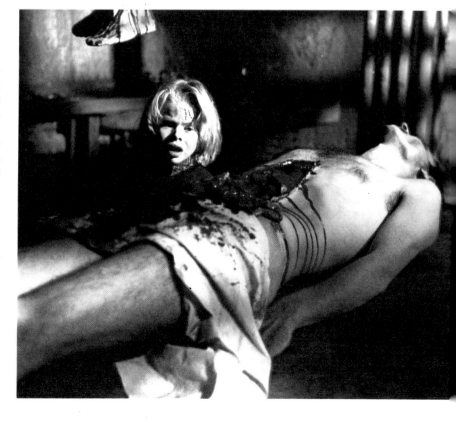

in droves. Isabelle Adjani stars as the house-wife who goes mad; from rage and sexual desire she breeds a tentacled, slimy monster with whom she lives in an apartment. Becoming pregnant by her own creation, she miscarries in a subway station amid loud screams, pus and ooze. At the end she is apparently more successful, and produces a creature that is an idealized version of her husband. It (or he) commits suicide.

It sounds dreadful, but after twenty or so minutes of my fidgeting uncomfortably about the pretentiousness of it all, the mad gallantry of Zulawski's ambition began to take effect. This is a film about mental disintegration, so what could be more appropriate than encouraging one's actors to go so far over the top they soar out of sight? The intensity with which abnormality is shown is theatrical, but it *is* intense. Nobody is normal, certainly not the husband (childishly jealous with a kind of petulant *machismo*), nor the homosexual private detectives he hires (they are killed), nor the bullying, psycho-babbling ex-lover (who is also killed). Only the young son is normal, and he gets so dejected about everyone else that he drowns himself in the bath. The film is overloaded with symbolism. The Berlin Wall is just outside the apartment. The local schoolteacher is Adjani's clone. The husband is a spy-assassin for mysterious politicos. When a door is opened at the very end, it is apparent that World War Three has begun.

Such spirited lunacy! The subtext, after all, is quite well achieved (sexual anguish and alienation breed monsters). It is a grotesquely overdone art-house movie, made by an intellectual, and not a sado-exploitation picture at all. It has something to say, and I would not be surprised if it lingered on to become a cult movie. The monster, incidentally, was the work of Carlo Rambaldi, who worked on *Alien*, *E.T.* and *The White Buffalo*. This must be the first of his monsters to be shown (in an enjoyably absurd scene) as being good in bed.

Parody horror
Possession is occasionally unintentionally funny. Some films, like *Flesh for Frankenstein*, intend to be funny but do not quite make it. Horror spoof is difficult to carry off well, though it is surprisingly often tried, as in *Bloodbath at the House of Death* (1984), or (discussed in the filmography) *Love at First Bite* (1979), *Dracula* (1979, the John Badham version), the vampire episode of *Immoral Tales* (1974), *Attack of the Killer Tomatoes* (1978), *Galaxina* (1980), *Mamma Dracula* (1980), *Schlock* (1971), *Son of Dracula* (1974) and *Big Meat Eater* (1982). One of the best of the lot, *Strange Invaders*, was discussed in Chapter Five.

Two of the most interesting were based on the Frankenstein myth. Mel Brooks' *Young Frankenstein* (1974) succeeds largely be-cause of the loving affection with which the parody is done. Gene Wilder plays the Frankenstein descendant, in America, who is called back to Europe and finds the family obsession beginning to infect him. Once created, his affable monster is even able to coax a soaring "Ah, sweet mystery of life" from Wilder's frigid fiancée (Madeline Kahn), in a scene that answers a rude question that many people have asked. Kenneth Strickfaden's electricals, as used in the original Frankenstein films, were exhumed with great success for this one. The funniest scene reprises the Monster's meeting with the old, blind hermit who, not being able to see, contrives to burn, scald, humiliate and render miserable the Monster in an extraordinary variety of ways. The film was, very sensibly, made in black and white.

The Rocky Horror Picture Show (1975), after a rocky start, became an enduring cult success in the USA at midnight-movie showings (though not in its home country of the UK), where the audience would dress up, chant the lines in unison, pull visual gags, dance and sing, talk back at the screen, and generally take part in a kind of mass group therapy. The film was based on a small-scale but very successful British stage musical, and many of the original players were used in the film, including your author's first cousin Little Nell as Columbia, the horror-groupie. Much of the film's success can be ascribed to the leering eroticism of Tim Curry as Dr Frank-N-Furter, the Transsexual from Transylvania, in black net stockings, garter belt and lots of sexy eye shadow.

The jokes are mainly to do with the arrival in his decadent mansion of deadly straight, boring Brad and Janet (Barry Bostwick and Susan Sarandon), just in time for Frank-N-Furter to unveil his new creation, a handsome but effeminate looking Creature, named Rocky Horror. The film's co-author, Richard O'Brien, plays Riff Raff, the sinister alien butler. Things progress complicatedly and rather feebly from there (the film is weaker than the stage show), but are laced with enjoyable in-jokes for genre horror and SF fans, especially in the words to some of the songs: "Science Fiction, Double Feature", and the horror-movies song performed in front of a replica of the RKO tower (RKO made many of the horror movies of the 1930s, notably *King Kong*).

The *Rocky Horror* cult is an extraordinary phenomenon. Something about the film's combination of elements from glam-rock and punk, along with the trendy emphasis on bisexuality (Curry makes it with both Brad and Janet, and is furious when Janet makes it with the effeminate Rocky), seems to have helped it along. Curry's strong resemblance to Mick Jagger may have been a factor. In any event, the film at its midnight showings bridges the gap between cinema and theatre in a way that has never happened before, for here the audience becomes the actors, and the auditorium the stage.

Nature's revenge

We have looked at *un*natural and *super*natural images of horror. But even the natural has some surprises to offer, creatures of the great outdoors who suddenly turn against humans. Not all of these creatures are entirely natural, however. The dominant theme of monster movies in the 1970s and 1980s has been the perversion of nature by man's ill treatment. The monsters in monster movies used mostly to be created by nuclear radiation, but these days they usually symbolize ecological outrage.

Few of the films in the period we are now considering were especially strong. It is with only mild regret that I consign *Frogs*, *Squirm*, *Bug*, *Prophecy*, *Willard*, *Kingdom of the Spiders*, *The Swarm* and *Night of the Lepus* to the filmography, even though some of them (especially *Squirm* and *Kingdom of the Spiders*) have undoubtedly effective moments. We can also, for the moment, forget *Jaws 2* and *Jaws 3-D*, though *Jaws 2* is in the top twelve box-office successes of fantastic cinema. Restricting ourselves to one-word titles only, let us glance – before saying goodbye to horror – at three examples of nature's revenge: *Piranha*, *Alligator* and *Wolfen*.

Piranha (1978) is a text-book example of good monster-movie direction. These tough, lethal mutants of the traditional piranha, created in a military experiment, are accidentally released in a Texas waterway. The military deny they have escaped. Downstream, kids are swimming in a summer-camp lake, and further down still, a new water-sports park is being opened. The film is taut, amusing, minatory and well directed by Joe Dante (*The Howling*) in his debut. John Sayles, king of B-movie writers, wrote the screenplay. My favourite line comes when the park proprietor tells his assistant that the piranha do not exist, that they have been dreamed up by hysterics. Assistant: "But sir, they're eating the guests." And so they are.

Little needs to be said about *Alligator* (1980) – a Sayles screenplay again – except to recommend it. The film was directed by Lewis Teague, who went on to make *Cujo*. The ecology theme is stronger here. Apparently people buy cute pet alligators from pet shops (only a few inches long), and then flush them down the toilet when they tire of them. Result in one case: a very large, very angry alligator in the sewers. (It gets big partly through eating the hormone-stuffed corpses of experimental dogs that have been secretly dumped.) Lots of shrewd social observation, an astonishingly fresh script, a fairly convincing alligator (he comes bursting up through the sidewalk in one good sequence, breaks up a top people's garden party in another, and lurks in the family swimming pool in a third) make the film a delight.

Wolfen (1981) is a more ambitious film than either of these. A new building project threatens the lair of the Wolfen, intelligent, telepathic wolves who prey on society's outcasts. They may be of supernatural origin, descendants of Red Indian shapeshifters, but they are not werewolves now. Most of the film's action takes place in the derelict South Bronx of New York, near to where a number of Red Indians (now construction workers) are living. Both wolves and Indians live on the fringes of urban society without belonging to it. Ecological messages abound. The director, Michael Wadleigh, after all, has impeccably hip liberal credentials; he was the man who made the film *Woodstock*. Not much peace and love here, though, in a grim story whose sociological significance is a little ponderously spelt out. Albert Finney is the tired, shabby police detective who figures out who is doing the killings (most cops reckon it's terrorists or urban guerrillas). He's an outcast too.

The film does have strong moments. The amazing perceptual abilities of the Wolfen are shared with us through an astonishing Dolby soundtrack and an optically enhanced visual process by which objects are coloured and magnified partly according to their emotional significance. When the Wolfen finally follow the detective to the heart of Manhattan (casually beheading one of his colleagues, in the only really gory sequence) their drifting, evasive figures really do create a chilling symbol. They seem not inappropriate to the urban setting, and for a moment it appears quite plausible that a violent, brutal city could be populated with a large number of huge wolves without anyone knowing. They follow Finney (magically?) to a high floor in a skyscraper, where, after a certain amount of mutally respectful sniffing, both parties (wolves and policeman) reach a kind of truce, and Finney agrees not to give away their secret. It is a powerful scene.

This is a strange film, and not the strongest of films with which to end the chapter, yet thoroughly appropriate all the same. For here we see the typical modern monster, first cousin to those that slunk around the nineteenth-century Transylvanian countryside, suddenly living among us ordinary people, in the big cities of the here-and-now. That trajectory, which we have explored, is the most significant change in modern horror.

Fantasy Films Since 1968

Previous two pages:
Rae Dawn Chong plays
the elusive Ika, one of
the more sophisticated
inhabitants of the
fantastic, prehistoric
world of Jean-Jacques
Annaud's Quest for Fire
(ICC Cine-Trail, 1981).

All attempts at genre definition end in frustration: no sooner do you build a pigeon hole than you find a pigeon that refuses to be stuffed into it. For convenience, this book has divided fantastic cinema into three main categories: science fiction, supernatural horror, and fantasy. We can make stabs at defining science fiction and supernatural horror and know that not *too* many exceptions will turn up. "Fantasy", though, is a word that means different things to different people. This book's definition is partly negative: if a film is clearly fantastic, but equally clearly is not horror or science fiction, then it must be fantasy. But there is something positive about fantasy films, too. They might have science fiction in them (*Superman*, for example), or scary ghosts (*Empire of Passion*), but the total impression will not be of SF or horror, but of something else. In a particular case a film may be mythic, or weird, or mysterious, or uncanny, or surrealist, or numinous, but none of these words touch the heart of the matter. The essence is that a fantasy film must contain a miracle: it might be the slaying of a dragon, or a cave man discovering how to make fire, or some schoolgirls disappearing into thin air at the top of a big hill, or even a little boy with a tin drum refusing to grow up. The *kind* of miracle does not matter. What does matter is that, at the film's heart, there is some sort of magic.

The film-maker as illusionist

Ingmar Bergman may be the cinema's premier illusionist. He stands squarely in the tradition that began right back around 1900 with Georges Méliès. All film-makers are illusionists, but Bergman is exceptional in taking illusion as the subject, and not just the method, of many of his films.

The old conjuror's allegedly final film, the valedictory *Fanny and Alexander* (1982), is appropriately enough about the small magics of everyday life, and specifically about a little boy who as he grows older becomes something of a conjuror himself. *Fanny and Alexander* must surely be autobiographical (there are many resemblances between the boy's youth and Bergman's own), and could easily have been titled "A Portrait of the Fantasist as a Young Man". It is a fantasy about fantasies – especially childhood fantasies, for they are the ones that stay with us the longest, and any fantastic film-maker must have something of the child about him.

As the film opens, Alexander is staring into a toy theatre and dreaming. He is in a big, beautiful old house, apparently empty for the moment. It is something of an old person's house, full of ticking clocks and polished floors and gracious furniture and bric-à-brac. He is interested in a statue, which turns to look at him.

But soon the house is throbbing with life; the complicated Ekdahl family: a grand-mother, her old Jewish lover, her three sons (all middle-aged), the wives of those two sons who are married, several children, and at least four maids. It is Christmas. One son philanders with a pretty maid. Another gives an exhibition to the children of spectacularly musical farting. People dance. It is rich with life and warmth, happiness, and a little unhappiness too.

Soon afterwards, however, Alexander's father, actor-manager of the theatre in this prosperous provincial town, collapses and dies during a rehearsal of *Hamlet*. Many months later, the lovely wife remarries, but her choice is bad. Bishop Vergerus, her new husband, is puritanical, stingy and spiteful (though extremely handsome). His household is a nightmare. When Alexander conjures up a story about how the Bishop murdered his first wife and children (who drowned), he is cruelly punished.

Alexander, of course, is a kind of Hamlet, and Vergerus a kind of Claudius. Indeed, his father's ghost – like the Ghost of Hamlet's father – returns several times, wearing the clothes of an Edwardian gentleman. The trouble is, his soulful gestures are not very helpful and, although Alexander loved his father, the ghost's spaniel-like eyes ultimately wear on his nerves. He tells it to go away, and we never see it again.

Alexander and Fanny (his sister) are saved by the old Jewish antique dealer, who spirits them away in an antique chest after having tricked Vergerus (an anti-Semite) by giving an immensely witty impersonation of Shylock and causing the Bishop to lose his self control.

The antique shop is very mysterious. Wandering through its labyrinthine rooms at night, Alexander hears God talking to him, but it turns out to be only a life-size puppet. Later, he meets the old Jew's mysterious son, who is kept locked up and is possibly dangerous. A beautiful man, he looks like a woman, and it may be that his androgynous magic is real (and cruel) for it seems that he causes the Bishop's death by fire that very night.

The film is intensely visual, and it is difficult to express in words its confident mingling of dream and solid reality. We feel that much of what we are witnessing is seen through the eyes of Alexander, who loves watching the flickering images of his magic lantern, and that his childhood vision draws no clear distinction between reality and imagination. The images of illusion are everywhere: the theatre, the toys, the primitive film projector, the rushing millstream, the many stories that are recounted, the allusions to *Hamlet* (itself a play that makes constant allusions to the theatre), the puppets, the magician.

All these metaphors have the effect of giving an aura of the fabulous, of make-believe, to even the realistic action. They remind us

·that we too are watching actors, and that all the vivid life of the film (it is more than three hours long, and has over forty characters) is, at the same time, something we are seeing on a screen, though it retains the power to move us both to laughter and to tears.

The ghost of make-believe behind the vigorous action is partly because the story is set in 1907, which for most of us is a period of "Once upon a time...". I believe the effect is deliberate, that Bergman wants us to see that this is a film coloured by the deceptive glow of memory (his own) as well as by the fantasies of childhood. (Memory is the conjuring trick that we can all perform.) *Fanny and Alexander* asks us, perhaps, to look back through the proscenium of the cinema screen to Bergman's own childhood. He may have changed some facts, but then, as the film shows us, memory and imagination are so intertwined that we cannot be sure where one leaves off and the other begins. The film's bustling world is as real as anything the cinema has ever given us, and that may be the most masterly illusion of all from the crafty old magician. It may be the greatest of his films, and it is certainly one of the greatest fantasy films ever made.

I deal with this film at some length because *Fanny and Alexander* directly concerns what the whole of fantastic cinema is about: the illusion of miracles being real, and the possibility that in one way they *are* just as real as our everyday lives, which are themselves subject to all the illusions of perception. We see what we want to see.

A domestic ghost

When Seki and her lover Toyoji join together in strangling Seki's husband in Oshima's *Empire of Passion* (1978), one might suppose that, if she saw what she wanted to see, she would never see him again. On the other hand, he was a good husband, and perhaps she *does* see what she wants to see when she returns home one night to find his ghost (perfectly solid-looking) sitting calmly by the fire and waiting for her to pour him his sake. She may have missed him. Japanese customs in a small rural village in 1895 have forbidden her to live with her lover, and she is lonely. She is upset, too, at her daughter's questions about what has happened to the father (his body is at the bottom of a well), and her story about his seeking work in Tokyo is beginning to wear thin. The villagers are talking.

What is remarkable about this tender and lovely film is the matter-of-factness of it all. The ghostly husband goes back to his job as rickshawman as if no more need be said. The seasons pass in their stately manner, the ghost occasionally reappears, and Seki becomes more distraught. Intimations of a more modern Japanese state appear even in this remote corner, and the village policeman is now convinced that Seki is a murderess.

Toyoji sees the ghost too, and this time, just for a moment, it has something of the demonic quality of the traditional vengeful ghosts of Kabuki theatre.

This is not really a horror film. It is, in part, a film about the constraints that a small, stable, conservative society place upon an obsessive love; in part, a film about being lost (the lover, twenty years younger than she, and an ex-soldier who does not quite fit into village life, is also lonely). The ghost is not threatening; he is merely a mute reminder of the simplicities of the life that she abandoned for so trivial a reason (he was murdered because she could not bear him to see that in a fit of passion she had shaved off her pubic hair). Finally the lovers go down to the well to retrieve the body; leaves are falling; Seki is struck blind by some unseen force. When they emerge they are taken by police and tortured. The body is raised from the well, Seki confesses, and for a moment she can see again.

It is a fine film, and along with *Fanny and Alexander* it serves as a reminder that ghosts need not be restricted to the conventions of the horror picture. They can symbolize memory and regret as well as menace and revenge.

Mythic quests

Ghosts, whose intrusion into the ordinary world suddenly make it seem fantastic, are one means of showing that our everyday reality may not be the whole story. A more direct means, of course, is to create an entirely fantastic world from the ground up. Until the 1980s, when the popularity of so-called "sword and sorcery" books became so great that film-makers could not afford to ignore it, there were very few producers who were prepared to take on the Herculean task of building an entirely "other" world of magic, with all the problems of sets and special effects that the work would entail.

Existing myths were the obvious source of such movies, though later on, as film-makers began to put greater trust in the audience's capacity to lose themselves in a story, it became quite common to invent new fantastic worlds altogether, usually in some unspecified, archaic past, or in some unspecified alternate universe. (*Star Wars* did both.)

Earlier in the 1970s, it was Ray Harryhausen (see Chapter Two) who persevered with the business of building fantasy worlds while others steered clear. Even if one has reservations about the quality of the end product, one has to admire the way Harryhausen, despite major obstacles, has always stuck to his fantastic guns. With co-producer Charles Schneer he made three magic-and-monsters films in ten years (doing the special effects himself, of course), of which the first was *The Golden Voyage of Sinbad* (1973).

At last Harryhausen's persistence was re-

The sinister fighting skeletons from Sinbad and the Eye of the Tiger *(Columbia, 1977). It is a good sequence, and so it should be, for the effects designer Ray Harryhausen had already used fighting skeletons in two previous films, and thus had plenty of practice.*

warded. After a series of semi-flops (*First Men in the Moon, Valley of Gwangi*, see filmography), this turned out to be his most successful film at the box-office yet. It even did better than its predecessor, *Seventh Voyage of Sinbad* (1958). *Golden Voyage*, with a screenplay by Brian Clemens (of *The Avengers* fame), and a score by Miklos Rozsa, succeeded in projecting an atmosphere of the uncanny more successfully than most of his other work, before or after. Sinbad, this time, was John Phillip Law (the blind angel from *Barbarella*), while Tom Baker (later to become Dr Who) played the wicked magician Koura. Although the film's title suggests a mythology from the Arabian Nights, the hotchpotch here take elements from Hindu mythology (a statue of the six-armed goddess Kali comes to life) and Greek (a wicked centaur battles with a griffin). Filmed in Spain, the story recounts a mythic quest for the third part of an amulet of which the first part is held by Sinbad and the second by the Grand Vizier whose face, destroyed by the evil magician, is hidden behind a forbidding golden mask. The quest takes them to Lemuria, but some of the better effects occur earlier on: the evil little winged homunculus that eavesdrops on their plans, the ship's figurehead that slowly turns from the prow, tears herself out of the wooden frame, snatches a vital map, and swims away. There is a real sense of wonder here, though in other parts of the film (especially the centaur-griffin battle) the fantasy is much more mechanical.

The sequel, *Sinbad and the Eye of the*

Tiger (1977), was disappointing. John Wayne's son Patrick starred as Sinbad, without any of his old man's charisma. There is, incidentally, no tiger, though there is a sabre-toothed lion. The script is amazingly vapid, and the film has a frowsty, old-fashioned look about it, and plods along at an unvarying pace, building very little tension. Thus Harryhausen's effects appear in a frame that does not set them off to advantage, though there is plenty of entertainment in the giant walrus, the giant bee, the minotaur and the horned troglodyte man. The most touching effects centre on the young man who is turned into a big baboon.

Clash of the Titans (1981), which was backed by MGM, gave Harryhausen the largest budget he ever had to work with. It is quite a lavish production, with cameos by big stars such as Laurence Olivier, Burgess Meredith and Maggie Smith, but there is something sad about it – as if Harryhausen has been trapped in some time warp every since *Seventh Voyage* in 1958, the same awkwardly shambling monsters and trite plot looking more old-fashioned with each new film. The story (Perseus's love for Andromeda and their many trials before her final rescue from the Kraken) is typically episodic – for Harryhausen, all stories run in straight lines – but his animation is as good as ever, the best things this time round being the winged horse, Pegasus; the fight with the melancholy monster, Calibos; the giant scorpions; the Kraken; and, best of all, the fiendish gorgon Medusa with her hair of writhing snakes, and her cave full of the stone bodies of previous victims, caught in postures of agony. But special effects in the outside world had been moving on, and the optical processing that unites animation with live action looks pretty weak alongside *Star Wars*; it has blue fringing around the models, fuzzy background plates and a generally grainy appearance. The best performance in the film is that of spirited and intelligent Judi Bowker as Andromeda; the worst may be that of the dopey owl, Bubo, a creature of metal whose mannerisms seem to be copied from R2D2 in *Star Wars*. *Clash of the Titans* is good fun, but could have been so much better. Have the imaginations of Harryhausen and Schneer been petrified by immersion in the numbing waters of some stagnant, mythic pond?

King Arthur

Perhaps the legend of King Arthur has a more immediate resonance for English-speaking people than the legends of the Greeks or the Indians. Certainly it had for John Boorman, who planned his production of *Excalibur* (1981) over more than ten years before he finally made it. It came out at the same time as *Clash of the Titans* and the two films make an interesting contrast.

Boorman understands that a myth is more

than a story packed with incident. The stories of myth are stories of the evolution of human consciousness, and symbolize our archetypal concerns. Whereas for Harryhausen a prince is just a brave young man, for Boorman King Arthur is literally the integrity and fertility of the land he rules. When, at the end, Arthur rides to cleansing battle, flowers spring up in the grass as he passes.

Excalibur is set between two worlds: a fragmented world of dark magic and mysterious powers, and a lighter world where technology and political unity are beginning to arise. Arthur himself is a transitional figure, bred by the first world in an act of rape presided over by a wizard, carrying a sword which seems to represent the brighter, colder powers of modernity. His mentor, Merlin, belongs to the first world (though the alchemy he practises will become the very science that supplants him). Arthur's task of reconciliation between two kinds of living, two kinds of imagination, is a difficult one. As in Boorman's films before, the sheer complexity of the mythic symbolism sometimes makes events seem fuzzy, and Arthur's role is not aways clear.

In the earlier part of the film, human life seems to spring naturally from the grass, the dark trees of the forest. The armour of the knights looks like the leathery hides of dinosaurs. When Arthur inherits a sword and a kingdom, and sets up the Round Table, the setting changes. The corridors of Camelot gleam spanking new; the armour of the knights is bright and shining; we have moved from a world of nature to a world of artifice. But older forms of magic (which are presented as potently attractive as well as dangerous) hinder progress. Arthur's half-sister seduces him (disguised as his wife) and she bears a son, Mordred – a baby-faced beauty whom we usually see, later on, in moulded body armour and a cruel beautiful mask. Merlin retires, but returns at the end to rob Morgana (Arthur's witch sister) of youth and beauty in a scene of foggy dissolution. Arthur and his son, Mordred, kill one another; Excalibur is returned to the Lady of the Lake; and we feel that beneath the surface of the world of rationality that will now prosper, magic is not dead but merely sleeping.

Excalibur is a badly flawed film (with a daft performance by Nicol Williamson as Merlin, using an unsatisfying funny voice); it often gives rise to audience laughter in the wrong place, but nevertheless it provides us with glimpses of the authentic magic which the cinema can create.

Sword and sorcery

"Sword and sorcery" is a label that is often applied to stories of heroic fantasy, usually set in archaic worlds (no technology in evidence), in which heroes use their muscles

and sometimes their wits to do battle against the forces of evil. The two main forms of sword and sorcery in books are those derived from Tolkien's *Lord of the Rings* (small hero against large opposition, with the emphasis on magic and myth), and those derived from Robert E. Howard's "Conan" stories of the 1930s (big hero, with the emphasis on swordplay and bloodshed).

When it became clear that such books were beginning to outsell science fiction, the film industry moved in. The best known of the sword and sorcery films, in a temporary boom that began in 1981 and was almost over by 1983 (because none of them made as much money as the producers had hoped), was *Conan the Barbarian* (see Chapter Four). One of the first, a disaster, was *Hawk the Slayer* (1980, see filmography).

Of the four most interesting sword and sorcery films that followed, the first, and probably the best, was *Dragonslayer* (1981). It was written by Matthew Robbins and Hal Barwood in the Tolkien mode, and directed by Robbins. (These two were comparatively junior members of the University of Southern California film-school "mafia", a group to which George Lucas, John Milius and Dan O'Bannon also belonged.) *Dragonslayer* was a Walt Disney co-production (with Paramount), but it avoided the Disney stereotypes.

The story is set in some unspecified Dark Age. A delegation of villagers asks the sorcerer Ulrich (Ralph Richardson) to protect them from the depredations of a monstrous dragon, which demands a diet of virgins. But

Harry Hamlin is the young hero of another fantasy epic with special effects created by Harryhausen, Clash of the Titans *(MGM, 1981). This battle against giant scorpions is one of the best animated sequences.*

Princess Elspeth (Chloe Salaman) is in trouble, for the local dragon demands a diet of virgins in Dragonslayer *(Disney/Paramount, 1981). The excellent special effects were created by Industrial Light and Magic, the same group that did the effects for the Star Wars films.*

Ulrich is killed, and the task is left to his innocent and inexperienced apprentice, Galen (Peter MacNicol). The film traces Galen's growth to maturity until, after many errors, he succeeds in his task. The plot is simple. It is the movie's texture that makes it interesting: muted, brooding colours for the coarse-flavoured peasant environment in which most of the story is set; excellent special effects for the more brightly-coloured dragon scenes (done by George Lucas's Industrial Light and Magic company, the group that creates the effects for the *Star Wars* films); a sense of real violence and misery in the life of the time; the vivid actuality of dragon life (especially when we see its offspring eating what is left of a princess); some crisp dialogue. As in *Excalibur*, there is a subtext about the death of the age of magic (symbolized by the mutual deaths of dragon and resuscitated sorcerer), a theme that is probably connected with a late twentieth-century feeling that our own world is becoming bleak, cold and mechanistic. *Dragonslayer*, while not a great film, is certainly an intelligent one.

The Sword and the Sorceror (1982) is, by contrast, in the Conan line of descent. A young princeling loses his kingdom, becomes a bandit chief, leads a revolt, is crucified, tears the nails out of his wrists, has a fight with the evil wizard and wins the girl. This is a real action-packed comic-strip swashbuckler, made at only a fraction of the cost of *Conan*, which probably gains vigour

from the very narrowness of its ambition. Unlike Milius, Boorman and Robbins, the director (a young unknown called Albert Pyun) is not remotely interested in making elegiac statements about the fading of an age, or the nature of manliness, or rites of passage. Pyun is interested in showing fights, tits and bums and the kind of evil that pops out and says "Boo!" It all works surprisingly well. The fantastic elements are well created, and while not subtle, are colourfully uncanny. Xusia the magician rises from a pool of blood within a tomb whose walls are encrusted with agonized, living, human faces; he rips a witch's heart from her chest (from a distance); and, much later, he spectacularly tears off his face, a human disguise, to reveal the demon beneath. There is a heroine who is constantly kneeing villains in the testicles, and a hero who very properly says at the finale, "We've a battle in the offing – kingdoms to save and women to love", before riding into the sunset. It is all very good-humoured.

I seem to have a critical blind spot about Don Coscarelli, director of the low-budget *Phantasm* (see Chapter Six). His sword and sorcery epic *The Beastmaster* (1982) pleased none of the critics and few of the fans, but I quite enjoyed it. Loosely based on a popular novel by André Norton, the film tells of a muscular young telepath in quest of revenge (his village, much as in *Conan*, has been wiped out). He can communicate with animals and is soon befriended by an eagle (through whose eyes he can see), two lively raccoons (who steal for him) and a black lion (who kills for him). The good people are handsome (Tanya Roberts from the television show *Charlie's Angels* is one of them) and the bad people are ugly, especially Rip Torn as wicked high-priest Maax. There are impressively savage bird people who turn out to be quite good, and a magic ring that flips open to reveal the high-priest's eye peering about. It has stark desert scenery and lots of action. It is all quite juvenile, but I prefer it to *Doctor Dolittle* in the talking-to-animals line.

Krull (1983) is much more ambitious. The distributors, however, did not seem too confident about the product, and delayed its release for a considerable time, possibly to prevent it clashing with *Return of the Jedi*. It is not exactly clear how everything went wrong. The director Peter Yates, the special-effects director Derek Meddings and the art director Stephen Grimes all have good track records. But the screenwriter, imposed by the studio, had only one previous credit (*Any Which Way You Can*), and this may partly explain the limpness of the narrative. Elements from every successful screen fantasy for several years have been taken and shuffled around like a pack of greasy cards. There is a hero orphaned at the outset (*Star Wars, Beastmaster*), a tetchy magician (*Dragonslayer, Excalibur*), a magic weapon

(*Sword and the Sorceror, Excalibur*), a blind seer (*Clash of the Titans*), and so on. The genuinely fantastic is always more than the sum of its parts; *Krull*, somehow, is less. There is also an awful performance from the petulant hero (Ken Marshall), who is supposed to be like Errol Flynn but looks like his soppy kid brother.

Yet there are many good moments: the delicate, lethal crystal spider on the great Web; the Fire Mares (no ordinary horses, but huge, magnificent Clydesdales); the organic, constricting passages of the Black Fortress; some of the most spectacular sets ever built at Pinewood Studios (a towering forest, a deadly swamp); and Lysette Anthony as the Princess is wonderfully spirited and lovely.

The sad point is that *Krull* has become the latest of a string of sword-and-sorcery financial disasters. It can be assumed that now no Hollywood producer will be prepared to touch the genre for years to come. Yet the fault is not in the genre, it is in the fantasy-by-numbers, film-making-by-committee syndrome, where every set-piece has to be an imitation of somebody else's proven set-piece, and originality is at a discount, for fear that the backers' money be lost. *Krull* cost a fortune – the exact figure is not available – and one can only feel angry at the people who botched the job so badly, overall, that it may have damaged the genre for many years to come.

Monsters in Muppet Land

More successful commercially, though not a great deal better, was a Tolkien-derivative film, *The Dark Crystal* (1982), made by the team who created the Muppets (the amusing puppet creatures who had a tremendous success on television). The Crystal is cracked, and until it is restored the magical world in which the film is set will be chaotic and full of evil. Jen, a pixie boy, is told by the slothful, shambling Mystics that he may, by recovering the Crystal's missing shard, restore creation to its former integrity. He does so, with the help of Kira, a pixie girl.

This fantastic world is created in loving (and extremely expensive) detail. Enormous effort and imagination has gone into creating a menagerie of strange creatures, both good and bad, of whom by far the most interesting are the doddering Skeksis: clawed, decaying, bent, vulture-like sophisticates who have all the best lines. The art of filmed puppetry here is infinitely more accomplished than anything that has been screened before.

Only one thing is missing – a story. A quest whose result we are told at the beginning is no quest at all. It is boring. Predestination does not make for nail-biting tension. It is true there is a brief moment of distress at the self-sacrifice of pretty little Kira, but the tragedy is perfunctory, since her apparent death is followed almost instantly by resur-

rection. In this world, Evil is nasty but also instantly deflatable. We do not see the night side of fantasy at all, and only a moment or so of twilight. The philosophy seems to be, Do nothing to upset the children! (Some of the most popular children's fairy tales, however, are infinitely bleaker and crueller than this). In other words, the film is bland.

The decision to use no human actors at all (and no stop-motion animation either) may be justifiable in terms of consistency, but I doubt it. The film was rumoured to have cost $30 million, and that is a lot to pay for artistic integrity. Indeed the use of real children as the pixie people might have proved more involving for the audience than the use of puppets whose main characteristic is cuteness.

Discovering civilization

It has often been observed – notably by the SF writer Arthur C. Clarke – that, to an unsophisticated mind, technology and magic are indistinguishable, which is one of the reasons why it can be difficult to distinguish between the genres of science fiction and straight fantasy.

The point is nicely made in a little movie directed by James Ivory, whose sensitive, worldly films are very popular at "arthouse" cinemas, but seldom reach the film-going public *en masse*. *Savages* (1972) begins with primitive tribesmen wearing body paint, some of them masked, about to undertake a human sacrifice in the woods. Then a croquet ball descends from the air like a message

Handsome, muscular, slightly wooden Marc Singer (a typical sword-and-sorcery hero) poses becomingly with one of his best friends, a curiously pigmented lion, in the enjoyably silly The Beastmaster *(Leisure Investment/Ecta, 1982), directed by the young Canadian Don Coscarelli.*

Things are coming to a climax in the colourfully menacing castle of the evil, doddering Skeksis towards the end of The Dark Crystal *(ITC, 1982). The object in the middle is the crystal – not very dark at all.*

from some angry god, and interrupts them. Following the direction of its trajectory they emerge onto a beautiful smooth lawn, in front of a great mansion. A luxurious 1930 Pierce-Arrow automobile is parked there, and they investigate it eagerly. Then they enter the house, awed and delighted at the pictures, the furnishings, the clothes they find. Soon they are dressing up, and using cosmetics.

In a series of amusing vignettes, we see these Mud People recapitulating the entire history of human civilization in a kind of parabolic arc. Infected by the house, they become instantly more sophisticated, and later we see them giving an upper-class dinner party, everybody in formal dress. The savages have become Julian Branch, a songwriter; Carlotta, a hostess; Iliona, a decadent; Mrs Emily Penning, a woman in disgrace; Archie, a bully; and so on. The milieu is 1920s; the dialogue is Noel Coward. Civilization has reached its peak, though intimations of war and depression can be heard over the radio, and in the conversation of unpleasant Otto Nürder, a capitalist. Somebody sings a witty, rather cruel dance number called "Steppin' on the Spaniel". A croquet ball rolls into the room.

From now on things go downhill: the party becomes wilder; people smoke dope in the basement; someone is drowned in the pool and nobody pays much attention. The next

morning they all rush outside to play a rough game of croquet. The ball rolls into the woods, and the savages follow it...

It is a poignant and witty fable, whose absurdist jokes and tongue-in-cheek anthropological observations were well received in Europe, but died the death in America, even though the film used American actors and settings.

Savages, as a joke, does what a sub-genre of fantastic cinema does, occasionally, in all seriousness. We have already referred to an example in *One Million Years BC* (see Chapter Two), and the same sub-genre is mercilessly parodied in *Caveman* (1981, see filmography). The best recent example is the French film *Quest for Fire* (1981), whose anthropological points can hardly be taken more seriously than those in *Savages*, despite the director's employment of sociobiologist Desmond Morris as advisor on primitive body language and gesture, and of Anthony Burgess on prehistoric words. The film is based on a book published in 1909, and hardly represents the latest thinking on matters prehistoric.

Just the same, it is enormous good fun, and seems to have a kind of symbolic truth about it. A primitive tribe, the Ulam, possess fire but do not know how to make it – they took their burning brands from a naturally occurring fire. In a fight with an even more primitive nearby tribe, the fire is put out, and everyone squats miserably in a chilly swamp. Three brave young men then go off to seek more fire; they are pursued by sabre-tooth tigers; attacked by cannibals (some gruesome bits here) who are scared off by a herd of convincing mammoths (elephants covered with hearth rugs); they meet a more sophisticated tribe who teach them the delights of sex in the missionary position as opposed to mounting from behind; they learn love; they learn more about language; they learn how to laugh; they learn how to make fire.

Beautifully photographed in Kenya and the Scottish Highlands, and intelligently scripted, the film is just as much about a fantastic quest as it would have been if the fire were the Holy Grail. It is not a profound film, but the depicted acquisition of the rudiments of civilization (not carried quite so far as in *Savages*) is funny, touching and exciting.

Archaic survivals

Behaviourists tell us that the brain of modern man carries within it a more primitive consciousness; the brain's hind-stem is the brain of the beast. Not so deeply hidden in the genetic code of human chromosomes is the whole of our evolutionary past. Our rituals of love and warfare may recapitulate the sexual and territorial lessons learned as our fruit-eating ancestors descended from the trees. Sociobiologists exaggerate the case at times, but few doubt that there is something in it.

It is no wonder, then, that (as in the previous two films) a central theme of fantasy is the encounter between the primitive and the sophisticated, for this is a psychodrama that is everyday stuff within our minds. It is a meeting in which not all the dice are loaded in favour of the sophisticated; our partial loss of the simple passions and appetites of animals is to be considered, perhaps, with a joy that is mingled with regret. Sometimes visibly, sometimes hidden just beneath the surface, this theme has run throughout most of the films previously looked at: heroic fantasies like *Excalibur*, SF movies like *Altered States*, horror movies like *Cat People*.

The caveman movie traditionally describes primitive people learning about civilization, but the precise obverse of this theme is even more popular: the encountering of archaic survivals by sophisticated people. It is the fundamental metaphor of horror films, and it is commonplace in fantasy cinema as well. A good example is *Malpertuis* (1971), directed by the same Belgian director, Harry Kumel, who made the cult horror film *Daughters of Darkness* (see filmography).

A sailor, Jan, is kidnapped as he reaches port, and taken to a rambling old house, Malpertuis, where his old uncle (Orson Welles) lies dying. A weird collection of grasping relatives lives there too; they had been told they can inherit a fortune only on condition they never leave the house. Susan Hampshire plays three roles: Jan's sister, Nancy, who plans to leave with her lover (but he is murdered); the dowdy Alice; and the sexy Euryale. The rambling old house has a strange geometry, with passages going in impossible directions. Jan inherits all this. One day, he finds a vulture tearing at the liver of one of the residents. He is mildly astonished as he comes to learn that they are all Greek Gods living in an age where nobody believes in them any more: they are therefore much weakened. A bowler-hatted creep tries to seduce Alice (who has a wonderful body beneath her dingy dress): he is Hermes, but she is Alecto, the Fury, and he comes to a nasty end. The uncle had captured all these divinities on a small Greek island and brought them here to make a kind of Olympian menagerie. Jan's love for Euryale, who demurely refuses to look at him for most of the film, proves his undoing. He kisses her and turns to stone, for she is the Gorgon.

The special effects, especially the stone figures, are mostly very amateurish, but the film's sumptuous colour and its omnivorous desire to fit everything in are appealing. The banal awfulness of the Gods – small-minded, bickering, a bit decadent – is well achieved. The film is a nice comment on the decline of mystery and, at the end, the petrification of myth.

Peter Weir's Australian film *The Last Wave* (1977) has a sophisticated Sydney lawyer (Richard Chamberlain) defending a downtrodden group of slum-dwelling, urban aborigines accused of murdering one of their number in a street brawl. He is slowly sucked into an enigmatic world of ancient myth as he learns that this was a ritual murder carried out by magic (bone-pointing), and that the aborigines are members of an ancient tribe whose homeland lies where the sprawling, vulgar city has been built. Beneath the sewers of the city lies their most secret holy place, a cave decorated with paintings that suggest links with the Easter Islanders, even perhaps with ancient visiting aliens.

The fantastic elements of the film are created with considerable subtlety, as tiny intimations of wrongness build up into a vision of nightmare and apocalypse. The tribal magicians have power over water, and the film's images of rain, overflowing baths, hailstones in the desert, have a cumulative effect that climaxes quite naturally in the great tidal wave, looming hundreds of feet high, that confronts the lawyer on a Sydney beach in the last scene. There is an extremely credible performance from the aboriginal actor Gulpilil (who also starred in Nicolas Roeg's *Walkabout*) that gives depth to what is basically an extremely melodramatic tale. His mobile, intense, dignified features are compelling.

An altogether cruder clash between middle-class man and ancient rituals occurs in *The Island* (1980), one of the less fortunate films of Michael Ritchie (whose *Downhill Racer* and *The Candidate* were much admired).

Michael Caine is the newspaper reporter sent to the Caribbean to investigate some Bermuda Triangle types of disappearance. A sceptical fellow, he does not expect any real trouble, and takes his young son along for the ride. They are quite rapidly catapulted into a

The expressive aboriginal actor Gulpilil holds up a magic stone, a sacred tribal relic, in Peter Weir's exotic fantasy about ancient survivals in modern Sydney, The Last Wave *(Ayer-McElroy/United Artists, 1977).*

melodramatic lost world, a small island inhabited by seventeenth-century buccaneers with (it is implied rather obliquely) cannibalistic tendencies. They quote the Bible a lot, talk in archaic slang and have strange ceremonies. The son is attracted by this life, and in no time at all becomes Tue-Barbe, a cold-blooded young killer. The twentieth century wins out in the end, but not before some bloody clashes and a spectacularly silly scene of karate expert versus cutlass-wielding pirate, not unlike the whip-versus-gun scene in *Raiders of the Lost Ark* the following year.

It is all dreadfully implausible, with amazingly hammy performances from David Warner as the pirate chief and Frank Middlemass as the corrupt doctor who is their link to the real world. But the film is not without ideas (much Freudian symbolism and sociobiological jokes about submission versus aggression) and has moments of visual flair.

Oases of enigma

Fantasy takes much of its vividness from dualisms, tensions between opposites, often symbolized by the meeting of two different kinds of world. A similar tension to that between modern and ancient is that between the rational and the irrational: the routine versus the mysterious. At the heart of many fantastic films is a pure mystery protruding into the banalities of everyday life. To enter such a mystery is often to find that the inside is bigger than the outside. One small item of irrationality opens a door to a maze, which becomes wilder the more deeply it is explored. That was the central image of Peter Weir's *The Last Wave*, and in a different way it is also the centre of his earlier film, *Picnic at Hanging Rock* (1975).

On St Valentine's Day 1900, a group of normal, chattering schoolgirls sets out on a picnic in a rural area of Victoria, Australia. They come from a rather posh boarding school (based on a real school where the present writer taught science as a young man). At Hanging Rock (a real place) they find that everybody's watches have stopped at exactly twelve. The door that leads out of the everyday has been opened. Four of the more active girls ascend to the weirdly contorted top of the hill. The first three disappear into thin air; the fourth, a struggling fat girl, is left behind.

The rest of the film circles, like some fluttering bird, around this oasis of enigma in the desert of routine. Its mystery is only deepened when one of the girls reappears, for she has lost her memory.

Why were these girls taken and not others? Was it something to do with sexuality? A series of blandly impervious images offers tantalising hints but no explanation; the camera explores the natural world near the school with grace and lyricism; vignettes of upper-class life are photographed to look like fin-de-siècle academy pictures by Tissot, all straw hats, long dresses, leaves and rippling water. Darker images intrude: schoolgirl propriety suddenly erupts into screaming hysteria; the relentless buzzing of blowflies portends the discovery of a suicide's body. The red of carnality obtrudes on the pastels of chastity.

It is a quite remarkable film, weaving its intricate, elegant variations, playing games with Freud and Marx and even the possibility of flying saucers, to tease us about a mystery whose whole point must be that it remains a mystery.

Magic houses

The notion that mysterious places may only open their doors to a special kind of person is also central to one of the most unusual fantasies of the century, Jacques Rivette's *Céline and Julie Go Boating* (1974). The film opens in a little garden square in Paris where we see a cat stalking something invisible. For the next three hours and twelve minutes we, the audience, are put into much the same position. The world is a strange place for the two girls, Céline and Julie (Juliet Berto and Dominique Labourier, by whom much of the film was improvised). They are hardly more than children, really, and the Paris they so spontaneously inhabit is full of the delightful surprises of childhood, little worlds within worlds, small moments of magic as when Julie (who has only just met Céline) drops in surprise the Bloody Mary she has already prepared when Céline requests her to make one. But telepathy between them becomes a commonplace. After all, Céline is a magician (in rather a cheap cabaret), and Julie is a librarian much involved in books of magic.

The film begins by summoning up the ghost of all the other films it might have been: "Most of the time it started like this..." At the very end it looks as if it might be going to begin again, only the other way around.

In another of Paris's secret gardens, Julie finds a strange old house (with cats outside) that she enters. Two hours later she leaves it looking stunned and holding a candy. She cannot remember anything. But when she and Céline eat the candy (is it LSD?) they both remember. What we are then shown is like a film-within-a-film. The house was full of ghosts; something was happening there. Was there a plot? Who were these elegant, claustrophobic spirits? (As Rivette confesses, they deliberately look like the mildly catatonic characters from some brightly coloured, late-1940s RKO woman's picture, and everything is in stylized deep focus.) Céline visits the house next and forgets what happened. They eat the candy again, and we have to make sense of more scenes from this film-within-a-film. All of this goes on for a long time, and we witness some of the action in this mysterious house three or four times over. Finally, in exasperation, both girls raid the house together, pull silly faces at the ghosts (who ignore them, as they continue their stately, repetitive melodrama) and save the child. Julie then confesses that she knew the house well when she was a little girl. Céline implies that she made the whole thing up; she is always fantasizing. But we, the audience, saw it all too

Are fantasies things we see because wo want to see them? Towards the end, Céline and Julie go boating, and on the tranquil water they drift past another boat on which are the three ghosts, the handsome man and the two women who hopelessly, helplessly love him, pale and impassive. The world of reality and the world of fantasy are, it seems, ships that pass not in the night, but in the middle of a gentle summer's day. Perhaps the title gives the game away. In an obscure French idiom, to go boating ("aller en bateau") is to be caught up in a tall story, and so we have been. To some people it is the most magical film ever made (I belong in this group); to others it is an irritating fable about narcissistic young women who are intrinsically boring and silly.

The screenplay was written by the remarkable Argentinian scenarist Eduardo de Gregorio. (He also wrote the story of Bertolucci's *The Spider's Stratagem.*) As he is steeped in the South American literary tradition that is often known today as "magic realism", it is perhaps not surprising that echoes of Borgesian labyrinths or Marquezian tricks with time should permeate his work. In a film that he himself directed, another fascinating oasis of enigma appears, and again it takes the form of a magic house.

Sérail (1976) is about a crumbling house which was clearly built by the same architect as the one in *Céline and Julie*. A sophisticated writer of detective novels, Eric Sange (Corin Regrave), arrives with the thought of buying it. Of the strange group of women who seem to live there, two are – by more than coincidence, one feels – ghosts from *Céline and Julie*: Bulle Ogier and Marie-France Pisier; the third, the housekeeper who tells him that the house has secret passages and two-way mirrors, is Leslie Caron. He begins to write a story about a young man visiting a strange house, but the words fade from the page. Two of the women deny the third exists. Attempting to possess the house, he makes sexual overtures to its women (or are they its spirits?) to which they tantalisingly respond. The looking glasses, somebody remarks, remind one of Lewis Carroll. Has he wandered into a Gothic romance, or is he dreaming one up to coax his creative juices into action? The riddle is resolved. The two young women were paid actresses, playing a part. They leave. He sits at his typewriter.

The house encloses him (the riddle returns), swallowing him up, with doors and windows banging shut, like a spider eating a fly. This is pre-eminently a film that asks the question, is the fantastic something real, or something invited by the fantasist? Or are both the same thing?

In training for magic

Light Years Away (1981), a French film made by Alain Tanner, shot in Ireland, and recorded in English, certainly suggests that miracles do not just happen to anyone. You have to cultivate them, like the discontented young barman (Mick Ford) who goes to work with a cantankerous old eccentric (a performance by Trevor Howard that shows how good an actor he really can be) at a tumbledown garage, no longer operating, way out in the country. Over a period of many weeks the boy is given useless tasks. He mans a petrol pump on a deserted road but it holds no petrol. He polishes all the decaying cars in the junkyard next door. He is not allowed to know what the old man is doing in his locked shed. But when the boy has almost burned himself to death in a fit of fury, he learns, having passed some obscure test, that Trevor Howard is making wings with which to fly. Howard sends the boy to trap an eagle, whose blood is needed for the final flight. The boy does this. It is all a very complicated rite of passage, some sort of Zen and the Art of Wing Maintenance.

Dominique Labourier, on the steps, is Julie, awaiting the arrival of her friend Céline (Juliet Berto) who has just erupted from a haunted house, and instantly forgotten what happened inside. It is just one of those days in the fantastic Paris of Jacques Rivette's imagination in Céline and Julie Go Boating *(Films du Losange, 1974).*

And then, after all this careful build-up of an old man's madness, his absurd aspirations, comes the miracle. He straps on his wings, smears himself with bird's blood, and without any fuss at all flies off into the night. It is superb. He had planned to fly over Light Years, but in fact he is brought down twenty miles away, by the eagle, who has pecked his eyes out. But that, curiously, does not matter. The boy inherits the garage and the obsession.

Woody Allen is the mild inventor in *A Midsummer Night's Sex Comedy* (1982) who can also fly. It is early this century, in a pleasant old rural farmhouse somewhere in New York State, and his helicopter works by pedal power. Two ill-assorted couples join him and his wife (Mary Steenburgen) for the weekend. One man (José Ferrer) is a distinguished professor, a ruthless pragmatist who thinks magic is nonsense. During the enchanted evening that follows, a protracted summer twilight with waving trees and little animals and mysterious will-o'-the-wisp lights (glowingly photographed by Gordon Willis), Ferrer is the first victim of magic, in a piece of gentle but obvious irony. Reverting to snorting, Neanderthal behaviour, he finally dies in the throes of orgasm with another man's girlfriend (couples are changing and melting into one another's arms throughout this erotic, suspended period of not-quite-dying day), only to float as yet another softly glowing sphere, hovering over the garden, which by now has become a Garden of Eden. All sexual difficulties and jealousies (some of them more 1980s than 1900s in style) are finally reconciled in this tenderest, most softly sentimental of modern fantasies, where the numinous fertility of nature is too strong to be overwhelmed by the distinctly urban one-liners that Allen cannot resist. It is all reminiscent, strangely enough, of J.M. Barrie's half-forgotten magic play *Dear Brutus*, though the more immediately obvious sources are the Shakespeare play, the Mendelssohn music, and Ingmar Bergman's *Smiles of a Summer Night*. It is a very likeable film.

Children's fantasy

Some adult fantasy, like *A Midsummer Night's Sex Comedy*, is more authentically child-like than the slightly mechanical fantasies that are specially designed for children. We have already considered one of the latter, *Chitty Chitty Bang Bang* (see Chapter Four). Many others of the same kind, of course, were Walt Disney films.

Two of the more notable Disneys were *The Love Bug* (1968) and *Bedknobs and Broomsticks* (1971). *The Love Bug* was an enormous success and had three sequels (see under "Herbie" in the filmography) but, as light fantasies go, it is rather heavyhanded. The central conceit of the intelligent VW beetle car with a mind of its own is well worked out, with some excellent special effects. The plot

about evil David Tomlinson trying to steal the car from nice Dean Jones, however, is strictly routine melodrama, over-acted, and the long race sequence at the end arouses no tension or anxiety at all. As every four-year-old in the audience knows, no matter what dirty tricks are pulled by Tomlinson, there's no way Herbie isn't going to win.

Bedknobs and Broomsticks has a slightly more resonant story. Angela Lansbury is the matronly witch on England's South Coast who has some irritating cockney children billeted with her during the war. Gradually she softens towards them, and together they perform lots of magic (involving a flying bed that travels to where you wish it when you twist the bedknob) and defeat a rather tiny Nazi invasion. The effects are well achieved, especially the showy last sequence where suits of armour which once belonged to ancient knights are brought to life, to do battle with the astonished Germans. The team of Danny Lee, Eustace Lycett and Alan Maley, three of Disney's top effects wizards, received an Academy Award for their work on the film.

The two Muppet films, *The Muppet Movie* (1979) and *The Great Muppet Caper* (1981), made by the team that went on to make the puppet sorcery epic *Dark Crystal*, did very well for Lord Lew Grade's British production company ITC. The Muppets were enormously popular on television, and there is no denying they are monstrously endearing little creatures—or, sometimes, endearingly monstrous. But *The Muppet Movie*, which tells of the odyssey of a number of Muppets to Hollywood where they intend to make good and sign "the standard rich and famous contract", leaves them oddly lonely, outside the cosy context of their shabby vaudeville theatre, and Kermit is terribly sentimentalised, singing marshmallow frog ditties of a nauseating kind.

The Great Muppet Caper is an altogether more delicately confident affair. Forget the plot (Muppets solve mysterious jewel robberies), and concentrate on the marvellous Hollywood parodies, in which Miss Piggy is especially appealing doing Busby Berkeley style musical numbers. Gonzo, the innocently sinister vulture, is here a newspaper photographer. Few will forget him leaning out of a window and saying "Smile!" to an astonished pigeon. The most notable guest-star cameo is from top-drawer John Cleese who lives at 17 Highbrow Street. It is all a bit crowded and frantic though; the Muppet movies tend to try too hard.

Unfortunately, the most memorable children's fantasy of the 1970s was a flop so great that the financing company (Quaker Oats, no less) never made another film. Now, however, it is showing signs of becoming a small-scale cult classic. This was *Willy Wonka and the Chocolate Factory* (1971), starring Gene

Wilder as the eponymous Wonka.

Enough candy for a lifetime can be won by the children who find the five golden tickets inside Wonka candy bars. Four particularly revolting children win tickets, and so does Charlie, a nice ordinary boy. The prize involves a trip round the factory, which proves to be a sinister fantasyland where literally sticky ends are a constant risk. Wonka is aggressive, mysterious and unpredictable; it is really quite a menacing performance, not at all what we expect in a children's film. The four nasty children receive bizarre and violent punishments for being greedy and spoiled. The chocolate factory is a place of surreal threat, with, for example, the image of a beheaded chicken cast on the walls of the tunnel traversed by the *S.S. Wonkatania*. Fortunately Charlie does not go through with his plan to steal an Everlasting Gobstopper and give it to Wonka's competitors. When he returns the candy, Wonka instantly becomes benign – becomes, indeed, the father Charlie never had. Charlie, when the time comes, will become the new king of the Chocolate Factory.

Leslie Bricusse's songs (as in the case of *Doctor Dolittle*) are unmemorable, but the lurid dangers of the factory (no patronizing of children by giving them only the sunny side of life here) are well worth watching.

Comic-book fantasies

There is quite a tradition of basing fantastic films on popular comics. (These are not necessarily children's films. After all, lots of grown-ups read comics too.) For examples, see *Barbarella* in Chapter Three, *Flash Gordon* and *Popeye* in Chapter Four, and *Buck Rogers*, *The Incredible Hulk*, *Dr Strange*, *Spider-Man* and *Swamp Thing* in the filmography. But of all such adaptations, by far the most successful were *Superman*, *Superman II* and *Superman III*.

All the *Superman* films are enjoyable (fans have arguments about which is the best – I slightly incline to the second), and so they should be, because they took astronomical amounts of money to make. The first two together cost 109 million dollars, and it was partly because of the wildly escalating budget that Richard Donner, the director of *Superman* (his previous big film was *The Omen*), was replaced by Richard Lester during the shooting of *Superman II*. Parts of *Superman II*, in fact, were filmed at the same time as *Superman*, but around 75% of the film consists of Lester's work, filmed later.

Many of Lester's previous films had contained fantasy elements, notably the two Beatles Movies, but his only fully fledged fantasy, *The Bed Sitting Room* (see below), had been a flop. Lester also made *Superman III*.

Superman (Christopher Reeve) has temporarily lost his superpowers in Superman III *(Dovemead/Cantharus 1983), and is not very happy about it. Richard Lester, the director, took some liberties with the dignity of America's national superhero in this film, and some of Supie's fans were appalled.*

Both Donner and Lester had had to learn a great deal about special-effects shooting. All three films make copious use of miniatures, and flying on wires against a back-projection screen. But the success of the three films owes more to a judicious compound of humorous and mythic elements than it does to special effects *per se*. What makes them such fun is that they take themselves just seriously enough; they are not parody or spoof in any obvious way, but there are tongue-in-cheek moments, many of the best arising out of the helpless lasciviousness felt by Lois Lane (a witty performance by Margot Kidder) whenever she is in Superman's company. The first time she flies with him, in *Superman* (1978) is, in fact, quite genuinely erotic, surprisingly so in this sort of film; one remembers Freud's insistence that dreams of flight are dreams of sexual intercouse, and it is precisely this blend of dreaminess and sensual excitement that Kidder's performance captures.

Christopher Reeve is superbly cast in the dual role of Superman and Clark Kent. He is a good actor, who not only projects handsomeness and sincerity; he also evokes the sense of the innocent abroad that was always part of Superman's characterisation, even in the original comics of the 1930s. Superman's arrival in the bustling big city of New York, the third sequence of the tri-partite *Superman*, is quite touchingly confusing for him: the Man of Steel as Candide, the kid from the sticks.

Both the directors, and the screenwriters too, are obviously sophisticates. There is no shame for intellectuals in enjoying these witty and intelligent movies. Take, for example, the visual pleasantry of the second part of *Superman*, in which we witness our hero's childhood in Norman Rockwell's Middle America. The visual homage to a way of life that is itself every bit as mythic as Superman, a glowing never-was land of decent folk and rolling prairies, is very well done.

When Lester took over, the emphasis shifted slightly from mythic resonance to an ironic humour, which recalls at times the pop-art gleefulness of *Hard Day's Night* and *Help!* The story line of *Superman II* (1980) involves the three imprisoned Kryptonite rebels from the previous film breaking free and planning to conquer Earth with their superpowers. Superman, unfortunately, has succumbed to the lure of Lois Lane, and potency in bed proves to be incompatible with potency of the supermuscular variety. He is like the magicians of yore whose magic was tied to celibacy: to become a lover, he has to relinquish his Superman image. (Some people hated this demystifying of America's great Icon.) But all ends well in the highly satisfying and protracted finale, where enormous chaos is wrought by all combatants in a sequence as close to the anarchic tab-leaux of comic-strip imagery as the cinema has ever reached.

Superman is humanized even further in *Superman III* (1983), a slightly incoherent concoction that has black comedian Richard Pryor becoming a super-villain against his own better judgement. Superman has a new romance this time, with the convincing Lana Lang (Annette O'Toole), who interestingly falls for Clark Kent, where Lois Lane had gone for the man in the blue and red underwear. But Superman is badly affected by synthetic Kryptonite, and goes bad. "I hope you don't expect me to save you, 'cos I don't do that nice stuff anymore" he sneers at a woman in trouble, and takes to brooding in bars. After a fight between his good and bad selves, everything turns out all right. We may feel a legitimate dismay at the distance we have travelled from Superman as a dignified incarnation of slightly priggish human decency, but there is no denying that Richard Lester has few equals as choreographer of comedy. The long opening sequence of escalating slapstick gags that begins with a pretty girl walking past and ends with total chaos is probably finer than anything since Mack Sennett.

Computer world

An alternative to adapting comic strips is creating them, and that is what Steven Lisberger, a young man previously known for his animated feature cartoon *Animalympics*, did with *Tron* (1982). It did not do very well at the box-office, but it was one of the best Disney films for years.

A brilliant young computer expert, seeking evidence that there is dirty work afoot in the communications outfit ENCOM, is attacked by the Master Control Program, atomized and inserted as an electronic simulation into the circuitry of the computer, where he is forced to become the target in a variety of sadistic computer game scenarios. He meets other sub-programs Tron and Yori, analogues created by programmer friends he had in real life. Together, overcoming many fiendish, comic-strip obstacles, they seek out the vicious Master Control Program and destroy it. (The structure of this film bears a marked resemblance to *The Wizard of Oz* in which Dorothy meets similar analogues.)

The landscapes inside the computer are a phantasmagoria of light and colour. Unfortunately, one early sequence – a chase on light-cycles which leave a wake of solid colour wherever they go – is so strong and beautiful that nothing later in the film can match it. All the scenes that take place within the computer were in real life computer-animated, we are told, though there is probably a publicity element in this (the main characters seem to be humans in suits with light-strip decorations). Certainly the computer scenes represent a breakthrough to new concepts of animation, though the success is a little uneven. It is the wit and good humour of the script that makes the film so pleasant – for example, the threat to an underling program that if he does not behave himself he'll finish up doing time in a pocket calculator.

The last scene of the film, in one brilliant stroke, proposes an entirely new, metaphysical subtext. We are back in the real world, looking down at the lights of Los Angeles. There is something very familiar about the grid patterns of light, the little moving dots of vehicles. Visually, this is the world of the computer all over again. Are we all sub-programs whose actions are controlled at the whims of some great Master Control Program in the sky? And if so, should we revolt? In retrospect, the entire film is a light-hearted text about determinism.

Charisma

Some of us, of course, are Master Control Programs in our own right. A recurrent figure of fantasy cinema is the charismatic, the miracle worker, the Rasputin. A new dualism of conjuror/magician, or fraudulence/candour, emerges here – yet another variation on the appearance/reality theme that we have seen so often already.

The cult movie *El Topo* (1971) presents one of the weirdest of all charismatic figures, the eponymous El Topo, The Mole, played by its eccentric writer-director, who appears in virtually every scene – a Chilean of Russian descent called Alexandro Jodorowsky. El Topo rides in black leather through the desert, accompanied by a naked little boy, his son. They enter a frontier town littered with disembowelled corpses, and encounter fetishistic bandits who fondle shoes, and monks, whose leader they castrate. The boy is abandoned. Taking a woman, El Topo goes back to the desert where he duels with the Four Masters, Zen gunslingers, who are said to be faster on the draw than he. Events acelerate. Mad with guilt at having used dirty tricks in these duels, he allows himself to be crucified, is resurrected, lives with dwarfs and cripples, meets homosexual cowboys, decimates a township, sets fire to himself, dies. His honeyed grave is covered with bees.

This cross between spaghetti western and religious allegory is pure surrealism. El Topo may be God or the Devil, but, whatever the case, Jodorowsky is obviously having a great time. He has an energetic visual sense, and while the film is often irritating, it is seldom boring. The film became an important cultural artefact for the Hippy movement in America, but never really caught on in Europe, despite its occasionally Buñuelian manner.

In Jerzy Skolimowski's *The Shout* (1978), filmed in North Devon, the charismatic figure is wild-eyed Alan Bates, who invites himself to the home of John Hurt, a composer of the kind of electronic music that incorporates all sorts of everyday sounds. Like the Man Who Came to Dinner, Bates stays on, humiliates his host, seduces his wife (Susannah York), perhaps by magic, and tells stories about the things he learned from his eighteen years with the Australian aborigines, notably how to kill with a magic shout. Hurt demands a demonstration, and down in the sand dunes he is given one. It seems to work, though Hurt is stunned, not killed. He awakes holding a stone which makes him hallucinate that he is a cobbler, but when he realizes it may be the secret repository of Bates's soul he smashes it open. Bates is then arrested for the murder of his four children.

This tall story, which we do not necessarily believe, is recounted by the Bates character during a gentle, lazy, sunlit cricket match which, it transpires, is taking place in the grounds of an insane asylum. About to demonstrate the killing shout again at the end, Bates is struck by lightning. This is a subtle, malicious, intricate film, with a complex subtext about sex and power, appearance and reality. Luminously photographed, edited with a series of enigmatic, sometimes lovely juxtapositions, it is more truly fantastic than almost any sword and sorcery film you care to name.

The Australian film *Harlequin* (1980) is more commonplace. It retells the story of Rasputin in the context of modern American politics. Robert Powell is the mysterious, aggressive healer of the Senator's child and seducer of the Senator's wife, who may be a confidence trickster (he dresses sometimes as a jester) and may be a magician. A scene where he beheads a live pigeon at a dinner party by hurling a cymbal at it with supernatural force suggests the latter, as does his effortless escape from prison. It is all rather incoherent, but contains some startling images amid all the hoop-la. There is rather a draggy sub-plot about political corruption.

The magic circus comes to town again

Something Wicked This Way Comes (1982) is the first fantasy film made by Jack Clayton since *The Innocents* (see Chapter Two). Co-produced by Disney, it went through tremendous upheavals during the production period, with Clayton being over-ruled on several key issues. A new, embarrassingly sentimental ending was shot, a lot of Disneyish special effects were inserted (also a new scene, which Clayton did quite like, about small boys being menaced in their bedroom by magical tarantulas), and a new musical score was commissioned. All this held up the film's release until 1983, and those who had heard the rumours were gloomily expecting the worst.

Actually, *Something Wicked* is very good. The visiting circus (see also *7 Faces of Dr*

David Warner plays a villain, as usual, in the otherwise unusual film Tron *(Disney, 1982), much of which takes place inside a computer. The spectaculously colourful computer sequences were, in real life, created by a computer: a movie breakthrough. Warner is an unscrupulous control program called Sark.*

Lao, Chapter Two, and *Vampire Circus*, Chapter Six) is a neat symbol of the entrance of fantasy into the routine lives of ordinary people, and the people in this film could hardly be more ordinary. The film is set in the 1930s in an idyllically peaceful, commonplace Mid-Western town. But the visiting carnival is run by Mr Dark, a seductive, strong personality (well played by Jonathan Pryce), who lures people to lose their souls by giving them the illusion that they have attained their dearest wish. Thus a spinster schoolmarm becomes young and beautiful, a maimed shopkeeper becomes an athlete. But two small boys see through the attactive facade of the carnival to the evil beneath. Symbolically they are fair and dark, wholly innocent in one case, but trembling on the brink of puberty in the other, and therefore more vulnerable to the adult-oriented seductions on display.

Clayton, a past master at creating atmosphere, adopts a low-key approach to his gradual revelations, but he was partially overruled, and there are some rather conventional horror-film set-pieces as well. It is a good story – certainly the best adaptation of a Ray Bradbury story on the screen – which is given a sad resonance by its sub-plot of children who do not feel close enough to their parents (to a father in one case, and to a mother in the other). But it is the father (a melancholy, attractive performance by Jason Robards) who finally saves the day, trapping Mr Dark on his own magic carousel (which travels through time) until he ages and decays into a mummified corpse.

Mr Dark is another personification of the Rasputin figure. There is, however, one interesting fantasy film whose hero is precisely the reverse: an anti-charismatic. The film is

Woody Allen's *Zelig* (1983). Zelig (Allen) is a man so intent on passing unnoticed that he has become a kind of human chameleon. Paradoxically, he becomes famous for this, and again we see a touch of the magic circus. His ability to blend in (we have already seen him as a baseball player and a Chinese) is discovered by Dr Eudora Fletcher (Mia Farrow), and he becomes an exploitable freak once this is known. Kidnapped (like the Elephant Man), he becomes a sideshow display, but he escapes, later turning up in the Vatican. Eudora finds him (they are now falling in love) but again he is lost, and the pair are not reunited until she locates him sitting just behind Hitler at a Nazi rally.

The whole complex parody sums up Woody Allen's career; the more he played the role of the barely visible *nebbish*, the more famous he became. It is a good joke, and the fantasy is strengthened by the extraordinary skill with which footage of Allen is seamlessly incorporated into newsreel footage of the 1920s (in which the film is set). But in the end it is a joke that (deliberately?) disappears up its own backside. If the magical little man does not exist except as a shadow, then history (which sees him as famous, as Susan Sontag, Bruno Bettelheim and Saul Bellow attest in their own persons in the movie) is itself fantasy. Perhaps the whole thing is an obscure critique of Charlie Chaplin. The skills of the anti-magician are just as mysterious as the skills of the magician.

Fantasies inside the head

Psychologists tell us that all fantasy springs from the mind. There is an interesting cinematic sub-genre whose only fantastic element is that the audience is allowed to share in the hallucinations of a tormented

mind, and each of us becomes a schizophrenic at first remove. It is interesting how readily we recognize these subjective nightmares of isolated people. Jung's theory of archetypes is, for the moment, vindicated.

One of the prototypes of this kind of film is Roman Polanski's *Repulsion* (1965, see filmography), but in the period we are now considering, the most distinguished example is Bergman's *Hour of the Wolf* (1968). This could well have figured as one of the key fantasies from 1968 that we discussed in Chapter Three, except that it is so far removed from genre fantasy that its direct relevance is limited.

Hour of the Wolf tells of a painter, Johan (Max von Sydow), and his wife, Alma (Liv Ullmann), arriving on a lonely island for a holiday. He feels that his creativity is fading, and is tormented by internal demons which, as the film progresses, begin to take external shape. Using character names borrowed from the Gothic writer E.T.A. Hoffman, and using visual imagery which owes a great deal to the B-movie traditions of horror cinema, Bergman builds to a climax in which Johan enters a castle and attends a nightmare dinner party, where he is attacked (both verbally and physically) by Gothic manifestations of his despair. Among them are a Birdman (earlier, as in the Hitchcock film, he was attacked by small birds), an old woman who peels off her face to reveal the skull beneath, and his ex-lover Veronica Vogler, now a member of the living dead; he couples with her to the jeers of the demons in the mud and the darkness. All of this takes place during the Hour of the Wolf, that hour of night when the psyche is at its weakest. Johan's final descent to a pit of abnormality from which there is no apparent escape is cruelly pictured.

Earlier we have seen the possibility of his becoming reconciled to life, especially through his pregnant wife, who is associated throughout with images of abundance, fertility and (less portentously) a wholly natural affection. On the other hand, the story of the film is told, at the beginning, as recalled by the wife, which confuses further the already baffling nature of the reality depicted. It is possible, for example, that the dinner-party of Hell, within the castle, was merely a distorted, expressionist version of a perfectly real dinner party attended by Johan. Because we see, apparently, through his eyes, we never know.

Polanski's *The Tenant* (1976) tells a comparable story. Polanski himself plays the central figure, a withdrawn, likeable, nervous young man who moves into an apartment (in a rather grim old building) which was previously occupied by a girl who tried to commit suicide. The longer he stays there, the more remote he becomes from everyday life, and after a time he is not even able to accept the sexual consolation offered to him by a generous, outgoing girl (Isabelle Adjani). Paranoid hallucinations (which we share) begin to multiply. Through his window (which overlooks a courtyard) we see a shadowy figure standing immobile in the communal lavatory for hours. He takes to dressing in the suicide girl's clothes, and wearing her makeup. When he buys cigarettes, he orders her brand. The pressure towards his repetition of her suicide is remorseless (immediately preceded by a vision of his own head bouncing through the air like a ball). Appallingly, when he hurls himself from the window he is not killed, and painfully he drags himself upstairs to do it again, surrounded by the other tenants (witches, or ordinary people, we no

The forces of oppression are gathering in the claustrophobic film Pink Floyd The Wall (Tin Blue – Goldcrest/ MGM, 1982). The movie has some exciting images, but the story it tells is – to put it politely – self-pitying and banal.

longer know). At the end he is lying in hospital, screaming from within the bandages that totally enwrap him, a mirror image of the opening shot of the suicide-girl, but this time the subjective camera angle suggest that he is us. Oddly, Polanski's inquisitive, roaming camera (much use of the Louma Crane), and his interest in the small mannerisms of people, give the film quite a lively feeling, mercifully at odds with its depressing content.

Pink Floyd The Wall (1982), a surrealist film made by Alan Parker to embody the music from Pink Floyd's album of the same title, shows how not to do this sort of thing. Looming expressionist scenery, masks, distorted faces, hallucinatory flashbacks to traumatic episodes of childhood and youth, and even sadistically Protean cartoon sequences animated from designs by caricaturist Gerald Scarfe, are meant to picture for us the disintegrating life of the rock star played by Bob Geldof. Such is the overkill effect of this prolonged, hysterical, self-pitying scream that we could not care less. If the hero, Pink, is trapped behind the big symbolic wall of the title, well, so what? We don't care, either, when he smashes it down. It is a film of staggering vulgarity.

Surrealism as social criticism

There has always been in surrealism a strong element of shocking the bourgeois. Conversely, those who want to put sacred cows through the meat-grinder are very apt to choose surrealist devices for setting about the job. Surrealism – a basically absurd form – is well adapted to puncturing pomposity and lampooning bombast. It is almost too well adapted to the job, because its devices can be used rather mechanically. A surrealist film is not necessarily an imaginative film.

Surrealism thrives on the escalation of small, disturbing incidents into full-bodied chaos. Most of us, in part of our minds, rather like the idea of seeing society blown magnificently apart. Half the fun of building a sand castle is seeing the tide come in and washing it away, when it is finished and frozen. Real society, of course, is not a sand castle, but the impulse remains, though it is naturally repressed in polite circles. It is this same impulse that has led to the ongoing tradition of anarchic, surrealist satire, sometimes comic, sometimes not, that has characterized fantastic cinema of the past two decades.

The master of this kind of film was the late Luis Buñuel, who was permitted, even encouraged by middle-class society all around the world, to play anarchic games. This was, perhaps, because so long as they could be perceived as games, they were distanced and not threatening. Thus arose his slightly equivocal position, over the last decades of his life (he died in 1983), as licensed jester to the courts of the bourgeoisie.

The Discreet Charm of the Bourgeoisie (1972) makes the point immediately in its ironic but not untruthful title. Guests arrive for dinner on the wrong evening; they are taken to a restaurant, but a funeral is about to take place there; the following day the guests arrive again, but their hosts have capitulated to uncontrollable erotic urges and are coupling in the garden; a Bishop arrives and asks for the post of gardener (after initial doubts he is hired); a young soldier tells a ghost story in a tea room (it is horrible and bloody – we see it ourselves); an adulterous assignation between two of the earlier dinner guests is interrupted; a third attempt at a dinner party is foiled by the arrival of billeted troops; a Sergeant tells another ghost story; the fourth attempt at dinner is a dream sequence where the poultry is made of plaster and a curtain lifts to reveal that the table is on the stage of a theatre; the Bishop hears a confession, absolves the sinner and shoots him; a third ghost story is told; at the fifth attempt at dinner, terrorists enter and shoot the guests. So far nobody in the film has managed to eat anything at all. A guest reveals himself by reaching to take some meat from a plate from beneath the table where he had crawled; he is shot; waking up from this nightmare, he goes to the refrigerator for a snack.

These crazy juxtapositions, where violence and intimations of death continually intrude on a group of elegant gourmets, whose lives are only minimally disturbed by these events, are created with calm panache. Society is corrupt but unflappable. At all levels it requires the satisfaction of its appetites for sex and food. The world of gentility and the world of horror do indeed collide, but somehow the impact is muffled. Perhaps one of these worlds is a dream, but which one?

Discreet Charm is a model of linear narration compared to the spiralling, contorted structure of Buñuel's next film, *The Phantom of Liberty* (1974). Unlike the previous film, this does actually end in social apocalypse, as open revolt breaks out at the zoo, observed by a curious ostrich that fails to bury its head in the sand, unlike another ostrich that appears in a man's bedroom earlier on. The film consists of a series of unfinished stories, a minor character in one becoming the protagonist of the next. They are tall stories, of the kind that get an immediate easy laugh, and then, when they sink in, a more choked, difficult laugh: as when, in one story, a doctor offers a patient, who has just been told that he is suffering from terminal lung cancer, a consolatory cigarette. In another episode, distraught parents search for their missing daughter, who is in fact there all the time, but she cannot attract their attention to let them know. A pervert gives dirty postcards to children in the park; the shocked parents confiscate them and then become excited themselves by what they show; the postcards are, in fact, landscapes. A police inspector is telephoned by his dead sister; rushing to the family crypt he finds that the phone is off the hook. At yet another Buñuelian dinner-party, the guests sit around the table on toilet bowls, into which they occasionally relieve themselves; conversation is sophisticated and unconcerned; every now and then one excuses himself and goes furtively off to a private cabinet to eat.

Social surfaces are more important than the realities that lie beneath. Beneath the surface of the film – not far beneath – the characters are half in love with death. A mad rooftop sniper becomes a popular hero. At the film's opening, an execution scene prettily parodying a Goya painting of the same subject, Buñuel himself has a walk-on part as a man patiently waiting to be shot. The film ends in gunfire. The surrealist disjunctions of *Phantom of Liberty* point in a darker direction than those in *Discreet Charm* (as does its title), which may be why this superficially affable, jokey film never had quite the popular success of its predecessor; it is probably the greater film of the two.

More surrealist satires

Many more surrealist satires of the recent period have aroused a good deal of discussion, though none can compete with Buñuel's work.

In opalescent, beautifully photographed imagery, Borowczyk's *The Beast* (1975) tells a bawdy story of a young American heiress who is to marry the scion of an aristocratic French family. At the family's chateau we see the husband-to-be brooding over his favourite stallion mating with a mare. The girl arrives. All is not well in the chateau. There is a family legend of a were-beast in the woods. The girl has a long, erotic dream of her rape by this beast, a cheerfully attractive creature midway between a bear and a wolf. She awakes and masturbates (this *is* a pornographic film). She dreams again. The beast dies in the throes of orgasm. Awake, she finds that her brutish fiancé lies dead. When he is laid out, we learn that he has a paw, a body covered with hair, a tail. Of few films can one say that the imagery is *literally* ravishing, but this is one. Again and again the camera lingers on an apparent irrelevance: a snail, for example, crawling over a delicate satin shoe. It all adds up to a remarkably light-hearted essay in eroticism (and, along the way, anti-clericalism), and is, perhaps, to be commended for confronting the issues that lie behind such fantastic classics as *Beauty and the Beast* and *Cat People*. The film's perversity is all in the spirit of a rather rude game.

Fellini Satyricon (1969) is also a film that features much eroticism (largely homosexual) as a central feature of its chastising of soci-

ety. The setting is ancient Rome, envisaged as a phantasmagoric place, inhabited (during the period of its decline) by persons so bizarre that they might as well be Martians. (Fellini has said that he saw the work as a science-fiction film about aliens.) The film is a glum masque, with almost no story, and tells rather ponderously how the death of the spirit cannot be compensated for by the febrile life of the body. The usual grossly fat women that haunt Fellini appear several times. Many of the characters in the film are bestial, appearing like birds, reptiles, insects.

Sexual satire takes a much more life-enhancing form in Woody Allen's collection of absurd anecdotes, *Everything You Always Wanted to Know About Sex* *But Were Afraid to Ask* (1972). This features a frigid woman who discovers she can find satisfaction by making love publicly in department stores; a medieval jester whose love for his lady is frustrated by her chastity belt; a psychiatrist treating a sodomite and then falling in love and finally eloping with the unfortunate man's partner, a particularly beautiful sheep; a teenage couple menaced by a giant breast created by mad scientist John Carradine; and other such fantasies. The film tells us little we do not already know about the factors that make anybody's sex life hardly worth pursuing, but it tells us engagingly.

British apocalypse

The English director Lindsay Anderson is fascinated by images of absurd apocalypse. One of his earlier films, *If...* (1968), goes one further than Vigo's *Zéro de Conduite* (see

The characters in Fellini Satyricon (Artistes Associés, 1969) are so exotically alien that the film – as Fellini himself remarked – could almost be taken as science fiction. Not all of them are as pretty as this.

filmography), and amusingly describes a boy's public school where repressive authoritarianism gets its comeuppance in the form of active revolt; machine-gun wielding students have a good time. One of the boys is played by Malcolm McDowell, who starred in a later Anderson film, *O Lucky Man!* (1973), another intransigently British piece of work that failed to win many friends across the Atlantic. McDowell plays the coffee salesman whose surrealist rise and fall the film chronicles, as he passes through a sinister landscape peopled by maniacal British stereotypes, mad scientists, warmongers. In a secret experimental hospital he stumbles across experiments in organ-grafting that include the creation of a man with the body of a pig. With sublime insouciance, McDowell, a lucky man, wins his way back to the top.

This kind of approach was beginning to look more like formula by the time of Anderson's *Britannia Hospital* (1982). The establishment of the symbolic title suffers from workers in revolt outside, loony trade unionists inside, an incipient Royal visit, and a doctor conducting more Frankenstein-style organ-grafting experiments of a peculiarly gory kind. Sometimes enjoyable but terribly messy, the film knocks over so many satirical targets in its surreal picture of Britain in a state of terminal disintegration that one cannot tell from what platform, what moral position if any, the satire is being conducted. The film is a prolonged hysterical scream; it flails about and collapses in exhaustion.

Richard Lester's *The Bed Sitting Room* (1969) is a sad comedy about a nation that has already suffered its apocalypse. In the ruins left after the holocaust, the gallant survivors attempt, against all the odds, to patch together workable lives. One character is mutating into a bed-sitting room, another into a parrot. The only person left to be Queen of England is Mrs Ethel Shroake. The police force drifts disconsolately overhead in a balloon. It was a brave attempt by Lester, but the jokes echo thinly in this scabby wasteland, and the film finally subsides limply into its own vision of bleakness, though it does linger in the memory.

Decay

Fantastic cinema has a great capacity for producing resilient, optimistic images. It was not planned that this survey, which has covered so much vigorous and ebullient work, should trail sadly away into a vista of decay. Only when one comes to consider the recent history of surrealism quite closely does its consistent pessimism become apparent. Perhaps it is appropriate that entropy – the tendency of stars to get colder, metal to rust, love to fade and people to die – should enter the picture here. Entropy is characteristic of endings rather than beginnings, though the thermodynamics experts tell us

that it was implicit in the first instants of the universe.

It is certainly very obvious in Volker Schlöndorff's *The Tin Drum* (1979), a quite literal adaptation of Günter Grass's famous novel, which is notable for its hero's refusal to grow up, its images of warfare and collapse, and a nasty picture of eels wriggling revoltingly in a decaying horse's head. From a child's or dwarf's eye view (it is never totally clear which of the two the hero is), even quite nice Germans, like the mother who dies from eating too much fish, tend to look gross and distorted. In some respects the hero does not remain entirely a child; his sex life is displayed to us with no tenderness, only disgust. His ability (like the hero of *The Shout*) to break things with his voice seems merely destructive. All the way through, to the beating of his little tin drum, Germany moves inexorably through anti-semitism to persecution and then holocaust. There is something a little spurious about this (the film, not the book) – a perversion of fantastic imagery into the kind of radical chic whose essence is grotesquerie and nausea. The performance of twelve-year-old David Bennent as the tantrum-prone, warped Peter Pan is staggeringly good.

Let us shrink from too close an analysis of Derek Jarman's *Jubilee* (1978), a film that was determined to crystallize everything that is wrong with Great Britain just in time for Queen Elizabeth's real-life Jubilee. The film is set in a future London, whose physical decay reflects the anti-heroic, punk ethos of its inhabitants, who seem to be largely in their early twenties. It is a bit like a punk *Fellini Satyricon* but the other way round. Here it is the past that was healthy (symbolized by Jenny Runacre's Queen Elizabeth I, who is given the power to glimpse episodes from the future), and the future that is decayed. A critic, Scott Meek, writes: "No synopsis could adequately convey the wealth of imaginative incident which fills *Jubilee* with a textual and thematic richness quite extraordinary in the field of British...production." I thought it stank: pretentious, theatrically decadent in an unreal sort of way, and boring. The much-touted punk ethos comes from the middle-class Chelsea fringe (several *Rocky Horror* alumni involved), not the street centre. Camp, adolescent cynicism abounds.

A happy ending

As a silly and feeble escape from the surrealist horrors of the present (and the recent past) there is the example of Billy Pilgrim, the optometrist who becomes unstuck in time in Kurt Vonnegut's novel *Slaughterhouse-Five*. This was filmed (1972) by George Roy Hill, sandwiched between his two successes of *Butch Cassidy* and *The Sting*.

Suburban Billy, nagged and pathetic, drifts back in time to the horrors of his incarcera-

tion in Dresden during the war and the saturation bombing of that murdered city, and forward to his ultimate and apparently pleasant incarceration as a kind of zoo display with sexpot actress Montana Wildhack in a glass cage on the planet Tralfamadore. In the book, this was a dark irony rather than a consummation devoutly to be wished, and the Tralfamadorians were aliens who believed that all cosmic reality runs in predestined grooves. Whatever dubious satirical point the book made (a nihilist one, it seems to me) is lost in the film, where Billy's ending is really something of a rest cure after everything else that has happened. It is merely flip, rather than satirical, and the vulgarity of comparing this *Playboy* fantasy with a real-life event of unfathomable horror (Dresden's bombing) shows exactly where fantastic cinema itself can become unstuck in time, or at least unrooted in any kind of value system. Satire about the lack of human values falls all too easily into the trap of displaying none itself.

Thus free-floating, fantastic images from the human psyche can appear on our cinema screens in contexts that trivialize, or contexts that deepen, our humanity. It has nowhere been the argument in this survey that the fantastic end of the cinematic spectrum has automatic claims on our attention that other types of movie do not have. But so long as the majority of film critics and film historians continue to regard fantastic cinema as the poor relation, as something of an embarrassment even now that it has come into money and dresses better (with all the vulgarity, of course, of the *nouveau riche*), then a survey of this kind will have a useful function. The function is to direct attention not just at the Buñuels and the Bergmans (we knew about those already), but at the Spielbergs and the Cronenbergs, the Larry Cohens, the Romeros and even the makers of films like *The Evil Dead*, who (to change the metaphor) toil in the same vineyards, and whose wine may be equally worth laying down in the cellars of the mind.

To the beat of little Oskar's tin drum, some dreadful things happen in The Tin Drum *(United Artists, 1979). Oskar, like Peter Pan, has decided never to grow up. The part is played with painfully convincing ferocity by a twelve-year-old actor, David Bennent.*

Chronology of 250

	1902	1919	1920	1922	1923	1924	1925	1926	1927	1929	1930	1931	1932	1933	1935	1936	1939	1940	1941
SCIENCE FICTION	• A TRIP TO THE MOON					• AELITA	• THE LOST WORLD	• METROPOLIS		• DIE FRAU IM MOND			• ISLAND OF LOST SOULS	• THE INVISIBLE MAN • KING KONG		• FLASH GORDON (SERIAL) • THINGS TO COME	• BUCK ROGERS (SERIAL)	• DR CYCLOPS	
HORROR		• THE CABINET OF DR CALIGARI	• DR JEKYLL & MR HYDE • THE GOLEM (REMAKE)	• NOSFERATU				• THE STUDENT OF PRAGUE	• LONDON AFTER MIDNIGHT		• DRACULA	• DR JEKYLL & MR HYDE (REMAKE) • FRANKENSTEIN • VAMPYR	• FREAKS • WHITE ZOMBIE		• THE BRIDE OF FRANKENSTEIN • MAD LOVE	• THE DEVIL-DOLL			• THE WOLFMAN
FANTASY					• DIE NIBELUNGEN • PARIS QUI DORT	• THE THIEF OF BAGDAD		• FAUST			• L'AGE D'OR					• THE WIZARD OF OZ	• THE THIEF OF BAGDAD (REMAKE)		• ALL THAT MONEY CAN BUY • HERE COMES MR JORDAN

	1959	1960	1961	1962	1963	1964	1965	1966	1967	1968	1969	1970	1971	1972	1973
SCIENCE FICTION		• JOURNEY TO THE CENTER OF THE EARTH • THE TIME MACHINE • THE VILLAGE OF THE DAMNED	• MYSTERIOUS ISLAND	• DR NO	• THE DAMNED • DR STRANGELOVE			• FAHRENHEIT 451 • FANTASTIC VOYAGE	• JE T'AIME, JE T'AIME • QUATERMASS & THE PIT	• BARBARELLA • CHARLY • PLANET OF THE APES • 2001: A SPACE ODYSSEY		• THE ANDROMEDA STRAIN • THE FORBIN PROJECT • THX 1138	• A CLOCKWORK ORANGE	• SILENT RUNNING • SOLARIS	• SLEEPER • SOYLENT GREEN • WESTWORLD • ZARDOZ
HORROR	• LES YEUX SANS VISAGE	• BLACK SUNDAY • THE CURSE OF THE WEREWOLF • HOUSE OF USHER • THE LITTLE SHOP OF HORRORS	• THE INNOCENTS		• THE BIRDS • THE HAUNTED PALACE • THE HAUNTING • X – THE MAN WITH X-RAY EYES	• KWAIDAN • THE MASQUE OF THE RED DEATH • TOMB OF LIGEIA	• REPULSION	• THE PLAGUE OF THE ZOMBIES		• NIGHT OF THE LIVING DEAD • ROSEMARY'S BABY • WITCHFINDER GENERAL			• VAMPIRE CIRCUS	• DEATH LINE • DUEL • SISTERS	• DON'T LOOK NOW • THE EXORCIST • IT'S ALIVE • THE WICKER MAN
FANTASY	• DARBY O'GILL & THE LITTLE PEOPLE		• LAST YEAR AT MARIENBAD		• JASON & THE ARGONAUTS • 7 FACES OF DR LAO	• MARY POPPINS	• THE SARAGOSSA MANUSCRIPT	• ONE MILLION YEARS BC	• DOCTOR DOLITTLE • WEEKEND	• FINIAN'S RAINBOW • HOUR OF THE WOLF	• FELLINI SATYRICON	• BREWSTER McCLOUD	• MALPERTUIS • EL TOPO	• THE DISCREET CHARM OF THE BOURGEOISIE • SLAUGHTERHOUSE-FIVE	• THE GOLDEN VOYAGE OF SINBAD • O LUCKY MAN!

Key Fantastic Films

1942–1958

1942
- CAT PEOPLE

1943
- I WALKED WITH A ZOMBIE
- THE SEVENTH VICTIM
- THE ADVENTURES OF BARON MUNCHAUSEN
- HEAVEN CAN WAIT

1944
- THE UNINVITED

1945
- DEAD OF NIGHT
- THE PICTURE OF DORIAN GRAY

1946
- BEAUTY & THE BEAST

1947
- THE GHOST & MRS MUIR

1948
- PORTRAIT OF JENNIE

1950
- DESTINATION MOON
- ORPHÉE

1951
- THE DAY THE EARTH STOOD STILL
- THE THING
- WHEN WORLDS COLLIDE
- THE TALES OF HOFFMAN

1952
- MONKEY BUSINESS
- LES BELLES DE NUIT

1953
- INVADERS FROM MARS
- IT CAME FROM OUTER SPACE
- THE WAR OF THE WORLDS
- THE 5,000 FINGERS OF DR T
- UGETSU MONOGATARI

1954
- THE CREATURE FROM THE BLACK LAGOON
- GODZILLA
- THEM!
- 20,000 LEAGUES UNDER THE SEA

1955
- QUATERMASS X-PERIMENT
- TARANTULA
- THIS ISLAND EARTH

1956
- FORBIDDEN PLANET
- INVASION OF THE BODY SNATCHERS

1957
- THE INCREDIBLE SHRINKING MAN
- THE CURSE OF FRANKENSTEIN
- NIGHT OF THE DEMON
- HERCULES
- THE SEVENTH SEAL

1958
- I MARRIED A MONSTER FROM OUTER SPACE
- DRACULA (REMAKE)
- THE FLY
- THE SEVENTH VOYAGE OF SINBAD

1974–1983

1974
- CELINE & JULIE GO BOATING

1975
- DARK STAR
- THE STEPFORD WIVES
- PHANTOM OF THE PARADISE
- SHIVERS
- YOUNG FRANKENSTEIN
- PICNIC AT HANGING ROCK
- TOMMY

1976
- A BOY & HIS DOG
- ROLLERBALL
- THE BEAST (LA BETE)
- JAWS
- THE ROCKY HORROR PICTURE SHOW

1977
- KING KONG (REMAKE)
- THE MAN WHO FELL TO EARTH
- CARRIE
- DEMON
- ERASERHEAD
- MARTIN
- THE OMEN
- SUSPIRIA
- JABBERWOCKY
- THE LAST WAVE
- SINBAD & THE EYE OF THE TIGER
- 3 WOMEN

1978
- CLOSE ENCOUNTERS OF THE THIRD KIND
- STAR WARS
- COMA
- DAWN OF THE DEAD
- THE MANITOU
- HEAVEN CAN WAIT (REMAKE)
- THE SHOUT
- SUPERMAN

1979
- THE BOYS FROM BRAZIL
- INVASION OF THE BODY SNATCHERS (REMAKE)
- THE FURY
- HALLOWEEN
- PHANTASM
- PIRANHA
- MONTY PYTHON'S LIFE OF BRIAN
- THE MUPPET MOVIE
- THE TIN DRUM

1980
- ALIEN
- THE BLACK HOLE
- MAD MAX
- MOONRAKER
- QUINTET
- STAR TREK THE MOTION PICTURE
- TIME AFTER TIME
- THE BROOD
- THE FOG
- NOSFERATU THE VAMPYRE
- POPEYE

1981
- ALTERED STATES
- THE EMPIRE STRIKES BACK
- SATURN 3
- SCANNERS
- THE ELEPHANT MAN
- THE HOWLING
- INFERNO
- THE SHINING

1982
- ESCAPE FROM NEW YORK
- MAD MAX 2
- AN AMERICAN WEREWOLF IN LONDON
- BASKET CASE
- GHOST STORY
- WOLFEN
- CLASH OF THE TITANS
- CONAN THE BARBARIAN
- DRAGONSLAYER
- EXCALIBUR
- QUEST FOR FIRE
- RAIDERS OF THE LOST ARK
- TIME BANDITS

1983
- ANDROID
- BLADE RUNNER
- E.T.
- THE THING (REMAKE)
- TRON
- VIDEODROME
- CAT PEOPLE (REMAKE)
- CREEPSHOW
- THE EVIL DEAD
- POLTERGEIST
- Q—THE WINGED SERPENT
- FANNY & ALEXANDER
- THE BEASTMASTER
- THE DARK CRYSTAL
- THE SWORD & THE SORCEROR
- BRAINSTORM
- RETURN OF THE JEDI
- STRANGE INVADERS
- WAR GAMES
- HALLOWEEN III
- THE HUNGER
- TWILIGHT ZONE THE MOVIE
- THE DEAD ZONE
- CHRISTINE
- KRULL
- SOMETHING WICKED THIS WAY COMES
- SUPERMAN III

Filmography

This is an alphabetical listing of 700 fantastic films, of which 300 have already been discussed in detail in the main text. The remaining 400 appear in this section only, where each now receives a brief critical description. The main listing is given under the title by which each film is best-known to viewers, or, if there is a title change between the USA and the UK, by the title used in the country of origin. Foreign-language films are normally indexed under their English title unless they are best known abroad under their original title as is the case, for example, with Buñuel's *L'Age d'Or*. Cross-references are given from variant titles (including original foreign title) to the main title. Alphabetical order is given as if the whole title were one word: thus *Alligator* precedes *All That Money Can Buy*.

Information is given in the following order:

TITLE (followed by variant titles)

STAR RATING (one to five stars) for quality (see Introduction)

SKULL RATING (one to three skulls) for Squeamish Factor (see Introduction)

MADE FOR TV (when relevant)

COUNTRY OR COUNTRIES OF ORIGIN AND DATE (see note below)

WHETHER BLACK-AND-WHITE (b/w) **OR COLOUR**

RUNNING TIME (see note (b) below)

PRODUCTION COMPANY AND/OR DISTRIBUTOR (Abbreviations are used here, as Warner for Warner Brothers, AIP for American International)

DIRECTOR (*D* is abbreviation)

PRODUCER (*P* is abbreviation)

WRITER (*W* is abbreviation; when screenplay is taken from an existing story, novel or play, this information is given)

MUSIC COMPOSER (*M* is abbreviation)

CINEMATOGRAPHER (*C* is abbreviation)

ART DIRECTOR or **PRODUCTION DESIGNER** (*AD* and *PD* are abbreviations)

SPECIAL EFFECTS (*SPFX* is abbreviation; these listings are selective, and some names are preceded by terms such as Visual, Make-up, Matte, when these credits are of some importance)

STARRING (a selective list of the main performers)

VIDEO AVAILABILITY (*V* is abbreviation; see Introduction for further details)

CAPSULE COMMENT (given only for films not covered in the main text; for the latter, consult the Index for page references)

Notes: (a) The date of a film can be problematical. One can take the copyright date or the date of first release. Where possible we have accepted the date given by the British Film Institute, which is normally copyright date. Where the date of release differs substantially from the copyright date, we have often noted this information. Students of film reference books will be familiar with this problem. It is amazing to see the variety of dates that can be given for a single film. Some American references, for example, give the date of American release for foreign films, rather than either the copyright date or original release date. (b) The length of a film is amazingly difficult to give with accuracy, and the figures provided here may not necessarily fit the version of the film you see yourself. It often happens that some minutes are cut from a film (especially in a foreign country whose standards are different) for reasons of censorship. Sometimes further editing of a film takes place before its overseas release or its second release, usually making it shorter but sometimes longer. Films on cable television are sometimes cut to fit them to specific time slots. Videotape lengths are almost invariably different from film lengths, because the system used to transfer films to tape speeds them up very slightly. As an example of the problems, the British videotape version of *Battle Beyond the Stars* runs six minutes shorter than the advertised original length. I do not know why, but the problem is unlikely to have been censorship. The cuts have a rather amusing effect. The film is based quite closely on *The Magnificent Seven* (itself based on the *The Seven Samurai*) but in the British videotape version it appears to be based on a film which, if it had a title, would have been *The Magnificent Six*. The seventh interstellar tough guy becomes visible for fewer than ten seconds at the end of the movie. When different and usually reliable sources give contradictory running times for a film, normally I have chosen the longer time. (c) In most cases we have given the credits listed above completely. In a very few cases the full information is no longer available. Credits for special effects, however, are selective, and given only when they seem relevant. We have often not given the author of an original story in cases where that story was never published.

THE ABOMINABLE DR PHIBES ★★★
UK 1971; colour; 94 mins; AIP/EMI; *D* Robert Fuest; *P* Louis M. Heyward; *W* James Whiton, William Goldstein; *M* Basil Kirchen, Jack Nathan; *C* Norman Warwick; *PD* Brian Eatwell; *SPFX* George Blackwell; *Starring* Vincent Price, Joseph Cotten, Hugh Griffith, Terry-Thomas; *V* Vestron (USA).

THE ABSENT-MINDED PROFESSOR ★★½
USA 1960; b/w; 97 mins; Disney; *D* Robert Stevenson; *P/W* Bill Walsh from the story "A Situation of Gravity" by Samuel W. Taylor; *M* George Bruns; *C* Edward Colman; *AD* Carroll Clark; *SPFX* Peter Ellenshaw, Eustace Lycett, (animation/photographic) Joshua Meador, also (photographic) Robert A. Mattey; *Starring* Fred MacMurray, Nancy Olson, Keenan Wynn, Tommy Kirk; *V* Disney (USA). One of the better Disneys. MacMurray, a likeable eccentric, invents anti-gravity substance. Witty and astonishing special effects sequences, especially with flying car. Inferior sequel was *Son of Flubber*, 1962.

THE ADVENTURES OF BARON MUNCHAUSEN (MÜNCHHAUSEN; aka BARON MUNCHAUSEN, THE AMAZING ADVENTURES OF BARON MUNCHAUSEN) ★★★★
Germany 1943; colour; 103 mins; Ufa; *D* Joseph von Baky; *W* Erich Kästner from the stories by Rudolph Erich Raspe; *M* G. Haentzschel; *C* Werner Krien; *AD* Werner Klein, (sets) Emil Hasler, Otto Gulstorff; *SPFX* Konstantin Jrmenin-Jschet; *Starring* Hans Albers, Brigitte Horney, Käthe Haack, Werner Scharf, Leo Slezak; *V* Thorn EMI (UK).

AELITA ★★★
USSR 1924; b/w; 78 mins; Mezhrabpom; *D* Jacob Protazanov; *W* Fyodor Otzep, Alexei Faiko from the novel by Alexei Tolstoy; *C* Yuri Zhelyabuzhky, E. Schoenemann; *AD* Victor Simov, Isaac Rabinovitch, Alexandra Exter, Sergei Kozlovsky; *Starring* Igor Ilinsky, Yulia Solntseva, Konstantin Eggert. Russian cosmonaut destroys corrupt Martian regime in the central sequence of this, one of the first interplanetary films. Stylized, expressionist sets, vigorous direction. Terribly dated now, but loonily entertaining still.

L'ÂGE D'OR ★★★★
France 1930; b/w; 65 mins; *D* Luis Buñuel; *P* Vicomte Charles de Noailles; *W* Salvador Dali, Luis Buñuel; *Starring* Gaston Modot, Lya Lys, Max Ernst, Pierre Prévert.

AI NO BOREI – *see* EMPIRE OF PASSION

THE ALCHEMIST ★ ☠
USA 1981; colour; 84 mins; Ideal; *D* Charles Band; *P* Lawrence Appelbaum; *W* Alan J. Adler; *C* Andrew W. Friend; *PD* Dale A. Pelton; *SPFX* (photographic) John Lambert and Paul Gentry; *Starring* Robert Ginty, Lucinda Dooling, John Sanderford; *V* Video Form (UK). Aaron, cursed with eternal life, meets reincarnation of the wife he accidentally killed in 1871; Hell opens (cut-price demons emerging), evil alchemist gets his. Typical aimless Charles Band low-budgeter.

ALIEN ★★★★ ☠
UK 1979; colour; 117 mins; Brandywine – Ronald Shusett/20th Century-Fox; *D* Ridley Scott; *P* Gordon Carroll, David Giler, Walter Hill; *W* Dan O'Bannon from a story by O'Bannon and Ronald Shusett, also Hill and Giler uncredited; *M* Jerry Goldsmith; *C* Derek Vanlint; *PD* Michael Seymour; *SPFX* (Alien design) H. R. Giger, (Alien head effects) Carlo Rambaldi, (small aliens) Roger Dicken; *Starring* Tom Skerritt, Sigourney Weaver, Veronica Cartwright, Harry Dean Stanton, John Hurt, Ian Holm, Yaphet Kotto; *V* CBS/Fox (UK and USA).

ALIEN ENCOUNTER – *see* STARSHIP INVASIONS

ALLIGATOR ★★★½ ☠
USA 1980; colour; 91 mins; Alligator Associates/Group 1; *D* Lewis Teague; *P* Brandon Chase; *W* John Sayles; *M* Craig Hundley; *C* Joseph Mangine; *SPFX* (Co-Ordinator) Richard O. Helmer; *Starring* Robert Forster, Robin Riker, Michael Gazzo, Dean Jagger, Henry Silva; *V* Intervision (UK), Catalina (USA).

ALL THAT MONEY CAN BUY (aka THE DEVIL AND DANIEL WEBSTER) ★★★
USA 1941; b/w; 112 mins; RKO; *D/P* William Dieterle; *W* Dan Totheroh, Stephen Vincent Benet from the story by Benet; *M* Bernard Herrmann; *C* Joseph August; *Starring* Walter Huston, Edward Arnold, Simone Simon.

ALMOST HUMAN – *see* SHOCK WAVES

ALPHAVILLE (UNE ÉTRANGE AVENTURE DE LEMMY CAUTION) ★★★★
France/Italy 1965; b/w; Chaumiane/Film Studio; *D/W* Jean-Luc Godard; *P* André Michelin; *M* Paul Misraki; *C* Raoul Coutard; *Starring* Eddie Constantine, Anna Karina, Akim Tamiroff; *V* Palace (UK), Vintage (USA). Intellectual New-Wave SF from France. Private eye Lemmy Caution outwits computer-ruled future city (locations in present-day Paris), defying authoritarian order with feeling and shrewdness. The future is a clinical version of now.

ALTERED STATES ★★★
USA 1980; colour; 102 mins; Warner; *D* Ken Russell; *P* Howard Gottfried; *W* Sidney Aaron (Paddy Chayefsky) from the novel by Chayefsky; *M* John Corigliano; *C* Jordan Cronenweth; *PD* Richard McDonald; *SPFX* Chuck Gaspar, (make-up) Dick Smith, Carl Fullerton; *Starring* William Hurt, Blair Brown, Bob Balaban, Charles Haid; *V* Warner (UK and USA).

THE AMAZING ADVENTURES OF BARON MUNCHAUSEN – *see* THE ADVENTURES OF BARON MUNCHAUSEN

THE AMAZING MR BLUNDEN ★★★★
UK 1972; colour; 99 mins; Hemisphere; *D/W* Lionel Jeffries from "The Ghosts" by Antonia Barber; *P* Barry Levinson; *M* Elmer Bernstein; *C* Gerry Fisher; *PD* Wilfred Shingleton; *SPFX* Pat Moore; *Starring* Lawrence Naismith, Lynne Frederick, Garry Miller, Diana Dors, James Villiers; *V* VCL (UK). Good children's film. In a ghost story (rationalized by time travel) two children put right an ancient wrong, despite opposition from fiendishly over-the-top Diana Dors. Occasionally moving and mysterious.

AN AMERICAN WEREWOLF IN LONDON ★★★★ 🍅

UK 1981; colour; 97 mins; Lycanthrope/Poly-Gram; D/W John Landis; P George Folsey Jr; M Elmer Bernstein; C Robert Paynter; SPFX (make-up) Rick Baker; Starring David Naughton, Jenny Agutter, Griffin Dunne; V PolyGram (UK), MCA (USA).

THE AMITYVILLE HORROR ★★ 🍅

USA 1979; colour; 118 mins; Cinema 77 – Professional Films/AIP; D Stuart Rosenberg; P Ronald Saland, Elliot Geisinger; W Sandor Stern from the book by Jay Anson; M Lalo Schifrin; C Fred J. Koenekamp; SPFX Delwyn Rheaume, (visual design) William Cruse; Starring James Brolin, Margot Kidder, Rod Steiger, Don Stroud, Murray Hamilton; V Guild (UK), Warner (USA).

AMITYVILLE II: THE POSSESSION ★★½ 🍅

USA 1982; colour; 105 mins; Dino De Laurentiis/Media Technology; D Damiano Damiani; P Ira N. Smith, Stephen R. Greenwald; W Tommy Lee Wallace from Murder in Amityville by Hans Holzer; M Lalo Schifrin; C Franco DiGiacomo; SPFX Glen Robinson, (make-up) John Caglione Jr; Starring James Olson, Burt Young, Jack Magner, Rutanya Alda; V Thorn EMI (UK), Embassy (USA).

...AND NOW THE SCREAMING STARTS! ★★½ 🍅

UK 1973; colour; 87 mins; Amicus; D Roy Ward Baker; P Max J. Rosenberg, Milton Subotsky; W Roger Marshall from Fengriffen by David Case; M Douglas Gamley; C Denys Coop; AD Tony Curtis; Starring Peter Cushing, Herbert Lom, Patrick Magee, Stephanie Beacham; V Guild (UK), Nostalgia (USA). Amicus shocker starring severed hand, ghostly revenge for bloody deeds, much screaming and truly nasty flashback. Crudely atmospheric (Gothic house and plot) with some good moments, but shrill and predictable.

ANDROID ★★★★

USA 1982; colour; 80 mins; Android/New World; D Aaron Lipstadt; P Mary Ann Fisher; W James Reigle, Don Opper from an idea by Will Reigle; M Don Preston; C Tim Suhrstedt; AD K. C. Scheibel, Wayne Springfield; SPFX (visual) New World Effects; Starring Don Opper, Klaus Kinski, Brie Howard, Kendra Kirchner; V Iver/CBS (UK).

THE ANDROMEDA STRAIN ★★★½

USA 1970; colour; 131 mins; Wise/Universal; D/P Robert Wise; W Nelson Gidding from the novel by Michael Crichton; M Gil Melle; C Richard H. Kline; PD Boris Leven; SPFX (photographic) Douglas Trumbull; Starring Arthur Hill, David Wayne, James Olson, Kate Reid; V CIC (UK), MCA (USA).

ANDY WARHOL'S DRACULA – see BLOOD FOR DRACULA

ANDY WARHOL'S FRANKENSTEIN – see FLESH FOR FRANKENSTEIN

EL ÁNGEL EXTERMINADOR – see THE EXTERMINATING ANGEL

L'ANNEÉ DERNIÈRE À MARIENBAD – see LAST YEAR AT MARIENBAD

ANSIKTET – see THE FACE

ARABIAN ADVENTURE ★★★

UK 1979; colour; 98 mins; Badger; D Kevin Connor; P John Dark; W Brian Hayles; M Ken Thorne; C Alan Hume; PD Elliot Scott; SPFX Richard Conway, David Harris, (supervision) George Gibbs; Starring Christopher Lee, Milo O'Shea, Oliver Tobias, Emma Samms, Mickey Rooney; V Thorn EMI (UK). This Arabian-Nights fantasy with a Prince, a wicked magician and a flying carpet is not nearly as good as Korda's 1940 Thief of Bagdad, which it strongly resembles. On the other hand, it is better than all subsequent remakes of Thief of Bagdad, and is really quite enjoyable. The young Indian boy, Puneet Sira, who plays the brave ophan, has a smile of the most transparent sweetness and pretty well steals the film. The

quest is for a magic rose. The genie who comes out of the bottle is not good at all, but watch out for Mickey Rooney's cameo as the Wizard-of-Oz-like guardian of the rose, with his three fire-breathing, mechanical monsters. Some of the nicest effects are very simple, like the sapphire that becomes a peach stone whenever the wrong person handles it.

THE ASPHYX ★★

UK 1972; colour; 99 mins; Glendale; D Peter Newbrook; P John Brittany; W Brian Comport; M Bill McGuffie; C Freddie Young; AD John Stoll; SPFX Ted Samuels; Starring Robert Stephens, Robert Powell, Jane Lapotaire, Ralph Arliss; V Intervision (UK). Psychic researcher photographs tiny screaming reptile (invisible to ordinary sight) that feeds on souls escaping bodies at moment of death; figures out that trapping creatures will ensure immortality, but disasters follow. Weirdly silly story, primitive effects, good performances.

ASYLUM (aka HOUSE OF CRAZIES) ★★★ 🍅

UK 1972; colour; 88 mins; Amicus – Harbor/CIC; D Roy Ward Baker; P Max J. Rosenberg, Milton Subotsky; W Robert Bloch; M Douglas Gamley; C Denys Coop; SPFX Ernie Sullivan; Starring Patrick Magee, Robert Powell, Herbert Lom ("Mannikins of Horror"); Barbara Parkins, Sylvia Syms, Richard Todd ("Frozen Fear"); Peter Cushing, Barry Morse, Ann Firbank ("The Weird Taylor"); Britt Ekland, Charlotte Rampling ("Lucy Comes To Stay"); V Guild (UK), Nostalgia (USA). Above-average horror anthology scripted by author of Psycho with linking story about new doctor trying to guess which mental patient is the asylum chief. Most bizarre episode has Lom making killer dolls.

L'ATLANTIDE (DIE HERRIN VON ATLANTIS; aka LOST ATLANTIS) ★★★

Germany 1932; b/w; 90 mins; Nero; D G. W. Pabst; P Seymour Nebenzal; W Ladislaus Vayda, Hermann Oberländer from the novel by Pierre Benoit; M Wolfgang Zeller; C Eugen Schüfftan; AD Erno Metzner; Starring Brigitte Helm, (German version) Gustav Diessl, (French version) Pierre Blanchar, (English version) John Stuart. Romantic adventure story with strong visual flair based on the best-selling 1919 novel about the Queen of Atlantis (here a city beneath the North African desert) who lures men to their doom, keeping their bodies in a trophy room. Brigitte Helm starred in all three versions, though the rest of the cast differed. She was the heroine/robot in Metropolis.

ATLANTIS, THE LOST CONTINENT ★★

USA 1960; colour; 90 mins; Galaxy/MGM; D/P George Pal; W Daniel Mainwaring from a play Atlanta, A Story of Atlantis by Gerald P. Hargreaves; M Russ Garcia; C Harold E. Wellman; AD George W. Davis, William Ferrari; SPFX A. Arnold Gillespie, Lee LeBlanc, Robert R. Hoág, (animation) Projects Unlimited (Jim Danforth et al.); Starring Anthony Hall, Joyce Taylor, John Dall. Colourful schlock from old-time fantasy maestro George Pal. This is one of his hack works. Ancient Greek fisherman stumbles on Atlantis which is destroyed by its corruption and super-science, none too convincingly.

ATTACK OF THE CRAB MONSTERS ★★★

USA 1957; b/w; 64 mins; Los Altos/Allied Artists; D/P Roger Corman; W Charles B. Griffith; M Ronald Stein; C Floyd Crosby; Starring Richard Garland, Pamela Duncan, Russell Johnson. Celebrated Corman cheapie with lunatically interesting story; two giant, intelligent crabs can absorb victims' brains, thus becoming group minds. Most unjustly awarded "Golden Turkey" by one not-very-good critic. The crabs look silly, but somehow believable as well.

ATTACK OF THE KILLER TOMATOES ★½

USA 1978; colour; 87 mins; Four Square; D John De Bello; P Steve Peace, De Bello; W Costa Dillon, Peace, De Bello; M Gordon Goodwin, Paul Sundfor; C John K. Culley; SPFX Greg Auer; Starring David Miller, George Wilson, Sharon Taylor, Rock Peace; V Media (UK and USA). Musical parody of monster-movie genre is certainly funny

at points; killer tomatoes (they even attack from underwater like Jaws) are vulnerable, we learn, to bad music. Slightly tiresome overall, with some jokes truly deplorable.

AT THE EARTH'S CORE ★★

UK 1976; colour; 90 mins; Amicus/British Lion; D Kevin Connor; P John Dark; W Milton Subotsky from the novel by Edgar Rice Burroughs; M Mike Vickers; C Alan Hume; PD Maurice Carter; SPFX Ian Wingrove; Starring Doug McClure, Peter Cushing, Caroline Munro; V Thorn EMI (UK), Warner (USA). Not the best of the Amicus Burroughs adaptations, though some people like the rubber-looking monsters, but bad script and unlovable Doug McClure take this prehistoric-civilisation story to literally abysmal depths after promising opening.

AUDREY ROSE ★★★½

USA 1977; colour; 113 mins; United Artists; D Robert Wise; P Joe Wizan, Frank De Felitta; W De Felitta from his novel; M Michael Small; C Victor J. Kemper; PD Harry Horner; SPFX Henry Millar Jr; Starring Marsha Mason, Anthony Hopkins, John Beck, Susan Swift.

THE AWAKENING ★★

UK 1980; colour; 105 mins; Solofilm/Orion – EMI/British Lion; D Mike Newell; P Robert Solo, Andrew Scheinman, Martin Shafer; W Allan Scott, Chris Bryant, Clive Exton from the novel The Jewel of Seven Stars by Bram Stoker; M Claude Bolling; C Jack Cardiff; PD Michael Stringer; SPFX John Stears; Starring Charlton Heston, Susannah York, Jill Townsend, Stephanie Zimbalist; V Thorn EMI (UK), Warner (USA). Extremely slow-moving and boringly respectable adaptation of Stoker more excitingly done in Blood from the Mummy's Tomb. Story of daughter possessed by mummy's spirit; pardon the pun, but there is a subdued incest theme with daddy as well. Brilliant cameraman Cardiff largely wasted.

BABES IN TOYLAND (aka REVENGE IS SWEET, MARCH OF THE TOYS and MARCH OF THE WOODEN SOLDIERS) ★★★½

USA 1934; b/w; 79 mins; Hal Roach/MGM; D Charles Rogers, Gus Meins; P Hal Roach; W Nick Grinde, Frank Butler from the operetta by Victor Herbert and Glen McDonough; M (additional) Ann Ronell, Frank Churchill; C Art Lloyd, Francis Corby; Starring Stan Laurel, Oliver Hardy, Charlotte Henry; V Thorn EMI (UK), IUD (USA). Attractive musical comedy (emphasis on the comedy) with Laurel and Hardy as workers in toy factory conquering evil toymaker and his monstrous cohorts with aid of wooden soldiers. Surprisingly, pretty scary in places. Classic fantasy, much better than Disney remake.

BABES IN TOYLAND ★

USA 1961; colour; 105 mins; Disney, D Jack Donohue; P Walt Disney; W Ward Kimball, Joe Rinaldi, Lowell S. Hawley from the operetta by Victor Herbert and Glen McDonough; Songs George Bruns, Mel Leven; SPFX (animation) Joshua Meador; Starring Ray Bolger, Tommy Sands, Annette Funicello, Ed Wynn; V Disney (USA). Probably Disney's biggest flop, with new songs no good, generally limp direction and soppy romance. See the 1934 version.

BARBARELLA ★★★★

France/Italy 1968; colour; 98 mins; Dino De Laurentiis – Marianne/Paramount; D Roger Vadim; P De Laurentiis; W Terry Southern, Brian Degas, Jean-Claude Forest and others from the comic strip by Forest; M Maurice Jarre; C Claude Renoir; PD Mario Garbuglia; AD Enrico Fea; SPFX Augie Lohman; Starring Jane Fonda, John Phillip Law, Anita Pallenberg, David Hemmings; V CIC (UK), Paramount (USA).

BARON BLOOD (GLI ORRORI DEL CASTELLO DI NORIMBERGA) ★½ 🍅

Italy/West Germany 1972; colour; 90 mins; AIP/Leone/Euro-America & Geissler; D Mario Bava; W Bava, Vincent Fotre; M Les Baxter; C Emilio Varriani; SPFX Franco Tocci; Starring Joseph Cotten,

Elke Sommer, Massimo Girotti. A restless camera fails to vitalise this limp tale of reincarnated sadistic baron (a very embarrassed-looking Cotten). Bava's much vaunted visual sense not at all in evidence, and as *giallos* go, it isn't even very horrid, the mutilations looking like papier-mâché and ketchup.

BARON MUNCHAUSEN – *see* THE ADVENTURES OF BARON MUNCHAUSEN

BASKET CASE ★★★½ 💀 💀
USA 1981; colour; 90 mins (two versions in circulation, censored version shorter); Basket Case Co.; *D/W* Frank Henenlotter; *P* Edgar Ievins; *M* Gus Russo; *C* Bruce Torbet; *SPFX* (make-up) Kevin Haney, John Caglione Jr; *Starring* Kevin VanHentenryck, Terri Susan Smith, Beverly Bonner; *V* Palace (UK), Media (USA, uncensored).

BATTLE BEYOND THE STARS ★★★
USA 1980; colour; 103 mins; New World; *D* Jimmy T. Murakami; *P* Roger Corman, Ed Carlin; *W* John Sayles from a story by John Sayles and Anne Dyer; *M* James Horner; *SPFX* (make-up) Steve Neill, Rick Stratton, (miniatures) M. Shallock; *Starring* Richard Thomas, Robert Vaughn, John Saxon, George Peppard, Sam Jaffe, Sybil Danning; *V* Warner (UK), Vestron (USA).

BATTLE FOR THE PLANET OF THE APES ★
USA 1973; colour; 86 mins; Apjac/20th Century-Fox; *D* J. Lee Thompson; *P* Arthur P. Jacobs; *W* John W. and Joyce H. Corrington from a story by Paul Dehn; *C* Richard H. Kline; *SPFX* (make-up) John Chambers; *Starring* Roddy McDowall, Claude Akins, Natalie Trundy; *V* CBS/Fox (UK). Fifth, last and worst of Apes series. Apes led by Caesar (from *Escape from the Planet of the Apes*) form Ape City; tripartite struggle ensues between radiation-scarred human survivors of the War, militant-tendency gorillas and moderate chimps. Social democrats win the day.

BATTLESTAR GALACTICA ★★
USA 1978; made for TV; colour; 122 mins; Universal; *D* Richard A. Colla; *P* John Dykstra; *W* Glen A. Larson; *M* Stu Phillips; *C* Ben Colman; *AD* John E. Chilberg II; *SPFX* (production co-ordinator) John Dykstra; *Starring* Lorne Greene, Richard L. Hatch, Dirk Benedict, Maren Jensen; *V* CIC (UK), MCA (USA). Telefilm cut from pilot episode of the TV series; 12 telefilms were cut from 17 of the original episodes, but the only other to have theatrical release was *Mission Galactica: The Cylon Attack*, 1979. Producer Dykstra was rumoured to have infuriated George Lucas by taking his special effects expertise from *Star Wars* to this imitative series. Colourful but childish space-opera melodrama, wooden acting, right-wing politics.

BATTLETRUCK ★★½
USA 1982; colour; 91 mins; New World; *D* Harley Cokliss; *P* Lloyd Phillips, Rob Whitehouse; *W* Irving Austin, Cokliss, John Beech; *M* Kevin Peek; *C* Chris Menges; *PD* Gary Hansen; *SPFX* Jonnie Burke; *Starring* Michael Beck, Annie McEnroe, James Wainwright. Set in attractive New Zealand scenery, this post-holocaust thriller occupies *Mad Max* territory in that it takes place after the Oil Wars. Villain Straker (Wainwright) terrorises rural communities with his 60-foot long battletruck; Beck plays the good guy (also motorised) who gets him. Lively, rather empty.

THE BEAST (LA BÊTE) ★★★½
France 1975; colour; 102 mins; *D/W* Walerian Borowczyk; *P* Anatole Dauman; *M* Domenico Scarlatti; *C* Bernard Daillencourt, Marcel Grignon; *AD* Jacques d'Ovidio; *Starring* Sirpa Lane, Lisbeth Hummel, Guy Tréjan, Pierre Benedetti; *V* VTC (UK).

THE BEAST FROM 20,000 FATHOMS ★★½
USA 1953; b/w; 80 mins; Mutual/Warner; *D* Eugene Lourié; *P* Hal E. Chester, Bernard W. Burton; *W* Lou Morheim, Fred Freiberger from the story (aka "The Foghorn") by Ray Bradbury; *M* David Buttolph; *C* Jack Russell; *AD* Horace Hough; *SPFX* Willis Cook, (animation) Ray Harry-

hausen; *Starring* Paul Christian, Paula Raymond, Cecil Kellaway. Director Lourié was once art director to Jean Renoir, but you wouldn't guess. A "rhedosaurus" on the loose was the star. One of the earliest 1950s monster movies, the film looks dated and wooden now, but there are atmospheric moments and vigorous stop-motion animation (Harryhausen's first solo effort).

THE BEASTMASTER ★★
USA 1982; colour; 118 mins; Leisure Investment/Beastmaster/Ecta; *D* Don Coscarelli; *P* Paul Pepperman, Sylvio Tabet; *W* Coscarelli, Pepperman, loosely based on characters from the novel by Andre Norton; *M* Lee Holdridge; *C* John Alcott; *PD* Conrad E. Angone; *SPFX* Roger George, Frank DeMarco, (make-up) William Munns, David B. Miller; *Starring* Marc Singer, Tanya Roberts, Rip Torn; *V* Thorn EMI (UK), MGM/UA (USA).

THE BEAST MUST DIE ★
UK 1974; colour; 93 mins; Amicus/British Lion; *D* Paul Annett; *P* Max J. Rosenberg, Milton Subotsky; *W* Michael Winder from "There Shall Be No Darkness" by James Blish; *M* Douglas Gamley; *C* Jack Hildyard; *AD* John Stoll; *SPFX* Ted Samuels; *Starring* Calvin Lockhart, Peter Cushing, Charles Gray, Anton Diffring; *V* Nostalgia (USA). Drearily old-fashioned and talky adaptation of Blish's O.K. story about a big-game hunter throwing a house party knowing one guest is a werewolf, but not which one. More detective story than supernatural thriller. The werewolf looks like a dog.

THE BEAST WITHIN ★★ 💀 💀
USA 1981; colour; 98 mins; MGM/United Artists; *D* Philippe Mora; *P* Harvey Bernhard, Gabriel Katzka; *W* Tom Holland from the novel by Edward Levy; *M* Les Baxter; *C* Jack L. Richards; *PD* David M. Haber; *SPFX* (make-up) Tom Burman; *Starring* Ronny Cox, Bibi Besch, Paul Clemens, Don Gordon, L. Q. Jones; *V* MGM/UA (USA). Bastard son of woman raped in swamp by animal exhibits bestial symptoms and becomes ferocious killer at regular intervals. Standard exploitation fare by Australian director, notable for well-achieved though disgusting transformation scenes.

BEAUTIES OF THE NIGHT – *see* LES BELLES DE NUIT

BEAUTY AND THE BEAST (LA BELLE ET LA BÊTE) ★★★★★
France 1946; b/w; 90 mins; Discina; *D/W* Jean Cocteau from his play and the fairy story; *P* André Paulvé; *M* Georges Auric; *C* Henri Alekan; *Starring* Jean Marais, Josette Day; *V* Thorn EMI (UK), Video Dimensions (USA).

BEDAZZLED ★★½
UK 1967; colour; 107 mins; Stanley Donen Enterprises/20th Century-Fox; *D/P* Stanley Donen; *W* Peter Cook from a story by Cook and Dudley Moore; *M* Dudley Moore; *C* Austin Dempster; *Animation* Bailey-Pettengell Design; *Starring* Peter Cook, Dudley Moore, Eleanor Bron, Raquel Welch, Barry Humphries; *V* CBS/Fox (UK and USA). Uneven satirical comedy featuring British comedy stars Cook and Moore as the Devil and the short-order cook who sells his soul for seven wishes. Raquel Welch is Lillian Lust. Director Donen (*Damn Yankees*) never makes his devil movies quite crisp enough.

BEDKNOBS AND BROOMSTICKS ★★
USA 1971; colour; 117 mins; Disney; *D* Robert Stevenson; *P* Bill Walsh; Don DaGradi from the book by Mary Norton; *M/Lyrics* Richard M. and Robert B. Sherman; *C* Frank Phillips; *AD* John B. Mansbridge, Peter Ellenshaw; *Animation* Ward Kimball; *SPFX* Alan Maley, Eustace Lycett, Danny Lee; *Starring* Angela Lansbury, David Tomlinson, Roddy McDowall, Sam Jaffe; *V* Disney (UK and USA).

THE BED SITTING ROOM ★★★
UK 1969; colour; 91 mins; Oscar Lewenstein/United Artists; *D/P* Richard Lester; *W* John Antrobus from the play by Spike Milligan and Antrobus; *M*

Ken Thorne; *C* David Watkin; *PD* Assheton Gorton; *SPFX* Phil Stokes; *Starring* Rita Tushingham, Ralph Richardson, Peter Cook, Dudley Moore, Spike Milligan, Michael Hordern, Roy Kinnear, Marty Feldman.

BELL, BOOK AND CANDLE ★★½
USA 1958; colour; 103 mins; Phoenix/Columbia; *D* Richard Quine; *P* Julian Blaustein; *W* Daniel Taradash from the play by John Van Druten; *M* George Duning; *C* James Wong Howe; *Starring* James Stewart, Kim Novak, Jack Lemmon, Hermione Gingold, Elsa Lanchester; *V* Columbia (USA). The film shows its theatrical origins in a mild staginess. James Stewart looks even more bemused than usual when, about to be married, he finds himself falling in love with a witch (Kim Novak) instead. It is all moderately engaging, but not very funny. Jack Lemmon tries very hard as a warlock; there is much business with a cat called Pyewacket; Novak is sexy but not very witchy. A minor fantastic comedy.

LA BELLE ET LA BÊTE – *see* BEAUTY AND THE BEAST

LES BELLES DE NUIT (aka NIGHT BEAUTIES, BEAUTIES OF THE NIGHT) ★★★½
France 1952; b/w; 87 mins; Franco London/Rizzoli; *D/W* René Clair; *M* Georges Van Parys; *C* Armand Thirard, Robert Juillard; *AD* Léon Barsacq; *Starring* Gérard Philipe, Martine Carol, Gina Lollobrigida. Delightful and witty farce by a near-great director about a young composer whose real life is undignified, but whose dream life is heroic and erotic (though also subject to pitfalls). The women in the dreams are idealised versions of those he knows in real life, and each occupies a different period of a romantic past; but these pasts come to overlap.

BEN ★★
USA 1972; colour; 94 mins; Bing Crosby Productions; *D* Phil Karlson; *P* Mort Briskin; *W* Gilbert A. Ralston from characters created by Stephen Gilbert; *M* Walter Scharf; *C* Russell Metty; *SPFX* Bud David, (photographic) Howard Anderson Co.; *Starring* Lee Harcourt Montgomery, Joseph Campanella. Difficult to take this sequel to *Willard* seriously; Ben, the chief rat from the previous movie, is befriended by a sickly little boy, but persecuted (with his rat army) by other humans. In many ways a reprise of the previous film, but more sentimental.

BENEATH THE PLANET OF THE APES ★★★
USA 1969; colour; 95 mins; Apjac/20th Century-Fox; *D* Ted Post; *P* Arthur P. Jacobs; *W* Paul Dehn, based on characters created by Pierre Boulle; *M* Leonard Rosenman; *C* Milton Krasner; *AD* Jack Martin Smith, William Creber; *SPFX* (photographic) L. B. Abbott, Art Cruickshank, (make-up) John Chambers; *Starring* James Franciscus, Charlton Heston, Kim Hunter, Linda Harrison, Victor Buono; *V* CBS/Fox (UK).

LA BÊTE – *see* THE BEAST

BEWARE! THE BLOB (aka SON OF BLOB) ★½
USA 1971; colour; 88 mins; Jack H. Harris Enterprises; *D* Larry Hagman; *P* Anthony Harris; *W* Jack Woods, Anthony Harris from a story by Richard Clair and Jack H. Harris; *M* Mort Garson; *C* Al Hamm; *SPFX* Tim Baar; *Starring* Robert Walker, Gwynne Gilford, Godfrey Cambridge; *V* Video Gems (USA). *The Blob* hardly needed a parody, but that is what this sequel is. Not a lot of people know that J. R. of *Dallas* fame made an SF movie. Mildly funny; the Blob (brought back to life) disposes of several small-time Hollywood stars in cameo roles. Cambridge drinks it in a beer!

THE BEYOND (...E TU VIVRAI NEL TERRORE! L'ALDILA aka THE SEVEN DOORS OF DEATH) ★★ 💀 💀
Italy 1981; colour; 88 mins; Fulvia Film; *D* Lucio Fulci; *P* Fabrizio De Angelis; *W* Fulci, Giorgio Mariuzzo, Dardano Sacchetti; *M* Fabio Frizzi; *C* Sergio Salvati; *SPFX (make-up)* Giannetto De Rossi; *Starring* Katherine McColl, David Warbeck, Sarah Keller; *V* Videomedia (UK).

BEYOND THE DOOR (CHI SEI? aka THE DEVIL WITHIN HER) ★½ 💀
Italy 1974; colour; 109 mins; Film Ventures International; *D* Oliver Hellman (Sonia Assonitis); *W* Richard Barrett (Piazzoli), Hellman; *M* (USA version) Riz Ortolani; *C* Piazzoli; *SPFX* Donn Davison, Wally Gentleman; *Starring* Juliet Mills, Richard Johnson, David Colin Jr; *V* Media (USA). Spaghetti *Exorcist* rip-off, subject of legal action from Warner Bros. The foetus inside Juliet Mills is possessed by a demon; she becomes disgusting; familiar nasty effects; toys come to life.

BEYOND THE DOOR II – *see* SHOCK

BIG MEAT EATER ★★½
Canada 1982; colour; 82 mins; BCD Entertainment; *D* Chris Windsor; *P* Laurence Keane; *W* Windsor, Keane, Phil Savath; *M* J. Douglas Dodd; *C* Doug McKay; *SPFX* Michael Dorsey, Iain Best, Jim Bridge; *Starring* George Dawson, Big Miller, Howard Taylor, Andrew Gillies, Ida Carnevali; *V* Virgin/Palace (UK). The plot of this musical SF lunacy, made on a low budget and proud of it, it seems, defies description. Aliens reanimate the corpse of Mayor Rigatoni, ordering him to build a plant on the site of the butcher's shop to tap the resources of the butcher's sewage tank, where baloneum has been formed. The butcher's murderous assistant, Abdulla, the big meat eater ...but I can't go on. The butcher has invented a universal language, and the robots who speak good English anyway are subtitled. It's warped, grotesque, mildly witty, in the same parodic, midnight-movie genre as *The Rocky Horror Picture Show*.

THE BIRDS ★★★½ 💀
USA 1963; colour; 119 mins; Hitchcock/Universal; *D/P* Alfred Hitchcock; *W* Evan Hunter from the story by Daphne Du Maurier; *M* Bernard Herrmann; *C* Robert Burks; *SPFX* Lawrence A. Hampton, (special photographic advisor) Ub Iwerks; *Starring* Tippi Hedren, Rod Taylor, Jessica Tandy, Suzanne Pleshette; *V* CIC (UK), MCA (USA).

THE BLACK CAT (IL GATTO NERO) ★ 💀
Italy 1980; colour; 90 mins; Selenia; *D* Lucio Fulci; *P* Giulio Sbarigia; *W* Biagio Proietti, Fulci from story by Proietti loosely based on the story by Edgar Allan Poe; *M* Pino Donaggio; *C* Sergio Salvati; *PD* Francesco Calabrese; *SPFX* Paolo Ricci; *Starring* Patrick Magee, Mimsy Farmer, David Warbeck; *V* VTC (UK). Remarkably demure not to say tepid thriller from goremeister Fulci, here setting a much changed Poe story in the UK and obviously unhappy about it. Magee is hammy hermit (recorder of graveyard sounds) in incoherent tale of ghost of murdered cat triggering bloody deaths.

THE BLACK HOLE ★★
USA 1979; colour; 98 mins; Disney; *D* Gary Nelson; *P* Ron Miller; *W* Jeb Rosebrook, Gerry Day; *M* John Barry; *C* Frank Phillips; *PD* Peter Ellenshaw; *SPFX* (mattes) Harrison Ellenshaw, (miniature effects) Peter Ellenshaw, (composite opticals) Eustace Lycett, (animation) Dorse A. Lanpher and Ted C. Kierscey; *Starring* Maximilian Schell, Anthony Perkins, Robert Forster, Joseph Bottoms, Yvette Mimieux, Ernest Borgnine; *V* Disney (UK and USA).

BLACK SABBATH (I TRE VOLTI DELLA PAURA) ★★½
USA/France/Italy 1963; 100 mins; Emmepi/Lyre/Galatea/AIP; *D* Mario Bava; *P* Salvatore Billitteri; *W* Marcello Fondato, also Alberto Bevilacqua, Bava, Ugo Guerra, from the stories "The Drop of Water" by Anton Chekhov, "The Telephone" by F. G. Snyder and "The Wurdalak" by Alexei Tolstoy; *M* Roberto Nicolosi, (English dubbed version) Les Baxter; *C* Ubaldo Terzano; *AD* Giorgio Giovannini; *Starring* Boris Karloff, Michele Mercier, Mark Damon; *V* Inter Ocean (UK). Nothing like as good as *Black Sunday* (also Bava). First story (the haunting of a corpse-robbing nurse) atmospheric, the other two feeble. Karloff looks rather unwell as a Russian vampire.

BLACK SUNDAY (LA MASCHERA DEL DEMONIO, aka REVENGE OF THE VAMPIRE, MASK OF THE DEMON) ★★★★ 💀
Italy 1960; b/w; 88 mins; Galatea/Jolly; *D* Mario Bava; *P* Massimo De Rita; *W* Ennio De Concini and others from "The Vij" by Nikolai Gogol; *M* Roberto Nicolosi, (English-dubbed version) Les Baxter; *C* Ubaldo Terzano, Bava; *AD* Giorgio Giovannini; *Starring* Barbara Steele, John Richardson, Andrea Checchi; *V* Videomedia (UK).

BLACULA ★
USA 1972; colour; 92 mins; Powers/AIP; *D* William Crain; *P* Joseph T. Naar; *W* Joan Torres, Raymond Koenig; *M* Gene Page; *C* John Stevens; *AD* Walter Herndon; *Starring* William Marshall, Vonetta McGee, Denise Nicholas. Feeble, tongue-in-cheek blaxploitation picture with a black vampire (a vampirised African prince) and some songs. There was, regrettably, a sequel: *Scream Blacula Scream*, 1973.

BLADE RUNNER ★★★★½ 💀
USA 1982; colour; 117 mins; Blade Runner Partnership – Ladd Company – Sir Run Run Shaw/Warner; *D* Ridley Scott; *P* Michael Deeley; *W* Hampton Fancher, David Peoples from *Do Androids Dream of Electric Sheep?* by Philip K. Dick; *M* Vangelis; *C* Jordan Cronenweth; *PD* Lawrence G. Paull; *Visual Future Designs* Syd Mead; *SPFX* (special photographic) Douglas Trumbull, Richard Yuricich and David Dryer, (matte artist) Matthew Yuricich; *Starring* Harrison Ford, Rutger Hauer, Sean Young, Daryl Hannah; *V* Warner (UK), Embassy (USA).

DIE BLECHTROMMEL *see* THE TIN DRUM

BLITHE SPIRIT ★★★½
UK 1945; colour; 96 mins; Cineguild/Two Cities; *D* David Lean; *P* Noel Coward; *W* Anthony Havelock-Allan, Lean, Ronald Neame from the play by Noel Coward; *M* Richard Addinsell; *C* Ronald Neame; *AD* C. P. Norman; *SPFX* Tom Howard; *Starring* Rex Harrison, Constance Cummings, Kay Hammond, Margaret Rutherford. Rutherford steals the show as Madam Arcati, the medium, in efficient adaptation of the classic Coward comedy. Harrison, recently remarried, is haunted and teased by the elegant ghost of his former wife. Howard won an Oscar for his special effects.

THE BLOB ★★★
USA 1958; colour; 86 mins; Tonylyn/Paramount; *D* Irvin S. Yeaworth Jr; *P* Jack H. Harris; *W* Kate Phillips, Theodore Simonson from a story by Irvine H. Millgate; *M* Ralph Carmichael; *C* Thomas Spalding; *SPFX* Barton Sloane; *Starring* Steve McQueen, Aneta Corsaut, Olin Howlin, Earl Rowe; *V* Mountain (UK), Video Gems (USA). Terrible film really, but such good fun it has to have three stars. McQueen in an early role stars as gutsy teenage leader trying to convince police about presence of amoeboid, ever-growing, carnivorous monster. Special effects ludicrous.

BLOEDVERWANTEN – *see* BLOOD-RELATIONS

BLOOD AND ROSES (ET MOURIR DE PLAISIR) ★★★
France/Italy 1960; colour; 100 mins; EGE – Documento/Paramount; *D* Roger Vadim; *P* Raymond Eger; *W* Vadim, Roger Vailland, Claude Brulé, Claude Martin from "Carmilla" by J. Sheridan Le Fanu; *M* Jean Prodromides; *C* Claude Renoir; *AD* Jean André; *Starring* Mel Ferrer, Elsa Martinelli, Annette Vadim, Marc Allégret. Mistily romantic and mildly erotic adaptation of classic vampire story (see also *Vampyr*, *The Vampire Lovers*). Slow, with sometimes beautiful use of colour (especially red), it emphasises the lesbian aspects of the story. More decadently titillating than substantial, but strong on atmosphere.

BLOOD FOR DRACULA (DRACULA VUOLE VIVERE: CERCA SANGUE DI VERGINE! aka ANDY WARHOL'S DRACULA) ★★ 💀💀
Italy/France 1973; 3-D; colour; 103 mins; C.C. Champion & 1/Yanne-Rassam; *D/W* Paul Morrissey; *P* Andrew Braunsberg; *C* Luigi Kuveiller; *PD* Enrico Job; *SPFX* Carlo Rambaldi; *Starring* Joe Dallesandro, Udo Kier, Vittorio De Sica, Maxime McKendry, Milena Vukotic; *V* Palace (UK), Video Gems (USA). Mildly pornographic horror spoof, made back-to-back with *Flesh For Frankenstein* by the same team. Udo Kier is Dracula, in bad trouble because he needs the blood of virgins and there aren't any left near his castle. He travels by limousine to Italy, where he moves in with a decadent aristocratic family (they see him as a potential husband for one of their many daughters) and attempts to vampirize the sisters, one by one, having been assured they are all virgins. Thanks to the heroic efforts, which we witness, of Joe Dallesandro, the gardener-stud, he is mistaken. The polluted blood makes Dracula frightfully sick – he acts as if he has terminal tuberculosis throughout – and there are extremely long scenes of him vomiting violently. There is also a very bloody finale (a bit like something from *Monty Python and the Holy Grail*) where Dallesandro chops his arms, legs and head off. In between the moments of nausea, and the sexual couplings, there are many *longueurs*, despite the implausible cameo role played by Vittoria De Sica.

BLOOD FROM THE MUMMY'S TOMB ★★★½
UK 1971; colour; 94 mins; Hammer/EMI; *D* Seth Holt, (uncredited) Michael Carreras; *P* Howard Brandy; *W* Christopher Wicking from *Jewel of the Seven Stars* by Bram Stoker; *M* Tristram Cary; *C* Arthur Grant; *AD* Scott Macgregor; *SPFX* Michael Collins; *Starring* Andrew Keir, Valerie Leon, James Villiers; *V* Thorn EMI (UK).

THE BLOOD OF DR JEKYLL (DR JEKYLL ET LES FEMMES) ★★★½ 💀
France 1981; colour; Whodunnit/Allegro/Multimedia; *D/W/C/PD* Walerian Borowczyk from *The Strange Case of Dr Jekyll and Mr Hyde* by Robert Louis Stevenson; *P* Robert Kuperberg, Jean-Pierre Labrande; *Starring* Udo Kier, Marina Pierro, Patrick Magee; *V* VTC (UK). Eccentric, surrealist, Polish pornographer Borowczyk, whose films are more interesting than good, here rewrites the Jekyll myth. (Two different actors play Jekyll and Hyde.) Jekyll is joined in the bath by his fiancée as he is changing into Hyde, and she changes too. Both go on a rampage of rape and murder; it is very obviously a film about schizophrenia and repressed desires.

BLOOD ON SATAN'S CLAW (aka SATAN'S SKIN) ★★★ 💀
UK 1970; colour; 93 mins; Chilton/Tigon; *D* Piers Haggard; *P* Peter L. Andrews, Malcolm B. Heyworth; *W* Robert Wynne-Simmons, Haggard; *M* Marc Wilkinson; *C* Dick Bush; *Starring* Patrick Wymark, Linda Hayden, Michele Dotrice; *V* Guild (UK), Paragon (USA).

BLOOD-RELATIONS (BLOEDVERWANTEN) ★★
Netherlands/France 1977; colour; 97 mins; Jaap van Rij/CTIS; *D* Wim Lindner; *P* Jaap van Rij; *W* John Brasom from a story by Belcampo; *M* Jean Manuel de Scarano; *C* Walter Bal; *AD* Hans Oosterhuis; *Starring* Sophie Deschamps, Maxim Hamel, Eddie Constantine; *V* Home Video (UK). Mildly amusing comedy. Young nurse arrives at hospital to find that Dr Steiger (Hamel) is stealing blood plasma because he is a vampire, with a large circle of rather sedate and respectable vampire friends. Claiming to be a vampire too, she infiltrates their group, but alas, her plans fail.

BLOOD SISTERS – *see* SISTERS

BLOW OUT ★★★ 💀
USA 1981; colour; 108 mins; Cinema 77 – Geria/Filmways; *D/W* Brian De Palma; *P* George Litto; *M* Pino Donaggio; *C* Vilmos Zsigmond; *PD* Paul Sylbert; *Starring* John Travolta, Nancy Allen, John Lithgow, Dennis Franz; *V* Rank (UK), Warner (USA).

BLUE THUNDER ★★★
USA 1982; colour; 110 mins; Rastar-Gordon Car-

roll/Columbia; *D* John Badham; *P* Gordon Carroll; *W* Dan O'Bannon, Don Jakoby; *M* Arthur B. Rubinstein; *C* John A. Alonzo; *SPFX* (supervision) Chuck Gaspar; *Starring* Roy Scheider, Warren Oates, Candy Clark, Daniel Stern; *V* RCA/Columbia (USA).

THE BOOGENS ★★ ☻

USA 1981; colour; 95 mins; Taft; *D* James L. Conway; *P* Charles E. Sellier Jr; *W* David O'Malley, Bob Hunt; *M* Bob Summers; *C* Paul Hipp; *PD* Paul Staheli; *SPFX* Jon Reeves, Doug Kramer, (Boogen) William Munns and Ken Horn; *Starring* Rebecca Balding, Fred McCarren, Anne-Marie Martin. Sharp-toothed, tentacled, scaly little creatures (Boogens) are the stars of this old-fashioned and rather predictable monster movie. They live in an abandoned silver mine, and by the end they have demolished most of the cast. Mediocre.

A BOY AND HIS DOG ★★★★

USA 1975; colour; 87 mins; LQJAF; *D/W* L. Q. Jones from the novella by Harlan Ellison; *P* Alvy Moore; *M* Tim McIntire; *C* John Arthur Morrill; *PD* Ray Boyle; *SPFX* Frank Rowe; *Starring* Don Johnson, Susanne Benton, Alvy Moore, Jason Robards, Charles McGraw; *V* Media (UK and USA).

THE BOYS FROM BRAZIL ★★½

USA 1978; colour; 125 mins; Producer Circle/ITC; *D* Franklin J. Schaffner; *P* Martin Richards, Stanley O'Toole; *W* Heywood Gould from the novel by Ira Levin; *M* Jerry Goldsmith; *C* Henri Decaë; *PD* Gil Parrondo; *Starring* Gregory Peck, Laurence Olivier, James Mason; *V* Precision (UK), CBS/Fox (USA).

BRAINSTORM ★½

USA 1983; colour; 106 mins; JF/MGM/UA; *D/P* Douglas Trumbull; *W* Robert Stitzel, Philip Frank Messina; *M* James Horner; *C* Richard Yuricich; *PD* John Vallone; *SPFX* (visual) Entertainment Effects Group, (supervisor) Alison Yerxa; *Starring* Christopher Walken, Natalie Wood, Louise Fletcher, Cliff Robertson; *V* MGM/UA (USA).

BREWSTER McCLOUD ★★★

USA 1970; colour; 104 mins; Adler – Phillips – Lion's Gate/MGM; *D* Robert Altman; *W* Doran William Cannon; *M* Gene Page; *C* Lamar Boren, Jordan Cronenweth; *SPFX* Marcel Vercoutere, (wings design) Leon Ericksen; *Starring* Bud Cort, Sally Kellerman, Michael Murphy, William Windom, Shelley Duvall, Rene Auberjonois.

THE BRIDE OF FRANKENSTEIN ★★★★

USA 1935; b/w; 75 mins; Universal; *D* James Whale; *P* Carl Laemmle Jr; *W* William Hurlbut, John L. Balderston; *M* Franz Waxman; *C* John Mescall; *SPFX* (make-up) Jack P. Pierce, (electrics) Kenneth Strickfaden; *Starring* Boris Karloff, Colin Clive, Elsa Lanchester, Ernest Thesiger, Dwight Frye.

THE BRIDES OF DRACULA ★★★☻

UK 1960; colour; 85 mins; Hammer-Hotspur/Universal; *D* Terence Fisher; *P* Anthony Hinds; *W* Jimmy Sangster, Peter Bryan, Edward Percy; *M* Malcolm Williamson; *C* Jack Asher; *AD* Bernard Robinson, Thomas Goswell; *Starring* Peter Cushing, Yvonne Monlaur, Freda Jackson, Martita Hunt. First sequel to Hammer's *Dracula* and slightly above the studio average, but they had to do without Christopher Lee (the title is misleading) though Cushing still plays Van Helsing. Sympathetic girl unchains nice young man – and then discovers why she was chained.

BRITANNIA HOSPITAL ★★☻

UK 1982; colour; 116 mins; Film & General/EMI; *D* Lindsay Anderson; *P* Davina Belling, Clive Parsons; *W* David Sherwin; *M* Alan Price; *C* Mike Fash; *PD* Norris Spencer; *SPFX* George Gibbs, also Peter Aston; *Starring* Leonard Rossiter, Graham Crowden, Joan Plowright, Jill Bennett, Malcolm McDowell; *V* Thorn EMI (UK and USA).

THE BROOD ★★★★☻

Canada 1979; colour; 91 mins; Mutual/Elgin; *D/W* David Cronenberg; *P* Claude Héroux; *M* Howard Shore; *C* Mark Irwin; *AD* Carol Spier; *SPFX* Allan Kotter, (make-up) Jack Young and Dennis Pike; *Starring* Oliver Reed, Samantha Eggar; *V* Intervision (UK), Embassy (USA).

THE BROTHERHOOD OF SATAN ★★★

USA 1970; colour; 92 mins; LQJAF-Four Star Excelsior/Columbia; *D* Bernard McEveety; *P* L. Q. Jones, Alvy Moore; *W* William Welch from a story by Sean MacGregor; *M* Jaime Mendoza-Nava; *C* John Arthur Morrill; *AD* Ray Boyle; *Starring* Strother Martin, L. Q. Jones, Alvy Moore; *V* RCA/Columbia (UK), Columbia (USA). Quite a taut, unpretentious little thriller from the team that made *A Boy and His Dog*, but too silly to take seriously. Couple supernaturally trapped in small town find parents being murdered, sinister children. Elderly satanists are seeking new bodies, and (ambiguous ending?) may find them.

BUCK ROGERS ★½

USA 1939; serial (12 episodes); b/w; Universal; *D* Ford Beebe, Saul Goodkind; *P* Barney Sarecky; *W* Norman S. Hall, Ray Trampe from *Armageddon 2419 AD* by Philip Francis Nowlan and the comic strip by Nowlan and Dick Calkins; *C* Jerry Ash; *AD* Jack Otterson, Ralph De Lacy; *Starring* Larry "Buster" Crabbe, Constance Moore, Jackie Moran, Jack Mulhall; *V* Rainbow (UK). Severely cut 1953 feature version *Planet Outlaws* aka *Buck Rogers Conquers the Universe* *V* CBS/Fox (USA). There is still amusement value in this SF period piece replete with unconvincing spaceships, death rays etc. Crabbe (who also starred in the *Flash Gordon* serials) was too pretty for real *machismo*, but he still defeats Killer Kane and the Saturnian Zuggs.

BUCK ROGERS IN THE 25TH CENTURY ★★

USA 1979; colour; 89 mins; Universal; *D* Daniel Haller; *P* Richard Caffey; *W* Glen A. Larson, Leslie Stevens from the comic strip; *M* Stu Phillips; *C* Frank Beascoechea; *AD* Paul Peters; *SPFX* Bud Ewing, Jack Faggard, (visual) David M. Garber and Wayne Smith, (matte artist) Syd Dutton; *Starring* Gil Gerard, Pamela Hensley, Erin Gray, Henry Silva, Joseph Wiseman; *V* CIC (UK), MCA (USA). Originally intended as a TV pilot by Larson (producer of *Battlestar Galactica*), this was given theatrical release first. Cheerful, rather coy space opera that does not really explore the quandary of a man catapulted forward into time; effects modest. A TV series followed.

BUG ★★☻

USA 1975; colour; 101 mins; Paramount; *D* Jeannot Szwarc; *P* William Castle; *W* Castle, Thomas Page from *The Hephaestus Plague* by Page; *M* (electronic) Charles Fox; *C* Michel Hugo; *AD* Jack Martin Smith; *SPFX* Phil Cory, Walter Dion; *Starring* Bradford Dillman, Joanna Miles, Richard Gilliland; *V* CIC (UK), Paramount (USA). Entertainingly silly monster movie. The monsters are big, black cockroach things that swarm out of a fissure in the earth after an earthquake. When they rub their tail appendages together they become incendiary, and they spend a lot of time setting fire to people and things. Mad scientist Bradford Dillman breeds a new carnivorous strain which, at one point, clusters in groups in such a way as to spell out a written message to him. Who says bugs are stupid? The attacks of the monstrous bugs (around eight inches long) are suitably nasty; they have an unpleasant tendency to lurk and jump out unexpectedly. Director Szwarc, most of whose work had been in TV, shows a visual flair for orchestrating absurdities, and went on to use it again in *Jaws 2* and, rather differently, *Somewhere in Time*.

BURNT OFFERINGS ★★½

USA 1976; colour; 115 mins; PEA-Dan Curtis/United Artists; *D/P* Dan Curtis; *W* William F. Nolan, Dan Curtis from the novel by Robert Marasco; *M* Robert Cobert; *C* Jacques Marquette, also Stevan Larner; *PD* Eugene Lourié; *SPFX* Cliff Wenger; *Starring* Karen Black, Oliver Reed, Bette Davis,

BURN, WITCH, BURN – *see* NIGHT OF THE EAGLE

THE CABINET OF DR CALIGARI (DAS KABINETT DES DR CALIGARI) ★★★★

Germany 1919; b/w; 6 reels; Decla-Bioscop; *D* Robert Wiene; *P* Erich Pommer; *W* Carl Mayer, Hans Janowitz, (uncredited) Fritz Lang; *SPFX* (production design) Walter Reimann, Hermann Warm, Walter Röhrig; *Starring* Werner Krauss, Conrad Veidt, Lil Dagover; *V* Thorn EMI (UK), Budget (USA).

CALTIKI – THE IMMORTAL MONSTER (CALTIKI, IL MOSTRO IMMORTALE) ★★★

Italy/USA 1959; b/w; 75 mins; Galatea/Bruno Vailati; *D* Richard Hampton (Riccardo Freda); *P* Samuel Schneider; *W* Philip Just (Filippo Sanjust); *M* Robert Nicholas (Roman Vlad); *C* John Foam (Mario Bava); *SPFX* Marie Foam (presumably Bava); *Starring* John Merivale, Daniela Rocca, Didi Sullivan (Didi Perego). The film that introduced the continuing Italian effort to break into the English-speaking market by using Anglo-Saxon pseudonyms on the credits. Rather a good, atmospheric monster movie about an amorphous thing (see also *The Blob* which is not as good) that rises from a subterranean lake in a Mayan city. Freda's visual sense is strong (unlike his sense for narrative) and he produces an eerie, imaginative, Lovecraftian feeling in several sequences. Freda was the father of the Italian *giallo* (sensational horror picture), helped train Bava, and stands at the head of a line including Argento and Fulci.

THE CANTERVILLE GHOST ★★★

USA 1944; b/w; 96 mins; MGM; *D* Jules Dassin; *P* Arthur Field; *W* Edwin Blum from the story by Oscar Wilde; *M* George Bassman; *C* Robert Planck; *Starring* Charles Laughton, Robert Young, Margaret O'Brien, Peter Lawford. Little-remembered, mildly amusing ghost film with good performances, especially Laughton as the cowardly ghost who cannot rest until his descendant does some great deed. Typical of the nervously jokey attitude Hollywood took to the fantastic in the 1940s.

CAPRICORN ONE ★★

USA 1977; colour; 124 mins; Capricorn One/Associated General; *D/W* Peter Hyams; *P* Paul N. Lazarus III; *M* Jerry Goldsmith; *C* Bill Butler; *PD* Albert Brenner; *Starring* Elliott Gould, James Brolin, Karen Black; *V* Precision (UK), CBS/Fox (USA). Hyams also made *Outland* which is better, but he has no real affinity for SF. The absurdly paranoid plot (NASA fakes a Mars landing and is prepared to kill to keep the secret) is too much even for the Watergate era, and makes it very strange that NASA co-operated in the filming! The science is terrible, but as a thriller it has exciting moments.

CAPTAIN KRONOS – VAMPIRE HUNTER ★★½ ☻

UK 1972 (released 1974); colour; 91 mins; Hammer; *D/W* Brian Clemens; *P* Albert Fennell, Clemens; *M* Laurie Johnson; *C* Ian Wilson; *PD* Robert Jones; *Starring* Horst Janson, John Carson, Caroline Munro, Ian Hendry; *V* Iver-CBS (UK), Paramount (USA). Brian Clemens was the driving force behind the popular TV series *The Avengers*, and this cross between swashbuckler and vampire movie has the same jokey bizarreness. High spots: vampires feeding on youth instead of blood, stakes through the heart that don't work, an affable hunchback assistant.

CAPTAIN NEMO AND THE UNDERWATER CITY ★★

UK 1969; colour; 106 mins; Omnia/MGM; *D* James Hill; *P* Bertram Ostrer, Steven Pallos; *W* Pip Baker, Jane Baker, R. Wright Campbell from characters created by Jules Verne; *M* Wally Stott; *C* Alan Hume, (underwater) Egil S. Woxholt; *AD* Bill Andrews; *SPFX* Jack Mills, George Gibbs, Richard Conway; *Starring* Robert Ryan, Chuck Connors, Nanette Newman. Run-of-the-mill mad scientist story. Nemo's underwater Utopia is visited inadvertently by shipwreck survivors who lust after the gold produced as a by-product of making oxygen! A giant manta almost demolishes the city.

THE CAR ★★½
USA 1977; colour; 98 mins; Universal; D Elliot Silverstein; P Marvin Birdt, Silverstein; W Dennis Shryack, Michael Butler, Lane Slate; M Leonard Rosenman; C Gerald Hirschfeld; SPFX Jack Faggard, Paul Hickerson, Ed Kennedy, Bill Aldridge, (photographic) Albert Whitlock; Starring James Brolin, Kathleen Lloyd, John Marley.

CARNE PER FRANKENSTEIN – see FLESH FOR FRANKENSTEIN

CARRIE ★★★★ ☻
USA 1976; colour; 98 mins; Red Bank/United Artists; D Brian De Palma; P Paul Monash; W Lawrence D. Cohen from the novel by Stephen King; M Pino Donaggio; C Mario Tosi; SPFX Gregory M. Auer; Starring Sissy Spacek, Piper Laurie, Amy Irving, William Katt, John Travolta, Nancy Allen; V Warner (UK), CBS/Fox (USA).

LA CASA DELL'EXORCISMO – see THE HOUSE OF EXORCISM

IL CASANOVA DI FEDERICO FELLINI – see FELLINI'S CASANOVA

THE CAT FROM OUTER SPACE ★½
USA 1978; colour; 103 mins; Disney; D Norman Tokar; P Ron Miller, Norman Tokar; W Ted Key; M Lalo Schifrin; C Charles F. Wheeler; AD John B. Mansbridge, Preston Ames; SPFX Eustace Lycett, Art Cruickshank, Danny Lee, (matte artist) P. S. Ellenshaw; Starring Ken Berry, Sandy Duncan, Harry Morgan, Roddy McDowall; V Disney (UK and USA). Intelligent alien cat with psychic powers enlists human assistance to repair damaged spaceship with opposition from the military. Comedy minimal, tension negligible, too cute for words, Disney Studios at their worst. Question: does the alien cat's lusting after Earth cats constitute bestiality? It seems somehow indecent.

CAT PEOPLE ★★★★
USA 1942; b/w; 71 mins; RKO; D Jacques Tourneur; P Val Lewton; W DeWitt Bodeen; M Roy Webb; C Nicholas Musuraca; Starring Simone Simon, Kent Smith, Tom Conway; V Nostalgia (USA).

CAT PEOPLE ★★★ ☻
USA 1982; colour; 118 mins; RKO-Universal; D Paul Schrader; P Charles Fries; W Alan Ormsby from the screenplay of the 1943 Cat People by DeWitt Bodeen; M Giorgio Moroder; C John Bailey; SPFX (visual) Albert Whitlock, (make-up) Tom Burman, (cat vision optical) Robert Blalack; Starring Nastassia Kinski, Malcolm McDowell, John Heard, Annette O'Toole; V CIC (UK), MCA (USA).

CAVEMAN ★★★
USA 1981; colour; 91 mins; Turman-Foster/United Artists; D Carl Gottlieb; P Lawrence Turman, David Foster; W Rudy De Luca, Carl Gottlieb; M Lalo Schifrin; C Alan Hume; PD Philip M. Jefferies; SPFX (animation) David Allen, (mechanical) Roy Arbogast, (abominable snowman) Christopher Walas; Starring Ringo Starr, Barbara Bach, Dennis Quaid; V Warner (UK), CBS/Fox (USA). Wonderfully dopey monsters done with stop-motion animation in this sophomoric, affectionate parody of One Million Years BC, with Ringo Starr as the sweet, resourceful hero. Likeable, good-humoured, often funny.

CELINE AND JULIE GO BOATING (CÉLINE ET JULIE VONT EN BATEAU) ★★★★½
France 1974; colour; 192 mins; Films du Losange; D Jacques Rivette; P Barbet Schroeder; W Eduardo de Gregorio, Rivette, improvisations from the main actors, (the "film" within the film, Phantom Ladies Over Paris derived from "The Other House" and "A Romance of Certain Old Clothes" by Henry James); M/Songs Jean-Marie

Sénia; C Jacques Renard; Starring Juliet Berto, Dominique Labourier, Bulle Ogier, Marie-France Pisier, Barbet Schroeder.

THE CHANGELING ★★½
Canada 1979; colour; 107 mins; Chessman Palk; D Peter Medak; P Joel B. Michaels, Garth H. Drabinsky; W William Gray, Diana Maddox; M Rick Wilkins; C John Coquillon; PD Trevor Williams; SPFX Gene Grigg; Starring George C. Scott, Trish Van Devere, Melvyn Douglas; V VTC (UK), Vestron (USA). It looks like a script-writing committee agonized over how to make this both scary and yet tasteful enough for middle-class audiences. George C. Scott is the classical pianist who moves into a mysterious old house where comparatively trivial manifestations include a lot of battering noises in the bathroom, an empty wheelchair that chases people, and a rather good seance scene where a medium suddenly tears off page after page of automatic writing. Scott's loss of wife and daughter in an accident at the beginning proves to have little bearing on this tale of the ghost of a drowned boy, which is confusingly presented as sometimes merely sad and lost, sometimes actively malevolent. All this is rather tediously drawn out.

CHARLY ★★★
USA 1968; 106 mins; Selmur-Robertson/Cinerama; D/P Ralph Nelson; W Stirling Silliphant from Flowers for Algernon by Daniel Keyes; M Ravi Shankar; C Arthur Ornitz; AD Charles Rosen; Starring Cliff Robertson, Claire Bloom; V Rank (UK), CBS/Fox (USA).

LE CHARME DISCRET DE LA BOURGEOISIE – see THE DISCREET CHARM OF THE BOURGEOISIE

CHIKYU BOEIGUN – see THE MYSTERIANS

THE CHILD (aka ZOMBIE CHILD, KILL AND GO HIDE) ★½ ☻
USA 1977; colour; 82 mins; BoxOffice International/Panorama; D Robert Voskanian; P Robert Dadashian; W Ralph Lucas; M Rob Wallace; C/AD Mori Alavi; SPFX (make-up/creatures) Jay Owens; Starring Laurel Barnett, Rosalie Cole, Frank Janson; V Video Network (UK), Monterey (USA). Fairly typical exploitation movie of the nasty-child genre, and it cashes in on the zombie boom as well. Eleven-year-old Rosalie uses supernatural powers to avenge her mother's death with the help of her "friends", cannibalistic living dead from the local cemetery. Mediocre and derivative.

THE CHILDREN ★ ☻
USA 1980; colour; 90 mins; Albright; D Max Kalmanowicz; P Carlton J. Albright, Kalmanowicz; W Albright, Edward Terry; M Henry Manfredini; C Barry Abrams; SPFX (make-up) Carla White; Starring Martin Shakar, Gil Rogers, Gale Garnett; V Intervision (UK). Laughably inept exploitation pic. Kids affected by radiation become malign zombies, kill parents, can only be destroyed by having hands cut off. It all looks like amateur theatricals. Special effects miracle: fingernails of zombies turn black.

CHILDREN OF THE DAMNED ★★
UK 1963; b/w; 90 mins; MGM; D Anton M. Leader; P Lawrence P. Bachmann, Ben Arbeid; W John Briley from characters created by John Wyndham; M Ron Goodwin; C Davis Boulton; SPFX Tom Howard; Starring Ian Hendry, Alan Badel, Barbara Ferris. More a repeat performance of Village of the Damned than a sequel, based loosely on the same Wyndham novel. Superintelligent, telepathic, mutant children found by UNESCO around the world are seen as menace by the military; final confrontation in a church ends badly for the kids. A sad but pedestrian little moral fable filmed with too much British restraint.

CHILDREN SHOULDN'T PLAY WITH DEAD THINGS ★ ☻
USA 1973; colour; 87 mins; Gold Key/Europix/

Geneni; D Benjamin Clark; P Clark, Gary Goch; W Clark, Alan Ormsby; M Carl Zittrer; C Jack McGowan; AD Forest Carpenter; SPFX (ghoul make-up) Alan Ormsby; Starring Alan Ormsby, Anya Ormsby; V Intervision (UK), Maljack (USA). Campy, amateurish, rambling tale of group of actors on lonely island egged on by leader to raise the dead (as a joke) which in fact they do. Derivative, flesh-eating zombies look as if covered in plaster of paris. Writer, star and make-up man Ormsby worked on Shock Waves (make-up), Cat People (screenplay) later on.

CHI SEI? – see BEYOND THE DOOR

CHITTY CHITTY BANG BANG ★★
UK 1968; colour; 145 mins; Warfield-Dramatic Features/United Artists; D Ken Hughes; P Albert R. Broccoli; W Roald Dahl, Ken Hughes with additional dialogue by Richard Maibaum from the novel by Ian Fleming; M and lyrics Richard M. and Robert B. Sherman; C Christopher Challis; PD Ken Adam; SPFX John Stears; Inventions Rowland Emett; Starring Dick Van Dyke, Sally Ann Howes, Lionel Jeffries, Gert Fröbe; V Warner (UK), CBS/Fox (USA).

THE CHOSEN – see HOLOCAUST 2000

CHOSEN SURVIVORS ★★½
USA/Mexico 1974; colour; 98 mins; Alpine-Churubusco Studios/Metromedia; D Sutton Roley; P Charles W. Fries, Leon Benson; W H. B. Cross, Joe Reb Moffly; M Fred Karlin; C Gabriel Torres; AD José R. Granada; SPFX (bats) Tony Urbano; Starring Jackie Cooper, Alex Cord, Richard Jaeckel, Bradford Dillman, Diana Muldaur. Eleven people are sealed in a bomb-shelter as chosen survivors from the nuclear holocaust about to take place; unfortunately a lot of vampire bats get to them from nearby caves. It turns out that the whole thing was a government hoax to test stress reactions, which has backfired. Not bad as unpretentious, paranoid horror flicks go.

CHRISTINE ★★★★ ☻
USA 1983; colour; 110 mins; Delphi/Columbia; D John Carpenter; P Richard Kobritz; W Bill Phillips from the novel by Stephen King; M Carpenter, Alan Howarth; C Donald M. Morgan; PD Daniel Lomino; SPFX (supervisor) Roy Arbogast; Starring Keith Gordon, John Stockwell, Alexandra Paul.

CIRCLE OF IRON – see THE SILENT FLUTE

CITY OF THE DEAD (aka HORROR HOTEL) ★★★
UK 1960; b/w; 78 mins; Vulcan; D John Moxey; P Donald Taylor, (uncredited) Milton Subotsky; W George Baxt from a story by Subotsky; M Douglas Gamley; C Desmond Dickinson; AD John Blezard; SPFX Cliff Richardson; Starring Christopher Lee, Betta St. John, Patricia Jessel, Venetia Stevenson, Valentine Dyall; V Intervision (UK), Thunderbird (USA). First and possibly best of Subotsky's many horror productions. Sombre, atmospheric tale of witchcraft and sacrifice in a foggy New England township, played straight; well done, modest movie. Heroine is killed shortly into the film, beating Hitchcock's Psycho to the punch.

CITY OF THE LIVING DEAD (PAURA NELLA CITTÀ DEI MORTI VIVENTI, aka GATES OF HELL) ★★★ ☻ ☻
Italy 1980; colour; 93 mins; Dania/Medusa/National Cinematografia; D Lucio Fulci; W Fulci, Dardano Sacchetti; M Fabio Frizzi; C Sergio Salvati; SPFX Gino De Rossi, (make-up) Franco Rufini; Starring Christopher George, Janet Agren, Katriona MacColl; V Inter-Light (UK), Paragon (USA).

CLASH OF THE TITANS ★★½
UK 1981; colour; 118 mins; Peerford/MGM; D Desmond Davis; P Charles H. Schneer, Ray Harryhausen; W Beverley Cross; M Laurence Rosenthal; C Ted Moore; PD Frank White; SPFX (visual) Ray Harryhausen, also Jim Danforth and Steven Archer, (opticals) Frank Van Der Veer and Roy Field; Starring Harry Hamlin, Judi Bowker, Burgess Meredith, Laurence Olivier, Claire Bloom, Maggie Smith, Ursula Andress; V MGM/UA (UK and USA).

A CLOCKWORK ORANGE ★★★★☺

UK 1971; colour; 136 mins; Polaris/Warner; *D/P/W* Stanley Kubrick from the novel by Anthony Burgess; *M* (electronic) Walter Carlos; *C* John Alcott; *PD* John Barry; *Starring'* Malcolm McDowell, Patrick Magee, Adrienne Corri, David Prowse; *V* Warner (USA).

CLOSE ENCOUNTERS OF THE THIRD KIND ★★★½

USA 1977; colour; 135 mins; Columbia/EMI; *D/W* Steven Spielberg; *P* Julia and Michael Phillips; *M* John Williams; *C* Vilmos Zsigmond, also William A. Fraker, Douglas Slocombe, John Alonzo, Laszlo Kovacs; *PD* Joe Alves; *SPFX* (photographic supervision) Douglas Trumbull, (matte artist) Matthew Yuricich, (extra-terrestrials) Carlo Rambaldi, (chief model maker) Gregory Jein; *Starring* Richard Dreyfuss, François Truffaut, Teri Garr, Melinda Dillon, Bob Balaban.

CLOSE ENCOUNTERS OF THE THIRD KIND (SPECIAL EDITION) ★★★★

USA 1980; 132 mins; *C* (additional) Allen Daviau; slightly revised version of preceding film with otherwise identical credits; *V* RCA/Columbia (UK), Columbia (USA).

COLOSSUS – THE FORBIN PROJECT – see THE FORBIN PROJECT

COMA ★★★

USA 1977; colour; 113 mins; MGM; *D/W* Michael Crichton from the novel by Robin Cook; *P* Martin Erlichman; *M* Jerry Goldsmith; *C* Victor J. Kemper, also Gerald Hirschfeld; *PD* Albert Brenner; *Starring* Genevieve Bujold, Michael Douglas, Elizabeth Ashley, Rip Torn, Richard Widmark; *V* MGM/UA (UK and USA).

THE COMPUTER WORE TENNIS SHOES ★★

USA 1969; colour; 90 mins; Disney; *D* Robert Butler; *P* Bill Anderson; *W* Joseph L. McEveety; *M* Robert F. Brunner; *C* Frank Phillips; *AD* John B. Mansbridge; *Starring* Kurt Russell, Cesar Romero, Joe Flynn, William Schallert. Very minor Disney, with the usual clean-cut middle-American cuteness. Campus comedy in which a student has a computer's memory bank accidentally (by way of a lightning bolt) transferred to his brain. He is subsequently very good at TV quizzes. Sequels were *Now You See Him, Now You Don't* and *The Strongest Man in the World.*

CONAN THE BARBARIAN ★★½☺

USA 1981; colour; 129 mins; Dino De Laurentiis/Edward R. Pressman; *D* John Milius; *P* Buzz Feitshans; *W* Milius, Oliver Stone from characters created by Robert E. Howard; *M* Basil Poledouris; *C* Duke Callaghan; *PD* Ron Cobb; *SPFX* (supervisor) Nick Allder, (visual) Frank Van Der Veer; *Starring* Arnold Schwarzenegger, James Earl Jones, Max von Sydow, Sandahl Bergman; *V* Thorn EMI (UK), MCA (USA).

CONDORMAN ★★★

USA 1981; colour; 90 mins; Disney; *D* Charles Jarrott; *P* Jan Williams; *W* Marc Stirdivant, Glen Caron, Mickey Rose, loosely based on *The Game of X* by Robert Sheckley; *M* Henry Mancini; *C* Charles F. Wheeler; *PD* Albert Witherick; *SPFX* Colin Chilvers, (animation) Jack Boyd, (photographic) Art Cruickshank; *Starring* Michael Crawford, Oliver Reed, Barbara Carrera; *V* Disney (UK and USA). Above-average Disney, amusing but rather wet. Bumbling British comedian Michael Crawford stars in James Bond parody about comic-strip author who insists on testing his inventions in real-life, and dresses as his own hero, Condorman. Main fantasy element is artificial wings that really almost work, and, of course, the idea of life being comparable to a comic strip.

THE CONQUEROR WORM – see WITCHFINDER GENERAL

THE CONQUEST OF SPACE ★½

USA 1955; colour; 81 mins; Paramount; *D* Byron Haskin; *P* George Pal; *W* James O'Hanlon, also Philip Yordan, Barré Lyndon and George Worthing Yates, adapted very remotely from the nonfiction book by Chesley Bonestell and Willy Ley; *M* Van Cleave; *C* Lionel Lindon; *AD* Hal Pereira, Joseph MacMillan Johnson; *SPFX* (photographic) John P. Fulton and others; *Starring* Walter Brooke, Eric Fleming, Mickey Shaughnessy. Planned as a realistic account of what the first landing on Mars might be like, this early space film is in fact a lurid melodrama; the captain goes mad because space flight is irreligious and is killed by his son. Clumsy special effects; rotten science; Pal's worst SF movie; it flopped.

CONQUEST OF THE PLANET OF THE APES ★½

USA 1972; colour; 85 mins; Apjac/20th Century-Fox; *D* J. Lee Thompson; *P* Arthur P. Jacobs; *W* Paul Dehn; *M* Tom Scott; *C* Bruce Surtees; *AD* Philip Jefferies; *SPFX* (make-up) John Chambers; *Starring* Roddy McDowall, Don Murray, Natalie Trundy, Ricardo Montalban; *V* CBS/Fox (UK). Fourth in the progressively deteriorating *Planet of the Apes* series which began so well. On Earth, not too far from our own time, slave apes led by Caesar (the baby ape in *Escape from the Planet of the Apes*) rebel against their human masters. *Spartacus* was much better; this is bland.

CONTES IMMOREAUX – see IMMORAL TALES

COUNT DRACULA ★★★½

UK 1977; made for TV; colour; 155 mins; BBC TV/WNET 13; *D* Philip Saville; *P* Morris Barry; *W* Gerald Savory from *Dracula* by Bram Stoker; *M* Kenyon Emrys-Roberts; *C* Peter Hall; *PD* Michael Young; *SPFX* (visual) Tony Harding; *Starring* Louis Jourdan, Frank Finlay, Susan Penhaligon, Judi Bowker. See this above-average BBC Television adaptation of Stoker's novel if you have a chance. By returning to the original book, rather than quoting from previous films, it takes on a remarkable freshness. Jourdan is a handsome, suave Dracula, a kind of Christlike Antichrist who smiles sweetly and is solicitous to his disciples; he even offers a form of perverted communion to his victim Mina (Judi Bowker) by using a long fingernail to cut open his own breast, and giving her the blood to lick. This image is at once religious and erotic, and these themes are the two main strands of the film. Frank Finlay's Van Helsing is intelligent and convincing. The visual effects when Dracula attacks are perhaps overdone (the picture goes into discoloured negative). The production was made on a mixture of videotape and film proper.

COUNT DRACULA AND HIS VAMPIRE BRIDE – see THE SATANIC RITES OF DRACULA

COUNTESS DRACULA ★★½☺

UK 1970; colour; 93 mins; Hammer; *D* Peter Sasdy; *P* Alexander Paal; *W* Jeremy Paul; *M* Harry Robinson; *C* Ken Talbot; *AD* Philip Harrison; *SPFX* Bert Luxford; *Starring* Ingrid Pitt, Nigel Green, Sandor Elès, Lesley-Anne Down; *V* Rank (UK) Based on true story of sadistic Hungarian countess who bathed in blood of murdered virgins (it also appears in Borowczyk's *Immoral Tales*). In this version the blood makes her temporarily young again. Interesting on cruel-but-pathetic mother imagery, but generally flat. Nothing to do with Dracula.

COUNT YORGA, VAMPIRE ★★★☺

USA 1970; colour; 92 mins; Erica/AIP; *D/W* Robert Kelljan; *P* Michael Macready; *M* William Marx; *C* Arch Archambault; *SPFX* James Tanenbaum; *Starring* Robert Quarry, Roger Perry, Michael Murphy, Donna Anders.

CRASH! ★★

USA 1977; colour; 78 mins; Group One; *D/P* Charles Band; *W* Marc Marais; *M* Andrew Belling; *C* Andrew Davis, Bill Williams; *Starring* Jose Ferrer, Sue Lyon, John Carradine; *V* VCL (UK). One of Band's many cheap horror movies – generally not too scary – this is a little better than most, though the theme of possessed vehicles is done better in *The Car*. Main effects are car crashes and glowing red eyes. Jealous, crippled, killer-husband Ferrer gets supernatural comeuppance mediated through persecuted wife, ex-Lolita Lyon.

THE CRAZIES ★★★½☺

USA 1973; colour; 103 mins; Pittsburgh Films; *D/W* George A. Romero from a script by Paul McCollough; *P* A. C. Croft; *M* Bruce Roberts; *C* S. William Hinzman; *SPFX* Regis Survinski, Tony Pantanello; *Starring* Lane Carroll, W. G. McMillan, Harold Wayne Jones; *V* Hello Video (UK).

THE CRAZY RAY – see PARIS QUI DORT

THE CREATURE FROM BLACK LAKE ★★★

USA 1975; colour; 95 mins; Cinema Shares/Howco/McCullough; *D* Joy Houck Jr; *P* Jim McCullough; *W* Jim McCullough Jr; *M* Jaime Mendoza-Nava; *C* Dean Cundey; *Starring* Jack Elam, Dub Taylor, John David Carson; *V* Replay (UK). This *really* low-budget, regional movie about search by college kids for Bigfoot-type monster in Louisiana swamp country is surprisingly vivid and racy; good, amusing script; piratical cameo by Elam as old trapper; creature wisely left in shadow throughout.

THE CREATURE FROM THE BLACK LAGOON ★★★

USA 1954; b/w 3-D; 79 mins; Universal; *D* Jack Arnold; *P* William Alland; *W* Harry Essex, Arthur Ross; *C* William E. Snyder; *SPFX* (photography) Charles S. Welbourne, (make-up) Bud Westmore, Jack Kevan; *Starring* Richard Carlson, Julie Adams, Ricou Browning; *V* MCA (USA).

THE CREEPING FLESH ★★★

UK 1972; colour; 91 mins; World Film/Tigon; *D* Freddie Francis; *P* Michael Redbourn; *W* Peter Spenceley, Jonathan Rumbold; *M* Paul Ferris; *C* Norman Warwick; *AD* George Provis; *Starring* Christopher Lee, Peter Cushing, Lorna Heilbron; *V* Videomedia (UK), Columbia (USA). More British horror from Tigon, a down-market version of Hammer Films. Victorian setting. Skeleton of ape-man grows new flesh when touched by water; subplot involves insanity-producing blood cells. Deftly handled, but too silly for words.

THE CREEPING UNKNOWN – see THE QUATERMASS XPERIMENT

CREEPSHOW ★★★

USA 1982; colour; 120 mins; Laurel Show/United Film Distribution; *D* George A. Romero; *P* Richard P. Rubinstein; *W* Stephen King, "The Crate" being based on his short story; *M* John Harrison; *C* Michael Gornick; *PD/SPFX* (make-up) Tom Savini; *Starring* ("Father's Day") Carrie Nye and Viveca Lindfors, ("The Lonesome Death of Jordy Verrill") Stephen King, ("Something to Tide You Over") Leslie Nielsen, ("The Crate") Hal Holbrook, Adrienne Barbeau, Fritz Weaver, ("They're Creeping Up on You") E. G. Marshall; *V* Intervision (UK), Warner (USA).

CRIMES OF THE FUTURE ★★★☺

Canada 1970; colour; 65 mins; Emergent; *D/P/W/C* David Cronenberg; *Starring* Ronald Mlodzik, Jon Lidolt, Tania Zolty.

THE CRIMSON CULT – see THE CURSE OF THE CRIMSON ALTAR

CRY OF THE BANSHEE ★½

UK 1970; colour; 87 mins; AIP; *D/P* Gordon Hessler; *W* Tim Kelly, Christopher Wicking; *M* Les Baxter; *C* John Coquillon; *AD* George Provis; *Starring* Vincent Price, Patrick Mower, Elisabeth Bergner, Essy Persson; *V* Guild (UK). Mower plays a werewolf spawn of Satan used by witch-cult members in Tudor period to revenge themselves upon sadistic squire (Price) and family. Narrative and moral confusion abound. Is setting England or Ireland? Where is the banshee? Are witches innocent flower people or bloody killers? Slow-moving and flaccid.

CUJO ★★★★☺

USA 1983; colour; 91 mins; Taft/Sunn Classic; *D*

Lewis Teague; *P* Daniel H. Blatt, Robert Singer; *W* Don Carlos Dunaway, Lauren Currier from the novel by Stephen King; *M* Charles Bernstein; *C* Jan De Bont; *PD* Guy Comtois; *SPFX* Rick Josephsen, (make-up) Peter Knowlton; *Starring* Dee Wallace, Daniel Hugh-Kelly, Danny Pintauro, Ed Lauter; *V* Warner (USA). Young genre director Teague (see *Alligator*) in excellent form with not especially promising source material, one of King's weaker novels, about an adulterous woman and her young son trapped by a killer St Bernard dog which may be possessed of evil. The film eliminates the depressing and not wholly necessary death of the child, and gets rid of the fantasy element too. Here the dog is simply rabid. Nonetheless, very much in the monster-movie genre, an object lesson in crisp, taut thriller-making. As in many monster films, the outside horror is partly an image of tensions within the family.

THE CURSE OF FRANKENSTEIN ★★½ ♥
UK 1957; colour; 82 mins; Hammer/Warner; *D* Terence Fisher; *P* Anthony Hinds; *W* Jimmy Sangster from the novel by Mary Shelley; *M* James Bernard; *C* Jack Asher; *SPFX* Phil Leakey, (make-up) Roy Ashton; *Starring* Peter Cushing, Christopher Lee.

THE CURSE OF THE CAT PEOPLE ★★★★½
USA 1944; b/w; 70 mins; RKO; *D* Gunther Von Fritsch, Robert Wise; *P* Val Lewton; *W* DeWitt Bodeen; *M* Roy Webb; *C* Nicholas Musuraca; *Starring* Simone Simon, Kent Smith, Jane Randolph; *V* Nostalgia (USA). Only a sequel to *The Cat People* in that the werecat of the previous film (Simone Simon) becomes the ghost of a little girl's dead mother, called up by the daughter as a playmate. The daughter is lonely, dreamy, easily frightened. Although the ghost seems protective (and may only be imaginary), she is still associated with a little of the aberrant cat imagery of the previous film. This skilful, delicate film about a child's fantasies and fears was Wise's first directorial assignment; he took over from Fritsch.

CURSE OF THE CRIMSON ALTAR (aka THE CRIMSON CULT) ★½
UK 1968; colour; 89 mins; Tigon/AIP; *D* Vernon Sewell; *P* Louis M. Heyward; *W* Mervyn Haisman, Henry Lincoln, also Gerry Levy, suggested by the story "The Dreams in the Witch-House" by H. P. Lovecraft; *M* Peter Knight; *C* John Coquillon; *Starring* Mark Eden, Boris Karloff, Christopher Lee, Barbara Steele; *V* Videomedia (UK). Karloff, who died about the time the film was released, looks old and sick in his wheelchair cameo. Loosely based on a Lovecraft story, the film has no Lovecraft atmosphere. Eden limply searches for missing brother in old Morley house (Lee as family head); has strange dreams; stumbles on witchcraft. Barbara Steele painted blue appears in witchcraft scenes, which are sexually fetishistic; the rest of the movie is mild, sluggish, too well bred by half.

CURSE OF THE DEMON – see NIGHT OF THE DEMON

THE CURSE OF THE MUMMY'S TOMB ★
UK 1964; colour; 81 mins; Hammer-Swallow/Columbia; *D/P* Michael Carreras; *W* Henry Younger (pseudonym of Carreras); *M* Carlo Martelli; *C* Otto Heller; *PD* Bernard Robinson; *Starring* Terence Morgan, Ronald Howard, Fred Clark, Jeanne Roland; *V* RCA-Columbia (UK). Thoroughly undistinguished sequel to Hammer's *The Mummy*. Performances terrible; not remotely scary. Story turns on resuscitated mummy seeking vengeance on immortal brother.

THE CURSE OF THE WEREWOLF ★★
UK 1960; colour; 88 mins; Hammer-Hotspur/Universal; *D* Terence Fisher; *P* Anthony Hinds; *W* John Elder (pseudonym of Anthony Hinds) from *The Werewolf of Paris* by Guy Endore; *M* Benjamin Frankel; *C* Arthur Grant; *SPFX* Les Bowie, (make-up) Roy Ashton; *Starring* Oliver Reed, Clifford Evans, Yvonne Romain. A mute servant girl is raped by a mad old beggar in prison and later

dies in childbirth on Christmas Day. The son, Leon (played as an adult by Oliver Reed), is adopted by a simple family, but there are problems. At his baptism the holy water in the font bubbles. When he reaches manhood, he battles against the taint in his blood, but, alas, he becomes a werewolf during the full moon. Afraid of hurting the girl he loves, he finally begs his stepfather to shoot him with a silver bullet, and dies in church. Highly praised by some, but really not up to much, the romantic love-story elements being done rather woodenly and melodramatically. Moderately restrained for Hammer, though. The supposed Spanish setting is not very convincing, and the story is directed at rather a torpid pace.

DALEKS – INVASION EARTH 2150 AD ★★½
UK 1966; colour; 84 mins; Amicus-Aaru; *D* Gordon Flemyng; *P* Max J. Rosenberg, Milton Subotsky; *W* Subotsky, also David Whitaker from the BBC Television serial *Dr Who* by Terry Nation; *M* Bill McGuffie; *C* John Wilcox; *AD* George Provis; *SPFX* Ted Samuels; *Starring* Peter Cushing, Bernard Cribbins, Ray Brooks, Andrew Keir; *V* Thorn EMI (UK). Affable movie spin-off from the celebrated TV series *Dr Who* is in fact sequel to earlier movie *Dr Who* and the *Daleks*. Mainly notable for yet another actor playing the good doctor: Peter Cushing. The Daleks as usual plan to conquer Earth, but they are sent packing. (Daleks are creatures inside machines that roll about on wheels shrilling "Exterminate! Exterminate!")

DAMIEN OMEN II ★★★ ♥
USA 1978; colour; 109 mins; 20th Century-Fox; *D* Don Taylor; *P* Harvey Bernhard, Charles Orme; *W* Stanley Mann, Michael Hodges from story by Bernhard and characters by David Seltzer; *M* Jerry Goldsmith; *C* Bill Butler, also Gil Taylor; *PD* Philip M. Jefferies, Fred Harpman; *SPFX* Ira Anderson Jr; *Starring* William Holden, Lee Grant, Jonathan Scott-Taylor, Robert Foxworth, Lew Ayres, Sylvia Sidney; *V* CBS/Fox (UK and USA).

DAMNATION ALLEY ★
USA 1977; colour; 91 mins; Landers-Roberts-Zeitman/20th Century-Fox; *D* Jack Smight; *P* Jerome M. Zeitman, Paul Maslansky; *W* Alan Sharp, Lukas Heller, very loosely adapted from the novel by Roger Zelazny; *M* Jerry Goldsmith; *C* Harry Stradling Jr; *PD* Preston Ames; *Starring* Jan-Michael Vincent, George Peppard, Dominique Sanda, Paul Winfield; *V* CBS/Fox (UK). Disastrously poor adaptation of good novel, in which the Hells Angels hero of the original becomes an air force officer, thus losing much of the punch of the basic situation. After the nuclear holocaust four men make a dash across America to the East through the now mutant-infested radioactive wasteland. Script terrible, special effects laughably bad, even carnivorous cockroaches disappointingly placid.

THE DAMNED (aka THESE ARE THE DAMNED) ★★★★
UK 1961 (released UK 1963, USA 1965); b/w; 87 mins; Hammer-Swallow/Columbia; *D* Joseph Losey; *P* Anthony Hinds; *W* Evan Jones from *The Children of Light* by H. L. Lawrence; *M* James Bernard; *C* Arthur Grant; *AD* Bernard Robinson; *Starring* Macdonald Carey, Shirley Ann Field, Viveca Lindfors, Alexander Knox, Oliver Reed.

DAMN YANKEES (aka WHAT LOLA WANTS) ★★★
USA 1958; colour; 110 mins; Warner; *D/P* George Abbott, Stanley Donen; *W* Abbott from the musical by Abbott and Douglas Wallop based on *The Year the Yankees Lost the Pennant* by Wallop; *M* Richard Adler, Jerry Ross; *C* Harold Lipstein; *AD* Stanley Fleischer; *Choreography* Bob Fosse, Pat Ferrier; *Starring* Gwen Verdon, Tab Hunter, Ray Walston. Ageing baseball fan sells soul to the Devil (roguish Ray Walston) to help the Washington Senators out of trouble; he is made young again (Tab Hunter) and becomes great baseball star, but fails to succumb to not-especially-luscious Lola (Verdon), thus allowing him to use an escape clause. All too bland and cute to have any real punch, and three good songs are not enough to save it.

DANCE OF THE VAMPIRES (aka THE FEARLESS VAMPIRE KILLERS OR, PARDON ME BUT YOUR TEETH ARE IN MY NECK) ★★★
UK 1967; colour; 107 mins; Cadre-Filmways/MGM; *D* Roman Polanski; *P* Gene Gutowski; *W* Gérard Brach, Polanski; *M* Krzysztof Komeda; *C* Douglas Slocombe; *Starring* Jack MacGowran, Roman Polanski, Alfie Bass, Sharon Tate, Ferdy Mayne. Polanski himself stars in this silly, enjoyable vampire story, which hovers between being a spoof and genuinely scary. He is the innocent, Candide-figure, assistant to an eccentric Van Helsing style master out to investigate a nest of vampires in the Transylvanian boondocks. The final score is vampires 2, vampire-killers 0. Goes on a lot too long in a self-indulgent way, but some of the funny bits are really funny (especially the Jewish vampire who is vastly amused when Polanski tries to ward him off with a crucifix), and the bits in the vampire castle have a kind of grotesque stateliness. The vampires do, in fact, hold a dance.

DANGER: DIABOLIK (DIABOLIK) ★★½
Italy 1968; colour; 105 mins; Dino De Laurentiis-Marianne/Paramount; *D* Mario Bava; *P* Dino De Laurentiis; *W* Dino Maiuri, Adriano Baracco, Bava, Brian Degas, Tudor Gates from the cartoon strip by Luciana and Angela Giussani; *M* Ennio Morricone; *C* Antonio Rinaldi; *Starring* John Phillip Law, Marisa Mell, Michel Piccoli, Adolfo Celi, Terry-Thomas.

DARBY O'GILL AND THE LITTLE PEOPLE ★★½
USA 1959; colour; 93 mins; Disney; *D* Robert Stevenson; *P* Walt Disney; *W* Lawrence E. Watkin from stories by J. T. Kavanagh; *M* Oliver Wallace; *C* Winton C. Hoch; *SPFX* Peter Ellenshaw, Eustace Lycett, (animation) Joshua Meador; *Starring* Albert Sharpe, Janet Munro, Sean Connery; *V* Disney (USA).

THE DARK CRYSTAL ★★★
UK 1982; colour; 93 mins; Henson Organisation/ITC; *D* Jim Henson, Frank Oz; *P* Henson, Gary Kurtz; *W* David Odell from a story by Henson; *M* Trevor Jones; *C* Oswald Morris; *PD* Harry Lange; *Creatures/Conceptual Design* Brian Froud; *SPFX* (visual) Roy Field, Brian Smithies, (scenic mattes) Mike Pangrazio, Chris Evans, Industrial Light & Magic, also Charles Stoneham; *Starring the voices of* Jim Henson (*Jen/Skeksis High Priest*), Kathryn Mullen (*Kira*), Frank Oz (*Aughra/Skeksis Chamberlain*); *V* RCA/Columbia (UK), Thorn EMI (USA).

DARK STAR ★★★★½
USA 1974; colour; 83 mins; Jack H. Harris Enterprises; *D/P/M* John Carpenter; *W* Carpenter, Dan O'Bannon; *C* Douglas Knapp; *PD/SPFX* O'Bannon, (paintings) Jim Danforth, (spaceship design) Ron Cobb, (miniatures) Greg Jein and Harry Walton; *Starring* Brian Narelle, Dre Pahich, Cal Kuniholm, O'Bannon, Joe Saunders; *V* Iver (UK), Video Communications and Budget (USA).

DAUGHTERS OF DARKNESS (LE ROUGE AUX LÈVRES) ★★★½
Belgium/France/West Germany/Italy 1970; Showking/Cine Vog/Maya/Roxy/Mediterranea; *D* Harry Kumel; *P* Alain Guilleaume, Paul Collet; *W* Kumel, Pierre Drouot; *M* François de Roubaix; *C* Eddy van der Enden; *AD* Françoise Hardy; *Starring* Delphine Seyrig, John Karlen, Danièle Ouimet, Andréa Rau. Stylish European vampire film, with the elegant Delphine Seyrig looking tired, lovely, a little bored, a little decadent, as the eternally youthful Countess Bathory (see also *Immoral Tales, Countess Dracula*). Asked how she manages to look so young she accurately responds, "a strict diet and lots of sleep". The film explores her encounter with a young couple. Kumel also made the interesting *Malpertuis*.

DAWN OF THE DEAD (aka ZOMBIES) ★★★½ ♥ ♥
USA 1977; colour; 127 mins; Laurel Group/Dawn Associates; *D/W* George A. Romero; *P* Richard P. Rubinstein; *W Consultant* Dario Argento; *M* The Goblins, Argento; *C* Michael Gornick; *AD* Josie

Caruso, Barbara Lifsher; *SPFX* (make-up) Tom Savini; *Starring* David Emge, Ken Foree, Scott H. Reininger, Gaylen Ross; *V* Intervision (UK), Thorn EMI (USA).

THE DAY THE EARTH CAUGHT FIRE ★★½
UK 1961; b/w; 99 mins; Melina-Pax/British Lion; *D/P* Val Guest; *W* Wolf Mankowitz, Guest; *C* Harry Waxman; *SPFX* Les Bowie; *Starring* Edward Judd, Janet Munro, Leo McKern; *V* Intervision (UK), Thorn EMI (USA). Nuclear tests knock Earth out of orbit and send it falling towards the Sun. Very British disaster movie, largely set in the offices of London's *Daily Express*. The documentary style does not conceal the silliness, bad science and melodrama of the story, but Les Bowie's special effects, especially the drying up of the Thames, are good.

THE DAY THE EARTH STOOD STILL ★★★½
USA 1951; b/w; 92 mins; 20th Century-Fox; *D* Robert Wise; *P* Julian Blaustein; *W* Edmund H. North from "Farewell to the Master" by Harry Bates; *M* Bernard Herrmann; *C* Leo Tover; *AD* Lyle Wheeler, Addison Hehr; *Starring* Michael Rennie, Patricia Neal, Hugh Marlowe, Sam Jaffe; *V* CBS/Fox (UK and USA).

DEAD AND BURIED ★★★ 👁 👁
USA 1981; colour; 95 mins; Shusett/Avco Embassy; *D* Gary A. Sherman; *P* Ronald Shusett, Robert Fentress; *W* Shusett, Dan O'Bannon from a story by Jeff Millar and Alex Stern; *M* Joe Renzetti; *C* Steve Poster; *SPFX* (make-up design) Stan Winston; *Starring* James Farentino, Melody Anderson, Jack Albertson; *V* Thorn EMI (UK), Vestron (USA). Competent director Sherman *(Death Line)* had a gratuitously nasty script to work from here, by the writers of *Alien*, about the living-dead citizens of a seafront township who brutally murder visitors. The zombies look quite normal. Quite well made, with scary moments and a good, quite amusing role for Albertson as the eccentric and mysterious local undertaker, but basically a sado-exploitation movie.

DEAD KIDS – *see* STRANGE BEHAVIOR

DEADLY BLESSING ★★★ 👁
USA 1981; colour; 102 mins; Inter Planetary/Poly-Gram; *D* Wes Craven; *P* Micheline and Max Keller, Pat Herskovic; *W* Glenn M. Benest, Matthew Barr, Craven; *M* James Horner; *C* Robert Jessup; *SPFX* Jack Bennett; *Starring* Maren Jensen, Ernest Borgnine, Lois Nettleton, Lisa Hartman; *V* PolyGram (UK), Embassy (USA).

DEAD OF NIGHT ★★★
UK 1945; b/w; 102 mins; Ealing; *P* Sidney Cole, John Croydon; *W* John V. Baines, Angus MacPhail, T. E. B. Clarke; *M* Georges Auric; *C* Douglas Slocombe and others; *AD* Michael Relph. *"Linking story" D* Basil Dearden, *W* from "The Room in the Tower" by E. F. Benson, *Starring* Mervyn Johns, Roland Culver. *"Christmas Party" D* Cavalcanti, *W* from story by MacPhail, *Starring* Sally Ann Howes. *"Hearse Driver" D* Basil Dearden, *W* from "The Bus Conductor" by E. F. Benson, *Starring* Miles Malleson. *"The Haunted Mirror" D* Robert Hamer, *W* from story by Baines, *Starring* Googie Withers. *"Golfing Story" D* Charles Crichton, *W* from "The Inexperienced Ghost" by H. G. Wells, *Starring* Basil Radford, Naunton Wayne. *"The Ventriloquist's Dummy" D* Cavalcanti, *W* from story by Baines, *Starring* Michael Redgrave. *V* Thorn EMI (USA).

THE DEAD ZONE ★★★½ 👁
USA 1983; colour; 103 mins; Dino De Laurentiis/Lorimar; *D* David Cronenberg; *P* Debra Hill; *W* Jeffrey Boam from the novel by Stephen King; *M* Michael Kamen; *C* Mark Irwin; *PD* Carol Spier; *SPFX* (co-ordinator) Jon Belyeu; *Starring* Christopher Walken, Brooke Adams, Herbert Lom, Anthony Zerbe, Martin Sheen.

DEATH LINE (aka RAW MEAT) **★★★★ 👁**
UK 1972; colour; 87 mins; K-L/Rank; *D* Gary Sherman; *P* Paul Maslansky; *W* Ceri Jones; *M* Jeremy Rose, Wil Malone; *C* Alex Thomson; *SPFX*

(make-up) Harry and Peter Frampton; *Starring* Donald Pleasence, Christopher Lee, Hugh Armstrong, David Ladd, Sharon Gurney; *V* Rank (UK).

DEATH RACE 2000 ★★★
USA 1975; colour; 79 mins; New World; *D* Paul Bartel; *P* Roger Corman; *W* Robert Thom, Charles Griffith from "The Racer" by Ib Melchior; *M* Paul Chihara; *C* Tak Fujimoto; *Car design* James Powers; *SPFX* Richard MacLean; *Starring* David Carradine, Sylvester Stallone, Simone Griffeth, Mary Woronov, John Landis; *V* Brent Walker (UK), Warner (USA).

DEATH SHIP ★
UK/Canada 1980; colour; 91 mins; Bloodstar/Lamitas; *D* Alvin Rakoff; *P* Derek Gibson, Harold Greenberg; *W* John Robins; *M* Ivor Slaney; *C* René Verzier; *SPFX* Mike Albrechtsen, Peter Hughes; *Starring* George Kennedy, Richard Crenna, Nick Mancuso, Sally Ann Howes, Kate Reid; *V* Thorn EMI (UK). So awful as to be almost funny. Nazi ghost ship rams passenger liner; survivors clamber aboard haunted ship; captain is possessed of evil; Kate Reid gets fatal case of facial boils; others die unconvincingly. Nazis are popular in low-budget exploitation movies; see also *Shock Waves*.

DEATH WATCH (LA MORT EN DIRECT) **★★★**
France/West Germany 1979; colour; 130 mins; Selta/Little Bear/Sara/Gaumont/Antenne 2/TV 15; *D* Bertrand Tavernier; *P* Jean-Serge Breton, Tavernier; *W* David Rayfiel, Tavernier from *The Continuous Katherine Mortenhoe* by D. G. Compton; *M* Antoine Duhamel; *C* Pierre-William Glenn; *PD* Tony Pratt; *Starring* Romy Schneider, Harvey Keitel, Harry Dean Stanton, Max Von Sydow; *V* VTC (UK).

DELUGE ★★½
USA 1933; b/w; 70 mins; Admiral/RKO; *D* Felix E. Feist; *P* Samuel Bischoff; *W* John Goodrich, Warren B. Duff from the novel by S. Fowler Wright; *C* Norbert Brodine; *SPFX* Ned Mann, (photography) William B. Williams; *Starring* Sidney Blackmer, Peggy Shannon, Fred Kohler. This seldom-seen, early SF disaster movie is celebrated for its scenes of the sea flooding in over New York. Effects director Mann later worked on *Things to Come*. Strange weather patterns are followed by earthquakes and floods. Most of the spectacle is early on; the rest is a disappointing love story between two of the shocked survivors.

DEMON (aka GOD TOLD ME TO) **★★★★**
USA 1976; colour; 89 mins; Larco; *D/P/W* Larry Cohen; *M* Frank Cordell; *C* Paul Glickman; *SPFX* (make-up) Steve Neill; *Starring* Tony Lo Bianco, Deborah Raffin, Sandy Dennis, Sylvia Sidney, Sam Levene; *V* VTC (UK).

THE DEMON – *see* ONIBABA

DEMON SEED ★★½
USA 1977; colour; 95 mins; MGM; *D* Donald Cammell; *P* Herb Jaffe; *W* Robert Jaffe, Roger O. Hirson from the novel by Dean R. Koontz; *M* Jerry Fielding; *C* Bill Butler; *PD* Edward Carfagno; *SPFX* Tom Fisher, (mechanical) Glen Robinson; *Starring* Julie Christie, Fritz Weaver, Gerrit Graham, Berry Kroger; *V* MGM/UA (UK).

DESTINATION MOON ★★½
USA 1950; colour; 92 mins; Pal/Eagle-Lion; *D* Irving Pichel; *P* George Pal; *W* Rip Van Ronkel, Robert A. Heinlein, James O'Hanlon very loosely derived from the novel *Rocketship Galileo* by Heinlein; *M* Leith Stevens; *C* Lionel Linden; *PD* Ernst Fegté; *SPFX* Lee Zavitz, (astronomical art) Chesley Bonestell; *Starring* John Archer, Warner Anderson, Dick Wesson, Erin O'Brien Moore, Tom Powers; *V* Nostalgia (USA). Historically important as the first major movie that ushered in the SF boom of the 1950s, and the first serious space movie since *Frau im Mond*. But flat dialogue, and a script curiously without incident (not to mention the fact of the real Moon-landing in 1969) have helped to date this fictional account of man's first trip to the Moon badly, although the special

effects are quite good and won an Oscar for Zavitz, and Heinlein insisted with some success on scientific accuracy.

THE DEVIL AND DANIEL WEBSTER – *see* ALL THAT MONEY CAN BUY

THE DEVIL AND MAX DEVLIN ★★
USA 1981; colour; 95 mins; Disney; *D* Steven Hilliard Stern; *P* Jerome Courtland; *W* Mary Rodgers from a story by Rodgers and Jimmy Sangster; *M* Buddy Baker; *C* Howard Schwartz; *AD* John B. Mansbridge, Leon R. Harris; *SPFX* Art Cruickshank, Danny Lee; *Starring* Elliott Gould, Bill Cosby, Susan Anspach; *V* Disney (UK and USA). Cosby, a black actor, has the best lines as the devil who offers to restore life to unscrupulous Max Devlin (killed in an accident) if he can persuade three innocents to sell their souls; they are a rock singer, a motor cyclist and (the really sentimental bit) a little boy who wants a daddy. Devlin (Gould) can help these three to their various hearts' desires with his newly-acquired magic powers, provided he stays within eyesight of them. Rather halting farce ensues, and decent American morality wins the day.

DEVIL DOG: THE HOUND OF HELL ★★½
USA 1978; made for TV; colour; 93 mins; Landers-Roberts-Zeitman; *D* Curtis Harrington; *P* Lou Morheim; *W* Stephen and Elinor Karpf; *M* Artie Kane; *C* Gerald Finnerman; *SPFX* Sam DiMaggio, Allen Blaisdell; *Starring* Richard Crenna, Yvette Mimieux; *V* VTC (UK). Likeably bad horror movie from director with small cult following. Friendly, lolloping Alsatian dog cast as Satanic villain; film gets quite good when kids and wife are taken over by demon dog and give husband bad time, but special effects laughable. Question, how does it profit Satanists to upset suburban families?

THE DEVIL-DOLL ★★★½
USA 1936; b/w; 79 mins; MGM; *D* Tod Browning; *P* E. J. Mannix; *W* Browning, Guy Endore, Garrett Fort, Erich von Stroheim from *Burn, Witch, Burn* by Abraham Merritt; *Starring* Lionel Barrymore, Maureen O'Sullivan, Frank Lawton. The director of *Dracula* and *Freaks* is in good but not top form in this tale of wicked Barrymore disguised as old-lady toymaker sending out people he has miniaturised to six inches tall to commit acts of revenge on his behalf. Would you buy a used doll from this man? Special effects very good, comparable with those of two films with similar central images: *Dr Cyclops* and *Incredible Shrinking Man*.

THE DEVIL RIDES OUT (aka THE DEVIL'S BRIDE) **★★★**
UK 1967; colour; 95 mins; Hammer/Seven Arts; *D* Terence Fisher; *P* Anthony Nelson-Keys; *W* Richard Matheson from the novel by Dennis Wheatley; *M* James Bernard; *C* Arthur Grant; *AD* Bernard Robinson; *Starring* Christopher Lee, Charles Gray, Nike Arrighi. Critic David Pirie thinks this is wonderful: "...melodrama is achieved so completely and so imaginatively that it ceases to be melodrama at all and becomes a full-scale allegorical vision". But it could be argued that despite some felicities along the way, notably a night within a pentacle where the heroes are besieged by satanic tempters and monsters, this tale of decent upper-class chaps versus witch cult led by urbane Charles Gray never transcends the absurdity of its best-selling pulp origin, and is rather thin compared with the dense detail of the original novel.

THE DEVIL'S BRIDE – *see* THE DEVIL RIDES OUT

THE DEVIL'S EYE (DJÄVULENS ÖGA) **★★★**
Sweden 1960; b/w; 90 mins; Svensk Filmindustri; *D/W* Ingmar Bergman; *P* Allan Ekelund; *M* Domenico Scarlatti; *C* Gunnar Fischer; *Starring* Jarl Kulle, Bibi Andersson, Nils Poppe. A weakish Bergman film is still pretty good by most standards. The Devil sends Don Juan to seduce the virgin daughter of a pastor, whose chastity is offensive

to Hell. The pastor's wife is attended to by Don Juan's servant with rather more success. Engaging light comedy, with scenes in Hell, but Bergman's serious hells are more interesting than this.

THE DEVIL'S MEN – *see* LAND OF THE MINOTAUR

THE DEVIL'S RAIN ★★
USA 1975; colour; 86 mins; Sandy Howard/20th Century-Fox; *D* Robert Fuest; *P* James V. Cullen, Michael S. Glick; *W* Gabe Essoe, James Ashton, Gerald Hopman; *M* Al De Lory; *C* Alex Phillips Jr; *PD* Nikita Knatz; *SPFX* Cliff and Carol Wenger, Thomas Fisher, Frederico Farfan, (make-up) Burman's Studio; *Starring* Ernest Borgnine, Eddie Albert, Ida Lupino, William Shatner; *V* Video Communications (USA). Rather inferior post-*Exorcist* devil film, celebrated for its closing sequence (not particularly well done) when all the satanic acolytes are gruesomely melted in the rain of the title. Set in American Southwest, the film tells (confusedly) of a sinister town run by eye-rolling Borgnine (who turns out to be a demon), and the search for a missing "Book of Names". Shatner is hero; John Travolta in bit part.

THE DEVIL'S WIDOW (aka TAM LIN) ★★★
UK 1971; colour; 106 mins; Winkast/Commonwealth United; *D* Roddy McDowall; *P* Alan Ladd Jr, Stanley Mann; *W* William Spier from the old ballad "Tam Lin"; *M* Stanley Myers; *C* Billy Williams; *PD* Don Ashton; *Starring* Ava Gardner, Ian McShane, Stephanie Beacham, Richard Wattis. McDowall's first film as director was sporadically praised when it appeared, but seems to have sunk without trace since. Based on the myth of Tam Lin, the human who was captured to be the lover of the Queen of Faerie, it sets a similar story in Scotland in modern times, with McShane the lover of mysterious rich woman Ava Gardner. Long, arty, it sets up its uneasy atmosphere rather well with the supernatural element very slowly becoming apparent, as the Hell Hounds draw closer.

THE DEVIL WITHIN HER – *see* BEYOND THE DOOR (also alternate title of I DON'T WANT TO BE BORN, aka MONSTER, UK, 1975)

DIABOLIK – *see* DANGER: DIABOLIK

DIE, MONSTER, DIE! – *see* MONSTER OF TERROR

THE DISCREET CHARM OF THE BOURGEOISIE (LE CHARME DISCRET DE LA BOURGEOISIE) ★★★★★
France 1972; colour; 105 mins; Greenwich; *D* Luis Buñuel; *P* Serge Silberman; *W* Buñuel, Jean-Claude Carrière; *C* Edmond Richard; *AD* Pierre Guffroy; *Starring* Fernando Rey, Delphine Seyrig, Stéphane Audran, Bulle Ogier, Jean-Pierre Cassel.

DJÄVULENS ÖGA – *see* THE DEVIL'S EYE

DOC SAVAGE – THE MAN OF BRONZE ★½
USA 1975; colour; 100 mins; Warner; *D* Michael Anderson; *P* George Pal; *W* Pal, Joseph Morhaim from the first of the pulp-magazine series by Kenneth Robeson; *C* Fred Koenekamp; *AD* Fred Harpman; *Starring* Ron Ely, Paul Wexler. Michael Anderson *(Logan's Run, Orca, Dominique, Martian Chronicles)* seems to have little feeling for fantastic cinema, though he keeps getting assignments. The essence of the original pulp stories was the speed at which they rattled along, and the fact that they took themselves seriously. This film, conversely, is sluggish and half-heartedly campy. High adventure in South America with fountains of liquid gold and mysterious native tribes sounds good but it was not; this sort of thing was done infinitely better in *Raiders of the Lost Ark*.

DR CYCLOPS ★★★
USA 1940; colour; 76 mins; Paramount; *D* Ernest B. Schoedsack; *P* Merian C. Cooper; *W* Tom Kilpatrick; *M* Ernest Toch, Gerard Carbonara, Albert

Hay Malotte; *C* Winton C. Hoch, Henry Sharp; *SPFX* (photography) Farciot Edouart, W. Wallace Kelley; *Starring* Albert Dekker, Janice Logan, Thomas Coley, Victor Kilian, Charles Halton.

DOCTOR DOLITTLE ★★
USA 1967; colour; 152 mins; APJAC/20th Century-Fox; *D* Richard Fleischer, (musical numbers) Herbert Ross; *P* Arthur P. Jacobs; *W/M* Leslie Bricusse from the novels by Hugh Lofting; *C* Robert Surtees; *SPFX* L. B. Abbott, (mechanical) A. D. Flowers; *Starring* Rex Harrison, Samantha Eggar, Anthony Newley, Richard Attenborough; *V* CBS/Fox (UK and USA).

DR JEKYLL AND MR HYDE ★★½
USA 1920; b/w; 7 reels; Famous Players-Lasky; *D* John S. Robertson; *P* Adolph Zukor; *W* Clara S. Beranger from the novel *The Strange Case of Dr Jekyll and Mr Hyde* by Robert Louis Stevenson and the play version by T. R. Sullivan; *C* Roy Overbaugh; *Starring* John Barrymore, Martha Mansfield, Brandon Hurst, Charles Lane, Nita Naldi; *V* PolyGram (UK), Blackhawk (USA). Barrymore's transformation from Jekyll to Hyde without camera tricks, using facial contortions only, remains remarkable, but the film is no classic. Static direction, and possibly the wordiest dialogue (all neatly printed out) in silent film history. The departures from Stevenson's plot were mostly followed in later versions.

DR JEKYLL AND MR HYDE ★★★★
USA 1931; b/w; 90 mins; Paramount; *P/D* Rouben Mamoulian; *W* Samuel Hoffenstein, Percy Heath from the novel by Robert Louis Stevenson; *C* Karl Struss; *AD* Hans Dreier; *SPFX* (make-up) Wally Westmore; *Starring* Fredric March, Rose Hobart, Miriam Hopkins.

DR JEKYLL AND MR HYDE ★★★★
USA 1941; colour; 127 mins; MGM; *D/P* Victor Fleming; *W* John Lee Mahin from the novel by Robert Louis Stevenson; *M* Franz Waxman; *C* Joseph Ruttenberg; *AD* Cedric Gibbons, Daniel B. Cathcart; *SPFX* Warren Newcombe, (make-up) Jack Dawn; *Starring* Spencer Tracy, Ingrid Bergman, Lana Turner, Donald Crisp, C. Aubrey Smith. Quite a good, glossy re-make, though Tracy is too nice a guy to be wholly convincing as Hyde. Transformation scenes so-so. Mainly notable for very appealing, sad and winsome performance by Bergman as the tart victimised by Hyde – her scenes are the emotional centre of the film.

DOCTOR JEKYLL AND SISTER HYDE ★★★
UK 1971; colour; 97 mins; Hammer/EMI; *D* Roy Ward Baker; *P* Albert Fennell, Brian Clemens; *W* Brian Clemens remotely suggested by the novel by Robert Louis Stevenson; *M* Philip Martell; *C* Norman Warwick; *AD* Robert Jones; *SPFX* (make-up) John Wilcox; *Starring* Ralph Bates, Martine Beswick, Gerald Sim, Dorothy Alison; *V* Thorn EMI (UK). There are one or two nice touches in this silly story about Jekyll experimenting with female hormones and becoming a female Hyde (also Jack the Ripper). Enjoyably decadent performance by Beswick as Sister Hyde; typically bizarre Clemens screenplay has some amusing sex-role jokes.

DR JEKYLL ET LES FEMMES – *see* THE BLOOD OF DR JEKYLL

DR MABUSE, DER SPIELER (DR MABUSE THE GAMBLER) (In two parts: *Der Grosse Spieler* and *Inferno*) ★★★★
Germany 1922; b/w; 20 reels (around 5 hours); UCO-Films/Decla-Bioscop; *D* Fritz Lang; *P* Erich Pommer; *W* Thea von Harbou from the novel by Norbert Jacques; *C* Karl Hoffmann; *AD* Otto Hunte, Stahl-Urach; *Starring* Rudolf Klein-Rogge, Aud Egede Nissen, Alfred Abel; *V* Thorn EMI (UK), Thunderbird (USA, as *Dr Mabuse: The Fatal Passion*). Classic mad genius movie, and very influential. Based on a pulp novel, it featured arch-criminal and hypnotist Mabuse (Klein-Rogge) who is also a master of disguise. Grotesque sets, drifting and affectless society victims – all build

up a claustrophobic atmosphere of evil. There are supernatural touches too, as when Mabuse is haunted by the spirits of his victims. He is the primal source for such later cinema villains as those in the James Bond movies. Videotape version is cut to 90 minutes.

DR NO ★★★
UK 1962; colour; 111 mins; Eon/United Artists; *D* Terence Young; *P* Harry Saltzman, Albert R. Broccoli; *W* Richard Maibaum, Johanna Harwood, Berkely Mather from the novel by Ian Fleming; *M* Monty Norman; *C* Ted Moore; *PD* Ken Adam; *SPFX* Frank George; *Starring* Sean Connery, Ursula Andress, Joseph Wiseman, Jack Lord; *V* Warner (UK), CBS/Fox (USA).

DR PHIBES RISES AGAIN ★★
UK 1972; colour; 89 mins; AIP; *D* Robert Fuest; *P* Louis M. Heyward; *W* Fuest, Robert Blees from characters created by James Whiton and William Goldstein; *M* John Gale; *C* Alex Thomson; *AD* Brian Eatwell; *Starring* Vincent Price, Robert Quarry, Peter Cushing, Valli Kemp. Slightly tired and strained sequel to *The Abominable Dr Phibes*, in which the sinister Quarry plays obsessive Egyptologist who, like the re-animated Phibes (Price), is searching in the desert for the lost elixir of life. People who enjoy Fuest's camp direction and Price's camp performances may rank this higher. Some grotesque deaths are contrived by the sympathetic Phibes whom one somehow never blames for his homicidal behaviour.

DR STRANGE ★★
USA 1978; made for TV; colour; 100 mins; Universal; *D/W* Philip DeGuere from the comic strip by Stan Lee and others; *P* Alex Beaton; *M* Paul Chihara; *C* Enzo A. Martinelli; *AD* William H. Tuntke; *SPFX* Van Der Veer Studios; *Starring* Peter Hooten, Clyde Kusatsu, Jessica Walter, John Mills; *V* CIC (UK). As possible pilots for TV series released as television movies goes, this is better than average, but that is not high praise. Tons of special effects, but none outstanding. Nice psychologist is groomed for stardom (to his annoyance) by elderly magician, finds himself in conflict (amorous and otherwise) with Jessica Walters' Morgan Le Fay; much fighting on the astral plane; ends up as superhero and Guardian of the Light with magical powers.

DR STRANGELOVE: OR, HOW I LEARNED TO STOP WORRYING AND LOVE THE BOMB ★★★★★
UK 1963; b/w; 94 mins; Hawk/Columbia; *D/P* Stanley Kubrick; *W* Kubrick, Terry Southern, Peter George from *Red Alert* by Peter George; *M* Laurie Johnson; *C* Gilbert Taylor; *PD* Ken Adam; *SPFX* Wally Veevers; *Starring* Peter Sellers, George C. Scott, Sterling Hayden, Keenan Wynn, Slim Pickens.

DR TERROR'S HOUSE OF HORRORS ★★★
UK 1964; colour; 98 mins; Amicus/Paramount; *D* Freddie Francis; *P* Milton Subotsky, Max J. Rosenberg; *W* Subotsky; *M* Elisabeth Lutyens; *C* Alan Hume; *AD* William Constable; *SPFX* Ted Samuels; *Starring* Peter Cushing, Christopher Lee, Roy Castle, Donald Sutherland, Max Adrian, Michael Gough. The first of many Amicus anthology horror films, this has a framing story about five train travellers having the cards read for them; they are in fact dead, but do not know it. Best stories are "Werewolf", "Voodoo", "Crawling Hand", but all are very derivative. Sutherland, in an early role, stars in the jokey "Vampire" episode.

DR WHO AND THE DALEKS ★★
UK 1965; colour; 85 mins; Amicus; *D* Gordon Flemyng; *P* Milton Subotsky, Max J. Rosenberg; *W* Subotsky from the BBC TV series; *M* Malcolm Lockyer; *C* John Wilcox; *AD* Bill Constable; *SPFX* Ted Samuels; *Starring* Peter Cushing, Roy Castle, Roberta Tovey, Jennie Linden; *V* Thorn EMI (UK). For kids, really, this first of two spin-offs from the deservedly popular BBC TV series; the film sequel was *Daleks – Invasion Earth 2150 AD*. The

Daleks, amoeboid creatures sheathed in metal casings, were one of the most popular features of the TV series around this time, and the rather bland plot takes Who (Cushing) with granddaughters on to the Daleks' planet, where he helps the human underdogs defeat them.

DOCTOR X ★★★
USA 1932; colour; 77 mins; First National; *D* Michael Curtiz; *W* Robert Tasker, Earl Baldwin from the play by Howard W. Comstock and Allen C. Miller; *C* Richard Tower, Ray Rennahan; *AD* Anton Grot; *Starring* Lionel Atwill, Fay Wray, Lee Tracy, Preston Foster. Lively blend of SF, horror and whodunnit genres by celebrated director; very early colour film. Maniac and cannibalistic murderer is thought to be a scientist in Doctor Xavier's research centre, or perhaps Xavier (Atwill) himself. Culprit turns out to be one-armed man who has invented synthetic flesh, whose effects madden him. Effects so-so, comic relief appalling, yet it keeps up the interest. Efficient potboiler.

DOMINIQUE ★
UK 1978; colour; 100 mins; Grand Prize/Sword & Sorcery; *D* Michael Anderson; *P* Milton Subotsky, Andrew Donally; *W* Edward and Valerie Abraham, from "What Beckoning Ghost" by Harold Lawlor; *M* David Whitaker; *C* Ted Moore; *AD* David Minty; *Starring* Cliff Robertson, Jean Simmons, Jenny Agutter, Simon Ward; *V* Guild (UK). Greedy man drives rich wife to suicide; her ghost haunts him. Or does it? Ghost peels off mask; it is all a fraud. Not technically a fantasy, then, but not rational either: interesting in a dreadful way for its failure to explain convincingly how the supernatural trick was carried off. Heavily cut? Lots of unexplained events including one murder. Waste of good actors. Directed at Anderson's usual snail's pace.

DON'T LOOK NOW ★★★★★
UK/Italy 1973; colour; 110 mins; Casey-Eldorado/British Lion; *D* Nicolas Roeg; *P* Peter Katz; *W* Allan Scott, Chris Bryant from the story by Daphne Du Maurier; *M* Pino Donaggio; *C* Anthony Richmond; *AD* Giovanni Soccol; *Starring* Julie Christie, Donald Sutherland, Hilary Mason, Clelia Matania; *V* Thorn EMI (UK), Paramount (USA).

DON'T OPEN THE WINDOW – see THE LIVING DEAD AT THE MANCHESTER MORGUE

DOOMWATCH ★★½
UK 1972; colour; 92 mins; Tigon; *D* Peter Sasdy; *P* Tony Tenser; *W* Clive Exton from the BBC TV series by Kit Pedler and Gerry Davis; *M* John Scott; *C* Kenneth Talbot; *AD* Colin Grimes; *Starring* Ian Bannen, Judy Geeson, George Sanders, Geoffrey Keen; *V* Guild (UK). The TV series of the same title dealt with a watchdog scientific group faced every week with ecocatastrophe of one kind or another, set off by mad scientists and capitalists. The movie spin-off has an offshore British island whose residents are secretive with strangers; the dumping of radioactive waste in the sea nearby, it turns out, is polluting fish, thus causing some islanders to develop acromegaly (giantism and bone deformity). Routine thriller, routinely directed.

DOPPELGANGER (aka JOURNEY TO THE FAR SIDE OF THE SUN) ★★
UK 1969; Century 21; *D* Robert Parrish; *P* Gerry and Sylvia Anderson; *W* the Andersons, Donald James; *M* Barry Gray; *C* John Read; *AD* Bob Bell; *SPFX* (visual director) Derek Meddings; *Starring* Ian Hendry, Roy Thinnes, Herbert Lom. The Andersons, who are mainly known for SF on TV, such as *Space 1999* and *Thunderbirds*, came up with this jolly but completely incredible extravaganza, told in flashback by a man in a lunatic asylum. Astronaut crashlands on an identical Earth hidden from the real Earth on the far side of the Sun. Even the people are the same – or at any rate, mirror images – of their Earth originals. His mind spins, and so does the audience's.

DRACULA ★★★
USA 1930; b/w; 84 mins; Universal; *D* Tod Browning; *P* Carl Laemmle Jr; *W* Garrett Fort, Dudley Murphy from the play by Hamilton Deane and John L. Balderston and the novel by Bram Stoker; *C* Karl Freund; *AD* Charles D. Hall; *SPFX* (make-up) Jack Pierce; *Starring* Bela Lugosi, Edward Van Sloan, Dwight Frye, Helen Chandler; *V* MCA (USA).

DRACULA (aka HORROR OF DRACULA) ★★★½ 🏆
UK 1958; colour; 82 mins; Hammer/Universal; *D* Terence Fisher; *P* Anthony Hinds; *W* Jimmy Sangster from the novel by Bram Stoker; *M* James Bernard; *C* Jack Asher; *SPFX* (make-up) Phil Leakey; *Starring* Peter Cushing, Christopher Lee, Michael Gough.

DRACULA ★★★
USA 1979; colour; 112 mins; Mirisch/Universal; *D* John Badham; *P* Walter Mirisch; *W* W. D. Richter from the usual sources; *M* John Williams; *C* Gilbert Taylor; *PD* Peter Murton; *SPFX* Roy Arbogast, Effects Associates, (photographic) Albert Whitlock; *Starring* Frank Langella, Laurence Olivier, Kate Nelligan, Donald Pleasence, Trevor Eve; *V* CIC (UK), MCA (USA). This screen adaptation of a successful Broadway stage production steers an uneasy course between genuine horror movie and camp parody. The main twist is to have Dracula as a suave, Valentino-like romantic hero, all burning, hypnotic eyes and sweeping women off their feet. It is frightfully theatrical. Laurence Olivier, as Van Helsing, is allowed to go completely over the top, his Dutch accent reminiscent of Peter Sellers in the Inspector Clouseau movies. The lavish sets seem to have been displaced in time; they look early twenties, and the women look like flappers, but elsewhere the time seems to be Edwardian. Some good special effects (at last we see the bit where Dracula climbs down a wall *head first*, one of the best touches in the novel), but only one scene of authentic horror, where Van Helsing meets his vampirized daughter (she looks absolutely *foul*) in old mineworkings, and she attacks him while chattering affectionately to him in Dutch. Flamboyant editing; great performance by Kat Nelligan as Lucy Harker; very unconvincing working-class Jonathan Harker (Trevor Eve). Badham went on to direct the SF movies *Blue Thunder* and *Wargames*.

DRACULA AD 1972 ★½
UK 1972; colour; 95 mins; Hammer/Warner; *D* Alan Gibson; *P* Josephine Douglas; *W* Don Houghton; *M* Michael Vickers; *C* Richard Bush; *PD* Don Mingaye; *SPFX* Les Bowie; *Starring* Christopher Lee, Peter Cushing, Stephanie Beacham. Interesting sociologically but boring in all other respects, this was Hammer's tired, uncertain, last-gasp attempt to give new life to the Dracula myth by updating the action to modern, swinging London. Nude, hip kids practising satanism are wholly unconvincing. *Count Yorga, Vampire* did the urban vampire with a much surer touch.

DRACULA HAS RISEN FROM THE GRAVE ★★★ 🏆
UK 1968; colour; 92 mins; Hammer/Warner-Seven Arts; *D* Freddie Francis; *P* Aida Young; *W* John Elder (pseudonym of Anthony Hinds); *M* James Bernard; *C* Arthur Grant; *SPFX* Frank George; *Starring* Christopher Lee, Rupert Davies, Veronica Carlson. The fourth of Hammer's nine Dracula films, this was the first to be directed by Freddie Francis (the ex-cameraman; he filmed *The Innocents*), who replaced Terence Fisher on the series. We are still in Transylvania, here, with this time a lot of talk about the Church and no Van Helsing. Rupert Davies plays the Monsignor. The erotic aspects are more forthright than before, and so are the scenes of graphic mutilation, notably where an atheist stakes Dracula through the heart. Because the action is performed without faith, Dracula is able to rise from his coffin, spouting blood, and tear the stake from his body. The ending, too, is violent (Dracula's death scene had become the high spot of each successive movie) with the vampire falling from the battlements to be impaled on a cross conveniently lying beneath.

DRACULA – PRINCE OF DARKNESS ★★★ 🏆
UK 1965; colour; 90 mins; Hammer/Seven Arts; *D* Terence Fisher; *P* Anthony Nelson Keys; *W* John Sansom; *M* James Bernard; *C* Michael Reed; *PD* Bernard Robinson; *SPFX* Bowie Films; *Starring* Christopher Lee, Barbara Shelley, Andrew Keir. This, the third Hammer *Dracula* film, is the one that ends with Dracula crashing through the ice of the frozen moat. Good stuff, as is the story about stuffy Victorian couple made victims – husband murdered so that his blood can revive Dracula, and wife vampirized (and eroticised as well – Hammer's sexist revenge on prudish women). Lee does not speak, just hisses. Hardly a classic, but crudely effective.

DRACULA VUOLE VIVERE: CERCA SANGUE DI VERGINE! – *see* BLOOD FOR DRACULA

DRAGONSLAYER ★★★½
USA 1981; colour; 110 mins; Disney/Paramount; *D* Matthew Robbins; *P* Hal Barwood; *W* Robbins, Barwood; *M* Alex North, (period) Christopher Page; *C* Derek Vanlint; *PD* Elliot Scott; *SPFX* (mechanical) Brian Johnson, (miniatures, opticals) Dennis Muren, (matte supervision) Alan Maley, (dragon design) David Bunnett; *Starring* Peter MacNicol, Caitlin Clarke, Ralph Richardson; *V* Disney (UK), Paramount (USA).

DUEL ★★★★
USA 1971-1972; made for TV; colour; 90 mins (cinema release version); Universal; *D* Steven Spielberg; *P* George Eckstein; *W* Richard Matheson from his short story; *M* Billy Goldenberg; *C* Jack A. Marta; *Starring* Dennis Weaver; *V* CIC (UK), MCA (USA).

DUELLE ★★★★
France 1976; colour; 118 mins; Sunchild/Gaumont; *D* Jacques Rivette; *P* Jacques Roitfeld; *W* Rivette, Eduardo De Gregorio, Marilù Parolini; *M* Jean Wiener; *C* William Lubtchansky; *Starring* Juliet Berto, Bulle Ogier, Jean Babilee, Elisabeth Wiener. You either like Rivette's wholly individual style, described by a romantic French critic as like "the beautiful corridors of a dream", or else its improvised, labyrinthine theatricality drives you mad with fury. This is the second of a projected tetralogy "Scenes of Parallel Life"; the third is *Noroît*; one and four have not been made. Leni (Berto) and Viva (Ogier) are the brunette daughter of the Moon and the blonde daughter of the Sun respectively, searching for a diamond on Earth at Carnival time, through nightclubs and subways and all over, and in mutual conflict. Surreal action; ruptured plot. Brilliant screenwriter De Gregorio made his own film, *Sérail*, in the same year.

THE DUNWICH HORROR ★★★
USA 1970; colour; 90 mins; AIP; *D* Daniel Haller; *P* James H. Nicholson, Samuel Z. Arkoff, Roger Corman; *W* Curtis Lee Hanson, Henry Rosenbaum, Ronald Silkosky from the story by H. P. Lovecraft; *M* Les Baxter; *C* Richard C. Glouner; *AD* Paul Sylos; *SPFX* Roger George; *Starring* Sandra Dee, Dean Stockwell, Ed Begley, Sam Jaffe; *V* Guild (UK). Haller's second shot at a good Lovecraft story (the first was *Monster of Terror*), and this is even less true to the atmosphere of the original. Anyone who puts Sandra Dee into a Lovecraft story has to be mad. Devil cult in New England; sacrifice threats; what lurks in the attic; invisible monster runs amuck. The film has its small moments.

THE ELEPHANT MAN ★★★★½
USA/UK 1980; b/w; 124 mins; Brooksfilms/EMI; *D* David Lynch; *P* Jonathan Sanger; *W* Christopher de Vore, Eric Bergren, Lynch from *The Elephant Man and Other Reminiscences* by Sir Frederick Treves and *The Elephant Man: A Study in Human Dignity* by Ashley Montagu; *M* John Morris; *C* Freddie Francis; *PD* Stuart Craig; *SPFX* Graham Longhurst, (Elephant Man make-up design) Christopher Tucker; *Starring* Anthony Hopkins, John Hurt, Anne Bancroft, John Gielgud, Wendy Hiller, Freddie Jones; *V* Thorn EMI (UK), Paramount (USA).

EMBRYO ★★
USA 1976; colour; 106 mins; Sandy Howard; *D* Ralph Nelson; *P* Arnold H. Orgolini, Anita Doohan; *W* Doohan,- Jack W. Thomas; *M* Gil Melle; *C* Fred Koenekamp; *AD* Joe Alves; *SPFX* Roy Arbogast, (make-up) John Chambers, Dan Striepeke, Mark Redall; *Starring* Rock Hudson, Barbara Carrera, Diane Ladd, Roddy McDowall; *V* Video Form (UK). Gothic horror tale with thin scientific gloss directed, perhaps surprisingly, by Ralph Nelson (see *Charly*). Dr Holliston (Hunter) uses new growth hormone to produce very quickly a full-grown, blank-minded woman (Carrera) from premature foetus – outside the womb. She turns out evil – a plot that was old seventy years ago – see *Homunculus*. Mediocre.

EMPIRE OF PASSION (AI NO BOREI, L'EMPIRE DE LA PASSION) ★★★★½
Japan/France 1978; colour; 105 mins; Argos/Oshima; *D/W* Nagisa Oshima from part of a biography of Takashi Nagatsuka by Itoko Nakamura; *M* Toru Takemitsu; *C* Yoshio Miyajima; *Starring* Kazuko Yoshiyuki, Tatsuya Fuji, Takahiro Tamura; *V* Palace (UK).

THE EMPIRE STRIKES BACK ★★★★
USA 1980; colour; 124 mins; Lucasfilm/20th Century-Fox; *D* Irvin Kershner; *2nd Unit D* Harley Cokliss, John Barry, Peter MacDonald; *Executive P* George Lucas; *P* Gary Kurtz; *W* Leigh Brackett, Lawrence Kasdan from a story by Lucas; *M* John Williams; *C* Peter Suschitzky; *PD* Norman Reynolds; *SPFX* (visual) Brian Johnson and Richard Edlund at Industrial Light and Magic, (additional optical) Van Der Veer Photo Effects and others, (matte painting supervision) Harrison Ellenshaw, (conceptual artist) Ralph McQuarrie, (make-up and creature design) Stuart Freeborn; *Starring* Mark Hamill, Harrison Ford, Carrie Fisher, Billy Dee Williams, Anthony Daniels, David Prowse, Frank Oz, Alec Guinness.

ENDANGERED SPECIES ★★★ ☻
USA 1982; colour; 97 mins; Alive/MGM/UA; *D* Alan Rudolph; *P* Carolyn Pfeiffer; *W* Rudolph, John Binder; *M* Gary Wright; *C* Paul Lohmann; *PD* Trevor Williams; *Starring* Robert Urich, JoBeth Williams, Paul Dooley, Hoyt Axton, Peter Coyote; *V* MGM/UA (UK and USA). Yet another film about US government conspiring to do nasty things. Post-Watergate paranoia rides on, and so perhaps it should. Mutilated cattle carcasses fall from the sky; police investigation reveals secret, illegal experiments on nerve gas. Characterization quite brisk.

THE END OF THE WORLD (1930) – *see* LA FIN DU MONDE

END OF THE WORLD ★
USA 1977; colour; 86 mins; Irwin Yablans; *D* John Hayes; *P* Charles Band; *W* Frank Ray Perilli; *M* Andrew Belling; *C* John Huneck; *Starring* Christopher Lee, Sue Lyon, Kirk Scott; *V* Intervision (UK), Media (USA). The closest thing this book has to a genuine Golden Turkey, the film will delight all connoisseurs of the truly appalling. Scientist discovers that six nuns and a priest (Lee) are really aliens, about to leave Earth and destroy it (seismically, in a wonderful effects shot of a tiny Earth breaking into pieces) because we are polluting "all the planets within light years" with our diseases. The script is almost totally incoherent – literally impossible to follow, and riddled with inconsistencies. Acting, effects, editing and sound quality all disastrous.

ENEMY FROM SPACE – *see* QUATERMASS II

THE ENTITY ★★½
USA 1981; colour; 125 mins; Pelleport Investors/American Cinema; *D* Sidney J. Furie; *P* Harold Schneider; *W* Frank DeFelitta from his novel; *M* Charles Bernstein; *C* Stephen H. Burum; *SPFX* Joe Lombardi, Special Effects Unlimited, (visual designer) William Cruse, (make-up) Stan Winston and James Kagel; *Starring* Barbara Hershey, Ron Silver, David Labiosa; *V* CBS/Fox (UK and USA).

EQUINOX ★½
USA 1969; colour; 82 mins; Tonylyn; *D/W* Jack Woods, Mark Thomas McGee; *P* Jack H. Harris; *M* John Caper; *C* Mike Hoover; *SPFX* (photographic) Dennis Muren, (model animation), David Allen and Jim Danforth; *Starring* Edward Connell, Barbara Hewitt, Jack Woods, Fritz Leiber; *V* Mountain (UK); Wizard (USA). This was a semi-amateur film shot on 16mm and then blown up for theatrical release with new scenes shot by Jack Woods. One of the stars is famous SF writer Fritz Leiber. Searching for missing professor, students find ancient book of magic which unleashes occult horrors. Pretty bad, but the stop-motion animation by Danforth and Allen of the monsters, including a strange blue giant, has been praised.

ERASERHEAD ★★★★★ ☻☻☻
USA 1976; b/w; 89 mins; David Lynch; *D/P/W/PD/SPFX* David Lynch; *C/SPFX* (photographic) Frederick Elmes; *C* also Herbert Cardwell; *Starring* John Nance, Charlotte Stewart, Allen Joseph, Jeanne Bates; *V* Palace (UK), Columbia (USA).

ERCOLE E LA REGINA DI LIDIA – *see* HERCULES UNCHAINED

ESCAPE FROM NEW YORK ★★★½
USA 1981; colour; 99 mins; International Film Investors/Goldcrest/Avco Embassy; *D* John Carpenter; *P* Larry Franco, Debra Hill; *W* Carpenter, Nick Castle; *M* Carpenter, Alan Howarth; *C* Dean Cundey; *PD* Joe Alves; *SPFX* (supervisor) Roy Arbogast, (visual effects) New World/Venice; *Starring* Kurt Russell, Lee Van Cleef, Ernest Borgnine, Donald Pleasence, Isaac Hayes; *V* Embassy (UK and USA).

ESCAPE FROM THE PLANET OF THE APES ★★½
USA 1971; colour; 97 mins; Apjac/20th Century-Fox; *D* Don Taylor; *P* Arthur P. Jacobs; *W* Paul Dehn; *M* Jerry Goldsmith; *C* Joseph Biroc; *AD* Jack Martin Smith, William Creber; *SPFX* (make-up design) John Chambers; *Starring* Roddy McDowall, Kim Hunter, Bradford Dillman, Ricardo Montalban, Natalie Trundy; *V* CBS/Fox (UK). Third in the *Apes* series, and the last of those worth watching. Three intelligent apes return to Earth of an earlier time (our time, in fact) in Charlton Heston's spaceship from *Planet of the Apes*. Some mildly amusing bits early on as psychologists are amazed to learn that Roddy McDowall in an apesuit is intelligent (actually, this was probably his best role); standard melodrama takes over when security services get worried, gun apes down (but baby ape Caesar survives after baby switch). A sad, gentle, slightly shoddy little film.

ESCAPE TO WITCH MOUNTAIN ★★½
USA 1974; colour; 97 mins; Disney; *D* John Hough; *P* Jerome Courtland; *W* Robert M. Young from the novel by Alexander Key; *M* Johnny Mandel; *C* Frank Phillips; *SPFX* Art Cruickshank, Danny Lee; *Starring* Eddie Albert, Ray Milland, Donald Pleasence; *V* Disney (UK and USA). John Hough's fantasy movies are seldom out of the ordinary (see *Incubus*, *Twins of Evil*, *The Watcher in the Woods* and *Legend of Hell House* for a selection), and this is no exception. Pleasant, slight tale of two kids with psychic powers seeking refuge from bullies, capitalist exploiters (Milland wicked as usual). Several of the levitation effects beloved of Disney Studios. The kids, by the way, turn out to be aliens, but ET they're not. Sequel was *Return from Witch Mountain*.

L'ETERNEL RETOUR (THE ETERNAL RETURN) ★★★½
France 1943; b/w; 111 mins; Discina; *D* Jean Delannoy; *P* Andre Paulvé; *W* Jean Cocteau; *M* Georges Auric; *C* Roger Hubert; *Sets* Wakhévitch; *Starring* Madeleine Sologne, Jean Marais, Jean Murat, Junie Astor, Piéral.

ET MOURIR DE PLAISIR – *see* BLOOD AND ROSES

UNE ÉTRANGE AVENTURE DE LEMMY CAUTION – *see* ALPHAVILLE

E.T. THE EXTRA-TERRESTRIAL ★★★★
USA 1982; colour; 115 mins; Universal; *D* Steven Spielberg; *P* Spielberg, Kathleen Kennedy; *W* Melissa Mathison; *M* John Williams; *C* Allen Daviau; *PD* James D. Bissell; *SPFX* (visual) Industrial light and Magic, (visual supervisor) Dennis Muren, (creator of E.T.) Carlo Rambaldi, (spaceship design) Ralph McQuarrie; *Starring* Dee Wallace, Henry Thomas, Peter Coyote, Robert MacNaughton, Drew Barrymore; *V* no official release at time of writing, but the most widely pirated videotape in history.

...E TU VIVRAI NEL TERRORE! L'ALDILA – *see* THE BEYOND

EVERYTHING YOU ALWAYS WANTED TO KNOW ABOUT SEX* *BUT WERE AFRAID TO ASK ★★★★
USA 1972; Rollins-Joffe-Brodsky-Gould/United Artists; colour; 87 mins; *D/W* Woody Allen, suggested by the book by Dr David Reuben; *P* Charles H. Joffe; *M* Mundell Lowe; *C* David M. Walsh; *PD* Dale Hennesy; *Starring* Woody Allen, Burt Reynolds, Gene Wilder, John Carradine, Lynn Redgrave, Tony Randall, Anthony Quayle, Louise Lasser; *V* Warner (UK), CBS/Fox (USA).

THE EVIL DEAD ★★★½ ☻☻☻
USA 1982; colour; 86 mins; Renaissance; *D/W* Samuel M. Raimi; *P* Robert G. Tapert; *M* Joe LoDuca; *C* Tim Philo; *SPFX* (make-up) Tom Sullivan; *Starring* Bruce Campbell, Ellen Sandweiss, Betsy Baker, Hal Delrich, Sarah York; *V* Palace (UK); Thorn EMI (USA).

THE EVIL OF FRANKENSTEIN ★★
UK 1964; colour; 84 mins (re-edited to 86 mins for US release); Hammer/Universal; *D* Freddie Francis; *P* Anthony Hinds; *W* John Elder (pseudonym of Hinds); *M* Don Banks; *C* John Wilcox; *AD* Don Mingaye; *SPFX* Les Bowie; *Starring* Peter Cushing, Peter Woodthorpe, Kiwi Kingston. Hammer's *Frankenstein* films did not generally reach the standard of their *Dracula* movies, and this, the third in the series, is fairly stodgy stuff (which unexpectedly reverts to a monster make-up not unlike that used in the James Whale version of 1931). Thawed-out Creature becomes psychically bonded to fairground mesmerist. A real potboiler.

EXCALIBUR ★★★½ ☻
USA 1981; colour; 140 mins; Orion/Warner; *D/P* John Boorman; *W* Rospo Pallenberg, Boorman from *Le Morte d'Arthur* by Thomas Malory; *M* Trevor Jones; *PD* Anthony Pratt; *C* Alex Thomson; *SPFX* (optical) Wally Veevers; *Starring* Nigel Terry, Helen Mirren, Nicholas Clay, Cherie Lunghi, Nicol Williamson; *V* Warner (UK and USA).

THE EXORCIST ★★★ ☻☻
USA 1973; colour; 122 mins; Hoya/Warner; *D* William Friedkin; *P/W* William Peter Blatty from his novel; *C* Owen Roizman, also Billy Williams; *PD* Bill Malley; *SPFX* Marcel Vercoutere, (optical) Marv Ystrom, (make-up) Dick Smith and Rick Baker; *Starring* Linda Blair, Ellen Burstyn, Max von Sydow, Lee J. Cobb, Jason Miller; *V* Warner (UK and USA).

EXORCIST II: THE HERETIC ★★★½ ☻
USA 1977; colour; 117 mins (re-edited version); Warner; *D* John Boorman; *P* Richard Lederer, Boorman; *W* William Goodhart from characters created by William Peter Blatty; *M* Ennio Morricone; *C* William A. Fraker; *PD* Richard MacDonald; *SPFX* Chuck Gaspar and others, (photographic) Albert Whitlock and Van Der Veer Photo, (make-up) Dick Smith; *Starring* Linda Blair, Richard Burton, Louise Fletcher, Max von Sydow, Kitty Winn, James Earl Jones; *V* Warner (UK and USA).

THE EXTERMINATING ANGEL (EL ÁNGEL EXTERMINADOR) ★★★★½
Mexico 1962; b/w; 95 mins; Uninci/Films 59/Alatriste; *D* Luis Buñuel; *P* Gustavo Alatriste; *W* Luis Alcoriza, Luis Buñuel from play *Los náufragos de la Calle de la Providencia* by José Bergamín; *M* from Alessandro Scarlatti, Pietro Domenico Para-

disi; *C* Gabriel Figueroa; *AD* Jesús Bracho; *SPFX* Juan Muñoz Ravelo; *Starring* Silvia Pinal, Enrique Rambal, Jacqueline Andere, José Baviera; *V* Budget (USA). Witty, black, surrealist comedy, with Buñuel near his top form. The guests arrive for a posh dinner party (in South America), but somehow nobody is able to leave the room and go home. The situation continues for days, with the guests regressing to near savages (the reverse of *Savages*) before they escape. Sheep play a prominent role. Then at a thanksgiving ceremony in the cathedral the same thing happens...

EYES OF LAURA MARS ★★

USA 1978; colour; 103 mins; Jon Peters/Columbia; *D* Irvin Kershner; *P* Jon Peters; *W* John Carpenter, David Zelag Goodman from a story by Carpenter as modified by (uncredited) Peters; *M* Artie Kane; *C* Victor J. Kemper; *PD* Gene Callahan; *SPFX* Edward Drohan, (photographic) James Liles; *Starring* Faye Dunaway, Tommy Lee Jones, Brad Dourif, Rene Auberjonois; *V* RCA/Columbia (UK), Columbia (USA). Slick and nasty slash movie with the rather irrelevant twist that fashionable photographer-of-violence Laura "sees" (telepathically) through the murderer's eyes – but still cannot identify him. Early (1974) work by Carpenter; he was not happy with what happened to his story. As it stands, the psychic powers part of the plot is hardly exploited. Lots of eye imagery, red herrings; empty and rather pretentious. Twist-ending revelation of murderer is cheap.

EYES WITHOUT A FACE – see LES YEUX SANS VISAGE

THE FACE (ANSIKTET, aka THE MAGICIAN) ★★★★½

Sweden 1958; b/w; 101 mins; Svensk Filmindustri; *D/W* Ingmar Bergman; *M* Erik Nordgren; *C* Gunnar Fischer; *AD* P. A. Lundgren; *Starring* Max von Sydow, Ingrid Thulin, Gunnar Björnstrand, Lars Ekborg, Bibi Andersson, Erland Josephson; *V* Budget (USA). Not strictly fantasy but, in terms of atmosphere, one of the most fantastic-seeming films ever made. Vogler (von Sydow) is a mesmerist showman, in one sense a pseudo-scientific fraud, in another sense a genuine magician. In brilliant imagery the film confronts the artistic imagination with science, fantasy with reality. Creators may be illusionists and partially corrupt; faces may be masks. Wonderfully Gothic moments. Can the inexplicable be explained?

FAHRENHEIT 451 ★★★½

UK 1966; colour; 111 mins; Vineyard-Anglo-Enterprise/Universal; *D* François Truffaut; *P* Lewis Allen; *W* Truffaut, Jean-Louis Richard, (additional dialogue) David Rudkin and Helen Scott, from the novel by Ray Bradbury; *M* Bernard Herrmann; *C* Nicolas Roeg; *AD* Syd Cain; *Starring* Oskar Werner, Julie Christie, Cyril Cusack, Anton Diffring.

THE FALL OF THE HOUSE OF USHER – see HOUSE OF USHER

FANNY AND ALEXANDER (FANNY OCH ALEXANDER) ★★★★★

Sweden 1982; colour; 189 mins (TV version 300 mins); Cinematograph/Swedish Television SVT 1/Gaumont; *D/W* Ingmar Bergman; *P* Jörn Donner; *M* Daniel Bell; *C* Sven Nykvist; *AD* Anna Asp; *SPFX* Bengt Lundgren; *Starring* Bertil Guve, Ewa Fröling, Gunn Wållgren, Jarl Kulle, Mona Malm, Pernilla Wallgren, Allan Edwall, Jan Malmsjö, Harriet Andersson, Erland Josephson, Stina Ekblad.

FANTASTIC VOYAGE ★★★

USA 1966; colour; 100 mins; 20th Century-Fox; *D* Richard Fleischer; *P* Saul David; *W* Harry Kleiner from a story by Otto Klement, J. L. Bixby adapted by David Duncan; *M* Leonard Rosenman; *C* Ernest Laszlo; *AD* Jack Martin Smith, Dale Hennesy; *SPFX* (photographic) L. B. Abbott, Art Cruickshank, Emil Kosa Jr; *Starring* Stephen Boyd, Raquel Welch, Edmond O'Brien, Donald Pleasence; *V* CBS/Fox (UK and USA).

LE FANTÔME DE LA LIBERTÉ – see THE PHANTOM OF LIBERTY

LE FATICHE DI ERCOLE – see HERCULES

FAUST ★★★★½

Germany 1926; b/w; 8110 ft, approx. 100 mins; Ufa; *D* F. W. Murnau; *W* Hans Kyser from folk tales; *C* Carl Hoffmann; *AD* Robert Herlth, Walter Röhrig; *Starring* Gösta Ekman, Emil Jannings, Camilla Horn, Wilhelm Dieterle; *V* Thunderbird (USA). Classic fantasy film from the director of *Nosferatu*. Even with the faded prints that we usually see of silent films, it is astonishing how strongly some still have the power to move us, especially this film, with its fabulous architectural settings; its flight by the Devil Mephisto (Jannings) over the world, his black cloak blotting out whole towns; its winged archangel; even the Four Horsemen of the Apocalypse riding across the sky. How were these effects achieved so well with such comparatively primitive equipment? It helps put the miracles of today's films into perspective.

THE FEARLESS VAMPIRE KILLERS OR, PARDON ME BUT YOUR TEETH ARE IN MY NECK – see DANCE OF THE VAMPIRES

FEAR NO EVIL ★★½ ☻

USA 1980; colour; 99 mins; LaLoggia Productions; *D/W* Frank LaLoggia; *P* Frank and Charles M. LaLoggia; *M* Frank LaLoggia, David Spear; *C* Fred Goodich; *AD* Carl Zollo; *SPFX* (animation) Chris Casady; *Starring* Stefan Arngrim, Elizabeth Hoffman, Kathleen Rowe McAllen, Frank Birney. This inventive, low-budget production is very much a one-man performance, as the credits show. Three archangels are incarnated as human beings, and their job is to fight Lucifer, the Devil, also (temporarily) in human form as a shy college student. At first none of these supernatural figures knows their true identity, but as they find out, murder and mayhem ensue, particularly from Andrew/Lucifer. Messy, immature, but also colourful and promising better things in the future.

FELLINI SATYRICON (aka SATYRICON) ★★½

Italy 1969; colour; 136 mins; PEA/Artistes Associés; *D* Federico Fellini; *P* Alberto Grimaldi; *W* Fellini, Bernardino Zapponi, Brunello Rondi from the *Satyricon* by Petronius Arbiter; *M* Nino Rota, Ilhan Mimaroglu, Tod Dockstader, Andrew Rudin; *PD* Danilo Donati; *SPFX* Adriano Pischiutta, (makeup) Rino Carboni; *Starring* Martin Potter, Hiram Keller, Salvo Randone; *V* Warner (UK).

FELLINI'S CASANOVA (IL CASANOVA DI FEDERICO FELLINI) ★★½

Italy 1976; colour; 163 mins; PEA/20th Century-Fox; *D* Federico Fellini; *P* Alberto Grimaldi; *W* Fellini, Bernardino Zapponi from *Histoire de Ma Vie* by Giacomo Casanova de Seingalt; *M* Nino Rota; *C* Giuseppe Rotunno; *PD* Danilo Donati, Fellini; *SPFX* Adriano Pischiutta; *Starring* Donald Sutherland, Tina Aumont, Cicely Browne; *V* CBS Fox (UK). Long, self-indulgent but sometimes enjoyable account of the great lover's life, done in typical Fellini style. Many people hated the film for its theatricality, but in a way this is the point: it is a film about fantasies (Sutherland plays Casanova as not nearly as romantic as he would like to be), which explains the fantasy studio settings: a billowing sea made out of plastic in the Venice sequence, for instance. Surrealism throughout, especially in the necromancy sequences.

FIEND WITHOUT A FACE ★★★

UK 1957; b/w; 74 mins; Amalgamated/Eros; *D* Arthur Crabtree; *P* John Croydon; *W* Herbert J. Leder from "The Thought-Monster" by Amelia Reynolds Long; *M* Buxton Orr; *SPFX* Puppel Nordhoff, Peter Nielson; *Starring* Marshall Thompson, Terence Kilburn, Kim Parker; *V* Kingston (UK), Blackhawk (USA).

THE FINAL CONFLICT ★

USA 1981; colour; 108 mins; Mace Neufeld/20th Century-Fox; *D* Graham Baker; *P* Harvey Bernhard; *W* Andrew Birkin from characters created by David Seltzer; *M* Jerry Goldsmith; *C* Robert

Paynter, Phil Meheux; *PD* Herbert Westbrook; *SPFX* Ian Wingrove; *Starring* Sam Neill, Rossano Brazzi, Don Gordon, Lisa Harrow; *V* CBS/Fox (UK and USA). Sequel to *The Omen* and *Damien Omen II*. Terrible script leaves Sam Neill, not a bad actor, quite helpless. The statutory satanic murders are over-contrived and without shock value, let alone point. Damien, now US Ambassador in London, sets about killing babies to prevent the Second Coming of Christ, which event ends the film quite farcically.

THE FINAL COUNTDOWN ★½

USA 1980; colour; 105 mins; Bryna/United Artists; *D* Don Taylor; *P* Peter Douglas; *W* David Ambrose, Gerry Davis, Thomas Hunter, Peter Powell; *M* John Scott; *C* Victor J. Kemper; *SPFX* (visual/storm sequence) Maurice Binder; *Starring* Kirk Douglas, Martin Sheen, James Farentino, Katharine Ross; *V* Vestron (USA). Good idea, bad screenplay, leaden direction. Strange-looking storm hits UK aircraft carrier *Nimitz* on manoeuvres, carries it back in time to the attack on Pearl Harbour. Captain Kirk Douglas faced with ethical problem of whether or not to take action and alter history, but cop-out ending avoids necessity. Other SF in book form deals much better with time-paradox questions. Terribly flat film, and a waste of a perfectly good aircraft carrier. (They used the real one.)

THE FINAL PROGRAMME (aka THE LAST DAYS OF MAN ON EARTH) ★★

UK 1973; colour; 89 mins; Goodtimes – Gladiole/EMI; *D/W/PD* Robert Fuest from the "Jerry Cornelius" novel by Michael Moorcock; *P* John Goldstone, Sandy Lieberson; *M* Paul Beaver, Bernard Krause; *C* Norman Warwick; *Starring* Jon Finch, Jenny Runacre; *V* Thorn EMI (UK and USA). Nothing has dated faster than the trendy, camp, swinging-sixties style Fuest used in several movies (see *The Abominable Dr Phibes*, *The Devil's Rain*). Moorcock, an excellent writer, hated the film, which completely failed to catch the eerie atmosphere of a world in which reality itself is crumbling. The film jettisoned structure in favour of disconnected jokes. Cornelius (Finch) searches for mysterious, "final" computer programme, up against Miss Brunner (Runacre – the best player in the film) who specializes in literally absorbing people. At the end the programme when run combines them into an ape-person – Fuest's wet idea of the new Messiah, not Moorcock's.

FIN DE SEMANA PARA LOS MUERTOS – see THE LIVING DEAD AT THE MANCHESTER MORGUE

LA FIN DU MONDE (aka THE END OF THE WORLD) ★★(?)

France 1930; b/w; 103 mins (English version 54 mins); L'Ecran d'Art; *D* Abel Gance; *W* Gance, André Lang from the 1893 novel by Camille Flammarion; *M* Arthur Honegger, Michel Lévine; *C* Jules Krüger, Nicolas Roudakoff, Forster, Roger Hubert; *AD* Lazare Meerson; *Starring* Gance, Victor Francen, Colette Darfeuil, Sylvie Grenade. Rare (if not lost) SF movie by talented director famous for his ambitious use of spectacle, as in *Napoleon*. Earth is menaced by a comet – orgies, panic etc. – which finally strikes; one of the earliest disaster movies, though in fact there is a 1916 version of the same story from Norway. This film is said to be not one of Gance's best. He repudiated the heavily-cut English version.

FINIAN'S RAINBOW ★★★★

USA 1968; colour; 145 mins; Warner/Seven Arts; *D* Francis Ford Coppola; *P* Joseph Landon; *W* E. Y. Harburg, Fred Saidy from the play by E. Y. Harburg and Burton Lane; *M and lyrics* Harburg and Lane; *PD* Hilyard Brown; *Starring* Fred Astaire, Petula Clark, Tommy Steele.

FIREFOX ★★

USA 1982; colour; 136 mins; Malpaso/Warner; *D/P* Clint Eastwood; *W* Alex Lasker, Wendell Wellman from the novel by Craig Thomas; *M* Maurice Jarre; *C* Bruce Surtees; *SPFX* Chuck Gaspar, Karl

Baumgartner, (mechanical) Bill Shourt, Don Trumbull and others, (visual) John Dykstra and Robert Shepherd; *Starring* Clint Eastwood; *V* Warner (UK and USA).

FIRST MEN IN THE MOON ★★

UK 1964; colour; 103 mins; Ameran/Columbia; *D* Nathan Juran; *P* Charles H. Schneer; *W* Nigel Kneale, Jan Read from the novel by H. G. Wells; *M* Laurie Johnson; *C* Wilkie Cooper; *AD* John Blezard; *SPFX* Ray Harryhausen, (technical staff) Les Bowie, Kit West; *Starring* Edward Judd, Lionel Jeffries, Martha Hyer, Miles Malleson. The only real reason for watching would be Harryhausen's good special effects – of insect-like Selenites (though some of these were children in suits), mooncalves and so on. Good sets (many of which were miniatures matted in), but the script! A classic novel reduced to low farce (only Jeffries copes successfully) and worse – leading players made into thuggish murderers who kill Selenites left, right and centre just because they are aliens! Science bad, too: gravitic effects in free fall, sound travelling in vacuum, all the usual blunders.

FIVE MILLION YEARS TO EARTH – see QUATERMASS AND THE PIT

THE 5,000 FINGERS OF DR T ★★★★

USA 1953; colour; 88 mins; Kramer/Columbia; *D* Roy Rowland; *P* Stanley Kramer; *W* Dr Seuss, Allan Scott from a story by Seuss; *M* Frederick Hollander; *C* Frank (Franz) Planer; *PD* Rudolph Sternad; *Starring* Peter Lind Hayes, Mary Healey, Hans Conried, Tommy Rettig.

FLASH GORDON (aka, in feature-film version, ROCKETSHIP, SPACESHIP TO THE UNKNOWN) ★★★

USA 1936; serial (13 episodes); feature-film version 82 mins; b/w; Universal; *D* Frederick Stephani; *W* Stephani, George Plympton, Basil Dickey, Ella O'Neill from the comic strip by Alex Raymond; *C* Jerry Ash, Richard Fryer; *Starring* Larry "Buster" Crabbe, Jean Rogers, Frank Shannon, Charles Middleton; *V* Home Video (UK), Media, Video Communications (USA). The celebrated SF serial, best of all the old space-opera serials. The story is similar to that of the Di Laurentiis 1980 version, which was based on it. Flash, Dale and Zarkov battle fiendish Ming the Merciless (Middleton) and various beasts and monsters on the planet Mongo. Death rays, monkey men, dragons, winged men, invisibility machine, much else. The serial retains an archaic charm, and is often replayed on TV and in theatres. (Two serials made as sequels were not quite as good: *Flash Gordon's Trip to Mars* [1938] and *Flash Gordon Conquers the Universe* [1940], both starring Crabbe.) A severely cut version was later given theatrical release as a feature (see alternate titles above), and it is this version available on videotape.

FLASH GORDON ★★½

UK 1980; colour; 115 mins; Starling-Famous; *D* Michael Hodges; *P* Dino De Laurentiis; *W* Lorenzo Semple Jr from the comic strip by Alex Raymond; *M* Queen; *C* Gil Taylor; *PD* Danilo Donati; *SPFX* (supervisor) George Gibbs, (models) Richard Conway, (flying) Derek Botell, (photographic) Frank Van Der Veer, Barry Nolan; *Starring* Sam J. Jones, Melody Anderson, Topol, Max von Sydow, Ornella Muti, Brian Blessed; *V* Thorn EMI (UK), MCA (USA).

FLESH AND FANTASY ★★★

USA 1943; b/w; 93 minutes; Universal; *D* Julien Duvivier; *P* Charles Boyer, Duvivier; *W* Ernest Pascal, Samuel Hoffenstein, Ellis St. Joseph from "Lord Arthur Savile's Crime" by Oscar Wilde and stories by Laslo Vadnay and Ellis St. Joseph; *M* Alexandre Tansman; *C* Paul Ivano, Stanley Cortez; *AD* John B. Goodman, Richard Riedel, Robert Boyle; *Starring* Edward G. Robinson, Charles Boyer, Barbara Stanwyck, Betty Field, Robert Cummings. This anthology film has three supernatural stories, presented as if they were tales recounted in a club. Visually elegant, but stories sentimental, stereotyped. First episode,

set in New Orleans at carnival time when a plain woman finds love and beauty, is visually very strong; third episode, starring Boyer, has best story, involving a circus wire-walker and an unnerving premonition. Typical 1940s fantasy in which the supernatural is domesticated, aiming at no more than a discreet *frisson*.

FLESH FOR FRANKENSTEIN (CARNE PER FRANKENSTEIN, aka ANDY WARHOL'S FRANKENSTEIN) ★★½ 👹 👹

Italy/France 1973; 3-D; colour; 95 mins; C. C. Champion & 1/Yanne-Rassam; *D/W* Paul Morrissey; *P* Andrew Braunsberg; *M* Claudio Gizzi; *C* Luigi Kuveiller; *PD* Enrico Job; *SPFX* Carlo Rambaldi; *Starring* Joe Dallesandro, Monique Van Vooren, Udo Kier; *V* Vipco (UK), Video Gems (USA).

FLESH GORDON ★★

USA 1974; colour; 90 mins (cut to 78); Graffiti; *D* Michael Benveniste, Howard Ziehm; *P* Ziehm, William Osco; *W* Benveniste suggested by the *Flash Gordon* comic strip by Alex Raymond; *M* Ralph Ferraro; *C* Ziehm; *AD* Donald Harris; *SPFX* Ziehm, Lynn Rogers, Walter R. Cichy, (visual) David Allen and Mij Htrofnad (i.e. Jim Danforth), (miniatures) Greg Jein, (props) Rick Baker; *Starring* Jason Williams, Suzanne Fields, Joseph Hudgins, John Hoyt; *V* Media (UK and USA). This oddity was originally planned as a pornographic parody of *Flash Gordon* (the starring roles are Flesh Gordon, Dale Ardor and Dr Jerkoff), but the many special-effects people who worked on the film got so carried away – with some rather good results – that the film was cut, cleaned up a bit and released as a fantasy (rather rude, but without the feared X-rating). Undergraduate humour and a very uneven script, but marvellous moments (a duel with an animated insect, the Great God Porno climbing a building in the style of King Kong).

THE FLY ★★★

USA 1958; colour; 94 mins; 20th Century-Fox; *D/P* Kurt Neumann; *W* James Clavell from the story by George Langelaan; *M* Paul Sawtell; *C* Karl Struss; *SPFX* L. B. Abbott; *Starring* Vincent Price, Al Hedison, Patricia Owens; *V* CBS/Fox (UK).

THE FOG ★★★½ 👹

USA 1979; colour; 89 mins; Avco Embassy; *D/M* John Carpenter; *P* Debra Hill; *W* Carpenter, Hill; *C* Dean Cundey; *PD* Tommy Lee Wallace; *SPFX* Richard Albain Jr, Rob Bottin, Cundey, (photographic) James F. Liles; *Starring* Adrienne Barbeau, Hal Holbrook, Janet Leigh, Jamie Lee Curtis, John Houseman; *V* Embassy (UK), CBS/Fox (USA).

THE FOOD OF THE GODS ★ 👹

USA 1976; colour; 88 mins; AIP; *D/P/W/SPFX* (visual) Bert I. Gordon from part of the novel by H. G. Wells; *M* Elliot Kaplan; *C* Reginald Morris; *SPFX* Tom Fisher and others; *Starring* Marjoe Gortner, Pamela Franklin, Ralph Meeker, Ida Lupino. Bert Gordon's fantasy films are generally tacky, and this (one of the few included in this book) is no exception. There's not much of Wells in the film whose sole point is to display menacing giant animals (dragonflies, chickens, rats) – the offspring of creatures which ate stuff oozing out of the ground. Larger budget than most Gordon films, but the effects remain unconvincing and the screenplay is ludicrous.

FORBIDDEN PLANET ★★★★½

USA 1956; colour; 98 mins; MGM; *D* Fred McLeod Wilcox; *P* Nicholas Nayfack; *W* Cyril Hume from a story by Irving Block and Allen Adler; *M* (electronic tonalities) Louis and Bebe Barron; *C* George Folsey; *SPFX* A. Arnold Gillespie, Warren Newcombe, Irving G. Reis, (animation) Joshua Meador; *Starring* Walter Pidgeon, Anne Francis, Leslie Nielsen; *V* MGM/UA (UK and USA).

THE FORBIN PROJECT (aka COLOSSUS – THE FORBIN PROJECT) ★★★

USA 1970; colour; 100 mins; Universal; *D* Joseph Sargent; *P* Stanley Chase; *W* James Bridges from

Colossus by D. F. Jones; *M* Michel Colombier; *C* Gene Polito; *AD* Alexander Golitzen, John J. Lloyd; *SPFX* Whitey McMahon, (photography) Albert Whitlock; *Starring* Eric Braeden, Susan Clark, William Schallert.

THE FOUR SKULLS OF JONATHAN DRAKE ★★½

USA 1959; b/w; 70 mins; Vogue/United Artists; *D* Edward L. Cahn; *P* Robert E. Kent; *W* Orville H. Hampton; *M* Paul Dunlap; *C* Maury Gertsman; *AD* William Glasgow; *Starring* Eduard Franz, Valerie French, Paul Wexler, Henry Daniell. Often spoken of as a real low-budget stinker, this is really not bad (it terrified me as a child). Voodoo curse by Ecuadorian medicine man (Wexler) leads to decapitation for men in accursed family, heads subsequently shrunken. Living-dead Wexler, lips sewn shut and 180 years old, was one of the memorable images from pulp horror movies of the fifties.

FRANKENSTEIN

USA 1910; b/w; 975ft (around 12 mins); Edison; *D/W* J. Searle Dawley from the novel by Mary Shelley; *SPFX* (make-up), Charles Ogle; *Starring* Charles Ogle, Augustus Phillips, Mary Fuller. This apparently lost piece of history – the first real horror movie with a monster – is included for the sake of completeness. Ogle, who did his own make-up, looks splendidly ghastly in the stills: furry hands and long, wild grey hair haloing a blank white face with sunken eyes. The film had a moral about true love triumphing.

FRANKENSTEIN ★★★★

USA 1931; b/w; 71 mins; Universal; *D* James Whale; *P* Carl Laemmle Jr; *W* Robert Florey, Garrett Fort, Francis Edward Faragoh, John L. Balderston from the novel by Mary Shelley and the play by Peggy Webling; *C* Arthur Edeson; *AD* Charles D. Hall; *SPFX* (make-up) Jack P. Pierce, (electrics) Kenneth Strickfaden; *Starring* Colin Clive, Boris Karloff, Edward Van Sloan, Dwight Frye; *V* CIC (UK), MCA (USA).

FRANKENSTEIN AND THE MONSTER FROM HELL ★★½ 👹

UK 1973; colour; 99 mins; Hammer/Avco Embassy; *D* Terence Fisher; *P* Roy Skeggs; *W* John Elder (Anthony Hinds); *M* James Bernard; *C* Brian Probyn; *AD* Scott MacGregor; *SPFX* (make-up) Eddie Knight; *Starring* Peter Cushing, Shane Briant, Madeline Smith, Dave Prowse. This is the seventh and last of the Hammer *Frankenstein* movies. Frankenstein, now running an asylum for the criminally insane, is still obsessively making monsters from dead people. Prowse (later Darth Vader in *Star Wars*) has the brain of a professor but a monstrous body. One feels sorry for him. More efficiently made than some of the previous films in the series.

FRANKENSTEIN MUST BE DESTROYED ★★★

UK 1969; colour; 97 mins; Hammer/Warner; *D* Terence Fisher; *P* Anthony Nelson Keys; *W* Bert Batt; *M* James Bernard; *C* Arthur Grant; *AD* Bernard Robinson; *SPFX* (make-up) Eddie Knight; *Starring* Peter Cushing, Simon Ward, Veronica Carlson. The fifth of Hammer's seven *Frankenstein* movies (praised by some Terence Fisher fans, of whom I am not one) is a tedious and squalid story of brain transplants, with the dandyish baron here almost wholly evil – a blackmailer, rapist (very embarrassing to see the dignified Cushing in this scene) and murderer, lacking almost all traces of his former idealism.

FRANKENSTEIN: THE TRUE STORY ★★★½

UK 1973; made for TV; colour; 200 minutes (shorter in theatrical version); Universal; *D* Jack Smight; *P* Hunt Stromberg Jr; *W* Christopher Isherwood, Don Bachardy from the novel by Mary Shelley; *M* Gil Melle; *C* Arthur Ibbetson; *AD* Wilfrid Shingleton; *Starring* James Mason, Leonard Whiting, David McCallum, Jane Seymour, Michael Sarrazin, Michael Wilding, Agnes Moorehead, Margaret Leighton, Ralph Richardson, John Gielgud, Tom Baker. One of the strangest versions of the Frankenstein story, with a very deceptive title.

In fact, the story is far removed from Mary Shelley's, though interestingly it does deploy some Shelley scenes which have not been used in other versions, notably the climactic trip to the Arctic. Amazingly up-market cast and Isherwood script might have pointed to a definitive version of the story, but it is more bizarre than classic, with Mason swanning about as an evil rival to Frankenstein in a kimono, a female Creature who is (in a stunning scene) decapitated, and a male creature (Sarrazin) who begins by being wholly beautiful but decays like an unpleasant memory as the story continues. Terribly slow and silly first hour, but then it picks up and in places is amazingly good, though Smight's direction (as usual) is less than first-class overall (see *Damnation Alley*, *The Illustrated Man*). Thought-provoking, with some strong images.

DIE FRAU IM MOND (THE WOMAN IN THE MOON) ★★★
Germany 1929; b/w; 155 mins; Lang/Ufa; *D/P* Fritz Lang; *W* Thea von Harbou from her novel; *C* Curt Courant, Oskar Fischinger, Otto Kanturek; *AD* Otto Hunte, Emil Hasler, Karl Vollbrecht; *SPFX* Konstantin Tschet (Tschetwerikoff); *Starring* Klaus Pohl, Willy Fritsch, Gustav von Wangenheim, Gerda Maurus. The first serious space-travel film, though not one of Lang's best. The two-stage rocket was designed by Hermann Oberth and Willy Ley; the former was involved in the development of the V-2 later on during the war. A melodramatic story weakens the film after the strong beginning, as do the unscientific sequences on the Moon (which has air, snow and lots of gold) where the young leading couple decide to live.

FREAKS ★★★★½ ⚑
USA 1932; b/w; 64 mins (cut from never-released 90 mins version); MGM; *D/P* Tod Browning; *W* Willis Goldbeck, Leon Gordon, Edgar Allan Woolf, Al Boasberg from "Spurs" by Tod Robbins; *C* Merritt B. Gerstad; *Starring* Wallace Ford, Leila Hyams, Olga Baclanova, Harry Earles, Daisy Earles.

FREAKY FRIDAY ★★★
USA 1976; colour; 100 mins; Disney; *D* Gary Nelson; *P* Ron Miller; *W* Mary Rodgers from her novel; *M* Johnny Mandel; *C* Charles F. Wheeler; *SPFX* Eustace Lycett, Art Cruickshank, Danny Lee; *Starring* Barbara Harris, Jodie Foster, John Astin; *V* Disney (UK and USA). New version of an old idea: mother and daughter, both dissatisfied with their roles in life, wish that things could be different. They find themselves in one another's bodies. Quite good performances, particularly from Barbara Harris as the mother/mother's body, but the opportunities for satire or even farce are largely squandered. The setting is middle-class Californian suburban.

FROGS ★★★
USA 1972; colour; 90 mins; AIP; *D* George McCowan; *P* George Edwards, Peter Thomas; *W* Robert Hutchison, Robert Blees; *M* Les Baxter; *C* Mario Tosi; *Starring* Ray Milland, Sam Elliott, Joan Van Ark, Adam Roarke, Judy Pace; *V* Guild (UK), Warner (USA). Ecological fable: nature revolts in Florida against ill-treatment by man; snakes, snapping turtles, spiders polish off upper-crust layabouts. Fun.

FROM BEYOND THE GRAVE (aka TALES FROM BEYOND THE GRAVE) ★★★
UK 1973; colour; 98 mins; Amicus/Warner; *D* Kevin Connor; *P* Max J. Rosenberg, Milton Subotsky; *W* Robin Clarke, Raymond Christodoulou from four stories by R. Chetwynd-Hayes; *M* Douglas Gamley; *C* Alan Hume; *SPFX* Alan Bryce; *Starring* Peter Cushing, David Warner, Donald Pleasence, Angela Pleasence, Margaret Leighton, Ian Carmichael, Ian Ogilvy, Lesley-Anne Down. One of the crisper Amicus anthology films, with a framework about antique dealer (Cushing) whom people cheat and the way they are punished. Second story about sexy, drab daughter of Donald Pleasence (played by Angela Pleasence) seducing, then killing by voodoo, seedy henpecked ex-soldier is well done. The third, about

an elemental on Ian Carmichael's shoulder, is distinguished by the lunatic playing of the psychic advisor who makes matters worse. First and last stories (magic mirror with Jack the Ripper; malevolent Cavalier behind antique door) are so-so.

FROM THE EARTH TO THE MOON ★½
USA 1958; colour; 100 mins; Waverly/RKO/Warner; *D* Byron Haskin; *P* Benedict Bogeaus; *W* Robert Blees, James Leicester from the novel by Jules Verne; *M* Louis Forbes; *C* Edwin DuPar; *SPFX* Lee Zavitz; *Starring* Joseph Cotten, George Sanders, Henry Daniell, Debra Paget. Extremely sluggish adaptation of an SF "classic" that was not too good to begin with (but Verne's work had just come out of copyright). At the time of the American Civil War, space travellers reach the Moon in projectile fired from huge gun. Haskin did better with *War of the Worlds*.

FUKKATSU NO HI – see VIRUS

FULL CIRCLE (aka THE HAUNTING OF JULIA) ★★
UK/Canada 1976; colour; 97 mins; Fetter/Classic Film Industries; *D* Richard Loncraine; *P* Peter Fetterman, Alfred Pariser; *W* Dave Humphries from *Julia* by Peter Straub; *M* Colin Towns; *C* Peter Hannan; *AD* Brian Morris; *SPFX* Thomas Clark; *Starring* Mia Farrow, Keir Dullea, Tom Conti, Samantha Gates; *V* Media (UK and USA). Disastrous British release; not released US until 1981. Based on good novel; convoluted story about accidental child-killer (Farrow) meeting Olivia (Gates), sadistic ghost-child lookalike of her dead daughter. Another evil child film, messily put together but with good moments.

THE FUNHOUSE ★★★½ ⚑
USA 1981; colour; 96 mins; Mace Neufeld/Universal; *D* Tobe Hooper; *P* Derek Power, Steven Bernhardt; *W* Larry Block; *M* John Beal; *C* Andrew Laszlo; *PD* Morton Rabinowitz; *SPFX* J. B. Jones, (make-up design) Rick Baker, (make-up execution) Craig Reardon; *Starring* Elizabeth Berridge, Cooper Huckabee, Miles Chapin, Largo Woodruff; *V* CIC (UK), MCA (USA). In one way, this is a very conventional stalk-and-slash movie, with teenagers at a carnival menaced by the appallingly deformed mutant son of the Funhouse barker. (His brother, we learn, is the ghastly foetus in a bottle in the freak show, and his mother – just conceivably – is a two-headed cow.) But Tobe Hooper is an unusually strong director *(Texas Chainsaw Massacre, Salem's Lot, Poltergeist)*, and he exploits this material intelligently and remorselessly. The teenagers, for example, are extremely credible: giggling, pot-smoking, irritating. The build-up of tension is good, and it allows a certain sympathy for the mutant (whom we see unmasked quite early, during a scene where he is offered sex in return for cash by the carnival's fortune teller, who taunts him and is murdered while the teenagers watch through a grille). Three of the four teenagers are gorily killed (stylishly frightening set-pieces) and the fourth escapes. It is a violent and scary film, lit with many flashes of black humour. The subtext, as with so many films in the lower echelons of the splatter genre, is the confrontation of the "normal" family with the "abnormal" family, and the asking of the question, how normal is normal? In addition, the tawdry carnival setting is used to make some interesting visual points about voyeurism, some of which constitute a criticism of the audience for sitting and watching this grisly stuff.

THE FURY ★★★½ ⚑
USA 1978; colour; 118 mins; Yablans/20th Century-Fox; *D* Brian De Palma; *P* Frank Yablans; *W* John Farris from his novel; *M* John Williams; *C* Richard H. Kline; *PD* Bill Malley; *SPFX* A. D. Flowers, (make-up) Rick Baker; *Starring* Kirk Douglas, John Cassavetes, Amy Irving, Carrie Snodgress, Andrew Stevens, Fiona Lewis; *V* CBS/Fox (UK and USA).

FUTUREWORLD ★★
USA 1976; colour; 107 mins; Aubrey/Paul N.

Lazarus III/AIP; *D* Richard T. Heffron; *P* Lazarus, James T. Aubrey; *W* Mayo Simon, George Schenck; *M* Fred Karlin; *C* Howard Schwartz, Gene Polito; *SPFX* Gene Grigg; *Starring* Peter Fonda, Blythe Danner, Arthur Hill; *V* Guild (UK), Warner (USA).

GALAXINA ★★★
USA 1980; colour; 95 mins; Crown/Marimar; *D/W* William Sachs; *P* Marilyn J. Tenser; *C* Dean Cundey; *PD* Tom Turlley; *Starring* Dorothy R. Stratten, Stephen Macht, James David Hinton; *V* Guild (UK), MCA (USA). Not really very good, but it has charm and tries hard. Space-opera parody, in which Sachs *(Incredible Melting Man)* is inventive as a writer, so-so as a director. Spoofs of *Alien*, *Star Trek*, *2001*, *Star Wars*; search for "blue star", lots of aliens (good make-up, especially grumpy rock-eater), cannibal restaurant. Dorothy Stratten showed real talent as the emotionless but sexy android who learns to have feelings. *Playboy's* 1979 Playmate of the Year, she was murdered soon afterwards by her husband, and became the subject of sentimental Bob Fosse movie *Star 80* (1983).

GAS-S-S-S (aka GAS), **OR IT BECAME NECESSARY TO DESTROY THE WORLD IN ORDER TO SAVE IT** ★★★★
USA 1970; colour; 79 mins; San Jacinto/AIP; *D/P* Roger Corman; *W* George Armitage; *M* Country Joe and the Fish; *C* Ron Dexter; *AD* David Nichols; *Starring* Robert Corff, Elaine Giftos, George Armitage. Amusing Corman cheapie, rumoured to have been recut by worried studio executives who disapproved of the story's iconoclasm. Black comedy: everyone in the world over twenty-five dies (of instant old age) when nerve gas is released. Hell's Angels become the new conservatives; Edgar Allan Poe rides around on motorcycle with raven on shoulder; cameo role for God. The kids don't do so badly running things. Satire crude but not bad.

GATES OF HELL – see CITY OF THE LIVING DEAD

IL GATTO NERO – see THE BLACK CAT

GAWAIN AND THE GREEN KNIGHT ★★★
UK 1973; colour; 93 mins; Sancrest/United Artists; *D* Stephen Weeks; *P* Philip Breen; *W* Breen, Weeks, also Rosemary Sutcliff, from the medieval poem; *M* Ron Goodwin; *C* Peter Hurst; *AD* Anthony Woollard; *SPFX* Les Hillman; *Starring* Murray Head, Ciaran Madden, Nigel Green, Robert Hardy. The greatest of all medieval British poems outside Chaucer is the basis of this slightly bloodless (literally and metaphorically) fantasy. The symbolic sexuality of the original is bowdlerized (the film may have been intended for children). Gawain goes on quest for gigantic Green Knight whom he beheaded at beginning; Knight (after restoring head) demands return bout. Some good mysterious moments in this very British film that makes no concessions to the international market, but effects rather weak.

THE GHOST AND MRS MUIR ★★★½
USA 1947; b/w; 104 mins; 20th Century-Fox; *D* Joseph L. Mankiewicz; *P* Fred Kohlmar; *W* Philip Dunne from the novel by R. A. Dick; *M* Bernard Herrmann; *C* Charles Lang; *AD* Richard Day, George Davis; *SPFX* Fred Sersen; *Starring* Rex Harrison, Gene Tierney, George Sanders. Sentimental, enjoyable light fantasy; widow Tierney moves into English seaside house haunted by Captain Gregg (Harrison); unusual romance blossoms between them. Harrison's droll, soft-centred swagger is mildly appealing. Sanders plays a cad, as usual. Tierney's slightly haunted life goes on, quite happily, and in tear-jerking close she dies peacefully (an old woman) and the spirit of the young woman rises up and goes off hand in hand into a foggy sunset with Gregg! A TV series followed years later (1968) with Hope Lange.

GHOST STORY ★★ ⚑
USA 1981; colour; 110 mins; Universal; *D* John Irvin; *P* Burt Weissbourd, Douglas Green; *W*

Lawrence D. Cohen from the novel by Peter Straub; *M* Philippe Sarde; *C* Jack Cardiff; *SPFX* (visual) Albert Whitlock, (make-up) Dick Smith; *Starring* Fred Astaire, Melvyn Douglas, Douglas Fairbanks Jr, John Houseman, Alice Krige, Craig Wasson; *V* CIC (UK), MCA (USA).

GIULIETTA DEGLI SPIRITI – *see* JULIET OF THE SPIRITS

GLADIATORERNA (aka THE PEACE GAME; THE GLADIATORS) ★★
Sweden 1969; colour; 105 mins; Sandrews; *D* Peter Watkins; *P* Göran Lindgren; *W* Nicholas Gosling, Watkins; *M* Mahler, Claes af Geijerstam; *C* Peter Suschitzky; *AD* William Brodie; *SPFX* Stig Lindberg; *Starring* Arthur Pentelow, Frederick Danner, Kenneth Lo, Björn Franzén; *V* Wizard (USA). To channel aggressive instincts, future society has organized warfare into a computer-controlled contest between special teams of soldiers: almost a sports contest. But in Game 256 in Sweden the computer breaks down. The war games are not well staged, technically, and the pacifist message, while admirable, is very crudely thumped home in this pseudo-documentary-styled fiction.

THE GLADIATORS – *see* GLADIATORERNA

GLEN AND RANDA ★★★
USA 1971; colour; 94 mins; *D* Jim McBride; *W* Lorenzo Mans, Rudolph Wurlitzer, McBride; *C* Alan Raymond; *Starring* Steven Curry, Shelley Plimpton, Garry Goodrow; *V* CBS/Fox (UK). Glen (Curry) and Randa (Plimpton) set off on a quest for the mythical city of Metropolis twenty-five years after an unspecified holocaust, their imaginations inflamed by the tales of a lustful magician (Goodrow). Through an oddly innocent, desolate landscape (filmed in Oregon), haunted by incomprehensible items of a fallen civilization's detritus, they drift. Metropolis is never reached, and Randa dies in childbirth, in this strange, gloomy, austere, hopeful fairy tale, blown up from a semi-amateur 16mm print, and given excellent reviews by the underground press.

THE GODSEND ★★★
UK 1980; colour; 90 mins; London Cannon; *D/P* Gabrielle Beaumont; *W* Olaf Pooley from the novel by Bernard Taylor; *M* Roger Webb; *C* Norman Warwick; *AD* Tony Curtis; *Starring* Malcolm Stoddard, Cyd Hayman, Angela Pleasence, Patrick Barr, Wilhelmina Green, Joanne Boorman; *V* Rank (UK), Vestron (USA). Angela Pleasence is the thoroughly sinister cuckoo who leaves a newborn baby in an idyllic nest, and then disappears. Blonde baby grows up to be innocent-looking killer of her adopted brothers and sisters. The basic premise suggests a supernatural origin for little Bonnie, but the horror is played straight, clean and non-exploitative, with no special effects. Of the four actresses who play Bonnie as she grows older, the second oldest is the most chilling, with a blank, angelic, homicidal stare. Nasty but efficient film, made by a woman (unusual in this genre), and apparently about the irrationality of the maternal instinct.

GOD TOLD ME TO – *see* DEMON

GODZILLA, KING OF THE MONSTERS (GOJIRA) ★★½
Japan 1954 (USA version 1956); b/w; 98 mins (USA version 80 mins); Toho (USA version Embassy); *D* Ishiro (Inoshira) Honda (added scenes USA version Terry Morse); *P* Tomoyuki Tanaka; *W* Honda, Takeo Murata from a story by Shigeru Kayama; *M* Akira Ifukube; *SPFX* Eiji Tsuburaya, Akira Watanabe and others; *Starring* Akira Takarada, Takashi Shimura, Momoko Kochi, (USA version only) Raymond Burr; *V* Vestron (USA).

GOG ★★½
USA 1954; colour; 3-D; 85 mins; Ivan Tors/United Artists; *D* Herbert L. Strock; *P* Ivan Tors; *W* Tom Taggart, also Richard G. Taylor, from a story by Tors; *M* Harry Sukman; *C* Lothrop Worth; *AD* Wil-

liam Ferrari; *SPFX* Harry Redmond Jr; *Starring* Richard Egan, Constance Dowling, Herbert Marshall, John Wengraf. Largely-forgotten, routine SF film, but quite advanced for its time, especially in its two non-humanoid robots Gog and Magog. Sabotage in scientific plant turns out to be the work of the controlling computer (the earliest version of this plot in movies, I believe), whose programming has been modified by foreign spy planes. Ingenious murders take place (involving centrifuges, cold-chambers, ultrasonics). A bit slow and talky. Made in colour and 3-D, but surviving prints seem to be black-and-white without the depth.

GOJIRA – *see* GODZILLA, KING OF THE MONSTERS

THE GOLDEN VOYAGE OF SINBAD ★★★
UK 1973; colour; 105 mins; Morningside/Columbia; *D* Gordon Hessler; *P* Charles H. Schneer, Ray Harryhausen; *W* Brian Clemens from a story by Clemens and Harryhausen; *M* Miklos Rozsa; *C* Ted Moore; *PD* John Stoll; *SPFX* (visual) Ray Harryhausen; *Starring* John Phillip Law, Caroline Munro, Tom Baker; *V* Columbia (USA).

THE GOLEM (DER GOLEM)
Germany 1914; b/w; 1250 metres; Bioscop; *D* Paul Wegener, Henrik Galeen; *W* from the novel by Gustav Meyrink; *C* Guido Seeber; *AD* R. A. Dietrich, Rochus Gliese, *Starring* Wegener, Lyda Salmonova, Henrik Galeen, Carl Ebert.

THE GOLEM (DER GOLEM, WIE·ER IN DIE WELT KAM) ★★★
Germany 1920; b/w; 1922 metres; Ufa; *D* Paul Wegener, Carl Boese; *W* Wegener, Henrik Galeen from the novel by Gustav Meyrink; *C* Karl Freund; *AD* Hans Poelzig, Kurt Richter; *Starring* Wegener, Lyda Salmonova, Hans Sturm, Lothar Müthel, Albert Steinrück.

GORGO ★★½
UK 1959; colour; 78 mins; King Bros; *D* Eugene Lourié; *P* Wilfred Eades; *W* John Loring, Daniel Hyatt; *M* Angelo Francesco Lavagnino; *C* Freddie Young; *AD* Elliot Scott; *SPFX* (photographic) Tom Howard; *Starring* Bill Travers, William Sylvester, Vincent Winter; *V* Nostalgia (USA). Another monster-movie from the director of *Beast from 20 000 Fathoms*. Thirty-foot monster caught off coast of Ireland is exhibited in London; its mother finds out and comes to collect it. Good location work; the monster is not bad (made using the man-in-a-suit technique); yet the film does not quite come off. Just too derivative.

THE GORGON ★★½
UK 1964; colour; 83 mins; Hammer/Columbia; *D* Terence Fisher; *P* Anthony Nelson Keys; *W* John Gilling from a story by J. Llewellyn Devine; *M* James Bernard; *C* Michael Reed; *PD* Bernard Robinson; *SPFX* Syd Pearson, (make-up) Roy Ashton; *Starring* Peter Cushing, Christopher Lee, Richard Pasco, Barbara Shelley; *V* RCA/Columbia (UK and USA). A Transylvanian·village, a wicked brain surgeon (Cushing), a series of villagers turned to stone, in short a Hammer costume drama. It seems that beautiful Carla (Shelley) is possessed by the spirit of the Gorgon. Atmospheric, rather slow, and we do not get to see much of the Gorgon at all, which is actually just as well, since she looks more like a stern headmistress than a mythological horror.

THE GREAT MUPPET CAPER ★★★
UK 1981; colour; 97 mins; ITC; *D* Jim Henson; *P* David Lazer, Frank Oz; *W* Tom Patchett, Jay Tarses, Jerry Juhl, Jack Rose; *C* Oswald Morris; *PD* Harry Lange; *Muppet design consultant* Michael K. Frith; *SPFX* (supervision) Brian Smithies, (make-up) Stuart Freeborn; *Starring the voices of* Jim Henson (Kermit the Frog etc.), Frank Oz (Miss Piggy etc.); *Also starring* Diana Rigg, John Cleese, Robert Morley, Peter Ustinov, Peter Falk; *V* Precision (UK), CBS/Fox (USA).

HALLOWEEN ★★★★♥
USA 1978; colour; 91 mins; Falcon International; *D/M* John Carpenter; *P* Debra Hill; *W* Carpenter, Hill; *C* Dean Cundey; *PD* Tommy Wallace; *Starring* Donald Pleasence, Jamie Lee Curtis, Nancy Loomis, P. J. Soles, Nick Castle; *V* VPD (UK), Media (USA).

HALLOWEEN III: SEASON OF THE WITCH ★★★½♥♥
USA 1983; colour; 98 mins; Dino De Laurentiis; *D/W* Tommy Lee Wallace; *P* Debra Hill, John Carpenter; *W* also Nigel Kneale and Carpenter (uncredited); *M* Carpenter, Alan Howarth; *C* Dean Cundey; *PD* Peter Jamison; *SPFX* Jon G. Belyeu, (make-up) Tom Burman; *Starring* Tom Atkins, Stacey Nelkin, Dan O'Herlihy; *V* Thorn EMI (UK, heavily cut), MCA (USA).

THE HAND ★½
USA 1981; colour; 105 mins; Orion/Warner; *D/W* Oliver Stone from *The Lizard's Tail* by Marc Brandel; *P* Edward R. Pressman; *M* James Horner; *C* King Baggot; *PD* John Michael Riva; *SPFX* (visual) Carlo Rambaldi, (make-up) Stan Winston, Tom Burman; *Starring* Michael Caine, Andrea Marcovicci, Annie McEnroe; *V* Warner (UK and USA). Comic-strip artist Lansdale (Caine) loses hand in accident, has mechanical replacement made, becomes very neurotic. Meanwhile, missing hand seems to take on life of its own (this being probably the seventh crawling-hand movie on record, another being *Dr Terror's House of Horrors*). Story deeply confused about whether hand is real or figment of Lansdale's imagination to remove guilt about murders he has committed himself.

THE HANDS OF ORLAC (ORLAC'S HÄNDE) ★★★½
Austria 1924; b/w; 7 reels; Pan-Film; *D* Robert Wiene; *W* Ludwig Nerz from *Les Mains d'Orlac* by Maurice Rénard; *C* Günther Krampf, Hans Androschin; *AD* S. Wessely; *Starring* Conrad Veidt, Alexandra Sorina, Fritz Strassny, Paul Askonas, Carmen Cartellieri. First version of often refilmed horror story (see also *Mad Love*), made by Wiene who earlier made *Cabinet of Dr Caligari*. Expressive performance by Veidt as concert pianist whose hands are lost in an accident, those of an executed murderer being grafted in their place. Veidt imagines subsequent murders are his own work via supernaturally powered hands, but in fact the whole thing is a plot against his sanity. Not strictly fantasy, therefore, unlike *Mad Love*.

HARLEQUIN ★★
Australia 1980; colour; 93 mins; F. G. Film Prod.; *D* Simon Wincer; *P* Antony I. Ginnane; *W* Everett De Roche, also Jon George, Neill Hicks; *M* Brian May; *C* Gary Hansen; *PD* Bernard Hides; *SPFX* Conrad C. Rothmann; *Starring* Robert Powell, David Hemmings, Carmen Duncan, Broderick Crawford; *V* VCL (UK).

HARVEY ★★★½
USA 1950; b/w; 104 mins; Universal; *D* Henry Koster; *P* John Beck; *W* Mary Chase, Oscar Brodney from the play by Mary Chase; *M* Frank Skinner; *C* William Daniels; *AD* Bernard Herzbrun, Nathan Juran; *Starring* James Stewart, Josephine Hull, Cecil Kellaway. Adapted from the stage hit. Stewart is wonderful as gentlemanly, whimsical drunk whose best friend is a six-foot-tall invisible rabbit called Harvey; Hull won an Oscar as the put-upon, respectable sister. At the time, I belonged (aged eleven) to the school of thought that believed the rabbit was real. Others didn't.

THE HAUNTED PALACE ★★★½
USA 1963; colour; 85 mins; Alta Vista/AIP; *D/P* Roger Corman; *W* Charles Beaumont from "The Case of Charles Dexter Ward" by H. P. Lovecraft; *M* Ronald Stein; *C* Floyd Crosby; *AD* Daniel Haller; *Starring* Vincent Price, Debra Paget, Lon Chaney (Jr), Leo Gordon, Elisha Cook (Jr); *V* Rank (UK).

THE HAUNTING ★★★½
UK 1963; b/w; 112 mins; Argyle/MGM; *D/P* Robert Wise; *W* Nelson Gidding from *The Haunting of Hill House* by Shirley Jackson; *M* Humphrey Searle; *C* Davis Boulton; *AD* Elliot Scott; *SPFX* Tom Howard; *Starring* Julie Harris, Claire Bloom, Richard Johnson, Russ Tamblyn, Fay Compton, Valentine Dyall.

THE HAUNTING OF JULIA – see FULL CIRCLE

HAUSER'S MEMORY ★★
USA 1970; made for TV; colour; 100 mins; Universal; *D* Boris Sagal; *P* Jack Laird; *W* Adrian Spies from the novel by Curt Siodmak; *M* Billy Byers; *C* Petrus Schloemp; *AD* Ellen Schmidt; *Starring* David McCallum, Susan Strasberg, Lilli Palmer, Helmut Kautner, Leslie Nielsen. The main interest is that the film was based on a novel by German film-maker Siodmak, most of whose many supernatural films were not among the best in the period 1937-56 when he did most of his American work (the only one of his films in this book is *Riders to the Stars*). *Hauser's Memory* has DNA from the brain of a dead Nazi scientist accidentally (!) injected into the brain of a Jewish-American scientist, who thus shares Hauser's dead memories. Promising idea becomes routine thriller/spy story involving the CIA.

HAWK THE SLAYER ★½
UK 1980; colour; 94 mins; Chips/ITC; *D* Terry Marcel; *P* Harry Robertson; *W* Marcel, Robertson; *M* Robertson; *C* Paul Beeson; *AD* Michael Pickwoad; *SPFX* Effects Associates; *Starring* Jack Palance, John Terry, Bernard Bresslaw, Cheryl Campbell; *V* Precision (UK). An early but disappointing entry in the sword-and-sorcery miniboom of 1980-82, which quickly fizzled out. More sword than sorcery in this cut-price epic, with lamentable special effects and a generally cheap look, about good and bad brothers (Terry and Palance) and a magical "mind-sword".

THE HEARSE ★★½
USA 1980; colour; 95 mins; Marimark/Crown International; *D* George Bowers; *P* Mark Tenser, Charles Russell; *W* Bill Bleich from an idea by Mark Tenser; *M* Webster Lewis; *C* Mori Kawa; *AD* Keith Michl; *Starring* Trish Van Devere, Joseph Cotten, David Gautreaux, Donald Hotton; *V* Media (UK and USA). Poor Trish Van Devere works hard and well in this loony story about an unfriendly village, a young schoolma'am, a deceased aunt, a ghostly hearse that keeps appearing from nowhere, a drunken greedy lawyer (Cotten), and a demon lover (Gautreaux) who has immortality. Less than brilliant, the film has a kind of schlock vigour.

HEARTBEEPS ★★★
USA 1981; colour; 79 mins; Universal; *D* Allan Arkush; *P* Michael Phillips; *W* John Hill; *M* John Williams; *C* Charles Rosher Jr; *PD* John W. Corso; *SPFX* (visual) Albert Whitlock, (mechanical) Jamie Shourt and Robbie Blalack, (make-up) Stan Winston; *Starring* Bernadette Peters, Andy Kaufman; *V* CIC (UK), MCA (USA). Amusing, gently satirical comedy about two robots who escape from the repair shop and fall in love. The effects are brilliant, the story less so. Effectively killed by bad distribution and the cutting of ten minutes (unauthorized by director Arkin) on the grounds that the film needed more action – but it is not that sort of movie.

HEAVEN CAN WAIT ★★★★
USA 1943; colour; 112 mins; 20th Century-Fox; *D/P* Ernst Lubitsch; *W* Samson Raphaelson from the play *Birthday* by Lazlo Bus-Feketé; *M* Alfred Newman; *C* Edward Cronjager; *AD* James Basevi, Leland Fuller; *SPFX* Fred Sersen; *Starring* Gene Tierney, Don Ameche, Charles Coburn, Laird Cregar, Spring Byington, Louis Calhern. Lubitsch's sophisticated way with light comedy works well in this gently sardonic story of Don-Juan type (Ameche) requesting admission to Hell, where he tells a self-chastising Rake's-Progress life story. Satan (Cregar) thinks he's too good for Hell, and packs him off. This is *not* the film remade as *Heaven Can Wait* (1978).

HEAVEN CAN WAIT ★★★
USA 1978; colour; 101 mins; Shelburne/Paramount; *D* Warren Beatty, Buck Henry; *P* Beatty; *W* Elaine May, Beatty from the play by Harry Segall (previously filmed as *Here Comes Mr Jordan*); *M* Dave Grusin; *C* William A. Fraker; *PD* Paul Sylbert; *Starring* Warren Beatty, Julie Christie, James Mason, Dyan Cannon, Jack Warden, Buck Henry; *V* CIC (UK), Paramount (USA). This pleasant remake (*not* of the film *Heaven Can Wait* but of the film called *Here Comes Mr Jordan*) proved remarkably popular. Beatty is the sportsman sent to heaven prematurely (a pro footballer this time) and returned in a new body – that of a millionaire. It is all rather heavy-footed compared to the original, though Dyan Cannon is fun as the murderous wife.

HERBIE RIDES AGAIN ★★
USA 1974; colour; 88 mins; Disney; *D* Robert Stevenson; *P/W* Bill Walsh; *M* George Bruns; *C* Frank Phillips; *AD* John B. Mansbridge, Walter Tyler; *SPFX* Art Cruickshank, Alan Maley, Eustace Lycett, Danny Lee; *Starring* Helen Hayes, Stefanie Powers, Ken Berry, John McIntire, Keenan Wynn; *V* Disney (USA). Sequel to Disney's successful *The Love Bug*, and itself followed by formula films *Herbie Goes to Monte Carlo* (1977) and *Herbie Goes Bananas* (1980). The car Herbie, a living VW beetle, is as irritatingly cute as any Disney animal. Sweet old lady (Hayes), Herbie's new owner, is menaced by greedy land-developer (Wynn), but Herbie saves the day. Both professional and routine; good special effects.

HERCULES (LE FATICHE DI ERCOLE) ★½
Italy 1957; colour; 107 mins; Oscar; *D* Pietro Francisci; *P* Federico Teti; *W* Ennio De Concini, Gaio Frattini, Francisci; *M* Enzo Masetti; *C* Mario Bava; *AD* Flavio Mogherini; *Starring* Steve Reeves, Sylva Koscina, Gianna Maria Canale; *V* Intervision (UK), Embassy (USA). Beginning of a seemingly interminable series of Italian blood-and-thunder mythological fantasies, most of them starring young men with spectacular muscles, usually Steve Reeves at first. Greek myth as watered down for this sort of film loses its magical qualities and becomes thunderously literal-minded – partly, of course, because magic is expensive to recreate. Hercules (with Jason and the Argonauts) retrieves the Golden Fleece, slays the Nemean lion (which looks like a child's soft toy) and restores the rightful king. Reeves looks good, but the film has no resonance.

HERCULES UNCHAINED (ERCOLE E LA REGINA DI LIDIA) ★
Italy 1959; colour; 101 mins; Lux Galatea; *D* Pietro Francisci; *P* Bruno Vailati; *W* Francisci, Ennio De Concini; *M* Enzo Masetti; *C/SPFX* Mario Bava; *AD* Massimo Tavazzi; *Starring* Steve Reeves, Sylva Koscina, Primo Carnera, Sylvia Lopez; *V* Intervision (UK). The second of the once-popular Italian *Hercules* series starring muscle-man Reeves, handsome but wooden. (There were a half-dozen more in the series, one of them, *Hercules in the Haunted World* [1961], directed by Mario Bava, the cinematographer here.) Hercules defeats Antaeus the Earth-ogre (played by Carnera), drinks from Lethe and becomes amnesiac, and falls for wicked Queen Omphale, forgetting his wife. Appalling dubbing in the English-language version, but the acting must have seemed pretty frightful in the original too. It is hard to see now why any of these films were successful.

HERE COMES·MR JORDAN ★★★½
USA 1941; b/w; 93 mins; Columbia; *D* Alexander Hall; *P* Everett Riskin; *W* Seton I. Miller, Sidney Buchman from the play *Heaven Can Wait* by Harry Segall; *M* Maurice W. Stoloff; *C* Joseph Walker; *AD* Lionel Banks; *Starring* Robert Montgomery, Claude Rains, Evelyn Keyes, Rita Johnson, Edward Everett Horton, James Gleason; *V* Columbia (USA). Enjoyable fantastic comedy, remade in 1978 as *Heaven Can Wait*, with the first version fractionally better. Professional boxer (Montgomery) is sent prematurely to Heaven be-

cause of bureaucratic confusion; he is sent back to Earth in a new body, and looked after by guardian angel (Rains). Amusing complications ensue. A very minor classic.

HERO ★★½
UK 1982; colour; 92 mins; Maya/Channel 4 TV; *D/W* Barney Platts-Mills from the stories *Tales of the Western Highlands* by J. F. Campbell; *M* Paul Steen with Al Fraser, Jimmy Davidson; *C* Adam Barker; *AD* Tom Paine; *Starring* Derek McGuire, Caroline Kenneil, Alastair Kenneil, Stewart Grant. Indeed an heroic effort, but ill-conceived. Low-budget Dark-Ages fantasy set in Scotland, with most dialogue spoken in Gaelic using amateur actors from Glasgow streets who do not speak Gaelic and therefore had to perform lines parrot fashion. The magic elements are matter-of-fact and only crudely achieved, in this strange attempt to demythologize myth and give it modern resonance. The complex story relates the stormy relationship between young Dermid and the legendary hero Finn MacCumhaill (McCool). It is reported that the TV company that commissioned the film were unaware it was to be in Gaelic!

DIE HERRIN VON ATLANTIS – see L'ATLANTIDE

HIGH PLAINS DRIFTER ★★★★
USA 1973; colour; 105 mins; Malpaso/Universal; *D* Clint Eastwood; *P* Robert Daley; *W* Ernest Tidyman; *M* Dee Barton; *C* Bruce Surtees; *AD* Henry Bumstead; *Starring* Clint Eastwood, Verna Bloom; *V* CIC (UK), MCA (USA). Eastwood, actor turned director, showed real talent in this bizarre spaghetti-style western, in which a laconic Man With No Name sadistically takes over a corrupt western township, renames it Hell, has it painted a sinister red, and arranges for most of its occupants' deaths. At the end he turns out to have been the avenging spirit of a murdered sheriff. Nasty, skilful film, with a well-achieved haunted atmosphere.

THE HOLE – see ONIBABA

HOLOCAUST 2000 (aka THE CHOSEN) ★★
UK/Italy 1977; Embassy/Aston; *D* Alberto De Martino; *P* Edmondo Amati; *W* De Martino, Michael Robson; *M* Ennio Morricone; *C* Erico Menczer; *AD* Uberto Bertacca; *SPFX* Gino De Rossi; *Starring* Kirk Douglas, Simon Ward, Agostina Belli, Anthony Quayle; *V* Rank (UK). Industrialist Kirk Douglas is warned by various portents that his building a nuclear plant may coincide with the seven-headed beast of the Apocalypse being unleashed by the Antichrist (whose hidden identity is all too obvious). This spaghetti version of *The Omen* is terrible tosh, redeemed by one splendid image in which monster and power plant coalesce in a truly apocalyptic vision.

THE HOLY MOUNTAIN ★★ ☻☻
Mexico/USA 1973; colour; 126 mins; ABKCO; *D/W* Alexandro Jodorowsky; *P* Alan Klein; *M* Jodorowsky, Ronald Frangipane, Don Cherry; *C* Rafael Corkidi; *Starring* Jodorowsky, Horacio Salinas, Ramona Saunders. This film – that counterculture hero Jodorowsky made in Mexico with a cast that had undergone mystical training – was a flop, despite the earlier success of his *El Topo*. Indescribable plot is crammed with surrealist and often unpleasant images (crucifixions, lizards, frogs, tarantulas, an armless dwarf, faeces transmuted into gold, mutilations, bleeding crotches, a sage with leopard-head breasts). Upon reaching the Mountain of the Nine Immortals, Jodorowsky and his disciples find the Immortals are dummies, and take their place. The deliberate shock tactics and blend of hippy religious and drug-taking mysticism have dated, and the film is seldom shown.

HOMUNCULUS ★★★
Germany 1916; b/w; serial (six episodes approx. one hour each); Deutsche Bioscop; *D* Otto Rippert; *W* Rippert, Robert Neuss from the novel by Robert Reinert; *C* Carl Hoffman; *AD* Robert A.

Dietrich; *Starring* Olaf Fönss, Friedrich Kühne, Theodor Loos, Mechthild Thein.

THE HORROR CHAMBER OF DR FAUSTUS – *see* LES YEUX SANS VISAGE

HORROR EXPRESS (PANICO EN EL TRANSIBERIANO) ★★½
Spain/UK 1972; colour; 90 mins; Scotia International/Granada & Benmar; *D* Eugenio Martin; *P* Bernard Gordon; *W* Arnaud d'Usseau; *M* John Cacavas; *C* Alejandro Ulloa; *SPFX* Pablo Perez, *Starring* Christopher Lee, Peter Cushing, Telly Savalas; *V* Media (USA). This British/Spanish co-production was filmed on a set (a posh train) left over from *Nicholas and Alexandra*. The well-preserved, mummified body of a prehistoric missing-link is brought on the train by aristocratic Christopher Lee. It comes to life in the luggage compartment and proceeds to wreak havoc, because it has the power, through staring at people, to possess them so that their bodies are vehicles for his consciousness. (It's like a dry run for Carpenter's *The Thing* – you never know which person is now a monster.) When he stares, his eyes glow bright red, in one of the amazingly cheapo special effects that give such joy to fans of this sort of thing. The ill-disciplined story rattles on in a jolly way, like the train, ending with a memorable cameo from Telly Savalas as a sadistic, whip- and wise-cracking Cossack.

HORROR HOTEL – *see* CITY OF THE DEAD

HORROR OF DRACULA – *see* DRACULA

HOUR OF THE WOLF (VARGTIMMEN) ★★★★★♥
Sweden 1968; b/w; 88 mins; Svensk Filmindustri; *D/W* Ingmar Bergman; *M* Lars-Johan Werle; *C* Sven Nykvist; *AD* Marik Vos-Lundh; *SPFX* Evald Andersson; *Starring* Liv Ullmann, Max von Sydow, Erland Josephson, Ingrid Thulin.

THE HOUSE BY THE CEMETERY (QUELLA VILLA ACCANTO AL CIMITERO) ★★★♥♥·
Italy 1981; colour; 86 mins; Fulvia; *D* Lucio Fulci; *P* Fabrizio De Angelis; *W* Dardano Sacchetti, Giorgio Mariuzzo, Fulci; *C* Sergio Salvati; *SPFX* Gino De Rossi, (make-up) Giannetto De Rossi, Maurizio Trani; *Starring* Katherine MacColl, Paolo Malco, Giovanni Frezza; *V* Videomedia (UK).

HOUSE OF CRAZIES – *see* ASYLUM

HOUSE OF DARK SHADOWS ★★
USA 1970; colour; 97 mins; MGM; *D/P* Dan Curtis; *W* Sam Hall, Gordon Russell from the TV series *Dark Shadows*; *M* Robert Cobert; *C* Arthur J. Ornitz; *PD* Trevor Williams; *SPFX* (make-up) Dick Smith; *Starring* Jonathan Frid, Joan Bennett, Grayson Hall, Thayer David. Movie spin-off from the TV soap opera which ran for over one thousand episodes. Lots of Gothic atmosphere, rather restrained shudders in conventional vampire story with much hammy over-acting, set in old New England estate. Julia (Grayson Hall) falls in love with mysterious visitor Barnabas (Frid) and does not live long to regret it. She knew he was a vampire, silly girl. Sequel was *Night of Dark Shadows*.

THE HOUSE OF EXORCISM (LA CASA DELL' EXORCISMO, aka LISA AND THE DEVIL) ★★♥
Italy 1975; Alfred Leone International; *D* Mickey Lion (pseudonym of Mario Bava and Alfred Leone); *P* Alfred Leone; *W* Alberto Cittini, Leone; *M* Carlo Savina; *C* Cecilio Paniagua; *AD* Nedo Azzini; *SPFX* Franco Tocci; *Starring* Telly Savalas, Elke Sommer, Sylva Koscina, Alida Valli, Robert Alda, Gabriele Tinti; *V* VTC (UK), Maljack (USA). Lollipop-sucking villain Savalas (irrelevant *Kojak* joke) is a demon in human shape, and under his influence Lisa (Sommer) is possessed in archetypal *The Exorcist* style (vomiting, levitation) but exorcised by priest (Alda) in climactic scene which amuses exploitation fans. Others may find the whole exercise merely crude. Leone re-edited the film after it was finished, and apparently the exorcism scenes were added by him.

HOUSE OF USHER (aka THE FALL OF THE HOUSE OF USHER) ★★★½
USA 1960; colour; 85 mins; Alta Vista/AIP; *D/P* Roger Corman; *W* Richard Matheson from the story by Edgar Allan Poe; *M* Les Baxter; *C* Floyd Crosby; *AD* Daniel Haller; *SPFX* Pat Dinga; *Starring* Vincent Price, Mark Damon, Myrna Fahey, Harry Ellerbe; *V* Guild (UK), Warner (USA).

THE HOUSE THAT DRIPPED BLOOD ★★★½
UK 1970; Amicus/Cinerama; *D* Peter Duffell; *P* Max J. Rosenberg, Milton Subotsky; *W* Robert Bloch; *M* Michael Dress; *C* Ray Parslow; *AD* Tony Curtis; *SPFX* (make-up) Harry and Peter Frampton; *Starring* Denholm Elliott, Peter Cushing, Christopher Lee, Jon Pertwee, Ingrid Pitt. One of the better Amicus compendium horror films, this has four episodes linked by a commonplace story about a policeman investigating an old house. The best episodes are "The Cloak", an amusing story of a horror star who buys a genuine vampire's cloak, and "Sweets to the Sweet" in which witches abound and a little girl uses a voodoo doll; other episodes involve waxworks and fictional mad strangler who comes to life.

THE HOWLING ★★★★♥
USA 1980; colour; 90 mins; International Film Investors-Wescom/Avco Embassy; *D* Joe Dante; *P* Michael Finnell, Jack Conrad; *W* John Sayles, Terence H. Winkless from the novel by Gary Brandner; *M* Pino Donaggio; *C* John Hora; *AD* Robert A. Burns; *SPFX* Roger George, (make-up) Rob Bottin, (make-up consultant) Rick Baker, (stop-motion animation) David Allen, (mechanical) Doug Beswick; *Starring* Dee Wallace, Patrick Macnee, Denis Dugan, Elisabeth Brooks, John Carradine; *V* Embassy (UK), CBS/Fox (USA).

HUMANOIDS FROM THE DEEP (aka MONSTER) ★★♥
USA 1980; colour; 81 mins; New World; *D* Barbara Peeters; *P* Martin B. Cohen; *W* Frederick James; *M* James Horner; *C* Daniel Lacambre; *AD* Michael Erler; *SPFX* Robert George, (humanoids creation/design) Rob Bottin; *Starring* Doug McClure, Ann Turkel, Vic Morrow; *V* Warner (USA). Typical exploitation movie of the Corman school has imitations of *Creature from the Black Lagoon* (the monsters), *Prophecy* (ecological carelessness that creates the monsters) and *Alien* (the womb-bursting climax). These monsters, who want to hurry up the evolutionary process, are killers and also sex-mad rapists. Jokes have been made about this film which degrades women being made by a woman, but it is rumoured that the most sexually exploitative scenes were directed by somebody else and edited in.

THE HUNGER ★★♥♥
USA 1983; colour; 99 mins; Richard Shepherd Co./MGM/UA; *D* Tony Scott; *P* Richard A. Shepherd; *W* Ivan Davis, Michael Thomas from the novel by Whitley Strieber; *M* Michel Rubini, Denny Jaeger; *C* Stephen Goldblatt, Tom Mangravite; *PD* Brian Morris; *SPFX* (monkey effects) David Allen and Roger Dicken, (make-up illusions) Dick Smith and Carl Fullerton; *Starring* Catherine Deneuve, David Bowie, Susan Sarandon, Cliff De Young; *V* MGM/UA (UK and USA).

HUNGRY WIVES – *see* JACK'S WIFE

IF... ★★★½
UK 1968; colour; 111 mins; Memorial/Paramount; *D* Lindsay Anderson; *P* Michael Medwin, Anderson; *W* David Sherwin from a script *Crusaders* by Sherwin and John Howlett; *M* Marc Wilkinson (with Sanctus from the *Missa Luba*); *C* Miroslav Ondricek; *PD* Jocelyn Herbert; *Starring* Malcolm McDowell, David Wood, Richard Warwick, Robert Swann; *V* Paramount (USA).

THE ILLUSTRATED MAN ★★½
USA 1969; colour; 103 mins; SKM/Warner-Seven Arts; *D* Jack Smight; *P* Howard B. Kreitsek, Ted Mann; *W* Kreitsek from three stories, "The Veldt", "The Long Rain" and "The Last Night of the World", in *The Illustrated Man* by Ray Bradbury;

M Jerry Goldsmith; *C* Philip Lathrop; *AD* Joel Schiller; *SPFX* Ralph Webb, (skin illustration design) James E. Reynolds; *Visual consultant* Richard Sylbert; *Starring* Rod Steiger, Claire Bloom, Robert Drivas, Don Dubbins. Appalling screenplay by producer Kreitsek and limp, literal-minded direction by Smight sunk this anthology film so that even some fair performances could not redeem it. Bradbury, whose stories are here adapted, hated it. Steiger's body is covered by mysterious tattoos, three of which tell stories about malign fate. "The Veldt" has nursery animals coming to life and disposing of parents; "The Long Rain" is set on Venus, where an umbrella is badly needed. Don't ask about the other one. The same actors are in each episode.

IMAGES ★★½♥
Eire 1972; colour; 101 mins; Lion's Gate/Hemdale; *D/W* Robert Altman (texts for *In Search of Unicorns* by Susannah York); *P* Tommy Thompson; *M* John Williams, (Sounds) Stomu Yamashta; *C* Vilmos Zsigmond; *PD* Leon Ericksen; *Starring* Susannah York, Rene Auberjonois, Marcel Bozzuffi; *V* VCL (UK).

I MARRIED A MONSTER FROM OUTER SPACE ★★½
USA 1958; b/w; Paramount; *D/P* Gene Fowler Jr; *W* Louis Vittes; *C* Haskell Boggs; *SPFX* John P. Fulton; *Starring* Tom Tryon, Gloria Talbott, Ken Lynch; *V* Paramount (USA).

I MARRIED A WITCH ★★★★
USA 1942; b/w; 76 mins; Paramount/Cinema Guild (United Artists); *D* René Clair; *P* (uncredited) Preston Sturges; *W* Robert Pirosh, Marc Connelly, (uncredited) Dalton Trumbo from *The Passionate Witch* by Thorne Smith (completed by Norman Matson); *M* Roy Webb; *C* Ted Tetzlaff; *AD* Hans Dreier, Ernst Fegté, *SPFX* (photographic) Gordon Jennings; *Starring* Fredric March, Veronica Lake, Robert Benchley, Susan Hayward, Cecil Kellaway. Typical forties approach to the supernatural: domesticated and made into light comedy. Not one of Clair's greatest, but still an amusing tale of witch who returns to be whimsically revenged on descendants of those who burnt her. Lake makes an implausibly sultry witch. Good effects.

IMMORAL TALES (CONTES IMMORAUX) ★★★
France 1974; colour; 103 mins; Argos; *D/W/AD* Walerian Borowczyk from in part (episode "La Marée"/"The Tide") a story by André Pieyre de Mandiargues; *M* Maurice Le Roux; *Starring* ("La Marée") Lise Danvers and Fabrice Luchini; ("Thérèse, Philosophe"/"Therese the Philosopher") Charlotte Alexandra; ("Erzsebet Bathory") Paloma Picasso and Pascale Christophe; ("Lucrezia Borgia") Florence Bellamy, Jacopo Berinizi and Lorenzo Berinizi; *V* Thorn EMI (UK), Force (USA). Stylish French pornography written and directed and designed by the Polish surrealist Walerian Borowczyk, whose fantasy classic is *The Beast*. The first, second and fourth episodes (sexual initiation of girl on beach, masturbatory fantasies of pious girl, the Borgias being libidinous) are not fantasy, but the third episode takes as its subject Elizabeth Bathory, the Hungarian vampire countess who bathed in the blood of virgin girls (see also *Countess Dracula*, *Daughters of Darkness*). This is picturesque and stylized, full of noisy frolicking village girls in the bath, who are joined by the ornately dressed Countess (a stern-faced lady played by, of all people, Paloma Picasso) whose pearls are fought for by the girls just prior to their slaughter by a pretty, androgynous page with a curved scimitar. It's all rosy flesh and stage blood, and not at all sadistic. On the other hand, it's not clear what its carefully composed tableaux and its strawberries-and-cream colour contrasts are supposed to add up to, though they are visually interesting. Some sort of surrealist taunting about eroticism and blood? The most spirited girl is held back from the slaughter for use in a Lesbian partnership, but she betrays the Countess to the seventeenth-century cops.

THE IMMORTAL ★★½

USA 1969; made for TV; colour; 75 mins; Paramount; *D* Joseph Sargent; *P* Lou Morheim; *W* Morheim, Robert Specht from *The Immortals* by James E. Gunn; *M* Dominic Frontiere; *C* Howard R. Schwartz; *AD* William Campbell; *Starring* Christopher George, Barry Sullivan, Jessica Walter, Ralph Bellamy, Carol Lynley. Slightly above average for TV film (pilot for a series that lasted only one season), based on interesting story. Young man (George) has blood condition that renders him immune from disease and ageing. Billionaire (Sullivan) finds out and tries to capture him. SF implications jettisoned in favour of routine chase sequences.

I, MONSTER ★★★

UK 1971; colour; 75 mins; Amicus; *D* Stephen Weeks; *P* Max J. Rosenberg, Milton Subotsky; *W* Subotsky from *The Strange Case of Dr Jekyll and Mr Hyde* by Robert Louis Stevenson; *M* Carl Davis; *C* Moray Grant; *AD* Tony Curtis; *Make-Up* Harry and Peter Frampton; *Starring* Christopher Lee, Peter Cushing, Mike Raven; *V* Thorn EMI (UK). Knowing script (which sees Freudian implications of Jekyll-and-Hyde story) is nevertheless limp, but Lee is good, especially as Blake (the Hyde figure), and the direction gets a period atmosphere nicely. Main twist to story is that as Blake's pleasures become more corrupt, his face turns more horrible: a clear pinch from Dorian Gray's portrait.

AN IMPOSSIBLE VOYAGE (LE VOYAGE À TRAVERS L'IMPOSSIBLE) ★★★

France 1904; b/w; 1410ft (about 20 mins); Star; *D/P/W/Starring* Georges Méliès.

THE INCREDIBLE HULK ★½

USA 1978; made for TV; colour; 104 mins; Universal; *D* Kenneth Johnson, Sigmund Neufeld Jr; *P* Johnson, Chuck Bowman; *W* Johnson, Thomas Szollosi, Richard Matheson from characters created by Stan Lee and others for Marvel Comics; *M* Joseph Parnell; *C* Howard Schwartz, John McPherson; *Starring* Bill Bixby, Lou Ferrigno, Susan Sullivan; *V* CIC (UK), MCA (USA). Pilot for TV series together with subsequent episode in re-edited theatrical version; uncut pilot episode alone (97 mins) in video version. Scientist researching abnormal strength deliberately gives himself heavy dose of gamma rays; his DNA is changed and he periodically metamorphoses into brutish green Hulk (Ferrigno). First change occurs (we all know the feeling) when he loses temper unable to loosen wheel nuts on car. Effects primitive. Hulk so ridiculous we do not care what happens to him. Attempt at pathos by imitating little-girl scene from *Frankenstein* does not work.

THE INCREDIBLE MELTING MAN ★★ 🍅

USA 1977; colour; 84 mins; Quartet/ AIP; *D/W* William Sachs; *P* Samuel W. Gelfman; *M* Arlon Ober; *C* Willy Curtis; *AD* Michel Levesque; *SPFX* Harry Woolman, (make-up) Rick Baker; *Starring* Alex Rebar, Burr DeBenning, Myron Healey. What saves this low-budget monster movie is the sense of humour of writer-director Sachs (see also *Galaxina*). Colonel West contracts strange infection on space flight to Saturn. Symptom: his body melts unless he can eat human flesh. At the end he melts into a pile of goo. Baker's effects look pretty primitive; not entirely his fault, one understands. Text-book example of silly exploitation horror pic.

THE INCREDIBLE SHRINKING MAN ★★★★

USA 1957; b/w; 81 mins; Universal-International; *D* Jack Arnold; *P* Albert Zugsmith; *W* Richard Matheson from his novel *The Shrinking Man*; *AD* Alexander Golitzen, Robert Clatworthy; *SPFX* Clifford Stine; *Starring* Grant Williams, Randy Stuart, April Kent, Paul Langton.

THE INCREDIBLE SHRINKING WOMAN ★½

USA 1981; colour; 88 mins; Lija/Universal; *D* Joel Schumacher; *P* Hank Moonjean, Jane Wagner; *W* Wagner, suggested by the novel *The Shrinking Man* by Richard Matheson; *M* Suzanne Ciani; *C* Bruce Logan; *PD* Raymond A. Brandt; *SPFX* Roy Arbogast, Guy Faria, David Kelsey, (creator/designer of Sidney) Rick Baker; *Starring* Lily Tomlin, Charles Grodin, Ned Beatty, Henry Gibson; *V* MCA (USA). Extraordinarily feeble situation-comedy type satire on the consumer society. Housewife shrinks after new perfume is spilt on her; wicked scientist (Gibson) plots to shrink the world; now-almost-entirely-shrunk housewife exposes plot. The gorilla who befriends her is the only decent bit of fantasy in a film that is thoroughly offensive to all who loved the classic original, *The Incredible Shrinking Man*.

THE INCREDIBLE TWO-HEADED TRANSPLANT ★★½

USA 1970; colour; 88 mins; Mutual General – Trident Enterprises/AIP; *D* Anthony M. Lanza; *P* John Lawrence, Wolodymyr Kowal; *W* James Gordon White, Lawrence; *M* John Barber; *C* John Steely, Glen Gano, Paul Hipp; *SPFX* (make-up and head design) Barry Noble; *Starring* Bruce Dern, Pat Priest, John Bloom, Berry Kroeger. Who can follow the thinking of down-market company AIP? They must have imagined Barnard's experiments on heart transplants had readied the world for this and *The Thing with Two Heads*, which they released the next year. Loony scientist Dern grafts head of insane killer onto body of gigantic, subnormal gardener (who keeps his own head as well). The surely unsurprising result 'is an insane subnormal killer. Bad-movie fans will enjoy the dialogue between the heads.

INCUBUS ★★ 🍅

Canada 1981; Guardian Trust/Mark/John M. Eckert; *D* John Hough; *P* Marc Boyman, Eckert; *W* George Franklin from the novel by Ray Russell; *M* Stanley Myers; *C* Albert J. Dunk; *PD* Ted Watkins; *SPFX* (Incubus design) Les Edwards, (make-up) Maureen Sweeney; *Starring* John Cassavetes, Kerrie Keane, Erin Flannery; *V* VTC (UK), Vestron (USA). Vast amounts of semen found in dead, raped women suggest presence of possible supernatural being in small town, thinks police doctor Cassavetes. Many red herrings later the incubus turns out to be the last person you'd ever expect, just as we expected. Sadly, the rather jolly incubus is glimpsed only briefly at the end. It is all done (honestly) in the best possible taste, with quite a low gore quotient and Cassavetes agonizing as convincingly as he can in these tawdry surroundings.

INFERNO ★★★ 🍅

Italy 1980; colour; 107 mins; Intersound/20th Century-Fox; *D/W* Dario Argento; *P* Claudio Argento; *M* Keith Emerson; *C* Romano Albani; *SPFX* Germano Natali, Mario Bava, Pino Leoni; *Starring* Leigh McCloskey, Irene Miracle, Eleonora Giorgi, Daria Nicolodi, Feodor Chaliapin, Alida Valli; *V* CBS/Fox (UK).

THE INNOCENTS ★★★★

UK 1961; b/w; 99 mins; Achilles/20th Century-Fox; *D/P* Jack Clayton; *W* Truman Capote, William Archibald from *The Turn of the Screw* by Henry James and the play *The Innocents* by Archibald adapted by John Mortimer; *M* Georges Auric; *C* Freddie Francis; *AD* Wilfred Shingleton; *Starring* Deborah Kerr, Martin Stephens, Michael Redgrave, Pamela Franklin, Peter Wyngarde.

INSEMINOID ★ 🍅 🍅

UK 1980; colour; 92 mins; Jupiter/Brent Walker; *D* Norman J. Warren; *P* Richard Gordon, David Speechley; *W* Nick and Gloria Maley; *M* John Scott; *C* John Metcalfe; *PD* Hayden Pearce; *SPFX* Oxford Scientific Films, Camera Effects, (make-up) Nick Maley; *Starring* Robin Clarke, Jennifer Ashley, Stephanie Beacham, Judy Geeson; *V* Brent Walker (UK). Yet another attempt to cash in on the success of *Alien*; Geeson plays (quite well) a crew member who is raped by an alien on a distant planet, becomes horribly changed, cannibalistic, murderous, gives birth to two monsters. Thoroughly violent and unpleasant film, aimed at the sado-porn audience, with the birth being especially exploitative and offensive.

INVADERS FROM MARS ★★★

USA 1953; colour; 78 mins; National/20th Century-Fox; *D/PD* William Cameron Menzies; *P* Edward L. Alperson Sr; *W* Richard Blake, (uncredited) John Tucker Battle and Menzies; *M* Raoul Kraushaar; *C* John Seitz; *SPFX* Jack Cosgrove, (opticals) Jack Rabin and Irving Block, (miniatures) Theodore Lydecker; *Starring* Jimmy Hunt, Leif Erickson, Helena Carter, Arthur Franz; *V* Intervision (UK), Nostalgia (USA).

INVASION OF THE BEE GIRLS ★★

USA 1973; colour; 85 mins; Centaur/Sequoia; *D* Denis Sanders; *W* Nicholas Meyer; *M* Chuck Bernstein; *C* Gary Graver; *SPFX* Joe Lambardi; *Starring* William Smith, Anitra Ford, Victoria Vetri; *V* Embassy (USA). Low-budget semi-parody, notable for a screenplay by subsequent director Meyer *(Time After Time, Star Trek II)*. Girls turned into beautiful "queen bees" (pun on B-girls – tarts), huge-breasted, who love willing male victims to death. Metamorphosis of housewives to erotic killers by scientist is well done. Tacky; quite amusing.

INVASION OF THE BODY SNATCHERS ★★★★½

USA 1956; b/w; 80 mins; Allied Artists, *D* Don Siegel; *P* Walter Wanger; *W* Daniel Mainwaring from *The Body Snatchers* by Jack Finney; *M* Carmen Dragon; *C* Ellsworth Fredericks; *SPFX* Milt Rice; *Starring* Kevin McCarthy, Dana Wynter, Carolyn Jones, King Donovan; *V* BBC (UK), Nostalgia (USA).

INVASION OF THE BODY SNATCHERS ★★★½

USA 1978; colour; 115 mins; Solofilm/United Artists; *D* Philip Kaufman; *P* Robert H. Solo; *W* W. D. Richter from *The Body Snatchers* by Jack Finney; *M* Denny Zeitlin; *C* Michael Chapman; *PD* Charles Rosen; *SPFX* Dell Rheaume, Russ Hessey, (make-up) Tom Burman and Edouard Henriques; *Starring* Donald Sutherland, Brooke Adams, Art Hindle, Leonard Nimoy; *V* Warner (UK), MGM/UA (USA).

THE INVISIBLE BOY ★★★

USA 1957; b/w; 90 mins; Pan/MGM; *D* Herman Hoffman; *P* Nicholas Nayfack; *W* Cyril Hume from the story by Edmund Cooper; *M* Les Baxter; *C* Harold Wellman; *PD* Merrill Pye; *SPFX* Jack Rabin, Irving Block, Louis DeWitt; *Starring* Richard Eyer, Philip Abbott, Diane Brewster, Harold J. Stone. Under-rated children's SF adventure, now seldom seen. It was primarily made as a vehicle for the popular Robby the Robot, one of the stars of *Forbidden Planet*. Slightly neglected boy befriended by Robby; both become tools of the father's evil super-computer (a kind of first draft for HAL in *2001: A Space Odyssey*) but eventually loyalty of Robby saves the day. Complex, literate screenplay neatly directed, full of amusing lines. But apart from the boy (Eyer) the actors are fairly negligible.

THE INVISIBLE MAN ★★★★½

USA 1933; b/w; 70 mins; Universal; *D* James Whale; *P* Carl Laemmle Jr; *W* R. C. Sherriff from the novel by H. G. Wells; *M* W. Franke Harling; *C* Arthur Edeson; *AD* Charles D. Hall; *SPFX* John P. Fulton with John Mescall; *Starring* Claude Rains, Gloria Stuart, Henry Travers, William Harrigan, Una O'Connor. Wonderfully vigorous version of Wells's classic, directed by James Whale *(Frankenstein)*, the greatest of the early American genre directors along with Tod Browning. Griffin (Rains) invents a drug that causes invisibility, but it also causes madness and megalomania as a side effect. Whale directs with a lot of sympathy for this outsider figure, and his death at the end (and return to visibility) is genuinely sad, even in the comparatively comic context of the film. The invisibility is superbly done by Fulton; for most of the film Rains is swathed in bandages with, apparently, nothing beneath. Few directors could blend farce and terror with Whale's skill.

THE ISLAND ★★ 🍅

USA 1980; colour; 114 mins; Zanuck-Brown/Universal; *D* Michael Ritchie; *P* Richard D. Zanuck, David Brown; *W* Peter Benchley from his novel; *M* Ennio Morricone; *C* Henri Decäe; *PD* Dale Hennesy; *SPFX* Cliff Wenger, (visual) Albert Whitlock, (make-up) José Antonio Sanchez and Bob Westmoreland; *Starring* Michael Caine, David Warner, Frank Middlemass, Angela Punch McGregor; *V* CIC (UK), MCA (USA).

THE ISLAND AT THE TOP OF THE WORLD ★★½

USA 1973; colour; 94 mins; Disney; *D* Robert Stevenson; *P* Winston Hibler; *W* John Whedon from *The Lost Ones* by Ian Cameron; *M* Maurice Jarre; *C* Frank Phillips; *PD* Peter Ellenshaw; *SPFX* Ellenshaw, Art Cruickshank, Danny Lee, (matte artist) Alan Maley; *Starring* Donald Sinden, David Hartman, Jacques Marin, Mako; *V* Disney (UK and USA). Conventional lost-race movie has aristocratic, over-acting Sinden seeking his lost son in the far north by means of an airship and a rather unwilling crew. They find an island with a lost Viking race, and the statutory erupting volcano. Rambling story, hammy acting; the airship is excellent, the many matte paintings only so-so.

THE ISLAND OF DR MOREAU ★★

USA 1977; colour; 98 mins; Cinema 77/AIP; *D* Don Taylor; *P* John Temple-Smith, Skip Steloff; *W* John Herman Shaner, Al Ramrus from the novel by H. G. Wells; *M* Laurence Rosenthal; *C* Gerry Fisher; *PD* Philip Jefferies; *SPFX* Cliff Wenger, (make-up) John Chambers, Dan Striepeke and Tom Burman; *Starring* Burt Lancaster, Michael York, Barbara Carrera, Nigel Davenport, Richard Basehart; *V* Guild (UK), Warner (USA). Rather wooden version of the Wells classic, which had been much better done as *Island of Lost Souls* in 1932. Lancaster plays the obsessive doctor, who here uses genetic manipulation rather than surgery (thus diminishing the point of the phrase "House of Pain" for his laboratory) to create humans from animals, and vice versa, rather implausibly in the case of clean-cut Michael York. Beast-people (with rather rubbery masks) finally revolt, and York runs off with a fetching cat-person (Carrera). Sloppily directed.

ISLAND OF LOST SOULS ★★★★½

USA 1932; b/w; 72 mins; Paramount; *D* Erle C. Kenton; *W* Waldemar Young, Philip Wylie from *The Island of Dr Moreau* by H. G. Wells; *C* Karl Struss; *SPFX* (make-up) Wally Westmore; *Starring* Charles Laughton, Richard Arlen, Leila Hyams, Bela Lugosi. Laughton in smoothly demented form as the doctor on a remote island who surgically transforms animals into men; the romantic sub-plot (a young couple are shipwrecked on the island) is not well done, but the Beast Men are effective, especially when they revolt and Laughton himself is operated on in "The House of Pain". Touching moment when Laughton's panther-woman reverts to type. Classic, even though Wells disliked it.

ISLE OF THE DEAD ★★★½

USA 1945; b/w; 71 mins; RKO; *D* Mark Robson; *P* Val Lewton; *W* Ardel Wray, Josef Mischel; *M* Leigh Harline; *C* Jack Mackenzie; *AD* Albert S. D'Agostino, Walter E. Keller; *Starring* Boris Karloff, Ellen Drew, Marc Cramer, Katherine Emery; *V* Kingston (UK), Nostalgia (USA). Opinions differ as to whether this is one of the best of the literate, Lewton-produced horror movies of the forties. I find the straining for an oppressive, doom-laden atmosphere all rather obvious, and the pacing excruciatingly slow. The story is set on a Greek island where a small, motley group is isolated by an outbreak of plague. One, a cataleptic, is mistakenly buried alive and re-emerges insane from the grave. There is much to-do about the possibility of another women being a vampire, but she is not. Not so much a fantasy as an attemptedly poetic examination of the nature of fantasies about death; the superstitious atmosphere, however, is itself fantastic.

IT! ★★

UK 1967; colour; 97 mins; Gold Star/Seven Arts; *D/P/W* Herbert J. Leder; *M* Carlo Martelli; *C* Davis

Boulton; *AD* Scott MacGregor; *Starring* Roddy McDowall, Jill Haworth, Allan Sellars. A modest but not completely ineffective English remake of *The Golem*, who is this time re-animated by a crazed museum curator (McDowall). The film's ambitions were higher than the budget, and this shows in the rather ludicrous special effects during the sequences of large-scale destruction.

IT CAME FROM OUTER SPACE ★★★

USA 1953; b/w; 3-D; 81 mins; Universal-International; *D* Jack Arnold; *P* William Alland; *W* Harry Essex, Ray Bradbury from a screen treatment by Bradbury; *M* Herman Stein; *C* Clifford Stine; *SPFX* (cinematography) David S. Horsley, (alien design) Millicent Patrick; *Starring* Richard Carlson, Barbara Rush, Charles Drake; *V* MCA (USA).

IT LIVES AGAIN ★★★½

USA 1978; colour; 91 mins; Larco/Warner; *D/P/W* Larry Cohen; *M* Bernard Herrmann; *C* Fenton Hamilton, also Danny Pearl; *SPFX* (make-up) Rick Baker; *Starring* Frederic Forrest, Kathleen Lloyd, John P. Ryan, John Marley.

IT'S ALIVE ★★★★

USA 1973; colour; 91 mins; Larco/Warner; *D/P/W* Larry Cohen; *M* Bernard Herrmann; *SPFX* (make-up) Rick Baker; *Starring* John Ryan, Sharon Farrell, Andrew Duggan; *V* Warner (UK).

IT! THE TERROR FROM BEYOND SPACE ★★

USA 1958; b/w; 69 mins; Vogue/United Artists; *D* Edward L. Cahn; *P* Robert E. Kent; *W* Jerome Bixby; *M* Paul Sawtell, Bert Shefter; *C* Kenneth Peach Sr; *AD* William Glasgow; *SPFX* (make-up) Paul Blaisdell; *Starring* Marshall Thompson, Shawn Smith, Ray Corrigan, Ann Doran. Low-budget horror movie about alien thing that sneaks aboard spaceship on Mars and starts draining blood from the crew one by one on the way back; at the end, the ship's oxygen is removed to kill it. Notable for its suspicious resemblance to A. E. van Vogt's story "The Black Destroyer" (1939), and the equally suspicious resemblance the later film *Alien* has to it, but not particularly interesting in itself. The monster works well while kept in shadow, but once revealed it is all too obviously a man (Corrigan) in a monster suit.

I WALKED WITH A ZOMBIE ★★★★

USA 1943; b/w; 68 mins; RKO; *D* Jacques Tourneur; *P* Val Lewton; *W* Curt Siodmak, Ardel Wray from a story by Inez Wallace; *M* Roy Webb; *C* J. Roy Hunt; *Starring* Frances Dee, Tom Conway, James Ellison, Sir Lancelot, Darby Jones; *V* Kingston (UK), Nostalgia (USA).

JABBERWOCKY ★★½ 👹

US 1977; colour; 101 mins; Umbrella/Columbia; *D* Terry Gilliam; *P* Sandy Lieberson; *W* Charles Alverson, Gilliam; *M* DeWolfe; *C* Terry Bedford; *PD* Roy Smith; *SPFX* John F. Brown, Effects Associates, (monster creation) Valerie Charlton, Clinton Cavers, Jen Effects; *Starring* Michael Palin, Max Wall, Deborah Fallender, John Le Mesurier, Dave Prowse, Bernard Bresslaw; *V* RCA/Columbia (UK and USA).

JACK'S WIFE (aka SEASON OF THE WITCH; HUNGRY WIVES) ★★★½

USA 1972; colour; 89 mins; Latent Image; *D/W/C* George A. Romero; *P* Nancy M. Romero, Gary Streiner; *M* (electronic) Steve Gorn; *SPFX* Rege Survinski; *Starring* Jan White, Ray Laine, Anne Muffly; *V* Astra (UK), Wizard (USA).

JACK THE GIANT KILLER ★★

USA 1962; colour; 94 mins; Edward Small/Zenith/United Artists; *D* Nathan Juran; *P* Edward Small; *W* Orville H. Hampton, Juran; *M* Paul Sawtell, Bert Shefter; *C* David S. Horsley; *AD* Fernando Carrere, Frank McCoy; *SPFX* Howard A. Anderson, Jim Danforth, David Pal; *Starring* Kerwin Mathews, Judi Meredith, Torin Thatcher, Barry Kelley. This magical fantasy was made in the hope of capturing the market that had recently made *Seventh Voyage of Sinbad* a success, with stop-motion animation by Danforth rather than

Harryhausen. The evil wizard Pendragon captures the Princess, and Jack, with the aid of a Viking and a leprechaun, ultimately saves her. Battles with giants, zombies, a tentacled sea-monster, a dragon. So-so acting and animation, though there are enough marvels for most fantasy fans, and some nice moments.

JASON AND THE ARGONAUTS ★★★½

UK 1963; colour; 104 mins; Morningside-Worldwide/Columbia; *D* Don Chaffey; *P* Charles H. Schneer; *W* Jan Read, Beverley Cross; *M* Bernard Herrmann; *C* Wilkie Cooper; *SPFX* Ray Harryhausen; *Starring* Todd Armstrong, Nancy Kovack, Gary Raymond, Laurence Naismith, Niall MacGinnis, Honor Blackman; *V* RCA/Columbia (UK and USA).

JAWS ★★★★ 👹

USA 1975; colour; 125 mins; Zanuck-Brown/Universal; *D* Steven Spielberg; *P* Richard D. Zanuck, David Brown; *W* Peter Benchley, Carl Gottlieb from the novel by Benchley; *M* John Williams; *C* Bill Butler; *PD* Joseph Alves Jr; *SPFX* Robert A. Mattey; *Starring* Roy Scheider, Richard Dreyfuss, Robert Shaw, Lorraine Gary, Murray Hamilton, Carl Gottlieb; *V* CIC (UK), MCA (USA).

JAWS 2 ★★

USA 1978; colour; 116 mins; Zanuck-Brown/Universal; *D* Jeannot Szwarc; *P* Richard D. Zanuck, David Brown; *W* Carl Gottlieb, Howard Sackler, Dorothy Tristan from characters created by Peter Benchley; *M* John Williams; *C* Michael Butler; *PD* Joe Alves; *SPFX* (mechanical) Bob Mattey, Roy Arbogast; *Starring* Roy Scheider, Lorraine Gary, Murray Hamilton; *V* CIC (UK), MCA (USA). Amazingly successful at the box-office despite its flaws, this sequel to *Jaws* has moments, but rides far too closely on the shirt-tails of its predecessor. Yet again police chief Brody (Roy Scheider) warns the Mayor and councillors of Amity that a monster shark is on the rampage, and yet again they take not a blind bit of notice (it might scare off property developers), and he is fired. The human episodes are just silly, but the shark sequences are choreographed quite nicely, although Bruce the mechanical shark looks a lot more artificial this time round. Set-pieces: shark alarm on crowded beach when no shark is there; teenagers in large numbers on small boats becoming shark bait. In this climactic scene Bruce even bites a helicopter, but clever Brody saves the day by persuading it to chew on an underwater power cable.

JAWS 3-D (aka JAWS 3) ★★½ 👹

USA 1983; colour; 3-D; 99 mins; Alan Landsburg/Universal; *D* Joe Alves; *P* Rupert Hitzig; *W* Richard Matheson, Carl Gottlieb from a story by Guerdon Trueblood, using characters from *Jaws* by Peter Benchley; *M* Alan Parker; *C* James A. Contner; *PD* Woods Mackintosh; *SPFX* (photographic/optical) Robert Blalack, Praxis Film Works, (visual consultant) Roy Arbogast, (miniatures, composites) Chuck Comisky and others; *Starring* Dennis Quaid, Bess Armstrong, Simon MacCorkindale, John Putch, Louis Gossett Jr; *V* MCA (USA). Sequel to *Jaws* and *Jaws 2* directed by Alves, production designer on the previous two films. Quite good 3-D effects in this moderately enjoyable, teenage-oriented, kitschy, predictable story about a Florida theme park, Sea World, which captures a baby Great White Shark. As in *Gorgo*, the much bigger mother comes looking for baby. The odd dismembered fish or body looms at us in 3-D. Completely empty of anything except instantly forgettable thrills, but better than *Jaws 2*.

JENNIE – see PORTRAIT OF JENNIE

JE T'AIME, JE T'AIME ★★★★

France 1967; colour; 94 mins; Parc/Fox Europa; *D* Alain Resnais; *P* Mag Bodard; *W* Jacques Sternberg; *M* Krzysztof Penderecki, Jean-Claude Pelletier, Jean Dandeny; *C* Jean Boffety; *AD* Jacques Dugied, (time-machine) Auguste Pace; *Starring* Claude Rich, Olga Georges-Picot, Anouk Ferjac, Bernard Fresson.

JOURNEY TO THE CENTER OF THE EARTH ★★★

USA 1959; colour; 132 mins; 20th Century-Fox; *D* Henry Levin; *P* Charles Brackett; *W* Brackett, Walter Reisch from the novel by Jules Verne; *M* Bernard Herrmann; *C* Leo Tover; *AD* Lyle R. Wheeler, Franz Bachelin, Herman A. Blumenthal; *SPFX* L. B. Abbott, Emil Kosa Jr, James Gordon; *Starring* Pat Boone, James Mason, Arlene Dahl, Peter Ronson. Worth seeing for the spectacular sets and effects inside the Earth: crystal caverns, giant mushrooms, prehistoric animals, fountains of lava, hurricanes and floods. There is a real sense of the fantastic here. On the other hand, direction is ponderous, the acting (except for Mason) less than inspired, and the film too long.

JOURNEY TO THE FAR SIDE OF THE SUN – see DOPPELGANGER

JUBILEE ★½

UK 1978; colour; 104 mins; Whaley-Malin/ Megalo-vision; *D/W* Derek Jarman; *P* Howard Malin, James Whaley; *M* Brian Eno, various pop groups; *C* Peter Middleton; *Starring* Jenny Runacre, Toyah Willcox, Jordan, Little Nell, Adam Ant, Orlando, Ian Charleson; *V* VCL (UK).

JULIET OF THE SPIRITS (GIULIETTA DEGLI SPIRITI) ★★★★

Italy 1965; colour; 150 mins; Rizzoli Films; *D* Federico Fellini; *P* Angelo Rizzoli; *W* Fellini, Tullio Pinelli, Ennio Flaiano, Brunello Rondi; *M* Nino Rota; *C* Gianni Di Venanzo; *AD* Piero Gherardi; *Starring* Giulietta Masina, Mario Pisu, Sandra Milo, Valentina Cortese. Inside dowdy housewife Giulietta (played brilliantly by Masina) is a free spirit trapped by circumstances: an unfeeling husband, the puritanism of the Church, the orthodoxy of her life. At a seance she meets two spirits, one alluring, one threatening. The alluring spirit (Milo) in her earthly incarnation becomes Giulietta's neighbour, and teaches her (through example) the delights of the flesh. At the end of this progressively more surreal allegory, all Giulietta's ghosts from the past and present return (both good and bad) and she is moved to make a fresh start. Astonishingly vivid imagery gives life and a kind of fantastic conviction to a fundamentally rather banal situation.

JUNGFRUKÄLLAN – see THE VIRGIN SPRING

DAS KABINETT DES DR CALIGARI – see THE CABINET OF DR CALIGARI

KAIDAN – see KWAIDAN

KILL AND GO HIDE – see THE CHILD

KINGDOM OF THE SPIDERS ★★★½

USA 1977; colour; 95 mins; Arachnid-Dimension; *D* John "Bud" Cardos; *P* Igo Kantor, Jeffrey M. Sneller; *W* Richard Robinson, Alan Caillou from a story by Sneller and Stephen Lodge; *C* John Morrill; *SPFX* Greg Auer, (matte artist) Cy Didjurgis; *Starring* William Shatner, Tiffany Bolling, Woody Strode; *V* Intervision (UK), Video Communications (USA). Near a small community in Arizona, tarantulas upset by ecological changes are emigrating north, and appearing to act with communal intelligence. The film modestly builds the scale of the spider appearances, arriving at an apocalyptic climax. The usual absurdities of the monster-movie genre are here moderated by a witty script that allows time for character building, good performances from the spiders, and a crisp precision in the pacing of the whole thing. (The panel was split between one and four stars on this one!)

KING KONG ★★★★★

USA 1933; b/w; 100 mins; RKO; *D* Ernest B. Schoedsack, Merian C. Cooper; *P* David O. Selznick; *W* James Creelman, Ruth Rose from a story by Cooper and Edgar Wallace; *M* Max Steiner; *C* Edward Linden, Verne Walker, J. O. Taylor; *SPFX* Willis O'Brien, E. B. Gibson, Marcel Delgado and others; *Starring* Fay Wray, Robert Armstrong, Bruce Cabot; *V* Thorn EMI (UK), Nostalgia, Vestron (USA).

KING KONG ★★

USA 1976; colour; 135 mins; Dino De Laurentiis; *D* John Guillermin; *P* Dino De Laurentiis; *W* Lorenzo Semple Jr from the screenplay for the 1933 version; *M* John Barry; *C* Richard H. Kline; *PD* Mario Chiari, Dale Hennesy; *SPFX* (Kong designer) Carlo Rambaldi, (photographic supervision) Frank Van Der Veer, (technical advisers) Rick Baker and William Shepard, (matte artist) Lou Lichtenfield; *Starring* Jessica Lange, Jeff Bridges, Charles Grodin, John Randolph, Rene Auberjonois; *V* Thorn EMI (UK), Paramount (USA).

KRIEMHILD'S REVENGE – see DIE NIBELUNGEN

KRULL ★★½

UK 1983; colour; 121 mins; Columbia; *D* Peter Yates; *P* Ron Silverman; *W* Stanford Sherman; *M* James Horner; *C* Peter Suschitzky; *PD* Stephen Grimes; *SPFX* (visual) Derek Meddings, (make-up) Nick Maley, (animation) Steven Archer; *Starring* Ken Marshall, Lysette Anthony, Freddie Jones, Francesca Annis, Bernard Bresslaw, David Battley.

KWAIDAN (KAIDAN) ★★★★ ✿

Japan 1964; colour; 164 mins (released in Europe minus "Yuki-Onna" 125 mins); Bungei-Ninjin Club/Toho; *D* Masaki Kobayashi; *P* Shigeru Wakatsuki; *W* Yoko Mizuki from "The Reconciliation", "Yuki-Onna", "The Story of Mimi-Nashi-Ho'ichi" and "In a Cup of Tea" by Lafcadio Hearn; *M* Toru Takemitsu; *C* Yoshio Miyajima; *AD* Shigemasa Toda; *Starring* Rentaro Mikuni, Keiko Kishi, Katsuo Nakamura, Ganemon Nakamura, Noburu Nakaya; *V* Palace (UK).

LAND OF THE MINOTAUR (aka THE DEVIL'S MEN) ★½

USA/UK 1976; colour; 94 mins; Poseidon/Getty; *D* Costas Carayiannis; *P* Frixos Constantine; *W* Arthur Rowe; *M* Brian Eno; *C* Aris Stavrou; *AD* Petros Copourallis; *Starring* Donald Pleasence, Luan Peters, Peter Cushing; *V* CBS/Fox (UK), Video Communications (USA). American tourists are being kidnapped in Crete for sacrifice to the minotaur by the bad guys, led by Cushing as the Baron. The good guys are led by Father Roche, played by Pleasence (reversing the usual role). Most of the supposed Americans look extremely Greek; dialogue is largely dubbed. Story rattles along but never manages a real scare.

THE LAND THAT TIME FORGOT ★★½

UK 1974; colour; 91 mins; Amicus/British Lion; *D* Kevin Connor; *P* John Dark; *W* James Cawthorne, Michael Moorcock from the novel by Edgar Rice Burroughs; *M* Douglas Gamley; *C* Alan Hume; *PD* Maurice Carter; *SPFX* Derek Meddings, (dinosaur sequences) Roger Dicken; *Starring* Doug McClure, Susan Penhaligon, John McEnery; *V* Thorn EMI (UK), Vestron (USA). Lost-world fantasy, probably the best of the low-budget, slightly feeble Burroughs trilogy made by Amicus. (The sequels were *At The Earth's Core* and *The People That Time Forgot*.) German U-boat with assorted nationalities on board finds Caprona, primeval undiscovered land near Antarctica with many monsters (basically puppets) and volcanic eruption (statutory in such films). What survives of the Moorcock script is quite good, but it was much altered; the volcano was not his, and not in the book.

LASERBLAST ★

USA 1978; colour; 80 mins; Irwin Yablans Co.; *D* Michael Rae; *P* Charles Band; *W* Franne Schacht, Frank Ray Perilli; *M* Joel Goldsmith, Richard Band; *C* Terry Bowen; *SPFX* Harry Woolman, (make-up) Steve Neill, (alien animation) Dave Allen; *Starring* Kim Milford, Cheryl Smith, Gianni Russo; *V* Intervision (UK), Media (USA). One of the very worst Charles Band horror cheapies, though not quite as abysmal as *End of the World*. Teenage wimp Billy finds laser and amulet left by alien in desert; amulet makes his eyes glow red every now and then; laser is useful for killing people who pick on him. Badly scripted, badly paced rubbish, with the only plus being Dave

Allen's o.k. aliens. Looks like a home movie directed by a dope fiend.

THE LAST CHASE ★★

USA 1981; colour; 101 mins; Crown; *D/P* Martyn Burke; *W* C. R. O'Christopher, Taylor Sutherland, Burke; *C* Paul Van Der Linden; *AD* Roy Forge Smith; *SPFX* Tom Fisher; *Starring* Lee Majors, Burgess Meredith, Alexandra Stewart, Chris Makepeace; *V* VTC (UK), Vestron (USA). Adventure story with ageing Majors a rebel in post-plague, post-technological, oppressive Eastern USA where the oil has run out and most machinery is regarded as evil. Seeking free society in the West, he drives the last car (a Porsche) pursued by Meredith in the last aeroplane (a Phantom), at the instigation of an appalled government who see Major's rebellion as setting off trouble. Sad to see a promising basic idea turn into a routine chase drama with a made-for-TV look.

THE LAST DAYS OF MAN ON EARTH – see THE FINAL PROGRAMME

THE LAST WAVE ★★★★

Australia 1977; colour; 106 mins; Ayer-McElroy & McElroy-Derek Power/United Artists; *D* Peter Weir; *P* Hal and James McElroy; *W* Weir, Tony Morphett, Petru Popescu; *M* Charles Wain; *C* Russell Boyd; *PD* Goran Warff; *SPFX* Monty Fieguth, Bob Hilditch; *Starring* Richard Chamberlain, Olivia Hamnett, Gulpilil, Nandjiwarra Amagula; *V* Warner (USA).

LAST YEAR AT MARIENBAD (L'ANNÉE DERNIÈRE À MARIENBAD) ★★★★½

France 1961; b/w; 99 mins; Terra/Cormoran/ Como/Précitel/Argos/Tamara/Cinétel/Silver/Cineriz; *D* Alain Resnais; *P* Pierre Coureau, Raymond Froment; *W* Alain Robbe-Grillet; *M* Francis Seyrig; *C* Sacha Vierny; *AD* Jacques Saulnier; *Starring* Delphine Seyrig, Giorgio Albertazzi, Sacha Pitoëff. Surrealist fantasy, surprisingly once described as great SF film by SF writer Brian Aldiss. Beautiful to look at; an intellectual puzzle. Man meets woman at spa hotel (symbolically Limbo? Hell? a psychiatrist's rooms?), claims to have met her there last year. She does not remember. Cross-cutting gives the illusion either of time travel between this year and last, or between memory and the fantasies of the imagination.

THE LATHE OF HEAVEN ★★★½

USA 1980; made for TV; colour; 120 mins; TV Laboratory WNET New York/Taurus-Film; *D/P* David R. Loxton, Fred Barzyk; *W* Roger Swaybill, Diane English from the novel by Ursula K. Le Guin; *M* Michael Small; *C* Robbie Greenberg; *PD* John W. Stevens, (additional design) Ed Emshwiller; *SPFX* Jack Bennett; *Starring* Bruce Davison, Kevin Conway, Margaret Avery. Probably the most sophisticated SF story to appear as a made-for-television film, this should be seen if you get a chance. Based on an excellent novel by Ursula Le Guin, one of the most powerful of SF writers, it tells of George Orr (Bruce Davison), who has the power to change our world by dreaming alternate realities into being. There is no way for the people in these changed worlds to know what has happened, because so all-embracing are the dreams that nobody has any memory of any other way of life. But a manipulative psychiatrist learns the truth and exploits it. Overpopulation is cured (by a plague), Earth is united (by fear of aliens who have appeared on the Moon); eventually the fundamental fabric of reality itself seems to be coming apart. Lots of good metaphysical fun here, with cheap but interesting effects – as when the entire human race turns grey. A nice, ambiguous ending.

THE LEGACY ★★

UK 1978; colour; 102 mins; Pethurst; *D* Richard Marquand; *P* David Foster; *W* Jimmy Sangster, Patrick Tilley, Paul Wheeler; *M* Michael J. Lewis; *C* Dick Bush, Alan Hume; *PD* Disley Jones; *SPFX* Ian Wingrove; *Starring* Katharine Ross, Sam Elliott, John Standing, Charles Gray; *V* Vipco (UK). Complicated story has American couple invited to British country estate where they cannot leave again (best effect in film: all roads lead back to the estate – there is no escape). Host gives Maggie (Ross) a ring, identical to those the other five guests are wearing. Other five all die nastily. Satanic explanation for all this involves reincarnation, immortality, sixteenth-century witch. Maggie inherits occult powers. Some good effects, but all rather tired and silly. Marquand later directed *Return of the Jedi*.

THE LEGEND OF BOGGY CREEK ★½
USA 1973; colour; 90 mins; Halco/Pierce-Ledwell; *D/P/C* Charles B. Pierce; *W* Earl E. Smith; *M* Jaime Mendoza-Nava; *Starring* Willie E. Smith, John P. Hixon, Travis Crabtree; *V* Iver (UK). One of the many low-budget movies about missing-link Bigfoot-type monsters, this is set in Arkansas, has sad songs, a lonely monster and some atmosphere.

THE LEGEND OF HELL HOUSE ★★★
UK 1973; colour; 94 mins; Academy; *D* John Hough; *P* Albert Fennell, Norman T. Herman; *W* Richard Matheson from his novel *Hell House*; *M/ electronic score* Brian Hodgson, Delia Derbyshire; *C* Alan Hume; *AD* Robert Jones; *SPFX* Roy Whybrow, (photographic) Tom Howard; *Starring* Pamela Franklin, Roddy McDowall, Clive Revill, Gayle Hunnicutt, Roland Culver. Psychologist (Revill) and wife (Hunnicutt) take two mediums (McDowall and Franklin) to investigate allegedly haunted house. Their scepticism is soon shaken; creepy events make first half scary, but the ultimate explanation is lame; the psychosexual doubletalk of the book translates rather embarrassingly on to the screen. Has its moments: good seance, seduction by cat, moving shadows. Slight SF slant: psychic energy can be counteracted by energy-nullifying machine.

THE LEGEND OF THE 7 GOLDEN VAMPIRES
(aka THE 7 BROTHERS MEET DRACULA) ★★ ☻
UK/Hong Kong 1974; colour; 89 mins; Hammer/ Shaw Bros; *D* Roy Ward Baker; *P* Don Houghton, Vee King Shaw; *W* Don Houghton; *M* James Bernard; *C* John Wilcox, Roy Ford; *AD* Johnson Tsau; *SPFX* Les Bowie; *Starring* Peter Cushing, David Chiang, Julie Ege, John Forbes-Robertson; *V* Electric (USA). Ninth and last of Hammer's *Dracula* films and the second to last of the feature films the company has made. Dracula (Forbes-Robertson) does not play a major role in this extraordinary mixture of two genres: the kung-fu movie and the vampire movie. Vampires raid a Chinese village and Van Helsing teams up with seven martial-arts experts who tackle the Dracula-led vampire team. These vampires are partially masked, rotting, zombie-like creatures, looking more dead than undead. Good moments set like raisins in a rather heavy cake.

LET'S SCARE JESSICA TO DEATH ★★★ ☻
USA 1971; colour; 89 mins; Jessica/Paramount; *D* John Hancock; *P* Charles B. Moss Jr, William Badalto; *W* Norman Jonas, Ralph Rose; *M* Orville Stoeber, (electronic) Walter Sear; *C* Bob Baldwin; *Starring* Zohra Lampert, Barton Heyman, Gretchen Corbett, Kevin O'Connor. This low-budget horror film, made by and starring mostly unknowns, is actually very scary indeed. Young woman (Lampert) recovering from breakdown in quiet village is beset by visiting girl/vampire (Corbett), assorted living dead. Less-than-supportive husband and friend get amply punished for whatever nefarious schemes they may have had.

THE LIFE OF BRIAN – *see* MONTY PYTHON'S LIFE OF BRIAN

LIGHT YEARS AWAY ★★★
France/Switzerland 1981; colour; 107 mins; LPA-Phénix/Slotint-SSR; *D+W* Alain Tanner from *La Voie sauvage* by Daniel Odier; *P* Pierre Heros; *M* Arié Dzierlatka; *C* Jean-François Robin; *AD* John Lucas; *Starring* Trevor Howard, Mick Ford.

LIQUID SKY ★★
USA 1982; colour; 112 mins; Z Films; *D/P* Slava Tsukerman; *W* Tsukerman, Anne Carlisle, Nina V. Kerova; *M* Tsukerman, Brenda I. Hutchinson,

Clive Smith; *C* Yuri Neyman; *PD* Marina Levikova-Neyman; *SPFX* Yuri Neyman, Oleg Chichilnitsky, (Margaret's mask, UFO design) Gennadi Osmerkin; *Starring* Anne Carlisle, Paula E. Sheppard, Bob Brady, Susan Doukas, Otto von Wernherr; *V* Media (USA). Strange film made by Russian ex-patriates in New York, clearly a product of, and designed for, the New Wave or Punk sensibility. Killer alien from flying saucer is attracted to chemical released by (a) taking heroin, and (b) achieving orgasm. Punk model Margaret is vehicle for alien, can kill with sexual intercourse, and often does. The film is a kind of loony documentary about freaked-out and posturing lifestyles, and the SF elements seem to be a metaphor to do with the kinds of pleasure available in this Punk world. "Liquid sky", apparently, is slang for heroin.

LISA AND THE DEVIL – *see* THE HOUSE OF EXORCISM

THE LITTLE PRINCE ★★
USA 1974; colour; 89 mins; Donen/Paramount; *D/P* Stanley Donen; *W* Alan Jay Lerner from *Le Petit Prince* by Antoine De Saint-Exupéry; *M/Lyrics* Frederick Loewe, Alan Jay Lerner; *C* Christopher Challis; *PD* John Barry; *SPFX* John Richardson, (photographic) Thomas Howard; *Starring* Richard Kiley, Steven Warner, Bob Fosse, Gene Wilder; *V* Paramount (USA). Disappointing musical adaptation of children's fantasy classic; songs unmemorable; some incidental pleasures, including Fosse as a snake, and the tiny asteroid with one flower (a talking rose) that is the Prince's birthplace. He has come to Earth (where he meets crashed pilot Kiley in the Sahara) to learn about life, and has visited various small planets (which we see in flashback) on the way. Cute, sentimental, moralising – but then the original story is not all that great either. Sad ending. The actor (Warner) who played the Prince was only six.

THE LITTLE SHOP OF HORRORS ★★★½
USA 1960; b/w; 71 mins; Santa Clara/Filmgroup; *D/P* Roger Corman; *W* Charles Griffith; *M* Fred Katz; *C* Archie Dalzell; *AD* Daniel Haller; *Starring* Jonathan Haze, Jackie Joseph, Mel Welles, Jack Nicholson, Dick Miller; *V* Budget (USA). Seymour Krelboined (Haze) is a dimwitted florist's assistant who discovers an exotic flower that eats people; it keeps shouting "Feed me!", so Seymour has to scour the area for victims. Various lunatics, notably Nicholson as a masochist who loves the dentist's chair, visit the shop in this film which contrives to be mindless and funny at the same time. Shot in two-and-a-half days by Corman on a budget apparently no more than a teenager's pocket money, it has become the centre-piece of the Corman legend. Twenty years later, the stage version was a Broadway hit.

LIVE AND LET DIE ★★★
UK 1973; colour; 121 mins; Eon/United Artists; *D* Guy Hamilton; *P* Harry Saltzman, Albert R. Broccoli; *W* Tom Mankiewicz from the novel by Ian Fleming; *M* George Martin; *C* Ted Moore; *AD* Syd Cain; *SPFX* Derek Meddings; *Starring* Roger Moore, Yaphet Kotto, Jane Seymour, Clifton James, Geoffrey Holder; *V* Warner (UK), CBS/Fox (USA).

THE LIVING DEAD AT THE MANCHESTER MORGUE (aka DON'T OPEN THE WINDOW) (FIN DE SEMANA PARA LOS MUERTOS) ★★★ ☻ ☻ ☻
Spain/Italy 1974; colour; 93 mins; Star/Flaminia; *D* Jorge Grau; *P* Edmondo Amati; *W* Sandro Continenza, Marcello Coscia; *M* Giuliano Sorgini; *C* Francisco Sempere; *PD* Carlo Leva; *SPFX* Luciano Bird, (photographic and make-up) Giannetto De Rossi; *Starring* Ray Lovelock, Arthur Kennedy, Christine Galbo; *V* VIP (UK, as *The Living Dead*). This Spanish exploitation of the zombie boom set off by *Night of the Living Dead* is not without merit. It is also very explicitly horrible (and anti-police), and several police departments in the UK have asked video dealers not to stock it. A new pest-killing machine has the side effect of re-animating corpses with its ultrasonic waves; right-wing authority figures try to suppress the

scandal, brutally. Interesting political dimension. Shot in Yorkshire with Italian/Spanish crew.

LE LOCATAIRE – *see* THE TENANT

LOGAN'S RUN ★★
USA 1976; colour; 118 mins; MGM; *D* Michael Anderson; *P* Saul David; *W* David Zelag Goodman from the novel by William F. Nolan and George Clayton Johnson; *M* Jerry Goldsmith; *C* Ernest Laszlo; *AD* Dale Hennesy; *SPFX* Glen Robinson, (photographic) L. B. Abbott and Frank Van Der Veer, (matte paintings) Matthew Yuricich; *Starring* Michael York, Richard Jordan, Jenny Agutter, Peter Ustinov, Farrah Fawcett-Majors; *V* MGM/UA (UK and USA). Sluggish adaptation of lively SF novel about society where the over-thirties go willingly (usually) to meet their deaths. Logan is a renegade "Sandman" (official elite of runners) who himself runs at age twenty-nine out of the domed city. The large budget was partly wasted – effects don't mean much in a vacuum – because the script is conceptually so weak (no explanation of any kind for how society got this way), morally simplistic, and sentimental. At best, SF adventure for kids, and indeed a TV series followed for one season.

LONDON AFTER MIDNIGHT
USA 1927; b/w; 5687ft (around 75 mins); MGM; *D/P* Tod Browning; *W* Browning, Waldemar Young, (titles) Joe Farnham, from *The Hypnotist* by Browning; *AD* Cedric Gibbons, Arnold Gillespie; *Starring* Lon Chaney, Henry B. Walthall, Marceline Day, Edna Tichenor.

LOOKER ★½
USA 1981; colour; 94 mins; Ladd Co./Warner; *D/W* Michael Crichton; *P* Howard Jeffrey; *M* Barry DeVorzon; *C* Paul Lohmann; *PD* Dean Edward Mitzner; *SPFX* Joe Day; *Starring* Albert Finney, James Coburn, Susan Dey, Leigh Taylor-Young; *V* Warner (USA). Barely comprehensible SF story seems to have been viciously cut before release, judging from loose ends. Crichton's previous track record fair to good (*Westworld*, *Coma* etc.), but he lapses here. Computer-generated 3-D human figures are used in advertising (they can hypnotise viewers!) by evil businessman Coburn. Plastic surgeon Finney finds models used in this process turning up dead; investigates; shock-horror revelations follow. The elaborate design and look of the movie are quite interesting, but in context not especially effective.

LOST ATLANTIS – *see* L'ATLANTIDE

THE LOST CONTINENT ★½
UK 1968; colour; 98 mins; Hammer/Seven Arts; *D/P* Michael Carreras; *W* Michael Nash from *Uncharted Seas* by Dennis Wheatley; *M* Gerard Schurmann; *C* Paul Beeson; *AD* Arthur Lawson; *SPFX* Robert Mattey, Cliff Richardson; *Starring* Eric Porter, Hildegard Knef, Suzanna Leigh, Nigel Stock. Utterly absurd adventure yarn, clumsily executed but with amusing passages. Tramp steamer breaks down in Sargasso Sea, carrying motley load of passengers who confront carnivorous seaweed, giant crabs, octopuses and lobsters, and finally a lost race (descended from Conquistadores) who travel by balloon. The continent of the title appears to have been lost; it isn't in the film.

LOST HORIZON ★★★★
USA 1937; b/w; 133 mins (usually 118); Columbia; *D/P* Frank Capra; *W* Robert Riskin from the novel by James Hilton; *M* Dimitri Tiomkin; *C* Joseph Walker; *AD* Stephen Goosson; *SPFX* (photographic) E. Roy Davidson, Ganahl Carson; *Starring* Ronald Colman, Jane Wyatt, Edward Everett Horton, John Howard, Thomas Mitchell, Margo, Sam Jaffe. This supposed classic has dated a little, and the sentimental elements seem marshmallowy now and the philosophy of the ever-youthful inhabitants of Utopian Shangri-La banal. But the story of the discovery of the lost valley in the Himalayas still grips, and Ronald Colman's struggling return through the snow to the hidden city still moves.

LOST HORIZON ★
USA 1972; colour; 143 mins; Columbia; *D* Charles Jarrott; *P* Ross Hunter; *W* Larry Kramer from the novel by James Hilton; *M* Burt Bacharach; *Lyrics* Hal David; *C* Robert Surtees; *AD* Preston Ames; *SPFX* (photographic) Butler-Glouner; *Starring* Peter Finch, Liv Ullmann, Sally Kellerman, George Kennedy, Michael York, Olivia Hussey, Charles Boyer, John Gielgud. Box-office failure. Empty-headed and unnecessary remake of fantasy classic, with all the magic drained away. The last thing it needed was to become a musical. Sets so-so, acting wooden, songs forgettable, far too long.

THE LOST WORLD ★★★
USA 1925; b/w; 9,700ft (approx 100 mins); First National; *D* Harry O. Hoyt; *P* Earl Hudson; *W* Marion Fairfax from the novel by Arthur Conan Doyle; *C* Arthur Edeson; *AD* Milton Menasco; *SPFX* Willis H. O'Brien, Marcel Delgado and others; *Starring* Bessie Love, Lloyd Hughes, Lewis Stone, Wallace Beery, Arthur Hoyt; *V* Thunderbird (USA, cut to 60 mins).

LOVE AT FIRST BITE ★★★
USA 1979; colour; 96 mins; Melvin Simon; *D* Stan Dragoti; *P* Joel Freeman; *W* Robert Kaufman; *M* Charles Bernstein; *C* Edward Rosson; *PD* Serge Krizman; *SPFX* Allen Hall; *Starring* George Hamilton, Susan Saint James, Richard Benjamin, Arte Johnson, Dick Shawn; *V* Guild (UK), Warner (USA). This parody of vampire movies did very well at the box-office, and it certainly does have funny moments, though basically only one joke: the irony of seeing Dracula as an old-fashioned, conservative gentleman (played with a heavy Lugosi accent by Hamilton), slightly bewildered by the hectic pace of life in New York (where he goes with the cockroach-chewing Renfield), but nonetheless contriving to find true love. The one-liners are often good: the migraine-suffering Count at the opening, shouting "Children of the night, shut up!"; or his experience in bed with Cindy (the woman he comes to love) where he cries out with exaltation to her, "Oh, that's so kinky! Are *you* biting *me*?" I'm not sure, though, whether 96 minutes of incongruity jokes might not be too many. *Young Frankenstein* is better than this.

THE LOVE BUG ★★
USA 1968; colour; 107 mins; Disney; *D* Robert Stevenson; *P* Bill Walsh; *W* Walsh, Don DaGradi from a story by Gordon Buford; *M* George Bruns; *SPFX* Robert A. Mattey, Howard Jensen and Danny Lee, (photographic) Eustace Lycett, Alan Maley and Peter Ellenshaw; *Starring* Dean Jones, Michele Lee, David Tomlinson, Buddy Hackett; *V* Disney (UK and USA).

LUST FOR A VAMPIRE ★★
UK 1971; colour; 95 mins; Hammer/EMI; *D* Jimmy Sangster; *P* Harry Fine, Michael Style; *W* Tudor Gates from characters created by J. Sheridan Le Fanu; *M* Harry Robinson; *C* David Muir; *AD* Don Mingaye; *Starring* Ralph Bates, Barbara Jefford, Suzanna Leigh, Michael Johnson, Yutte Stensgaard, Pippa Steel; *V* Thorn EMI (UK and USA). Sequel to Hammer's *The Vampire Lovers*; the third in this Kárnstein series was *Twins of Evil*. Made in the period when Hammer, anxious to retain audiences, was becoming much more overtly sexy, there is a lot of lesbianism and nudity in this feeble exploitation film about Mircalla, a female vampire (Stensgaard) at a girl's finishing school. Teacher/writer Lestrange (Johnson) falls in love with her; he writes horror stories himself, so should have known better.

MACABRE (MACABRO) ★★★ ☠
Italy 1980; colour; 90 mins; AMA/Medusa; *D* Lamberto Bava; *P* Gianni Minervini, Antonio Avati; *W* Pupi and Antonio Avati, Roberto Gandus, Bava; *M* Ubaldo Continiello; *C* Franco Delli Colli; *SPFX* Tonino Corridori, Angelo Mattei; *Starring* Bernice Stegers, Stanko Molnar; *V* GO (UK). This is the film that was temporarily celebrated in the UK by being held up at the Conservative Party Conference in 1983 as an example of all that was most

disgusting in what is available on videotape. In fact, it is a well-made and not too unpleasant study in neurosis, in some ways tender, mostly set in an old house in New Orleans. The part of the film that people find offensive shows a woman keeping the head of her dead lover in the fridge, but this is a Grand Guignol image with almost classical associations, and used well here. Malicious daughter hates mother; mother rejects blind suitor; at the end of this archetypal *giallo*, the blind man (the other two are dead) is savaged by the teeth of the severed head – the only truly fantastic element, and probably ill-judged in a film that otherwise explores the psyche and not the supernatural. This is Bava Jr's first solo film, though in fact he directed most of *Shock*.

MAD LOVE ★★★★
USA 1935; b/w; 70 mins; MGM; *D* Karl Freund; *P* John W. Considine Jr; *W* Guy Endore, P. J. Wolfson, John L. Balderston from the novel *Les Mains d'Orlac* by Maurice Renard; *M* Dimitri Tiomkin; *C* Chester Lyons, Gregg Toland; *Starring* Peter Lorre, Frances Drake, Colin Clive, Edward Brophy. Remake of *The Hands of Orlac* by celebrated cameraman Freund acting this time as director; he also made *The Mummy* (1932). In this version, the emphasis is shifted to insane plastic surgeon Gogol, brilliantly played by Peter Lorre who had only recently reached the USA from Germany and went on to become one of the greatest of horror stars. This stylized version of the story, deeply melodramatic, does not shrink from the supernatural, unlike its predecessor, though most of the Grand Guignol touches result from Gogol's madness.

MAD MAX ★★★★ ☠
Australia 1979; colour; 100 mins; Mad Max Pty; *D* George Miller; *P* Byron Kennedy; *W* James McCausland, Miller from a story by Miller and Kennedy; *M* Brian May; *C* David Eggby; *Stunt co-ordinator* Grant Page; *Vehicle designer* Ray Beckerley; *SPFX* Chris Murray; *Starring* Mel Gibson, Joanne Samuel, Hugh Keays-Byrne, Steve Bisley; *V* Warner (UK), Vestron (USA).

MAD MAX 2 (aka THE ROAD WARRIOR) ★★★★ ☠
Australia 1981; colour; 96 mins; Kennedy Miller Entertainment; *D* George Miller; *P* Byron Kennedy; *W* Terry Hayes, Miller, Brian Hannant; *M* Brian May; *C* Dean Semler; *AD* Graham Walker; *Stunt co-ordinator* Max Aspin; *SPFX* Jeffrey Clifford, (props design) Melinda Brown, (make-up) Bob McCarron; *Starring* Mel Gibson, Bruce Spence, Kjell Nilsson, Emil Minty; *V* Warner (UK and USA).

MAGIC ★★½
USA 1978; colour; 107 mins; Joseph E. Levine Presents/20th Century-Fox; *D* Richard Attenborough; *P* Joseph E. and Richard P. Levine; *W* William Goldman from his novel; *M* Jerry Goldsmith; *C* Victor J. Kemper; *PD* Terence Marsh; *SPFX* Robert MacDonald Jr; *Starring* Anthony Hopkins, Ann-Margret, Burgess Meredith, Ed Lauter; *V* Intervision (UK), Embassy (USA). Hopkins plays a ventriloquist whose personal inadequacies are compensated for by his dummy, Fats, onto whom he projects a cruder and more aggressive personality. At a small lakeside motel, run by an old girl-friend, his chance for happiness is ruined by Fats' murderous intervention. Not really fantasy, since the far-fetched explanation is schizophrenia, but it certainly feels fantastic. Good, edgy performance from Hopkins, but all rather routine alongside the ventriloquist episode from *Dead of Night*, upon which Goldman's novel seems clearly modelled.

THE MAGIC DONKEY – see PEAU D'ÂNE

THE MAGICIAN – see THE FACE

THE MAGIC SWORD ★½
USA 1962; colour; 80 mins; Bert I. Gordon/United Artists; *D/P* Bert I. Gordon; *W* Bernard Schoenfeld from a story by Gordon; *M* Richard Markowitz; *C* Paul C. Vogel; *AD* Franz Bachelin; *SPFX* (mechanical) Milt Rice, (make-up) Dan Striepeke;

Starring Basil Rathbone, Estelle Winwood, Gary Lockwood; *V* EVC (UK), Video Yesteryear (USA). Bert Gordon is one of the characters who lurk down in the bargain basement of the horror-flick business (see *Food of the Gods*) but he emerged with a slightly bigger budget than usual to make this fairy tale about George, a dragon, a wicked sorcerer (Rathbone) and a princess. It sounds like a wonderfully magical fantasy in synopsis: ogres, vampires, shrunken people and so on. But old habits die hard, and as usual, a rotten script and monsters that look like (and are) people in suits sink the whole endeavour.

MALEVIL ★★★
France/West Germany 1981; colour; 119 mins; NEF-Diffusion/Stella/Antenne 2/Gibe Telecip; *D* Christian de Chalonge; *P* Claude Nedjar; *W* de Chalonge, Pierre Dumayet from the novel by Robert Merle; *M* Gabriel Lared; *C* Jean Penzer; *AD* Max Douy; *Starring* Michel Serrault, Jacques Dutronc, Robert Dhéry, Jacques Villeret, Jean-Louis Trintignant. Moderately expensive-looking French SF movie is based on impressive post-holocaust novel by Merle (who also wrote *Day of the Dolphin*). In a French village a group of people are tasting the new vintage in a cellar when the Bomb goes off. Strong opening, and good work by the designers when the now blasted landscape outside is revealed. But the story is not about destruction, it is about building a new society from scratch, and this it achieves slowly, sentimentally, and with bags of symbolism about life reasserting itself. Trintignant good but hammy as leader of nearby group of survivors ordered along totalitarian lines. In twist ending, the new pastoralism is threatened by a helicopter relief mission, years later, so goodbye the paternalist, feudal society we've grown to love.

MALPERTUIS (MALPERTUIS: HISTOIRE D'UNE MAISON MAUDITE) ★★★
Belgium/France/West Germany 1971; colour; 124 mins; SOFIDOC-Artistes Associés-Societé d'Expansion du Spêctacle-Artemis; *D* Harry Kumel; *P* Pierre Levie, Paul Laffargue; *W* Jean Ferry from the novel by Jean Ray; *M* Georges Delerue; *C* Gerry Fisher; *AD* Pierre Cadiou; *SPFX* (photographic) Michel Bernard, Jean Percriáux; *Starring* Orson Welles, Susan Hampshire, Michel Bouquet, Mathieu Carrière, Jean-Pierre Cassel; *V* Intervision (UK).

MAMMA DRACULA ★★
France/Belgium 1980; colour; 90 mins; Valisa/SND; *D/P* Boris Szulzinger; *W* Szulzinger, Pierre Sterckx, M.-H. Wajnberg (English dialogue by Tony Hendra); *M* Roy Budd; *C* Willy Kurant; *Starring* Louise Fletcher, Maria Schneider, Marc-Henri Wajnberg, Alexander Wajnberg. Crude but sometimes funny *National Lampoon* style parody of the *Countess Dracula* genre (lady vampire stays always young by drinking blood of virgins), from Belgium of all places. Director Szulzinger had previously made an animated Tarzan parody released abroad as *Jungleburger*. Mamma has two sons, Vlad and Lad, one too shy to bite, the other a gay dress designer. Mamma runs a boutique as an easy way of attracting victims. Oh dear.

THE MAN IN THE STEEL MASK – see WHO?

THE MAN IN THE WHITE SUIT ★★★★
UK 1951; b/w; 85 mins; Ealing; *D* Alexander Mackendrick; *P* Michael Balcon, Sidney Cole; *W* Roger Macdougall, Mackendrick and John Dighton from the play by Macdougall; *M* Benjamin Frankel; *C* Douglas Slocombe; *AD* Jim Morahan; *Starring* Alec Guinness, Joan Greenwood, Cecil Parker, Ernest Thesiger; *V* Thorn EMI (UK and USA). Classic SF comedy from the great days of Ealing Studios. Everyone remembers the burping, bubbling scientific equipment in the laboratory in which a young scientist (Guinness) invents a fabric that repels all dirt (it cannot even be dyed, but remains a glowing, pristine white). The film confronts problems (such as a textile would put thousands out of work as well as damaging a lot of capitalists) that are seldom tackled in more overtly serious SF movies. Guinness is wonderful-

ly naive and touching in his part, which involves a protracted chase sequence as everyone tries to capture him.

THE MANITOU ★★½ ☻
USA 1977; colour; 105 mins; Manitou/Avco Embassy; *D/P* William Girdler; *W* Girdler, Jon Cedar, Thomas Pope from the novel by Graham Masterton; *M* Lalo Schifrin; *C* Michel Hugo; *PD* Walter Scott Herndon; *SPFX* Gene Grigg, Tim Smythe, (optical supervision) Dale Tate, Frank Van Der Veer, (make-up) Tom Burman; *Starring* Tony Curtis, Michael Ansara, Susan Strasberg, Burgess Meredith; *V* Embassy (UK), CBS/Fox (USA).

THE MAN WHO CHEATED LIFE – *see* THE STUDENT OF PRAGUE

THE MAN WHO COULD WORK MIRACLES ★★★
UK 1937; b/w; 82 mins; London Films; *D* Lothar Mendes; *P* Alexander Korda; *W* H. G. Wells and (uncredited) Lajos Biro from the story by Wells; *M* Mischa Spoliansky; *C* Harold Rosson; *PD* Vincent Korda; *SPFX* Ned Mann, Lawrence Butler, Edward Cohen; *Starring* Roland Young, Ralph Richardson, Edward Chapman, Ernest Thesiger. Amusing fantasy about timid shop assistant who is granted by capricious gods the power to bring about whatever he thinks. Notable for the co-operation of Wells, who usually despised the cinema, and for the superb crescendo of special effects, ending with the great world-destroying hurricane created when our hero (Young) stops Earth on its axis. These were largely created by special-effects pioneer Ned Mann, who later worked on *Things to Come*, and had begun his career in the silent days with *Thief of Bagdad*, among others.

THE MAN WHO FELL TO EARTH ★★★★★
UK/USA 1976; colour; 138 mins; British Lion; *D* Nicolas Roeg; *P* Michael Deeley, Barry Spikings; *W* Paul Mayersberg from the novel by Walter Tevis; *M* John Phillips; *C* Anthony Richmond; *AD* Brian Eatwell; *SPFX* (photographic) P. S. Ellenshaw, Camera Effects; *Starring* David Bowie, Rip Torn, Candy Clark, Buck Henry; *V* Thorn EMI (UK), RCA/Columbia (USA).

MAN WITHOUT A FACE – *see* WHO?

THE MAN WITH THE X-RAY EYES – *see* X – THE MAN WITH X-RAY EYES

MARCH OF THE TOYS – *see* BABES IN TOYLAND (1934)

MARCH OF THE WOODEN SOLDIERS – *see* BABES IN TOYLAND (1934)

MAROONED ★★★
USA 1969; colour; 133 mins; Frankovich/Columbia; *D* John Sturges; *P* M. J. Frankovich; *W* Mayo Simon from the novel by Martin Caidin; *C* Daniel Fapp; *PD* Lyle R. Wheeler; *SPFX* (visual) Lawrence W. Butler, Donald C. Glouner, Robie Robinson; *Starring* Gregory Peck, Richard Crenna, David Janssen, James Franciscus, Gene Hackman, Lee Grant; *V* RCA/Columbia (UK and USA). Honest, low-key, rather slow SF film – made in semi-documentary style – about three astronauts trapped in orbit, and the rescue mission that saves them. Not very fantastic; indeed, notable for accuracy of the science and special effects. Slightly sterile, it suffered from being released just after the much better *2001: A Space Odyssey*.

MARTIN ★★★★☻
USA 1976; colour; 95 mins; Braddock Associates/ Laurel; *D/W* George A. Romero; *P* Richard Rubinstein; *M* Donald Rubinstein; *C* Michael Gornick; *SPFX/make-up* Tom Savini; *Starring* John Amplas, Lincoln Maazel, Christine Forrest, Tom Savini; *V* Hello Video (UK).

THE MARTIAN CHRONICLES ★★
UK/West Germany/USA 1980; 3-episode miniseries; made for TV; colour; three × 110 mins; Charles Fries/Stonehenge/NBC; *D* Michael Anderson; *P* Andrew Donally, Milton Subotsky; *W* Richard Matheson from the story-collection by Ray Bradbury; *M* Stanley Myers; *C* Ted Moore; *PD* Assheton Gordon; *SPFX* John Stears, (mattes) Ray Caple, (make-up) George Frost; *Starring* Maggie Wright, Rock Hudson, Gayle Hunnicutt, Bernie Casey, Darren McGavin, Fritz Weaver, Barry Morse; *V* Videoform (UK, on three cassettes). The leaden hand of director Michael Anderson seems to have put paid to this one, just as it did with *Logan's Run*. Bradbury may often be prosey, but he is seldom prosaic. To be fair to screenwriter Matheson, Bradbury's alleged lyricism (it is sometimes over-flowery) is extremely difficult to adapt, and the themes of the book – the Martian ability to create illusion, the amazing fragility of their society, and so on – are more sophisticated than is customary for TV. Bradbury's dreamlike, magical vision of Mars, whose images haunt in a variety of ways the Earth people who come to settle there (it is all more fantasy than SF), is here only briefly glimpsed: the mask a Martian wears to kill in, the resuscitated ghost-youth who changes shape according to the yearnings of the humans he meets, the gliding sandships. The Rock Hudson part, all desperate sincerity, is terrible. The screenplay substitutes windy dialogue (the miniseries is almost six hours long!) for action and visual imagination. But then it must be accepted that part of the hackneyed quality is true to the over-rated original book.

MARY POPPINS ★★★
USA 1964; colour; 140 mins; Disney; *D* Robert Stevenson; *P* Bill Walsh; *W* Walsh, Don DaGradi from the books by P L. Travers; *Songs* Richard M. and Robert B. Sherman; *D of animation* Hamilton S. Luske; *SPFX* (optical) Eustace Lycett, (mechanical) Danny Lee, (mattes) Peter Ellenshaw; *Starring* Julie Andrews, Dick Van Dyke, Karen Dotrice, Matthew Garber, David Tomlinson, Glynis Johns, Elsa Lanchester, Jane Darwell; *V* Disney (UK and USA).

LA MASCHERA DEL DEMONIO – *see* BLACK SUNDAY

THE MASK OF FU MANCHU ★★★½
USA 1932; b/w; 72 mins; Cosmopolitan/MGM; *D* Charles Brabin, Charles Vidor; *P* Irving Thalberg (uncredited); *W* Irene Kuhn, Edgar Allan Woolf, John Willard from the novel by Sax Rohmer; *C* Tony Gaudio; *AD* Cedric Gibbons; *Starring* Boris Karloff, Lewis Stone, Karen Morley, Myrna Loy.

MASK OF THE DEMON – *see* BLACK SUNDAY

THE MASQUE OF THE RED DEATH ★★★
UK 1964; colour; 90 mins; Alta Vista/Anglo Amalgamated-AIP; *D/P* Roger Corman; *W* Charles Beaumont, R. Wright Campbell from the story of the same name and "Hop-Frog", both by Edgar Allan Poe; *M* David Lee; *C* Nicolas Roeg; *AD* Robert Jones; *Starring* Vincent Price, Hazel Court, Jane Asher, Patrick Magee.

MASTER OF THE WORLD ★
USA 1961; colour; 104 mins; Alta Vista/AIP; *D* William Witney; *P* James H. Nicholson; *W* Richard Matheson from the novel of the same name, and also *Robur the Conqueror*, both by Jules Verne; *M* Les Baxter; *C* Gilbert Warrenton; *PD* Daniel Haller; *SPFX* Tim Barr, Wah Chang, Gene Warren, (photographic) Butler-Glouner and Ray Mercer; *Starring* Vincent Price, Charles Bronson, Henry Hull; *V* Guild (UK). Hammy Vincent Price is 18th-century mad scientist, with flying machine, out to end war with his own weaponry. Absurdly cheap special effects are fun for connoisseurs: London from the air is stock footage from Olivier's *Henry V*.

MAUSOLEUM ★½ ☻
USA 1981 (released 1983); colour; 96 mins; Western International; *D* Michael Dugan; *P/W* Robert Barich, Robert Madero; *M* Jaime Mendoza-Nava; *C* Robert Barich; *AD* Robert Burns; *SPFX* Roger George, (make-up) John Buechler,

Maurice Stein; *Starring* Marjoe Gortner, Bobbie Bresee, Norman Burton; *V* Filmtown Videospace (UK). Down-market story of nice housewife suffering demonic possession (which runs in the family) and disposing of her nearest and dearest, and also the gardener. Pretty dire, with cardboard characters, but Ms Bresee is attractive (as the many nude shots take pains to show us), and Buechler's demon effects are enjoyably post-*Exorcist*.

THE MAZE ★★
USA 1953; b/w; 3-D; 80 mins; Allied Artists; *D/PD* William Cameron Menzies; *P* Richard Heermance; *W* Dan Ullman from the novel by Maurice Sandoz; *M* Marlin Skiles; *C* Harry Neumann; *Starring* Richard Carlson, Veronica Hurst, Michael Pate, Hillary Brooke. Seldom shown, eccentric horror film made in primitive 3-D by great designer and sometimes good director Menzies (*Things to Come, Invaders from Mars*) towards the end of his career. Nobody ever believes the story when it is recounted to them: basically, it tells of young Scot, Gerald (Carlson), inheriting a castle, only to find that the real laird, who is still alive, is a 200-year-old frog – quite a big frog, who lives in the castle maze, and is referred to by the loyal servants as "The Old Gentleman". The story of his freakish birth from normal parents, and his tormented life, is quite sad, really. Very peculiar film – atmospheric, studio-bound and very cheap.

THE MEDUSA TOUCH ★★
UK/France 1978; colour; 109 mins; Bulldog/ Citeca/ITC; *D* Jack Gold; *P* Gold, Anne V. Coates; *W* John Briley from the novel by Peter van Greenaway; *M* Michael J. Lewis; *C* Arthur Ibbetson; *AD* Peter Mullins; *SPFX* Brian Johnson, (photographic) Doug Ferris; *Starring* Richard Burton, Lino Ventura, Lee Remick; *V* Precision (UK), CBS/Fox (USA). Burton plays a tortured, obsessive, apparently unkillable novelist who since boyhood has been able to destroy people and things by the power of thought, working his way up from a schoolteacher and his parents, through a Jumbo crash, to toppling cathedrals. Melodramatic and hammy.

THE MEPHISTO WALTZ ★★★
USA 1971; colour; 109 mins; Q.M./20th Century-Fox; *D* Paul Wendkos; *P* Quinn Martin; *W* Ben Maddow from the novel by Fred Mustard Stewart; *M* Jerry Goldsmith; *C* William W. Spencer; *AD* Richard Y. Haman; *SPFX* (photographic) Howard A. Anderson Co.; *Starring* Alan Alda, Jacqueline Bisset, Barbara Parkins, Curt Jurgens, Bradford Dillman; *V* CBS/Fox (UK). Enjoyable hokum, gaudily directed with a constantly moving camera by Wendkos. Warlock-classical pianist (Jurgens) transfers his spirit into the body of a younger man (Alda) at moment of death. Alda's wife (Bisset) slowly realizes something is wrong with husband; quite creepy; good use of romantic music by Goldsmith and Liszt. Ambiguous ending suggests the wife may also have learned a trick or two about spirit-transference. Lots of satanists, magic, eerie effects.

MESSAGE FROM THE FUTURE ★★★
Israel 1981; MMF/Thirtieth Century; *D/W* David Avidan; *P/AD* Jacob Kotzky; *M* Jan Pulsford, Tom Blades; *C* Amnon Salomon; *SPFX* Butch Lee, (time machine) Kuly Sander; *Starring* Joseph Bee, Avi Yakir, Irit Meiry. Probably Israel's first SF movie. Future Man (Bee) arrives in strife-torn world of 1985, attempts to arrange (partly by telepathic powers) for World War III to be held soon for future health of world. Scientist (Yakir) disputes this, taken to future (3005 AD) to find sting-in-tail climax. Shot in English. Interesting though wordy.

METALSTORM: THE DESTRUCTION OF JARED-SYN ★★
USA 1983; colour; 3-D; 84 mins; Band/Universal; *D* Charles Band; *P* Alan J. Adler, Band; *W* Adler; *M* Richard Band; *C* Mac Ahlberg; *AD* Pamela B. Warner; *Conceptual Designer* Douglas J. White; *SPFX* (make-up) Douglas J. White, Allan A. Apone, Francis X. Carrisosa; *Starring* Jeffrey

Byron, Tim Thomerson, Kelly Preston, Mike Preston, David Smith. Probably the lowest budget of all the films in the 1983 3-D boom – less than a third of what most of the others spent – and it shows, though there are some enjoyable effects in this sword-and-sorcery/space opera/western. Evil Jared-Syn (Preston) and his cyborg son Baal (Smith) wield death crystals on their desert planet to drain the life force of their victims. The good guys go after them. Mutants, skycycles, nomads. It has much the same ambitions as *Spacehunter*, and similar settings, but is a cruder effort altogether.

METEOR ★
USA 1979; colour; 107 mins; Paladium; *D* Ronald Neame; *P* Arnold Orgolini, Theodore Parvin; *W* Stanley Mann, Edmund H. North; *M* Laurence Rosenthal; *C* Paul Lohmann; *PD* Edward Carfagno; *SPFX* Robert Staples, Glen Robinson, (visual) William Cruse; *Starring* Sean Connery, Natalie Wood, Brian Keith, Martin Landau, Karl Malden; *V* Warner (UK and USA). Perhaps the worst big-budget SF disaster movie ever made. The science would fail any high-school exam, the script is perfunctory, the special effects ludicrous, and the scenes of disaster and panic around the world almost as funny as Martin Landau's acting. The story, such as it is, involves an asteroid heading towards Earth, and a Russian/American team's blasting it away with secret space-mounted nuclear weapons, thus leading to a new era of mutual trust.

METROPOLIS ★★★★½
Germany 1926; b/w; 10,400ft (around 118 mins); Ufa; *D* Fritz Lang; *P* Erich Pommer; *W* Thea von Harbou from her novel; *C* Karl Freund, Günther Rittau; *AD* Otto Hunte, Erich Kettelhut, Karl Vollbrecht; *SPFX* Eugen Shuftan; *Starring* Alfred Abel, Gustav Frölich, Brigitte Helm, Rudolf Klein-Rogge; *V* Thorn EMI (UK), Thunderbird/Budget/Video Yesteryear (USA).

A MIDSUMMER NIGHT'S SEX COMEDY ★★★½
USA 1982; colour; 88 mins; Orion/Rollins-Joffe; *D/W* Woody Allen; *P* Robert Greenhut; *M* Felix Mendelssohn; *C* Gordon Willis; *PD* Mel Bourne; *Flying Machines and Inventions* Eoin Sprott Studio; *Starring* Woody Allen, Mia Farrow, Jose Ferrer, Julie Hagerty, Tony Roberts, Mary Steenburgen; *V* Warner (UK and USA).

MILLION DOLLAR DUCK ★★★
USA 1971; colour; 92 mins; Disney; *D* Vincent McEveety; *P* Bill Anderson; *W* Roswell Rogers from a story by Ted Key; *M* Buddy Baker; *C* William Snyder; *AD* John B. Mansbridge, Al Roelofs; *SPFX* (photographic) Eustace Lycett; *Starring* Dean Jones, Sandy Duncan, Tony Roberts, James Gregory; *V* Disney (UK). Better than average for a Disney live-action movie, though the usual sentimental reverence for small-town values is still central. Experimental, irradiated duck lays golden eggs when frightened. Dean Jones is the put-upon father who exploits the situation; the US Treasury becomes upset; jolly, low-brow political satire; the wife (Duncan) is seen as comic in an extremely sexist portrait (women as narcissistic idiots). Well-mounted chase sequence.

THE MIND OF MR SOAMES ★★
UK 1970; colour; 98 mins; Amicus/Columbia; *D* Alan Cooke; *P* Max A. Rosenberg, Milton Subotsky; *W* John Hale, Edward Simpson from the novel by Charles Eric Maine; *M* Michael Dress; *C* Billy Williams; *PD* Bill Constable; *Starring* Terence Stamp, Robert Vaughn, Nigel Davenport. Minor little SF/horror film, starring Stamp as the man in a coma since birth who is brought back to life in his twenties; a blank slate to be written on, he gives a modestly touching performance, turning violent when society treats him violently. Not much in it, and it suffers, perhaps, from comparison with *Charly*, though it is probably less sentimental.

MIRACLE IN MILAN (MIRACOLO A MILANO) ★★★
Italy 1951; b/w; 101 mins; De Sica/L'ENIC; *D/P* Vittorio De Sica; *W* Cesare Zavattini, De Sica,

Adolfo Franci, Mario Chiari from *Toto il Buono* by Zavattini; *M* Alessandro Cicognini; *C* Aldo Graziati; *AD* Guido Fiorino; *SPFX* Ned Mann; *Starring* Emma Gramatica, Francesco Golisano, Paolo Stoppa. It caused a stir at the time, being – paradoxically – a fantasy film at the heart of the Italian neorealist movement; terribly soft-centred, though. A boy belonging to society's victims, the poor and the outcast (there were millions of displaced persons in Europe after the war), is given a magic dove with which he can work miracles. Capitalists want to exploit the humble people when oil is found beneath their shanty town. At the end, they all fly happily away on broomsticks. Whimsically satirical.

THE MOLE – see EL TOPO

THE MONITORS ★½
USA 1969; colour; 92 mins; Wilding/Second City; *D* Jack Shea; *P* Bernard Sahlins; *W* Myron J. Gold from the novel by Keith Laumer; *C* William (Vilmos) Zsigmond; *AD* Roy Henry; *Starring* Guy Stockwell, Susan Oliver, Avery Schreiber, Sherry Jackson, Keenan Wynn, Ed Begley. Hippy-oriented movie made by a Chicago cabaret troupe, about aliens in overcoats and dark glasses who try to enforce peaceful behaviour on earthlings by spraying them with a special gas; there is a successful revolt. Lots of cameo roles by big names. The film flopped badly – a forgotten SF curiosity, which was not sure if it was a satirical comedy or a moral fable.

MONKEY BUSINESS ★★★★
USA 1952; b/w; 97 mins; 20th Century-Fox; *D* Howard Hawks; *P* Sol C. Siegel; *W* Ben Hecht, I. A. L. Diamond, Charles Lederer; *M* Leigh Harline; *C* Milton Krasner; *AD* Lyle Wheeler, George Patrick; *Starring* Cary Grant, Ginger Rogers, Charles Coburn, Marilyn Monroe, Hugh Marlowe. Daft Howard Hawks comedy, with Cary Grant the scientist who believes he has formulated a fluid which restores youth (actually, a laboratory monkey did it). First he, then his wife (Ginger Rogers), and finally his employers take the substance, and all behave in a zestfully but irritatingly adolescent fashion. Quick-fire farce; good performances; even a serious point to be made (remotely) about hormone treatments. Marilyn Monroe, in an almost forgotten bit part, plays the predatory Grant's first sexy victim, though not a lot happens.

THE MONOLITH MONSTERS ★★★
USA 1957; b/w; 77 mins; Universal; *D* John Sherwood; *P* Howard Christie; *W* Norman Jolley, Robert M. Fresco from a story by Jack Arnold and Fresco; *C* Ellis W. Carter; *SPFX* (photographic) Clifford Stine; *Starring* Grant Williams, Lola Albright, Les Tremayne. Despite weaknesses in the execution, this bizarre, immortal fifties film deserves to be ranked with some of the more discussed monster movies of the period. A fallen meteor releases strange crystals which grow (in contact with water) into great, lurching towers of stone. Extraordinary effects as they advance loomingly across a moodily photographed desert to menace a small township. (All the wooden acting can be forgiven in the face of this grotesque image.) As a bonus, anyone they touch is turned to stone. Terrific!

MONSTER – see HUMANOIDS FROM THE DEEP

THE MONSTER CLUB ★★
UK 1980; colour; 97 mins; Chips-Sword & Sorcery/ITC; *D* Roy Ward Baker; *P* Milton Subotsky; *W* Edward and Valerie Abraham from the collection of short stories by R. Chetwynd-Hayes; *C* Peter Jessop; *PD* Tony Curtis; *SPFX* (monster masks) Vic Door, (make-up) Roy Ashton; *Starring* Vincent Price, John Carradine, Barbara Kellerman, Simon Ward, James Laurenson, Donald Pleasence, Richard Johnson, Britt Ekland, Stuart Whitman, Patrick Magee; *V* Precision (UK). Extremely silly trilogy of stories linked by tale of a special club for monsters into which a horror-story writer (Carradine) is taken. Very bad rock music is interpolated between each story. Stories

are gaudy, comic-book style, the most original being about a Humgoo (a cross between a human and a ghoul) who can kill or disfigure with its dreadful whistle. Other stories feature vampire family (weak) and ghoul-infested village (middling).

MONSTER OF TERROR (aka DIE, MONSTER, DIE!) ★★½
UK 1965; colour; 80 mins; Alta Vista/AIP; *D* Daniel Haller; *P* Pat Green; *W* Jerry Sohl from "The Colour Out of Space" by H. P. Lovecraft; *M* Don Banks; *C* Paul Beeson; *AD* Colin Southcott; *SPFX* Wally Veevers, Ernie Sullivan; *Starring* Boris Karloff, Nick Adams, Freda Jackson, Patrick Magee. Art director for Roger Corman on most of the Poe adaptations, Haller had a disappointing debut as director, not assisted by a very clumsy adaptation of the bizarre original story, nor by Nick Adams, disastrous as the juvenile lead. A meteor falls from space and is carried to the Whitley mansion, where it mutates animals into nasties, Mrs Whitley into something bloated, rotting, and half-glimpsed, and Nahum Whitley (Karloff) into a metallic Thing. Filmed in England instead of New England, it had some atmospheric moments, but was mostly dire.

MONTY PYTHON AND THE HOLY GRAIL ★★★
UK 1974; colour; 90 mins; Python-Michael White/EMI; *D* Terry Gilliam, Terry Jones; *P* Mark Forstater, John Goldstone; *W/Starring* Graham Chapman, John Cleese, Gilliam, Eric Idle, Jones, Michael Palin; *M* Neil Innes, also De Wolfe; *C* Terry Bedford; *PD* Roy Smith; *SPFX* John Horton, (photographic) Julian Doyle; *Animation* Gilliam; *V* Brent Walker (UK), Columbia (USA).

MONTY PYTHON'S LIFE OF BRIAN (aka THE LIFE OF BRIAN) ★★★★
UK 1979; colour; 93 mins; HandMade/Universal; *D* Terry Jones; *P* John Goldstone; *W/Starring* Graham Chapman, John Cleese, Terry Gilliam, Eric Idle, Jones, Michael Palin; *M* Geoffrey Burgon; *C* Peter Biziou; *AD* Roger Christian; *Design/Animation* Gilliam; *V* Thorn EMI (UK), Warner (USA).

MONTY PYTHON'S THE MEANING OF LIFE ★★★☠☠
UK 1983; Celandine-Monty Python Partnership/Universal; *D* Terry Jones; *P* John Goldstone; *W/Starring* Graham Chapman, John Cleese, Terry Gilliam, Eric Idle, Jones, Michael Palin; *C* Peter Hannan; *PD* Harry Lange; *SPFX* George Gibbs, (optical) Kent Houston and others; *Animation* Gilliam; *V* MCA (USA).

MOONRAKER ★★½
UK/France 1979; colour; 126 mins; Eon/Artistes Associés; *D* Lewis Gilbert; *P* Albert R. Broccoli; *W* Christopher Wood from the novel by Ian Fleming; *M* John Barry; *C* Jean Tournier; *PD* Ken Adam; *SPFX* John Evans, John Richardson, René Albouze, Serge Ponvianne, (visual effects supervision) Derek Meddings; *Starring* Roger Moore, Lois Chiles, Michel Lonsdale, Richard Kiel; *V* Warner (UK), CBS/Fox (USA).

MOON ZERO TWO ★½
UK 1969; colour; 100 mins; Hammer/Warner; *D* Roy Ward Baker; *P/W* Michael Carreras from a story by Gavin Lyall, Frank Hardman and Martin Davison; *M* Don Ellis; *C* Paul Beeson; *AD* Scott MacGregor; *SPFX* Les Bowie, (photographic) Kit West, Nick Allder; *Starring* James Olson, Catherina von Schell, Warren Mitchell, Adrienne Corri. Hammer spent more than usual on this space western, but their timing was bad. The real Moon landing in 1969 made this melodramatic hokum look pretty silly, which it was, though the special effects were all right. A space pilot (Olson) is forced to help space bandits steal an asteroid made of sapphire! When will film-makers learn that SF does not have to be infantile?

LA MORT EN DIRECT – see DEATH WATCH

MOST DANGEROUS MAN ALIVE ★★½
USA 1958 (released 1961); b/w; 82 mins; Trans-

Global/Columbia; *D* Allan Dwan; *P* Benedict Bogeaus; *W* James Leicester, Phillip Rock from a story by Rock and Michael Pate; *M* Louis Forbes; *C* Carl Carvahal; *Starring* Ron Randall, Debra Paget, Elaine Stewart, Anthony Caruso. The last movie of ex-silent film director Dwan, whose career has recently been evaluated upwards. He was 73 when he made this. (Curiously, this forgotten SF movie surfaced again in 1982, in Wim Wenders' *The State of Things*, which is an intellectual film about shooting a remake of *Most Dangerous Man Alive*.) Very low-budget film, with interesting tough quality, tells of wrongly-convicted prisoner escaping, being caught in nuclear blast, slowly turning to steel (mentally and physically), revenging himself on his betrayers, destroyed by flame-throwers, turning to dust.

THE MUMMY ★★★½
USA 1932; b/w; 72 mins; Universal; *D* Karl Freund; *P* Carl Laemmle Jr, Stanley Bergerman; *W* John L. Balderston from a story by Nina Wilcox Putnam and Richard Schayer; *C* Charles Stumar; *SPFX* John P. Fulton, (make-up) Jack P. Pierce; *Starring* Boris Karloff, Zita Johann, David Manners, Edward Van Sloan, Bramwell Fletcher, Noble Johnson. Universal's follow-up to *Frankenstein*, with Karloff as The Mummy, proved after a time extremely influential and much imitated (though seldom well). Universal made five more *Mummy* movies, beginning with *The Mummy's Hand* in 1940. Hammer Films made four, the best being *Blood from the Mummy's Tomb*. Various unknown Mexicans made at least seven, with the mummies being Aztec or Mayan. A recent Anglo-American attempt was *The Awakening*. The original is not quite a classic, but well photographed, restrained: a film of atmosphere rather than horror. Karloff's role as the unwrapped mummy posing as an archaeologist is interesting. Good flashback to ancient Egypt.

THE MUMMY ★★★ 👹
UK 1959; colour; 88 mins; Hammer/Universal; *D* Terence Fisher; *P* Michael Carreras; *W* Jimmy Sangster from the screenplays for *The Mummy's Hand* (1940) and *The Mummy's Tomb* (1942); *M* Frank Reizenstein; *C* Jack Asher; *AD* Bernard Robinson; *SPFX* (make-up) Roy Ashton; *Starring* Peter Cushing, Christopher Lee, Yvonne Furneaux. Universal gave Hammer the copyright release on their entire *Mummy* series, so there were no problems here. Archaeologists who disturb a princess's tomb in Egypt are pursued to England by the guardian mummy (Lee), who revenges himself – largely in well-photographed marshland settings. Lee is a good, lurching, ominous mummy. Nasty scene in flashback where tongue is torn out.

MÜNCHHAUSEN – see THE ADVENTURES OF BARON MUNCHAUSEN

THE MUPPET MOVIE ★★
UK 1979; colour; 97 mins; ITC; *D* James Frawley; *P* Jim Henson; *W* Jerry Juhl, Jack Burns; *M* Paul Williams, Kenny Ascher; *C* Isidore Mankofsky; *PD* Joel Schiller; *Creative consultant* Frank Oz; *Muppet design consultant* Michael Frith; *SPFX* Robbie Knott; *Starring the voices of* Jim Henson (Kermit the Frog etc.), Frank Oz (Miss Piggy etc.), Dave Goelz (The Great Gonzo etc.); *Also starring* Edgar Bergen, Milton Berle, Mel Brooks, James Coburn, Dom DeLuise, Elliott Gould, Madeline Kahn, Orson Welles and others in cameos; *V* Precision (UK), CBS/Fox (USA).

THE MUTATIONS ★½
UK 1973; colour; 92 mins; Getty/Columbia; *D* Jack Cardiff; *P* Robert D. Weinbach; *W* Weinbach, Edward Mann; *M* Basil Kirchin, Jack Nathan; *SPFX* Mike Hope, (photographic) Ken Middleham, (make-up) Charles Parker; *Starring* Donald Pleasence, Tom Baker, Julie Ege. Freak-show proprietor Baker provides mad scientist Pleasence with freaks (some real freaks were used) for experiments in combining human life with plant life. Pleasence's daughter's fiancé, now half fly-trap, gets revenge. Nasty and not even very efficient SF/horror pic.

THE MYSTERIANS (CHIKYU BOEIGUN) ★★
Japan 1957; colour; 89 mins; Toho; *D* Inoshiro Honda; *P* Tomoyuki Tanaka; *W* Takeshi Kimura, also S. Kayama, from a story by Jojiro Okami; *M* Akira Ifukube; *C* Hajime Koizumi; *AD* Teruaki Abe; *SPFX* Eiji Tsuburaya; *Starring* Kenji Sahara, Yumi Shirakawa; Akihiko Hirata; *V* Kingston (UK), Video Communications (USA). One of the better SF movies from Toho, which is not saying a whole lot. Effects man Tsuburaya was the creator of *Godzilla*. Pulp-style melodrama about aliens, wanting to breed with Earth women, attacking with death rays from the Moon. They are driven off. Good giant robot. Colourful, and quite typical of the Japanese input to the SF genre.

MYSTERIOUS ISLAND ★★★
UK 1961; colour; 101 mins; Ameran/Columbia; *D* Cy Endfield; *P* Charles H. Schneer; *W* John Prebble, Daniel Ullman, Crane Wilbur from the novel by Jules Verne; *M* Bernard Herrmann; *C* Wilkie Cooper; *AD* Bill Andrews; *SPFX* Ray Harryhausen; *Starring* Michael Craig, Joan Greenwood, Michael Callan, Gary Merrill, Herbert Lom; *V* Columbia (USA). The sixth collaboration between effects wizard Harryhausen and producer Schneer is among the more enjoyable of their early efforts, though not really very good. As ever, wooden acting and an uninspired script fail to give a proper context for Harryhausen's stop-motion animated monsters, which include giant crabs, bees and a chicken. The story is a sequel to *20,000 Leagues Under the Sea*, and re-introduces Captain Nemo, who is trying to help the world by introducing new food sources. Lom is not a patch on James Mason in the role. Colourful and amusing, however, despite routine and predictable volcanic explosion at end.

NEITHER THE SEA NOR THE SAND ★
UK 1972; colour; 94 mins; Portland/Tigon; *D* Fred Burnley; *P* Jack Smith, Peter Fetterman; *W* Gordon Honeycombe from his novel; *M* Nahum Heiman; *C* David Muri; *AD* Michael Bastow; *Starring* Susan Hampshire, Michael Petrovitch, Frank Finlay; *V* Guild (UK). First half-hour is especially disastrous, as Hampshire and Petrovitch go through the (slow) motions of an adulterous love affair. There is then some (laughable) action when the Petrovitch character dies of a heart attack but continues as her animated-corpse lover: he seems more at home being dead and no longer required to show human qualities (such as acting ability). Almost incredibly badly made, and the necrophiliac theme, apparently envisaged as romantic, is merely disgusting.

DIE NIBELUNGEN (in two parts: SIEGFRIEDS TOD, aka SIEGFRIED; and KRIEMHILDS RACHE, aka KRIEMHILD'S REVENGE) ★★★★
Germany 1923-24; b/w; nearly six hours (in recently restored version projected at 16 fps); Decla-Bioscop/Ufa; *D* Fritz Lang; *P* Erich Pommer; *W* Lang, Thea von Harbou; *C* Carl Hoffmann, Günther Rittau; *AD* Otto Hunte, Erich Kettelhut, Karl Vollbrecht; *Animation* Walther Ruttmann; *Starring* Gertrud Arnold, Margarete Schön, Paul Richter, Rudolf Klein-Rogge, Hanna Ralph. This important classic is based directly on myth rather than on the Wagnerian version. *Siegfried* is magical, fantastic, stylized; *Kriemhild's Revenge* is epic rather than romantic, and deals coldly with the warfare (involving Attila the Hun) that results from Siegfried's murder at the end of Part I. The beautiful, ritualistic images of *Siegfried* include the dream of circling hawks, the slaying of the dragon (an early piece of monster animation involved here), the dwarfs turned to stone, the cathedral-like forest, and an extraordinary grandeur of setting.

NIGHT BEAUTIES – see LES BELLES DE NUIT

NIGHTMARES ★★
USA 1983; colour; 99 mins; Universal; *D* Joseph Sargent; *P* Christopher Crowe; *W* (chapters 1, 2 and 3) Crowe, (chapter 4) Jeffrey Bloom; *M* Craig Safan; *C* (chapters 1 and 2) Gerald Perry Finnerman, (chapters 3 and 4) Mario DiLeo; *AD* Jack Taylor; *SPFX* (optical) John Nogle, (matte) Dwight S. Land, (aka SIEGFRIED; *Starring* ("Terror in Topanga") Cristina Raines, Joe Lambie; ("Bishop of Battle") Emilio Estevez; ("The Benediction") Lance Henriksen; ("Night of the Rat") Richard Masur, Veronica Cartwright; *V* MCA (USA). Anthology film, with all episodes but the first fantastic. In the second, video-game obsessive fights computer-generated monsters; in the third, priest losing faith is haunted by black car that bursts, spectacularly, from the ground; in the last, a monster rat retrieves its trapped baby. All stories pretty predictable, and most of the special effects (the video-game creatures for example) rather mediocre. Experienced director Sargent *(The Forbin Project)* does nothing much with the material, but there is some atmospheric photography.

NIGHT OF DARK SHADOWS ★★
USA 1971; colour; 97 mins; MGM; *D/P* Dan Curtis; *W* Sam Hall; *M* Robert Cobert; *C* Richard Shore; *AD* Trevor Williams; *SPFX* (make-up) Reginald Tackley; *Starring* David Selby, Lara Parker, Kate Jackson, Grayson Hall. Sequel to *House of Dark Shadows*, but this time there is no vampire. Spin-off from popular Gothic TV soap opera *Dark Shadows*. Quentin (Selby), an artist, takes his bride to an old house he has inherited; it is haunted by Angelique (Parker); it seems he is the re-incarnation of her lover, an executed witch, whose spirit comes to possess his body. Rather feeble genre piece with a stronger and soppier romantic element than usual; confused story.

NIGHT OF THE DEMON (aka CURSE OF THE DEMON) ★★★★
UK 1957; b/w; 83 mins; Sabre/Columbia; *D* Jacques Tourneur; *P* Hal E. Chester; *W* Charles Bennett, Chester from "Casting the Runes" by M. R. James; *M* Clifton Parker; *C* Ted Scaife; *AD* Ken Adam; *SPFX* George Blackwell, Wally Veevers, (photographic) S. D. Onions; *Starring* Dana Andrews, Peggy Cummins, Niall MacGinnis.

NIGHT OF THE EAGLE (aka BURN, WITCH, BURN) ★★★½
UK 1962; b/w; 90 mins; Independent Artists; *D* Sidney Hayers; *P* Albert Fennell; *W* Charles Beaumont, Richard Matheson, George Baxt from *Conjure Wife* by Fritz Leiber; *M* William Alwyn; *C* Reginald Wyer; *AD* Jack Shampan; *Starring* Janet Blair, Peter Wyngarde, Margaret Johnston, Anthony Nicholls, Kathleen Byron. Based on an excellent occult novel about college professor who finds signs of witchcraft on campus, with his wife involved. Low-key thriller in the Val Lewton style, featuring bravura sequence when hero is chased by stone eagle come to life. Modest and enjoyable.

NIGHT OF THE LEPUS ★
USA 1972; colour; 88 mins; MGM; *D* William F. Claxton; *P* A. C. Lyles; *W* Don Holliday, Gene R. Kearney from *The Year of the Angry Rabbit* by Russell Braddon; *M* Jimmie Haskell; *C* Ted Voigtlander; *PD* Stan Jolley; *SPFX* (photographic) Howard A. Anderson Co.; *Starring* Stuart Whitman, Janet Leigh, Rory Calhoun, DeForest Kelley. Connoisseurs of truly terrible horror films cherish this one. It contains the immortal line: "I don't want to alarm you, folks, but there's a herd of killer rabbits on the way", spoken by Whitman as the sheriff. Try as they might, the effects men could not make the carnivorous rabbits (bred from an experimental rabbit full of hormones) look menacing. This is probably the most enjoyable one-star movie in this book. The original novel, incidentally, was a satire set in Australia; the film is set in Arizona.

NIGHT OF THE LIVING DEAD ★★★★ 👹👹
USA 1968; b/w; 90 mins; Image Ten; *D/C* George A. Romero; *P* Russell Streiner, Karl Hardman; *W* John A. Russo from a story by Romero; *SPFX* Regis Survinski, Tony Pantanello; *Starring* Judith O'Dea, Russell Streiner, Duane Jones, Karl Hardman; *V* Intervision (UK), Media, Video Communications, others (USA).

THE NIGHT STALKER ★★
USA 1971; made for TV; colour; 74 mins; ABC; *D* John Llewellyn Moxey; *P* Dan Curtis; *W* Richard Matheson from a story by Jeff Rice; *M* Robert Colbert; *C* Michel Hugo; *AD* Trevor Wallace; *Starring* Darren McGavin, Carol Lynley, Simon Oakland, Ralph Meeker; *V* Guild (UK), 20th Century-Fox (USA). Very successful TV movie led to sequel *(The Night Strangler)* and TV series *(Kolchak: The Night Stalker)*. Vampire with superhuman strength terrorizes Las Vegas; hard-bitten reporter McGavin tries to convince police force of its supernatural origins. Strong stuff for TV perhaps, but feeble by any other standard; vampire disappointing.

THE NIGHT STRANGLER ★★★
USA 1972; made for TV; colour; 74 mins; ABC Circle; *D/P* Dan Curtis; *W* Richard Matheson from characters created by Jeff Rice; *M* Robert Colbert; *C* Robert B. Hauser; *AD* Trevor Williams; *SPFX* (monster make-up) William J. Tuttle; *Starring* Darren McGavin, Jo Ann Pflug, Simon Oakland, Scott Brady, John Carradine; *V* Guild (UK). Sequel to *The Night Stalker*, and more interesting. Jokey tough-guy reporter McGavin locates semi-immortal doctor and murderer of women (he leaves rotting flesh around the wounds) in creepy underground settings beneath Seattle.

NIGHTWING ★★½
USA/Netherlands 1979; colour; 105 mins; Polyc/Columbia; *D* Arthur Hiller; *P* Martin Ransohoff; *W* Steve Shagan, Bud Shrake, Martin Cruz Smith from the novel by Cruz Smith; *M* Henry Mancini; *C* Charles Rosher (Jr); *SPFX* Milt Rice, (special visual) Carlo Rambaldi; *Starring* Nick Mancuso, David Warner, Kathryn Harrold; *V* RCA-Columbia (UK and USA). Based on an interesting novel by the man who wrote *Gorky Park*, this disappoints, though Rambaldi's mechanical bats (radio controlled) are quite good. The director, Hiller, is more used to comedy than horror, and here he plays down the horrific possibilities in favour of the sociology of detribalized Indians. Vampire bats carrying bubonic plague invade Indian reservation country in eastern Arizona; they may have been called up by an ancient medicine man who schemes to end the corrupt world; this fantastic element is ambiguous, since the medicineman scenes involve chewing datura, which brings on hallucinations. Warner less hammy than usual in good role as obsessive bat-hunting naturalist.

NIPPON CHINBOTSU (aka THE SUBMERSION OF JAPAN, TIDAL WAVE) ★★★★
Japan 1974; colour; 140 mins (81 mins as *Tidal Wave*); Toho; *D* Shiro Moritani; *W* Shinobu Hashimoto from *Japan Sinks* by Sakyo Komatsu; *M* Masaru Sato; *C* Hiroshi Murai, Daisaku Kimura; *SPFX* Teruyoshi Nakano; *Starring* Keiju Kobayashi, Tetsuro Tamba, Hiroshi Fujioka, Aymui Ishida, Shogo Shimada. The most successful movie ever made in Japan, this disaster story (based on a good novel, available in the West) has an epic scope. Geophysical changes (their gradual discovery is carefully traced in the film) lead to the gradual submersion of the Japanese island chain, rendering many millions homeless. Other countries are reluctant to take them in (though quite a few finish up in Australia's Northern Territory). The special effects are fairly routine in the Toho style, but they are not the main point. They became the main point, however, in the vandalised version put out in the USA by Roger Corman's New World. This had additional scenes with Lorne Greene, written and directed by Andrew Meyer and photographed by Eric Saarinen, with clumsy dubbing elsewhere. All the careful build-up of character is gone here, and the semi-coherent result is thoroughly tawdry – a one-star (★) movie. Over an hour had been cut from the original, which was very briefly shown in the USA as *Submersion of Japan*.

NOROÎT (aka NORTHWEST WIND) ★★½
France 1977; colour; 142 mins; Sunchild; *D* Jacques Rivette; *P* Stephen Tschalgadjieff; *W* Eduardo de Gregorio, Maria Ludovica Parolini; *C* William Lubschansky; *Starring* Bernadette Lafont, Geraldine Chaplin, Kika Markham, Anne-Marie Reynaud. Sequel to *Duelle*; see the comment there for further details. Moon ghost (Chaplin) struggles against sun fairy (Lafont) and her pirate band. Cyril Tourneur's *The Revenger's Tragedy*, a Jacobean drama, is in there somewhere. Abstract, ritualistic, weird, irritating and opaque.

NORTHWEST WIND – see NOROÎT

NOSFERATU ★★★★½
Germany 1922; b/w; circa 70 mins; Prana Film; *D* F. W. Murnau; *W* Henrik Galeen from *Dracula* by Bram Stoker; *C* Fritz Arno Wagner, Günther Krampf; *AD* Albin Grau; *Starring* Max Schreck, Alexander Granach, Greta Schroder, Ruth Landshoff; *V* Thorn EMI (UK), Blackhawk, Thunderbird (USA).

NOSFERATU THE VAMPYRE (NOSFERATU: PHANTOM DER NACHT) ★★★½
West Germany 1979; colour; 107 mins; Werner Herzog/Gaumont; *D/P/W* Werner Herzog from the film *Nosferatu*, 1922; *M* Popol Vuh, Florian Fricke; *C* Jörg Schmidt-Reitwein; *PD* Henning von Gierke, Ulrich Bergfelder; *SPFX* Cornelius Siegel, (make-up) Reiko Kruk and Dominique Colladant; *Starring* Klaus Kinski, Isabelle Adjani, Bruno Ganz, Roland Topor, Walter Ladengast; *V* CBS/Fox (UK).

NOTHING BUT THE NIGHT ★
UK 1972; colour; 90 mins; Charlemagne/Rank; *D* Peter Sasdy; *P* Anthony Nelson Keys; *W* Brian Hayles from the novel by John Blackburn; *M* Malcolm Williamson; *C* Ken Talbot; *SPFX* Les Bowie; *Starring* Christopher Lee, Peter Cushing, Diana Dors, Georgia Brown; *V* Rank (UK). Lacklustre performances all around in this confused, badly developed, laborious movie, especially from the children who are so important to the plot. Trustees of an orphanage mysteriously die; Diana Dors overplays the mother with a criminal record whose homicidal tendencies (presumed) are the main red herring. Turns out that trustees have surgically transplanted their personalities into the kids, who behave fiendishly at the end – too late to save an otherwise placid film.

NOW YOU SEE HIM, NOW YOU DON'T ★½
USA 1972; colour; 88 mins; Disney; *D* Robert Butler; *P* Ron Miller; *W* Joseph L. McEveety from a story by Robert L. King; *M* Robert F. Brunner; *C* Frank Phillips; *AD* John B. Mansbridge, Walter Tyler; *SPFX* (photographic) Eustace Lycett, Danny Lee; *Starring* Kurt Russell, Cesar Romero, Jim Backus. Sequel to *The Computer Wore Tennis Shoes*; the third in the series was *The Strongest Man in the World*. It does one's heart good to see Kurt Russell, now a snarling tough guy in John Carpenter films *(Escape from New York, The Thing)*, back in his Disney days of innocence as a goofy teenage genius. In this one he invents an invisibility formula. The film is pretty formulaic too.

THE NUTTY PROFESSOR ★★★★
USA 1963; colour; 107 mins; Jerry Lewis Enterprises/Paramount; *D* Jerry Lewis; *P* Ernest D. Glucksman; *W* Lewis, Bill Richmond; *M* Walter Scharf; *C* W. Wallace Kelley; *AD* Hal Pereira, Walter Tyler; *SPFX* Paul K Lerpae; *Starring* Jerry Lewis, Stella Stevens, Del Moore, Kathleen Freeman, Henry Gibson. Some people can't stand him, of course, but the French think he's a genius,' and his fans think this is Jerry Lewis's most accomplished film. A rewrite of the Jekyll-and-Hyde story, it has wimpish professor who changes into revolting, sexually-charged smoothie, and it certainly has funny moments. Some people see Buddy Love (Professor Kelp's lounge-lizard alter ego) as Lewis's revenge on long-time colleague Dean Martin. Well-made, mounting to a comic crescendo and a good pay-off.

THE OBLONG BOX ★½
UK 1969; colour; 101 mins; AIP; *D/P* Gordon Hessler; *W* Lawrence Huntingdon, also Christopher Wicking, from the story by Edgar Allan Poe; *M* Harry Robinson; *C* John Coquillon; *AD* George Provis; *Starring* Vincent Price, Christopher Lee; *V* Guild (UK). Fruity period melodrama. Price plays world-weary aristo with dreadful secret – horribly deformed brother kept in chains, his condition the result of torture by African tribesmen. For reasons too boring to go into, a witchdoctor brews up a substance that causes suspended animation, and brother is whisked away apparently dead. But he's not. Seldom has a film foundered so badly on ineffective make-up; when the hideous brother is finally revealed, his leprous condition appears like a mild acne, thus rendering all the previous screaming completely inexplicable. Creepy only for the first half hour.

OH, GOD! ★★★½
USA 1977; colour; 104 mins; Warner; *D* Carl Reiner; *P* Jerry Weintraub; *W* Larry Gelbart from the novel by Avery Corman; *M* Jack Elliott; *C* Victor Kemper; *AD* Jack Senter; *Starring* George Burns, John Denver, Teri Garr, Donald Pleasence, Ralph Bellamy, William Daniels; *V* Warner (UK and USA). Whimsical, rather soft-centred comedy, in which John Denver meets God (George Burns), who asks him to act as a missionary on His behalf. God is an eccentric wise-cracking old gentleman; Denver surprisingly good as the embarrassed young man who doesn't quite know how to cope with the situation. Promising basis for satire largely squandered through easy laughs; God for example, is not entirely happy with his invention of the avocado (the stone is too big). The established Churches are given a hard – but not *very* hard – time.

O LUCKY MAN! ★★★
UK 1973; colour; 174 mins (later cut by director to 165 mins); Memorial-Sam/Warner; *D* Lindsay Anderson; *P* Michael Medwin, Anderson; *W* David Sherwin from an idea by Malcolm McDowell; *M* Alan Price; *C* Miroslav Ondricek; *PD* Jocelyn Herbert; *Starring* McDowell, Ralph Richardson, Rachel Roberts, Arthur Lowe, Helen Mirren; *V* Warner (UK and USA).

THE OMEGA MAN ★★½
USA 1971; colour; 98 mins; Seltzer/Warner; *D* Boris Sagal; *P* Walter Seltzer; *W* John William Corrington, Joyce H. Corrington from *I Am Legend* by Richard Matheson; *M* Ron Grainer; *C* Russell Metty; *AD* Arthur Loel, Walter M. Simonds; *Starring* Charlton Heston, Anthony Zerbe, Rosalind Cash. Second version of good, scientifically-rationalized vampire novel (vampirism is caused by anaerobic bacteria). The first version, which was dreadful, was *The Last Man on Earth* (Italy, 1964), but at least that remained faithful to the story, which *The Omega Man* does not. Heston plays the sole survivor in Los Angeles of a plague which turns its victims into albino zombies; in the book he pursues a mad vendetta against the vampire/zombies, but in the film he is much nicer, and experiments with an antidote serum. Thus the irony of the only human left being much more violent than the monsters is quite lost. The vampirism theme has almost disappeared, and the whole thing is a rather weak adventure story, though there are some good, moody sequences in the empty, garbage-strewn city.

THE OMEN ★★½ ☻
USA 1976; colour; 111 mins; 20th Century-Fox; *D* Richard Donner; *P* Harvey Bernhard; *W* David Seltzer; *M* Jerry Goldsmith; *C* Gilbert Taylor; *AD* Carmen Dillon; *SPFX* John Richardson, (make-up) Stuart Freeborn; *Starring* Gregory Peck, Lee Remick, David Warner, Billy Whitelaw, Leo McKern; *V* CBS/Fox (UK and USA).

ONE MILLION YEARS BC ★★½
UK 1966; colour; 100 mins; Hammer-Seven Arts/Associated British-Pathe–20th Century-Fox; *D* Don Chaffey; *P/W* Michael Carreras from the screenplay of *One Million B.C.* (1940) by Mickell Novak, George Baker and Joseph Frickert; *M* Mario Nascimbene; *C* Wilkie Cooper; *AD* Bob Jones; *SPFX* (visual) Ray Harryhausen; *Starring* Raquel Welch, John Richardson, Martine Beswick; *V* Thorn EMI (UK).

ON HER MAJESTY'S SECRET SERVICE ★★
UK 1969; colour; 140 mins; Eon-Danilaq/United Artists; D Peter Hunt; P Harry Saltzman, Albert R. Broccoli; W Richard Maibaum, also Simon Raven, from the novel by Ian Fleming; M John Barry; C Michael Reed; PD Syd Cain; SPFX John Stears; Starring George Lazenby, Diana Rigg, Telly Savalas, Gabriele Ferzetti; V Warner (UK).

ONIBABA (aka THE DEMON; THE HOLE) ★★★
Japan 1964; b/w; 105 mins; Kindai Eiga Kyokai-Tokyo Eiga/Toho; D/W Kaneto Shindo; P Toshio Konya; M Hikaru Hayashi; C Kiyomi Kuroda; Starring Nobuko Otowa, Jitsuko Yoshimura, Kei Sato; V Palace (UK).

ORCA...THE KILLER WHALE (aka ORCA) ★½
USA 1977; colour; 92 mins; Famous (Dino De Laurentiis); D Michael Anderson; P Luciano Vincenzoni; W Vincenzoni, Sergio Donati; M Ennio Morricone; C Ted Moore; PD Mario Garbuglia; SPFX Alex C. Weldon, (photographic) Frank Van Der Veer; Starring Richard Harris, Charlotte Rampling, Will Sampson, Bo Derek, Keenan Wynn; V Thorn EMI (UK), Paramount (USA).

ORLAC'S HÄNDE – see THE HANDS OF ORLAC

ORPHÉE (ORPHEUS) ★★★★½
France 1950; b/w; 112 mins; Films du Palais Royal; D/M Jean Cocteau; P André Paulvé; M Georges Auric; C Nicolas Hayer; AD Jean d'Eaubonne; Starring Jean Marais, Maria Casarès, François Périer, Edouard Dermit; V Thorn EMI (UK), Video Yesteryear, Budget, Sheik (USA).

GLI ORRORI DEL CASTELLO DI NORIMBERGA – see BARON BLOOD

THE OTHER ★★★
USA 1972; colour; 100 mins; Rex-Benchmark/20th Century-Fox; D/P Robert Mulligan; W Thomas Tryon from his novel; M Jerry Goldsmith; C Robert L. Surtees; PD Albert Brenner; Starring Uta Hagen, Diana Muldaur, Chris and Martin Udvarnoky. An interesting category of fantasy, not much represented in this book for lack of space, is the ambiguous fringe-fantasy where the explanation for events can be either supernatural or psychological. Here, in a nostalgically-seen rural America of the 1930s, are twin brothers, one dark and perhaps evil, one blonde and perhaps innocent. There are a series of murders. The revelation is not made until an hour into the film that the dark brother has been dead for years (when we see the blonde brother talking, apparently, to thin air). Is this a story of schizophrenia or possession by a spirit of the dead? Or perhaps these are two names for the same thing. Yet another film in the curiously popular, Gothic evil-child genre, but innocence is played off against knowingness better here than in most.

OUTLAND ★★★
UK 1981; colour; 109 mins; Ladd/Warner; D/W Peter Hyams; P Charles Orme; M Jerry Goldsmith; C Stephen Goldblatt; PD Philip Harrison; SPFX John Stears, Bob Harman, John Markwell, (optical) Roy Field; Starring Sean Connery, Peter Boyle, Frances Sternhagen, James B. Sikking; V Warner (UK and USA).

PANDORA AND THE FLYING DUTCHMAN ★★★★
UK 1950; colour; 122 mins; Romulus/Independent-British Lion; D/P/W Albert Lewin; M Alan Rawsthorne; C Jack Cardiff; PD John Bryan; Starring Ava Gardner, James Mason, Nigel Patrick, Sheila Sim, Harold Warrender, Mario Cabre. Atmospheric love story, haunted and deeply romantic, about mysterious stranger (Mason) who has love affair with Ava Gardner. She turns out to be the double of the woman for whom the Flying Dutchman was condemned to sail the oceans of the world eternally. Guess who the mysterious stranger is, and don't forget to take a clean handkerchief. Well-made and interesting.

PANICO EN EL TRANSIBERIANO – see HORROR EXPRESS

PARASITE ★½ ☻
USA 1982; colour; 3-D; 85 mins; Charles Band Productions; D/P Charles Band; W Alan Adler, Michael Shoob, Frank Levering; M Richard Band; C Mac Ahlberg; AD Pamela B. Warner; SPFX Doug White, (parasite) Stan Winston, James Kagel and Lance Anderson; Starring Robert Glaudini, Demi Moore, Luca Bercovici; V Entertainment in Video (UK), Wizard (USA). Post-holocaust America; scientist develops and is then infected by parasite; he is pursued by paramilitary and a gang who want it; it destroys various people in a kind of weak Alien style. Hard to judge the special effects because of the bad 3-D process; Winston's effects are sometimes good. Monthly Film Bulletin comments "...an under-budgeted monster which resembles a hamburger with teeth"

THE PARASITE MURDERS – see SHIVERS

PARIS QUI DORT (aka THE CRAZY RAY; PARIS ASLEEP) ★★★
France 1923; b/w; 61 mins; Films Diamant; D/W René Clair; P Henri Diamant-Berger; C Maurice Desfassiaux, Paul Guichard; PD André Foy; Starring Henri Rolland, Madeleine Rodrigue, Albert Préjean, Charles Martinelli, Marcel Vallée; V Video Archives (USA). Eccentric inventor accidentally freezes Paris in time, with almost everyone immobile; those who escape the effects of this strange ray have a thoroughly good time. One of the first SF feature films, this silent comedy is still charming, and the social comment witty.

PARSIFAL ★★★★
France/West Germany 1982; colour; 255 mins; Gaumont/TMS; D Hans Jürgen Syberberg; W/M (the opera by Richard Wagner); C Igor Luther; PD Werner Achmann; Starring Michael Kutter, Karin Krick (sung by Reiner Goldberg), Edith Clever (sung by Yvonne Minton), Armin Jordan (sung by Wolfgang Schöne). Extraordinary version of the Wagner opera, over four hours long. Although theatrical, it has been claimed as the best cinematic version of an opera ever made. The story, of course, is a myth that lies at the heart of the fantastic genre: that of the wounded King who keeps the Holy Grail, and Parsifal, the innocent saviour who heals him. Syberberg's version is part homage to Wagner, and part critique. Many vital changes are made, notably the shocking moment when Parsifal becomes a woman. The film is very post-Freudian (as any story made today, in which bleeding wounds and magic spears play a central role, is bound to be); Kundry, sorceress and seducer (powerfully played by Clever) represents a femininity against which the aggressive male world seems unnatural and neurotic. Very interesting film by one of the most controversial directors of the new German cinema.

PATRICK ★★½
Australia 1978; colour; 110 mins; Australian International/Filmways Australasia; D Richard Franklin; P Antony I. Ginnane, Franklin; W Everett de Roche; M Brian May; C Don McAlpine; SPFX C. C. Rothman; Starring Susan Penhaligon, Robert Helpmann; V VCL (UK), Vestron (USA). Hospital nurse Kathy (Penhaligon) comes to suspect that comatose patient Patrick, who has been unconscious for three years, is influencing events by powers of the mind. Various psionic phenomena take place, some frightening, as Patrick attempts to make Kathy (whom he loves) commit suicide and join him. Australian attempt to cash in on the genre success of Carrie, The Fury etc. Director Franklin shows some promise; he went make Psycho II (1983) in the USA – rather well, most critics felt.

PAURA NELLA CITTÀ DEI MORTI VIVENTI – see CITY OF THE LIVING DEAD

THE PEACE GAME – see GLADIATORERNA

PEAU D'ÂNE (THE MAGIC DONKEY) ★★★
France 1970; colour; 89 mins; Parc/Marianne; D/W Jacques Demy from the story by Charles Perrault; P Mag Bodard; M/Songs Michel Legrand; C Ghislain Cloquet; AD Jacques Dugied, Jim Léon; Starring Catherine Deneuve, Jean Marais, Delphine Seyrig, Jacques Perrin, Michelin Presle. Charming, saucy, slightly sentimental, musical fairy tale for adults. The King (Marais) has a donkey that defecates jewels and keeps the kingdom solvent. He wishes to marry his daughter (Deneuve). Unnerved by this suggestion, she fends him off with help of fairy godmother (Seyrig), asking him to grant ever more excessive wishes, and finally the donkey's skin of the title. She dresses in this and escapes to another kingdom disguised as a humble nobody, where she marries the Prince. Great play is made with the magical use of very bright colours, and the occasional modern touch (travel by helicopter, for example).

THE PEOPLE THAT TIME FORGOT ★½
UK 1977; colour; 90 mins; Amicus/AIP; D Kevin Connor; P John Dark; W Patrick Tilley, also Connor and Maurice Carter, from the novel by Edgar Rice Burroughs; M John Scott; C Alan Hume; PD Maurice Carter; SPFX John Richardson, Ian Wingrove; Starring Patrick Wayne, Sarah Douglas, Dana Gillespie, Thorley Walters, Dave Prowse, Doug McClure, Milton Reid; V Embassy (USA). The third and last of the Amicus lost-world films adapted from Edgar Rice Burroughs, this was the direct sequel to The Land That Time Forgot. (The other was At the Earth's Core.) The films were moderately popular, but were all pot-boilers. Well, this one was more a pot-simmerer, with perfunctory monsters (pterodactyl, giant spider etc.), fat cavemen (Milton Reid is good here), and that damned volcano again.

PERCEVAL LE GALLOIS ★★★★
France 1978; colour; 140 mins; Films du Losange-FR3-ARD-RAI/Gaumont; D/W Eric Rohmer from the twelfth-century romance by Chrétien De Troyes; M Guy Robert; C Nestor Almendros; AD J. Pierre Kohut-Svelko; Starring Fabrice Luchini, André Dussolier, Ariel Dussolier Dombas, Marc Eyraud, Marie-Christine Barrault. A real oddity, this very stylized version of an old Arthurian legend, in which a naive, innocent knight becomes a great champion and comes to understand the meaning of the Grail and the Passion of Christ. "My aim...was to visualize the events Chrétien narrated as medieval paintings or miniatures might have done", said Rohmer. The décor, with its metal trees and gilded, cardboard toy castles, has a strange conviction after a while, as does the curious literary device whereby the actors comment on their own actions, much like a Chorus in a Greek tragedy. Most critics found the assumed naivety of the film false and pretentious, but others found moments of true, moving poetry.

THE PERFECT WOMAN ★★★
UK 1949; b/w; 89 mins; Two Cities/Eagle-Lion; D Bernard Knowles; P George and Alfred Black; W George Black, Knowles, also J. B. Boothroyd, from the play by Wallace Geoffrey and Basil Mitchell; M Arthur Wilkinson; C Jack Hildyard; AD J. Elder Wills; Starring Patricia Roc, Stanley Holloway, Nigel Patrick, Miles Malleson, Irene Handl. Early British SF comedy, now mostly forgotten. Surprisingly indecent for the period, with confusion between a robot and the woman (the inventor's niece) it was modelled on leading to sexual hi-jinks of a farcical kind, when the niece (Roc) takes the robot's place during testing. Enterprisingly fetishistic underwear is a feature; good malfunction sequence at the end when damaged robot, sparking and emitting smoke, causes chaos in a hotel.

PHANTASM ★★★ ☻
USA 1978; colour; 89 mins; New Breed; D/P/W/C Don Coscarelli; M Fred Myrow, Malcolm Seagrove; PD S. Tyer; SPFX Paul Pepperman, (silver sphere) Willard Green; Starring Angus Scrimm, Michael Baldwin, Bill Thornbury; V VCL (UK), CBS/Fox (USA).

THE PHANTOM OF LIBERTY (LE FANTÔME DE LA LIBERTÉ) ★★★★½
France 1974; colour; 104 mins; Greenwich; *D* Luis Buñuel; *P* Serge Silberman; *W* Buñuel, Jean-Claude Carrière; *C* Edmond Richard; *AD* Pierre Guffroy; *SPFX* François Sune; *Starring* Bernard Verley, Jean-Claude Brialy, Monica Vitti, Michel Lonsdale, Marie-France Pisier, Jean Rochefort, Michel Piccoli.

PHANTOM OF THE PARADISE ★★★
USA 1974; colour; 91 mins; Pressman Williams-Harbor/20th Century-Fox; *D/W* Brian De Palma; *P* Edward R. Pressman; *M/Songs* Paul Williams; *C* Larry Pizer; *PD* Jack Fisk; *SPFX* Greg Auer; *Starring* Paul Williams, William Finley, Jessica Harper.

PHASE IV ★★½
UK 1973; colour; 91 mins (cut to 84 mins); Alced-PBR/Paramount; *D* Saul Bass; *P* Paul B. Radin; *W* Mayo Simon; *M* Brian Gascoigne, also Yamashta and David Vorhaus; *C* Dick Bush, (ants) Ken Middleham; *AD* John Barry; *SPFX* John Richardson; *Starring* Nigel Davenport, Lynne Frederick, Michael Murphy; *V* CBS/Fox (USA). Excellent insect photography does not quite compensate for the silliness of the concept, in this tale of intelligent ants in the desert waging a battle with obsessive scientist (Davenport) and girlfriend (Frederick). She is psychically taken over, and at the end both are transformed into the first of a new slave-form of life to serve the ants. A 2001-like surrealist montage at the end, showing evolutionary upheaval (to rhythms by Yamashta) was cut by the studio after the initial release. Sad that brilliant designer Bass did not do better in his directorial debut.

PICNIC AT HANGING ROCK ★★★★
Australia 1975; colour; 115 mins; Picnic/BEF; *D* Peter Weir; *P* Hal and Jim McElroy; *W* Cliff Green from the novel by Joan Lindsay; *C* Russell Boyd; *AD* David Copping; *Starring* Rachel Roberts, Dominic Guard, Helen Morse; *V* Home Video (UK), Vestron (USA).

THE PICTURE OF DORIAN GRAY ★★★★
USA 1945; b/w (colour inserts); 110 mins; MGM; *D/W* Albert Lewin from the novel by Oscar Wilde; *P* Pandro S. Berman; *M* Herbert Stothart; *C* Harry Stradling; *AD* Cedric Gibbons, Hans Peters; *Portrait* Ivan Albright; *Starring* Hurd Hatfield, George Sanders, Donna Reed, Lowell Gilmore, Angela Lansbury, *voice of* Sir Cedric Hardwicke. Elegant version of the Wilde classic, with Hatfield's frozen, haughty, Adonis-like features oddly appropriate for Gray, the ever more wicked man who stays young while his portrait ages. Lewin's idea of decadence looks a little romantic and old-fashioned now, but then so does the novel's. Albright's splendidly twisted, Gothic portrait develops interestingly through the film, and at the powerful climax is seen in colour, though the film has been in black-and-white. Lewin went on to direct another sinister, romantic fantasy: *Pandora and the Flying Dutchman*.

THE PIED PIPER ★★★½
UK 1971; colour; 90 mins; Sagittarius/Goodtimes; *D* Jacques Demy; *P* David Puttnam, Sanford Lieberson; *W* Andrew Birkin, Demy, Mark Peploe; *M/Songs* Donovan; *C* Peter Suschitzky; *PD* Assheton Gorton; *SPFX* John Stears; *Starring* Donovan, Donald Pleasence, Jack Wild, Michael Hordern, John Hurt; *V* Home Video Merchandisers (UK). The old story of the town plagued with rats, and saved by a mysterious piper who then spirits away the children, is here done as a musical, with rather forgettable songs. It has surprisingly sinister moments, though, for a film presumably made mainly for children. French director, but British film.

PINK FLOYD THE WALL ★½
UK 1982; colour; 95 mins; Tin Blue-Goldcrest/MGM; *D* Alan Parker; *P* Alan Marshall; *W* Roger Waters from the album *The Wall* by Pink Floyd; *M* Roger Waters, played by Pink Floyd; *C* Peter Biziou; *PD* Brian Morris; *SPFX* Martin Gutteridge, Graham Longhurst; *Animation D/designer* Gerald Scarfe; *Starring* Bob Geldof, Bob Hoskins; *V* Thorn EMI (UK), MGM/UA (USA).

PIRANHA ★★★ 🐟
USA 1978; colour; 94 mins; Piranha/New World; *D* Joe Dante; *P* Jon Davison, Chako Van Leeuwen; *W* John Sayles; *M* Pino Donaggio; *C* Jamie Anderson; *SPFX* Jon Berg, (creature design and animation) Phil Tippett, (make-up) Rob Bottin, Vincent Prentice; *Starring* Bradford Dillman, Heather Menzies, Kevin McCarthy, Keenan Wynn, Barbara Steele, Dick Miller; *V* Warner (UK and USA).

THE PIT AND THE PENDULUM ★★★½
USA 1961; colour; 85 mins; Alta Vista/AIP; *D/P* Roger Corman; *W* Richard Matheson from the story by Edgar Allan Poe; *M* Les Baxter; *C* Floyd Crosby; *AD* Daniel Haller; *SPFX* (photographic) Butler-Glouner, Ray Mercer; *Starring* Vincent Price, Barbara Steele, John Kerr, Luana Anders; *V* Guild (UK), Warner (USA). The familiar formula for Corman's Poe adaptations: the slow tracks through the old house, the bluish pastel colours, the epicene, haunted presence of Vincent Price hamming it up. There is undeniable style, but whether or not it is good style is another question. Kerr is the young Englishman who comes to Price's castle in the sixteenth century, looking for his sister. Price believes himself to be his own father, a Spanish inquisitor. The stagey torture chamber with the razor-edged pendulum is quite good. So is Barbara Steele, whose face is a sort of huge-eyed icon of the whole horror genre.

THE PLAGUE OF THE ZOMBIES ★★★½ 🐟
UK 1966; colour; 91 mins; Hammer/Associated British-Pathe–20th Century-Fox; *D* John Gilling; *P* Anthony Nelson-Keys; *W* Peter Bryan; *M* James Bernard; *AD* Bernard Robinson; *SPFX* Bowie Films; *Starring* André Morell, Diane Clare, Jacqueline Pearce, John Carson.

PLANET OF BLOOD – *see* PLANET OF THE VAMPIRES

PLANET OF THE APES ★★★★
USA 1968; colour; 112 mins; Apjac/20th Century-Fox; *D* Franklin J. Schaffner; *P* Arthur P. Jacobs; *W* Michael Wilson, Rod Serling from *La Planète des Singes* by Pierre Boulle; *M* Jerry Goldsmith; *C* Leon Shamroy; *AD* Jack Martin Smith, William Creber; *SPFX* (make-up design) John Chambers, (photography) L. B. Abbott, Art Cruickshank, Emil Kosa Jr; *Starring* Charlton Heston, Roddy McDowall, Kim Hunter, Maurice Evans, Linda Harrison; *V* CBS/Fox (UK and USA).

PLANET OF THE VAMPIRES (TERRORE NELLO SPAZIO, aka PLANET OF BLOOD) ★★★½ 🐟
Italy 1965; colour; 100 mins; Italian International/Castilla Cinematográfica Cooperativa; *D* Mario Bava; *P* Fulvio Lucisano; *W* Alberto Bevilacqua, Cosulich, Bava, Antonio Roman, Rafael J. Salvia (English version by Louis M. Heyward and Ib Melchior) from "Una notte di 21 ore" by Renato Pestriniero; *M* Gino Marinuzzi Jr; *C* Antonio Rinaldi; *AD* Giorgio Giovannini; *Starring* Barry Sullivan, Norma Bengell, Angel Aranda. Visually lush blend of horror and SF, shot with the restless, swooping camera that Bava habitually favours. One of his better films. Barry Sullivan's spaceship has no sooner landed than his crew starts acting homicidally. Three corpses are buried only to emerge mysteriously from the soil in a wonderful moment a little later, wrapped in their polythene shrouds. Vampiric disembodied spirits take over the crew; blood is spilt; the ultimate plan is to use zombie-astronauts to conquer Earth. All quite colourful.

POLTERGEIST ★★★½ 🐟
USA 1982; colour; 114 mins; SLM/MGM; *D* Tobe Hooper; *P* Steven Spielberg, Frank Marshall; *W* Spielberg, Michael Grais, Mark Victor from a story by Spielberg; *M* Jerry Goldsmith; *C* Matthew F. Leonetti; *PD* James H. Spencer; *SPFX* (visual) Industrial Light and Magic, (visual supervision) Richard Edlund, (animation supervision) John Bruno, (mechanical) Michael Wood, (make-up) Craig Reardon; *Starring* Jobeth Williams, Craig T. Nelson, Oliver Robbins, Heather O'Rourke, Beatrice Straight, Dominique Dunne; *V* MGM/UA (UK and USA).

POPEYE ★★★★½
USA 1980; colour; 114 mins; Disney/Paramount; *D* Robert Altman; *P* Robert Evans; *W* Jules Feiffer from characters created in the comic strip by E. C. Segar; *M and lyrics* Harry Nilsson; *C* Giuseppe Rotunno; *PD* Wolf Kroeger; *SPFX* Allen Hall, (make-up) Giancarlo Del Brocco, (animation) Ellis Burman and others; *Starring* Robin Williams, Shelley Duvall, Ray Walston, Paul Dooley, Paul L. Smith, Wesley Ivan Hurt; *V* Disney (UK), Paramount (USA).

PORTRAIT OF JENNIE (aka JENNIE) ★★★
USA 1948; part colour; 86 mins; Selznick; *D* William Dieterle; *P* David O. Selznick; *W* Paul Osborn, Peter Berneis from the novel by Robert Nathan adapted by Leonardo Bercovici; *M* Dimitri Tiomkin (based on themes by Claude Debussy); *C* Joseph August; *AD* J. McMillan Johnson; *SPFX* Paul Eagler, Johnson and others; *Starring* Jennifer Jones, Joseph Cotten, Ethel Barrymore, Cecil Kellaway; *V* Guild (UK).

POSSESSION ★★★ 🐟🐟
France/West Germany 1981; colour; 127 mins; Oliane/Marianne/Soma; *D* Andrzej Zulawski; *P* Marie-Laure Reyre; *W* Zulawski, also Frédéric Tuten; *M* Andrzej Korzynski; *C* Bruno Nuytten; *SPFX* Daniel Braunschweig, Charles-Henri Assola, (creature) Carlo Rambaldi; *Starring* Isabelle Adjani, Sam Neill, Heinz Bennent; *V* VTC (UK).

THE POSSESSION OF JOEL DELANEY ★★½
USA 1971; colour; 108 mins; Haworth/ITC; *D* Waris Hussein; *W* Matt Robinson, Grimes Grice from the novel by Ramona Stewart; *M* Joe Raposo; *C* Arthur J. Ornitz; *PD* Peter Murton; *Starring* Shirley MacLaine, Perry King, Michael Hordern; *V* Precision (UK).

THE POWER ★★★
USA 1967; colour; 109 mins; Galaxy/MGM; *D* Byron Haskin; *P* George Pal; *W* John Gay from the novel by Frank M. Robinson; *M* Miklos Rozsa; *C* Ellsworth Fredricks; *AD* George W. Davis, Merrill Pye; *SPFX* (visual) J. McMillan Johnson, Gene Warren, Wah Chang; *Starring* George Hamilton, Suzanne Pleshette, Michael Rennie, Earl Holliman, Aldo Ray. SF movie whose narrative interestingly anticipates Cronenberg's *Scanners* and De Palma's *The Fury*. A scientist (Hamilton) realizes that one of his colleagues has frighteningly strong mental powers and much of the film is devoted to figuring out which one; the idea of somebody who can kill by thought is quite well and frighteningly expressed. A bit slow overall, with fewer special effects than usual in a Pal film (he was in conflict with MGM at the time), but atmospheric, gripping, and ahead of its time. Good twist ending. It also anticipates later films dealing with the next step in human evolution. All this was commonplace in fiction, but unusual in movies (which tend to simplify SF plots to the infantile level, for fear that otherwise nobody will understand them).

THE PREMATURE BURIAL ★★★
USA 1962; colour; 81 mins; Santa Clara-Filmgroup/AIP; *D/P* Roger Corman; *W* Charles Beaumont, Ray Russell from the story by Edgar Allan Poe; *M* Ronald Stein; *C* Floyd Crosby; *AD* Daniel Haller; *SPFX* Pat Dinga; *Starring* Ray Milland, Hazel Court, Richard Ney, Heather Angel; *V* Guild (UK). Either you like Corman's Poe adaptations or you don't. The Gothic paraphernalia, dreamlike slowness and claustrophobic atmosphere remain fairly constant from film to film (the first was *House of Usher*; the best include *Tomb of Ligeia* and *Masque of the Red Death*). Milland plays the man with a terror of being buried alive. Guess what happens? Not recommended for cataleptics.

PRISONER OF THE SKULL – *see* WHO?

PROPHECY ★★
USA 1979; colour; 102 mins; Paramount; *D* John Frankenheimer; *P* Robert L. Rosen; *W* David Seltzer; *M* Leonard Rosenman; *C* Harry Stradling Jr; *SPFX* Robert Dawson, (creature design and make-up) Tom Burman; *Starring* Talia Shire, Robert Foxworth, Armand Assante, Richard Dysart; *V* CIC (UK), Paramount (USA). Ecological horror, like *Frogs*, *Kingdom of the Spiders*, *Piranha* or *Wolfen*, but not nearly as good. Bigname director Frankenheimer proves that you cannot make a good monster movie by formula alone; the result is merely patronizing. Paper-mill effluent (a mercuric fungicide) is poisoning waterways, and causing abortions in the local Indians. It also somehow creates a large, bear-like thing with two curiously repugnant babies. This hangs about in the woods and eats people, including several of the cast. The sub-plot of the heroine's pregnancy ("Will my baby be born deformed?") is crassly executed, and the whole film has the cynical air of trying to cash in on an area of legitimate public concern without any real conviction. The ending – the tiredest of horror cliches – always gets an unintended laugh.

PROVIDENCE ★★★★½ ☻
France/Switzerland 1977; colour; 107 mins; Action/Société Française/FR3/Citel; *D* Alain Resnais; *P* Klaus Hellwig, Yves Gasser, Yves Peyrot; *W* David Mercer; *M* Miklos Rozsa; *C* Ricardo Aronovitch; *AD* Jacques Saulnier; *Starring* Dirk Bogarde, Ellen Burstyn, David Warner, John Gielgud, Elaine Stritch; *V* RCA/Columbia (USA). We move through dim parkland and shrubbery to a rambling house where an old writer (Gielgud), in pain, is apparently remembering incidents involving his children, but some of these are very strange; for example, his son Claud (Bogarde) prosecutes a soldier in court whose defence is that his victim was a werewolf; later Claud shoots Woodford (Warner), a shambling fellow who is also becoming animal-like. Other incidents have a subtle wrongness about them; the jigsaw puzzle is very complex. Only at the end do we see Gielgud relaxing with his ordinary-seeming family (including Claud and Woodford), and we realize that everything that has gone before was as much fantasy as memory, the old writer's last fiction, which may have contained some metaphorical truth. A very good, subtle film *about* fantasies and the fantastic.

THE PSYCHIC (SETTE NOTTE IN NERO) **★★ ☻**
Italy 1979 (made 1977); colour; 89 mins; Cinecompany; *D* Lucio Fulci; *P* Fulvio Frizzi; *W* Dardano Sarchetti; *M* Fabio Frizzi; *C* Sergio Salvati; *Starring* Jennifer O'Neill, Gabriele Ferzetti, Marc Porel, Gianni Garko; *V* Catalina (USA). More story and less sensation than usual from the king of Italian nasties; dream and reality mingle (with a few brutal shocks) in this rather pedestrian suspense story about a female psychic who foresees her own murder without at first realizing it.

PSYCHOMANIA ★★½
UK 1972; colour; 91 mins; Benmar; *D* Don Sharp; *P* Andrew Donally; *W* Arnaud D'Usseau; *M* David Whitaker; *C* Ted Moore; *AD* Maurice Carter; *SPFX* Patrick Moore; *Starring* George Sanders, Beryl Reid, Nicky Henson, Mary Larkin, Robert Hardy; *V* Home Video (UK), Media (USA). Hardcore fans of the more absurd aspects of pop horror love this ridiculous mixture of living-dead and hell's-angel genres whose amusing script goes way over the top. Dead biker returns to convince his gang that life is more fun when you're dead; they all get dead too (except for nice girlfriend) and commit anti-social acts. There is a magic frog, a satanic butler, people literally turning to stone and a motorcycle roaring up out of the ground. The bikers tend to have up-market, middle-class accents.

PUNISHMENT PARK ★★
USA 1971; colour; 89 mins; Chartwell/Françoise; *D* Peter Watkins; *P* Susan Martin; *W* Peter Watkins and cast; *M* Paul Motian; *C* Joan Churchill; *AD* David Hancock; *Starring* Paul Alelyanes, Carmen Argenziano, Stan Armsted. Strident, counterculture, SF propaganda piece by angry left-wing film-maker (see also *Gladiatorerna*) whose fictions tend to be presented in a *cinéma-vérité* style as if they were documentary. Young dissidents and undesirables are given a choice between prison and a three-day ordeal in the desert where they have to avoid being picked up by assault forces before they reach home base. All this is being recorded by a TV crew, who are appalled (standing in for us, no doubt, as voyeurs, just in case we've missed the point). Even the winners lose in this grim fable set in a near-future USA – and, one must say, a USA envisaged by a particularly humourless foreigner. Scary movie, though.

Q – THE WINGED SERPENT (aka THE WINGED SERPENT) **★★★★ ☻**.
USA 1982; Larco; *D/P/W* Larry Cohen; *M* Robert O. Ragland; *C* Fred Murphy; *SPFX* (visual) Randy Cook, David Allen, Peter Kuran, Lost Arts, Roger Dicken; *Starring* Michael Moriarty, Candy Clark, David Carradine, Richard Roundtree; *V* Hokushin (UK).

QUATERMASS AND THE PIT (aka FIVE MILLION YEARS TO EARTH) **★★★**
UK 1967; colour; 98 mins; Hammer/Seven Arts; *D* Roy Ward Baker; *P* Anthony Nelson Keys; *W* Nigel Kneale from his BBC TV serial; *M* Tristram Cary; *SPFX* Bowie Films; *Starring* James Donald, Andrew Keir, Barbara Shelley. The third and, some think, the best of Hammer's Quatermass films, and the only one in colour. The story of a Martian spaceship dug up during building works in London – first thought to be an unexploded bomb – is excellent. It turns out (in a complex and subtle plot) that our racial memories – Jungian archetypes – were programmed by Martians millions of years ago, and the ship contains a dormant device (now reactivated) to reinforce them, including a Lemming-like desire for destruction. The final scenes, as London starts to go crazy, are imaginative, though generally the execution of the film is not as good as its screenplay. Well above average, though.

QUATERMASS II (aka ENEMY FROM SPACE) **★★★**
UK 1957; b/w; 85 mins; Hammer; *D* Val Guest; *P* Anthony Hinds; *W* Guest, Nigel Kneale from the BBC/TV serial by Kneale; *M* James Bernard; *C* Gerald Gibbs; *AD* Bernard Robinson; *Starring* Brian Donlevy, John Longden, Sidney James, Bryan Forbes. This is the movie sequel to *The Quatermass Xperiment*. Nigel Kneale repudiated it, disliking Donlevy's performance as Professor Quatermass, and Guest's rewriting of his screenplay. When the rights reverted to him in 1965, he withdrew the film from circulation. Actually, this story about humans (including some in government) being taken over by aliens – hive-minds – who have landed in hollow meteorites is not bad, though not nearly as good as *Invasion of the Body Snatchers* the year before.

THE QUATERMASS XPERIMENT (aka THE CREEPING UNKNOWN) **★★★**
UK 1955; b/w; 82 mins; Hammer/Exclusive-United Artists; *D* Val Guest; *P* Anthony Hinds; *W* Guest, Richard Landau, from the BBC TV serial by Nigel Kneale; *M* James Bernard; *C* Walter Harvey; *AD* J. Elder Wills; *SPFX* Les Bowie; *Starring* Brian Donlevy, Jack Warner, Margia Dean, Richard Wordsworth; *V* Walton (UK).

THE QUEEN OF SPADES ★★★★
UK 1948; b/w; 96 mins; World Screen Plays/Associated British; *D* Thorold Dickinson; *P* Anatole de Grunwald; *W* Rodney Ackland, Arthur Boys from the story by Alexander Pushkin; *M* Georges Auric; *C* Otto Heller; *AD* Oliver Messel; *Starring* Anton Walbrook, Edith Evans, Ronald Howard, Yvonne Mitchell; *V* Thorn EMI (UK). Modest, crisp atmospheric version of Pushkin's often filmed story. (There are eight silent versions, four more recent versions.) Russia in 1806: Walbrook plays the impoverished, likeable young army officer who learns of the countess (Edith Evans) who has sold her soul for the secret of winning at cards; he is determined to get the secret from her, but she dies of fright when he breaks into her home. The macabre story does not quite end there, however. Elegantly mounted, well played, rather literary in style.

QUELLA VILLA ACCANTO AL CIMITERO – see THE HOUSE BY THE CEMETERY

QUEST FOR FIRE ★★★
France/Canada 1981; colour; 100 mins; ICC-Cine-Trail/Belstar/Stephan; *D* Jean-Jacques Annaud; *P* John Kemeny, Denis Héroux; *W* Gérard Brach from *La Guerre du Feu* by J. H. Rosny, prehistoric language created by Anthony Burgess; *M* Philippe Sarde; *C* Claude Agostini; *PD* Guy Comtois, Brian Morris; *SPFX* Martin Malivoire, (mammoth costume) Colin On, (creative make-up consultant) Christopher Tucker, (body language and gestures) Desmond Morris; *Starring* Everett McGill, Ron Perlman, Nameer El-Kadi, Rae Dawn Chong; *V* CBS/Fox (UK and USA).

THE QUESTOR TAPES ★★★
USA 1974; made for TV; colour; 100 mins; Universal; *D* Richard A. Colla; *P* Gene Roddenberry, Howie Hurwitz; *W* Roddenberry, Gene L. Coon; *M* Gil Melle; *C* Michael Margulies; *AD* Phil Barber; *SPFX* Albert Whitlock; *Starring* Robert Foxworth, Mike Farrell, John Vernon, Lew Ayres, Dana Wynter. Produced by Gene Roddenberry, creator of *Star Trek*, it was to be the pilot for a TV series which NBC cancelled, believing that Farrell (who went on to play Dr Hunnicutt in *M★A★S★H*) would not be popular. Probably Roddenberry's best work after *Star Trek*, this SF melodrama features an android (Foxworth) with great powers, left on Earth as a guardian to humanity by an alien race. His programming was faulty, however, and the story involves his attempts to rediscover his purpose and origins. Questor's not-quite-human behaviour leads to some good, amusing sequences.

QUINTET ★★★★
USA 1979; colour; 118 mins; Lion's Gate/20th Century-Fox; *D/P* Robert Altman; *W* Frank Barhydt, Altman, Patricia Resnick; *M* Tom Pierson; *C* Jean Boffety; *PD* Leon Ericksen; *SPFX* Tom Fisher, John Thomas, (designer) David Horton; *Starring* Paul Newman, Vittorio Gassman, Brigitte Fossey, Fernando Rey, Bibi Andersson; *V* CBS/Fox (UK).

RABID ★★★½ ☻ ☻
Canada 1976; colour; 91 mins; Cinepix/Dibar Syndicate; *D/W* David Cronenberg; *P* John Dunning; *M* Ivan Reitman; *C* René Verzier; *AD* Claude Marchand; *SPFX* Al Griswold, (make-up) Joe Blasco; *Starring* Marilyn Chambers, Frank Moore, Joe Silver; *V* Intervision (UK), Warner (USA).

RACE WITH THE DEVIL ★★★
USA 1975; colour; 88 mins; Saber-Maslansky/20th Century-Fox; *D* Jack Starrett; *P* Wes Bishop; *W* Lee Frost, Bishop; *M* Leonard Rosenman; *C* Robert Jessup; *SPFX* Richard Helmer; *Starring* Peter Fonda, Warren Oates, Loretta Swit, R. G. Armstrong. *V* CBS/Fox (UK). Trivial but amusing story that rushes along at a great pace, and keeps the interest up. Two couples accidentally witness sacrifice by witch cult while camping in Texas; they are seen and their recreational vehicle followed; most of the film is a protracted chase sequence in which it seems that the whole of North Texas (including the cops) are secret cult members. Only real fantasy element is in downbeat ending where, just as they think they've got away, magic is used against them. Standard exploitation fare, but the crossing of genres between road movie and horror film is quite well done.

RADON – see RODAN

RAIDERS OF THE LOST ARK ★★★★½
USA 1981; colour; 115 mins; Lucasfilm/Paramount; *D* Steven Spielberg; *P* George Lucas, Howard Kazanjian, Frank Marshall; *W* Lawrence Kasdan from a story by George Lucas and Philip

Kaufman; *M* John Williams; *C* Douglas Slocombe; *PD* Norman Reynolds; *SPFX* (visual supervision) Richard Edlund, (visual) Industrial Light & Magic, (mattes) Alan Maley, (mechanical) Kit West, (models) Keith Short, (make-up) Christopher Walas; *Starring* Harrison Ford, Karen Allen, Paul Freeman, Ronald Lacey, Denholm Elliott; *V* CIC (UK), Paramount (USA).

THE RAVEN ★★★

USA 1963; colour; 86 mins; Alta Vista/AIP; *D/P* Roger Corman; *W* Richard Matheson suggested remotely by the poem by Edgar Allan Poe; *M* Les Baxter; *C* Floyd Crosby; *AD* Daniel Haller; *SPFX* Pat Dinga; *Starring* Vincent Price, Peter Lorre, Boris Karloff, Hazel Court, Jack Nicholson. After doing well with four ''serious'' Poe adaptations *(House of Usher, Pit and the Pendulum, Premature Burial, Tales of Terror)* Corman decided to make a Poe spoof, with three famous horror actors; Peter Lorre, who when he first appears has been turned into a raven by evil Karloff, carries off the acting honours as the least efficient of the three sorcerers conducting a duel of magic in sixteenth century England. Jack Nicholson, in an early performance as Lorre's son, keeps a commendable poker face. Terribly hammy, but quite funny in a grotesque way – though not like anything in Poe.

RAW MEAT – *see* DEATH LINE

THE RED SHOES ★★★★

UK 1948; colour; 133 mins; Archers/Rank; *D/P/W* Michael Powell, Emeric Pressburger from a story by Pressburger; *M* Brian Easdale; *C* Jack Cardiff; *PD* Hein Heckroth; *Choreographer* Robert Helpmann; *Starring* Moira Shearer, Anton Walbrook, Marius Goring, Helpmann, Leonide Massine; *V* Rank (UK).

THE REINCARNATION OF PETER PROUD ★★

USA 1974; colour; 104 mins; Bing Crosby Productions/AIP; *D* J. Lee Thompson; *P* Charles A. Pratt; *W* Max Ehrlich from his novel; *M* Jerry Goldsmith; *C* Victor Kemper; *Starring* Michael Sarrazin, Margot Kidder, Jennifer O'Neill, Cornelia Sharpe. Very low-key story about young male teacher with nightmares slowly coming to realize he is reincarnation of man who was murdered in 1946 by his wife. Seeks out the wife (now in her fifties), falls in love with daughter (his daughter in a sense). Rather a dull story, honestly but routinely told; good performance from Kidder aged 28 and 53 fails to compensate.

REKOPIS ZNALEZIONY W SARAGOSSIE – *see* THE SARAGOSSA MANUSCRIPT

THE REPTILE ★★★★

UK 1966; colour; 90 mins; Hammer/Seven Arts; *D* John Gilling; *P* Anthony Nelson Keys; *W* John Elder (Anthony Hinds); *M* Don Banks; *C* Arthur Grant; *PD* Bernard Robinson; *SPFX* Bowie Films; *Starring* Noel Willman, Jennifer Daniel, Jacqueline Pearce. Above average Hammer director shot this one back-to-back with *Plague of the Zombies*, using the same sets. Both are primarily studio films, though both are set in nineteenth-century Cornwall. This is the one where Pearce, the unfortunate daughter of the local doctor, has been cursed by an Eastern sect and periodically becomes a killer-snake (particularly horrid make-up by Roy Ashton here). Curiously sad film: it is not the poor girl's fault. An interesting father-daughter relationship, with the father (Willman) showing ambiguous feelings for the daughter, for whose plight he bears some guilt. Famous scene of snake-woman writhing on a bed to the chanting of her sinister Malay servant. The whole thing is made with surprising dignity.

REPULSION ★★★★½ ☻

UK 1965; b/w; 104 mins; Compton/Tekli; *D* Roman Polanski; *P* Gene Gutowski; *W* Polanski, Gerard Brach; *M* Chico Hamilton; *C* Gilbert Taylor; *AD* Seamus Flannery; *Starring* Catherine Deneuve, Yvonne Furneaux, John Fraser, Ian Hendry, Patrick Wymark; *V* Zodiac (UK), Video Dimensions (USA). The panel is divided on the

virtues of this film, assessments ranging from two to five stars – presumably because there is a question as to whether or not the bravura effects are pretentious. Neurotic girl (excellent performance by Deneuve) isolates herself, fears contact especially with men, stops going to work, starts hallucinating, murders both landlord and suitor in hysterics of fear when they come calling, finishes curled up in foetal position. The hallucinations are quite disturbing: expanding cracks in walls; loud, inexplicable sounds; imaginary rapist; hands bursting through the wall and reaching for her. Worst of all is the (quite real) progressively rotting carcass of a rabbit in the kitchen. Like Polanski's later film *The Tenant*, this belongs to the category of subjective-fantasy-shared-by-audience. The film has other reverberations, too: the fantasy world of the beauty parlour which shows up Deneuve's lack of contact with the real world; the sexual narcissism of the two murdered men, which is itself a form of madness, and deeply aggressive: that is to say, Deneuve's madness is not entirely without motivation. This is a feminist film in that respect.

RETURN FROM WITCH MOUNTAIN ★★

USA 1978; colour; 93 mins; Disney; *D* John Hough; *P* Ron Miller, Jerome Courtland; *W* Malcolm Marmorstein; *M* Lalo Schifrin; *C* Frank Phillips; *AD* John B. Mansbridge, Jack Senter; *SPFX* Eustace Lycett, Art Cruickshank, Danny Lee; *Starring* Bette Davis, Christopher Lee, Kim Richards, Ike Eisenmann; *V* Disney (UK). Inferior sequel to *Escape to Witch Mountain* is rather a mechanical follow-up. The two children with strange mental powers are taken (by flying saucer) to Los Angeles on a trip; Tony (Eisenmann) is kidnapped and harnessed by Bette Davis and Christopher Lee to a mind-control device; Tia (Richards) saves him with the help of a street gang. Various not-too-spectacular displays of telekinesis take place.

THE RETURN OF COUNT YORGA ★★☻

USA 1971; 97 mins; Peppertree/AIP; *D* Robert Kelljan; *P* Michael Macready; *W* Kelljan, Yvonne Wilder; *M* W. Marx; *C* Bill Butler; *SPFX* Roger George; *Starring* Robert Quarry, Mariette Hartley, Roger Perry, Yvonne Wilder. Sequel to successful low-budget shocker *Count Yorga, Vampire*, this (without explanation) resuscitates the vigorous count and his evil brides, and havoc is wreaked at an orphanage on the fringes of modern San Francisco. There is an evil boy orphan, and a repeat of the twist ending used first time round. Pretty silly, but Quarry performs with relish.

RETURN OF THE JEDI ★★★½

UK 1983; colour; 132 mins; Lucasfilm/20th Century-Fox; *D* Richard Marquand; *P* George Lucas, Howard Kazanjian; *W* Lawrence Kasdan, Lucas from a story by Lucas; *M* John Williams; *C* Alan Hume; *PD* Norman Reynolds; *Conceptual artist* Ralph McQuarrie; *SPFX* (supervision) Roy Arbogast, (miniature/optical) Industrial Light & Magic and others, (visual) Richard Edlund, Dennis Muren and Ken Ralston, (creature design/make-up) Phil Tippett and Stuart Freeborn, (mattes) Michael Pangrazio; *Starring* Mark Hamill, Harrison Ford, Carrie Fisher, Billy Dee Williams, Ian McDiarmid, Frank Oz, David Prowse, Alec Guinness, Kenny Baker.

REVENGE IS SWEET – *see* BABES IN TOYLAND (1934)

THE REVENGE OF FRANKENSTEIN ★★★

UK 1958; colour; Hammer/Columbia; *D* Terence Fisher; *P* Anthony Hinds; *W* Jimmy Sangster, also H. Hurford Janes; *M* Leonard Salzedo; *C* Jack Asher; *PD* Bernard Robinson; *SPFX* (make-up) Phil Leakey; *Starring* Peter Cushing, Francis Matthews, Eunice Gayson, Michael Gwynn, Lionel Jeffries. A number of critics believe that this sequel to *Curse of Frankenstein* is the best of the generally disappointing *Frankenstein* series from Hammer. It did not do terribly well, however, and there was a six-year wait for the next, the inferior *Evil of Frankenstein*. In *Revenge* Frankenstein (Cushing), masquerading as Dr Stein, is working

on behalf of the underprivileged in a workhouse hospital, which is a convenient source of body parts. (Frankenstein's liberality and sadism are neatly balanced in this film.) His hunchback assistant (Gwynn) is given a new body, but when he is subsequently injured, his body reverts and he stumbles screaming into a local posh party, thus giving his master away. Frankenstein is then beaten horribly by his own patients, but in a twist ending he, too, comes to inhabit a new body. The mythic machinery of the Frankenstein story was quite finely tuned this time around.

THE REVENGE OF THE BLOOD BEAST (LA SORELLA DI SATANA, aka SHE BEAST) ★★½

Italy 1965; colour; 76 mins; Leith; *D* Mike Reeves; *P* Paul M. Maslansky; *W* Michael Byron (Reeves); *M* Ralph Ferraro; *C* G. Gengarelli; *Starring* Barbara Steele, Ian Ogilvy, John Karlsen. Extremely low-budget Italian horror pic, about young woman on holiday in Transylvania possessed by long-dead witch's spirit, is of interest as being the first film by Reeves; he was the Keats (so to speak) of low-budget horror, an *enfant terrible* who died young. (See also *The Sorcerers, Witchfinder General*.) His depressing theme – the way evil and cruelty can permeate the lives of quite ordinary, decent people – is foreshadowed here. The decaying features of the drowned witch become a symbol of the process. (This has nothing to do with *Night of the Blood Beast*, a hack SF movie of 1958.)

REVENGE OF THE CREATURE ★★

USA 1955; b/w; 3-D; 82 mins; Universal-International; *D* Jack Arnold; *P* William Alland; *W* Martin Berkeley from a story by Alland; *M* Herman Stein; *C* Charles S. Welbourne; *SPFX* (make-up) Bud Westmore; *Starring* John Agar, Lori Nelson John Bromfield.

REVENGE OF THE VAMPIRE – *see* BLACK SUNDAY

RIDERS TO THE STARS ★½

USA 1954; colour; 81 mins; A-Men/United Artists; *D* Richard Carlson; *P* Ivan Tors; *W* Curt Siodmak; *M* Harry Sukman; *C* Stanley Cortez; *AD* Jerome Pycha Jr; *SPFX* Harry Redmond Jr, (photographic) Jack R. Glass; *Starring* William Lundigan, Herbert Marshall, Richard Carlson, Martha Hycr, Dawn Addams. This is included in the book for nostalgic reasons, as being almost certainly the silliest SF film ever made; this paradoxically gives it a high entertainment value for anybody scientifically literate – for them, it's a laugh a minute. The premise is that cosmic rays will make space travel dangerous, because they destroy metals outside the Earth's atmosphere. But meteors make it safely to Earth. Therefore meteors must be coated with an anti-cosmic-ray substance. Three men must be chosen to go up in rockets with great scoops attached and catch meteors, thus saving the space programme. With many grim-jawed heroics this is done, and the miracle substance turns out (not very usefully) to be diamond. This is absurd on too many counts to be enumerated here. Tors produced many fantasy films (see *Gog*), and Siodmak wrote many (see *Hauser's Memory*); it was, however, actor Carlson's only film as director.

THE ROAD WARRIOR – *see* MAD MAX 2

ROBINSON CRUSOE ON MARS ★★★½

USA 1964; colour; 110 mins; Devonshire/Paramount; *D* Byron Haskin; *P* Aubrey Schenck; *W* Ib Melchior, John C. Higgins from novel *The Life and Strange Surprising Adventures of Robinson Crusoe* by Daniel Defoe; *M* Nathan Van Cleave; *C* Winton C. Hoch; *AD* Hal Pereira, Arthur Lonergan; *SPFX* (photographic) Lawrence W. Butler; *Starring* Paul Mantee, Vic Lundin, Adam West. One of the best SF films made by experienced but not brilliant SF director Haskin (*War of the Worlds, From the Earth to the Moon, The Power*, among others). Good special effects, as in all his films. Astronaut (Mantee), crashlanded on Mars with only a monkey as companion (his co-pilot – West – is killed), is amazed to find alien humanoid Man

Friday (Lundin), who has escaped from cruel alien slave owners. The best part of the film may be the astronaut's solitary struggle to survive, rather than the space-opera melodrama that follows. Death Valley plays the role of Mars convincingly.

ROCKETSHIP – *see* FLASH GORDON (1936)

THE ROCKY HORROR PICTURE SHOW ★★★
UK 1975; colour; 101 mins; 20th Century-Fox; *D* Jim Sharman; *P* Michael White, John Goldstone; *W* Jim Sharman, Richard O'Brien from the stage musical by O'Brien; *M/Songs* O'Brien; *C* Peter Suschitzky; *AD* Terry Ackland Snow; *SPFX* Wally Veevers, (make-up) Pierre La Roche; *Starring* Tim Curry, Susan Sarandon, Barry Bostwick, Richard O'Brien, Patricia Quinn, Little Nell, Meat Loaf, Charles Gray, Jonathan Adams, Peter Hinwood.

RODAN (RADON) **★★**
Japan 1956; colour; 99 mins; Toho; *D* Inoshiro Honda; *W* Takeshi Kimura, Takeo Murata from a story by Takashi Kuronumura; *M* Akira Ifukube; *C* Isamu Ashida; *AD* Tatsuo Kita; *SPFX* Eiji Tsuburaya; *Starring* Kenji Sawara, Yuri Shirakawa, Akihiko Hirata; *V* Vestron (USA). Toho Studio's follow-up to *Godzilla* differed in being shot in a somewhat virulent colour rather than black-and-white. The American version was cut to 79 mins, with dialogue by David Duncan. H-bomb tests cause growth of huge insect larvae in a mine but, in the best scene, an egg hatches and the reptile that emerges eats the man-eating larvae. It grows into Rodan (Radon in Japanese), a kind of badly designed pterodactyl that flies with supersonic speed and damages cities; later it joins with another flying reptile; both perish in a volcano, though one (which one?) was resuscitated for later sequels. It is a bad film, but the monsters excited enough people for Toho to be sure they were on to a good thing, and dozens of monster movies followed.

ROLLERBALL ★★ ☻
USA 1975; colour; 129 mins; United Artists; *D/P* Norman Jewison; *W* William Harrison from his short story; *C* Douglas Slocombe; *PD* John Box; *SPFX* Sass Bedig, John Richardson, Joe Fitt; *Starring* James Caan, John Houseman, Maud Adams, Ralph Richardson; *V* Intervision (UK), CBS/Fox (USA).

ROSEMARY'S BABY ★★★★ ☻
USA 1968; colour; 137 mins; William Castle Enterprises/Paramount; *D/W* Roman Polanski from the novel by Ira Levin; *P* William Castle; *M* Krzysztof Komeda; *C* William A. Fraker; *PD* Richard Sylbert; *SPFX* (visual) Farciot Edouart; *Starring* Mia Farrow, John Cassavetes, Ruth Gordon, Sidney Blackmer, Maurice Evans, Ralph Bellamy, Elisha Cook Jr; *V* Paramount (USA).

LE ROUGE AUX LÈVRES – *see* DAUGHTERS OF DARKNESS

RUBY ★★½
USA 1977; colour; 85 mins; Steve Krantz; *D* Curtis Harrington; *P* George Edwards; *W* Edwards, Barry Schneider from a story by Kranz; *M* Don Ellis; *C* William Mendenhall; *Starring* Piper Laurie, Stuart Whitman, Roger Davis, Janit Baldwin; *V* Brent Walker (UK), Video Communications (USA). Ruby (Laurie) runs a drive-in cinema at which *Attack of the 50ft Woman* seems constantly to play; her employees (ex-gangsters) get rubbed out supernaturally one by one. Her mute daughter is possessed by the spirit of her long-ago murdered ex-lover, the daughter's father. Lots of blood but all done so stagily that the squeamish need not worry. Quite exceptionally ludicrous screenplay, in weakly post-*Exorcist* style.

SALEM'S LOT ★★★
USA 1979; made for TV; colour; 180 mins; Warner; *D* Tobe Hooper; *P* Richard Kobritz; *W* Paul Monash from the novel by Stephen King; *M* Harry Sukman; *PD* Mort Rabinowitz; *SPFX* Frank Torro, (make-up) Jack Young; *Starring* David Soul, James Mason, Lance Kerwin, Bonnie Bedelia,

Lew Ayres, Elisha Cook, Reggie Nalder; *V* Warner (USA).

THE SARAGOSSA MANUSCRIPT (REKOPIS ZNALEZIONY W SARAGOSSIE) **★★★½ ☻**
Poland 1965; b/w; 180 mins; Kamera/Film Polski; *D* Wojciech Has; *W* Tadeusz Kwiatkowski from the collection of linked stories by Count Jan Potocki; *M* Krzysztof Penderecki; *C* Mieczyslaw Jahoda; *Starring* Zbigniew Cybulski, Kazimierz Opalinski, Leon Niemczyk, Iga Cembrzyńska, Joanna Jędryka. Based on a very weird Polish classic little known in the West, this haunting, mysterious black comedy – which is quite true to its original – tells of the strange encounters that a brave, innocent young man has in the late eighteenth century in the deserted high-mountain country of Spain. The film consists of six or seven stories, often stories within stories, that comment upon one another in a hallucinatory, dreamlike fashion. Even at the end, when he appears to have reached safety, he sees through a window the windswept, barren hills with a gibbet on them from which he thought he had escaped. All the stories keep circling back to the same story, which involves the ghosts of hanged bandits, sexual experiences with Moorish succubi who disappear in daylight, aristocratic duellists, Casanovas, sinister hermits. The visual imagery is striking, and sometimes unpleasant (as in the plucking out of an eye). The film has faults, but it is a genuine, bizarre original – like no other fantasy film ever made. Cybulski, who stars, was one of the most popular and accomplished Polish actors of the period.

THE SATANIC RITES OF DRACULA (aka COUNT DRACULA AND HIS VAMPIRE BRIDE) **★**
UK 1973; colour; 88 mins; Hammer/Columbia; *D* Alan Gibson; *P* Roy Skeggs; *W* Don Houghton; *M* John Cacavas; *C* Brian Probyn; *SPFX* Les Bowie; *Starring* Christopher Lee, Peter Cushing, Joanna Lumley, Michael Coles, William Franklyn. The last Dracula movie Lee made for Hammer, immediate sequel to *Dracula AD 1972*, is set in modern London. British Intelligence incompetently investigates a satanist group which turns out to be headed by Dracula himself, intent on spreading bubonic plague worldwide (which will leave him with no victims – perhaps he was getting tired). Van Helsing's statutory victory is quite perfunctory, like the entire, crippled film.

SATAN'S SKIN – *see* BLOOD ON SATAN'S CLAW

SATURN 3 ★½ ☻
UK 1980; colour; 87 mins; Transcontinental/ITC; *D/P* Stanley Donen; *W* Martin Amis from a story by John Barry; *M* Elmer Bernstein; *C* Billy Williams; *PD* Stuart Craig; *SPFX* Colin Chilvers, Roy Spencer, Terry Schubert, Jeff Luff, (optical) Wally Veevers, Roy Field and Peter Parks; *Starring* Farrah Fawcett, Kirk Douglas, Harvey Keitel; *V* Precision (UK), CBS/Fox (USA).

SATYRICON – *see* FELLINI SATYRICON

SAVAGES ★★★½
USA 1972; colour; 106 mins; Angelika/Merchant-Ivory; *D* James Ivory; *P* Ismail Merchant; *W* George Swift Trow, Michael O'Donoghue from an idea by Ivory; *M* Joe Raposo; *C* Walter Lassally; *AD* James D. Rule, Jack Wright; *Starring* Louis Stadlen, Anne Francine, Thayer David, Susie Blakely, Russ Thacker, Salome Jens; *V* Home Video (UK).

SCANNERS ★★★½ ☻☻
Canada 1980; colour; 103 mins; Filmplan International; *D/W* David Cronenberg; *P* Claude Héroux; *M* Howard Shore; *C* Mark Irwin; *AD* Carol Spier; *SPFX* Gary Zeller, (make-up) Dick Smith, Chris Walas and others; *Starring* Jennifer O'Neill, Stephen Lack, Michael Ironside, Patrick McGoohan; *V* Guild (UK), CBS/Fox (USA).

THE SCARS OF DRACULA ★½ ☻
UK 1970; colour; 96 mins; Hammer/EMI; *D* Roy Ward Baker; *P* Aida Young; *W* John Elder

(Anthony Hinds); *M* James Bernard; *C* Moray Grant; *AD* Scott MacGregor; *SPFX* Roger Dicken; *Starring* Christopher Lee, Dennis Waterman, Jenny Hanley; *V* Thorn EMI (UK and USA). Very little originality in Hammer's sixth *Dracula* movie, here reduced to very tired formula. Emphasis on young couple seeking missing brother; good wall-climbing bit from Lee; bad bit where Lee uses a knife (aren't his teeth enough?); final demise of Lee from lightning bolt.

SCHLOCK ★★★
USA 1971 (released 1973); colour; 77 mins; Gazotskie; *D/W* John Landis; *P* James C. O'Rourke; *M* David Gibson; *C* Bob Collins; *SPFX* (creature) Rick Baker; *Starring* Landis, Saul Kahan, Joseph Piantadosi, Eliza Garrett, Eric Allison; *V* Astra (UK), Wizard (USA). Landis's first film (he was twenty-two at the time, and made it in two weeks) stars himself as the Schlockthropus, the thawed-out missing link, in an ape suit designed by another beginner, effects man Rick Baker. (They worked together again on *An American Werewolf in London*.) The undergraduate humour of this spoof on monster movies (especially *Trog*) is reflected in the film posters, one of which reads "Due to the horrifying nature of this film, no one will be admitted to the theatre". It's all a bit amateurish, but a lot of the jokes work well: the "erotic" scene between Schlock and the blind girl, the scene where he plays boogie on the piano, and the scene where he gets frightened at the dinosaurs in an old movie, etc. It all anticipates *National Lampoon's Animal House*, Landis's first real hit.

SCREAM AND SCREAM AGAIN ★★★
UK 1970; colour; 94 mins; Amicus/AIP; *D* Gordon Hessler; *P* Max J. Rosenberg, Milton Subotsky; *W* Christopher Wicking from *The Disoriented Man* by Peter Saxon; *M* David Whitaker; *C* John Coquillon; *PD* Bill Constable; *Starring* Vincent Price, Christopher Lee, Peter Cushing, Judy Huxtable, Alfred Marks. Critical opinions are divided on this one; most think it's dreadful, but some think it's very good. Part of the trouble is the storyline, which leaves the audience feeling (perhaps deliberately) like the title of Saxon's original novel, *The Disoriented Man*. Mysterious mutilations turn out to be connected with the creation of monstrously powerful androids who are systematically being used to take over key posts throughout the UK. (Christopher Lee, the Prime Minister, is one.) But the intricate plot takes its time in revealing all this, with apparent vampirism, Scotland Yard investigations, and all sorts of complications.

SCROOGE ★★½
UK 1970; colour; 118 mins; Waterbury/20th Century-Fox; *D* Ronald Neame; *P* Robert H. Solo; *W* Leslie Bricusse from "A Christmas Carol" by Charles Dickens; *M/Songs* Leslie Bricusse; *C* Oswald Morris; *PD* Terry Marsh; *SPFX* Wally Veevers, (photographic) Jack Mills; *Starring* Albert Finney, Alec Guinness, Edith Evans, Kenneth More. Quite enjoyable musical version of the Dickens fantasy classic, which had been filmed at least nine times before, three times in the sound era. Finney is a vigorous Scrooge, Guinness an impressive Marley. The music is nothing special, on the other hand, and the direction uninspired; the film relies almost wholly on the performances of experienced old troupers, including Evans and More as Ghosts of Christmas Past and Present.

SEASON OF THE WITCH – *see* JACK'S WIFE

SEIZURE ★★★ ☻
USA 1974; colour; 93 mins; Euro-American-Intercontinental Leisure/Cinerama; *D* Oliver Stone; *P* Garrad Glenn, Jeffrey Kapelman; *W* Edward Mann, Stone; *M* Lee Gagnon; *C* Roger Racine; *SPFX* Thomas Brumberger; *Starring* Jonathan Frid, Martine Beswick, Joe Sirola, Christine Pickles, Henry Baker, Herve Villechaize; *V* Astra (UK). Little-screened horror-fantasy, that appeared on one critic's top films of the decade list (in *Cinefantastique*). Convoluted, violent story goes over the top with author of supernatural novels perse-

cuted by his own characters coming to life: Beswick as the Queen of Evil, Villechaize as a malevolent dwarf, and Baker as a sadistic giant. These nightmares finally kill him. This was director Stone's debut. He went on to make *The Hand*, and to win an Oscar for the screenplay of *Midnight Express*.

THE SENDER ★★★
UK/USA 1982; colour; 91 mins; Kingsmere/Paramount; *D* Roger Christian; *P* Edward S. Feldman; *W* Thomas Baum; *M* Trevor Jones; *C* Roger Pratt; *AD* Steve Spence, Charles Bishop; *SPFX* Nick Allder, (make-up) Sarah Monzani; *Starring* Zeijko Ivanek, Kathryn Harrold, Shirley Knight, Paul Freeman; *V* Paramount (USA). Modest horror film, based on a similar premise to Franklin's *Patrick*: young man in hospital has telepathic and telekinetic powers. This one (Ivanek) can project images, and (as in *Videodrome*) the hallucinations are seamlessly linked to the "real" action. The intelligent but complicated story gets so confused at the end that everybody in the audience argues about what it all means; it is something to do with the Sender's possibly incestuous relationship with his mother (Knight). Always interesting, sometimes disturbing, well-acted movie, with good effects (bleeding mirrors and so on) by Allder. This was Roger Christian's debut as director; he was art director on *Alien* and *Star Wars*, and won an Oscar for the latter.

SENGOKU JIEITAI – *see* TIME SLIP

THE SENTINEL ★★ 😮
USA 1976; colour; 92 mins; Universal; *D* Michael Winner; *P/W* Winner, Jeffrey Konvitz from the novel by Konvitz; *M* Gil Melle; *C* Dick Kratina; *PD* Philip Rosenberg; *SPFX* (photographic) Albert Whitlock, (make-up) Dick Smith, Bob Laden; *Starring* Chris Sarandon, Cristina Raines, John Carradine, Ava Gardner, Burgess Meredith, Sylvia Miles, Eli Wallach, Christopher Walken; *V* CIC (UK).

SÉRAIL ★★★½
France 1976; colour; 87 mins; Filmoblic/Openfilm/Institut National de l'Audiovisuel; *D* Eduardo de Gregorio; *P* Hubert Niogret, Hugo Santiago, Jacques Zajdermann; *W* de Gregorio, Michael Graham; *M* Michel Portal; *C* Ricardo Aronovitch; *AD* Eric Simon; *SPFX* Jean-Pierre Lelong; *Starring* Leslie Caron, Bulle Ogier, Marie-France Pisier, Corin Redgrave.

SETTE NOTTE IN NERO – *see* THE PSYCHIC

THE 7 BROTHERS MEET DRACULA – *see* THE LEGEND OF THE 7 GOLDEN VAMPIRES

THE SEVEN DOORS OF DEATH – *see* THE BEYOND

7 FACES OF DR LAO ★★★
USA 1963; colour; 100 mins; Galaxy-Scarus/MGM; *D/P* George Pal; *W* Charles Beaumont from *The Circus of Dr Lao* by Finney; *M* Leigh Harline; *SPFX* (visual) Paul Byrd, Wah Chang, Jim Danforth, Ralph Rodine and Robert R. Hoag, (make-up) William Tuttle; *Starring* Tony Randall, Barbara Eden, Arthur O'Connell.

THE SEVENTH SEAL (DET SJUNDE INSEGLET) ★★★★
Sweden 1957; b/w; 95 mins; Svensk Filmindustri; *D/W* Ingmar Bergman; *M* Erik Nordgren; *C* Gunnar Fischer; *AD* P. A. Lundgren; *Starring* Max von Sydow, Gunnar Björnstrand, Bibi Andersson, Nils Poppe, Gunnel Lindblom.

THE SEVENTH VICTIM ★★★★½
USA 1943; b/w; 71 mins; RKO; *D* Mark Robson; *P* Val Lewton; *W* Charles O'Neal, DeWitt Bodeen; *M* Roy Webb; *C* Nicholas Musuraca; *AD* Albert S. D'Agostino, Walter E. Keller; *Starring* Tom Conway, Jean Brooks, Isabel Jewell, Kim Hunter, Hugh Beaumont, Evelyn Brent; *V* Nostalgia (USA). This is often regarded as the best of the short horror-thrillers that Lewton produced for RKO (see also *Cat People, Curse of the Cat People, Isle of the Dead, I Walked with a Zombie*). For a short film the story is remarkably labyrinthine. Mary (Kim Hunter) goes to New York in search of her missing sister Jacqueline (a haunted, waif-like performance from Jean Brooks). Jacqueline, it turns out, belongs to a witch cult. It is not completely clear whether or not they have genuinely occult powers, but at the end they brainwash Jacqueline into suicide, fearing she has disclosed their secrets to her psychiatrist (Conway). Synopsis does not begin to convey the atmosphere of disquiet and tension that can be conjured up in a big city. The film is very dark and pessimistic; its subtext is that for many lonely people (and cruel people too, of course) life has little value. The epigraph is from John Donne: "I run to Death, and Death meets me as fast, and all my Pleasures are like Yesterday" – itself an extraordinary touch in a low-budget thriller. Only a fringe fantasy, but it has exerted tremendous influence in the genre, and upon *film noir* generally.

THE SEVENTH VOYAGE OF SINBAD ★★★½
USA 1958; colour; 89 mins; Morningside/Columbia; *D* Nathan Juran; *P* Charles H. Schneer; *W* Kenneth Kolb from a story by Ray Harryhausen; *M* Bernard Herrmann; *C* Wilkie Cooper; *SPFX* Ray Harryhausen; *Starring* Kerwin Mathews, Kathryn Grant, Richard Eyer, Torin Thatcher; *V* Columbia (USA).

THE SHAGGY D.A. ★★
USA 1976; colour; 92 mins; Disney; *D* Robert Stevenson; *P* Bill Anderson; *W* Don Tait from *The Hounds of Florence* by Felix Salten; *M* Buddy Baker; *C* Frank Phillips; *AD* John B. Mansbridge, Perry Ferguson; *SPFX* Eustace Lycett, Art Cruickshank, Danny Lee, (mattes) P. S. Ellenshaw; *Starring* Dean Jones, Suzanne Pleshette, Tim Conway. Disney's first slapstick comedy (live action) was *The Shaggy Dog*, a big hit in 1959. It starred Tommy Kirk as the boy who periodically turned into a sheepdog through the powers of a magic ring. *The Shaggy D.A.*, almost two decades later, was the sequel, with Dean Jones as the unfortunate weredog, now grown up, and a district attorney. The usual comic romp, moderately well done. Fans of this sort of thing have said it is better than the original.

SHE BEAST – *see* THE REVENGE OF THE BLOOD BEAST

THE SHINING ★★★★ 😮
UK 1980; colour; 146 mins (often cut to 119 mins); Hawk – Peregrine – Producer Circle/Warner; *D/P* Stanley Kubrick; *W* Kubrick, Diane Johnson from the novel by Stephen King; *M* from various classical sources; *C* John Alcott; *PD* Roy Walker; *Make-up* Tom Smith, Barbara Daly; *Starring* Jack Nicholson, Shelley Duvall, Danny Lloyd, Scatman Crothers; *V* Warner (UK and USA).

SHIVERS (aka THE PARASITE MURDERS and THEY CAME FROM WITHIN) ★★★★ 😮😮😮
Canada 1974; colour; 87 mins; *D/W* David Cronenberg; *P/M* Ivan Reitman; *C* Robert Saad; *AD* Erla Gliserman; *SPFX* Joe Blasco; *Starring* Paul Hampton, Joe Silver, Lynn Lowry, Barbara Steele; *V* Intervision (UK).

SHOCK (SHOCK TRANSFERT-SUSPENCE-HYPNOS, aka BEYOND THE DOOR II) ★★★ 😮
Italy 1977; colour; 95 mins; Laser; *D* Mario Bava; *P* Juri Vasile; *W* Lamberto Bava, Francesco Barbieri, Paolo Brigenti, Dardano Sacchetti; *M* I libra; *C* Alberto Spagnoli; *AD* Francesco Vanorio; *Starring* Daria Nicolodi, John Steiner, David Collin Jr; *V* Videomedia (UK). Strong return to form in the last film Bava made before his death, perhaps because most of it was in fact shot by his son Lamberto (see *Macabre*). Scary story of woman experiencing bizarre nightmare events: her son is possessed by her dead first husband. The frights are stylishly achieved, but in between time the dialogue and performances are limp. No connection beyond the title with *Beyond the Door*.

SHOCK TREATMENT ★½
UK 1981; colour; 94 mins; 20th Century-Fox; *D* Jim Sharman; *P* John Goldstone; *W* Richard O'Brien, Sharman, also Brian Thomson; *M* Richard Hartley, O'Brien; *C* Mike Molloy; *PD* Thomson; *Starring* Cliff De Young, Jessica Harper, Patricia Quinn, Richard O'Brien, Charles Gray, Nell Campbell, Barry Humphries; *V* CBS/Fox (UK). Inferior sequel to *Rocky Horror Picture Show* clearly misses the charismatic presence of Tim Curry. Extremely normal Brad and Susan Majors (both played by new actors, the latter by Jessica Harper who was so effective in *Suspiria*) suffer through the obsessive live-TV orientation of their township Denton, Susan becoming a star, Brad locked away in the asylum run by Cosmo (O'Brien). Terribly limp all around, with only a few moments amid all the ham, and the strangely attenuated satire which constantly fails to focus on any real target other than the excesses of TV game shows. The punk style that made the earlier film so successful as a midnight movie is here both watered down and (already) dated. Pretentious. Weak songs.

SHOCK WAVES (aka ALMOST HUMAN) ★★
USA 1976; colour; 86 mins; Zopix/Lawrence Friedricks; *D* Ken Wiederhorn; *P/C* Reuben Trane; *W* John Harrison, Wiederhorn; *M* Richard Einhoen; *SPFX* (make-up) Alan Ormsby; *Starring* Peter Cushing, John Carradine, Brooke Adams; *V* Guild (UK). Strong opening with ghost ship looming up in the Caribbean (see also *Death Ship*), and good cameo from Carradine as captain of broken-down steamer, but it soon degenerates into absolute tosh about living-dead SS soldiers stalking marooned passengers and crew across small island, but really not doing much beyond looking goggled, pale and menacing, though they are effectively creepy when we see them walking under water. Cushing good as still living SS leader waiting for the resuscitation of his crew (who then dispose of him). It has a kind of lunatic charm.

THE SHOUT ★★★½
UK 1978; colour; 86 mins; Recorded Picture/Rank; *D* Jerzy Skolimowski; *P* Jeremy Thomas; *W* Michael Austin, Skolimowski from the story by Robert Graves; *M* Anthony Banks, Michael Rutherford, (electronic) Rupert Hine; *C* Mike Molloy; *AD* Simon Holland; *Starring* Alan Bates, Susannah York, John Hurt, Robert Stephens, Tim Curry; *V* Rank (UK), Columbia (USA).

SIEGFRIED – *see* DIE NIBELUNGEN

THE SILENT FLUTE (aka CIRCLE OF IRON) ★★
USA 1978; colour; 95 mins; Volare; *D* Richard Moore; *P* Sandy Howard, Paul Maslansky; *W* Stirling Silliphant, Stanley Mann from story by James Coburn, Bruce Lee and Silliphant; *M* Bruce Smeaton; *C* Ronnie Taylor; *PD* Tambi Larsen; *Starring* David Carradine, Jeff Cooper, Roddy McDowall, Eli Wallach, Christopher Lee; *V* Rank (UK). Sword-and-sorcery martial-arts movie, with Carradine as blind flautist uttering wise but incomprehensible epigrams, Cooper as earnest but thuggish novice on quest for Book of Enlightenment who inherits Carradine's mantle and flute. Carradine also plays three other roles. All good fun, with creepy monkey people, a were-panther, and attractive settings in timeless Orient (actually Israel). But the dialogue is stiff, and the spirituality banal. They do these things better in Hong Kong.

SILENT RUNNING ★★
USA 1972; colour; 89 mins; Universal; *D* Douglas Trumbull; *P* Michael Gruskoff, Mike Cimino, Steve Bochco; *M* Peter Schickele; *C* Charles F. Wheeler; *Sets* F. Lombardo; *SPFX* Richard O. Helmer and others, (photographic) Trumbull, John Dykstra and Richard Yuricich, (designs) Wayne Smith and others; *Starring* Bruce Dern; *V* MCA (USA).

SIMON ★★
USA 1980; colour; 97 mins; Orion/Warner; *D/W* Marshall Brickman from a story by Brickman and Thomas Baum; *P* Martin Bregman; *M* Stanley

Silverman; *C* Adam Holender; *PD* Stuart Wurtzel; *SPFX* Ed Drohan, (visual) Werner Koopman; *Starring* Alan Arkin, Madeline Kahn, Austin Pendleton, Judy Graubert, William Finley; *V* Warner (UK and USA). Rather feeble satire written and directed by one-time writer for Woody Allen. Arkin, a good actor, tries hard in difficult role as psychology lecturer brainwashed in sensory deprivation tank by bored, malicious scientists into thinking he is an alien from the Orion nebula. In subsequently fractured narrative, various gags don't work – the main thread is that Arkin becomes a successful guru, upset by the fact that everybody likes junk. Easy satirical targets are picked off with overkill.

SINBAD AND THE EYE OF THE TIGER ★★
UK 1977; colour; 113 mins; Andor/Columbia; *D* Sam Wanamaker; *P* Charles H. Schneer, Ray Harryhausen; *W* Beverley Cross from a story by Cross and Harryhausen; *M* Roy Budd; *C* Ted Moore; *PD* Geoffrey Drake; *SPFX* Harryhausen; *Starring* Patrick Wayne, Taryn Power, Jane Seymour, Margaret Whiting, Patrick Troughton; *V* RCA/Columbia (UK and USA).

SINBAD THE SAILOR ★★½
USA 1947; colour; 116 mins; RKO; *D* Richard Wallace; *P* Stephen Ames; *W* John Twist; *M* Roy Webb; *C* George Barnes; *AD* Albert S. D'Agostino, Carroll Clark; *SPFX* Vernon L. Walker, Harold Wellman; *Starring* Douglas Fairbanks Jr, Maureen O'Hara, Walter Slezak, Anthony Quinn; *V* Kingston (UK), Nostalgia, King of Video, VidAmerica (USA). Perhaps trying to emulate his father in *Thief of Bagdad* (1924), Fairbanks Jr plays Sinbad as a devil-may-care swashbuckler, but lacks some of his old man's charisma. Arabian Nights fantasies retained a minor popularity, especially in the USA, right through from the original Fairbanks film to the Harryhausen films of the 1950s-70s. This was one of the most lavishly mounted, with treasure-seeking adventure and romance pushing fantasy proper into a comparatively minor role – that is, there is not much magic.

SISTERS (aka BLOOD SISTERS) ★★★½ 👻
USA 1972; colour; 92 mins; Pressman-Williams Enterprises; *D* Brian De Palma; *P* Edward R. Pressman; *W* De Palma, Louisa Rose from a story by De Palma; *M* Bernard Herrmann; *C* Gregory Sandor; *PD* Gary Weist; *Starring* Margot Kidder, Jennifer Salt, Charles Durning, Bill Finley; *V* Poly-Gram (UK), Warner (USA).

DET SJUNDE INSEGLET – see THE SEVENTH SEAL

THE SKULL ★★★
UK 1965; colour; 90 mins; Amicus/Paramount; *D* Freddie Francis; *P* Milton Subotsky, Max J. Rosenberg; *W* Subotsky from "The Skull of the Marquis de Sade" by Robert Bloch; *M* Elisabeth Lutyens; *C* John Wilcox; *AD* Bill Constable; *SPFX* Ted Samuels; *Starring* Peter Cushing, Christopher Lee, Patrick Wymark, Jill Bennett, Nigel Green, Michael Gough, George Coulouris, Patrick Magee. Offbeat horror from Amicus, more praised than most of that company's productions. Cushing is the collector of occult objects who gets hold of the skull of the Marquis de Sade (envisaged here as the cruel madman of legend), which exerts a malign influence over him, driving him to murder and grief. The skull itself floats not too convincingly about the house, but the famous scenes shot as if from within the skull (looking through its eyes) work well. Very much a film of images, with not much dialogue, it is one of Francis's more stylish films, with music by a celebrated British composer.

SLAUGHTERHOUSE-FIVE ★★★
USA 1972; colour; 103 mins; Vanadas/Universal; *D* George Roy Hill; *P* Paul Monash; *W* Stephen Geller from the novel by Kurt Vonnegut Jr; *M* Glen Gould; *C* Miroslav Ondricek; *PD* Henry Bumstead; *SPFX* (make-up) Mark Reedall, John Chambers; *Starring* Michael Sacks, Ron Leibman, Eugene Roche, Valerie Perrine; *V* MCA (USA).

SLEEPER ★★★½
USA 1973; colour; 88 mins; Rollins-Joffe/United Artists; *D/M* Woody Allen; *P* Jack Grossberg; *W* Allen, Marshall Brickman; *C* David M. Walsh; *PD* Dale Hennesy; *SPFX* A. D. Flowers; *Starring* Woody Allen, Diane Keaton; *V* CBS/Fox (USA).

THE SLIPPER AND THE ROSE ★★
UK 1976; colour; 146 mins; Paradine; *D* Bryan Forbes; *P* Stuart Lyons; *W* Forbes, Robert B. and Richard M. Sherman; *M/Songs* Shermans; *PD* Raymond Simm; *Starring* Richard Chamberlain, Gemma Craven, Annette Crosbie, Edith Evans; *V* Iver (UK). Knowingly aimed at the family market, at a time when complaints were rife that movies were not catering for families, this musical version of the fairy tale *Cinderella* did quite well in the UK, rather badly in the USA. Lavishly mounted, it was not in fact very imaginative, though Gemma Craven did her best as Cinderella opposite a slightly implausible Chamberlain as the Prince. This sort of movie-making to a calculated formula was not going to revive the British film industry.

SOLARIS ★★★★½ 👻
USSR 1972; colour; 165 mins; Mosfilm; *D* Andrei Tarkovsky; *W* Tarkovsky, Friedrich Gorenstein from the novel by Stanislaw Lem; *M* Eduard Artemyev; *C* Vadim Yusov; *AD* Mikhail Romadin; *Starring* Natalya Bondarchuk, Donatas Banionis, Anatoli Solonitsin.

SOMETHING WICKED THIS WAY COMES ★★★★
USA 1982 (released 1983); colour; 95 mins; Bryna/Disney; *D* Jack Clayton; *P* Peter Vincent Douglas; *W* Clayton (uncredited), Ray Bradbury from Bradbury's novel; *M* James Horner; *C* Stephen H. Burum; *PD* Richard MacDonald; *SPFX* (consultant) Harrison Ellenshaw, (mechanical) Roland Tantin, (special photographic) Art Cruickshank, Peter Anderson and Phil Meador, (special visual) Lee Dyer, (make-up) Robert J. Schiffer and (uncredited) Stan Winston; *Starring* Vidal Peterson, Shawn Carson, Jason Robards, Jonathan Pryce, Pam Grier, Royal Dano; *V* Disney (USA).

SOMEWHERE IN TIME ★★½
USA 1980; colour; 104 mins; Rastar/Universal; *D* Jeannot Szwarc; *P* Stephen Deutsch; *W* Richard Matheson from his novel *Bid Time Return*; *M* John Barry; *C* Isidore Mankofsky; *JPD* Seymour Klate; *SPFX* Jack Faggard; *Starring* Christopher Reeve, Jane Seymour, Christopher Plummer, Teresa Wright; *V* CIC (UK), MCA (USA). Romantic, time-travelling weepie fantasy, based on a novel by Richard Matheson which has much in common with Jack Finney's book *Time and Again* (this may explain why the time-travel expert in the film is called Dr Finney). Christopher Reeve (who has now spent years trying to duck his Superman image) plays the modern playwright who meets an old lady; she gives him an old watch, whispering "come back to me". Later, in a posh hotel, he sees a portrait with which he falls in love, of a beautiful young actress; he learns (prematurely – it gives the game away) that she is the old lady as a girl. By an effort of will (involving dressing up in Edwardian clothes), he steps into the past, glowingly photographed and redolent of nostalgia (which, when you think of it, the past is unlikely to be if you're actually in it) and fulfils his predestined tryst. Alas he is accidentally propelled back to the present, and it's broken-heart time. It's all enjoyable, but not terribly good.

SON OF BLOB – see BEWARE! THE BLOB

SON OF DRACULA ★½
UK 1974; colour; 90 mins; Cinemation/Apple; *D* Freddie Francis; *P* Ringo Starr; *W* Jay Fairbank; *M* Harry Nilsson; *C* Norman Warwick; *Starring* Harry Nilsson, Ringo Starr, Dennis Price, Freddie Jones, Suzanna Leigh. Seldom-seen musical parody of horror genre, not very successfully loony. Dracula's son is a pop star. Not to be confused with *Son of Dracula* (1943), an inferior Universal offering.

THE SORCERERS ★★★★
UK 1967; colour; 87 mins; Curtwel-Global/Tigon British; *D* Michael Reeves; *P* Patrick Curtis, Tony Tenser; *W* Reeves, Tom Baker from an idea by John Burke; *M* Paul Ferris; *C* Stanley Long; *AD* Tony Curtis; *Starring* Boris Karloff, Catherine Lacey, Ian Ogilvy, Susan George; *V* Walton (UK). Second film of young director Reeves who went on to make *Witchfinder General* before his early death. Karloff and Lacey play an elderly couple who have invented a machine which gives them hypnotic powers over other people, even at a distance. They start to control a young man, and the old woman especially becomes more and more voyeuristically excited at her powers, finally in a kind of sensual hysteria forcing Mike (Ogilvy) into a series of murders. The corrupting effect of vicarious emotions, of course, can relate also to the audiences at horror movies, and even though this is a cheap and in some ways tatty film, it is very interesting for this metaphor at its centre. The obvious comparison is with the classic *Peeping Tom*, 1959, which is not fantasy.

LA SORELLA DI SATANA – see THE REVENGE OF THE BLOOD BEAST

SOYLENT GREEN ★★½
USA 1973; colour; 97 mins; MGM; *D* Richard Fleischer; *P* Walter Seltzer, Russell Thacher; *W* Stanley R. Greenberg from *Make Room! Make Room!* by Harry Harrison; *M* Fred Myrow; *C* Richard H. Kline; *AD* Edward C. Carfagno; *SPFX* A. J. Lohman, (photographic) Robert R. Hoag, Matthew Yuricich; *Starring* Charlton Heston, Edward G. Robinson, Leigh Taylor-Young, Chuck Connors, Joseph Cotten; *V* MGM/UA (UK and USA).

THE SPACE CHILDREN ★★★
USA 1958; b/w; 69 mins; Paramount; *D* Jack Arnold; *P* William Alland; *W* Bernard C. Schoenfeld from a story by Tom Filer; *M* Van Cleave; *C* Ernest Laszlo; *AD* Hal Pereira, Roland Anderson; *SPFX* John P. Fulton; *Starring* Michel Ray, Adam Williams, Peggy Webber, Jackie Coogan, John Crawford. This was the last of the exotic B-grade pictures Arnold made with producer Alland. (Others were *It Came from Outer Space*, *Creature from the Black Lagoon* and *Tarantula*.) In this, the most seldom screened, a gigantic alien brain lands on Earth and makes telepathic contact with a group of children, whom it controls, with the aim of putting an end to nuclear missile testing ("Plus ça change…"). Like most of Arnold's best work, this is moody and atmospheric, making much of its isolated beach and cave locations. It is perhaps his most pessimistic film, with the children's parents (who are involved with the missile project) seeming more alien and unsympathetic than the affable, glowing alien himself. Special effects only so-so, but it doesn't matter. In some ways the film points forward to *E.T.*

SPACEHUNTER: ADVENTURES IN THE FORBIDDEN ZONE ★★★
USA 1983; colour; 3-D; 90 mins; Delphi/Columbia; *D* Lamont Johnson; *P* Don Carmody, André Link, John Dunning; *W* David Preston, Edith Rey, Dan Goldbert, Len Blum; *M* Elmer Bernstein; *C* Frank Tidy; *3-D Consultant* Ernest McNabb; *PD* Jackson De Govia; *SPFX* (visual) Fantasy II Film Effects, (optical) Image 3, (visual supervision) Peter Kleinow, Gene Warren Jr, (make-up) Thomas R. Burman; *Starring* Peter Strauss, Molly Ringwald, Grant Alianak, Michael Ironside, Ernie Hudson, Andrea Marcovicci; *V* RCA/Columbia (USA).

THE SPACEMAN AND KING ARTHUR – see UNIDENTIFIED FLYING ODDBALL

SPACESHIP TO THE UNKNOWN – see FLASH GORDON (1936)

SPIDER-MAN ★
USA 1977; made for TV; colour; 92 mins; Danchuck; *D* E. W. Swackhamer; *P* Edward J. Montagne; *W* Alvin Boretz from the Marvel Comics character; *M* Johnnie Spence, (electronic) Greg

Hundley; *C* Fred Jackman; *AD* James Hulsey; *SPFX* Don Courtney; *Starring* Nicholas Hammond, Lisa Eilbacher, Michael Pataki, Thayer David; *V* RCA/Columbia (UK). Very bland comic strip adaptation, lacking even the moderate wit of the original, though true enough to its essentials. Story concerns villains using mind control to programme respectable citizens as bank robbers. Spiderman (who got that way after a bite from a radioactive spider) climbs up a lot of walls, and after watching him once, there's no fun in it anymore. Only the bad-tempered police captain (Pataki) gives a real performance. This was a pilot for a TV series; two more films from edited later episodes were also given theatrical release.

THE SPY WHO LOVED ME ★★½
UK 1977; colour; 125 mins; Eon/United Artists; *D* Lewis Gilbert; *P* Albert R. Broccoli; *W* Christopher Wood, Richard Maibaum, based extremely remotely on the novel by Ian Fleming; *M* Marvin Hamlisch; *C* Claude Renoir; *SPFX* Ken Adam; *SPFX* Derek Meddings, John Evans, (photographic) Alan Maley; *Starring* Roger Moore, Barbara Bach, Curt Jurgens, Richard Kiel, Caroline Munro; *V* Warner (UK), CBS/Fox (USA).

SQUIRM ★★★ ☻
USA 1976; colour; 92 mins; Squirm Company; *D/W* Jeff Lieberman; *P* George Manasse; *M* Robert Prince; *C* Joseph Mangine; *SPFX* Bill Milling, Don Farnsworth, Lee Howard, (make-up design) Rick Baker; *Starring* John Scardino, Patricia Pearcy; *V* Rank (UK), Vestron (USA). The archetypal low-budget monster movie of the last decade; makes *Frogs* look like bunnies. Fallen power line in American South turns worms into flesh-eating horrors. For the rest of the film they do their thing. Sharp direction, and a witty script in which, for a change, the hero is a weakling and not a tough guy, make this the ultimate in killer-worm films, especially as (low budget or not) Lieberman did not skimp on worms. There are thousands of them. He went on to make two more goodish low-budget horror films, only fringe fantasy at most, so not in this book: *Blue Sunshine* (in which a hallucinogenic drug makes its victims bald and homicidal), and *Just Before Dawn*, a nasty but well achieved splatter movie in the same rural-killer genre as *The Hills Have Eyes*.

SSSSSSS (aka SSSSNAKE!) ★★
USA 1973; colour; 99 mins; Zanuck-Brown/Universal; *D* Bernard L. Kowalski; *P* Dan Striepeke; *W* Hal Dresner from a story by Striepeke; *M* Pat Williams; *C* Gerald Perry Finnerman; *AD* John T. McCormack; *SPFX* (make-up) John Chambers, Nick Marcellino; *Starring* Strother Martin, Dirk Benedict, Heather Menzies, Richard B. Shull. With a title like that you'd expect a one-star movie, but it makes it to two stars for taking its idiotic premise seriously and playing it straight. Mad scientist (Strother Martin) is convinced that snakes will do better than people at resisting pollution and other disasters, so with the best will in the world he tries to turn people into king cobras. Early unsuccessful experiments (they look awful) get sold to carnivals as freaks, but he finally succeeds with his daughter's boyfriend (Benedict). Then along comes a mongoose...

STALKER ★★★½
USSR 1979; colour; 161 mins; Mosfilm; *D/PD* Andrei Tarkovsky; *P* Alexandra Demidova; *W* Arkady and Boris Strugatsky from their novel *Roadside Picnic*; *M* Eduard Artemyev; *C* Aleksandr Knyazhinsky; *Starring* Aleksandr Kaidanovsky, Anatoly Solonitsin, Nikolai Grinko, Alisa Freindlikh. Long, hypnotic, rather inaccessible science fantasy by the brilliant director of *Solaris*. The Russian SF novel from which this is loosely adapted was set in America, but the unidentified, rather grim country where the action of the film takes place is very Russian in feeling. The English title, incidentally, was also used in Russia. Stalker is a shaven-headed smuggler-saint, who acts as a guide to people (in this case Scientist and Writer) who wish to visit the forbidden wasteland of the Zone, an area where, it is rumoured, a room exists which can grant the heart's desire of those

who visit it. Reaching the room is difficult, for the Zone (photographed in colour, as opposed to the black-and-white world outside) is riddled with invisible labyrinths, lethal booby-traps, areas where no matter in which direction you travel, you end up where you started. On reaching the Room, neither of the world-weary intellectuals carries out his intention (Scientist to destroy it, Writer to suck creativity from it). The Zone is no beautiful wonderland; it is polluted with chemicals, littered with the detritus of an industrial landscape, neglected and desolate. The ugliness is photographed with some beauty. This opaque allegory seems to be about the difficulty of maintaining faith in a world where so much is unknowable, but it certainly has a political dimension also, and says more about modern Russia than any other film released in the West. Oddly, although the film is bleak, and the Zone (whether created by God, aliens or a police state) offers no transcendence, Tarkovsky allows one minor miracle at the end, when Stalker's daughter moves a small object by the power of her mind alone.

STARCRASH ★½
USA 1979; colour; 92 mins; Columbia/AIP; *D* Lewis Coates (Luigi Cozzi); *P* Nat and Patrick Wachsberger; *W* Coates, Nat Wachsberger; *M* John Barry; *C* Paul Beeson, Roberto D'Ettore; *PD* Aurelio Crugnolla; *Starring* Marjoe Gortner, Caroline Munro, Joe Spinell, Christopher Plummer; *V* Vipco (UK). Second-rate special effects in Italian-American attempt to cash in on *Star Wars* boom, mainly notable for glamorous Caroline Munro in black bikini as ace space pilot Stella Star pitted against evil Zarth Arn (Spinell) in rather terrible space opera.

STARSHIP INVASIONS (aka ALIEN ENCOUNTER) ★
Canada 1977; colour; 89 mins; Warner; *D/W* Ed Hunt; *P* Norman Glick, Hunt, Ken Gord; *M* Gil Melle; *C* Mark Irwin; *AD* Karen Bromley; *SPFX* Warren Keillor; *Starring* Robert Vaughn, Christopher Lee, Daniel Pilon; *V* VCL (UK). There's something almost charming about trying to exploit the market created by *Close Encounters of the Third Kind* without a workable script or budget; commendable endeavour but no marks. Vaughn plays UFO expert contacted by friendly alien group who live in Bermuda Triangle; they are worried about the bad aliens led by Lee who are coming in flying saucers to take over Earth; ends in aerial battle with some of the worst special effects on record. Christopher Lee has said – and he knows a thing or two about bad movies – that this is the worst film he's ever been in.

STAR TREK THE MOTION PICTURE ★★★½
USA 1979; colour; 132 mins; Paramount; *D* Robert Wise; *P* Gene Roddenberry; *W* Harold Livingstone from a story by Alan Dean Foster and the TV series created by Roddenberry (especially the episodes "The Changeling" by John Meredith Lucas, and "The Doomsday Machine" by Norman Spinrad); *M* Jerry Goldsmith; *C* Richard H. Kline, Richard Yuricich; *PD* Harold Michelson; *SPFX* (photographic director) Douglas Trumbull, (matte paintings) Matthew Yuricich, (photographic effects supervision) John Dykstra, (miniatures) Greg Jein, Russ Simpson and Jim Dow; *Starring* William Shatner, Leonard Nimoy, DeForest Kelley, Persis Khambatta, Stephen Collins; *V* CIC (UK), Paramount (USA).

STAR TREK THE WRATH OF KHAN ★½
USA 1982; colour; 114 mins; Paramount; *D* Nicholas Meyer; *P* Robert Sallin; *W* Jack B. Sowards from a story by Sowards and Harve Bennett based on the TV series created by Gene Roddenberry (especially the episode "Space Seed" by C. Wilbur and Gene Coon); *M* James Horner; *C* Gayne Rescher; *PD* Joseph R. Jennings; *SPFX* (visual) Industrial Light and Magic, Modern Film Effects; *Starring* William Shatner, Leonard Nimoy, DeForest Kelley, Ricardo Montalban; *V* CIC (UK), Paramount (USA).

STAR WARS ★★★★½
USA 1977; colour; 121 mins; Lucasfilm/20th Century-Fox; *D/W* George Lucas; *P* Gary Kurtz; *M* John Williams; *C* Gilbert Taylor; *PD* John Barry; *Set decorator* Roger Christian; *SPFX* (photographic supervision) John Dykstra and Industrial Light & Magic, (planet and satellite artist, production illustration) Ralph McQuarrie, (matte artist) P. S. Ellenshaw, (production/mechanical supervision) John Stears, (make-up) Stuart Freeborn, with Rick Baker and Douglas Beswick; *Starring* Mark Hamill, Harrison Ford, Carrie Fisher, Peter Cushing, Alec Guinness, Anthony Daniels, Kenny Baker, Peter Mayhew, David Prowse; *V* CBS/Fox (UK and USA).

THE STEPFORD WIVES ★★
USA 1974; colour; 115 mins; Fadsin-Palomar/Columbia; *D* Bryan Forbes; *P* Edgar J. Scherick; *W* William Goldman from the novel by Ira Levin; *M* Michael Small; *C* Owen Roizman; *PD* Gene Callahan; *Starring* Katharine Ross, Paula Prentiss, Peter Masterson, Nanette Newman, Patrick O'Neal, Tina Louise; *V* VCL (UK).

STRANGE BEHAVIOR (aka DEAD KIDS) ★★★ ☻
New Zealand/USA 1981; colour; 105 mins; Hemdale-Richwhite/South Street; *D* Michael Laughlin; *P* William Condon; *W* Laughlin, Condon; *C* Louis Horvath; *PD* Susanna Moore; *SPFX* (make-up) Craig Reardon; *Starring* Michael Murphy, Louise Fletcher, Dan Shor, Fiona Lewis, Scott Brady, Arthur Dignam, Dey Young; *V* Iver (UK), RCA/Columbia (USA). Witty and promising directorial debut of Laughlin who was previously a producer *(Two Lane Blacktop)*, and went on to make the excellent SF movie *Strange Invaders*, the second of his proposed "strange" trilogy. This low-budget horror film is also, in part, SF. In a small, midwestern college town a government research centre is investigating the effect of mental conditioning (using drugs injected through the eye socket straight into the brain, among other things) on local college students. This turns out to be connected with a bizarre series of gory murders. The explanation, involving a supposedly-dead mad scientist, is conventional genre nonsense, but the conditioning theme is well done, and the script is consistently lively and believable.

STRANGE INVADERS ★★★★½
USA 1983; colour; 94 mins; Orion/EMI; *D* Michael Laughlin; *P* Walter Coblenz; *W* Laughlin, William Condon; *M* John Addison; *C* Louis Horvath; *PD* Susanna Moore; *SPFX* (visual design) John Muto and Robert Skotak, (special alien effects) Margaret Beserra, Stephan Dupuis, Bill Sturgeon, others including, uncredited, Henry Golas, James Cummins; *Starring* Paul LeMat, Nancy Allen, Diana Scarwid, Louise Fletcher, Kenneth Tobey; *V* Vestron (USA).

THE STRONGEST MAN IN THE WORLD ★½
USA 1975; colour; 92 mins; Disney; *D* Vincent McEveety; *P* Bill Anderson; *W* Joseph L. McEveety, Herman Groves; *M* Robert F. Brunner; *C* Andrew Jackson; *AD* John B. Mansbridge, Jack Senter; *SPFX* Art Cruickshank, Danny Lee; *Starring* Kurt Russell, Joe Flynn, Eve Arden, Cesar Romero, Phil Silvers. Sequel to *The Computer Wore Tennis Shoes* and *Now You See Him, Now You Don't*. Disney formula film, the sort described as funpacked. In this one, teenage genius Kurt Russell comes up with a potion for superhuman strength. More routine campus comedy.

THE STUDENT OF PRAGUE (DER STUDENT VON PRAG, aka THE MAN WHO CHEATED LIFE) ★★★
Germany 1926; b/w; approx 60 mins; Sokal; *D/W* Henrik Galeen from screenplay by Hans Heinz Ewers for *Der Student von Prag*, 1913, taken in turn from "William Wilson" by Edgar Allan Poe; *C* Günther Krampf, Erich Nitzschmann; *AD* Hermann Warm; *Starring* Conrad Veidt, Agnes Esterhazy, Werner Krauss. A silent film, almost the last gasp of German romantic Gothic cinema; quite stylish, with wild, slightly expressionist sets. Scapinelli (Krauss) is the umbrella-wielding bourgeois devil who buys the soul of Baldwin (Veidt) in exchange for his reflection in a mirror.

The reflection then becomes a Doppelgänger, a phantom double, which haunts Baldwin until his suicide.

THE SUBMERSION OF JAPAN – see NIPPON CHINBOTSU

SUPERMAN ★★★½
UK 1978; colour; 143 mins; Dovemead/International Film; *D* Richard Donner; *P* Ilya Salkind, Pierre Spengler; *W* Mario Puzo, David Newman, Leslie Newman, Robert Benton, also Norman Enfield, (creative consultant) Tom Mankiewicz, from characters in the comic strip by Jerry Siegel and Joe Shuster; *M* John Williams; *C* Geoffrey Unsworth; *PD* John Barry; *SPFX* John Richardson, Bob MacDonald, (supervision) Colin Chilvers, (flying systems/process projection) Wally Veevers, (supervision mattes and composites) Les Bowie, (model effects) Derek Meddings, (supervision opticals) Roy Field, (visual design) Denis Rich, (visuals supervision) Stuart Freeborn; *Starring* Christopher Reeve, Margot Kidder, Gene Hackman, Valerie Perrine, Ned Beatty, Marlon Brando, Glenn Ford, *V* Warner (UK and USA).

SUPERMAN II ★★★★
UK 1980; colour; 127 mins; Dovemead/International Film; *D* Richard Lester; *P* Ilya Salkind, Pierre Spengler; *W* Mario Puzo, David Newman, Leslie Newman; *M* Ken Thorne; *C* Geoffrey Unsworth, Bob Paynter; *PD* John Barry, Peter Murton; *SPFX* Colin Chilvers, Zoran Perisic, (flying effects) Bob Harman, (miniature effects direction/additional flying sequences) Derek Meddings, (mattes) Doug Ferris and Ivor Beddoes, (make-up) Stuart Freeborn; *Starring* Christopher Reeve, Gene Hackman, Ned Beatty, Margot Kidder, Sarah Douglas, Jack O'Halloran, Terence Stamp; *V* Warner (UK and USA).

SUPERMAN III ★★★½
UK 1983; colour; 125 mins; Dovemead/Cantharus; *D* Richard Lester; *P* Ilya Salkind, Pierre Spengler; *W* David Newman, Leslie Newman; *M* Ken Thorne; *C* Robert Paynter; *PD* Peter Murton; *SPFX* Colin Chilvers, Martin Gutteridge, Brian Warner, (mattes) Dennis Bartlett, Peter Melrose and Charles Stoneham, (optical) Optical Film Effects, (make-up) Paul Engelen and Stuart Freeborn; *Starring* Christopher Reeve, Richard Pryor, Annette O'Toole, Pamela Stephenson, Robert Vaughn, Margot Kidder; *V* Thorn EMI (UK), Warner (USA).

SUSPIRIA ★★★★ ☻
Italy 1976; colour; 97 mins; Seda Spettacoli; *D/M* Dario Argento; *P* Claudio Argento; *W* Dario Argento, Dario Nicolodi; *M* also Goblin; *C* Luciano Tovoli; *PD* Guiseppe Bassan; *SPFX* Germano Natali; *Starring* Jessica Harper, Stefania Casini, Udo Kier, Alida Valli, Joan Bennett; *V* Thorn EMI (UK).

SWAMP THING ★½
USA 1982; colour; 92 mins; Melnicker–Uslan/Embassy; *D/W* Wes Craven from the DC Comics written by Len Wein and drawn by Berni Wrightson; *P* Benjamin Melnicker, Michael Uslan; *M* Harry Manfredini; *C* Robin Goodwin; *SPFX* (make-up) William Munns; *Starring* Louis Jourdan, Adrienne Barbeau, Ray Wise, Dick Durock; *V* Embassy (USA). The original comic books are collector's items now, valued for their moody, Gothic appearance, but this inferior film captures almost nothing of that style. Craven's previous work, which included the extraordinary unpleasant *Last House on the Left*, as well as *The Hills Have Eyes* and *Deadly Blessing*, led people to expect something sharper and darker than this. The extremely low budget led to Swamp Thing looking absurd – a man in a badly fitting costume, rather than a looming, horrible avenger. Barbeau, as usual, is quite good, but here she acts in a vacuum.

THE SWARM ★½
USA 1978; colour; 116 mins; Warner; *D/P* Irwin Allen; *W* Stirling Silliphant from the novel by Arthur Herzog; *M* Jerry Goldsmith; *C* Fred J. Koenekamp; *PD* Stan Jolley; *SPFX* Howard Jensen, (photographic) L. B. Abbott and Van Der Veer Photo Effects; *Starring* Michael Caine, Katharine Ross, Richard Widmark, Richard Chamberlain, Olivia De Havilland, Ben Johnson, Jose Ferrer, Fred MacMurray, Henry Fonda; *V* Warner (UK and USA). Swarms of African killer bees invade an Air Force missile base in Texas, and subsequently most of Houston. Clever entomologist Michael Caine tries to cope with the disaster despite interference from the thick-headed military. Irwin Allen (producer/director) has built a career out of disaster movies (and the occasional SF piece, such as *Voyage to the Bottom of the Sea*), and they have been almost invariably implausible, ill-acted and terribly silly. This, however, must be just about the worst (despite all the cameos from big-name stars) – to the point where TV personality Clive James contrived to make a running gag about the film for over a year on British television, getting hoots of laughter whenever he mentioned it. One of the many things wrong about the film is that it concentrates on the boring people rather than the interesting bees.

THE SWORD AND THE SORCERER ★★★ ☻
USA 1982; colour; 99 mins; Sorcerer-Group 1; *D* Albert Pyun; *P* Brandon Chase, Marianne Chase; *W* Tom Karnowski, John Stuckmeyer, Pyun; *M* David Whitaker; *C* Joseph Mangine; *AD* George Costello; *SPFX* John Carter, Harry Woolman, (make-up) Gregory Cannom; *Starring* Lee Horsley, Kathleen Beller, Simon MacCorkindale, George Maharis, Richard Lynch, Richard·Moll; *V* Rank (UK), MCA (USA).

TALES FROM BEYOND THE GRAVE – see FROM BEYOND THE GRAVE

TALES FROM THE CRYPT ★★½
UK 1972; colour; 92 mins; Amicus/Metromedia; *D* Freddie Francis; *P* Max J. Rosenberg, Milton Subotsky; *W* Milton Subotsky from stories in the comic books *Tales from the Crypt* and *The Vault of Horror* by Al Feldstein, Johnny Craig and William Gaines; *M* Douglas Gamley; *C* Norman Warwick; *Starring* Ralph Richardson, "And All Through the House" Joan Collins, "Reflection of Death" Ian Hendry, "Poetic Justice" Peter Cushing, "Wish You Were Here" Richard Greene and Barbara Murray, "Blind Alleys" Nigel Patrick and Patrick Magee. Based, like *The Vault of Horror* (1972), on the popular and later banned E.C. horror comics of the 1950s. A linking story has Ralph Richardson as the cowled figure hearing the story of five tourists who have wandered into some catacombs; at the end they come to realize they are all dead and in Hell, a twist ending that would come as no surprise since most of the individual episodes have twist endings as well. The best stories have Peter Cushing as the sweet old man, persecuted by neighbours, who returns from the grave to wreak vengeance; Barbara Murray as the wife who uses three wishes to bring her husband back to life, but the embalming fluid in his veins causes such pain that she has to chop him up with a cleaver (the bits keep crawling about); and Patrick Magee as the blind man in a nursing home who constructs an unlit labyrinth of razor blades for the nasty director to crawl through. This all sounds sicker than it actually is. The bright colours, and Francis's jolly directorial style, make it something of a boisterous romp, but it is not really very interesting.

THE TALES OF HOFFMAN ★★★½
UK 1951; colour; 115 mins; Archers/London Films; *D/P/W* Michael Powell, Emeric Pressburger from the opera by Offenbach adapted by Dennis Arundell, libretto by Jules Barbier; *M* Jacques Offenbach; *C* Christopher Challis; *Choreography* Frederick Ashton; *PD* Hein Heckroth; *Starring* Moira Shearer, Robert Rounseville, Pamela Brown, Ludmilla Tcherina, Robert Helpmann, Leonid Massine.

TALES OF TERROR ★★★½
USA 1962; colour; 90 mins; Alta Vista/AIP; *D/P* Roger Corman; *W* Richard Matheson from the stories "Morella", "The Black Cat", "The Cask of Amontillado" and "The Facts in the Case of M. Valdemar" by Edgar Allan Poe; *M* Les Baxter; *C* Floyd Crosby; *AD* Daniel Haller; *SPFX* Pat Dinga; *Starring* Vincent Price, Peter Lorre, Basil Rathbone, Joyce Jameson, Debra Paget; *V* Guild (UK), Warner (USA). Another of the Corman adaptations of Poe, but hardly true to the original stories. "Morella" is the weakest (dying girl possessed by the spirit of dead mother); the third, "Valdemar" sequence, about a man hypnotised at the moment of death, and his subsequent dissolution into slime some months later, falls down through hammy acting and rotten special effects; but everybody remembers with affection Peter Lorre's over-the-top performance as the henpecked, murderous husband in the second episode, which is played moderately successfully for laughs.

TALES THAT WITNESS MADNESS ★½
UK 1973; colour; 90 mins; World Film Services; *D* Freddie Francis; *P* Norman Priggen; *W* Jay Fairbank (pseudonym of Jennifer Jayne); *M* Bernard Ebbinghouse; *C* Norman Warwick; *AD* Roy Walker; *Starring* Jack Hawkins, Donald Pleasence, Georgia Brown, Donald Houston, Suzy Kendall, Peter McEnery, Joan Collins, Michael Jayston, Kim Novak. Low-budget attempt by another small company to exploit the market created by such Amicus compendium films as *Tales from the Crypt*. Good cast was not much help with bad script, in these four stories (boy creates tiger out of his own mind, antique dealer goes back in time to meet girlfriend's double, carnivorous tree, ritual of human sacrifice by native tribe) linked by psychiatrist (Pleasence) discussing cases in his mental clinic.

TAM LIN – see THE DEVIL'S WIDOW

TANYA'S ISLAND ★½
Canada 1980; colour; 90 mins; Fred Baker-Rainier Energy Resources; *D* Alfred Sole; *P/W* Pierre Brousseau; *C* Mark Irwin; *SPFX* (beast make-up) Rob Bottin; *Starring* D. D. Winters, Richard Sargent, Don McCleod; *V* VTC (UK). Model Tanya (Winters) has erotic fantasies about life on island inhabited by jealous boyfriend and first-of-all tender but later randy, apelike beast. Shot in Puerto Rico. Beast good, but silly softcore pornography not as interesting as Borowczyk's in *The Beast*.

TARANTULA ★★★
USA 1955; b/w; 80 mins; Universal-International; *D* Jack Arnold; *P* William Alland; *W* Martin Berkeley, Robert M. Fresco from a story by Arnold, Fresco; *M* Henry Mancini; *AD* Alfred Sweeney, Alexander Golitzen; *SPFX* (cinematography) Clifford Stine, David S. Horsley; *Starring* John Agar, Mara Corday, Leo G. Carroll, Nestor Paiva.

TASTE THE BLOOD OF DRACULA ★★½
UK 1969; colour; 95 mins; Hammer; *D* Peter Sasdy; *P* Aida Young; *W* John Elder (pseudonym of Anthony Hinds); *M* James Bernard; *C* Arthur Grant; *AD* Scott MacGregor; *SPFX* Brian Johncock, (make-up) Gerry Fletcher; *Starring* Christopher Lee, Geoffrey Keen, Gwen Watford, Linda Hayden, Isla Blair. The fifth of Hammer's nine *Dracula* movies, and probably the last of any quality. Set in Victorian England it has Dracula becoming father-figure to the children of three appalling, rich thrill-seekers. The subtext (as in one or two previous films in the series) is the Victorian family flying apart under the strains of its own hypocrisies and internal pressures. Nothing special, but as Sasdy's debut it suggested he might go on to do more in the future of interest, though by and large he has not.

THE TEMPEST ★★
UK 1979; colour; 95 mins; Boyd's Co.; *D/W* Derek Jarman – an edited version of the play by William Shakespeare; *P* Guy Ford, Mordecai Schreiber; *M* Wavemaker (Brian Hodgson, John Lewis); *C* Peter Middleton; *PD* Yolanda Sonnabend; *Starring* Heathcote Williams, Karl Johnson, Toyah Willcox, Jack Birkett, Ken Campbell, Peter Bull; *V* Palace (UK). Having directed a punk SF movie,

Jubilee, Derek Jarman (whose style, not to put too fine a point on it, is extremely camp) went on to do punk Shakespeare. He treats the text like so many jigsaw pieces to be re-arranged, with most of the great speeches there, but in a different order. Prospero fails to abjure his "rough magic"; Miranda says "O brave new world" vis-à-vis a group of dancing matelots. At the end, a black lady sings "Stormy Weather". The updating (Ariel wears a boiler suit) makes the fantasy less, not more – a pity, since this may be the greatest work ever written about magic. Toyah Willcox is a lively, cockney Miranda. Caliban (here a rather handsome, bald, black man) could have been more monstrous. Best fantasy image is him suckling at the breast of the hugely fat, nude witch, Sycorax.

THE TENANT (LE LOCATAIRE) ★★★½
France 1976; colour; 126 mins; Marianne; *D* Roman Polanski; *P* Andrew Braunsberg; *W* Gerard Brach, Polanski from *Le Locataire Chimérique* by Roland Topor; *M* Philippe Sarde; *C* Sven Nykvist; *PD* Pierre Guffroy; *SPFX* (photographic) Jean Fouché; *Starring* Roman Polanski, Isabelle Adjani, Shelley Winters, Melvyn Douglas, Jo Van Fleet; *V* Paramount (USA).

THE TERMINAL MAN ★★★
USA 1974; colour; 104 mins; Warner; *D/P/W* Mike Hodges from the novel by Michael Crichton; *M* J. S. Bach; *C* Richard H. Kline; *AD* Fred Harpman; *Starring* George Segal, Joan Hackett, Richard A. Dysart, Jill Clayburgh, Donald Moffat.

THE TERROR ★★★
USA 1963; colour; 81 mins; Filmgroup/AIP; *D/P* Roger Corman; *W* Leo Gordon, Jack Hill; *M* Ronald Stein; *C* John Nickolaus, (exteriors) Monte Hellman; *Starring* Boris Karloff, Jack Nicholson, Sandra Knight; *V* Media, King of Video (USA). One of Corman's celebrated shoot-a-movie-in-three-days efforts, made when the sets from *The Raven* were still around, and so was Karloff. Sandra Knight plays the mysterious woman tracked to Karloff's castle by young soldier (Nicholson) whose life he has saved. Karloff is mad, and she is not all she seems to be. Somewhat confused, but surprisingly vigorous.

TERRORE NELLO SPAZIO – *see* PLANET OF THE VAMPIRES

EL TESORO DE LAS CUATRO CORONAS – *see* TREASURE OF THE FOUR CROWNS

THEATRE OF BLOOD ★★½ ☻
UK 1973; colour; 102 mins; Cineman/United Artists; *D* Douglas Hickox; *P* John Kohn, Stanley Mann; *W* Anthony Greville-Bell; *M* Michael J. Lewis; *C* Wolfgang Suschitzky; *PD* Michael Seymour; *SPFX* John Stears; *Starring* Vincent Price, Diana Rigg, Ian Hendry, Harry Andrews, Coral Browne, Jack Hawkins, Robert Morley, Dennis Price, Diana Dors. Vincent Price plays hammy Shakespearean actor who fakes his suicide and then contrives a series of gory revenges against the critics who have slighted his performances, each murder corresponding to the action of a particular Shakespeare play. Not strictly a fantasy, since the explanation is rational, but included here because of its loony Gothic jollity, and because it is Price's own favourite among his many films. (Actually, he's much better in *Witchfinder General*, but people who enjoy his tongue-in-cheek, over-the-top performances will like this one.)

THEM! ★★★½
USA 1954; b/w; 93 mins; Warner; *D* Gordon Douglas; *P* David Weisbart; *W* Ted Sherdeman, Russell Hughes from a story by George Worthing Yates; *M* Bronislau Kaper; *C* Sid Hickox; *AD* Stanley Fleisher; *SPFX* (ants) Dick Smith; *Starring* Edmund Gwenn, James Whitmore, James Arness.

THESE ARE THE DAMNED – *see* THE DAMNED

THEY CAME FROM WITHIN – *see* SHIVERS

THE THIEF OF BAGDAD ★★★
USA 1924; b/w; 11,230ft (over two hours); Fairbanks/United Artists; *D* Raoul Walsh; *W* Lotta Woods, Elton Thomas (pseudonym of Fairbanks); *C* Arthur Edeson; *AD* William Cameron Menzies; *Starring* Douglas Fairbanks, Julanne Johnson, Anna May Wong, Sojin; *V* PolyGram (UK), Budget (USA).

THE THIEF OF BAGDAD ★★★★
UK/USA 1940; colour; 106 mins; London Films/United Artists; *D* (UK) Michael Powell, Tim Whelan and Ludwig Berger, (USA, uncredited) Alexander Korda, Zoltan Korda and William Cameron Menzies; *P* Alexander Korda; *W* Lajos Biro, Miles Malleson; *M* Miklos Rozsa; *C* Georges Périnal and others; *AD* Vincent Korda; *SPFX* (mechanical) Lawrence Butler, (optical) Tom Howard, (miniatures) Johnny Mills; *Starring* John Justin, Conrad Veidt, Sabu, June Duprez, Rex Ingram, Miles Malleson; *V* PolyGram (UK).

THE THIEF OF BAGDAD ★
UK/France 1978; colour; 102 mins; Palm-Victorine/NBC; *D* Clive Donner; *P* Aida Young; *W* A. J. Carrothers, also Andrew Birkin; *M* John Cameron; *C* Denis Lewiston; *AD* Edward Marshall; *SPFX* (optical) Zoran Perisic, (magic carpet) John Stears and Dick Hewitt; *Starring* Roddy McDowall, Kabir Bedi, Peter Ustinov, Terence Stamp; *V* Video Gems (UK and USA). Why bother to make it again when it has been done so well before? This production, orginally intended for television, is truly terrible: a totally wooden prince (Bedi), an offensively charmless thief (McDowall), and a cast that simply does not bother to act.

THE THING (aka THE THING FROM ANOTHER WORLD) ★★★★
USA 1951; b/w; 86 mins; Winchester/RKO; *D* Christian Nyby, (uncredited) Howard Hawks; *P* Hawks; *W* Charles Lederer from "Who Goes There?" by Don A. Stuart (John W. Campbell Jr); *M* Dimitri Tiomkin; *C* Russell Harlan; *AD* John J. Hughes, Albert S. D'Agostino; *SPFX* Donald Stewart, (photographic) Linwood Dunn; *Starring* Kenneth Tobey, Margaret Sheridan, Robert Cornthwaite, John Dierkes, James Arness; *V* Kingston (UK), Nostalgia, Vestron (USA).

THE THING ★★★★½ ☻☻☻
USA 1982; colour; 109 mins; Universal; *D* John Carpenter; *P* David Foster, Lawrence Turman, Stuart Cohen; *W* Bill Lancaster from "Who Goes There?" by Don A. Stuart (John W. Campbell Jr); *M* Ennio Morricone; *C* Dean Cundey; *PD* John J. Lloyd; *SPFX* Roy Arbogast and others, (visual) Albert Whitlock, (make-up) Rob Bottin with crew of 30, including Stan Winston, uncredited; *Starring* Kurt Russell, A. Wilford Brimley, Charles Hallahan, David Clennon, T. K. Carter, Keith David, Richard Dysart; *V* CIC (UK), MCA (USA).

THINGS TO COME ★★★½
UK 1936; b/w; 130 mins (cut to 113); London Films/United Artists; *D* William Cameron Menzies; *P* Alexander Korda; *W* H. G. Wells from his novel *The Shape of Things to Come*; *M* Arthur Bliss; *C* Georges Périnal; *AD* Vincent Korda, John Bryan, Menzies, Frederick Pusey; *SPFX* Ned Mann, Lawrence Butler, Edward Cohen, Harry Zech, Wally Vaevers (Veevers), Ross Jacklin; *Starring* Raymond Massey, Ralph Richardson, Cedric Hardwicke, Edward Chapman; *V* PolyGram (UK, cut to 102 mins), Media, Video Yesteryear, Budget (USA, cut to 92 mins).

THE THING WITH TWO HEADS ★★
USA 1972; colour; 86 mins; Saber; *D* Lee Frost; *P* Wes Bishop; *W* Frost, Bishop, James Gordon White; *M* Robert O. Ragland, also David Angel, Porter Jordan; *C* Jack Steely; *SPFX* (heads creation) Dan Striepeke, Tom Burman and others; *Starring* Ray Milland, "Rosey" Grier, Don Marshall, Roger Perry. Not quite the "Golden Turkey" it has been described as, in a well-known but not-very-good book, but still a good example of the lowest stratum of exploitation movies. The premise – a schlock remake of *The Defiant Ones* – is that white bigot (Milland) has his head transplanted to body of black criminal (played by celebrated footballer Grier). A really on-the-skids performance from Milland, but it has its likeable moments.

THIS ISLAND EARTH ★★★½
USA 1955; colour; 86 mins; Universal-International; *D* Joseph M. Newman; *P* William Alland; *W* Franklin Coen, Edward O'Callaghan from the novel by Raymond F. Jones; *M* Herman Stein; *C* Clifford Stine; *AD* Alexander Golitzen, Richard H. Riedel; *SPFX* (optical) Stine, David S. Horsley, (mutant) Millicent Patrick and others; *Starring* Jeff Morrow, Rex Reason, Faith Domergue; *V* MCA (USA).

3 WOMEN ★★★★
USA 1977; colour; 123 mins; Lion's Gate/20th Century-Fox; *D/PW* Robert Altman; *M* Gerald Busby; *C* Charles Rosher (Jr); *AD* James D. Vance; *Starring* Shelley Duvall, Sissy Spacek, Janice Rule, Ruth Nelson, John Cromwell.

THE 3 WORLDS OF GULLIVER ★★½
UK/Spain 1959; colour; 99 mins; Morningside Worldwide/Columbia; *D* Jack Sher; *P* Charles H. Schneer; *W* Arthur Ross, Sher from *Gulliver's Travels* by Jonathan Swift; *M* Bernard Herrmann; *C* Wilkie Cooper; *AD* Gil Parrondo, Derek Barrington; *SPFX* Ray Harryhausen; *Starring* Kerwin Mathews, June Thorburn, Jo Morrow. Slightly stodgy film adapts the Lilliput and Brobdingnag sequences of Swift's fierce satire, which here (as in almost all modern versions) is not fierce at all. Harryhausen's forte, of course, is stop-motion animation, and there is not much of that here (apart from a fight with a giant squirrel). Most of the effort has gone into making Gulliver appear very big or very small (lots of mattes, and special sets). The end result is likeable enough, but a shade drab.

THX 1138 ★★★★
USA 1970; colour; 95 mins; American Zoetrope/Warner; *D* George Lucas; *P* Francis Ford Coppola, Lawrence Sturhahn; *W* Lucas, Walter Murch from a story by Lucas; *M* Lalo Schifrin; *C* Dave Meyers, Albert Kihn; *AD* Michael Haller; *Starring* Rovert Duvall, Donald Pleasence, Maggie McOmie, Ian Wolfe; *V* Warner (UK and USA).

TIDAL WAVE – *see* NIPPON CHINBOTSU

TIME AFTER TIME ★★
USA 1979; colour; 112 mins; Orion/Warner; *D/W* Nicholas Meyer from a story by Karl Alexander and Steve Hayes; *P* Herb Jaffe; *M* Miklos Rozsa; *C* Paul Lohmann; *PD* Edward C. Carfagno; *SPFX* Larry Fuentes, Jim Blount; *Starring* Malcolm McDowell, David Warner, Mary Steenburgen; *V* Warner (UK and USA).

TIME BANDITS ★★★½ ☻
UK 1981; colour; 113 mins; HandMade; *D/P* Terry Gilliam; *W* Michael Palin, Gilliam; *M* Mike Moran; *C* Peter Biziou; *PD* Millie Burns; *SPFX* (supervision) John Bunker, (opticals) Kent Houston, Paul Whitbread and others, (mattes) Ray Caple; *Starring* John Cleese, Sean Connery, Shelley Duval, Michael Palin, Ralph Richardson, David Warner, David Rappaport, Kenny Baker, Craig Warnock; *V* Thorn EMI (UK), Paramount (USA).

THE TIME MACHINE ★★½
USA 1960; colour; 103 mins; Galaxy/MGM; *D/P* George Pal; *W* David Duncan from the novel by H. G. Wells; *M* Russell Garcia; *C* Paul C. Vogel; *AD* George W. Davis, William Ferrari; *SPFX* Gene Warren, Tim Barr, Wah Chang, (make-up) William Tuttle; *Starring* Rod Taylor, Yvette Mimieux, Alan Young; *V* MGM/UA (USA).

TIMERIDER – THE ADVENTURE OF LYLE SWANN ★½
USA 1982; colour; 94 mins; Zoomo; *D* William Dear; *P* Harry Gittes; *W* Dear, Michael Nesmith; *M* Nesmith; *C* Larry Pizer; *AD* Linda Pearl; *SPFX* (visual) Computer Camera Service; *Starring* Fred Ward, Belinda Bauer, Peter Coyote, Ed Lauter, L. Q. Jones; *V* Thorn EMI (UK), MCA (USA).

Motorcycle racer Lyle Swann (Ward) is time-warped in the desert and finds himself up against bandits in the old Wild West. Really, that's all there is to it; the film does nothing much with the basic idea of putting up a motorcyclist against horsemen, and all the possible ironies of twentieth versus nineteenth century are pretty well thrown away. His new sexy girlfriend turns out to be his great grandmother. Ho hum.

TIME SLIP (SENGOKU JIEITAI) ★★ � 🌎
Japan 1981; colour; 139 mins; Toho; *D* Kosei Saito; *P* Haruki Kadokawa; *W* Toshio Kaneda from a novel by Ryo Hanmura; *M* Kentaro Haneda; *C* Iwao Isayama; *SPFX* Hiyoshi Suzuki; *Starring* Sonny Chiba, Isao Natsuki, Miyuki Ono, Jana Okada; *V* Astra (UK, cut by 40 mins). Fairly gory war film in which a modern Japanese military patrol group is transported into the past through a "timeslip" and finds itself in the middle of sixteenth-century samurai conflicts. The commander theorizes that, if he can change history, they will somehow be returned to their own time, so unlike the conscience-racked captain in *The Final Countdown* he goes to it with a will.

THE TIN DRUM (DIE BLECHTROMMEL) ★★★ 🌎
West Germany/France 1979; colour; 142 mins; Franz Seitz-Bioskop-GGB 14 KG-Hallelujah Artemis-Argos/United Artists; *D* Volker Schlöndorff; *P* Franz Seitz; *W* Jean-Claude Carrière, Seitz, Schlöndorff from the novel by Günter Grass; *M* Maurice Jarre; *C* Igor Luther; *PD* Nicos Perakis; *SPFX* Georges Jaconelli; *Starring* David Bennent, Mario Adorf, Angela Winkler, Daniel Olbrychski; *V* Warner (USA).

THE TINGLER ★★½
USA 1959; b/w (colour sequence); 82 mins; William Castle Productions/Columbia; *D/P* William Castle; *W* Robb White; *M* Von Dexter; *C* Wilfrid M. Cline; *AD* Phil Bennett; *Starring* Vincent Price, Judith Evelyn, Philip Coolidge, Darryl Hickman. Castle was the Gimmick King, and this his most gimmicky movie – at least in big American cities where it was first released. Vincent Price, the mad medico, opines that we all have parasites at the base of the spine that feed on fear unless we relieve tension by screaming. The story revolves around a cruel experiment (perpetrator not revealed until the twist ending) on the mute wife (she cannot scream) of a cinema owner to drive her mad with fear. (The film changes to colour in the much-imitated scene where blood runs from the taps.) She dies, and during the autopsy the tingler escapes. Here, Price turns to the audience and warns that it is now loose among them and they had better scream. To reinforce this illusion, in some theatres, selected seats were wired up to give patrons a small electric charge at this point. Price told them the tingler was "like a lobster, but flat, and instead of claws it has long slimy feelers". In areas that did not use this audience-participation gimmick, the film was reckoned only mediocre.

THE TOMB OF LIGEIA ★★★★
UK 1964; colour; 81 mins; Alta Vista; *D* Roger Corman; *P* Pat Green, Corman; *W* Robert Towne from "Ligeia" by Edgar Allan Poe; *M* Kenneth V. Jones; *C* Arthur Grant; *AD* Colin Southcott; *SPFX* Ted Samuels; *Starring* Vincent Price, Elizabeth Shepherd. The last and in some ways the best of Corman's Poe adaptations, it sums up the feeling of all of them: the shadow that death casts over the living; the feeling of rot and decay not just in the outside world, but also in the mind; the middle-aged obsessive living in the past unable to come to terms with youth or freshness. It is a handsome production, with a bigger budget than most of the earlier films in the series, and produces some striking imagery, not least in Vincent Price's appearance. It is the only Corman version of Poe that actually reminds the viewer of what Poe's writing is like. The story tells of a widower, Price, who has remarried, but believes his first wife is still alive; possession, magic, and a gloomy necrophilia permeate this slow-moving, atmospheric piece.

TOMMY ★★
UK 1975; colour; 108 mins; Robert Stigwood; *D/W* Ken Russell from the rock opera by Pete Townshend and The Who with additional material by John Entwhistle and Keith Moon; *P* Robert Stigwood, Russell; *M/Songs* Pete Townshend and The Who, Sonny Boy Williamson; *C* Dick Bush, Ronnie Taylor; *AD* John Clark; *SPFX* Effects Associates, Nobby Clarke, Camera Effects, (photographic) Robin Lehman; *Starring* Roger Daltrey, Ann-Margret, Oliver Reed, Elton John, Eric Clapton, Keith Moon, Jack Nicholson; *V* Thorn EMI (UK), RCA/Columbia (USA). The film version of The Who's rock opera starts off at the top of its visual voice, so to speak, and keeps going that way. Admirers of Ken Russell's flamboyant pyrotechnics will enjoy the film, but some people find the constant straining for grotesque effect rather wearisome, and musically there is a case for arguing that the original Who record was superior. The story, of course, is true fantasy. Tommy (Roger Daltrey) is traumatised as a child and becomes deaf, dumb and blind. He retains his sense of touch, and becomes an expert at pinball, defeating the pinball wizard (Elton John). He experiments with drugs (the Acid Queen is Tina Turner). He regains his senses, starts his own religion, and is eventually discarded by his disciples.

TOMORROW I'LL WAKE UP AND SCALD MYSELF WITH TEA (ZITRA VSTANU A OPARIM SE CAJEM) ★★★
Czechoslovakia 1977; colour; 93 mins; Filmové Studio; *D* Jindrich Polak; *P* Jan Suster; *W* Milos Macourek, Polak from a story by Josef Nesvadba; *M* Karel Svoboda; *C* Jan Kalis; *AD* Milan Nejedly; *Starring* Petr Kostka, Jiri Sovak, Vladimir Mensik. See this one if you ever have the chance. I am not aware of any theatrical release in English-speaking countries, but it has had a TV showing in the UK. One aspect of science fiction that English/American movies have always shied away from, except in the most simplistic way, is time paradox. But this Czech comedy is full of it. The wildly convoluted story, which involves going back in time to give the H-bomb to Hitler, throws up paradox after paradox. By going back to the past, can one change the present?

TOM THUMB ★★
UK 1958; colour; 98 mins; Galaxy/MGM; *D/P* George Pal; *W* Ladislas Fodor from the story by the Brothers Grimm; *M* Douglas Gamley, Ken Jones; *C* Georges Périnal; *AD* Elliot Scott; *SPFX* Tom Howard; *Animation* Gene Warren, Wah Chang; *Starring* Russ Tamblyn, Alan Young, Peter Sellers, Terry-Thomas, Jessie Matthews, June Thorburn. Family movie with so-so story, but good special effects, for which British effects veteran Howard won an Oscar. Pal is mainly remembered for his SF movies rather than his fantasy, but the success of this one led to *The Wonderful World of the Brothers Grimm* (1962), and later he made *The 7 Faces of Dr Lao*. *Tom Thumb* starred cheerful, freckled Tamblyn as the tiny hero, Terry-Thomas and Sellers as villainous thieves who wish to exploit his size. It is a pity that effects specialists like Harryhausen and Pal so seldom have screenplays worthy of their talents.

TOOMORROW ★½
UK 1970; colour; Sweet Music-Lowndes; *D/W* Val Guest; *P* Harry Saltzman, Don Kirshner; *M* Hugo Montenegro; *Songs* Ritchie Adams, Mark Barkan; *C* Dick Bush; *PD* Michael Stringer; *SPFX* John Stears, (photographic) Ray Caple, Cliff Culley; *Starring* Olivia Newton-John, Benny Thomas, Roy Dotrice, Viv Cooper, Karl Chambers. You can't see this curiosity, a "space musical" with songs by the people who wrote for the Monkees, and then unknown star Newton-John: writer-director Guest took out an injunction against the picture being shown because he had not been paid. A pop group is kidnapped by aliens who are worried about a galactic shortage of certain sound vibrations.

EL TOPO (aka THE MOLE) ★★★½ 🌎 🌎
Mexico 1971; colour; 124 mins; Producciones Panic; *D/W/M/AD* Alexandro Jodorowsky; *P* Roberto Viskin; *C* Raphael Corkidi; *Starring* Jodorowsky, Robert John, Mara Lorenzio, Brontis Jodorowsky.

TOPPER ★★★½
USA 1937; b/w; 98 mins; Hal Roach Studios; *D* Norman Z. McLeod; *P* Milton H. Bren; *W* Jack Jevne, Eric Hatch, Eddie Moran from the novel by Thorne Smith; *M* Arthur Morton; *C* Norbert Brodine; *SPFX* (photographic) Roy Seawright; *Starring* Cary Grant, Constance Bennett, Roland Young, Billie Burke. Based on a very popular, saucy, fantastic novel of the time, this was the first and best of three successful *Topper* films: the other two were *Topper Takes a Trip* (1938) and *Topper Returns* (1941). Roland Young is the unfortunate Cosmo Topper whose life is made a misery by the ghosts of a mischievous, sophisticated couple killed in a car crash (Grant and Bennett), who resent the staid banker having moved into their old home. Most of the humour comes from the fact that (as in *Ghost and Mrs Muir*) nobody else can see them.

TORTURE GARDEN ★★★
UK 1967; colour; 93 mins; Amicus/Columbia; *D* Freddie Francis; *P* Max J. Rosenberg, Milton Subotsky; *W* Robert Bloch from his stories "Enoch", "The Man Who Collected Poe", "Mr Steinway" and "Terror Over Hollywood"; *M* Don Banks, James Bernard; *C* Norman Warwick; *Starring* Jack Palance, Burgess Meredith, Peter Cushing, Maurice Denham, Robert Hutton, Niall MacGinnis, Michael Bryant, Beverly Adams. The second of the seven Amicus horror film anthologies, based on stories by notable horror writer Bloch (who wrote the book on which *Psycho* was based). There is no torture and no garden. Disquieting Dr Diabolo (Meredith), a carnival performer, shows the future to four visitors: episodes include man whose head is eaten by cat, bringing Poe back to life, a jealous piano, and a long-lasting Hollywood star who turns out to be a robot. This latter SF episode is probably the best. Overall not too hot.

TO THE DEVIL A DAUGHTER ★★½ 🌎
UK/West Germany 1976; colour; 93 mins; Hammer-Terra Filmkunst; *D* Peter Sykes; *P* Roy Skeggs; *W* Chris Wicking, also John Peacock, from the novel by Dennis Wheatley; *M* Paul Glass; *C* David Watkin; *AD* Don Picton; *SPFX* Les Bowie; *Starring* Richard Widmark, Christopher Lee, Honor Blackman, Denholm Elliott, Nastassia Kinski; *V* Thorn EMI (UK), Planet (USA).

TREASURE OF THE FOUR CROWNS
(EL TESORO DE LAS CUATRO CORONAS) ★½
Spain/USA 1982; colour; 3-D; 100 mins; MTG-Lotus/Cannon; *D* Ferdinando Baldi; *P* Tony Anthony, Gene Quintano; *W* Lloyd Battista, Jim Bryce, Jerry Lazarus; *M* Ennio Morricone; *C* Marcello Masciocchi, Giuseppe Ruzzolini; *AD* Luciano Spadoni; *SPFX* Freddy Unger, Germano Natali, (make-up) Carlo de Marchis; *Starring* Tony Anthony, Ana Obregon, Gene Quintano, Jerry Lazarus, Francisco Rabal; *V* Guild (UK), MGM/UA (USA). Enterprising but ill-made imitation of *Raiders of the Lost Ark* is doomed from the outset by the casting of Tony Anthony whose face seems incapable of registering any emotion at all, with the result that the whole thing is unintentionally like a zombie movie. If you like special effects in 3-D, then this is for you: they make up in vast quantity for what they lack in quality. The story confusedly tells of superhero's search for Visigothic crowns (they could apparently only afford two) with occult powers. Mummies come to life, booby-trap medieval weapons spring in all directions, objects levitate, faces dissolve, and at the end a totally irrelevant monster is born. Truly terrible, but kind of fun.

I TRE VOLTI DELLA PAURA – *see* BLACK SABBATH

TRILOGY OF TERROR ★★★
USA 1975; made for TV; colour; 78 mins; ABC Circle; *D/P* Dan Curtis; *W* "Julie" and "Millicent and Therese" by William F. Nolan from "The Like-

ness of Julie'' and ''Therese'' by Richard Matheson, ''Amelia'' by Richard Matheson from his own short story ''Prey''; *M* Robert Cobert; *C* Paul Lohmann; *AD* Jan Scott; *SPFX* (puppet) Erik M. Von Bluelow; *Starring* Karen Black. Generally spoken of as the best, and possibly the only, scary movie ever made for TV. Karen Black efficiently plays all the leads, including both personalities of the schizophrenic (or are they sisters?) in ''Millicent and Therese''. The first two episodes are commonplace, but the third, ''Amelia'', is unusually good: a mother-dominated young woman buys a Zuni fetish doll for her boyfriend, but it comes to life quite horribly (excellent effects, a bit like the Tasmanian Devil in a popular Warner Bros cartoon series), shrieking, moving at amazing speed and snapping its horrible teeth.

A TRIP TO THE MOON (LE VOYAGE DANS LA LUNE) ★★★★
France 1902; b/w; silent; 285 metres (around 15 mins); Star; *D/P/W/AD/Starring* Georges Méliès, acrobats of the Folies-Bergère.

TROG ★★
UK 1970; colour; 91 mins; Herman Cohen/Warner; *D* Freddie Francis; *P* Herman Cohen; *W* Aben Kandel from a story by Peter Bryan and John Gilling; *M* John Scott; *C* Desmond Dickinson; *AD* Geoffrey Tozer; *Trog Design* Charles Parker; *Starring* Joan Crawford, Michael Gough, Bernard Kay. Not to put too fine a point on it, Joan Crawford's career had reached its nadir when she played the lady scientist who introduces missing-link, Trog, found in an old cave system in England, to polite society. Trog doesn't like it, and turns nasty. Trouper Crawford tried hard to give value for money. The film was well parodied by *Schlock*.

TRON ★★★½
USA 1982; colour; 96 mins; Disney; *D/W* Steven Lisberger from a story by Lisberger and Bonnie MacBird; *P* Donald Kushner, Harrison Ellenshaw; *M* Wendy Carlos; *C* Bruce Logan; *PD* Dean Edward Mitzner; *SPFX* (visual concept) Steven Lisberger, (supervision) Richard Taylor, Harrison Ellenshaw, (mechanical) R. J. Spetter, (animation compositing photography supervision) Jim Pickel, (effects animation supervisor) Lee Dyer, (conceptual artists) Syd Mead, Jean ''Moebius'' Giraud, Peter Lloyd; *Starring* Jeff Bridges, Bruce Boxleitner, David Warner, Cindy Morgan; *V* Disney (UK and USA).

TURKEY SHOOT ★ 💀 💀
Australia 1981; colour; 93 mins; FGH/Hemdale; *D* Brian Trenchard-Smith; *P* Antony I. Ginnane, William Fayman; *W* Jon George, Neill Hicks; *M* Brian May; *C* John McLean; *SPFX* John Stears, (make-up) Bob McCarron; *Starring* Steve Railsback, Olivia Hussey, Michael Craig, Carmen Duncan; *V* Guild (UK). This represents the soft, white underbelly of the renascent Australian film industry: a cynical exploitation film with no redeeming features at all, and not even seeming very Australian in the version released abroad, in which some voices were redubbed. Future dissident young people are herded into concentration camps; some are used in human hunts, but this backfires and the hunters are bloodily slaughtered. Violent, schlock version of *Punishment Park/The Most Dangerous Game*, designed to show maximum mutilation, but censored in UK version to 87 mins. Extremely badly made, and negligible as SF.

TWENTY MILLION MILES TO EARTH ★★★
USA 1957; b/w; 84 mins; Morningside/Columbia; *D* Nathan Juran; *P* Charles H. Schneer; *W* Bob Williams, Christopher Knopf from a story by Charlotte Knight; *C* Irving Lippman, Carlos Ventigmilia; *AD* Cary Odell; *Animation* Ray Harryhausen; *Starring* William Hopper, Joan Taylor, Frank Puglia. Conventional monster movie lifted a little out of the ordinary by Harryhausen's good stop-motion animation of the creature. A rocket returning from a survey of Venus crashes in the sea off Sicily; there is one survivor (Hopper) and a jelly-like substance, out of which hatches a small, lizard-like creature. This grows with extreme rapidity

(though it's actually more interesting while still small) and by the end is tearing things up (in its search for food, which is sulphur), having a gigantic struggle with an implausible elephant, and being destroyed by the army in the Colosseum. Bad screenplay.

20,000 LEAGUES UNDER THE SEA ★★★½
USA 1954; colour; 127 mins; Walt Disney; *D* Richard Fleischer; *W* Earl Felton from the novel by Jules Verne; *M* Paul J. Smith; *C* Franz Planer; *AD* John Meehan; *SPFX* (photography) Ralph Hammeras, (mattes) Peter Ellenshaw, (special processes) Ub Iwerks, John Hench and Joshua Meador, (squid) Bob Mattey; *Starring* Kirk Douglas, James Mason, Paul Lukas, Peter Lorre; *V* Disney (UK and USA).

TWILIGHT ZONE THE MOVIE ★★★
USA 1983; colour; 101 mins; Warner; *P* Steven Spielberg, John Landis; *M* Jerry Goldsmith; *PD* James D. Bissell. *Prologue and Segment 1:D/W* John Landis; *C* Stevan Larner; *SPFX* Paul Stewart, (make-up) Craig Reardon; *Starring* Dan Aykroyd, Albert Brooks, Vic Morrow. *Segment 2: D* Steven Spielberg; *W* George Clayton Johnson, Richard Matheson, Josh Rogan from the 1962 *Twilight Zone* episode ''Kick the Can'' by Johnson; *C* Allen Daviau; *SPFX* (supervision) Mike Wood; *Starring* Scatman Crothers, Bill Quinn. *Segment 3: D* Joe Dante; *W* Richard Matheson from the 1961 *Twilight Zone* episode ''It's a GOOD Life'' by Richard Matheson from the story by Jerome Bixby; *C* John Hora; *SPFX* (supervision) Mike Wood, (mattes) Rocco Gioffri, Dreamquest Images, (make-up) Rob Bottin, (cartoons) Sally Cruikshank; *Starring* Kathleen Quinlan, Jeremy Light, Kevin McCarthy. *Segment 4: D* George Miller; *W* Richard Matheson from his 1963 *Twilight Zone* episode ''Nightmare at 20,000 Feet'' based on his own short story; *C* Allen Daviau; *SPFX* (visual) Peter Kuran, VCE, Industrial Light and Magic and David Allen, (monster conceptual design) Ed Verreaux, (make-up) Craig Reardon; *Starring* John Lithgow. *V* Warner (USA).

TWINS OF EVIL ★½ 💀
UK 1971; colour; 87 mins; Hammer/Rank; *D* John Hough; *P* Harry Fine; *W* Tudor Gates; *M* Harry Robinson; *C* Dick Bush; *AD* Roy Stannard; *SPFX* Bert Luxford; *Starring* Madeleine Collinson, Mary Collinson, Peter Cushing, Kathleen Byron, Dennis Price; *V* Rank (UK). The third of Hammer's *Karnstein* trilogy, which began with *The Vampire Lovers* and went on to *Lust for a Vampire*. Puritan bigot Cushing is out to destroy good times and vampires alike, and briskly executes witches. But it is one of his own twin nieces who gets vampirized by Count Karnstein – a hedonistic girl, and indeed the only point of interest is the subtext which reads sex/fun/vampires will always be destroyed by repression/gloom/Christianity, which, come to think of it, equates sex with death and where does that leave us? Morally very confused. The direction is ordinary, and the lunatic subtext really requires a more full-blooded treatment.

2001: A SPACE ODYSSEY ★★★★★
UK 1968; colour; 160 mins; MGM; *D/P* Stanley Kubrick; *W* Kubrick, Arthur C. Clarke from ''The Sentinel'' by Clarke; *M* from the works of Khachaturian, Ligeti, Johann Strauss and Richard Strauss; *C* Geoffrey Unsworth, also John Alcott; *PD* Tony Masters, Harry Lange, Ernest Archer; *AD* John Hoesli; *SPFX* (photography) Kubrick, Wally Veevers, Douglas Trumbull, Con Pederson, Tom Howard, (make-up) Stuart Freeborn; *Starring* Keir Dullea, Gary Lockwood, William Sylvester; *V* MGM/UA (UK and USA).

THE UFO INCIDENT ★★★
USA 1975; made for TV; colour; 100 mins; Universal; *D* Richard A. Colla; *P* Colla, Joe L. Cramer; *W* S. Lee Pogostin, Hesper Anderson from *The Interrupted Journey* by John G. Fuller; *M* Billy Goldenberg; *C* Rexford Metz; *AD* Peter M. Wooley; *SPFX* (optical) Magicam; *Starring* James Earl Jones, Estelle Parsons, Barnard Hughes, Dick O'Neill. Effective TV movie, partly financed by black actor James Earl Jones (Darth Vader's voice) who

plays well with Parsons. They are Barney and Betty Hill, in a supposedly true story about a disturbed couple who seek psychiatric help. Hypnosis reveals that years ago they had been kidnapped by aliens and taken aboard their spacecraft. It makes for a good story, with the emphasis on the human drama of amnesia. Highly praised at the time, and it looks forward interestingly to the wholly fictional *Close Encounters of the Third Kind*.

UGETSU MONOGATARI ★★★★★
Japan 1953; b/w; 94 mins; Daiei; *D* Kenji Mizoguchi; *P* Masaichi Nagata; *W* Matsutaro Kawaguchi from ''Asaji Ga Yado'' and ''Jasei No In'' in the collection *Tales of a Pale and Mysterious Moon After the Rain* by Akinari Ueda; *M* Fumio Hayasaka; *C* Kazuo Miyagawa; *AD* Kisaku Ito; *Starring* Masayuki Mori, Machiko Kyo, Sakae Ozawa, Mitsuko Mito. One of the great classics of fantastic cinema, made by a great director, the film is notable for the poetic mystery and eeriness it summons up without any overt special effects. Set in sixteenth-century Japan, the film tells of a simple villager, Genjuro, straying into the ghost castle of the Princess Wakasa (a memorable performance from Machiko Kyo), and the illusory love he comes to feel for this shadowy being, part sad woman, part Lamia (the eternally alluring, eternally cruel vampire woman). His return home, finally, where his wife is now dead, leads to an extraordinary supernatural sequence. (She matter-of-factly welcomes him back.) The visual imagery is beautiful throughout, as is the relation of these mysterious events to quite ordinary human life, and the delicacy with which the women characters are presented.

THE ULTIMATE WARRIOR ★★½ 💀
USA 1975; colour; 94 mins; Warner; *D/W* Robert Clouse; *P* Fred Weintraub, Paul Heller; *M* Gil Melle; *C* Gerald Hirschfeld; *AD* Walter Simonds; *SPFX* Gene Griggs, (photographic) Van der Veer Photo Effects; *Starring* Yul Brynner, Max von Sydow, Joanna Miles; *V* Warner (UK). Director Clouse had previously made kung fu movies, and it shows. Set in a post-holocaust New York where rival groups struggle to survive amid the ruins of a once-great civilization, the film stars Brynner as, in effect, a Samurai warrior, hired to protect one such group. He ends by escorting pregnant Joanna Miles and a packet of desperately important unmutated plant seeds through the wreckage of the subway system to freedom. As an action movie, conventional enough, with indifferent acting, but at moments it provides quite hard-edged images of what society might look like after a terrible plague. It flopped badly.

THE UNCANNY ★★ 💀
UK/Canada 1977; colour; 85 mins; Cinévidéo-Tor-Subotsky and Héroux/Rank; *D* Denis Héroux; *P* Claude Héroux, René Dupont; *W* Michel Parry; *M* Wilfred Josephs; *C* Harry Waxman, James Bawden; *PD* Wolf Kroeger, Harry Pottle; *SPFX* Michael Albrechtsen; *Starring* Peter Cushing, Ray Milland, Susan Penhaligon, Joan Greenwood, Roland Culver, Alexandra Stewart, Donald Pleasence, Samantha Eggar, John Vernon; *V* Rank (UK), Nostalgia (USA). Trio of horror stories with framing device about cat-researcher (Cushing) trying to sell anti-cat book to unconvinced publisher (Milland), whose cats (with others) get Cushing in the end. In first story Joan Greenwood is an old lady eaten by her cats; the second features an incredible shrinking girl (and is not well done); the third has Pleasence as a horror star who demolishes his wife with a pit-and-pendulum device, and is punished by her cat. This has the one good line: ''What's wrong? Has the cat got your tongue?'' To which the answer, I'm afraid, is Yes. Of real interest only to cat-haters. All stories banal and conventional. Good cast, though.

UNIDENTIFIED FLYING ODDBALL (aka THE SPACEMAN AND KING ARTHUR) ★★½
USA 1979; colour; 93 mins; Disney; *D* Russ Mayberry; *P* Ron Miller; *W* Don Tait from *A Connecticut Yankee in King Arthur's Court* by Mark Twain; *M* Ron Goodwin; *C* Paul Beeson; *AD*

Albert Witherick; *SPFX* Ron Ballanger, Michael Collins, (photographic) Cliff Culley, (make-up) Roy Ashton and Ernie Gasser; *Starring* Dennis Dugan, Jim Dale, Sheila White, Ron Moody, Kenneth More, John Le Mesurier, Rodney Bewes. Astronaut Tom Trimble (Dugan) and his robot double Hermes are unexpectedly thrown back in time to the sixth century at King Arthur's court. Most of the humour is tailored primarily for children, but some scenes are done with flair, the best being where Hermes (who everybody thinks is Tom) gets chopped to pieces in a joust with Sir Mordred (Dale).

THE UNINVITED ★★★½
USA 1944; b/w; 98 mins; Paramount; *D* Lewis Allen; *P* Charles Brackett; *W* Dodie Smith, Frank Partos from the novel by Dorothy Macardle; *M* Victor Young; *C* Charles Lang; *AD* Hans Dreier, Ernst Fegté; *SPFX* (optical) Farciot Edouart; *Starring* Ray Milland, Ruth Hussey, Donald Crisp, Gail Russell.

THE VALLEY OF GWANGI ★★
USA/Spain 1969; colour; 95 mins; Morningside/Warner-Seven Arts; *D* Jim O'Connolly; *P* Charles H. Schneer; *W* William E. Bast, additions by Julian More; *M* Jerome Moross; *C* Erwin Hillier; *AD* Gil Parrando; *SPFX* Ray Harryhausen; *Starring* James Franciscus, Gila Golan, Richard Carlson, Laurence Naismith. One of the less interesting vehicles for Harryhausen's special effects, the film was originally to be made back in 1942 by RKO, with Harryhausen's mentor Willis O'Brien doing the special effects, but the project was axed. The story tells of a group of cowboys discovering a hidden valley in Mexico populated with dinosaurs; they capture Gwangi (an allosaurus – the film's best scene shows the cowboys roping him like a steer) and take him to civilization where, like King Kong, he escapes and goes on a rampage, but is finally cornered in a church. Very derivative, but it's fair to say some critics differ and see the film as one of Harryhausen's most underrated.

VAMPIRE CIRCUS ★★★½ ☻
UK 1971; colour; 87 mins; Hammer/Rank; *D* Robert Young; *P* Wilbur Stark; *W* Judson Kinberg from a story by George Baxt and Stark; *M* David Whittaker; *C* Moray Grant; *AD* Scott MacGregor; *SPFX* Les Bowie, (make-up) Jill Carpenter; *Starring* Adrienne Corri, Laurence Payne, Thorley Walters, John Moulder Brown, Lynne Frederick, Dave Prowse, Lalla Ward; *V* Rank (UK).

THE VAMPIRE LOVERS ★½ ☻
UK 1970; colour; 91 mins; Hammer/AIP; *D* Roy Ward Baker; *P* Harry Fine, Michael Style; *W* Tudor Gates from an adaptation by Fine, Gates and Style of "Carmilla" by J. Sheridan Le Fanu; *M* Harry Robinson; *C* Moray Grant; *AD* Scott MacGregor; *Starring* Ingrid Pitt, Pippa Steel, Madeleine Smith, Peter Cushing, George Cole, Dawn Addams, Kate O'Mara. With their *Dracula* series running out of steam, and also wanting an opportunity for some overt sexuality, Hammer began a new vampire trilogy with an adaptation of one of the best vampire stories ever written, Le Fanu's "Carmilla". But the haunting atmosphere of the original is lost here, and all that remains (very much more crudely) is the lesbian proclivities of the Karnstein's strange and dangerous house-guest, played by Ingrid Pitt. Confused script. This tits-and-teeth film looks pretty bad when compared with two other films based on the same story; *Vampyr* and *Blood and Roses*. Sequels (quite unnecessary) were *Lust for a Vampire* and *Twins of Evil*.

VAMPYR ★★★★★
France/Germany 1931/32; b/w; 83 mins; Tobis-Klangfilm; *D* Carl Dreyer; *P* Dreyer, Baron Nicolas de Gunzburg; *W* Dreyer, Christen Jul loosely based on "Carmilla" by J. Sheridan Le Fanu; *M* Wolfgang Zeller; *C* Rudolph Maté, Louis Née; *AD* Hermann Warm, Hans Bittmann, Cesare Silvagni; *Starring* Julian West (pseudonym of de Gunzburg), Sybille Schmitz, Henriette Gérard, Jan Hieronimko; *V* Budget, Thunderbird, Video Yesteryear (USA).

VARGTIMMEN – *see* HOUR OF THE WOLF

VAULT OF HORROR ★★½
UK 1973; colour; 86 mins; Amicus/Metromedia; *D* Roy Ward Baker; *P* Max J. Rosenberg, Milton Subotsky; *W* Subotsky from five stories by Al Feldstein and William Gaines in EC Comics; *M* Douglas Gamley; *C* Denys Coop; *AD* Tony Curtis; *SPFX* (make-up) Roy Ashton; *Starring* Daniel Massey, Anna Massey, Terry-Thomas, Glynis Johns, Curt Jurgens, Dawn Addams, Michael Craig, Edward Judd, Tom Baker, Denholm Elliott; *V* Nostalgia (USA). The sixth of seven horror anthologies from Amicus, and the second adapted from the celebrated horror comics brought out by EC Comics in the 1950s. The first of these *(Tales from the Crypt)* was better though *Vault*, too, was successful. (By far the best attempt to recreate EC Comics' atmosphere was *Creepshow*.) In *Vault*, five men are trapped in a mysterious room (which turns out to be a vault in a cemetery – they're dead) and tell stories; prissy husband neatly dismembered; murderer attacked by vampires; ironic Indian rope trick tale; insurance fraud with pretended death; voodoo artist making his paintings come true. Vaguely unpleasant, but too mediocre to be really scary.

VIDEODROME ★★★★½ ☻ ☻
Canada 1982; colour; 89 mins; Filmplan International/Universal; *D/W* David Cronenberg; *P* Claude Héroux; *M* Howard Shore; *C* Mark Irwin; *AD* Carol Spier; *SPFX* (physical) Frank Carere, (video) Michael Lennick, (make-up) Rick Baker, with a crew of five uncredited for obscure reasons; *Starring* James Woods, Deborah Harry, Sonja Smits, Peter Dvorsky, Les Carlson; *V* CIC (UK), MCA (USA).

VILLAGE OF THE DAMNED ★★★
UK 1960; b/w; 77 mins; MGM; *D* Wolf Rilla; *P* Ronald Kinnoch; *W* Stirling Silliphant, Rilla, George Barclay from *The Midwich Cuckoos* by John Wyndham; *M* Ron Goodwin; *C* Geoffrey Faithfull; *AD* Ivan King; *SPFX* Tom Howard, (make-up) Eric Aylott; *Starring* George Sanders, Barbara Shelley, Martin Stephens, Michael Gwynne, Laurence Naismith; *V* MGM/UA (USA). Low-key, uneven, sometimes very effective translation of the Wyndham classic to the screen. In a small English village a mysterious force renders everyone unconscious for some time. Upon recovery, they think that nothing has happened, but it turns out that twelve women have become pregnant. The children are born, and prove to be extraordinary: telepathic, and super-intelligent. Though human in appearance, they represent a form of alien invasion. They never smile, and seem preternaturally adult; this is in fact more disquieting than the slightly cheap trick that makes their eyes glow when they act as a group-mind. Good performance from Sanders as their mentor, a kindly man who has finally (with great difficulty) to destroy them. It is in small, imaginative, almost domestic touches that the strength of this slightly paranoid film lies.

THE VIRGIN SPRING (JUNGFRUKÄLLAN) ★★★★ ☻
Sweden 1960; b/w; 85 mins; Svensk Filmindustri; *D* Ingmar Bergman; *W* Ulla Isaksson from a medieval legend; *M* Erik Nordgren; *C* Sven Nykvist; *Starring* Max von Sydow, Birgitta Valberg, Gunnel Lindblom, Birgitta Pettersson; *V* Longman (UK).

VIRUS (FUKKATSU NO HI) ★½
Japan 1980; colour; 155 mins (cut to 108); Kadokawa/Toho; *D* Kinji Fukasaku; *P* Haruki Kadokawa; *W* Koji Takada, Gregory Knapp, Fukasaku from a novel by Sakyo Komatsu; *M* Teo Macero; *C* Daisaku Kimura; *SPFX* (miniatures) Gregory Jein, (mattes) Mike Minor; *Starring* Masao Kusakari, Chuck Connors, Glenn Ford, Olivia Hussey, George Kennedy, Henry Silva, Robert Vaughn; *V* Intervision (UK), Media (USA). Difficult to judge this Japanese disaster film, which was extremely successful there, because the Western export version is severely cut. It is hard to believe it could ever have been very good. The story:

germ-warfare virus is stolen and accidentally released on the world; only those in extremely cold areas survive. Then lunatic American Chief of Staff (Henry Silva) sets off nuclear strike. Poor special effects, laughably stereotyped performances (especially Chuck Connors, of all people, as a vewwy British submarine commander); in the Antarctic there are 8 women for 864 men, and much talk about the necessity for sharing. The whole story told as flashback, with bearded scarecrow Japanese about to walk (with amazing implausibility) from Washington D.C. to the Antarctic. (In the full version he makes it all the way to Tierra del Fuego, and is re-united with his buddies.) The film has nothing serious to say.

LE VOYAGE À TRAVERS L'IMPOSSIBLE – *see* AN IMPOSSIBLE VOYAGE

LE VOYAGE DANS LA LUNE – *see* A TRIP TO THE MOON

VOYAGE TO THE BOTTOM OF THE SEA ★★½
USA 1961; colour; 105 mins; Windsor/20th Century-Fox; *D/P* Irwin Allen; *W* Allen, Charles Bennett; *M* Paul Sawtell, Bert Shefter; *C* Winton C. Hoch; *SPFX* (photographic) L. B. Abbott; *Starring* Walter Pidgeon, Joan Fontaine, Peter Lorre, Barbara Eden; *V* CBS/Fox (UK and USA). Irwin Allen did lots of SF for TV and then moved on to disaster movies like *Towering Inferno* and, more typically bad, *The Swarm*. When he puts his hands on an SF idea, one thing is fairly certain – the science will be illiterate (or innumerate?). In this early example the Van Allen belt in the upper atmosphere has caught fire (!) and unless Walter Pidgeon, commander of a glass-nosed, experimental nuclear submarine, can fire a nuclear missile at it, then the fire won't go out. All sorts of incidental pleasures include sabotage and a giant octopus. Colourful hokum.

WARGAMES ★★½
USA 1983; colour; 113 mins; Sherwood/MGM/UA; *D* John Badham; *P* Harold Schneider; *W* Lawrence Lasker, Walter F. Parkes; *M* Arthur B. Rubinstein; *C* William A. Fraker; *PD* Angelo P. Graham; *SPFX* Joe Digaetano, (computer graphics design consultant) Colin Cantwell, (visuals supervision) Mike Fink; *Starring* Matthew Broderick, Dabney Coleman, John Wood, Ally Sheedy; *V* CBS/Fox (USA).

WARLORDS OF ATLANTIS ★½
UK 1978; colour; 96 mins; EMI; *D* Kevin Connor; *P* John Dark; *W* Brian Hayles; *M* Mike Vickers; *C* Alan Hume; *PD* Elliot Scott; *SPFX* John Richardson, George Gibbs, (monsters) Roger Dicken, (mattes) Cliff Culley; *Starring* Doug McClure, Peter Gilmore, Shane Rimmer, Cyd Charisse, Lea Brodie; *V* Thorn EMI (UK). Producer Dark and director Connor had been mining the low-grade ore of lost-world melodrama for some time (as in *Land that Time Forgot* and its sequels) and by now the vein looked played out. Why did they always star the inexpressive Doug McClure? Nineteenth-century expedition in diving bell is seized by giant octopus and dumped on shore of Atlantis (in a kind of vast cave under the seabed). The autocratic Atlanteans (ex-Martians, it seems) try to subvert scientist Peter Gilmore into their slave-oppressing ways, planning an attack on the upper Earth. Meanwhile, dinosaurs attack from all directions. And so on. The monsters are more animated than the screenplay and human performances.

THE WAR OF THE WORLDS ★★★½
USA 1953; colour; 85 mins; Paramount; *D* Byron Haskin; *P* George Pal; *W* Barré Lyndon from the novel by H. G. Wells; *M* Leith Stevens; *C* George Barnes; *AD* Hal Pereira, Albert Nozaki; *SPFX* Gordon Jennings, Wallace Kelley and others, (optical) Paul K. Lerpae and others, (mattes/paintings) Chesley Bonestell and others; *Starring* Gene Barry, Ann Robinson, Les Tremayne, Robert Cornthwaite; *V* CIC (UK), Paramount (USA).

THE WASP WOMAN ★★½
USA 1959; b/w; 66 mins; Santa Clara-Filmgroup/Allied Artists; D/P Roger Corman; W Leo Gordon; M Fred Katz; C Harry Newman; AD Daniel Haller; Starring Susan Cabot, Fred Eisley, Barboura Morris. A vigorous, early Corman monster cheapie, and not one of his best. Cosmetician Susan Cabot tries rejuvenating cream made from wasp enzymes. Result? "It works for a while, until her innate waspishness takes over and she buzzes about with a black mask and wobbling antenna, sucking blood (a new departure for wasps but not, of course, for horror films)." So said Philip Strick in Science Fiction Movies.

THE WATCHER IN THE WOODS ★★½
USA 1982; colour; 100 mins; Disney; D John Hough; P Ron Miller, Tom Leetch; W Brian Clemens, Harry Spalding, Rosemary Anne Sisson from the novel by Florence Engel Randall; M Stanley Myers; C Alan Hume; PD Elliot Scott, (final sequence) Harrison Ellenshaw; SPFX John Richardson, (photographic) Art Cruickshank and Bob Broughton, (visual effects) David Mattingly, Dick Kendall and Don Henry; Starring Bette Davis, Carroll Baker, David McCallum, Lynn-Holly Johnson, Kyle Richards, Ian Bannen; V Disney (USA). A horror story for children, and there are not many of those. Very mild, of course, opening with a haunted house, and ending with an SF denouement featuring an alien trapped with a thirty-years missing human in another dimension. The film was endlessly delayed, and rumours suggested that the original ending (with an alien planet) was met with hoots of laughter at previews in 1980, and had to be junked. Director Hough (Incubus, Legend of Hell House) is hardly brilliant, but he is experienced at this sort of thing, and Clemens' contribution to the script no doubt spiced up the bizarre elements. The new ending is said to have been shot (uncredited) by Vincent McEveety. As always with Disney, there is a fundamental cosiness, and the potentially real scares are never permitted to be more than frissons.

WEEKEND ★★★★ 🕱
France 1967; colour; 103 mins; Comacico/Copernic/Lira/Ascot Cineraid; D/W Jean-Luc Godard; M Antoine Duhamel; C Raoul Coutard; Starring Mireille Darc, Jean Yanne, Jean-Pierre Kalfon, Valérie Lagrange, Jean-Pierre Léaud.

WELCOME TO BLOOD CITY ★★½
Canada/UK 1977; colour; 96 mins; Blood City-EMI; D Peter Sasdy; P Marilyn Stonehouse; W Stephen Schenck, Michael Winder; M Roy Budd; C Reginald H. Morris; PD Jack McAdam; Starring Jack Palance, Keir Dullea, Samantha Eggar, Barry Morse; V Thorn EMI (UK). Clumsy direction and a script that does not make the most of its premise prevent this ingenious film from being as good as it should have been. A group of amnesiacs wake up in the desert; they carry cards telling them they are convicted murderers. They enter a small, typically nineteenth century Wild West township where, it transpires, the only way to climb up the hierarchy is through violence. The top man, and most efficient gunslinger, is Jack Palance. Unlike most of his group, Dullea cannily and viciously starts a process of upwards social mobility, and then we are suddenly back in a laboratory watching the whole thing on TV. It turns out to be a psychological test, seeking the most promising killers for potential military use. But the testers themselves get emotionally and then literally involved. The ending, where Dullea, sickened by what he has now learned about the project but choosing to return to his violent township-of-the-mind, is in a way touching.

THE WEREWOLF OF LONDON ★★★
USA 1935; b/w; 75 mins; Universal; D Stuart Walker; P Stanley Bergerman; W John Colton, also Harvey Gates, from a story from Robert Harris; C Charles Stumar; AD Albert S. D'Agostino; SPFX (optical) John P. Fulton, (make-up) Jack Pierce; Starring Henry Hull, Warner Oland, Valerie Hobson. There were a few hesitant stabs at the theme in silent movie days, but for all practical purposes this was the first werewolf movie, and some think Universal did better first time around than six years later with The Wolfman. Henry Hull is the botanist attacked in Tibet and later followed by the mysterious Yogami (Oland) who turns out to have been the beastly attacker. Some "mariphasa" flowers Hull has gathered are a specific against lycanthropy, and the two werewolves (for Hull has now succumbed to the infection) struggle for possession of the specimens he found in Tibet. Hull wins, but cannot stave off the illness and is finally killed by policemen. Thus began the legend of the werewolf, who unlike the vampire or the zombie is usually seen as a victim rather than a monster. (The theme, of course, is closely related to Dr Jekyll and Mr Hyde: that within us lurks a beast waiting to get out.)

THE WEREWOLF OF WASHINGTON ★★
USA 1973; colour; 90 mins; Millco; D/W Milton Moses Ginsberg; P Nina Schulman; M Arnold Freed; C Bob Baldwin; AD Nancy Miller-Corwin; SPFX (make-up) Bob Obradovich; Starring Dean Stockwell, Biff McGuire, Clifton James, Michael Dunn; V Vipco (UK), Monterey (USA). Watergate-era satire on Nixon administration and, in a piece of genre-crossing which is not quite as funny as it sounds, a parody of monster movies. Stockwell is the press attaché of the President who becomes a werewolf and proceeds to infect the Executive. All a bit undergraduate, but quite well told, with good end when he gets to bite the President (McGuire).

WESTWORLD ★★★★
USA 1973; colour; 89 mins; MGM; D/W Michael Crichton; P Paul N. Lazarus III; M Fred Karlin; C Gene Polito; AD Herman Blumenthal; SPFX Charles Schulthies, (visual) Brent Sellstrom; Starring Yul Brynner, Richard Benjamin, James Brolin, Victoria Shaw; V MGM/UA (UK and USA).

WHAT LOLA WANTS – see DAMN YANKEES

WHEN DINOSAURS RULED THE EARTH ★★
UK 1970; colour; 100 mins; Hammer/Warner; D/W Val Guest from a story by J. G. Ballard; M Mario Nascimbene; C Dick Bush; AD John Blezard; SPFX Jim Danforth, with David Allen, Allan Bryce, Roger Dicken and Brian Johnstock; Starring Victoria Vetri, Robin Hawdon, Patrick Allen. One of Hammer's prehistoric cycle, others being Slave Girls (1968), One Million Years BC and Creatures the World Forgot. Very little remains of the treatment commissioned (amazingly, since he is among the most literate and difficult of SF writers) from J. G. Ballard. Victoria Vetri (no Raquel Welch, she) is the Rock-tribe woman who escapes sacrifice and falls for the Sea-tribe man (Hawdon); forced to flee (again) she makes friends with a baby dinosaur. Animated monsters (not quite up to Harryhausen's standard, but he was not available) include a plesiosaur, a pterodactyl and giant crabs. At the end, the sudden arrival of the Moon (still gaseous!) in orbit conveniently kills the bad guys with huge tides.

WHEN WORLDS COLLIDE ★★½
USA 1951; colour; 83 mins; Paramount; D Rudolph Maté; P George Pal; W Sydney Boehm from the novel by Philip Wylie and Edwin Balmer; M Leith Stevens; C John F. Seitz, N. Howard Green; AD Hal Pereira, Albert Nozaki; SPFX Gordon Jennings, Harry Barndollar, (process) Farciot Edouart; Starring Richard Derr, Barbara Rush, John Hoyt; V Paramount (USA).

THE WHITE BUFFALO ★
USA 1977; colour; 97 mins; Dino De Laurentiis; D J. Lee Thompson; P Pancho Kohner; W Richard Sale from his novel; M John Barry; C Paul Lohmann; PD Tambi Larsen; SPFX Richard M. Parker, Roy Downey, (buffalo) Mario Chiari and Carlo Rambaldi; Starring Charles Bronson, Jack Warden, Will Sampson, Kim Novak, Clint Walker; V Guild (UK).

WHITE ZOMBIE ★★★½
USA 1932; b/w; 73 mins; Amusement Securities/United Artists; D Victor Halperin; P Edward Halperin; W Garnett Weston from The Magic Island by William Seabrook; M Abe Meyer; C Arthur Martinelli; AD Ralph Berger; SPFX (make-up) Jack Pierce; Starring Bela Lugosi, Madge Bellamy, Joseph Cawthorn, Robert Frazer, Clarence Muse; V Budget (USA). Based on a best seller about supposedly magic practices in Haiti, this was the first film about zombies. Bellamy goes to Haiti to marry her fiancé, but a plantation owner (Frazer) falls in love with her, and enlists the help of the sinister Murder Legendre (Lugosi) who uses zombie slave labour on his sugar-cane plantation. Legendre uses voodoo to cause the apparent death of the unfortunate woman, but in fact she becomes one of his servants, a cataleptic, wraith-like figure (but not by contemporary definitions a proper zombie, since she is not actually dead). All ends well. There are "real" zombies in the film, including an ex-pirate and an ex-judge, all played by white actors, and they are eerie, but also rather silly. It is in the sequences with the young woman that the film most successfuly adopts its stylized, Gothic atmosphere.

WHO? (aka MAN WITHOUT A FACE, PRISONER OF THE SKULL and THE MAN IN THE STEEL MASK) ★★★
UK 1974; colour; 93 mins; Lion International/Hemisphere/Maclean & Co.; D Jack Gold; P Barry Levinson; W John Gould from the novel by Algis Budrys; M John Cameron; C Petrus Schloemp; AD Peter Scharff; SPFX Richard Richtsfeld, (make-up) Colin Arthur; Starring Elliott Gould, Joseph Bova, Trevor Howard, Ivan Desny; V Home Video (UK).

THE WICKER MAN ★★★★
UK 1973; colour; 102 mins (usually cut); British Lion; D Robin Hardy; P Peter Snell; W Anthony Shaffer; M Paul Giovanni; C Harry Waxman; AD Seamus Flannery; Starring Edward Woodward, Christopher Lee, Diane Cilento, Britt Ekland, Ingrid Pitt; V Thorn EMI (UK), Media (USA).

WILD IN THE STREETS ★★★
USA 1968; colour; 97 mins; AIP; D Barry Shear; P Burt Topper, William J. Immerman; W Robert Thom from his story "The Day It All Happened, Baby"; M Les Baxter; C Richard Moore; AD Paul Sylos; Starring Christopher Jones, Hal Holbrook, Shelley Winters, Diane Varsi, Ed Begley, Richard Pryor. Rapidly dated but still quite amusing movie from the youth-protest era of the late 1960s. Jones plays the rock idol who promises support for a politician (Holbrook) in return for the voting age being lowered, but this allows himself to be elected President (with the help of LSD judiciously administered to various politicians). Compulsory retirement at thirty and force-feeding of older persons with drugs play a prominent role in the new administration. But rebellion is brewing among the thirteen-year olds... A curate's egg – funny in parts. On a similar theme, Gas-s-s-s (1970) is better.

WILLARD ★★
USA 1970; colour; 95 mins; Bing Crosby Productions; D Daniel Mann; P Mort Briskin; W Gilbert A. Ralston from Ratman's Notebooks by Stephen Gilbert; M Alex North; C Robert B. Hauser; AD Howard Hollander; SPFX Bud David; Starring Bruce Davison, Sondra Locke, Elsa Lanchester, Ernest Borgnine. A rather shy and creepy young man, whose domineering mother has just died (shades of Psycho), Willard makes friends with a group of rats. He uses these to revenge himself on people who are mean to him, notably wicked mortgage-forecloser Borgnine. But they come between him and a chance for normal life with his girlfriend (Locke). The chief rat, Ben, is now unnervingly intelligent, and when Willard plans to exterminate them, Ben makes his move first. Very average direction, and rats not as scary as they might have been. The slightly diseased, mausoleum-like house is not bad. Sequel was Ben.

WILLY WONKA AND THE CHOCOLATE FACTORY ★★★
USA 1971; colour; 100 mins; Wolper-Quaker Oats/Paramount; D Mel Stuart; P David L. Wolper,

Stan Margulies; *W* Roald Dahl from his book *Charlie and the Chocolate Factory*; *M and Lyrics* Anthony Newley, Leslie Bricusse; *C* Arthur Ibbetson; *AD* Harper Goff; *SPFX* Logar R. Frazee; *Starring* Gene Wilder, Jack Albertson, Peter Ostrum.

THE WINGED SERPENT – *see* Q – THE WINGED SERPENT

WITCHCRAFT ★★★
UK 1964; b/w; 80 mins; Lippert/20th Century-Fox; *D* Don Sharp; *P* Robert L. Lippert, Jack Parsons; *W* Harry Spalding; *M* Carlo Martelli; *C* Arthur Lavis; *Starring* Lon Chaney Jr, Jack Hedley, Jill Dixon, Yvette Rees. It may be that the career of director Don Sharp needs re-evaluation upwards. Most of his films were made on very low budgets, but there are usually touches of originality and bizarreness that make them worth watching (see, for example, *Psychomania*). In *Witchcraft*, a duel between the Whitlock and Lanier families (the Whitlocks being, secretly, warlocks and witches) is compounded by the digging up of an old cemetery and subsequent return of 300-year-old Whitlock witch (Rees). Standard occult plot, but some nice atmospheric happenings.

WITCHFINDER GENERAL (aka THE CONQUEROR WORM) ★★★★ ☠
UK 1968; colour; 87 mins; Tigon; *D* Michael Reeves; *P* Arnold L. Miller, Louis M. Heyward; *W* Reeves, Tom Baker, Heyward from the book by Ronald Bassett; *M* Paul Ferris; *C* Johnny Coquillon; *AD* Jim Morahan; *SPFX* Roger Dicken; *Starring* Vincent Price, Ian Ogilvy, Hilary Dwyer, Rupert Davies, Patrick Wymark; *V* Video Movies/Hokushin (UK).

THE WIZ ★★½
USA 1978; colour; 134 mins; Motown/Universal; *D* Sidney Lumet; *P* Rob Cohen; *W* Joel Schumacher from the stage musical by William Brown (book) and Charlie Smalls (music & lyrics) based on *The Wonderful Wizard of Oz* by L. Frank Baum; *M* Charlies Smalls, Quincy Jones; *C* Oswald Morris; *PD* Tony Walton; *SPFX* Al Griswold, (visual) Albert Whitlock, (make-up) Stan Winston; *Starring* Diana Ross, Michael Jackson, Nipsey Russell, Ted Ross, Richard Pryor; *V* CIC (UK), MCA (USA). This curious rock musical is an all-black remake of *The Wizard of Oz*. Diana Ross is very beautiful, but young enough to be Dorothy she ain't. The now enormously successful pop star Michael Jackson is the Scarecrow. Laid-back comedian Richard Pryor is the Wiz. In this version of the story, Dorothy, normally scared stiff about leaving the house and facing the world, finds herself transported to a fantasy New York (it is still recognizably Manhattan rather than the Emerald City) in which she faces various trials and learns how to accept life. The moralising is ponderous, and so is the direction. It's all surprisingly stodgy, the main point of interest being the witty sets designed by Tony Walton.

THE WIZARD OF OZ ★★★★
USA 1939; colour; 101 mins; MGM; *D* Victor Fleming, (uncredited) King Vidor; *P* Mervyn LeRoy; *W* Noel Langley, Florence Ryerson, Edgar Allan Woolf from the novel by L. Frank Baum; *M* Herbert Stothart, songs by E. Y. Harburg and Harold Arlen; *AD* Cedric Gibbons, William A. Horning; *SPFX* Arnold Gillespie, (character make-ups) Jack Dawn; *Starring* Judy Garland, Frank Morgan, Ray Bolger, Bert Lahr, Jack Haley, Billie Burke, Margaret Hamilton; *V* MGM/UA (UK and USA).

WOLFEN ★★★½ ☠
USA 1981; colour; 115 mins; King-Hitzig/Orion-Warner; *D* Michael Wadleigh; *P* Rupert Hitzig; *W* David Eyre, Wadleigh from the novel by Whitley Strieber; *M* James Horner; *C* Gerry Fisher; *PD* Paul Sylbert; *SPFX* (photographic) Robert Blalack, (Praxis – Wolfen vision) Betzy Bromberg and others, (make-up) Carl Fullerton; *Starring* Albert Finney, Diane Venora, Edward James Olmos, Gregory Hines; *V* Warner (UK and USA).

THE WOLFMAN ★★★
USA 1941; b/w; 71 mins; Universal; *D/P* George Waggner; *W* Curt Siodmak, Gordon Kahn; *M* Charles Previn; *C* Joseph Valentine; *AD* Jack Otterson; *SPFX* (make-up) Jack Pierce; *Starring* Claude Rains, Lon Chaney Jr, Ralph Bellamy, Evelyn Ankers, Bela Lugosi, Maria Ouspenskaya.

THE WOMAN IN THE MOON – *see* DIE FRAU IM MOND

XANADU ★★
USA 1980; colour; 96 mins; Universal; *D* Robert Greenwald; *P* Lawrence Gordon, Joel Silver; *W* Richard Christian Danus, Marc Reid Rubel; *M* Barry DeVorzon; *Songs* John Farrar, Jeff Lynne; *C* Victor J. Kemper; *PD* John W. Corso; *SPFX* Andy C. Evans, Burt Dalton, Dorse Lanpher, (visual) Richard Greenberg, (optical) Joel Hynek, (animation) Don Bluth; *Starring* Olivia Newton-John, Gene Kelly, Michael Beck; *V* CIC (UK), MCA (USA). Valiant attempt at a truly fantastic musical never survives the disco-dancing ambience of the setting, which manages to make the fantastic elements merely implausible and a bit tacky. Newton-John is the mysterious girl, Kira, who persuades commercial painter Sonny (Beck) and old-time band leader Danny (Kelly) to open a magnificent club, just like Xanadu, the "stately pleasure dome" of Coleridge's poem. The ever-changing Kira turns out to be a genuine Muse sent by her father Zeus to inspire Xanadu. Despite endless make-up and costume changes, a goddess Olivia Newton-John isn't, and the songs are not up to much either.

X – THE MAN WITH X-RAY EYES (aka THE MAN WITH THE X-RAY EYES) ★★★½
USA 1963; colour; 80 mins; Alta Vista/AIP; *D/P* Roger Corman; *W* Robert Dillon, Ray Russell; *M* Les Baxter; *C* Floyd Crosby; *SPFX* Butler-Glouner; *Starring* Ray Milland, Diana Van Der Vlis, Harold J. Stone, John Hoyt, John Dierkes; *V* Warner (USA).

XTRO ★★★ ☠ ☠
UK 1982; colour; 86 mins; Ashley-Amalgamated Film Enterprises; *D/M* Harry Bromley Davenport; *P* Mark Forstater; *W* Iain Cassie, Robert Smith, from a screenplay by Michel Parry and Davenport; *C* John Metcalfe; *AD* Andrew Mollo; *SPFX* Tom Harris, (creature) Francis Coates, (make-up) Robin Grantham and John Webber; *Starring* Bernice Stegers, Philip Sayer, Danny Brainin; *V* PolyGram (UK), Thorn EMI (USA) (video versions have new ending). This film deserves full credit for trying hard on a fairly minimal budget. Basically a rather unpleasant exploitation horror movie (the rape of a woman by a monster, followed closely by her giving birth to a full-sized man, has to be seen to be believed), it is all done with such lurid comic-strip gusto that it contrives to be remarkably inoffensive. The story begins with the abduction of a man by flying saucer, which returns three years later to deposit a nasty alien whose back legs are jointed the wrong way round. After a spot of murder and rape, it disappears, to be replaced by its fully grown child who is the man that disappeared in the first place. He rejoins his wife (now living with a lover) and bad things happen, with some black humour, especially involving the son (grass snakes in an old lady's salad, instantly dispatched with steak mallet; subsequent murder of old lady by boy using telekinetically animated toy clown). The high spots in this farrago of nonsense are the *au pair* girl turned into an ovipositing cocoon, and the love-making scene between husband and wife where the husband starts to decay halfway through. It is all quite loony and arbitrary, but packed with incident. The randomness of it all is demonstrated by the director's having shot an entirely different ending for the videotape version. The film ends with lots of clones of son Tony. The tape ends with mother being killed by thing from *au-pair*-laid egg.

LES YEUX SANS VISAGE (aka EYES WITHOUT A FACE, aka THE HORROW CHAMBER OF DR FAUSTUS) ★★★★½ ☠ ☠
France 1959; b/w; 95 mins; Champs-Elysées/Lux; *D* Georges Franju; *P* Jules Borkon; *W* Jean Redon, Franju, Claude Sautet, Pierre Boileau and Thomas Narcejac, Pierre Gascar from the novel by Redon; *M* Maurice Jarre; *C* Eugen Schüfftan; *Starring* Pierre Brasseur, Alida Valli, Edith Scob, Juliette Mayniel; *V* Intervision (UK).

YOUNG FRANKENSTEIN ★★★
USA 1974; b/w; 108 mins; Gruskoff-Venture-Crossbow-Jouer/20th Century-Fox; *D* Mel Brooks; *P* Michael Gruskoff; *W* Gene Wilder, Brooks from characters in *Frankenstein, or a Modern Prometheus* by Mary Shelley; *M* John Morris; *C* Gerald Hirschfeld; *AD* Dale Hennesy; *Laboratory equipment* Kenneth Strickfaden; *SPFX* Hal Millar, Henry Miller Jr, (make-up) William Tuttle; *Starring* Gene Wilder, Peter Boyle, Marty Feldman, Madeline Kahn, Cloris Leachmann, Teri Garr, Gene Hackman; *V* CBS/Fox (UK and USA).

YOU ONLY LIVE TWICE ★★½
UK 1967; colour; 116 mins; Eon-Danjaq/United Artists; *D* Lewis Gilbert, (action sequences) Bob Simmons; *P* Harry Saltzman, Albert R. Broccoli; *W* Roald Dahl, very loosely adapted from the novel by Ian Fleming; *M* John Barry; *C* Freddie Young; *PD* Ken Adam; *SPFX* John Stears; *Starring* Sean Connery, Akiko Wakabayashi, Mie Hama, Karin Dor, Donald Pleasence; *V* Warner (UK and USA).

ZARDOZ ★★★★
UK 1973; colour; 105 mins; John Boorman; *D/P/W* John Boorman (story associate Bill Stair); *M* David Munrow; *C* Geoffrey Unsworth; *PD* Anthony Pratt, Bill Stair; *SPFX* Gerry Johnson, (optical) Charles Staffell, (make-up) Basil Newall; *Starring* Sean Connery, Charlotte Rampling, Sara Kestelman; *V* CBS/Fox (UK).

ZELIG ★★★★
USA 1983; Orion/Warner; b/w & colour; 79 mins; *D/W* Woody Allen; *P* Roger Greenhut; *M* Dick Hyman; *C* Gordon Willis; *PD* Mel Bourne; *SPFX* (optical) Joel Hynick, Stuart Robinson, R/Greenberg Associates, (make-up) John Caglione; *Starring* Woody Allen, Mia Farrow, John Buckwalter, Mary Louise Wilson.

ZÉRO DE CONDUITE (ZERO FOR CONDUCT) ★★★★½
France 1933; b/w; 44 mins; Argui-Films; *D/W* Jean Vigo; *P* J.-L. Nounez; *M* Maurice Jaubert; *C* Boris Kaufman; *AD* Vigo, Kaufman, Henri Storck; *Starring* Louis Lefebvre, Gilbert Pruchon, Constantin Kelber, Delphin; *V* Budget (USA). Short, surrealist feature by brilliant, eccentric young filmmaker, made on a minimal budget with largely amateur actors – especially the schoolboys. It describes rebellion at a strict boys' boarding school, of a joyously anarchic and spontaneous kind; slow-motion pillow fights, a headmaster who is a dwarf, teachers who are in part cardboard cut-outs. Lindsay Anderson, who must have had the film in mind when he made *If...*, did not capture the same sense of freedom destroying repression.

ZITRA VSTANU A OPARIM SE CAJEM – *see* TOMORROW I'LL WAKE UP AND SCALD MYSELF WITH TEA

ZOMBIE – *see* ZOMBIE FLESH-EATERS

ZOMBIE CHILD – *see* THE CHILD

ZOMBIE FLESH-EATERS (ZOMBI 2, aka ZOMBIE) ★★ ☠ ☠ ☠
Italy 1979; colour; 91 mins; Variety; *D* Lucio Fulci; *P* Ugo Tucci, Fabrizio De Angelis; *W* Elisa Briganti; *M* Fabio Frizzi, Giorgio Tucci; *C* Sergio Salvati; *PD* Walter Patriarca; *SPFX* (including make-up supervision) Giannetto De Rossi, (make-up) Maurizio Trani; *Starring* Tisa Farrow, Ian McCulloch, Richard Johnson; *V* Vipco (UK), Wizard (USA).

ZOMBIES – *see* DAWN OF THE DEAD

ZOMBI 2 – *see* ZOMBIE FLESH-EATERS

Index

We regret that it is not practical – it would quadruple the length – to index the Filmography. We realize that it would be useful to look up, for example, all the films for which Rob Bottin did the make-up, or which were directed by Terence Fisher, but even if we were to provide page references to the Filmography, the reader would still be left with the problem of not knowing whether the name appeared once or more than once on a given page.

FURTHER REFERENCE

This list is selective, not comprehensive. It contains books and magazines that I have personally found useful or interesting.

Magazines

Cinefantastique (bi-monthly), Box 270, Oak Park, Illinois 60303, USA.
Cinefex (quarterly), Box 20027, Riverside, California 92516, USA.
L'Ecran Fantastique (monthly), Média Presse Edition, 92 avenue des Champs-Elysées, 75008 Paris, France.
Fangoria (eight issues a year), O'Quinn Studios, 475 Park Avenue South, New York, NY 10016, USA.
Monthly Film Bulletin (monthly), British Film Institute, 81 Dean Street, London W1V 6AA, UK.
Starburst (monthly), Marvel Comics, 23 Redan Place, London WC2, UK.

Of these L'Ecran Fantastique is excellent for those who read French, Monthly Film Bulletin gives a full filmography and review for every film released in the UK, Cinefex is a specialist magazine about special effects in fantasy movies, Fangoria is the ultimate sleaze magazine about visceral horror, vigorously written, and Cinefantastique and Starburst are by far the best of the general fantasy magazines.

Books – Primarily Reference

Lee, Walt, Reference Guide to Fantastic Films: Science Fiction, Fantasy and Horror, 3 vols, Chelsea-Lee Books, Los Angeles, 1972-4.
Maltin, Leonard, ed., TV Movies 1983-84 Edition (annual), New American Library, New York, 1982.
Naha, Ed, The Science Fictionary, Wideview Books, USA, 1980.
Nicholls, Peter, ed., The Encyclopedia of Science Fiction, Granada, London, 1979.
Pickard, Roy, The Hamlyn Book of Horror and S.F. Movie Lists, Hamlyn, Feltham, UK, 1983.
Scheuer, Steven H. ed., Movies on TV 1982-1983 Edition (annual), Bantam, New York, 1981.
Willis, Donald C. Horror and Science Fiction Films: a Checklist, Scarecrow, New Jersey, 1972.
Willis, Donald C. Horror and Science Fiction Films II, Scarecrow, New Jersey, 1982.

Of these, Lee's three volumes were the great pioneering work; Willis's two volumes are the most informatively up-to-date.

Books – Critical, Historical and Special Effects

Baxter, John, Science Fiction in the Cinema, A. S. Barnes, New York, 1970.
Brosnan, John, Future Tense: The Cinema of Science Fiction, Macdonald and Jane's, London, 1978.
Brosnan, John, James Bond in the Cinema (second edition), A. S. Barnes, San Diego, and Tantivy, London, 1981.
Clarens, Carlos, Horror Movies: an Illustrated Survey, Secker & Warburg, London, 1968.
Crawley, Tony, The Steven Spielberg Story, Zomba, London, 1983.
Culhane, John, Special Effects in the Movies: How They Do It, Ballantine, New York, 1981.
Derry, Charles, Dark Dreams: a Psychological History of the Modern Horror Film, A. S. Barnes, New Jersey, 1977.
Everson, William K. Classics of the Horror Film, Citadel, New Jersey, 1974.
Gifford, Denis, A Pictorial History of Horror Movies, Hamlyn, Feltham, UK, 1973, revised 1983.
Harryhausen, Ray, Film Fantasy Scrapbook (third Edition), A. S. Barnes, San Diego, and Tantivy, London, 1981.
Hoberman, J. and Rosenbaum, Jonathan, Midnight Movies, Harper & Row, New York, 1983.
Johnson, W. ed., Focus on the Science Fiction Film, Spectrum, New Jersey, 1972.
King, Stephen, Danse Macabre, Everest, New York, 1981.
Meyers, Richard, For One Week Only: The World of Exploitation Films, New Century, New Jersey, 1983.
Meyers, Richard, The World of Fantasy Films, A. S. Barnes, New Jersey, 1980.
Peary, Danny, Cult Movies, Delta, New York, 1981.
Pirie, David, A Heritage of Horror: the English Gothic Cinema 1946-1972, Gordon Fraser, London, 1973.
Pohl, Frederik, and Pohl, Frederik IV, Science Fiction Studies in Film, Ace, New York, 1981.
Pollock, Dale, Skywalking: the Life and Films of George Lucas, Harmony (Crown), New York, 1983.
Prawer, S. S., Caligari's Children: the Film as Tale of Terror, Oxford University Press, Oxford, 1980.
Rovin, Jeff, The Fabulous Fantasy Films, A. S. Barnes, New Jersey, 1977.
Savini, Tom, Grande Illusions: a Learn by Example Guide to the Art and Technique of Special Make-Up Effects from the Films of Tom Savini, Imagine Inc., USA, 1983.
Soren, David, The Rise and Fall of the Horror Film: an Art Historical Approach to Fantasy Cinema, Lucas Brothers, Missouri, 1977.
Strick, Philip, Science Fiction Movies, Octopus, London, 1976.
Warren, Bill, Keep Watching the Skies! American Science Fiction Movies of the Fifties Volume 1 1950-1957, McFarland, North Carolina, 1982.
Wood, Robin, and Lippe, Richard, eds., American Nightmare: Essays on the Horror Film, Festival of Festivals, Toronto, 1979.

The books that I have found most stimulating critically are those by Clarens, Hoberman and Rosenbaum, Prawer, Strick, Warren, and Wood and Lippe.

ACKNOWLEDGMENTS

Thanks go first of all to the publicity departments of the various film companies, the ultimate source of most of the illustrations used here. Studios are individually credited in the captions.

Very special thanks go to Phil Edwards and Alan Mackenzie who helped in more than one way, and to Allen Eyles who worked valiantly to produce the technical data for the filmography.

Thanks to the British Film Institute, the Kobal Collection, Stephen Jones and PSA Public Relations Ltd for help in acquiring visual material: to Philip Strick, Ramsey Campbell and Tom Milne for forming a panel of judgement with me for rating all the films discussed in this book; to BBC Radio 4 (Kaleidoscope) for allowing me to quote from a radio interview with David Cronenberg; to the following British-based videotape distribution companies for the loan of various films in videotape format: CBS/Fox, CIC, Guild Home Video, Intervision, MGM, Palace, Rank (and Disney), RCA, Replay/Media (Video Programme Distributors), Spectrum/PolyGram, Thorn EMI, VCL, Videomedia, VIPCO, VTC, Warner Home Video.

Thanks to Dave Marshall of Marshall Discount Video Service, 3130 Edsel Drive, Box 328, Trenton, Michigan 48183, USA, for helping me with information about video availability (up to February 1984) in the USA.

Finally, thanks to Zivia Desai for secretarial help throughout the planning stages, and my daughter Sophie Cunningham for putting up with my vagueness during the finishing stages.

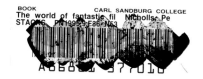

BOOK   CARL SANDBURG COLLEGE
The world of fantastic fil   Nicholls, Pe
STACKS   PN 1995.9.F86 N53

A 060   97 018

40301
PN WITHDRAWN N53

NICHOLLS   P

WORLD OF FANTASTIC FILMS

Carl Sandburg College
Learning Resources Center
2232 South Lake Storey Road
Galesburg, Illinois   61401